Early Rome to 290 BC

The Edinburgh History of Ancient Rome
General Editor: J. S. Richardson

Early Rome to 290 BC: The Beginnings of the City and the Rise of the Republic
Guy Bradley

Rome and the Mediterranean 290 to 146 BC: The Imperial Republic
Nathan Rosenstein

The End of the Roman Republic 146 to 44 BC: Conquest and Crisis
Catherine Steel

Augustan Rome 44 BC to AD 14: The Restoration of the Republic and the Establishment of the Empire
J. S. Richardson

Imperial Rome AD 14 to 192: The First Two Centuries
Jonathan Edmondson

Imperial Rome AD 193 to 284: The Critical Century
Clifford Ando

Imperial Rome AD 284 to 363: The New Empire
Jill Harries

From Rome to Byzantium AD 363 to 565: The Transformation of Ancient Rome
A. D. Lee

Visit the series web page at edinburghuniversitypress.com/series-the-edinburgh-history-of-ancient-rome.html

Early Rome to 290 BC
The Beginnings of the City and the Rise of the Republic

Guy Bradley

EDINBURGH
University Press

Edinburgh University Press is one of the leading university presses in the UK. We publish academic books and journals in our selected subject areas across the humanities and social sciences, combining cutting-edge scholarship with high editorial and production values to produce academic works of lasting importance. For more information visit our website: edinburghuniversitypress.com

© Guy Bradley, 2020

Edinburgh University Press Ltd
The Tun – Holyrood Road
12(2f) Jackson's Entry
Edinburgh EH8 8PJ

Typeset in 11/13 Adobe Sabon
IDSUK (DataConnection) Ltd

A CIP record for this book is available from the British Library

ISBN 978 0 7486 2109 5 (hardback)
ISBN 978 0 7486 2934 3 (webready PDF)
ISBN 978 0 7486 2110 1 (paperback)
ISBN 978 1 4744 8068 0 (epub)

The right of Guy Bradley to be identified as the author of this work has been asserted in accordance with the Copyright, Designs and Patents Act 1988, and the Copyright and Related Rights Regulations 2003 (SI No. 2498).

Contents

Illustrations	vi
Preface and acknowledgements	xii
Series editor's preface	xiv
Abbreviations	xv
1. Sources and approaches	1
2. Early Italy, from the Bronze Age to the classical era	35
3. Myths and legends of the foundation of Rome	81
4. Kingship	103
5. Urbanism and city foundation	138
6. Economy and society in archaic Rome and central Italy	192
7. Rome in the early Republic	237
8. Roman foreign relations in the sixth, fifth and fourth centuries BC	263
9. Rome and Italy 338–290 BC: conquest and accommodation	305
10. Rome around 300 BC	334
11. Conclusion	360
Chronology	365
Guide to further reading	367
Bibliography	370
Index	400

Illustrations

Maps

1 Map of central Italy (drawing: I. Dennis)   xvi
2 Map of northern Italy (drawing: I. Dennis)   xvii
3 Map of south Italy (drawing: I. Dennis)   xviii
4 Map of south Etruria and Latium (drawing: K. Harding)   xix
5 Map of Rome (drawing: K. Harding)   xx

Figures

Unless otherwise noted, illustrations are by the Cardiff archaeological drawing team.

Figure 1.1 Years covered by Livy's books 2–10   22
Figure 2.1 Map of key Bronze Age sites   37
Figure 2.2 Map of Villanovan sites   41
Figure 2.3 Biconical cinerary urn belonging to a child from Tomb 64, Monterozzi necropolis, Tarquinii (photo: G. Bradley)   42
Figure 2.4 Early Iron Age findspots from proto-urban centres in Etruria and Latium (after Carandini, *Nascita*, figs 26–7)   45
Figure 2.5 Map of Greek and Phoenician settlement in the Mediterranean, with the key Etruscan trade routes (after Lulof and van Kampen (eds), *Etruscans*, 17)   48
Figure 2.6 Greek colonisation in Sicily and southern Italy (after Forsythe, *Critical History*, map 5)   50
Figure 2.7 Banquet scene on architectural terracotta plaque from Murlo, northern Etruria, early sixth century BC (drawing: R. Sponer Za, for Winter, *Symbols*, 153–9, Roof 3–8, Plan 9)   53
Figure 2.8 *Patera baccellata* from Tomb 600, Osteria dell'Osa (Sciacca, 'Circolazione', fig. 1. Courtesy of Soprintendenza Speciale Archeologia Belle Arti e Paesaggio di Roma)   55

Illustrations   vii

Figure 2.9 The entrance to the Tomb of the Greek Vases in Tumulus 2, Banditaccia cemetery, Caere (photo: G. Bradley)   56

Figure 2.10 Gilded silver plate from Regolini-Galassi Tomb, *c.*675–650 BC, of probable Phoenician production (from Grifi, *Monumenti*, 214, Tav. V)   58

Figure 2.11 Large gold fibula from Regolini-Galassi Tomb, *c.*675–650 BC (from Grifi, *Monumenti*, 205, Tav. II)   59

Figure 2.12 Plan of Tomb 70, Acqua Acetosa Laurentina (from Bedini, 'La tomba 70 dell'Acqua Acetosa Laurentina', in Carandini and Cappelli (eds), *Roma*, 356. Courtesy of Soprintendenza Speciale Archeologia Belle Arti e Paesaggio di Roma)   60

Figure 2.13 Bronze fan from Tomb 70, Acqua Acetosa Laurentina (by concession of the Ministero per i beni e le attività culturali e per il turismo – Museo Nazionale Romano)   61

Figure 2.14 Impasto flask with graffito, from female Tomb 482 of Osteria dell'Osa, dating to *c.*825–770 BC (by concession of the Ministero per i beni e le attività culturali e per il turismo – Museo Nazionale Romano)   62

Figure 2.15 Murlo, roof system of second phase of palace complex, *c.*580–575 BC (drawing: R. Sponer Za, for Winter, *Symbols*, 153–9, Roof 3–8, Plan 9)   67

Figure 2.16 Murlo, plan of second phase of palace complex, *c.*580–575 BC (drawing: R. Sponer Za, for Winter, *Symbols*, 153–9, Roof 3–8, Plan 9)   68

Figure 2.17 Anchor with dedication to Apollo by Sostratos, Gravisca (photo: G. Bradley)   73

Figure 2.18 Plan of the sanctuary at Pyrgi (after Baglione et al., 'Pyrgi', fig. 12.2)   75

Figure 2.19 The Pyrgi tablets. The two tablets with Etruscan texts flank the tablet with the Phoenician text in the middle (drawing: K. Harding)   76

Figure 2.20 Ivory hospitality token with Etruscan inscription from the sanctuary of the Forum Boarium (after *GRT*, fig. 1.6)   79

Figure 3.1 Bronze mirror from Bolsena, Etruria, with scene of twins suckled by a wolf, late fourth century BC (from Roscher, *Ausführliches Lexikon*, I 1465)   95

Figure 3.2 The lupa Capitolina (photo: Guy Bradley)   96

Figure 4.1 The four sides of the Lapis Niger inscription with RECEI visible in line 5 (after *GRT*, fig. 3.1.39)   113

Figure 4.2 The frescoes from the François Tomb, Vulci, c.350–325 BC (drawing: H. Mason)   121

Figure 4.3 The Tarquin dynasty (after Cornell, *Beginnings*, fig. 14)   126

Figure 5.1 The topography of the site of Rome (after Momigliano and Schiavone (eds), *Storia di Roma*, I 577)   140

Figure 5.2 Funerary goods from Tomb 98, Esquiline cemetery (drawing: R. Hook, for Sekunda and Northwood, *Early Roman Armies*, 7; reproduced with kind permission of the authors)   144

Figure 5.3 The Domus Regia (after Filippi, 'Domus Regia', 101–21)   147

Figure 5.4 Sector 9 of the first phase of the Palatine wall, c.730–720 BC, showing the threshold identified as the Porta Mugonia and an associated wooden structure (after Carandini and Carafa, *Palatium e Sacra Via*, fig. 106)   149

Figure 5.5 The stratigraphy of the Roman Forum (after Filippi, 'Velabro', fig. 5)   153

Figure 5.6 Comitium, general plan of the excavated remains (after Cifani, *Architettura*, fig. 94)   157

Figure 5.7 The four phases of the monarchic Regia according to F. Brown (after *GRT*, 59)   158

Figure 5.8 Terracotta roof of the third phase of the Regia with disc acroteria (drawing: R. Sponer Za, for Winter, *Symbols*, 144–7, Roof 3-2)   159

Figure 5.9 Architectural terracotta plaque from the third phase of the Regia with felines and minotaur (drawing: R. Sponer Za, for Winter, *Symbols*, Ill. 3.5.1)   160

Figure 5.10 The two phases of the temple at Sant'Omobono (after Cifani, *Architettura*, 168, fig. 164)   161

Figure 5.11 Temple acroterion with Heracles and Athena, second phase of the temple at Sant'Omobono (drawing: R. Sponer Za, for Winter, *Symbols*, Ill. 5.16.2)   164

Figure 5.12 Architectural terracotta decoration of the second phase of the temple at Sant'Omobono (drawing: R. Sponer Za, for Winter, *Symbols*, 316–18, Roof 5-4, Plan 12.2)   165

Figure 5.13 Satricum, roof of sacellum or temple of Mater Matuta (drawing: R. Sponer Za, for Winter, *Symbols*, 398–400, Roof 6-1, Plan 15)   166

Illustrations

Figure 5.14 The foundations of the Capitoline temple visible in the Capitoline Museum (photo: G. Bradley) — 168

Figure 5.15 The foundations of the Capitoline temple (after Cifani, *Architettura*, fig. 70) — 169

Figure 5.16 The Capitoline temple: a reconstruction of the plan (after Cifani, *Architettura*, fig. 85) — 170

Figure 5.17 A comparison of the Capitoline temple with other temples in central Italy (after Mura Sommella, 'Tempio di Giove', fig. 26) — 172

Figure 5.18 The cappellaccio wall underneath Termini station (photo: G. Bradley) — 175

Figure 5.19 The Servian Walls outside Termini station (photo: G. Bradley) — 176

Figure 5.20 Surviving and reused sections of cappellaccio walling in the Servian Walls (after Carandini, *Nascita*, pl. 33) — 177

Figure 5.21 The distribution of tombs in the Esquiline cemetery, eighth and seventh centuries BC (after Cifani, *Architettura*, fig. 235) — 178

Figure 5.22 The distribution of archaic and Republican tombs in the Esquiline cemetery (after Cifani, *Architettura*, fig. 236) — 179

Figure 5.23 The comparative sizes of central Italian cities (drawing: H. Mason, after Momigliano and Schiavone (eds), *Storia di Roma*, I 586) — 181

Figure 5.24 City areas in hectares (figures from Cifani, *Architettura*, 257; Cornell, *Beginnings*, 204; Ampolo, 'Città riformata', 168) — 182

Figure 5.25 Architectural terracotta decoration of the temple of SS. Stimmate, Velitrae (drawing: R. Sponer Za, for Winter, *Symbols*, 320–3, Roof 5–7, Plan 18) — 185

Figure 5.26 Plan of atrium house (Domus 3) on the slopes of the Palatine (after *GRT*, fig. 4.2) — 188

Figure 5.27 The Comitium and associated monuments in the Archaic and Republican period (after Carafa, *Comizio*, 152, fig. 95) — 189

Figure 6.1 Plan of the Auditorium villa annex, c.500–350 BC (after Cifani, *Architettura*, fig. 191) — 196

Figure 6.2 Architectural terracotta decoration of the temple at Caprifico di Torrecchia (Cisterna di Latina) (drawing: R. Sponer Za, for Winter, *Symbols*, 323–4, Roof 5–8) — 200

Figure 6.3 Genucilia plates, Ashmolean Museum
(photo: G. Bradley) 202
Figure 6.4 Trading vessel from the Tomb of the Ship at
Tarquinii, mid 5th century BC (after Minetti, *Pittura*, 74) 205
Figure 6.5 Faience vase with cartouche naming the Pharoah
Bocchoris, from a tomb in Tarquinii, late eighth century
BC (photo: G. Bradley) 223
Figure 6.6 Illustration of banqueting on an architectural
terracotta plaque from the temple of SS. Stimmate,
Velitrae, produced in Rome, *c.*530 BC (drawing:
R. Sponer Za, for Winter, *Symbols*, Ill. 5.14.1) 225
Figure 7.1 The sites of the plebeian secessions
(after Wiseman, *Remus*, 115) 247
Figure 8.1 Map of Roman monarchic conquests, based on the
literary sources, using Thiessen polygons for hypothetical
city territories (reproduced with kind permission of the
author from Fulminante, *Urbanisation*, fig. 33) 276
Figure 8.2 The Lapis Satricanus (after *GRT*, fig. 1.10) 284
Figure 9.1 Roman territory and colonies in Italy, 302, 290
and 241 BC (after Cornell and Matthews, *Atlas*, 40–1) 313
Figure 10.1 Republican roads and colonies near Rome
(after Salmon, *Roman Colonization*, fig. 5) 344
Figure 10.2 Denarius of L. Marcius Censorinus, 82 BC,
with the head of Apollo and the statue of Marsyas with
a wineskin, from the Comitium (from Classical
Numismatic Group, LLC, www.cngcoins.com) 345
Figure 10.3 Francesco Piranesi, 'Prospetto del Sarcofago di
Scipione Barbato, e del Monumento d'Aula Cornelia'
(View of the sarcophagus of Scipio Barbatus and the
Monument of Aula Cornelia) (from *Monumenti degli
Scipioni* (1785), Tav. 3, via Wikimedia Commons) 349
Figure 10.4 Fresco from the Tomb of the Fabii, Esquiline,
of *c.*300–280 BC (drawing: R. Hook, for Sekunda and
Northwood, *Early Roman Armies*, 44; reproduced with
kind permission of the authors) 351

Tables

Table 1.1 The earliest Roman historians 19
Table 1.2 The character of the literary record 28
Table 2.1 Eras of Italian prehistory 36

Table 2.2 Foundation dates of Greek colonies in Italy and Sicily	52
Table 3.1 Various founders of Rome in Festus, Plutarch and Dionysius	92
Table 3.2 Foundation dates of Rome	100
Table 4.1 The list of kings in the ancient sources	110
Table 4.2 The arrangement of centuries in the centuriate assembly	127
Table 5.1 Archaeological phases, late seventh to sixth century BC	156
Table 6.1 The Roman census figures from the monarchy and early Republic	211
Table 6.2 Roman exiles in the early Republic	234
Table 7.1 Patricians of presumed foreign origin	246
Table 8.1 Latin colonies in the early Republic	289
Table 9.1 Roman voting tribes	314
Table 9.2 Roman treaties 390–264 BC	321
Table 10.1 Temple foundations attested by literary sources 509–264 BC	342

Preface and acknowledgements

This book has been long in the making, and I am grateful to the editor of the series and the publisher for their enduring patience and faith that the book would finally materialise. In joining the other volumes of this series, I hope that their authors had not completely despaired of the first volume ever appearing! The early stages of research were conducted whilst I held a Visiting Fellowship in the Institute of Classical Studies Library. The School of History, Archaeology and Religion at Cardiff University aided the production of the book through providing research leave in 2015–16, when much of the research and writing was done. I would also like to thank my colleagues in the Ancient History department for creating a supportive and congenial environment in which to work on the project.

Work on the book has been encouraged and influenced by conversations with many friends and colleagues in academia, and invitations to try out sections of the work in various fora: I'd particularly like to thank Jeremy Armstrong, Ed Bispham, Corey Brennan, Gabriele Cifani, Emma Dench, Gary Farney, Rebecca Flemming, Elena Isayev, Luuk de Ligt, Kathryn Lomas, Oliva Menozzi, Jeremia Pelgrom, Louis Rawlings, James Richardson, Corinna Riva, Roman Roth, Celia Schultz, Tesse Stek, Nicola Terrenato, Alex Thein, James Whitley, and my research students working on related topics, David Colwill, Joshua Hall, Daniel Morgan, Chiara Strazzulla and Alun Williams. John Richardson, the series editor, provided valuable comments on the full typescript which have greatly improved it, and has handled a delinquent contributor with admirable humour and patience. I also want to express my thanks to Carol MacDonald and the team at Edinburgh University Press, who have made publishing with them a very positive experience, and to Jane Burkowski for meticulous copyediting. The drawings have been produced by the illustration team in the School of History, Archaeology and Religion at Cardiff University, Kirsty Harding, Ian Dennis and Howard Mason. Kirsty in particular has been largely responsible for the figures and maps, producing excellent work under very tight deadlines and coping expertly with my complex requests.

My interest in this subject was first stimulated by the teaching of Tim Cornell, one of a stellar group of tutors that I was lucky to have overseeing my undergraduate and postgraduate education at UCL. In particular, Tim's brilliant third-year classes on early Rome introduced me to the fascinating nature of this topic, and I hope to convey some of that fascination in what follows. Michael Crawford taught me to appreciate that the history of Rome is also the history of Italy, both in classes and through eye-opening (and occasionally hair-raising) trips all over central Italy. John North was an inspirational lecturer and constructively critical reader of my work as a postgraduate student. Riet van Bremen was the key influence in encouraging me to follow postgraduate studies, and has provided friendly support during and after my time at UCL.

I also owe an enormous debt of gratitude to Christopher Smith, whose encouragement and wise counsel have been fundamental to finishing this project. Christopher read the full manuscript at short notice and provided detailed input just when I needed it. His mastery of the subject has meant that many of his penetrating observations remain unanswered, but the book is undoubtedly much the better for his input. Finally, my wife Fay Glinister has put her work aside to help with the book at more vital moments than I care to remember, bringing her profound knowledge of the topic to bear on many different points. She will be more pleased than anyone that the project is finally complete. Naturally, none of the above should be supposed to agree with any of the views expressed here, and given the nature of studying early Rome may in fact strongly disagree! All errors that remain are mine alone.

Series editor's preface

Rome, the city and its empire, stands at the centre of the history of Europe, of the Mediterranean and of lands which we now call the Middle East. Its influence through the ages which followed its transformation into the Byzantine Empire down to modern times can be seen across the world. This series is designed to present for students and all who are interested in the history of Western civilisation the changing shape of the entity that was Rome, through its earliest years, the development and extension of the Republic, the shift into the Augustan empire, the development of the imperial state which grew from that, and the differing patterns of that state which emerged in East and West in the fourth to sixth centuries. It covers not only the political and military history of that shifting and complex society but also the contributions of the economic and social history of the Roman world to that change and growth and the intellectual contexts of these developments. The team of contributors, all scholars at the forefront of research in archaeology and history in the English-speaking world, present in the eight volumes of the series an accessible and challenging account of Rome across a millennium and a half of its expansion and transformation. Each book stands on its own as a picture of the period it covers and together the series aims to answer the fundamental question: what was Rome, and how did a small city in central Italy become one of the most powerful and significant entities in the history of the world?

John Richardson, General Editor

Abbreviations

Abbreviation of primary sources follows the *Oxford Classical Dictionary*, 4th edition.

CIL   *Corpus inscriptionum Latinarum*
FGrH Jacoby, F. (ed.) 1923–, *Die Fragmente der griechischen Historiker*, Berlin: Weidmann
FRH   Cornell, T. J. (ed.) 2013, *The Fragments of the Roman Historians*, 3 vols, Oxford: Oxford University Press
GRT   Cristofani, M. (ed.) 1990, *La grande Roma dei Tarquini*, Rome: 'L'Erma' di Bretschneider
ILLRP Degrassi, A. (ed.) 1957–65, *Inscriptiones Latinae liberae rei publicae*, Florence: La Nuova Italia
ILS   Dessau, H. (ed.) 1892–1916, *Inscriptiones Latinae selectae*, Berlin: Weidmann
TLE   Pallottino, M. 1968, *Testimonia linguae Etruscae*, 2nd edn, Florence: La Nuova Italia

Translations follow the Loeb Classical Library editions, with minor adaptations, except where stated.

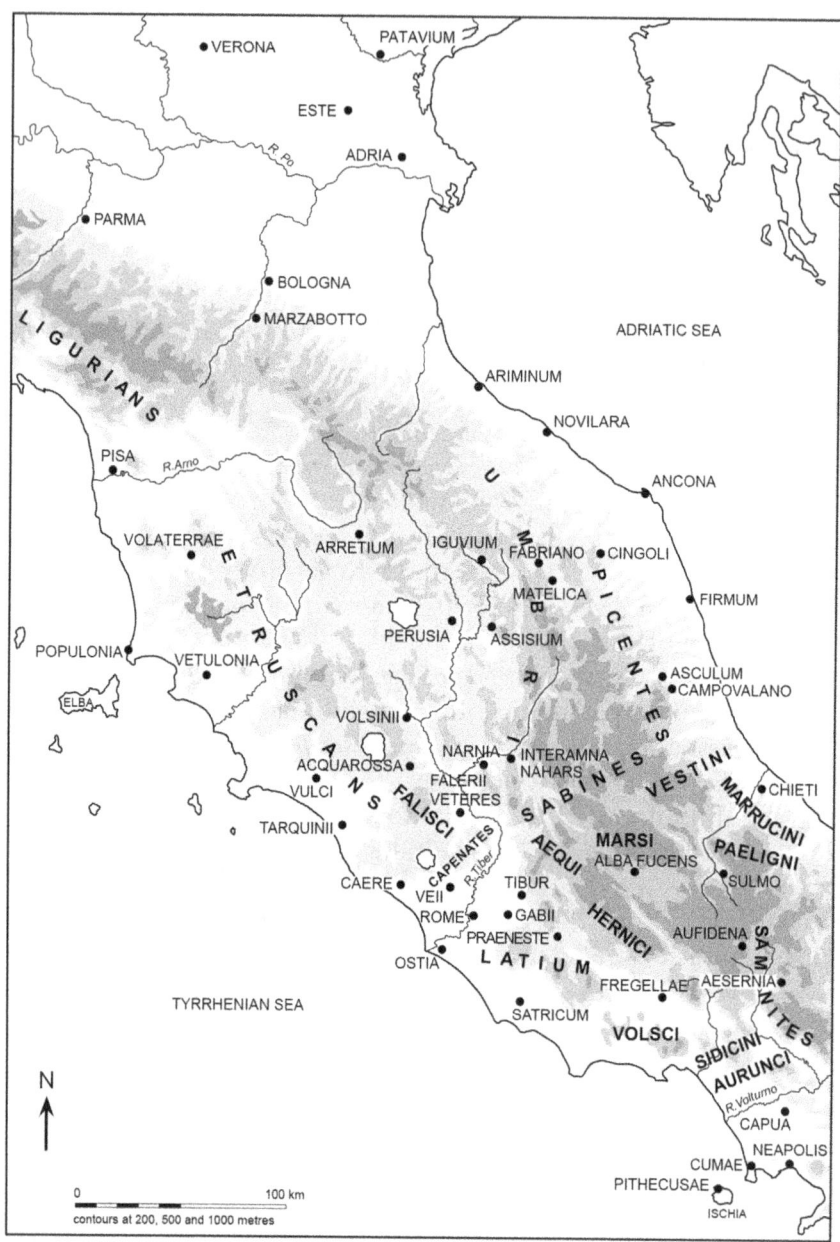

Map 1 Map of central Italy (drawing: I. Dennis)

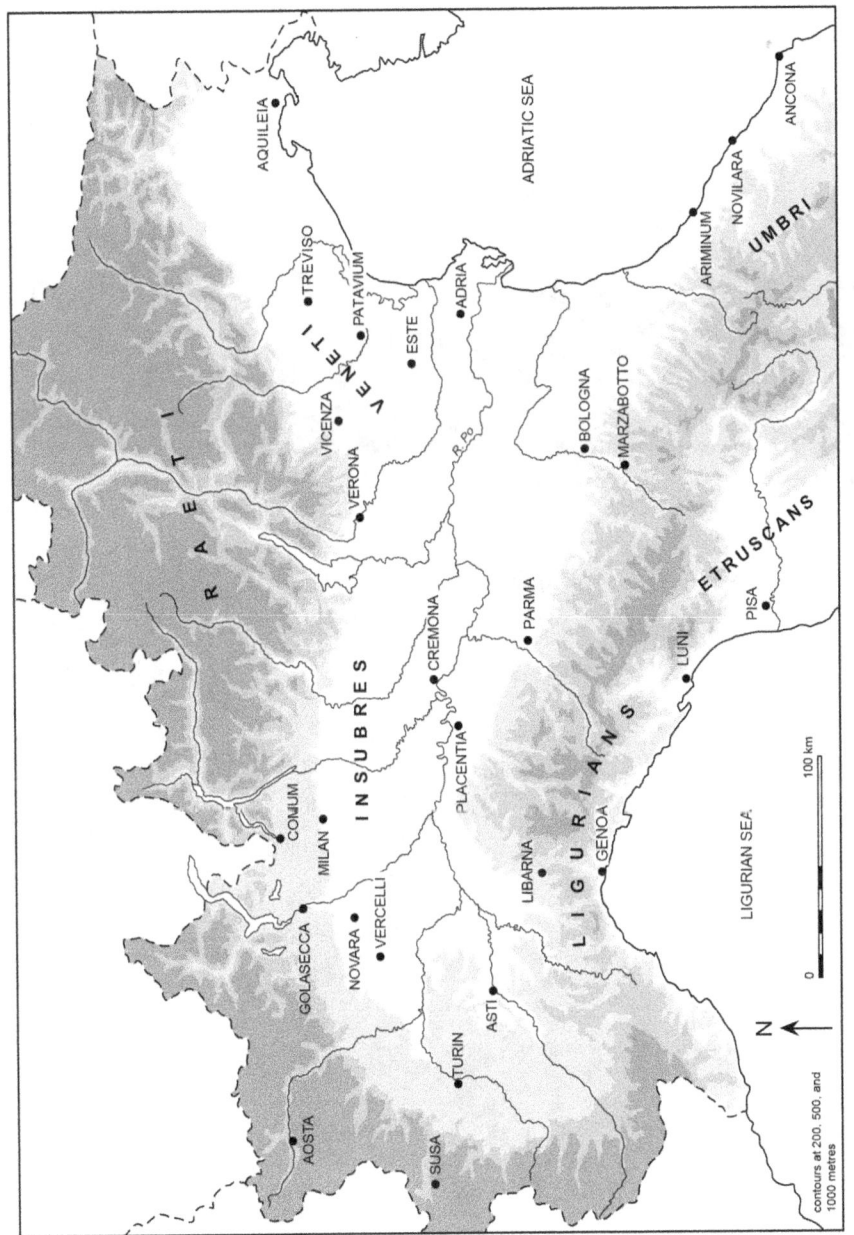

Map 2 Map of northern Italy (drawing: I. Dennis)

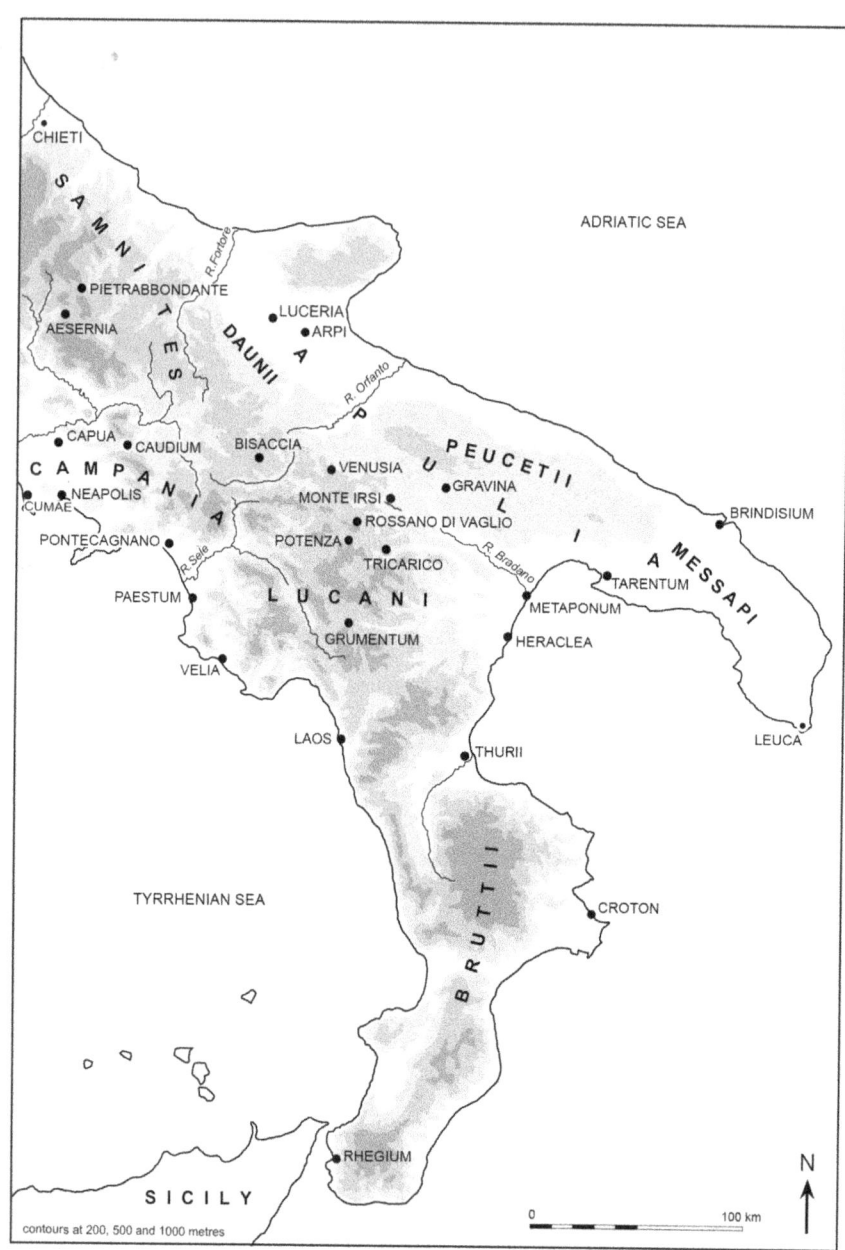

Map 3 Map of south Italy (drawing: I. Dennis)

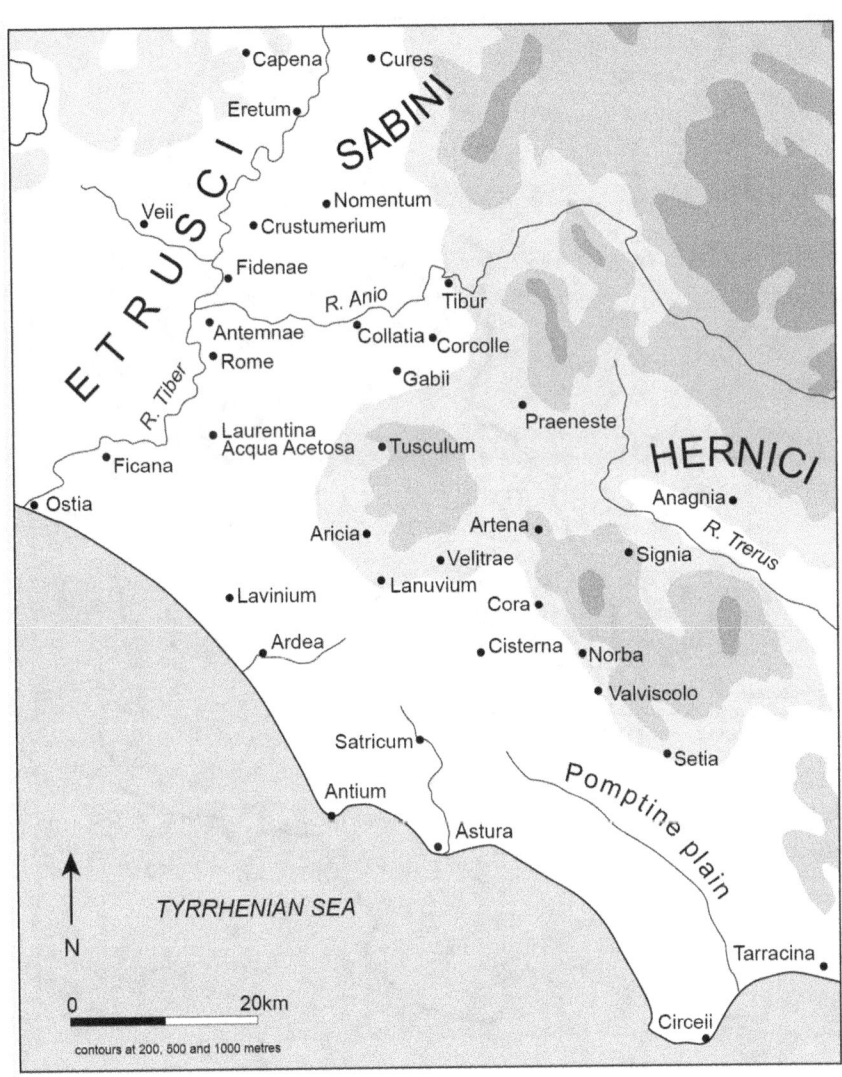

Map 4 Map of south Etruria and Latium (drawing: K. Harding)

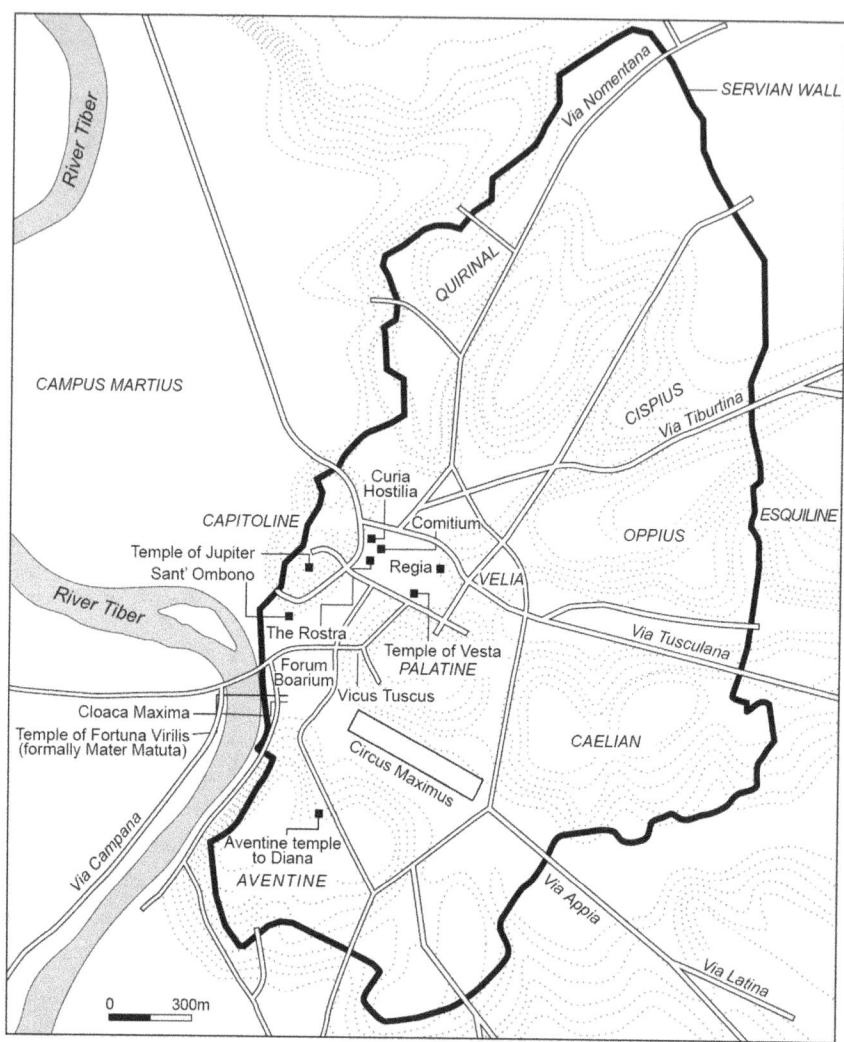

Map 5 Map of Rome (drawing: K. Harding)

CHAPTER 1

Sources and approaches

Introduction

Ancient Rome has left an indelible mark on our world, and historians of antiquity have an obligation to tackle its earliest phases, from the foundation down to the middle Republic. This is without doubt a formative phase of Roman history, when most of Rome's characteristic features in politics, imperialism, social structures and religion, to name but a few areas, appeared or were created.

Early Roman history remains a challenging topic to study. The wide range of previous approaches are a product of the uncertainties of the evidence, and a series of well-rehearsed problems are often seen as insurmountable obstacles to a rigorous history of the period. There is an enormous gap in time between the extant literary sources, notably our key source, Livy, writing in the late first century BC, and the events of *c.*750–290 BC. The historical tradition that preceded Livy and other late Republican writers is of uncertain quality, although we know that it dates back to at least 200 BC, and that some historical details were recorded as early as the sixth century BC. We are poorly informed on how the information used by our sources was preserved, and can be sure that much was rendered in the malleable forms of oral tradition. Furthermore, ancient authors, although ostensibly concerned with getting at the truth of events, were prone to anachronism in their handling of earlier history. They lacked the conceptual toolkit and the emphasis on distance that characterise the modern practice of history, and actively sought legitimation from their understanding of their distant past. This led to potential distortion of the information they conveyed. As a result, despite centuries of debate, even fundamental parts of the information preserved in literary sources, such as the fall of the monarchy at Rome, remain disconcertingly uncertain.

Previous scholarly approaches to early Rome are myriad, and a full discussion of its historiography is well beyond the scope of this book.[1] But it is worth drawing attention to two features of this debate: its antiquity, and its continuing focus on methodological questions. The study of early Rome stretches back beyond the two great German nineteenth-century historians Barthold Niebuhr and Theodore Mommsen, to eighteenth-century figures such as Louis de Beaufort, author of the 1738 work *Dissertation sur l'incertitude des cinq premiers siècles de l'histoire romaine* ('Dissertation on the Uncertainty of the First Five Centuries of Roman History').[2] The debate over the reliability of the literary sources has been long and heated. There have been many changing fashions, from the scepticism of De Beaufort, Niebuhr, Pais, and Alföldi, to the cautious optimism of De Sanctis and Momigliano.[3] In my view, the traditional, sterile, division between pessimists and optimists should be avoided as far as possible, given that the root lies in philosophical differences in individual historians' approaches to the evidence, and usually involves an almost dogmatic adherence to a particular view. In fact, all these approaches have something to offer the study of early Rome, whatever their outlook.

Furthermore, the impact of new archaeological material is now increasingly being felt, with many recent works making comprehensive use of it to provide new perspectives on early Rome.[4] Important research has also shed new light on the literary tradition, such as the project to compile the *Fragments of the Roman Historians* (*FRH* from here on). The increasing body of evidence available, literary and material, makes the study of early Roman history more important than ever. Integrating the study of the literary evidence with the archaeological material should thus be a key aim. As Michel Gras has put it, what counts is not the nature of the documentation utilised, but the rigour of the interpretation proposed.[5]

---

1. See, for instance, Bianchi, *Greci ed Etruschi*.
2. For useful discussions see Momigliano, 'Perizonius', 104–14; Richardson and Santangelo, 'Introduction', in Richardson and Santangelo (eds), *Roman Historical Tradition*, 1–5.
3. As Poucet, *Rois de Rome*, 18–20, points out, the terminology used by scholars to characterise their opponents in this debate (such as 'hyper-sceptical', or 'credulous') is often unfairly slanted.
4. E.g. Fulminante, *Urbanisation*, and Lomas, *Rise of Rome*, to cite just two recent works in English.
5. Gras, *Méditerranée archaïque*, 8, citing Lucian Febvre.

Collective memory and written records

As the historical accounts of early Rome date to centuries later than the events, the raw material for these histories would have had to have been preserved for hundreds of years. This length of time raises questions about how the information could be preserved and how accurate it is likely to be. There were three main conduits through which historical information on early Rome may have been preserved: family records, oral traditions and written documents. Assessing their nature is thus essential to understanding the reliability of the literary sources.

Family records

The keeping of family records was a vital activity for the aristocratic families that dominated the Republican political system. A family's prestige depended heavily on its past history and the achievements of its ancestral members. Having lineage connections with the great men of the past justified the domination of the state by the nobility and helped individuals win elections. We can see how these historical records were used in speeches and public displays at funerals from the famous description given by Polybius (6.53). It is clear that some written family records were available to historians from elite families such as Fabius Pictor, writing in the late third century BC. How reliable they were is open to question. According to Cicero, they encouraged distorted claims:

> Some of these funeral orations are extant, the families of the deceased having preserved them as trophies of honour and for use on the death of a member of the same family, whether to recall the memory of past glories of their house, or to support their own claims to noble origins. Yet by these laudatory speeches our history has become distorted; for much is set down in them which never occurred, false triumphs, too large a number of consulships, false relationships and transitions of patricians to plebeian status. (Cicero, *Brut.* 62)

Livy similarly reckoned that these records had had a negative influence, making it difficult to identify the real person responsible for a notable victory in 322 BC:

> It is not easy to choose between the facts or the authorities. The record has been falsified, I believe, by funeral eulogies and fictitious inscriptions on portrait busts, when families try to appropriate to

themselves the tradition of exploits and titles of office by means of inventions calculated to deceive. This has undoubtedly led to confusion both in individual achievements and in public records of events. (Livy, 8.40, trans. Radice)

It is worth remembering that as a 'new man' Cicero had an interest in denigrating noble family records, because such records were the source of aristocratic claims of legimacy.[6] By the Augustan era it seems that family histories had become obsolete as a source of historical information. This probably reflects their eclipse by literary history (most notably the publication of Livy's great work), and by antiquarian scholarship, with its implicit claims to being an authoritative source of information about the past. But it was also a consequence of the broader discrediting of the automatic right of Republican nobles to dominate high office that had resulted from the civil wars of the first century BC.[7]

Distortions probably were common in material originating from the great families, but their extent and exact nature – bias, 'spin' or straight falsehood – is ultimately unknowable. On the other hand, there are some more positive grounds to suggest that historians should not discard this material. For example, it is noteworthy that instances of different elite families claiming different (or the same) victories are rare. It also must have been difficult to invent wholesale new stories about episodes well known to fellow nobles and the wider Roman population of the day. The examples of funerary eulogies and tomb *elogia*, which must reflect the content of family histories, seem on the whole valid sources of information that might otherwise not have been preserved, allowing for the natural positivity of the genre.[8]

Oral traditions and collective memory

Oral traditions, or collective memory, are the second means by which information might have come down to the historians of the last two centuries BC. Cato in the *Origines* (cited by Cicero, *Brut.* 75) referred to songs performed at banquets which celebrated the deeds of the

---

6. Blösel, 'Geschichte'.
7. On antiquarianism see Wallace-Hadrill, 'Mutatas formas'; Glinister, 'Constructing the past'.
8. E.g. the eulogy of Lucius Metellus preserved by Pliny, *HN* 7.139–40 (discussed in Chapter 10).

great figures of the past. However, he does not say that this was a living tradition in his day (the early second century BC); the custom seems to have been confined to the archaic period, as part of the 'symposium culture' of that era.[9] Nevertheless, Habinek has made the case for a rich Roman tradition of song, associated particularly with convivial contexts, predating the Hellenisation of the second century BC.[10] There are traces of more public performances of such celebratory songs in other contexts, particularly in association with festivals and sacrifices. Dionysius of Halicarnassus mentions Faunus, Romulus and Remus, and Coriolanus as subjects, and claims that they continued to his own day.[11] Cicero (*Tusc.* 4.4) notes that the XII Tables prohibited invective-laden songs that harmed other citizens (450 BC), and the philosopher Panaetius commended a Pythagorean song of Appius Claudius Caecus, perhaps from the early third century BC. Oral traditions about historical figures and events may also have found their way into dramatic productions. We know of about fifteen plays on historical themes, called *fabulae praetextae*, six of which relate to the regal or early Republican periods.[12] Although they were written in the third or second centuries BC, Peter Wiseman has made a strong case that dramatic performances based on historical episodes are very likely to have informed the Roman tradition from an early date.[13] Drama at Rome is known to have dated back at least as far as the fourth century BC.

The reliability of oral tradition as a conduit for historical information is notoriously questionable. Critics point to examples like Homer's epics on the Trojan War and to anthropological studies of oral poetic composition.[14] As in archaic Greece, 'collective memory' at Rome was very rich and long-lasting, given the city's (largely) unbroken history of successful expansion.[15] The complexity of the ways that collective memory was constructed has been highlighted in recent approaches. These include not only written history and the retelling of historical events in plays and banquet songs, but also the customs and habits

---

9. Symposium culture: Zorzetti, 'Carmina convivalia'; Wiseman, 'Prehistory', 236.
10. Habinek, *World of Roman Song*, especially 269 n. 19.
11. Dion. Hal. 1.31.2, 1.79.11, 8.62.3, with Wiseman, 'Prehistory', 236; Habinek, *World of Roman Song*, 76; cf. Cornell, 'Coriolanus', 73–97.
12. Oakley, *Commentary*, IV 478.
13. Wiseman, *Roman Drama*; Flower, '*Fabulae praetextae*', for a more sceptical view.
14. Oakley, *Commentary*, I 22–4, IV 478–9.
15. Discussion in Gallia, *Remembering*.

governing everyday behaviour, the Roman *habitus*.[16] This included Roman reverence for *mos maiorum*, 'ancestral custom', as well as the way that the city of Rome itself came to serve as a kind of national 'museum'. A typical breakdown of the Roman *habitus* might thus cover community and clan records, the conservatism of institutions and rituals, stories and festivals, and monuments and statuary (stories in stone, if you like). At Rome the physical space of the city, as well as its political life and sacred and profane rituals, provided constant reminders of the archaic past. Archaic monuments – such as the Capitoline temple – dominated the city until the first century BC.[17]

The coherence of the surviving written histories suggests that a common tradition about the Roman past had built up before the first Roman historian, Fabius Pictor, came to write his work. This tradition was sustained by the proliferation of monuments, trophies and other physical memory aids such as paintings and object iconography, and by the regular memorialising of past events in the form of funerary processions and speeches, or annual rituals marking significant religious events such as temple foundations. Flower argues that a 'rich memory world' was fundamental to Roman self-identity throughout the Republic, and that the commemoration of history in literary form was a late and contingent development.[18] Written and oral forms of memory sustained and fed into one another.[19] The separation of 'literary' and 'oral' traditions as reliable versus unreliable forms of preservation of ideas about the past is therefore somewhat crude and artificial. We need to think more imaginatively about the Roman construction of the past (a process that was ongoing for most of Roman history).[20]

It is worth reflecting here on the cultural context of Rome as an emerging state within the ancient Mediterranean. Neighbouring cities and peoples had their own historical traditions in the form of family records (exemplified by the *Elogia Tarquiniensia*, imperial inscriptions commemorating the Etruscan Spurinna family at Tarquinii), lists of eponymous magistrates (evident in Etruscan, Campanian, Samnite, Lucanian, Umbrian and Greek communities), and literary history

---

16. A concept coined by the French sociologist P. Bourdieu: see *Outline*, especially 78–87.
17. Cornell, 'Formation'.
18. Flower, 'Alternatives', especially 69–70; cf. Purcell, 'Becoming historical', 17; Feeney, 'The beginnings of a literature in Latin', 229–31.
19. Thomas, *Oral Tradition and Written Record*, ch. 1.
20. Habinek, *Politics*, 36–7.

(Etruscan, Greek and perhaps also Oscan, Sabine and Venetic).[21] All these traditions are now lost, with only brief references to them preserved. But as Bourdin points out, they demonstrate that 'the Roman historical tradition was not an isolated phenomenon'.[22] More widely, Romans would certainly have been well aware of ancient societies with much deeper collective memories in the Near East and in Egypt from at least the late fourth century, and may even have been reading about their history from the fifth century BC in Greek authors such as Herodotus.[23] It is intriguing to reflect that in fixing the foundation date of their city at 753 BC (or thereabouts), Roman authors must have been well aware of the comparative 'youth' that this lent their city, in comparison with other central Italian societies and the renowned antiquity and extraordinarily deep 'memory worlds' of more distant lands such as Egypt.[24]

The broader context for Roman history is also evident through the echoes in Roman history of episodes from other Mediterranean societies. Many scholars have pointed out parallels between Roman and Near Eastern or Greek history at this time.[25] There are many examples, such as the analogies between the story of Romulus and Remus and those of other ancient Mediterranean founder figures. Perhaps the most famous instance is the story of Sextus Tarquinius and the poppies. The Roman king Tarquinius Superbus instructed his son Sextus on how to deal with the nobility of the city of Gabii (where Sextus was living in pretended exile) by cutting off the heads of the tallest poppies, a coded message sent through an uncomprehending intermediary (Livy, 1.54, Dion. Hal. 4.56). This story is nearly identical to that of Periander, the tyrant of Corinth, who according to Herodotus (5.92–3) received a similar message from Thrasybulus of Miletus.

It is clear that many episodes in early Roman history, especially from the regal period, have been affected by these borrowings: stories of kingship and tyranny, of figures destined for future greatness, and of divine retribution for betrayal.[26] Until recently scholars tended to attribute the existence of these parallels to the earlier Roman annalists,

---

21. Bourdin, *Peuples*, 23–4, with references.
22. Bourdin, *Peuples*, 23.
23. Purcell, 'Becoming historical', 26.
24. See Cornell, 'Livy's narrative', 251 for the Romans trying to match the foundation date with the canonical king list.
25. Oakley, *Commentary*, I 85–8; Scapini, 'Literary archetypes', with earlier references.
26. Scapini, 'Literary archetypes'.

particularly Fabius Pictor, straightforwardly copying Greek histories as a way of filling in the bare bones of the sketchy information on Rome provided by ancient documents. However, it is now apparent that many of these stories are more ancient than that, and may in fact be shared at a deeper folktale level: Cornell has argued, for instance, that the parallels between Romulus and a wide variety of founder stories from the ancient world reflect similar ways in which societies independently came to terms with their origins.[27] It is also often difficult to tell apart the copying of a story from the contemporary replication of similar traits amongst well-connected Mediterranean societies. Tales about the tyrannical nature of the last Roman kings may be similar to contemporary Greek tyrants because these rulers shared many traits in reality, and 'structural similarities' produced 'convergent development' of the two areas.

Literacy and written documents

Written documents are the most important of the three means of preserving historical facts in the period before Fabius Pictor. Documentary evidence clearly lies behind the repetitive list-type entries for each year which are a regular feature of the 'annalistic' histories of the Republic.[28] Its presence can also be detected in the regal period, from when various treaties and other epigraphic documents are reported by our sources, or in a few cases actually still exist. Their existence is not surprising, given that Rome was a state with a record-keeping habit from at least the sixth century BC, even if only a tiny proportion of the material survives.[29] Traces of this habit include the archaic calendar, the *Annales Maximi* (discussed below), and various archaic laws and ritual regulations. Many such documents were recorded by Roman historians, including the following:[30]

1. The inscription(s) of the Volcanal (i.e. the Lapis Niger, referred to as an inscription by ancient sources: Dion. Hal. 2.54.2; Plut. *Rom*. 24.3), early sixth century BC.
2. Bronze law from the temple of Diana on the Aventine (Dion. Hal. 4.26.5; perhaps also Fest. 164 L), sixth century BC.

---

27. Cornell, 'The foundation of Rome'.
28. Lendon, 'Historians without history'.
29. Habinek, *Politics*, 37; Coarelli, *Le origini di Roma*, 43.
30. This list is taken from Ampolo, C. 1983, 'La storiografia', 15–16, with additions.

3. Treaty with Gabii on the skin covering of a wooden shield in the temple of Dius Fidius, late sixth century BC (Dion. Hal. 4.58.4; Hor. *Epist.* 2.1.25–6; Fest. 48 L.).
4. Rome–Carthage treaty preserved in the *Aerarium* (Treasury) of the aediles near the Capitoline temple, late sixth century BC (Polyb. 3.22–6).
5. Cassian Treaty with the Latins on a bronze column, seen also by Cicero behind the Rostra, of 493 BC (Cic. *Balb.* 23.53; Livy, 2.33.9; cf. Dion. Hal. 6.95; Livy, 2.22; Fest. 276 L.).
6. *Lex Icilia de Aventino publicando*, on a bronze column in the temple of Aventine Diana, 456 BC, which 'regulated private settlement on Aventine hill' (Dion. Hal. 10.32.4).[31]
7. *Foedus Ardeatinum*, mentioned by the historian Licinius Macer (fr. 13 ap. Livy, 4.7.10; Dion. Hal. 11.62) of 444 BC.
8. Inscription on the linen corselet of Tolumnius dedicated in the temple of Jupiter Feretrius by A. Cornelius Cossus, allegedly read by Augustus (Livy, 4.20.7; Prop. 4.10), going back to 437, 428 or 426 BC.
9. The *lex Furia-Pinaria* of 472 or 432 BC concerning intercalation (correction of the calendar), on a bronze column (Varro, *Ant. hum.* 16 fr. 5 ap. Macrob. *Sat.* 1.13.21).
10. *Lex vetusta ... priscis literis verbisque scripta* ('an ancient law written in early letters and words') relating to the praetor maximus (Livy, 7.3.5, drawing on the antiquarian writer Cincius).
11. The inscription *ex Cassia familia datum* ('gift of the Cassian family') on a statue consecrated to Ceres, erected from the proceeds of goods confiscated from Sp. Cassius, 485 BC (Livy, 2.41.10).
12. List of Latin peoples who were accustomed to share in the meat from the sacrifice at the *Feriae Latinae* (Pliny, *HN* 3.68–9).
13. Dedication at Aricia by Egerius Baebius (Cato, *FRH* F36 a and b).
14. The laws of the XII Tables: 'After the legislation they had undertaken had been concluded, the consuls engraved the laws on twelve bronze tablets and affixed them to the Rostra before the Senate house. And the legislation as it was drawn up, since it is couched in such brief and pithy language, has continued to be admired by men down to our own day' (Diod. Sic. 12.26; cf. Livy, 3.34).

---

31. Forysthe, *Critical History*, 72.

These references show that our sources were aware of ancient documents which survived from the sixth century BC onwards. This type of material is likely to have been difficult to understand (as in the case of the Lapis Niger monument, whose significance was lost on our sources, and the Rome–Carthage treaty, which Polybius notes was challenging to read).[32] Nevertheless, in principle, documentary information clearly could and did survive for the historians of the late Republic to see (sometimes) and use. From the early Republic onwards bald reports of factual items that appear to derive from documentary sources, such as the following example from Livy, begin to appear:

> The same year [495 BC] the colony of Signia, which the king Tarquinius had founded was supplemented with new colonists and established for the second time. At Rome twenty-one tribes were formed. The temple of Mercury was dedicated on 15 May. (Livy, 2.21.7)

These brief notices are sparse at first, but become more extensive as time goes on.

A surprisingly wide range of documents underlie the detailed information conveyed about each year for the Republic in Livy and in other accounts, but two sources stand out. The first is the *Fasti*, lists of consuls and triumphs. This information is listed under each year of the Republic in Livy and Dionysius, beginning with the consuls. There is an inscribed copy of the list of consuls and of the list of triumphators from the Forum in the Augustan era, which largely agrees with the lists in our literary sources. Although some writers have doubted their authenticity, most scholars now accept that the lists are for the most part genuine.[33]

The second critical documentary source for Roman history is the priestly record known as the *Annales Maximi* (or *Annales Pontificorum*). These records are referred to quite commonly by Roman sources. The clearest references are:

> a) Servius Danielis, *Aen*. 1.373: *Annales* were compiled in the following way. Every year, the Pontifex Maximus had a whitewashed tablet, on which, with the names of the consuls and the other magistrates

---

32. Forysthe, *Critical History*, 74; Polybius, 3.26 on the Rome–Carthage treaty.
33. Their authenticity is fully discussed by Cornell, *Beginnings*, 13–15, 218–23 and Forsythe, *Critical History*, 155–7; doubts expressed by Wiseman, 'Prehistory', 235; Richardson, 'The Roman Nobility'.

written first, he was accustomed to note the things worthy of mention which had been done at home and abroad, by land and sea, day by day. Thanks to his diligence men of a former time put the annual records into eighty books, and they called them the *Annales Maximi* from the *Pontifices Maximi* by whom they were composed.

b) Cicero, *Orat.* 2.52: The Greeks used once to write history as did Cato, Pictor or Piso among us: for their history was no more than the compilation of annals, for the sake of which, and to maintain a public record, from the beginning of Roman history until Publius Mucius was Pontifex Maximus [*c.*133–114 BC], the Pontifex Maximus used to commit to writing all the events of each year, copy them out on a white board, and display the tablet at his home, to enable the people to get informed; and even now these are called *Annales Maximi*. (Trans. Cornell)

So according to Cicero they covered a timescale that ran from the beginning of Roman history down to the late second century BC. Servius records the publication of the *Annales* in eighty books. Beyond this, much remains obscure. The date of publication has been proposed as the pontificate of Mucius Scaevola (130–*c.*115 BC), or under Augustus;[34] but other periods are possible, given that the annals seem to have influenced early historians like Fabius Pictor.[35]

[Atticus speaking] For after the annals of the Pontifices Maximi (*post annales pontificum maximorum*), than which nothing could be more arid, when you come to Fabius, or to Cato, whose name is constantly on your lips, or to Piso, Fannius, or Vennonius, although one of these might have more vigour than another, yet what could be as thin as the whole lot of them? (Cic. *Leg.* 1.6) (see further below)

The nature of the record in its published form is also controversial. Most ancient authors regard it as bald, unelaborated reportage of events (e.g. Gellius, *NA* 5.18.8–9; Cato, *FRH* T1; Cicero above: 'thin'). However, the need for eighty books for the period 753–133/114 BC implies a surprising level of detail.[36] The starting

---

34. Scaevola: Mommsen, *History of Rome*, 469; Augustus: Frier, *Libri annales*, 179–200; Rich, 'Annales Maximi', 151–6.
35. That the *Annales* were a fundamental source for early history is also implied by Dion. Hal. 1.73.1: 'each of their historians has taken something out of ancient accounts that are preserved on sacred tablets', and by Gellius, *NA* 5.18.8–9, Cicero, *Orat.* 2.52 and *Leg* 1.6.
36. Cf. Livy's sixty-one books for this period, although it should be noted that there was no standard ancient book length.

point is another problem. Ostensibly the *Annales* went back to the beginning of Roman history, as Cicero asserts above. There seem to have been four books on the mythical Alban dynasty and the period before Romulus.[37] This raises the question of how genuine the information conveyed was. The office of Pontifex Maximus is certainly very ancient, so this provides no obstacle to the records stretching back early in time. But the presence of information about the mythical prehistory of the city must mean that extraneous material was invented and added at some point. This sort of uninhibited 'tidying up' of ancient documents is quite typical of the ancient world.[38]

The question then becomes one of when the information can be trusted as genuine. Some scholars assert that the genuine part of the record was mid Republican at the earliest. It was commonly believed that most such documents had perished in the Gallic sack in 390 BC, based on comments in Livy (6.1.2), but there are good reasons for believing some fifth-century notices to be genuine. It is likely, for instance, that an eclipse around 400 BC was recorded in the *Annales* (Cic. *Rep.* 1.25 = *FRH*, *Annales Maximi* F5). Most authors assume it is early Republican rather than regal in origin.[39] But there is no practical obstacle to thinking that the source could predate the fifth century, and the presence of accurate records about new tribal designations and about monarchic temple foundations make it possible that such records were kept earlier.[40] The sophisticated nature of Rome by the sixth century BC certainly encourages the idea that record-keeping would have been something that its rulers and others looked to undertake.

Judging by our surviving histories, the records included all sorts of important public events both at home and abroad.[41] There would also have been material of religious significance, such as the foundation of temples, the occurrence of prodigies and omens (such as the eclipse mentioned above), and the death and subsequent replacement of priests. In fact, the Roman mentality that all major civic initiatives and decisions needed divine approval meant that pretty

---

37. *FRH*, *Annales Maximi* F1–3. There were records in the original tablets about the foundation of the city (Dion. Hal. 1.74.3 = *FRH* T5), presumably invented.
38. Oakley, *Commentary*, I 97–8, citing invented documents referred to by annalists.
39. Rich, 'Annales Maximi', 149.
40. See Livy, 2.8.6–9 on the dedication of the Capitoline temple (509 BC), and 2.21.7 (495 BC), cited above.
41. See below for a list of likely types of information.

much everything entered within the Pontifex Maximus' purview. Again, judging at second hand through our sources, the quantity of documentary evidence that the *Annales* provided is fairly sparse in the fifth century, but it increases notably in the fourth century until by the latter part of this century there is a considerable amount for each year. This suggests that the record-keeping habit developed over time, and presumably some *Pontifices* were more diligent than others.[42]

Besides the *Fasti* and the *Annales Maximi*, other types of written records were also available, and must have influenced the historical record. As we have seen, the Roman state kept records of treaties going back into the regal period, of which various examples survived inscribed on bronze or written on materials such as textiles (noted above; the *liber linteus* is a surviving example of a textile base, though from an Etruscan context). The calendar, in its pre-Julian form, preserved a great deal of ancient religious information, including the days of the foundation of temples, the holding of festivals, and the *dies atri*, 'black days', on which disastrous events had occurred. The priestly college of the augurs kept *commentarii* (records) of its individual seats and who filled them. The extension of these records to other colleges of priests, such as the *pontifices*, is uncertain but probable. How ancient such records were is debated, but a fifth-century date seems likely for the records of the augurs.[43] In addition, records of the decrees of the Senate are attested as having been kept from 449 BC by the aediles in the temple of Ceres (Livy, 3.55.13). Records of the Roman census were, according to Dionysius, held by individuals in the censors' families, and could be consulted (Dion. Hal. 1.74.5). Finally, Livy refers to mysterious 'ancient annals and the books of the magistrates, made from linen and deposited in the temple of Moneta, cited by Licinius Macer'.[44] The contribution to the mix of all these sources is uncertain, and probably unrecoverable; but it is worth noting the variety of possible records that we know about; probably many other categories of records are unattested. It is likely that all of these contributed at some point to the Roman 'memory world', even if it is impossible to reconstruct the way that this worked.

---

42. Rich, 'Annales Maximi', 144–9.
43. See Livy, 3.7.6, 3.32.3 for the death notices of augurs and other priests in the context of plagues (Vaahtera, 'Livy and the priestly records'); Rüpke, *Fasti Sacerdotum*, 27–30 provides a more negative assessment.
44. Livy, 4.7.11–12; 4.13.7; 4.20.8; 4.23.1; Dion. Hal. 11.62.3. Oakley, *Commentary*, I 27–8.

Ultimately the importance of these types of records is clear because of the documentary basis of the historical record evident through the Republican period. This provides an enormous quantity of routine information that makes up a significant part of the story of each year in Livy's account, providing a chronological framework for the more elaborated stories that Livy inserts into it. The following types of information in Livy (and when they begin to be recorded) have been identified by Oakley as coming from archival sources:[45]

Magistrates:
- Consuls (from 509 BC).
- Consular tribunes (from 444 BC).
- Dictators (Oakley provides a list 'arbitrarily' from 420, but they are attested from the early fifth century).
- *Magistri equitum* (from 389 BC).
- *Interreges* (Republican examples from 482 BC).
- Censors (from 443 BC).
- Praetors (from 366 BC, selectively; elections first reported in book 10).
- Aediles (from 454 BC).
- Minor magistracies: *iiviri* (from 467 BC); *vviri* to assess debt (352 BC); *iivir navalis* (310/309 BC).
- Prorogations (from 327 BC).
- Augurs (from 463 BC).
- Tribunes (from 495 BC).
- Legates (from 499 BC).
- Generals who have triumphed (from start of Republic).

General 'annalistic' notices:
- Routine civic business.
- President of consular elections.
- Shortages of food and *pestilentiae* (from 496 BC).[46]
- *Lectisternia* (from 399 BC).
- Consultation of Sibylline books.
- Votive games.
- *Supplicationes* (from 449 BC).

---

45. Oakley, *Commentary*, I 38–72 (with full lists of many of these); cf. Cornell, *Beginnings*, 12–16; Lendon, 'Historians without history', 49. For a contrasting view, see Wiseman, *Unwritten Rome*, 14–15.
46. Accepted as authentic by Garnsey, *Famine and Food Supply*, 167ff.

- Prodigies (from 461 BC).
- Vowing and dedication of temples (from 509 BC).
- Creation of all new tribes (from 495 BC).
- Foundation of colonies.[47]
- Grants of citizenship.
- Military information, e.g. *deditiones*, number of enemy killed, standards captured, prisoners taken, legions numbered (common from book 10).
- Obscure place names (from 469 BC, though more common in books 9–10).
- Consular provinces.

Oakley observes that there is clearly much official information available to annalists for the period 509–292 BC; this information increases in quantity over the first decade of Livy, and particularly deepens in the period of book 10 (303–293 BC); Livy is selective in his use of it.[48] Much of this information goes back to the fifth century BC. Some of this type of information was probably recorded for the regal period (temples, *interreges*, triumphs, colonies, perhaps priests), although Livy's extreme compression of the regal narrative makes this uncertain. Some of the fifth-century information is demonstrably authentic (consuls, augurs, food shortages, temples, religious notices such as *supplicationes*, new tribes, colonies and obscure place names). A minority of items are problematic (such as early fifth-century tribunes, legates, dictators and triumphs; later fourth-century consular provinces). Some aspects are difficult to judge one way or another, but the authenticity of the solid information supports the credibility of the rest. This core of largely reliable material thus provided the accepted framework for the Roman historical tradition, and helped to explain the presence of some variants. There is a surprising level of unanimity amongst our sources.

Early historians (Greek and Roman)

The development of a literary tradition of history and other historical genres of literature (historical poetry, historical drama) at Rome comes relatively late, in the third century BC. This is often regarded as a fatal hindrance for reconstructing early Roman history. But the

---

47. Livy details many colonies, although he omits Saticula, founded in 313 BC, known from other sources.
48. Oakley, *Commentary*, I 38–9, 72.

situation is complex. First, it is important to remember, as Purcell and Flower have recently reminded us, that there was a rich Roman memory world beyond written histories.[49] It is very difficult to appreciate the depth of material making this up, given its almost complete loss. Written history, a late and contingent development, was perhaps never central to Roman collective memory; but it should not be regarded in artificial isolation from the broader world of Roman memory of which it formed a part.

Secondly, historical works on Rome have a very ancient past. The first historians to write about Rome and Italy were Greek. Their works largely survive as fragments, parts of their text cited by later, surviving writers.[50] The story of Evander, who in later versions settled on the site of Rome, was mentioned by the poet Stesichorus from Sicily in the early sixth century. The foundation of Rome was discussed by Greek writers from the fifth century BC, including the historians Hecataeus of Miletus and Hellanicus of Lesbos. In the fourth century we know that aspects such as the foundation of the city and the Gallic sack were covered by Heraclides of Pontus, Aristotle, Alcimus of Sicily and Theophrastus, and the Roman victory at Sentinum in 295 BC was noted by the contemporary Duris of Samos.[51] It is also quite likely that Greek references to 'Tyrsenoi' or 'Tyrrhenoi' in early Greek sources include references to Rome as a city of the Tyrrhenian seaboard.[52] But it is not until the early third century that Roman history received a more comprehensive treatment, as the completion of Rome's control over the whole peninsula and the defeat of the powerful Hellenistic Greek king Pyrrhus meant that histories of the western Greeks came to include that of Rome. Hieronymus of Cardia and Timaeus are both known to have covered Rome in their broader histories, and Timaeus was described by Gellius as writing 'about the affairs of the Roman people'.[53] We know that Timaeus linked the foundation of Rome to Carthage, and used local sources to discuss details of rituals in Rome and Lavinium.[54]

---

49. Flower, 'Alternatives'; Purcell, 'Becoming historical'; Oakley, *Commentary*, I 22–4, IV 478–9; Habinek, *Politics*, 35 on Rome's 'culture of verbal performance'.
50. Wiseman, 'Prehistory', 231–42.
51. Note also Cleitarchus (ap. Pliny, *HN* 3.57) on a Roman embassy to Alexander; see further, Chapter 10.
52. Dion. Hal. 1.25.5, 1.29.1–2 for the Greek conflation of Tyrrhenian seaboard dwellers under the name; see further Chapter 6 on seafaring, below.
53. Dion. Hal. 1.5.6; Gellius, *NA* 11.1.1.
54. Timaeus frr. 36, 59, 60, 61 Jacoby; Baron, *Timaeus*, 45. Purcell, 'Becoming historical', 29, reporting that Timaeus linked the foundation of Rome to Carthage as part of a scheme developed by Duris of Samos, which placed Alexander a thousand years after the Trojan War.

The focus of these Greek sources seems to be on the foundation legend and on their own day.[55] A wide range of different versions of the foundation story were outlined by Dionysius (1.72) and by Plutarch (*Rom.* 1–3). Given that the legend of Romulus and Remus was probably a local Roman tradition, its discussion suggests that Greek writers had consulted Romans at first or second hand about their own version of events.

Roman historical writing about their own past did not begin until the late third century. When the first Roman, Fabius Pictor, came to write a history of his own state, he was able to draw on a range of earlier Greek discussions of Rome. He wrote in Greek, both because this was the language of history at this time and because he would have been interested in presenting a Roman version of events to a Greek audience. He was writing at the end of the Second Punic War, and must have been conscious of the fact that Hannibal had the support of some Greek historians; his work must thus have aimed in part to counter the perspective provided by these sources.[56] Nevertheless it is clear from subsequent references to his work by authors such as Polybius that Fabius was regarded as an authoritative source, and although he drew on the historical records of his own family, the Fabii, he was not overly biased towards them.[57] We know that he disagreed with Timaeus on the date of the foundation of Rome, although he seems to have closely followed a version of the foundation story already reported by another Greek source, Diocles of Peparethus.[58] Modern scholars have often presented this development as a step change. Fabius, as a Roman, presumably had easier access to official and family records than his Greek predecessors.[59] But Purcell has cogently questioned the emphasis placed on the 'Fabian moment', as it unnecessarily privileges the ethnicity of the author.[60] Fabius was the first Roman author on Rome, but not the first historian, and it is not as if ancient historians have to come from the same city that they write about. Most modern historians, for instance, see little reason to worry about the background of Greek writers about Athens in a similar way. It is also worth remembering that the Greek

---

55. Oakley, *Commentary*, I 38 on the lack of influence on Livy's books 6–10.
56. Habinek, *Politics*, 44–5 for the national purpose of Latin literature, under senatorial control.
57. Bispham and Cornell, 'Q. Fabius Pictor', 176–8.
58. Plutarch says Fabius 'follows him in most points' (*Rom.* 3.1).
59. Bispham and Cornell, 'Q. Fabius Pictor', 175.
60. 'Becoming historical', 24.

historical tradition on Rome continues seamlessly from at least the fifth century BC to the late imperial period, something evident from Dionysius' discussion of his predecessors (Dion. Hal. 1.5.4).

Fabius was rapidly followed by other Romans writing their own histories, also in Greek, but the next crucial development in Roman history writing comes with Ennius (239–c.169 BC). Around 600 lines of an original eighteen books survive of his Latin epic poem, the *Annales*, which is enough to convey some of its character. Written from around 187 BC, this was evidently a substantial work on the history of the Roman people, although its main focus was on the third and early second century. Soon after, Marcus Porcius Cato, the famously strict censor of 184 BC, wrote the first history in Latin, the *Origines*. This was innovative not only in its language, but also in its treatment of the origins of other Italian cities besides that of Rome. His work had a dual focus, like that of the Greek historians who had gone before him, on both the mythical period of origins, and then on the history of his own day, and in particular the period of the Punic Wars and the Roman conquest of Greece. The lack of material on the early Republican period, which seems apparent from the fragments that remain to us, is striking.[61]

The historians who followed Cato in the later second and early first century are little known until we reach the archetypal 'annalists'[62] cited regularly by Livy: Valerius Antias, Licinius Macer, Claudius Quadrigarius, and Q. Aelius Tubero. These men are widely credited with a dishonest inflation of the narrative of the early Republic, filling in the copious gaps left by earlier authors. Valerius Antias especially is criticised by Livy on a number of occasions, amongst other things for exaggerated figures of combatants in famous battles.[63] The evidence for wholesale dishonesty on the part of these writers is controversial, however, chiefly because we know so little about their work. At least one of them, Licinius Macer, is known to have made extensive use of the Linen Books with magisterial lists. This would seem to indicate some propensity for original research, but he is also accused by Livy of invention (Table 1.1).

---

61. *FRH* II 134–243.
62. The term comes from their habit of writing histories in a year by year pattern, modelled on the annals of the *pontifices*.
63. E.g. Livy, 26.49.3; 33.10.8; 36.38.7; 38.23.8; Oakley, *Commentary*, I 89–92; Rich, 'Annales Maximi', 300–1.

Sources and approaches

Table 1.1 The earliest Roman historians

Q. Fabius Pictor: a senator, active in the Second Punic War; wrote a history of Rome from the origins, in Greek.
L. Cincius Alimentus, praetor 210 BC: wrote a history of Rome from the origins, in Greek.
A. Postumius Albinus, consul 151 BC: wrote a history of Rome from the origins, in Greek.
C. Acilius, a senator in the 150s–140s BC: wrote a history of Rome from the origins, in Greek.
Quintus Ennius, 239–169 BC, from Rudiae in Calabria: wrote an eighteen-book hexameter epic history of Rome, the *Annales*, from the origins to 171 BC. Also wrote tragedies and comedies in Latin, on Greek models.
M. Porcius Cato (the Elder), 234–149 BC, consul 195 BC, censor 184 BC: wrote the Origines (in seven books), the first history of Rome in Latin. His work *On Agriculture* (*De re rustica*) is preserved.
L. Cassius Hemina, writing c. 146 BC: wrote *Annales* in Latin, from the origins to his own time.
Q. Fabius Maximus Servilianus, consul 142 BC: wrote *Annales* in Latin, from the origins to his own time.
L. Calpurnius Piso Frugi, censor 120 BC: anti-Gracchan; wrote *Annales* in Latin, from the origins to his own time.
Cn. Gellius, Gracchan period: wrote *Annales* in ninety-seven books to 146 BC.
Q. Claudius Quadrigarius, Sullan period: wrote *Annales* from the sack of Rome (390 BC) to his own day, in at least twenty-three books.
Valerius Antias, Sullan period: wrote *Annales* from Rome's origins to his own times, in at least seventy-five books. A vital source for Livy, though thought to be unreliable.
C. Licinius Macer, tribune 73 BC: wrote *Annales*, probably with a strong populist stance.
Q. Aelius Tubero, writing 46 BC: wrote *Annales* from Rome's origins in at least fourteen books; later won fame as a jurist.

Surviving literary sources

The literary works that survive to our day were largely based on the now lost histories detailed above. Of the literary sources available to us, the most important is undoubtedly Titus Livius, known as Livy. He was born in Patavium (Padua) in northern Italy, but moved to Rome, where he became well known. His history of Rome went from the foundation (hence its Latin title, *Ab Urbe condita*, 'From the foundation of the city') to 9 BC in 142 books. Books 1–10 and 21–45 survive. The books which concern us are 1–5, covering 753–390 BC, and 6–10, covering 390–292 BC. References in the first pentad to Augustus (not Octavian) and to the second closing of the doors of the temple of Janus suggest a publication date of 27–25 BC. But it is now thought quite likely that he started writing just before the battle of Actium (31 BC), perhaps in 33/32 BC, which fits much better with the profoundly pessimistic tone of his preface.[64] The first book covers the period from the origins of the city down to the fall of the monarchy, traditionally 509 BC. This is a resonant topic, as he was writing about kings and about the end of the monarchy just as Augustus was establishing himself as an emperor, whilst proclaiming that the Republic continued.[65]

Although Livy's is our best account of early Rome, Livy himself frequently expressed scepticism about the historical value of the stories he told. When recounting mythical or controversial episodes he frequently adds 'it is said', or similar qualifications.[66] In his preface, he states:

> Events before the city was founded or planned (*ante conditam condendamve urbem*) which have been handed down more as pleasing poetic fictions than as reliable records of historical events, I intend neither to affirm nor to refute.[67] (Livy, Preface 6–7)

Livy seems to have done little original research in the modern historical sense of seeking out original sources.[68] But he generally made sound use of the previous writers on whom he based his account, and was certainly capable of pointing out their faults by comparing them against each other. Livy's aims were didactic, and he was a great moraliser: in the preface he recommends using exemplary figures from the past (*exempla*) as guides to behaviour, good and bad: 'The special and salutary benefit of the study of history is to see evidence of every sort of behaviour set forth as on a splendid memorial; from it you may select for yourself and for your country what to emulate, from it what to avoid, whether basely begun or basely concluded.'

Scholars writing on Livy in the nineteenth and for most of the twentieth century shared a rather negative perception of Livy, regarding him as little more than a copyist of earlier sources, and as a writer who prioritised entertainment over truth. Recent work has supported

---

64. See Luce, 'Dating'; Burton, 'Last Republican historian'.
65. Luce in fact argues that the pentad was complete by 27 BC.
66. Cornell, 'Livy's narrative', 246.
67. This is sometimes taken to indicate Livy's scepticism about early Roman history per se (cf. 6.1), but his phrase *condendam* (planning) would seem to refer to the Romulean period of the foundation.
68. Wiseman, *Unwritten Rome*, 14–15 for this as a general characteristic.

a dramatic rehabilitation of his work.[69] Livy certainly strove to enthral and engage the reader, and operated with different historical principles from those of today (including, as all ancient historians did, copious speeches and details of the feelings of his historical characters that he cannot have known). But he aimed to achieve these objectives through a claimed accuracy in reporting Roman events from the past; he at least strives to appear as a conscientious and diligent historian, who was essentially aiming to create an accurate as well as an inspiring account.

The most significant problems posed by Livy's history are different. He has the limitations of any ancient historian trying to write a history of up to seven hundred years earlier; his source material is patchy and unreliable; his account is inherently Romanocentric, seeing Rome as a virtual island within central Italy; he is anachronistic, and has a limited understanding of the different social and economic conditions of early Rome; and he operates within the constrictions imposed by the peculiar genre of Hellenistic historiography that flourished at Rome.[70]

Three features are typical of his extensive account. First, that he adopted an annalistic format, covering Roman Republican history year by year. This allowed him to follow the structure of the Roman annals. He used book divisions, however, in a sophisticated way, not neatly coinciding with each year.[71] Secondly, he gradually expanded the breadth of the account, slowly decreasing the number of years covered in each book (Fig. 1.1). This may show his awareness of the way that the quality and quantity of information available to him slowly increased as his history proceeded.[72] Thirdly, despite the great length of his work, Livy substantially compressed the information available to him, and was selective in what he used.[73]

Our other main surviving narrative of the monarchic and early Republican period is the *Roman Antiquities* of Dionysius of Halicarnassus, a Greek scholar and rhetorician who came to Rome in 30 BC. Published from 7 BC onwards, the *Roman Antiquities* covered the period down to 264 BC, with the first four books on the origins of Rome and the monarchy. His work is similar to Livy's as it used many of the same sources, but with overlong speeches and greater emphasis

69. See e.g. Chaplin and Kraus (eds), *Livy*, and Mineo (ed.), *Companion to Livy*.
70. Momigliano, 'Fabius Pictor'.
71. Levene, *Livy*, 35–6. Oakley, *Commentary*, I 122ff.
72. Cornell, 'Livy's narrative', 247.
73. Oakley, *Commentary*, I 39.

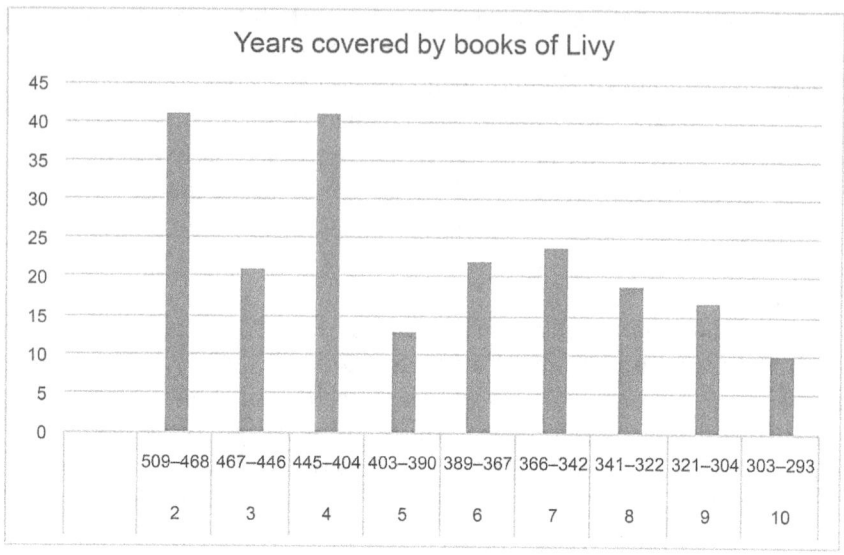

Figure 1.1 Years covered by Livy's books 2–10

on the era of Roman history for which there was least evidence, Dionysius' history can be heavy going, and so has lacked the scholarly attention afforded to Livy.[74] On the other hand, he seems to have been more interested in using antiquarian research than Livy (who largely compares previous accounts with one other), and cites a wider range of sources.[75] Dionysius' main aims were to correct mistaken views of early Rome in previous Greek sources, and to emphasise the Greek nature of the city.

There are a wide range of other sources available to the historian of early Rome, which provide a useful supplement to and contrast with the major authors. There are several other extant historical works of this period, most notably Diodorus Siculus,[76] who wrote a universal history published in the 30s BC, and Cassius Dio, whose history of Rome (early third century AD) included ten books on the period down to the Punic Wars, and which survives in a summary made by the Byzantine monk Zonaras. Cicero provided a particular

---

74. Cornell, 'Livy's narrative', 247 on the contrasting shape of Dionysius' history to Livy's.
75. Dion. Hal. 1.6–7, emphasising the shortcomings of his Greek sources, and the implicitly greater authority of the 'approved Roman authors' whom he follows. Schultze, 'Authority', 22–3 for a list of the sources he cites.
76. Oakley, *Commentary*, I 108 compares Diodorus on the fourth century to Livy.

take on early Roman history in the dialogue of his *Republic*, written in the 40s BC.[77] Polybius was a Greek historian living in Rome 168–c.145 BC. His histories, in forty books, focus on the wars in the period 220–164 BC (books 1–5 survive in full, the rest in excerpts). A fundamental source for Roman history later on, Polybius also provides some useful asides on earlier history and a valuable digression on the Roman wars against the Gauls. Finally, Plutarch (AD 46–120) wrote a series of Parallel Lives of famous Greeks and Romans. They include many important figures from our era – Romulus, Numa, Publius Valerius Publicola, Coriolanus, Camillus and Pyrrhus – but the mythical character of the Roman figures means they are short on plausible historical detail. All these works are useful comparanda to Livy and Dionysius as they use some different sources and sometimes contain variant traditions.

Few historians made direct use of documentary evidence: investigation of this kind was more characteristic of 'antiquarian' writers. Antiquarians were interested in the investigation of archaic and obsolete survivals from earlier eras; they studied traditions, institutions, language, monuments and documents. The two most important figures of this movement, which had begun in the second century BC, were Varro, working in the mid to late first century BC, and Verrius Flaccus, working under Augustus. Among an enormous number of works, Varro produced the forty books of *Human and Divine Antiquities* in 47 BC. Cicero dedicated his *Academica* to him, recording that 'your books led us home, when we were wandering like strangers in our own city . . . You have revealed to us the names, types, duties and origins of all things divine as well as human' (*Academica* 1.9). Verrius' semi-alphabetically organised lexicon was preserved in an abbreviated form by Festus, probably in the second century AD.[78] Only small portions of their work survive, but much of their material was used by later writers, and has consequently come down to us. Their studies seem to have uncovered a huge amount of neglected information, and potentially provided a more substantial basis to the accounts of contemporary and later writers on early Rome. The extent of their influence is uncertain. We can see their direct impact most clearly in Augustan works such as Dionysius' *Histories* and Ovid's *Fasti*, and later on in Pliny's *Natural History* and Plutarch's biographies.[79] Their

77. Cornell, 'Cicero'.
78. Glinister and Woods (eds), *Verrius, Festus, and Paul*.
79. Smith, 'Pliny the Elder'.

influence on other historians is less clear, although there is some evidence, for instance, that Livy used them.[80]

Archaeological evidence

The contribution of archaeology towards our understanding of early Rome is now very substantial, and it is increasing all the time. Rome occupies a geographically central site in Italy, at the intersection of the Tiber with various important land routes (Map 4). As there has been settlement here for over three millennia, there has been a huge accumulation of stratigraphy on the site, both as a result of the archaeological remains of the city's history and of the repeated alluviation that has affected the site.[81] This makes excavation very challenging, and the areas that can be investigated are usually very restricted. It is particularly difficult for excavations to reach the lower levels of occupation just above virgin soil, as it normally requires the removal of earlier monuments, such as in the Forum. Much material has been lost in successive phases of urban development, both ancient and modern, as with the dispersal of most of the cemetery material from the Esquiline during the development of the hill for housing in the nineteenth century. By the end of antiquity, much archaic material had in any case already been reworked, pillaged, or built over (the destruction of the Capitoline temple by fire on two occasions, and its subsequent rebuilding in later materials, is a case in point).[82]

Excavations in the city go back to Renaissance times, when central areas such as the Forum were explored by the Papacy in order to recover ancient statuary. Protection for the monuments of the city, and their proper excavation, was delayed until the Unification of Italy in 1871, and the work on the Forum by Giacomo Boni, around 1900.[83] Boni oversaw the large-scale clearance of later monuments and a series of excavations across the Forum site. He undertook carefully documented excavations of critical areas such as the early burials found in the Forum 'Sepulcretum', a burial ground of the ninth and eighth centuries BC, and the Comitium, one of the key meeting

---

80. Oakley, *Commentary*, I 33–4; Cornell, *FRH* I 84; Hickson Hahn, 'Livy's liturgical order', 97–8; Stadter, *Plutarch*, 11.
81. E.g. Carandini, *Rome: Day One*, 7, notes that there are 13 m of subsoil over the earliest phases of the Palatine slopes excavations; cf. also the depth of the recent excavations at the Forum Boarium.
82. See below, Chapter 5.
83. Ross Holloway, *Archaeology*, 5.

Sources and approaches

places in Rome. Excavations would not come close to the scale and importance of Boni's work until the 1980s.

Important excavations and reappraisals continued through the twentieth century, clarifying many aspects of the great monuments of the city centre, and the dates of the creation of the monumental Forum. Parts of the Forum Boarium under the church of Sant'Omobono were excavated, and a major reassessment of burials and collation of evidence was undertaken by Einar Gjerstad from the 1950s to the 1970s. He re-examined Boni's stratigraphy of the Forum pavements and collated all the archaeological material hitherto known, although advancing a controversial chronology that won few adherents.[84]

Modern excavation accelerated in the 1980s, and has become very wide ranging under the modern government agency, the Soprintendenza. Much attention has been paid to revisiting earlier work, as with Carafa's reassessment of the Comitium and the stratigraphy of the Forum, dating the paving to an earlier phase of urbanisation. Key new excavations have taken place on the Capitoline, on the Palatine, in the Colosseum area, and on the Caelian hill, amongst many others. Important excavations have also been conducted on the north-west slopes of the Palatine, and in the area of the temple of Vesta. These have turned up settlement remains from the eighth century, the famous Palatine wall of the mid eighth to sixth century BC and some huge atrium houses along the Sacra Via. Further significant finds of domestic structures have recently been uncovered on the Quirinal hill.[85] The Forum Boarium is currently undergoing further excavation. In addition, our understanding of the geology of the site of Rome has been transformed by a programme of taking coring samples, and research on architectural terracottas has clarified the nature of archaic building programmes at Rome and more widely in central Italy.[86] Outside of Rome, critical new archaeological evidence of rural settlement in the suburbium of the city has been thrown up by the excavation of the Auditorium villa site and by the continuing reassessment of survey evidence, such as the Tiber Valley Survey Project run by the British School at Rome. Further important

---

84. Gjerstad, *Early Rome*, IV.1–2.
85. www.beniculturali.it/mibac/export/MiBAC/sito-MiBAC/Contenuti/MibacUnif/Comunicati/visualizza_asset.html_1704181619.html.
86. E.g. Ammerman, 'On the origins'; Ammerman, 'Comitium'; Ammerman et al., 'Clay beds'; Winter, *Symbols*; Lulof, 'Reconstructing'.

archaeological investigation is ongoing in many Etruscan and Latin towns such as Tarquinii and Gabii.

This great back catalogue of material, and ongoing excavation, means that there is now an unprecedented level of archaeological information for the early city and its surroundings. It is important to retain a sense of perspective, however. The recent excavations of the north-west slopes of the Palatine uncovered an area of only one hectare (within an area of the ancient city of approximately 427 ha); within this area, deep excavation to archaic levels was possible only at a very small number of restricted points. Furthermore, perhaps the key source of evidence from other cities in central Italy, that of the cemeteries, is severely compromised in Rome. This is due to two factors: the devastation of the Esquiline cemetery in redevelopment, and the change to a more austere form of burial at the end of the Orientalising period, around 580 BC, a cultural change that Rome shared with other Latin cities. These factors, along with the better preservation of material in many Etruscan cities, has led to the growing importance of comparable material from elsewhere in central Tyrrhenian Italy, namely Etruria, Latium and Campania.

Much of the evidence that has come to light in the last few decades is yet to be properly assimilated into historical works on early Rome. For instance, it is now much more difficult to maintain that the Roman city state was not formed until 625 BC, when the first Forum paving (or second by Carafa's reckoning) was laid. This view, common to many historical overviews, is essentially based on tiny fragments of data from Boni's excavations. Recent work has provided a more optimistic picture of developments in the eighth and seventh centuries, and of a more gradual period of state formation leading up to this point. Nevertheless, it should be remembered that we are still at a very early stage in the archaeological investigation of early Rome and, given that so little of the archaic city has been properly excavated, debate over the significance of these earlier finds remains heated.[87]

A key issue with the archaeological material for early Rome is how far it can be integrated with the literary evidence, without which our knowledge would be greatly impoverished.[88] There are some striking and reassuring coincidences between the archaeological and literary

---

87. For discussion see Carandini, *Nascita*; Carandini, *Remo e Romolo*; Ampolo, 'Problema delle origini'; Fulminante, *Urbanisation*, 66–104; Hopkins, *Genesis*, 20–38.
88. For discussions of what Rome might look like without literary material, see Momigliano, 'Interim report', 107.

record for archaic Rome, stretching back into the regal period.[89] For instance, the archaeological remains of the temples of Jupiter Optimus Maximus on the Capitol and the temple of Castor in the Forum match the literary record for the foundation of these temples with varying degrees of neatness. The discovery of the Pyrgi tablets in the 1960s provided strong support for Polybius' dating of the Rome–Carthage treaty of 509 BC, as they provided corroborating evidence for a Phoenician-speaking presence in central Italy at precisely this time.[90] Even more strikingly, the legendary tale of the Demaratus, the father of Tarquinius Priscus, who moved to Rome from Corinth, shows extraordinary parallels with migrating individuals attested in the contemporary epigraphic record.[91] Similarly, the name of the legendary Etruscan adventurer Aulus Vibenna, who is said to have played a role in the later monarchy, features on an inscription of c.580 BC found at Veii.[92]

Nevertheless, it is vital to use archaeological data to address the right questions. Coincidences with the literary evidence such as those above are very fortunate. There are enormous perils in seeking to marry text and archaeological sources – what Snodgrass has called the 'positivist fallacy'.[93] This approach is very common, and many scholars using archaeological material still operate within a culture-historical paradigm that is based on searching for ethnic groups within the material record. Much more significant is the independent story that the archaeological evidence tells us about the nature of Roman economy, society and culture, and this requires a reshaping of what has normally passed for early Roman history.

The value of our evidence for early Rome and the Roman construction of the past

My general aim has been to clarify the current state of knowledge, rather than to provide a definitive judgement on the state of our sources. One critical factor that is apparent is the increasing value of our literary tradition over time. There are distinct phases evident

---

89. Poucet, 'Grands travaux', is very insistent on caution in archaeology 'confirming' tradition.
90. In fact, as we shall see below (Chapter 2), recent linguistic studies have complicated this picture somewhat.
91. Ampolo, 'Demarato: osservazioni'.
92. See Chapter 4.
93. Cited in Hall, *Artifact*, 207.

in our source material, which can be broken down into a schematic approximation in Table 1.2.

However, the shifts between these phases are not clean breaks but rather represent gradual changes in the nature of our evidence. The most important break in the nature of the evidence is probably with the Republic, but even here we need to think of a progression in our

Table 1.2 The character of the literary record

	Character of historical record	Some notable elaborations	Comments
Pre-foundation phase	Mythical	Aeneas; Evander; Hercules visits site of Rome	Mythical stories that may possibly preserve small elements of useful information
Foundation stories	Largely mythical	Romulus and Remus; Alban kings; the asylum; the Rape of the Sabine Women	Some useful information likely; much mythical material; very difficult to disentangle myth and history
Early monarchy	Semi-mythical	Numa and Egeria	Record changes: Numa substantially mythical; Ancus has substantial historical elements[a]
Later monarchy (the 'Tarquin dynasty')	Mythical and historical	Origins of Tarquinius Priscus; death of Priscus; origins of Servius Tullius; fall of monarchy	Substantial historical elements; frequent mythological elements; biographical focus on the kings; greater sense of chronological development
Republic before 367 BC	Quasi-historical with mythological elements	Porsenna's siege; Lake Regillus; Cincinnatus; Decemvirate and story of Virginia; Camillus; siege of Veii; Gallic sack of Rome; Licinio-Sextian laws	Substantial historical elements; lessening mythological elements; still many biographical characteristics; clearer chronological structure and framework of historical fact
Republic c.367–310 BC	Substantially historical	The Caudine Forks	
Republic c.310–290 BC	Very substantially historical	Omen of victory and death of Decius at Sentinum	More substantial detail provided; low percentage of elaboration

[a] See Camous, *Ancus Marcius*.

evidence, given that there are still distinctly legendary elements in the early Republic. As we have seen in the case of Livy above (Fig. 1.1), the detail in our sources steadily increases over time.

Tabulating the historical data in this way provides a reassuring means of assessing the sources, yet recent work has given us a much better appreciation of how much the particular agendas of our sources affect all the eras they discuss. In many ways this is even more critical than the much more widely discussed reliability of the sources. The most serious challenge in those terms is the issue of anachronism: a lack of understanding of archaic social conditions, and an idealised view of the past (both interconnected conditions).[94]

In describing the opening salvos of the war with the Samnites in 327 BC, Livy has a Samnite leader say, 'let us sort out whether Samnite or Roman is to have power over Italy' (8.23.8). The hindsight implicit in Livy's view, written when Rome had established Mediterranean hegemony, is a fundamental problem with our sources. These writers were conditioned by their 'teleological' understanding of Roman history, the idea that Rome's future path to greatness was mapped out. In addition, our sources must be read against the background of the enormous changes Rome underwent in the Republic. For instance, the period of the fourth and third centuries BC, with its costly wars against the Samnites, Pyrrhus and Carthage, was entirely different to the situation in the second to first centuries BC, when Rome undertook vast and rapid conquests of other Mediterranean societies, garnering huge economic resources, and extending its political control over the whole Mediterranean basin. In similar terms, the Roman state was exponentially larger in 264 BC than it had been only seventy years before. It was therefore a massive challenge for late Republicans in a time of world empire to reimagine the city-state conditions of the sixth to early third centuries BC.[95] As a result, our sources tend to underestimate the change that Rome underwent during the Republic. Furthermore, most of the surviving sources had never experienced a properly working Republican system, having lived only through its catastrophic demise in the second half of the first century BC. Thus, they tend to be coloured by an unrealistic nostalgia, and to be preoccupied with a moralising perspective on what went wrong.

---

94. Purcell, 'Becoming historical', 13–14; Cornell, 'Rome: the history of an anachronism'; Fox, *Roman Historical Myths*.
95. Cornell, 'Rome: the history of an anachronism' on the consequences. See also Rutledge, *Ancient Rome as a Museum*.

It is therefore crucially important to question the ideological constructions in our sources of the austere, patriarchal, patriotic and noble nature of early Romans. Such images were formed in implicit contrast to the dynamic and heterogenous society of the late Republic, which was so disturbing to contemporaries. Modern historical studies of nostalgia and the 'invention of the past' provide useful analogies here.[96] Much of the Roman self-image of their archaic past is deeply problematic, and is as much a reflection of contemporary anxieties of the late Republican and early imperial writers as it is of real information about the past. This idealisation was not naïve: the Roman view of the past should not be seen as a neutral recovery of past truths, such as modern historians like to imagine themselves performing, but a politicised and ideological construction to serve the purposes of particular groups.[97]

We should thus be alert for the common motifs in this idealised and nostalgic view. Roman authors looked back on early Rome as agricultural, uncommercial and unadulterated from the viewpoint of their highly urban-based society, where the impact of a 'global' imperial economy was becoming increasingly evident. Early Romans were regarded as austere in an era of debilitating luxury.[98] They were seen as militarily successful in an era of increasing anxiety about Roman military performance (a not altogether misleading conception). Early Roman society was envisaged as conservatively patriarchal from the viewpoint of a society where elite women were experiencing increased influence and freedoms, due to yawning wealth disparities, the greater concentration of power in dynastic families and higher rates of divorce. Early Romans were seen as devoted to the gods and committed to the sanctity of oaths in an era of greater philosophical secularisation of thought (at least amongst the elite, whose views are the only ones we can properly assess), and a (perceived) increase in the manipulation of religion for political purposes. And finally, the patrician families of early Rome were regarded as having had primordial origins in Rome, although in reality social mobility was prevalent throughout Roman history.[99]

---

96. Lowenthal, *The Past is a Foreign Country*; Hobsbawm and Ranger, *The Invention of Tradition*.
97. For Habinek, *Politics*, the aristocracy.
98. Rosenstein, *Rome and the Mediterranean*, 248–9; for attempts to regulate luxury see the sumptuary legislation recorded in Habinek, *Politics*, 61.
99. For an attempt to question these 'aristocratic myths', see Bradley, 'Investigating aristocracy'.

These motifs were surprisingly ancient and durable. They certainly go back beyond Livy, and perhaps beyond Polybius and Fabius Pictor. They are evident in antiquarians as well as historians: we can think here of Varro, who claimed in his *Divine Antiquities* to be recovering the past in order to prevent the 'forgetting' of old practices.[100] This type of nostalgia seems inherent in the historical consciousness of Rome; for instance, stories about prohibitions on women drinking wine under Romulus were evident from Fabius Pictor in the third century BC (*FRH* F25) to Valerius Maximus in the first century AD and beyond. Such moralising ideals seem not just to be characteristic of literary works but form a trend that is embedded in Roman historical memory. The backward-looking tendencies of oral culture are clear from Cato's banqueting songs (*FRH* F113) about 'the merits and glorious deeds of famous men'. This is probably even true of 'documentary' sources such as the *Annales Maximi*, where nostalgic tendencies are evident in several passages.[101]

This is a rather schematic simplification of the Roman archaising view of the past, which was much more complex in reality. These motifs are perhaps most characteristic of our stories from the early Republic, with exemplary heroes like Cincinnatus, Camillus and Fabricius, who combine many of these characteristics.[102] The situation for the monarchy is a little different, as the last four kings are not straightforwardly treated as exemplars. In addition, many of the stories inherited by historians from older tradition (both documentary and oral) contradicted these ideals. Our historians' image of early Rome is not an idealised museum, but a battleground of good and bad, where ambiguity is possible and frequent (for instance, the version of the foundation that has Romulus killing his brother Remus, and Romulus' own possible murder by senators rather than his apotheosis). Nor was it a given that later Romans would follow the good precedents, rather than the bad.

Writers were aware that these images had been propagated by elite Republican families and the Augustan regime for political gain, and were thus open to potential mockery and questioning. So Plautus likes to poke fun at pompous soldiers, pretentious nobles and preening triumphators (e.g. *Epidicus* 158–60); Propertius suggests that it is better to watch a triumph than take part in one (*Elegy* 3.4), and as

---

100. Varro, *Ant.* fr. 2a Cardauns.
101. E.g. *FRH* F 6 and 10.
102. Roller, *Models from the Past*.

we have seen, Livy and Cicero both question elite records relating to their families. These images were thus debated and challenged in the vibrant intellectual and literary culture of late Republic, and were by no means monolithic. This is perhaps a sign of the way that the full Roman community had a stake in the tradition, which was meaningful to plebeians as well as to nobles. Early Roman history was not just a glorious parade of wooden stereotypes. All these aspects were core features of Roman 'values', which together contributed to the constructed ideal of Roman self-identity in the late Republican and Augustan period. They were a way that Romans could contrast their earlier selves with contemporary society, with their neighbours, and with 'weaker' conquered states like Carthage and the Greek *poleis*.

These views are very influential and pervasive; they colour many of our stories. A reader of early Roman sources thus needs to be continually alert to them, and to the use of *exempla* by historians such as Livy to make moralising points. Many aspects of this Roman ideological worldview will be questioned in this book, such as the image of Rome as a self-sufficient, uncommercialised state, with little experience of the sea; or the image of a self-regulating, austere, scarcely wealthy elite which was mainly concerned with duty to the state.[103] Recent revisionist approaches to another ancient state with a somewhat mythologised reputation, Sparta, are methodologically instructive. Many aspects of Sparta are primarily known from later sources, such as Plutarch's *Life of Lycurgus*. The distorted perspective that was created has been called the 'Spartan mirage'.[104] Both Sparta and Rome were outward-looking states that came ideologically to overlook their debt to their neighbours and to cultivate a history of their own isolationism. Both societies have a mix of democratic, monarchic and oligarchic constitutional features. Their elites share ideals of austerity, military service and sacrifice to the state. Both go on in the aftermath of expansion to experience anxiety about population decline, and unsuccessful attempts at land reform (it is sometimes speculated that the Roman Gracchi were inspired by their Spartan counterparts). Unlike Sparta, Rome has no real surviving literature from the archaic period (unless we count the archaic song culture discussed by Habinek and Wiseman). Nevertheless, it is helpful to

---

103. Habinek, *Politics*, 53; Bradley, 'Investigating aristocracy'. For a more positive approach to the Roman self-image, see MacMullen, *Earliest Romans*.
104. Hodkinson and Macgregor Morris, 'Introduction', viii–x; Hall, *History*, 203–9.

think of a 'Roman mirage' along Spartan lines. Properly escaping from these distorting agendas requires a considerable rethink.

Approaching early Rome

There is something of a paradox at the heart of Roman history. Historians over the centuries since the Renaissance have traced the 'rise' of Rome from a village of huts with a small, rustic population, to the great city of the late Republic, dominating a European and Mediterranean empire. This is a story based around the Romans' own highly positive image of early Rome and how far it has changed in seven centuries. Writing Roman history implies an acceptance of the framework first provided by Roman historians such as Livy, and it is important to be aware of the constraints of this approach. Historians of archaic Greece, in contrast, whilst still writing within a chronological framework, have been more successful in escaping from a source-based agenda. They have tended to make greater use of anthropological and sociological concepts such as state formation, urbanisation, ritual and ethnicity to provide a more thematic approach to archaic history.[105]

In methodological terms, this work endeavours to approach both archaeological and literary material in equally critical fashion, although it is more concerned with the coherency of the broader picture than with establishing the historicity of each individual piece of evidence. As we have seen in this chapter, the complexity of the ways that information was preserved from the archaic period to the late Republic makes recovering its transmission almost impossible, and in most cases we are unable to verify or refute the historicity of events with complete certainty. The resultant uncertainty of most of the evidence is disconcerting. But it should not discourage us from undertaking the history of early Rome, as this methodological situation is typical for the study of most societies in the ancient world, apart from classical Greece and late Republican to early imperial Rome.

A further methodological principle is that we should aim for a more contextualised understanding of Roman history. Comparative approaches between Rome and other ancient societies help us to counteract the Romanocentricity of Roman tradition. This tends to

---

105. For Greek histories, see e.g. Hall, *History*, or Osborne, *Greece in the Making*. Fulminante, *Urbanisation*, discusses the applicability of anthropological models to early Rome.

mean prioritising archaeology and epigraphy as much as the literary sources, and the contemporary nature of material evidence allows us to control the anachronism of our literary sources. One aspect of the comparative approach is setting Rome into the context of central Italy. Methodologically, I take it that Rome is for many purposes the product of its central Italian milieu, and will therefore use evidence from neighbouring societies to discuss aspects of Rome such as its economy and society.[106] There are some risks in this project, notably of making Rome too much like its surroundings and failing to identify its exceptional characteristics. But there are also benefits, such as being able to set Rome's economy on a proper archaeologically determined footing, that outweigh the risks.

A second aspect of the comparative approach is to consider Rome as part of a wider Mediterranean world. A comparative approach with archaic Greece is particularly helpful in this sense. Vlassopolous has recently argued for the importance of adopting a plurality of approaches to Greek history, recognising the dominant role of nationalist and imperialist narratives of the nineteenth and early twentieth century, and seeing the *polis* not as self-sufficient but as part of a Mediterranean and Near Eastern world system.[107] His call for the nationalist emphasis on ancient Greece to be superseded by an interlinked history of the wider Mediterranean and Near East has important lessons for Rome too.[108] Furthermore, the interconnected nature of the ancient Mediterranean world, based on myriad networks and multiple types of mobility, has been illuminated by recent studies by Purcell and Horden, Malkin, and Isayev.[109] Overall, therefore, such comparisons offer as much as, if not more than, the implicit contrast drawn in our sources between Rome in its early period and in its late Republican and early imperial state.

---

106. For a similar approach see Smith, *Early Rome and Latium*.
107. Vlassopoulos, *Unthinking*, 13–67.
108. Vlassopolous, *Unthinking*, 1–10.
109. Horden and Purcell, *Corrupting Sea*; Malkin, *Small Greek World*; Isayev, *Migration*.

CHAPTER 2

Early Italy, from the Bronze Age to the classical era

Introduction

This chapter is designed to provide an overview of the wider Italian context for early Roman history. It is obvious that Rome is part of the wider Italian world, and closely connected to neighbouring regions at all points during its history. Yet this is frequently obscured by the capital-centred outlook that pervades the ancient sources, and hence is often forgotten in modern accounts of Roman history. The archaeological evidence for Rome's neighbours is often much more revealing than that for the city itself. For instance, there are around 600 graves dating from the ninth to sixth centuries BC at the cemetery of ancient Gabii (Osteria dell'Osa), far more than survive in the various cemeteries of Rome.

Bronze Age background

The Italian Bronze Age (c.1800–900 BC) forms an important background to the developments of the historical period. The Bronze Age is so called because bronze (an alloy of copper and tin) was widely used in manufacturing utensils, weapons and ornaments. Bronze remained the major metal in use through this period and even during much of the subsequent Iron Age. The Bronze Age is conventionally divided into four phases, the Early, Middle, Recent and Final (Table 2.1). Many of the trends in Italian history characteristic of the later era begin here. In particular, we see the first signs of stable settlement on many of the important later city sites. We can also trace the beginnings of burials with grave goods, which reach a pinnacle in the seventh century BC. The first signs of a developing commercial economy emerge, with new ceramic and metalworking traditions, and trade connections with Europe and the Mediterranean. In addition, clear differences between the later ethnic regions of Italy are visible for the first time. All this

Table 2.1 Eras of Italian prehistory

Eras (with their associated cultures)	Dates BC (all approximate)
Early Bronze Age	1800–1600
Middle Bronze Age (Appennine culture phases 1A and 1B)	1600–1300
Recent Bronze Age (Appennine culture phase 2)	1300–1200
Final Bronze Age (Proto-Villanovan)	1200–900
Early Iron Age (Villanovan culture)	900–730
Orientalising period	730–580
Archaic period	580–480

evidence allows us, tentatively, to trace some critical developments that we will examine in detail later back to the early first millennium BC and perhaps the late second millennium BC, notably state formation, the emergence of social classes, the impact of a Mediterranean 'world system', and the formation of ethnic identities.

The Bronze Age was characterised by the establishment of stable settlements, during the early Bronze Age in northern Italy, and during the middle Bronze Age in central and southern Italy (Fig. 2.1). Uninterrupted habitation of the great centres of later Italy such as Bologna, Rome, Bari and Taranto began in this era. In northern Italy the Terramare settlements of the Middle Bronze Age typically ranged between 1 and 10 ha in size, and probably had inhabitants in the hundreds. Settlements in central Italy were smaller, around a hectare, until sites of multiple hectares began to appear in the Recent Bronze Age.[1] The Middle and Recent Bronze Age saw considerable demographic expansion, but with the passage to the Final Bronze Age there was something of a crisis in established sites in the Padane area, which witnessed the collapse of the Terramare settlements. This is likely to have been connected to the disruption around 1200 BC of the Mycenaean kingdoms, with which the Padane settlements were closely linked. New sites arose and flourished in the Final Bronze Age in areas peripheral to the Terramare zone: the best known is Frattesina in the delta of the Po river, which prospered due to long-distance trade and the crafting of products such as metals, ceramics and glass.[2] Continuity is more evident over the Bronze–Iron Age transition in central Italy, although there was also

1. Peroni, 'Comunità', 9.
2. Smith, *Early Rome and Latium*, 26; Blake, *Social Networks*, 130–2.

Early Italy, from the Bronze Age to the classical era 37

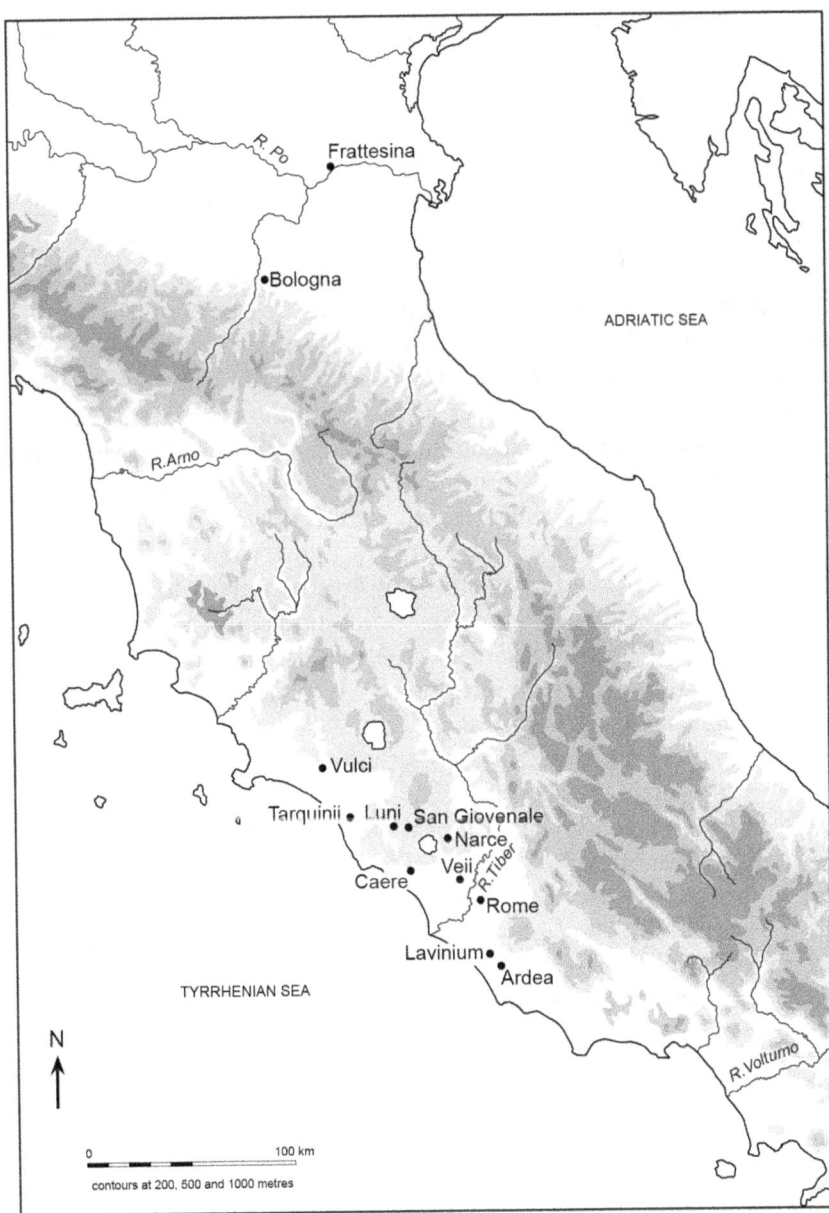

Figure 2.1 Map of key Bronze Age sites

selection and consolidation of sites. Less defendable sites disappeared, whereas sites on higher ground persisted and indeed grew, such as Luni sul Mignone, San Giovenale and Narce in southern Etruria, and Rome (Capitolium/ Sant'Omobono), Ardea and Lavinium in Latium.

The culture characteristic of central Italy in the Middle and Recent Bronze Age (c.1600–1200 BC) is known as Apennine culture. The distinctive pottery of this period was burnished, with incised decoration. It is found widely across Italy, mostly from settlement contexts, and together with metalwork shows a striking degree of cultural uniformity.[3] It is found in considerable quantities in settlement sites – the Biferno Valley Survey identified 10,000 or so sherds.[4] The egalitarian graves of this era seem to reflect a largely undifferentiated society. However, it was one with trading links to other areas of the Mediterranean. Sherds of Mycenaean pottery from the Aegean, particularly from the second half of the fifteenth to the thirteenth century BC, have been found in substantial numbers in sites in southern Italy, but are rarer in central Italy, with only five examples found in the largest group, at Luni sul Mignone.[5] Some finds have also occurred at a limited number of sites in northern Italy, mostly in the later stages of this trade. Local imitations of Mycenaean pottery, known as Italo-Mycenaean ware and dated to the thirteenth century, have been found at a large number of southern Italian sites.[6] They may have been produced in workshops set up by Mycenaean potters. By the end of the thirteenth century local imitations predominated over imported Mycenaean ware, and by the late twelfth century Mycenaean imports had declined dramatically. Aegean pottery imports did not resume until the eighth century, although metalworking suggests it is possible that contacts continued in the intervening years.[7]

Other imported items found across the peninsula include amber, ivory, glassy faience, and bronze items such as swords and fibulae. Metalworking flourished in the Bronze Age, and substantial metal hoards are found dating to the Final Bronze Age. The 1.5 kg of

---

3. Cornell, *Beginnings*, 31.
4. Barker et al., *Mediterranean Valley*, 132.
5. Smith, *Early Rome and Latium*, 27: one each at San Giovenale, Monte Rovello; five at Luni sul Mignone; none from Latium. However, Cifani (unpublished paper) reports that a fragment is known from Sant'Omobono in Rome. Blake, 'Mycenaeans', 1 notes that there are ninety-three sites across the western Mediterranean with 9,600 sherds (including 4,000 from Roca Vecchia in Apulia).
6. Blake, *Social Networks*, 43.
7. Blake, *Social Networks*, 44.

bronze objects from the Rimessone hoard, near Ardea, consisted of twenty items, all fragmentary, dating to the late eleventh and early tenth century. They demonstrate the existence of specialised artisans at this time, making use of metal ores from Etruria as well as from Sardinia, where there may have been Phoenician involvement in mining and smelting.

The Bronze Age is also important for the first signs of ethnic identity. This aspect of human mentality remains very difficult to trace without written texts. However, Blake has recently made the case that the distribution networks evident from mapping certain categories of artefact must relate to regional grouping, known from the Iron Age onwards and attested in later written sources. There are clear traces of networks during the Final Bronze Age encompassing the future area of the Etruscans and the Veneti, and somewhat less clear traces of networks in the zones of the Marche/Umbria (connected to Etruria), Apulia and Basilicata.[8] Some areas (Molise, Campania and Liguria) show no clear sign of regional networks.

This work is more methodologically sound than identifications of regional culture groups across Italy based on later ethnic categories,[9] and suggests ethnic identities emerged before the Iron Age in some areas of Italy. This would accord with the evident great antiquity of some markers of ethnicity in later history: the festival of the Latin peoples on the Alban Mount, the *Feriae Latinae*, has a strong claim to date back well into prehistory, and priesthoods such as the Vestal Virgins, fundamental to the identity of Rome, have prehistoric aspects.[10] Nevertheless, this line of research, which may well be supplemented in future by DNA studies, is still preliminary and fragile, given that some of these networks are currently attested by very small numbers of objects.[11]

The earliest towns in Etruria and Latium

A major shift takes place in the transition from the Final Bronze Age to the early Iron Age. Developments in Etruria suggest that this region has primacy in central Italy. In Etruria, in the related

---

8. Blake, *Social Networks*, 241–2.
9. For the problems with such approaches see Bradley, 'Tribes, states and cities'; for the validity of this approach for Latium see Fulminante, 'Ethnicity'; cf. Fulminante, *Urbanisation*, 226.
10. Discussed below, Chapters 6, 10.
11. G. J. van Wijngaarden, review of Blake, *Social Networks*, BMCR 2015.09.16.

region of Campania, and in the area of Bologna, there is a clear break in settlement patterns, corresponding to the shift from so-called Proto-Villanovan to Villanovan culture. Latium by contrast sees more continuity, particularly at Rome, where continuous settlement can be observed. Burial evidence appears widely in central Italy from around 1000 BC, allowing us to trace the development of social differentiation, with the articulation of society into separate classes. In particular we can track the development of luxurious lifestyles and the emergence of a consuming elite.

The most dramatic changes took place in Etruria, where there were key social, political, territorial and economic developments in the transition from the Proto-Villanovan to Villanovan periods.[12] These changes affected various spheres of life, including funerary culture, the economy and settlement structure. From the twelfth century we see the emergence of Proto-Villanovan culture in Etruria. This is typically characterised by cremation, which takes over from the previously prevalent practice of inhumation, and may have been influenced by the Urnfield cultures of Continental Europe spreading down from beyond the Alps. It is also marked by other distinctive cultural elements, such as the use of a biconical ossuary, covered by a bowl or helmet, pottery marked with distinctive decorative motifs, and particular types of sword, axe, razor and fibula (though not all of these elements necessarily occur together). In its fullest expression, Villanovan culture is found in Etruria, northern Italy around Bologna and the Adriatic coast, at Verruchio and Firmum in the Marche, and at Capua and Pontecagnano in Campania (Fig. 2.2).

From the ninth century the size and longevity of Villanovan cemeteries becomes much greater, and demonstrates an unprecedented degree of stable settlement on such sites. The ashes of the deceased were typically placed in impasto or bronze urns (often either biconical or in the shape of a hut), which were then interred in small pit-like shafts (Fig. 2.3). The burials of this period had few grave goods. By *c*.800 BC inhumation burial in trench graves (*tombe a fossa*) appear too, and this soon becomes the predominant burial rite in south Etruria.

---

12. 'Villanovan' is a term that derives from the first example of such a cemetery to be excavated, by Gozzadini near Villanova in northern Italy (1853–5); 'Protovillanovan' was coined by Patroni in 1937 to designate the earlier phase of this culture (Bartoloni, *Cultura villanoviana* 101).

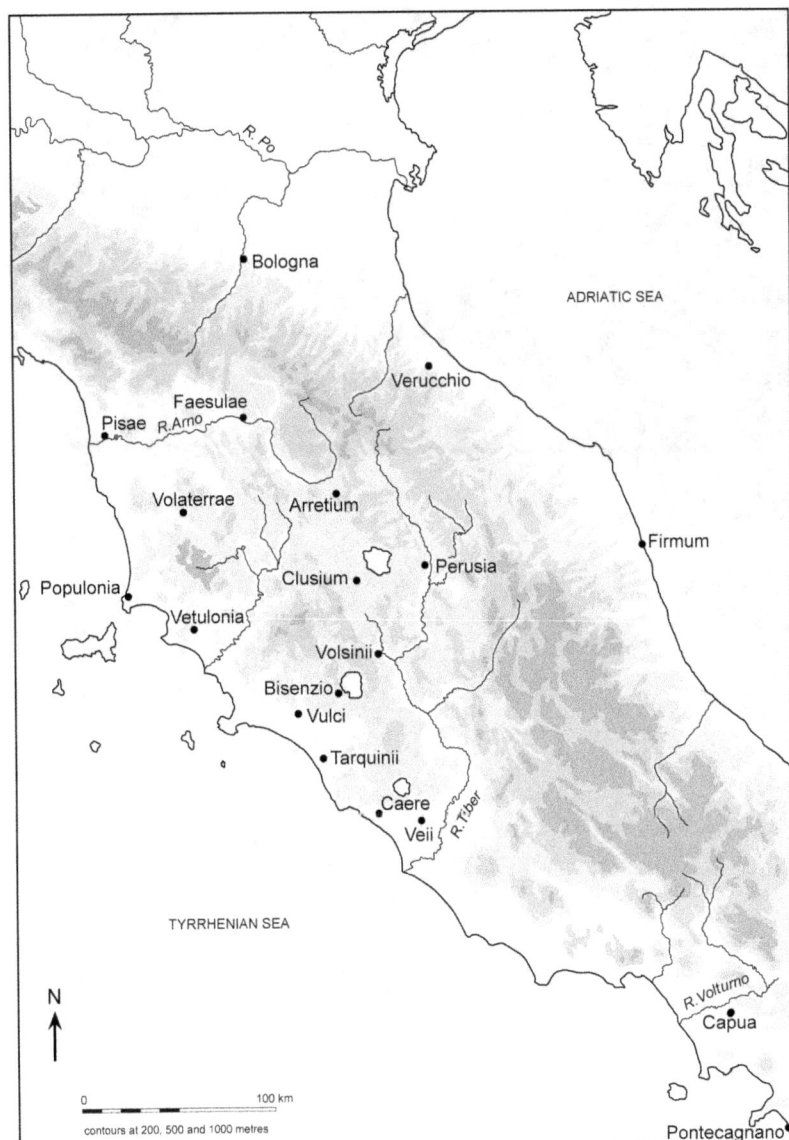

Figure 2.2 Map of Villanovan sites

Figure 2.3 Biconical cinerary urn belonging to a child from Tomb 64, Monterozzi necropolis, Tarquinii (photo: G. Bradley by concession of the Polo Museale del Lazio – Tarquinia (VT). Museo Archeologico Nazionale')

Early Italy, from the Bronze Age to the classical era 43

There is a dramatic rise in the quantity and quality of grave goods in the eighth century, and the appearance of exceptional wealth in a few tombs documents the emergence of a dominant elite manifested in the burial record. A clear example is Tomb AA1 from the Quattro Fontanile cemetery at Veii (third quarter of the eighth century), consisting of a cremation in an urn covered by a bronze helmet and accompanied by a wide range of impressive grave goods. These include a chariot, a sign of great status, an iron horse bit, weaponry such as a bronze shield, spearheads and axe, and an enormous array of banqueting equipment. This tomb is typical in showing increasing signs of warfare such as swords, spears, helmets, though in some cases these are of such intricate design and so thin they may be parade items, or else were designed solely for the funerary sphere.

Latial culture is similar to the Villanovan culture of south Etruria. There are early Iron Age cemeteries at Osteria dell'Osa (the future territory of Gabii), Rome, the Alban Hills (initially the key centre) and along the coast. Burials in Latial period I are typically marked by a hut urn, a dolium (into which the hut urn would be placed), miniaturised pottery vessels, metalwork (such as fibulae with serpentine whorls) and armour. The hut urns and miniaturisation are typical of this area, if not exclusive to it.

The main focus of settlement in Etruria shifted in the Final Bronze Age (tenth century BC) from dispersed villages to the large plateaux that would become the sites of the great historical Etruscan cities, such as Veii, Caere, Tarquinii, Vulci, Bisenzio, Vetulonia and Populonia. There were similar developments in Campania, at Capua (in the final Bronze Age and early Iron Age transition) and at Pontecagnano (in the early Iron Age). All these sites had much larger potentially habitable areas, averaging 126 ha rather than the 4–5 ha typical for the Bronze Age. Vulci and Veii were particularly large sites, at 180 and 190 ha respectively.[13] Most of these centres show no continuity with the earlier Bronze Age, but were new sites rapidly adopted by the population, a development that seems linked to the abandonment of villages in the surrounding territory. These new sites were not only larger, but also had much greater economic potential. Typically, they had large agricultural territories (averaging $c.1000$ km^2 in comparison to the 20–70 km^2 of Bronze Age settlements), were near

---

13. Peroni, 'Comunità', 12. Final Bronze Age remains are much more prevalent in Vulci and Tarquinii than Veii, where there is one Bronze Age sherd from the plateau, and a handful of burials (Moretti Sgubini (ed.), *Veio, Cerveteri, Vulci*, 91).

to the coast, and were accessible via rivers.[14] The size of these communities grew, and the villages coalesced into a single urban centre, which was then sometimes fortified.

This process is termed 'proto-urbanisation' by Peroni and his followers, a concept invented to express the importance of the developments in this period, although it is dependent on hindsight. It is important to realise that the urban nature of such sites is qualified. Habitation was patchy rather than unified. As the separate elements of the settlements grew they came to produce a 'leopard-skin' pattern of habitation interspersed with areas of cultivation and occasional burials (Fig. 2.4).[15] It is also uncertain how far they controlled the great extent of the territory we can theoretically assign to them. Hypothetically they had territories equivalent to those of the cities of classical Etruria, which archaeologists have identified using Thiessen polygons, but it is very uncertain to what extent the surrounding smaller settlements in the putative territory were actually abandoned, given the limitations of the ceramic chronologies. Many centres, such as Veii, Caere and Rome, may in fact have bucked the trend, seeing small rural sites increasing in the early Iron Age.[16]

Whether all this means that such settlements were politically unified is a point much debated by scholars. Some prefer to envisage separate groups, along the lines of Roman *gentes* (clans), collaborating, rather than a unified political authority, a state.[17] There is certainly some evidence for large, extra-familial groups in the burial record. Tumuli are used for multiple burials at Caere and many other cemeteries in central Tyrrhenian Italy, and in the distinct groups of tombs observable at Osteria dell'Osa, which have been linked to clans.[18] It is also striking that many city sites are initially ringed by multiple tomb groups or cemeteries, as at Veii.[19] Nevertheless, primordial social organisation based around clans rather than the state may be as much a modern construct as it was an ancient reality.[20] Ancient historical sources largely talk of power-

---

14. Fulminante, *Urbanisation*, 46.
15. Barker and Rasmussen, *Etruscans*, 65–70; Schiappelli, 'Veii', 334–6; Fulminante, *Urbanisation*, 47.
16. Barker and Rasmussen, *Etruscans*, 63; Patterson (ed.), *Bridging the Tiber*.
17. Bartoloni, *Cultura villanoviana*, 110; Barker and Rasmussen, *Etruscans*, 68.
18. Torelli, *Storia degli Etruschi*, 90, for Caere; Guidi et al., 'Confini', for Lazio; Bietti Sestieri, *Iron Age Community*, 241, for Osteria dell'Osa.
19. Tabolli and Cerasuolo (eds), *Veii*, 47–87.
20. Smith, *Roman Clan*, 165; Riva, *Urbanisation*, 4; cf. Bradley, 'Investigating aristocracy'.

Early Italy, from the Bronze Age to the classical era 45

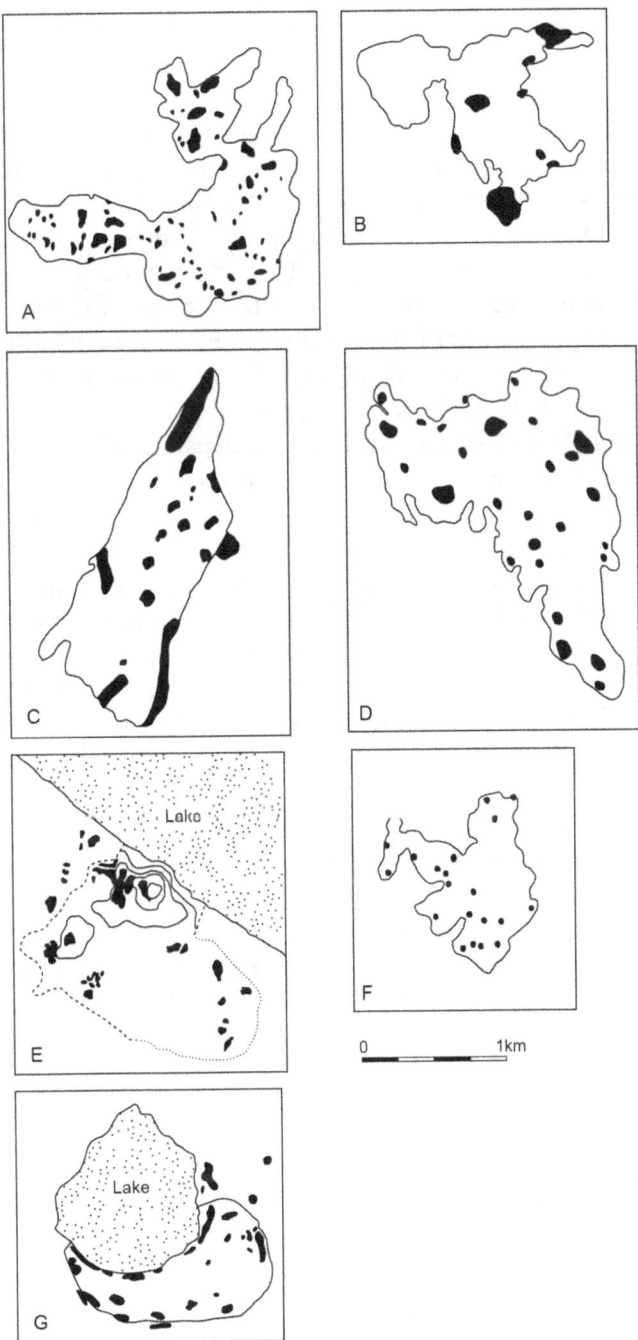

Figure 2.4 Early Iron Age findspots from proto-urban centres in Etruria and Latium. A: Tarquinii; B: Vulci; C: Caere; D: Veii; E: Bisenzio; F: Crustumerium; G: Gabii (after Carandini, *Nascita*, figs 26–7)

ful single leaders in the pre-urban phase, rather than collaborating groups of mafiosi-like clan elders. Clans are attested as influential institutions in early Rome by Roman legal and antiquarian sources, but there is little clear evidence that such groups predate the state.

We also need to avoid applying overly modern preconceptions about urbanism and the state to these entities. Ancient cities typically took a hugely long time to reach the type of full urban consistency represented by early imperial Pompeii. The city states of the archaic and classical Mediterranean were very far from this developed type. For example, large swathes of most major cities in this period probably remained unoccupied.[21] Similarly, ancient states took a long time to coalesce and strengthen, and we should probably think of an ongoing process of 'state organisation' as much as 'state formation'.[22] It remains likely that the beginnings of political organisation precede the urban dimension, and it is quite possible that an emerging political authority coerced or encouraged people to live together as much as economic or social forces operated to bring people together.[23]

In Latium, settlements in the early Iron Age were smaller and more numerous. Continuity of settlement from the Final Bronze Age to the Early Iron Age is more common than in south Etruria, and is attested at sites such as Rome, Ardea, Lavinium, Satricum, Gabii and Ficana.[24] This early occupation centred on the acropolis areas of the future city sites, and did not encompass the main living space until later. Proto-urbanisation seems to begin a century or so later, in the ninth rather than tenth century BC. As in south Etruria, there is also a process of agglomeration, as smaller sites disappear, probably due to migration, c.900 BC in Latial period IIA/IIB.[25] Latin cites were smaller in extent than Villanovan ones, generally with an area of between 20–50 ha, and a territory of 200–300 km².[26] This is evident from hypothetical

---

21. Hansen, *Shotgun Method*, 22.
22. Bradley, 'Tribes, states and cities'.
23. For J. C. Scott's argument that the state can be seen as a coercive apparatus that many try to escape rather than join, see Woolf, 'Moving peoples'. For what it's worth, forced movement of surrounding town populations to Rome is a critical feature of the narrative of the growth of the city under the early kings (defended as authentic by Bayet, 'Tite-Live et la précolonisation romaine').
24. Peroni, 'Comunità', 16.
25. Fulminante, *Urbanisation*, 46.
26. Peroni, 'Comunità', 16. Fulminante gives slightly different figures: settlements are mostly 20–50 ha, with a few 50–80 ha; they have territories of 100–150 km².

reconstructions of the likely territory of the extant centres, based on Thiessen polygons.[27]

There is a similar process of urbanisation to south Etruria. Settlement sites coalesce around plateaux, as at Ardea, where three distinct areas eventually merge with the acropolis occupied from the Bronze Age. As in Etruria, this is a gradual process that does not immediately result in unified urban centres.

Greek and Phoenician settlement and trading in the Tyrrhenian sea

In this context, we begin to get the first foreign settlements on the shores of Italy. The key stimulus is likely to be the presence of mineral deposits, with metals passing out of Italy, in exchange for Greek and Near Eastern products and pottery.

Between the eighth and sixth centuries BC both the Greeks and the Phoenicians had a very significant influence on western Italy (Fig. 2.5). One reason for their presence was the geology of Etruria. The region was very rich in mineral ores, with copper, tin and iron ore the main draw. In fact, it had an unusually strong concentration of these resources in comparison with much of the Mediterranean – sources were poor in Greece and Phoenicia, for example. Even today the northern coastal area of Etruria is recognised for these resources, being known as the Colline Metallifere ('metal-bearing hills').

Metal resources were therefore part of the reason why in the eighth century BC Tyrrhenian Italy began to be visited more regularly by foreign merchants travelling by ship. But we also need to take into account local developments. The thriving centres of Tyrrhenian Italy were also part of the draw, perhaps even the main part. Metal ores had probably been exploited locally from an early era, and it is likely that they were under Etruscan control.

There were two main reasons for increased interaction at this time. The first was the Phoenician diaspora to the western Mediterranean that occurred in the ninth and eighth century BC. This is traditionally attributed to Assyrian pressure on the coastal cities of the Levant, which was associated with the conquests in the area of Syria and Lebanon by the Assyrian empire. But more recently scholars have emphasised other factors engendering a wave of emigration to the west.[28] These include the new economic imperatives and opportunities in the west

---

27. Bartoloni, *Cultura villanoviana*, fig. 6.15.
28. Aubet, *Phoenicians and the West*, 70–1; Botto, 'Primi contatti', 145.

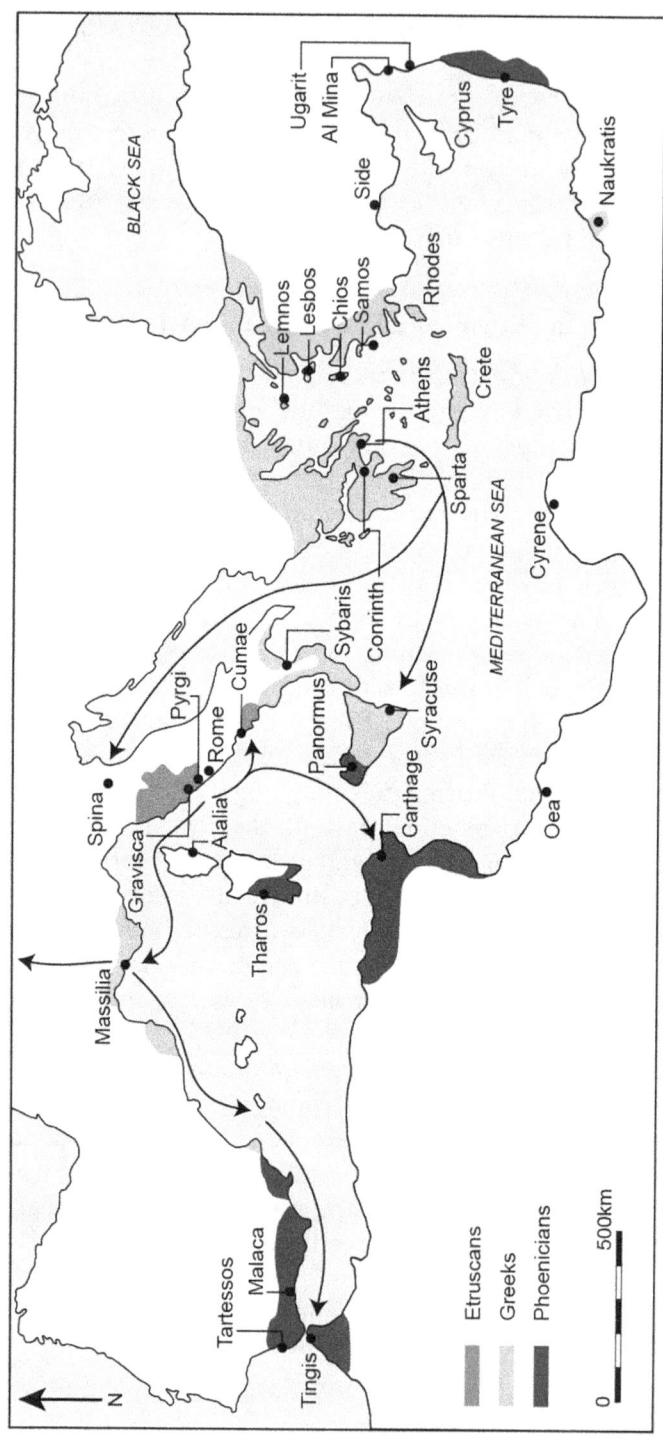

Figure 2.5 Map of Greek and Phoenician settlement in the Mediterranean, with the key Etruscan trade routes (after Lulof and van Kampen (eds), *Etruscans*, 17)

in terms of agricultural land (such as at Carthage) and metal resources (for example in southern Spain). Carthage was probably founded at this point (traditionally in 814 BC), and many Phoenicians settled in Africa, Spain, Sicily and Sardinia. Some must have come to Italy too, as we shall see; but typically it is their influence rather than their presence that is visible in the evidence.[29]

The second reason for increasing foreign contact is the foundation of Pithecusae on the island of Ischia, and subsequent Greek settlements on the mainland of Italy (Fig. 2.6).[30] Pithecusae occupies a promontory with a harbour on each side. It seems to have been part habitation, part trading-station (so in ancient terminology somewhere between an *emporion* and *apoikia*). Important information on the life of the settlement comes from a large rubbish dump on the acropolis (Monte Vico), from an 'industrial' quarter of the town (the area of Mezzavia), and from its cemetery, which stretched around the neck of the promontory. Around 1300 graves have been excavated, dating from the mid eighth century onwards, yet making up only 10 per cent of the cemetery area. The earliest pottery, middle geometric chevron skyphoi from Euboea and Corinth, dates to before 750 BC, around 770 BC.[31] Some graves contain eastern goods, such as Phoenician transport amphorae, Egyptian scarabs, and semi-precious stone seals of the so-called Lyre-player group (also found in Falerii, and many Greek sanctuaries), possibly from north Syria. Ridgway estimated the inhabitants in the mid eighth century to be *c.*5–10,000 people.[32] This shows the intensity of contact that had already developed by around 750 BC, as the settlement, and therefore its residents, were almost totally dependent on trade and industry. The excavators have discovered workshops that probably undertook metalsmithing at Mezzavia, and evidence for the production of pottery and ornaments such as fibulae. Strabo (5.4.9) attests to the presence of goldsmithing, a largely Phoenician skill according to Cristofani, and analysis of iron slag from the acropolis identifies it as coming from Elba.[33]

---

29. For early Phoenician contacts, see Botto, 'Primi contatti'.
30. Pithecusae may be a manifestation of increasing trade rather than a cause.
31. This is the traditional dating (Ridgway, *First Western Greeks*, 87; Tandy, *Warriors into Traders*, 66). However, a revised chronology proposed by Nijboer, based on radiocarbon dating, moves this to *c.*815 (see Janko, 'From Gabii and Gordion', 14).
32. Osborne, *Greece in the Making*, 41 for further estimates.
33. Cristofani, *Etruschi del mare*, 20; Ridgway, *First Western Greeks*, 34–5, 91–6; the Elban provenance is questioned by Tandy, *Warriors into Traders*, 66 n. 30.

Figure 2.6 Greek colonisation in Sicily and southern Italy (after Forsythe, *Critical History*, map 5)

Pithecusae was a Euboean foundation, although there was a mixed population, with Phoenicians and perhaps Etruscans settled alongside Greeks. The evidence for Phoenicians is strong, consisting of a handful of Semitic inscriptions, including a Phoenician religious symbol, and the widespread use of Phoenician imports in burials, particularly aryballoi (perfume containers), items of ritual significance in the Levant.[34] In addition, the similarity of ornaments in burials here with those in south Etruscan cemeteries encouraged Buchner to hypothesise the presence of women from the mainland wearing their native dress and fibulae to adorn it. The picture is quite complex: the particular fibula types (leech, navicella, serpentine, and bone and amber)

---

34. Cristofani, *Etruschi del mare*, 20–1; Ridgway, *First Western Greeks*, 111–18. The proportions are unknown; Ridgway hypothesises a Levantine presence of between 15 and 30 per cent, if the proportion of burials with Phoenician items is representative.

do match female burials, but serpentine fibulae also turn up in male burials, normally hypothesised to be Greek.[35] Nevertheless contacts with south Etruria were clearly intense. The near-contemporaneous importation and local production of chevron skyphoi of Euboean origin and type in Veii and Campania demonstrate the connections made through Pithecusae, from where fragments of similar cups have been found.[36]

Pithecusae thrived on exchange, quickly developing a substantial population and playing a major role in the distribution of goods across the Mediterranean, such as the wine jug made there which turned up in Carthage (North Africa) in 740–730 BC. The settlement flourished until around 700 BC. By then new Greek centres were developing in southern Italy and Sicily on more promising sites with greater agricultural potential. The first settlement on the mainland is at Cumae, around 750 BC, and the first Sicilian settlement at Zancle and Naxos appears very soon after (Table 2.2).[37]

Intense debate rages over the extent of the influence of these developments. The impact of this settlement was considerable, but it can no longer be seen as a case of a more advanced region (Greece) influencing a more primitive one (Tyrrhenian Italy).[38] As our knowledge of the proto-urban centres of early Iron Age central Italy has improved, it has become evident that the first Greek traders and settlers in central Italy encountered sophisticated societies with well-organised economies. Metal resources in Etruria, for instance, were certainly controlled and exploited locally. Thus, we need to think in terms of mutual interaction rather than a key spark, and in terms of multi-polar networks, rather than centre and periphery models.

The Orientalising period in central Italy

The result of these intense, early contacts was a very rich and thoroughly Mediterranean culture developing along the entire western coast of Italy from the fourth quarter of the eighth century onwards.

---

35. Assessed by Shepherd, 'Fibulae and females'; Osborne, *Greece in the Making*, 43.
36. Ridgway, *First Western Greeks*, 131–2. Note also the eighth-century Euboean pottery from Rome, discussed by La Rocca, 'Ceramica'.
37. D'Agostino, 'Euboean colonisation', argues that the earliest ceramic evidence from Pithecusae and Cumae is contemporaneous, though it is difficult to fix on any particular date for Cumae; cf. Demand, *Mediterranean Context*, 118.
38. E.g. Tandy, *Warriors into Traders*, 66: 'primitive but materially affluent Etruscans'; corrective in Osborne, *Greece in the Making*.

Table 2.2 Greek settlements in mainland Italy[a]

Settlement	Founders	Date BC	Literary evidence from Eusebius or other sources	Earliest archaeological evidence (from Osborne)
Pithecusae	Euboeans (Eretria/Chalcis)	c.770	Before Cumae (Livy)	Pre-750
Cumae	Euboeans and Pithecusae	c.725	Oldest Italiote city (Strabo)	Just after 725
Rhegium	Chalcis and Zancle	c.720	Time of the first Messenian war	720s
Sybaris	Achaea	c.720	709–708 (Dionysius of Halicarnassus)	720s
Croton	Achaea	c.710	709 (Eusebius)	7th c.
Taras (Latin Tarentum)	Sparta	c.700	706 (Eusebius)	c.700
Metapontum	Achaea	c.700	775/4 (Eusebius)	c.725–700
Neapolis	Cumae, Syracuse, Athens	c.700–600		c.470
Caulonia	Croton	c.700–675	After Croton	c.700
Laos	Sybaris	c.700–600		
Temesa	Croton	c.700–600		
Terina	Croton	c.700–600		
Poseidonia (Latin Paestum)	Sybaris/Achaea	c.700–675	After Sybaris	c.600
Locri Epizephirii	Locri	c.675	673–672 (Eusebius)	c.700
Siris	Colophon	c.650		c.700
Hipponion	Locri Epizephirii	c.625–600		c.620
Nicotera	Locri Epizephirii	c.600		
Medma	Locri Epizephirii	c.600		c.600
Elea (Latin Velia)	Phocaea and Massalia	c.535		6th c.
Dicaearchia (Latin Puteoli)	Samos	c.531	531 (Eusebius)	
Pyxus	Rhegium	c.471		
Thurii	Athens/Panhellenic colony	444–443		
Heraclea	Taras	433		Late 5th c.

[a]After Lomas, *Rise of Rome*, table 2, 29; Bartoloni, *Cultura villanoviana*, table 7.1, 199; Osborne, *Greece in the Making*, table 5, 121–5.

Early Italy, from the Bronze Age to the classical era 53

The wealth to be made from this trade is evident from the cemeteries of Etruria, Latium and Campania, although one should not discount the contribution of agricultural resources. From the end of the early Iron Age (the Villanovan period in Etruria), *c.*730 BC, the quality and quantity of the material in tombs rapidly increased. The characteristically eastern style of much of this material gives the period 730–580 the name 'Orientalising'. This term derives from art history, and expresses the strong foreign influence on Greek art in this period. It is visible in Etruria, Latium and Campania too, on a very substantial scale. This was a Mediterranean-wide phenomenon, involving deep interaction between the cities of Tyrrhenian Italy, mainland Greece and the Aegean, and the cities and kingdoms of the eastern Mediterranean, and perhaps direct personal relationships and migration between the Near East and Italy.[39]

The Orientalising period was an era of great change in central Italy. We see the first clear manifestations of a fully articulated social hierarchy, with the emergence of a high elite and rulers/kings in some communities. The elite adopted new lifestyles, based around banqueting and wine-drinking (Fig. 2.7). Craftworking developed in many areas, including extraordinarily impressive work in gold and ivory (developed from Near Eastern contacts) and the production of local finewares such as thin-walled bucchero pottery, using the

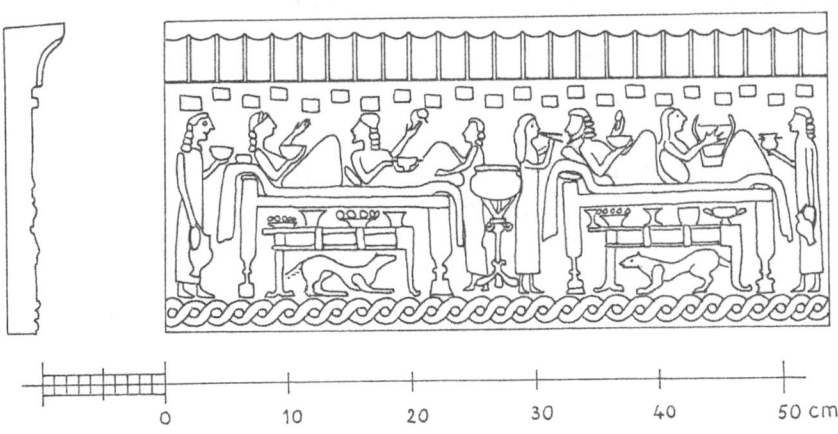

Figure 2.7 Banquet scene on architectural terracotta plaque from Murlo, northern Etruria, early sixth century BC (drawing: R. Sponer Za, for Winter, *Symbols*, 153–9, Roof 3–8, Plan 9)

39. Sannibale, 'Orientalizing Etruria'.

wheel. Large sculptural representations were undertaken for the first time, and decorative architecture flourished. Much of this happened under the impetus of contacts with Greeks and Phoenicians, and the settlement of master artisans from these areas in Tyrrhenian Italy. City living began to develop on a substantial scale, as these societies underwent urbanisation. Monumental architecture was attempted for the first time. Etruscan exploitation of metal resources developed considerably, and more intensive agricultural techniques were employed, producing olive oil, wine and grain. Imported goods expanded exponentially, especially from Greece and the Near East.[40]

In the last quarter of the eighth century BC very rich burials begin to appear, reaching a peak in the seventh century BC.[41] They are characterised by items of jewellery and treasure in precious metals, the accoutrements of banqueting and wine-drinking, weaponry and vehicles for transport. We find much material (often imported) in the form of bronze tripods, cauldrons, perfume flasks, armour and chariots. Imported ceramics are also common. The importance of banqueting and wine-drinking is quite evident from the range of items such as spits and skewers, wine cups and cauldrons, graters (for cheese mixed with wine, a Greek practice), and tripod bowls for mixing aromatic ingredients (a Near Eastern practice).[42] Status symbols abound: chariots and funerary wagons; parade weaponry, particularly shields; and symbolic items such as fans and sceptres, typical of monarchic iconography in the contemporary Near East.

Particularly striking are the class of ribbed bronze drinking bowls (*patera baccellata*), of which some 300 examples have been found in Tyrrhenian Italy.[43] Their decorated bases were designed to catch the sediment from the aromatics added to wine in this era. The earliest examples, of the late eighth century, are imports from Uratu and Assyria in the Near East, and are found in tombs of the highest rank (such as the example, one of four, from Tomb 600 in Osteria dell'Osa, which has direct parallels in Assur, Assyria) (Fig. 2.8).[44] They are then produced locally in much greater numbers. In the Near East they are closely associated with the figure of the king, and their

---

40. Steingraber, *Abundance of Life*, 31–2 provides a convenient list of such items. Fuller discussions are provided by Sannibale, 'Orientalizing Etruria', and Gunter, 'Etruscans'.
41. Fulminante, *Sepolture*.
42. Riva, *Urbanisation*, 144–6.
43. Catalogued by Sciacca, *Patere baccellate*.
44. Sciacca, 'Circolazione', 282.

Early Italy, from the Bronze Age to the classical era 55

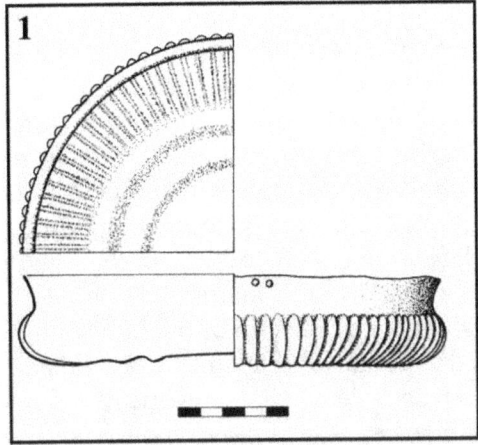

Figure 2.8 *Patera baccellata* from Tomb 600, Osteria dell'Osa (Sciacca, 'Circolazione', fig. 1. Courtesy of Soprintendenza Speciale Archeologia Belle Arti e Paesaggio di Roma)

use in Tyrrhenian tombs implies a close assimilation of Oriental elite ideology.

Some of this material is imported from the eastern Mediterranean, from areas such as Cyprus, and some is produced by Syrian or Phoenician artisans who have settled in Italy. Goldsmithing is one of the most distinctive and easily recognised areas, with the introduction of complex techniques such as granulation, filigree and knurling (*godronatura*).[45] Other important fields include the working of ivory and amber, metal, glass, faience, pottery, architecture, sculpture and wall-painting.[46] It is also evident that Greek potters were active in the mid eighth century in Tyrrhenian Italy, given the production of Greek-style chevron skyphoi at Veii, and painted local pottery using Greek forms in Campania (Capua and Pontecagnano), southern Etruria and Latium.[47] Syrian sculptors are attested by stone statuary in Etruria in the seventh century BC at the Tomb of the Statues in Relief, Caere, and at Vetulonia. This shows that there is a strong Near Eastern presence in central Italy well before the Pyrgi tablets attest Phoenician speakers in the sixth century.

---

45. Naso, 'Influssi', 434.
46. Naso, 'Influssi'.
47. Ridgway, *First Western Greeks*, 129; Tabolli and Cerasuolo, *Veii*, 160; Naso, 'Influssi', 444 notes that Greek ceramicists were active at Vulci, Tarquinii and Caere in the eighth century BC.

In the seventh century tomb styles change, with large chamber tombs appearing in the first half of the century at Caere. These closely parallel near-contemporary Lydian and Phrygian examples, suggesting that inspiration was drawn directly from there.[48] These tombs were often used over a long period of time, and could contain several generations of the same family. An example is Tumulus 2 in the Banditaccia cemetery of Caere, some 40 m across, containing four chamber tombs (Fig. 2.9). These date from *c.*680–450 BC, so the tomb is in use over two hundred years (perhaps with hiatuses). Although we cannot be certain they were all in the ownership of the same family, these tombs seem to have served as claims of the family's permanency and wealth, and as such are often considered characteristic of the emergence of an elevated elite within society. Cults celebrating family ancestors were associated with these tombs, which sometimes incorporated monumental staircases and platforms for such rituals, or contained statuary

Figure 2.9 The entrance to the Tomb of the Greek Vases in Tumulus 2, Banditaccia cemetery, Caere (photo: G. Bradley)

48. Naso, 'Influssi', 444, with more examples.

representing ancestors.[49] Nevertheless, these elites were for the most part highly mobile, fluid, and permeable to outsiders.[50]

The earliest tomb paintings and architectural iconography survive from this era. Chamber tombs appear from the late eighth century at Veii, and in the early seventh century we see the first painted tombs. The earliest examples are the Tomb of the Roaring Lions (discovered as recently as 2006), dating to 700–690 BC, the Tomb of the Ducks (680–670 BC), and the Campana Tomb of c.650 BC. There are also early painted tombs from Caere, such as the Mengarelli Tomb and the tombs of the Sorbo necropolis (c.675–650 BC).[51]

Of the so-called 'princely tombs' of this era, the most famous example is the Regolini-Galassi Tomb (Caere), whose contents are now displayed in the Vatican. It contained two burials, the most important of which may be female. The tumulus cut into rock is typical. It is preserved here as the original tumulus was covered by a later one with five further burial shafts. It contained luxurious gold ornaments and banqueting equipment (Figs 2.10, 2.11). Much of the metalwork has an orientalising style, and is likely to have been produced in Phoenician workshops. This includes three large gilded silver plates with Egyptianising motifs in relief, including one with a scene of lion hunts, typical of Near Eastern art, and processions of armed men (Fig. 2.10).[52] Very similar accoutrements are found in the Bernardini Tomb at Praeneste in Latium.

Particularly revealing for Near Eastern influences is another Latin burial, Tomb 70 from Laurentina, in a pseudo-chamber tomb (a very large trench grave, a transitional form on the way to a full chamber tomb cut into the rock) (Fig. 2.12). It dates to the mid seventh century BC and is attributed to a woman. Among the immensely rich equipment, there was a chariot, a wooden throne, a bronze footstool and a bronze fan (Fig. 2.13), associated with items for the consumption of wine (two wine-serving tables, mixing basins and drinking cups). This collection of items closely recalls Near Eastern iconography relating to sovereigns. Botto draws attention to the similar emphasis apparently placed in both societies on the

---

49. Bartoloni, 'Tomba', 167–8, with illustrations of Tumulus II at Cerveteri; Riva, *Urbanisation*. Note also the Tumulus II del Sodo at Cortona (Bartoloni (ed.), *Principi*, cat. no. 109).
50. Bradley, 'Investigating aristocracy'.
51. Bartoloni, 'Necropoli', 89; Steingraber, *Abundance of Life*, 33.
52. Sannibale, 'Ori'.

Figure 2.10 Gilded silver plate from Regolini-Galassi Tomb, *c.*675–650 BC, of probable Phoenician production (from Grifi, *Monumenti*, 214, Tav. V)

Figure 2.11 Large gold fibula from Regolini-Galassi Tomb, *c*.675–650 BC (from Grifi, *Monumenti*, 205, Tav. II)

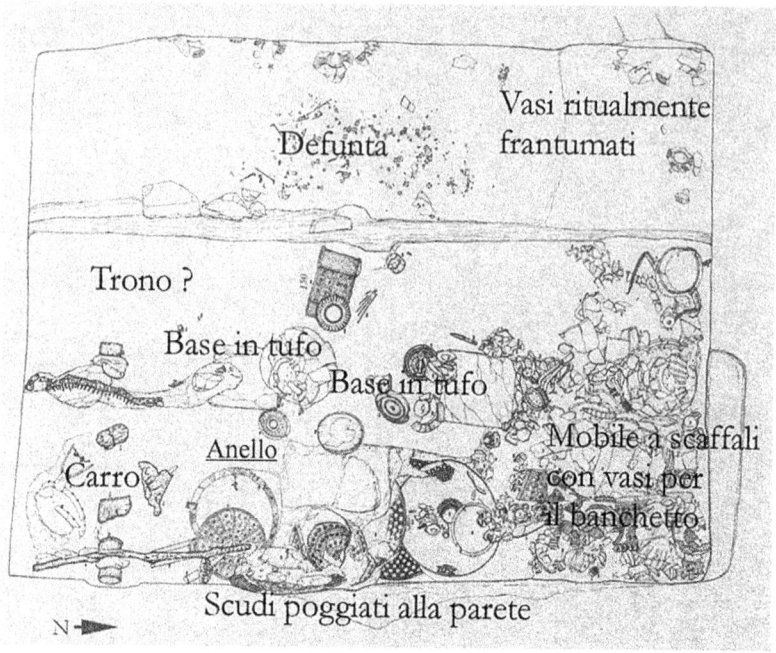

Figure 2.12 Plan of Tomb 70, Acqua Acetosa Laurentina. Labelled are the deceased ('defunta'), ritually broken vases ('vasi ritualmente frantumati'), a possible throne ('trono?'), pillars in tufa ('base in tufo'), chariot ('carro'), ring ('anello'), funerary equipment on shelves with banqueting vases ('mobile a scaffali con vasi per il banchetto'), and shields placed on the walls ('scudi poggiati alla parete') (from Bedini, 'La tomba 70 dell'Acqua Acetosa Laurentina', in Carandini and Cappelli (eds), *Roma*, 356. Courtesy of Soprintendenza Speciale Archeologia Belle Arti e Paesaggio di Roma)

role of powerful women, and argues for the direct influence on central Italy 'from Phoenician city states and Neo-Hittite and Aramaic kingdoms in the Syrio-Palestinian area' without Greek mediation (where a quite different iconography and ideology was prevalent).[53] A similarly complex array of material comes from another Latin pseudo-chamber tomb, Tomb XV at Castel di Decima, of the last quarter of the eighth century BC. This was a single male inhumation in a chamber of 5.3 × 4.8 m (much larger than the others), containing a possible sceptre, a silver fibula and cup, a fan, bronze vases, iron weapons, horse bits and wagon fragments, and pottery

---

53. Botto, 'Considerazioni'.

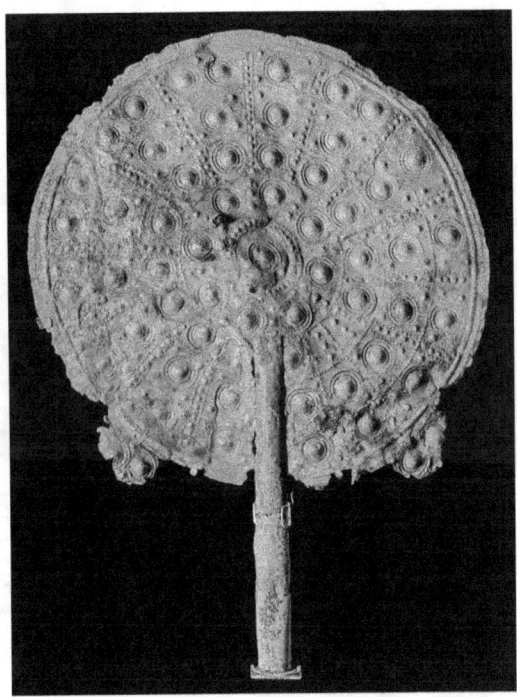

Figure 2.13 Bronze fan from Tomb 70, Acqua Acetosa Laurentina
(by concession of the Ministero per i beni e le attività culturali e per il turismo – Museo Nazionale Romano)

(including three Thapsos cups, and a Phoenician wine amphora).[54] This material reveals the strong influences of the eastern Mediterranean on central Italy in this period.

Another critical development is the adoption of the alphabet in central Italy. At some point in the ninth or early eighth century the Greek alphabet was created by adding vowels to the Phoenician alphabet. This must have occurred at a place where Greeks and Phoenicians mixed. Curiously, the oldest known Greek inscription actually comes from a Latin context: the town of Gabii, just to the south of Rome. This is a graffito on a local impasto flask of Latial period IIB2 from female Tomb 482 of Osteria dell'Osa, originally dated to c.770 BC (Fig. 2.14). In fact, the inscription may be considerably older, c.825 BC, if we accept the redating of Greek geometric pottery sequences

---

54. Winther, 'Princely tombs'. The closeness of the parallels implies familiarity with Syrian practices (Botto, 'Considerazioni', 70); and probably individual relationships (Sannibale, 'Ori').

Figure 2.14 Impasto flask with graffito, from female Tomb 482 of Osteria dell'Osa, dating to c.825–770 BC (by concession of the Ministero per i beni e le attività culturali e per il turismo – Museo Nazionale Romano)

suggested by dendrochronology. The script is Euboean Greek, and reads *eulin(os)* 'good at spinning'. An alternative reading has been suggested by Colonna, taking it to be Latin and therefore reading in the other direction as *ni lue* 'do not pay', but this is less plausible.[55] The presence of the Euboean script suggests that Pithecusae could be the place where the alphabet was invented.

The alphabet was soon copied and diffused through central Italy. The earliest Etruscan inscriptions, dating to around 700 BC, have three Phoenician sibilants (consonants with *s* or *sh* sounds) which were lost in Greek.[56] Alphabetaria such as the ivory example from Marsiliana d'Albegna from before the mid seventh century, show that the full alphabet was borrowed and retaught as a unit. The earliest inscription in Latin is *salvetod tita* of *c*.670 BC, from Tomb 115 of Gabii. Normally the script is thought to have been transmitted from Etruscan to Latin rather than directly from Greek. But Janko has recently shown that there was a more direct Latin (and indeed Sabine) borrowing of the alphabet from the Euboeans, due to the parallel pronunciation of X as *ks*, rather than as *sh*, as in south Etruscan.[57] The 'epigraphic habit' became widely diffused through central Italy, although far more evidence comes from Etruria than from Latium and Campania. Before 600 BC we have only four to five Latin inscriptions, in comparison to over 150 Etruscan examples; before 100 BC the proportions are *c*.3000 to *c*.9000.[58] This has encouraged some scholars to hypothesise that the Etruscans were more literate than the Romans and Latins, who have been presented very much as the secondary partners in this process. But the disparity is once more strongly conditioned by the different patterns of the recovery of evidence from the two regions, which is skewed towards the survival of evidence from Etruscan chamber tombs, and by the greater extent of Etruria.[59]

Thus, the very active trade of the Tyrrhenian seaboard in the Orientalising period had a profound influence on the social structures of Etruscan, Latin and Campanian societies. Near Eastern links are evident in a huge range of features in lifestyles, funerary ritual, architecture,

---

55. Janko, 'From Gabii and Gordion', 15 with references.
56. The earliest example is a graffito on a Protocorinthian kotyle from Tarquinii (Agostiniani, 'Etruscan language', 457).
57. Janko, 'From Gabii and Gordion', 22, with additional arguments.
58. Clackson and Horrocks, *Blackwell History of the Latin Language*, 10.
59. Stoddart and Whitley, 'Social context'; Harris, *Ancient Literacy*; Cornell, 'Tyranny of the evidence' for a corrective.

and production and the economy.⁶⁰ These influences were mixed with Greek cultural links, that accelerated after the foundation of Pithecusae and Cumae. The importation of foreign items in the eighth century was typically followed by local production of imitations, especially from the mid seventh century. Artisans from both regions must have been present in central Italy in this era, and are particularly evident in the spheres of metalworking (Phoenician artisans) and ceramics (Greek potters). The workshops they must have helped to set up were responsible for a wide range of products that fed into a long history of local art, artisanship and architecture. These influences do not neatly coincide with the period, and, as many scholars have pointed out, in fact predate it, particularly as archaeological knowledge of the ninth and eighth centuries proceeds. Nevertheless, the significance of the increased impetus in these trends from the last quarter of the eighth century is still evident.

Urbanisation in central Italy

Perhaps the most critical development of the Orientalising period is urbanisation, the development of cities. The evidence for this is complex, given that we know much more about cemeteries than we do about urban centres, a bias that is only slowly being corrected through the increasing focus of research projects on the latter. Urbanisation as a phenomenon develops out of the proto-urbanisation of the early Iron Age. By the late seventh and sixth centuries it affects the whole of the Etrusco-Latial-Campanian area. It sees the creation of designated spaces for collective activities (though these are yet to be uncovered in many cities), contiguous living spaces, more densely occupied than the patchy settlement in the early Iron Age, and monumental buildings.

When a proto-urban settlement becomes urban is heavily debated, but it remains a somewhat arbitrary point.⁶¹ In a famous article published in 1950, the archaeologist Gordon Childe, who introduced innovative social concepts into archaeological synthesis, posited the following ten-point checklist for an urban settlement: '1. concentration of a relatively large number of people in a restricted area; 2. craft specialization; 3. appropriation by a central authority of an economic surplus; 4. monumental public architecture; 5. developed

---

60. Naso, 'Influssi', for an overview.
61. Peroni, 'Formazione'; Pacciarelli, *Dal villaggio alla città*; Pacciarelli, 'Forme di complessità sociale'; Osborne, 'Urban sprawl'.

social stratification; 6. emergence of sciences; 7. use of writing [or the invention of scripts]; 8. naturalistic art; 9. foreign trade; 10. group membership [in a state organization] based on residence rather than kinship'.[62]

Nevertheless, it has become clear from the expansion of the dataset of urban centres worldwide, and through the work of new world archaeology and anthropology in particular, that some of these features are by no means typical, and requiring them imposes modernising preconceptions. For instance, cities occur without alphabetic literacy in Central America (as Childe perceptively noted), and naturalistic art existed in the Neolithic period before cities, as did monumental architecture (think of Stonehenge), foreign trade and astronomical science.[63] In addition, the absence of urbanisation in these conventional terms has not necessarily been a barrier to state formation, even in Italy.[64] In fact, traces of early urban centres are notably exiguous in the eighth and seventh centuries BC, before the great expansion of monumental building.[65] What is important is the process and the implications of urbanisation for the emergence of the 'state', in terms of political authority, collective social organisation, economy and religion.[66]

One key development is the appearance of monumental buildings. This is an important manifestation of power and is readily visible in archaeological terms. Monumentalisation can be defined as an increasing scale of structures beyond the utilitarian, and the deliberate display of the expenditure of human energy for symbolic purposes.[67] But although monumentalisation is eminently obvious in archaeological terms, it is a manifestation of, rather than a substitute for, pre-existing social organisation.[68] It is made possible by the employment of stone foundations and tiled roofs from around the

---

62. E.g. Childe, 'Urban revolution', 10–16; I here reproduce with minor adaptation the summarised version in Osborne, 'Urban sprawl'. Compare Smith, 'V. Gordon Childe', 21, emphasising Childe's model of the 'variability and political nature of ancient planning'.
63. Smith, 'V. Gordon Childe', 13–14.
64. Bradley, 'Tribes, states and cities'; Isayev, *Inside Ancient Lucania*, 55–8; Scopacasa, *Ancient Samnium*.
65. Polignac, 'Forms and processes' on Greek colonial sites; Ampolo, 'Problema delle origini' on Rome.
66. Bradley, *Ancient Umbria*, 29–41; Smith, 'Beginnings', 102; Hopkins, *Genesis*, 26–7.
67. For this 'thermodynamic theory' of monumentalisation see Meyers, 'Experience of monumentality'; Hopkins, *Genesis*, 38.
68. Müller-Karpe, *Vom Anfang Roms*; Smith, 'Beginnings'; Fulminante, *Urbanisation*, especially 220–1; Hopkins, *Genesis*, 24.

mid seventh century BC.[69] These developments were probably linked, as the strength of stone foundations was needed for supporting the new heavy roofs of terracotta tiles.

Tiled roofs had been used in Greece as early as the third millennium BC (e.g. at the 'House of Tiles', Lerna). But it is only with the development of new production techniques allowing standardised production of tiles that the technology came to be spread widely across the Mediterranean. The earliest examples of this new type of tiled roof come from the area of Corinth, notably the temple of Apollo of *c.*675 BC. The technology then spread rapidly to central Italy, where the earliest examples are found at Acquarossa, San Giovenale, Murlo and Rome in the second half of the seventh century.[70] This new building technique was adapted to western conditions: whereas Greek tiles were gently curved, Italian sites used flat pan-tiles with raised edges, which provided better protection against the heavy rain more common in Italy. In Rome the clay beds in the Velabrum were widely exploited from the late seventh century. Rome has a tiled building on the Sacra Via from *c.*650–625 BC, and the first phase of the Regia, which dates from *c.*620 BC.[71] These first stone, wood and terracotta structures were then rapidly followed by buildings on the site of the Comitium, the site of the temple of Castor, and on the northern slope of the Palatine in the last quarter of the seventh century BC. These early Roman roofs used the same type of tile structure as Acquarossa, but employed a different clay source, showing how new technological ideas were shared between Rome and Etruria.[72]

It is clear that these buildings evolve from large wooden buildings, often misleadingly called 'huts' given their relatively sophisticated construction and continued existence for multiple centuries.[73] This type of larger wooden building was typical of the early Iron Age, and has been found at many sites, such as the Palatine, the acropolis at Satricum, and San Giovenale. The most distinctive early buildings were long structures, with several interconnected rooms arranged linearly. The most elaborate buildings were large courtyard complexes known from six sites in central Italy, and epitomised by

---

69. Drews, 'Coming of the city'; Potts, *Religious Architecture*, 31; Hopkins, *Genesis*, 39.
70. Ammerman et al., 'Clay beds', 9.
71. The Domus Regia dated by Filippi, 'Domus Regia' (but not confirmed yet) would be the earliest in central Italy.
72. Ammerman et al., 'Clay beds', 26.
73. Colantoni, 'Straw to stone'.

the second phase of the Murlo complex (Figs 2.15, 2.16) and the Montetosto sanctuary outside Caere.[74] Sometimes called 'palaces', these structures were characterised by their huge scale, decorative roofs and associations with cult, particularly of ancestors.

The earliest temples appear in the early sixth century BC, and were distinguished by decorative roof schemes. The first is the Sant'Omobono temple of around 580.[75] Sant'Omobono sets the trend for the standardised type of Italic temple, marked by a high podium and a wooden superstructure decorated with terracottas. Although derived from Greek examples, in Italy a different form was ultimately settled on. The building of temples seems to represent a widely shared shift in aristocratic expenditure. Wealth was now spent in a public context, on temples, instead of a private one (tombs), a sign of a new 'civic' mentality.[76] In a parallel development we shall see that at Rome urbanisation was connected to the figure of the king, who needed the prestige of great building projects.

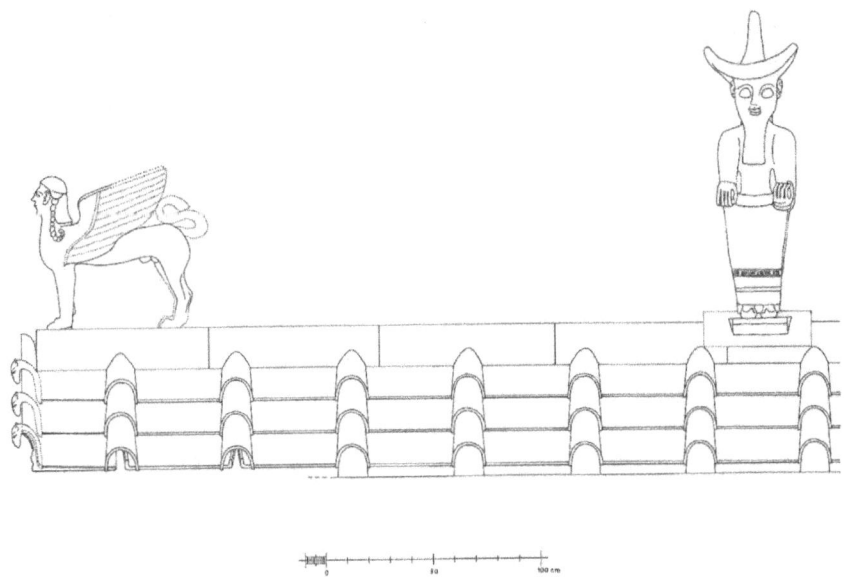

Figure 2.15 Murlo, roof system of second phase of palace complex, c.580–575 BC (drawing: R. Sponer Za, for Winter, *Symbols*, 153–9, Roof 3–8, Plan 9)

74. Potts, *Religious Architecture*, 141–3.
75. Potts, *Religious Architecture*, 40. See further details in later chapters.
76. Smith, *Early Rome and Latium*, 187.

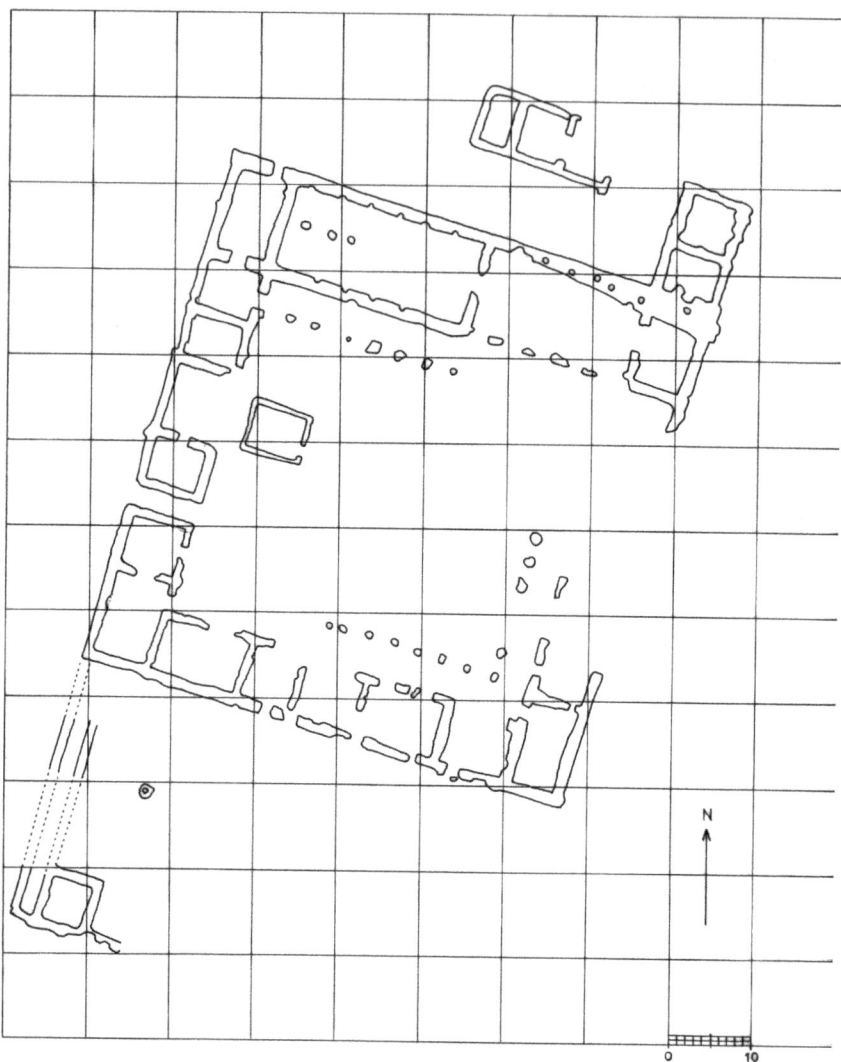

Figure 2.16 Murlo, plan of second phase of palace complex, *c*.580–575 BC (drawing: R. Sponer Za, for Winter, *Symbols*, 153–9, Roof 3–8, Plan 9)

Later developments in cemeteries in central Italy can be linked in to these processes. In Latium, burials with grave goods decline from around 600 BC, and end almost entirely by 550 BC. Colonna showed in an influential article that this was probably a product of new ideals of equality (or at least *isonomia*, equality before the law), drawn from Greek cities. The practice is generally different in Etruria, where later tombs in the fifth century continue to receive huge quantities of precious items such as Attic vases. There are, however, indications in Etruscan tomb architecture that these ideals had some effect. From 550 BC onwards the circular style of tombs becomes less fashionable, and tombs are increasingly regularised and organised into rectilinear streets, visible at Caere and Volsinii. This implies that the political community was developing more control over its citizens, and superseding the family groups which were hitherto dominant. In Tarquinii painted frescoes were common in tombs from the sixth century. At least some of these paintings were executed by Greek artists, commissioned by Etruscan nobles. The scenes represented are clearly symbolic of the common values shared by the elites of this period, with an emphasis on competition and athleticism, banqueting and celebration, and the importance of married couples (however, the presence of women here is strikingly different from Greek iconography of the banquet).

Later developments in Tyrrhenian connectivity: trading places and shipwrecks

Pithecusae is one of the earliest symptoms of the Mediterranean-wide trade network that becomes particularly active in the seventh and sixth centuries BC.[77] There is increasingly good evidence for this trade and mobility in the western Mediterranean.[78] We are best informed about Etruscan participation in Tyrrhenian trade, and it is usually assumed that the Etruscan cities participated more enthusiastically in seaborne trade, naval expeditions and piratical activities than Rome and the Latins. There is some truth to this, but it is not the whole story. Participation in Mediterranean-wide trade networks is well documented through the copious evidence from Etruscan cemeteries. But the more negative picture of Rome and Latium is in part the product of distorting factors: an undue reticence in Roman historiography about recognising the role Rome and the Latins must have played in this commercial activity; the diversion of resources in Latium away from cemeteries from the early sixth century (Orientalising burials in Latium show myriad foreign links before the virtual closing down of burials by 580 BC); and the particularly disturbed conditions of Rome's archaeological remains from the archaic period. It is sobering to consider how difficult it would be to recover the full extent of the foreign links of

---

77. Malkin, *Small Greek World* discusses network theory.
78. Cristofani, *Etruschi del mare*; Della Fina, *Etruschi e il Mediterraneo*; Della Fina, *Etruschi, greci, fenici e cartaginesi*.

Etruscan cities in the period before the beginnings of coastal *emporia* around 600 BC without the evidence of their cemeteries. Studies of Roman architecture are finally starting to address this imbalance, and to stress the city's integration into wider Mediterranean currents.[79] It thus seems justified to pay considerable attention to this evidence for Etruria, without wishing to directly apply it to Rome, and also to maintain awareness of the convergent trajectories of Etruscan and Romano-Latin societies in the Orientalising and archaic periods.

From the ninth century, coastal communities engaged in exchanges with the Nuraghic peoples of Sardinia and Oenotrian communities in southern Italy. Small Sardinian bronzes are widespread in Etruria and Campania, such as the distinctive form of bronze boats found at Vetulonia, Populonia, Vulci and Pithecusae in the seventh century. More broadly, Etruscan imports include metal ornaments, figurines, weapons, metal bowls and ceramic askoid jugs, and Etruscan objects were also traded in the opposite direction.[80] It is likely that migrants from Sardinia are responsible for some bronze and ceramic production in Villanovan contexts.

Etruscan trade is also known from finds across Mediterranean and Continental Europe. Links between Gaul and Villanovan and Etruscan Italy sustained Celtic elites in France. Many of the traded goods have left little trace, such as slaves, cloth and salt (for instance, from the major salt workings of Lorraine and Jura). But the more durable evidence of pottery, particularly the distinctive Etruscan product of bucchero, makes these connections very evident. Particularly striking is the oppidum of Saint-Blaise, overlooking a sheltered lagoon on the Rhône delta, and active from the late seventh century until around 520 BC, when it was side-lined by Massalia. The earliest dated amphorae are Corinthian and Attic SOS transport amphorae of the seventh century. The main bulk of the amphorae is Etruscan (some three quarters), and Sant Blaise has also produced the largest assemblage of bucchero anywhere outside Etruria. Other important evidence comes from the oppidum of Pech Macho in Languedoc. An inscribed plaque from this oppidum has Ionic Greek on one side and an older Etruscan text (first half of the fifth century) on the other, detailing a contract involving a deposit and official witnesses.

---

79. Cifani, *Architettura romana arcaica*; Potts, *Religious Architecture*; Hopkins, *Genesis*.
80. Bonfante, *Etruscan Life*, 74; Lo Schiavo and Milletti, 'Nuragic heritage', especially fig. 11.4.

Early Italy, from the Bronze Age to the classical era 71

There are also a number of small Etruscan wrecks dating to this period off the coast of both France and Italy. These show that Etruscans had early and direct involvement in maritime trade, and their contents are very informative about how interconnected these peoples were. This is exemplified by a shipwreck off the island of Giglio of c.580, whose varied cargo shows a wide range of trade links.[81] The contents include money (in the form of two bronze bars), and numerous lead and copper ingots; produce such as wine, resin and olives; Etruscan, Greek and Phoenician amphorae; Greek pottery (Laconian, Ionian, Corinthian) and Etruscan bucchero; aryballoi with perfumed oil; amber; a bronze olpe; a Corinthian helmet; numerous lamps; fishing equipment; and prestige items including a waxed tablet with a stylus, the remains of a kline (a couch or bed), vases relating to a drinking service, a krater and musical instruments. The best hypothesis is that this ship had an East Greek provenance and a halt at Corinth, at least for provisions, and undertook a series of mercantile operations in Etruria. At any stage on the voyage the crew must have had numerous contacts, all of which would have offered possibilities for the fertile exchange of goods and ideas.

Another important wreck, that of Grand Ribaud F, contained a thousand Etruscan amphorae, and may have had an Etruscanised Latin as a captain. Trade in wine with south Gaul was intense, as has been established by the high proportions of Etruscan amphorae found in the excavations of the archaic port at Massilia, and the enormous numbers dredged up from the Rhône. So it is clear that by the sixth century Etruscan activity had a properly mercantile character on a vast scale in the western Mediterranean, a phenomenon that had already begun in the seventh century. All this makes Etruscan populations now appear less the passive beneficiaries of Greek goods and ideas, and more as active participants in the economic circuits of the Tyrrhenian area.

Traders sailing this type of ship could meet native populations at mutually recognised places, called *emporia* (trading ports) by the Greeks. These were always associated with important sacred sites; sanctuaries seem to have played an important role in mediating relations between locals and outside traders, who were after supplies of metal, wood, agricultural products and other materials. These sanctuaries must also have been the site of periodic fairs and markets. The major Etruscan coastal *emporia* get going around 600 BC. Two examples have been thoroughly excavated on the Etruscan coast,

---

81. Spivey, *Etruscan Art*, 17–19; Bruni, 'Seafaring'.

Gravisca (connected to Tarquinii) and Pyrgi (the port of Caere). Both began to be frequented around 590 BC and thrived in the sixth and fifth centuries BC. They were notably cosmopolitan trading centres. It is worthwhile noting that Rome lies only 30–40 miles away from these sites: these are developments that certainly will have impacted on the city there.[82]

Gravisca was a very important *emporion* on the Etruscan coast, with many Greek features. It was the port of the major city of Tarquinii. The site was excavated from 1969, with key finds comprising votive materials which reveal the diversity and intensity of interactions occurring here. Its first phase dates to *c*.600–480 BC, and is notable for the Greek character of the cult here: a sanctuary was established to the Greek deities Aphrodite, Hera and Demeter in the early sixth century. The sanctuary shows that strong commercial contacts existed between Etruscan cities and the Greek world, and also points to links with Egypt. The first phase of the sanctuary featured an open-air precinct with three earth altars. The pottery recovered from the site is very cosmopolitan, including material from Massilia, Corinth, Laconia, Samos, Miletus, Chios and Etruria. There are large numbers of lamps (typical dedications to Demeter) from Ionia, the predominant source, Athens and Etruria. Most amphorae come from Ionia, but there are also examples from a wide range of other Mediterranean sources.[83]

Initially Gravisca was frequented almost exclusively by Eastern Greeks, as attested by the large number of dedications to Hera as graffiti on potsherds in the Ionian dialect and East Greek alphabet.[84] The earliest dedications are to Aphrodite, then Demeter and Hera. We know from the earliest Etruscan inscription, a dedication to Turan (*c*.560 BC), that the equivalence had been made between these Greek deities and their Etruscan counterparts already in an early phase of the sanctuary's existence.[85] The rich epigraphic haul reveals the presence of merchants from Samos, Ephesus and Miletus in Ionia, from Naucratis (an important Greek *emporion* in Egypt), and from Corinth, Aegina and Athens. The most famous example is a stone anchor dedicated to Apollo by Sostratos of Aegina, said to be the most successful merchant of all time by Herodotus (4.152) (Fig. 2.17).[86] Many Greek vases in

---

82. Coarelli, *Foro Boario*, 117–27; 'Santuari'.
83. Demetriou, *Negotiating identity*, 76.
84. Demetriou, *Negotiating identity*, 77 (noting that there are forty-three to Hera, six to Aphrodite, three to Apollo, one to Demeter, one to the Dioscuri or Zeus).
85. Cristofani, *Etruschi del mare*, 123. Turan was the Etruscan Aphrodite.
86. 'I belong to the Aeginetan Apollo. Sostratos, son of . . . . . had me made.' Demetriou, *Negotiating identity*, 80.

Early Italy, from the Bronze Age to the classical era

Figure 2.17 Anchor with dedication to Apollo by Sostratos, Gravisca (photo: G. Bradley, by concession of the Polo Museale del Lazio – Tarquinia (VT). Museo Archeologico Nazionale)

Etruria were found with SO marked on the bottom, almost certainly relating to him.[87] The quantities of material imply a very substantial and probably permanent Greek presence in this period.

Judging by the epigraphy, from the end of the sixth century the Greek presence in the sanctuary declines. The Etruscan presence predominates from c.480 BC, when we find only Etruscan epigraphy. The sanctuary nevertheless continues to flourish, being rebuilt at points in the fifth century, and remaining orientated around the cults (Turan–Aphrodite, Vei–Demeter and Uni–Hera) established in its Greek phase.[88] It finally disappears in the early third century, probably as a result of the Roman colonisation of the area. Thus Gravisca reveals intense interaction and interchange between local Etruscans and other areas of the Mediterranean only a little up the coast from Rome and Latium, and precisely at a critical period in its development. In this richly interconnected context it is worth remembering the story of Demaratus, the wealthy Corinthian trader who settled in Tarquinii at the time of the tyranny of Cypselus, and whose offspring migrated to Rome to assume the throne.[89]

The nearby site of Pyrgi is of similar interest, and shows very strong links with eastern and probably Carthaginian areas of the Mediterranean. It occupies a coastal zone some 13 km from Caere, and was connected to the city by a 10 m wide monumental paved road (Fig. 2.18). Its key evidence lies in its monumental buildings, rather than votive dedications (which are scarcer than at Gravisca). A complex of two temples was built in the northern sector of the sanctuary in the sixth century BC. The earlier temple (Temple B) dates to around 500 BC, and was dedicated to Uni–Astarte (the Etrusco-Phoenician version of Latin Juno). The temple has a typically Greek peripteral style (i.e. surrounded by a colonnade), and a decorative series of plaques and statuary celebrating the myth of Heracle (Hercules) and his association with Uni. The temple is situated in a courtyard complex with a line of at least seventeen small cells, widely but speculatively identified as rooms for the supposedly Phoenician practice of sacred prostitution.[90]

---

87. Demetriou, *Negotiating identity*, 64.
88. Cristofani, *Etruschi del mare*, 123; Jannot, *Religion*, 91–2.
89. Further discussed below, Chapter 4. The traditional date of Demaratus' migration is linked to the fall of the Bacchiads at Corinth; other dynasties of Bacchiad descent were thought to have been established across the Mediterranean.
90. Baglione, 'Sanctuary of Pyrgi', 618 with earlier bibliography; discussed in Glinister, 'Rapino bronze'; Budin, *Myth of Sacred Prostitution*, 247–54; Demetriou, *Negotiating identity*, 90–1. If the latter are right this interpretation tells us more about professorial mindsets in the late twentieth century than it does about classical antiquity.

Early Italy, from the Bronze Age to the classical era

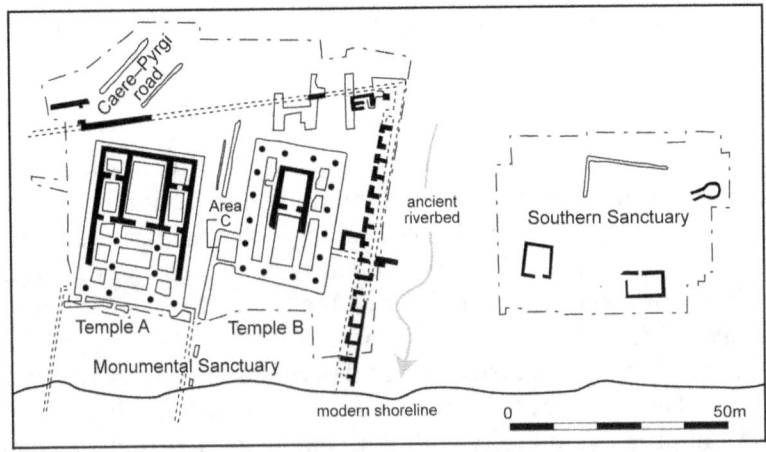

Figure 2.18 Plan of the sanctuary at Pyrgi (after Baglione et al., 'Pyrgi', fig. 12.2)

Adjacent to its north wall, a sacred precinct (Area C) was constructed, contemporary with Temple B. This had two altars, one with a perforation leading to an underground cavity, and a well, for worship of chthonic deities.

A few decades later, the sanctuary was further embellished by another temple. Temple A was dedicated to Thesan (Dawn, Greek Leucothea), known to have been worshipped here from accounts of the port's sack by Syracuse in 384 BC. This deity is particularly associated with seafaring and other journeys in Greek religion, and would be an appropriate choice for a sanctuary designed to welcome seafaring visitors. Built around 480–470 BC, Temple A was in more typical central Italian style – 'Tuscan', in Vitruvian terminology. Its most extraordinary feature is the superb high-relief sculpture group on the rear pediment, facing the entrance to the sanctuary from the city of Caere, representing the Greek (or perhaps better, Mediterranean) myth of the Seven Against Thebes. The sculptural style is similar to examples from Cyprus, influence also evident in contemporary architecture at Rome, although some scholars discern a particularly Etruscan take on the story.

Another area of the sanctuary, excavated from 1983, stretched to the south. This was not monumentalised in the same way as the northern section, and instead was characterised by small monuments and altars on a more individualistic pattern. In total, the sanctuary area was around 14,000 m², and it would have presented a very dramatic appearance to seaborne visitors.⁹¹

The most famous find from Pyrgi comes from Area C and relates to Temple B: the famous Pyrgi tablets, discovered in 1963. These comprise three gold tablets, found wrapped up in ritual fashion and placed in the well.⁹² They consist of a bilingual inscription in Phoenician/Punic and Etruscan. There is one tablet in Phoenician and two in Etruscan (Fig. 2.19). The Phoenician text is paralleled by the longer of the Etruscan texts, and both describe the foundation of the temple by the ruler of Caere, Thefarie Velianas, at the request of the goddess Uni–Astarte. The shorter Etruscan text describes rituals to be followed in the cult. The fact that the texts are 'idiomatic' bilinguals (and not identical) implies a familiarity with both language environments, and suggests that the population of the sanctuary were speakers of both

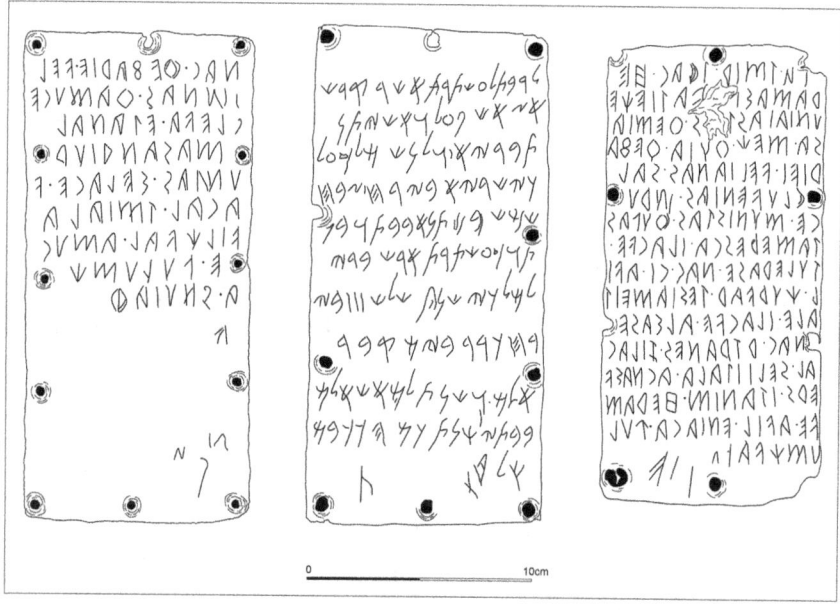

Figure 2.19 The Pyrgi tablets. The two tablets with Etruscan texts flank the tablet with the Phoenician text in the middle (drawing: K. Harding)

---

91. Baglione, 'Sanctuary of Pyrgi', 616.
92. Another bronze sheet was associated with them. For a discussion of their reading see Bonfante, *Etruscan Language*, 65–8; see also Adams, *Bilingualism*, 203–4 for linguistic aspects.

languages.[93] Historians have tended to assume that the Phoenicians were Punic-speakers from Carthage, and that this reinforces the reference to very close relations between Carthage and Etruscan cities reported by Aristotle (3.9.6–7 1280a). But the language is the 'Mediterranean dialect of Phoenician' (used for instance in Iberia, Sardinia, Cyprus and Lebanon) rather than Punic. It shares most similarities with the dialect of Cyprus, which indicates more direct connections between Etruria and the eastern Mediterranean.[94] This would not prohibit the likely frequentation of the sanctuary by Carthaginians, but it suggests that the Phoenicians who took part in the drafting of the text were Cypriot, and probably therefore that they were the more significant presence. Further aspects of the text will be considered later, but it is worth noting that the ruler of Caere is clearly in control of Pyrgi, and must have overseen the production of the text.[95]

Further emporic sanctuaries are found at intervals along the Tyrrhenian coastline. There is, for instance, Punicum between Gravisca and Pyrgi, attested only from literary evidence, and whose name suggests it was heavily frequented by Phoenicians. Another site to the north is Regisvilla, a probable port of Vulci. Surface survey and a brief excavation have revealed a residential quarter, much Attic and Etruscan pottery, and two phases of life covering 550–450 BC.[96] The regular spacing of such sites along the Tyrrhenian coast is indicative of a network that encompasses coastal or riverine sites in Latium (including Rome, Lavinium, Antium, Ardea, Circeii and Anxur–Tarracina) and Campania, as well as the western Tyrrhenian islands (Elba, Giglio, Lipari islands).[97] This reflects the ancient Mediterranean practice of *cabotage*, tramping from one port to another and exchanging goods on the way, producing the sort of complex assemblage of goods that we see in the Giglio wreck.[98] In south Etruria it also reflects the emergence of political authority in this part of Etruria, with *emporia* generally corresponding to the major Villanovan centres.

---

93. Adams, *Bilingualism*, 203.
94. Schmitz, 'Phoenician text'; Adams, *Bilingualism*, 202; Xella and Bellelli (eds), *Lamine di Pyrgi*.
95. Note that Carthage has material from south Etruria in this era.
96. Cristofani, *Etruschi del mare*, 124–5.
97. For Ardea, see now Bernard, 'In search of Aeneas'.
98. Horden and Purcell, *Corrupting Sea*, 137–43; Malkin, *Small Greek World*, 154 (long-distance trading routes are also critical).

The implications of Mediterranean traders visiting Etruria in such substantial numbers that they must be catered for with special trading places and through public notices in their own language are fundamental for our understanding of the development of Rome. Just off the coast, of necessity passing the mouth of the Tiber that led to Rome, was a highly developed trading network that encompassed the far reaches of the Mediterranean. Rome was an obvious stopping point on the way from the southern Tyrrhenian to the Etruscan coast. The Tiber was easily navigable for archaic ships such as the typical Greek pentecounter, and by central Italian standards relatively accessible. Veii, for instance, was further inland and some 7 km from the Tiber, and yet already shows a prominent Greek presence around 750 BC, as we have seen.[99] Vulci was another city like Rome, well connected to the sea via a navigable river.[100] In fact, Coarelli has argued that an *emporion* similar to those in Etruria developed at the Forum Boarium, the harbour on the river. The material found here also implies a strong Greek and Phoenician presence. In the mid eighth to early seventh century BC there is a substantial quantity of Greek pottery, then in the sixth century many imported votives, such as amber, ivories, bucchero ware, and Laconian and Corinthian pottery. The most famous find is an ivory lion, dated to the sixth century, and inscribed with the Etruscan name Spurinna (Fig. 2.20). So Rome is clearly participating in Mediterranean networks, although the nature of the evidence is wholly different at the Forum Boarium, where only small excavation pits could be dug, compared to Pyrgi and Gravisca, sites where the lack of subsequent building enabled much fuller-scale excavation to be carried out.

This was a formative period for Greek as well as Italian city states; interaction between the two was probably vital to both parties. For instance, some scholars propose Pithecusae as the most likely place for the invention of the Greek alphabet.[101] The peoples of Tyrrhenian Italy were not passive recipients in this process. We have noted Etruscan control of Pyrgi, and Etruscans were well known for their own sea-going, and regarded by Greeks as archetypal pirates.[102] In addition, evidence from Greek federal sanctuaries implies that Etruscans

---

99. Schiappelli, 'Veii', 334 notes that the quality of its agricultural land made up for its distance from the sea.
100. Cristofani, *Etruschi del mare*, 125.
101. Janko, 'From Gabii and Gordion', 15.
102. Cristofani, *Etruschi del mare*; Bruni, 'Seafaring'.

Early Italy, from the Bronze Age to the classical era

Figure 2.20 Ivory hospitality token with Etruscan inscription from the sanctuary of the Forum Boarium (after *GRT*, fig. 1.6)

were regular visitors to the east. The broader extent of the Etruscan role in Tyrrhenian trade is still controversial, and evidence is still thinner for the seafaring of other central Italian peoples. But recent reassessments have pointed to the predominance of Etruscan amphorae and other products on ships such as the Grand Ribaud F, Giglio and Antibes wrecks as indicative of Etruscan control, and epigraphic evidence confirms central Italian participation.[103] Thus it is slowly becoming clearer that the Etruscans and probably other Tyrrhenian peoples played an active role in the Mediterranean commerce that was at the root of this interchange.

Conclusion

In conclusion, the Villanovan, Orientalising and archaic periods see a wide range of extremely important processes occurring in central

---

103. Bruni, 'Seafaring', 767: Colonna ('Il commercio') thinks 'Maniie' on the Ionian-Massiliote amphora from the Grand Ribaud F wreck is an Etruscanised version of the Latin name Manios, and that letter forms from Tarquinii indicate the provenance of this merchant. Many scholars have doubted Etruscan responsibility for the Giglio wreck (despite Etruscan amphorae making up 90 per cent of the examples on board) and for the Antibes wreck (where 98 per cent of the amphorae are Etruscan); in fact, according to Colonna, the Etruscan presence in trade along the south Gallic coast was well established. For further discussion, see below p. 204.

Italy. These are linked to the vigourous trade of this era, though the cause and effect are not easily separable. We see the introduction of eastern goods and practices like literacy. An elite emerges in central Italian societies, distinguished by their tomb furnishings. Urban sites emerge which experience rapid demographic growth. All these changes were signs of state formation and a much greater political organisation in Italian communities. The development of Rome under the kings is just one aspect of these wider developments, something we should not lose sight of in following chapters.

CHAPTER 3

Myths and legends of the foundation of Rome

Introduction

This chapter addresses the period preceding the foundation of Rome and the stories of its foundation, starting first with the myths in early Greek literature, and then moving onto later Roman versions. These myths should certainly not be taken literally, and so scholars have instead tried to identify when and why these myths emerge. We can trace the appearance of particular stories such as that of Romulus and Remus in fragments of lost authors. This is challenging as most of the surviving authors are rather late. In addition, the fragmentary nature of the earlier evidence makes arguments from silence about their subjects perilous.[1] Scholars have then been tempted to identify particular periods and motives for 'myth-making'. But this is an exercise with many pitfalls. In the first place, fragments rarely allow a detailed idea of what an author wrote to be built up, and the vast majority of these works have been irretrievably lost. Secondly, the idea of political or religious motivations for myth creation has been overplayed by historians. Most myths probably formed through a long process of retelling in oral form, rather than springing fully formed from an individual propagandist's head.

But the myths do reflect widespread Greek settlement in the west in the eighth and seventh centuries BC, and the stories told of their adventures. This is not just through Greek initiative; myth is often regarded as a peculiarly Greek thing, but it is clear from the example of Rome and of other Italian cities that the locals participate fully in the process. As a result, it might be better to term it Mediterranean rather than Greek myth. Myths of figures like Hercules were widely shared across ethnic boundaries and were adapted and reworked locally, melding with indigenous stories. Some useful perspective on the whole process is provided by contemporary archaeology, particularly in the form of architectural terracottas ('gods on the roof'),

1. Wiseman, *Remus*, 42.

even if we are still ignorant of the decorative schemes of some key monuments such as the Capitoline temple.

Myths about Rome before its foundation

The canonical version of the foundation story occurs in Livy, but there are many other sources. Like most authors, Livy begins his story not with Romulus but with the Trojan War, and the flight of Aeneas to the west. He is rather thin on the period before Romulus, and makes comparatively little of the legend of Aeneas. Livy then moves briskly into a narrative of the reigns of the kings, beginning with the founder Romulus. Clearly a detailed discussion of the mythical period before the foundation did not hold much interest for him, despite his purported Augustan agenda. As he states, 'events before the city was founded or planned, which have been handed down more as pleasing poetic fictions than as reliable records of historical events, I intend neither to affirm nor to refute' (Livy, Preface 6).

A much more elaborate narrative is found in Livy's near contemporary, the Greek historian Dionysius of Halicarnassus, who takes this period much more seriously. He was concerned to emphasise the various Greek contributions towards the city, and this led him to cite a much wider range of earlier (predominantly Greek) material, including fourteen versions of the foundation of the city. Plutarch (*Rom.* 1–2) cites thirteen versions of why the city was named Rome, only some of which intersect with Dionysius' catalogue. A number of other versions are cited in Festus and Servius on the *Aeneid*, as well as other isolated versions. Thus, when we look beyond the canonical version, the most striking feature is the extraordinary variety of versions of the foundation of the city.

It has long been apparent that the early history of Rome was of great interest to Greek writers from the period of Pyrrhus onwards. This is not surprising, given that Rome came to control the major Greek cities of south Italy. But more recently scholars have increasingly taken seriously the idea that there was considerable Greek interest in the city well before this, and that the growing evidence of intense foreign contacts in the archaeological record ties in with this picture.

Various myths associated with the earliest history of Rome before the city was founded are preserved in our sources. Three figures are most widely attested, and occur in both Livy and Dionysius of Halicarnassus: Evander, Hercules and Aeneas. Evander was an exile from

Pallantion in Arcadia in Greece. He is said to have settled Palatium (the Palatine) before the arrival of Aeneas, and (in some versions) was a 'culture hero' who brought letters to Italy. Hercules passed through Latium with the cattle of Geryon, on the way from Iberia to Greece. He defeated Cacus, who was a local bandit operating from a cave. Recognising his divine form, Evander instituted a cult to Hercules in his honour at the Ara Maxima, with noble priests. Aeneas was a Trojan hero who escaped from the sack of Troy with the sacred objects, the Penates. He travelled around the Mediterranean, visiting Sicily (Livy), Carthage (Virgil), and eventually settling in Latium. He married the daughter of the local king Latinus and established the Latin peoples after the death of Latinus. He or his offspring founded Lavinium and Alba Longa, and in some versions Rome.[2]

It was a common feature of myth about the central ancient Mediterranean that cities were founded by heroes who had dispersed in the diaspora following the Trojan War. The archetype of such wandering heroes is of course Homer's *Odyssey*, but a huge variety of other mythical stories circulated, particularly in association with the Greek settlement of the western Mediterranean. Particular heroes became associated with particular places. So, Odysseus was said to have been linked to Circeii in Latium (where he met Circe, and by some accounts was buried), and was a popular myth in cities across Etruria. Diomedes was particularly associated with cities in Apulia and along the Adriatic coast.[3] Stories about Aeneas placed him in Etruria, Rome and Latium, and Sicily. We typically call these myths 'Greek', as they were recorded by Greek writers (particularly in the west) and involved demi-gods and heroes from 'Achaea' (that is, the later areas of mainland Greece and the Aegean) or Troy characteristic of later Greek religion. But there is a case to be made for regarding them as not exclusively 'Greek' and more broadly 'Mediterranean'. Many of the stories have Near Eastern precedents or parallels,[4] and it is clear that these stories were retold and adapted with little consciousness of their ethnic origins. The question of whether Hercules, for instance, is ultimately a Greek, Phoenician or Italian deity is difficult to resolve, and it may be best to reserve judgement on such questions.

It is clear that at least some of these myths are very early, and were circulating the western Mediterranean in the eighth century BC, not

---

2. According to Hellanicus of Lesbos (*FGrH* 4 F84).
3. Malkin, *Returns*, 234–57.
4. West, *East Face*.

far after the traditional foundation date of Rome. We know that stories of the Homeric heroes (if not the text itself) were familiar to the residents of Pithecusae in the eighth century BC. This is because an epigram on the so-called 'Nestor's cup' of *c.*740–720 BC, found in the burial of a 10-year-old boy, references a similar object in the *Iliad*. It reads, 'I am the drink-worthy cup of Nestor; whosoever should drink from this cup, desire for fair-crowned Aphrodite shall seize'.[5] Also potentially eighth century is a reference in Hesiod (*Theogony* 1011–16) to Agrios (the wild man) and Latinos (the progenitor of the Latins), the ruler of the Tyrsenians (Tyrrhenians), who were the offspring of Circe and Odysseus.[6] In the early sixth century the legend of the Greek hero Evander is mentioned by Stesichorus of Himera in Sicily. Stesichorus also seems to have covered the voyage west of Aeneas, as attested in the representation of Aeneas' embarking on the *Tabula Iliaca Capitolina*, a Roman marble relief perhaps of the first half of the first century BC, which cites him as an authority.[7] The key figures in the foundation of Rome were thus known to educated Greeks in the archaic era.

Later in the sixth or early in the fifth century Hecataeus of Miletus covered western Italy in his 'circuit of the earth', and recorded the foundation of Capua by the Trojan Capys.[8] We know that Rome cropped up in two further Greek authors of the fifth century. Antiochus of Syracuse discussed a certain Sicelus who was exiled from Rome to southern Italy in the era before Aeneas. And Hellanicus of Lesbos (*FGrH* 4 F84, F111, Dion. Hal. 1.72.2), provided the first clear version of the foundation legend of Rome, that it was founded by Aeneas with Odysseus, after the ships had been burnt by the Trojan women they had taken with them. The city was named after the Trojan woman Rhome.[9] The same legend of the city's foundation was reported a little later, around

---

5. Ridgway, *First Western Greeks*, 116, noting that the family may be Levantine in origin.
6. Often seen as a later (sixth century) addition to Hesiod, the authenticity of this text as Hesiodic is defended by Malkin, *Returns*, 180ff.
7. Regarded as inauthentic by Horsfall, 'Stesichorus at Bovillae?', but see the discussions in Malkin, *Returns*, 191–4. On the *Tabula Iliaca*, see Squire, *Iliad*; Petrain, *Homer in Stone*; Cappelli in Carandini and Cappelli (eds), *Roma*, 198. See now Wiseman, *House of Augustus*, 66–9.
8. *FGrH* 1 F62.
9. Rejected as an authentic quote by Gruen, *Culture*, 14–15, but only on the weak basis that no other contemporary Greek texts reflect this interest. Its authenticity is affirmed by Malkin, *Returns*, 196.

400 BC, by Damastes of Sigeum, a contemporary of Hellanicus (Dion. Hal. 1.72.2).[10]

In the fourth century BC the Sicilian historian Alcimus (*FGrHist* 560 F4 = Fest. 326, 35–328, 2 L.) provides the first mention of Romulus, saying that he was the son of Aeneas and Tyrrhenia, and his grandchild Rhodius (or perhaps Rhomus, if that is a legitimate correction of the text) founded Rome. Aristotle claimed that Rome was founded by Achaeans blown off course on their return from Troy (Plut. *Cam.* 22.3), and Theophrastus reported that Elpenor, the companion of Odysseus, was buried at Circeii, in southern Latium, following information from the inhabitants (*Hist. pl.* 5.8.1–3). In the third century Lycophron (1226ff.) has apparent references to the myths of both Romulus and Remus and of Aeneas' foundation of Lavinium; his traditional date in the 270s is controversial, given that he describes Rome as ruling earth and sea and seems to foretell the defeat of Macedon by Rome, but a third-century date has been defended by Momigliano.[11] The foundation of Rome was also discussed by Eratosthenes and (probably in considerable detail) by Timaeus.

The significance of these myths is that they indicate considerable knowledge of central Italy by Greek travellers, who appreciated the importance of key centres such as Rome, and attempted to locate them within the shared universe of the Mediterranean mythological world (usually but not necessarily to be seen as Greek). Whether this reflects the Roman view (and Greek knowledge of their views) is controversial. Greek authors were notorious for freely inventing origin myths for the peoples with whom they came into contact.[12] Romulus is not mentioned before Alcimus in the fourth century, which might be taken to indicate Greek ignorance of the story of the twins, normally regarded as an 'indigenous' myth. Aeneas is often seen as a Greek myth grafted onto the indigenous story of Romulus and Remus, with Aeneas particularly emphasised as part of the story only with Augustus.

In fact, there is plenty of evidence to show that the myth of Aeneas was adopted very early in central Italy. It appears in Etruria on a number of Greek vases from the sixth and fifth centuries, on an Etrusco-Corinthian oenochoe from Caere in the sixth century, and various

---

10. Fowler, *Early Greek Mythography*, II 644–6.
11. Lycophron's work is very hard to interpret and often obscure. For the date, see Momigliano, 'Terra marique'; cf. Erskine, *Troy*, 154–6.
12. Bickerman, 'Origines gentium'.

Etruscan objects of the fifth century (two scarabs, and a red-figure amphora from Vulci).[13] Furthermore, statuettes of Aeneas carrying Anchises were also found in Veii at the Campetti and Portonaccio sanctuaries. Although the identification of Aeneas is relatively secure, their date is disputed. Torelli thought that they were brought from Rome by Roman colonists, but Colonna has recently dated them to the fifth century and therefore pertinent to the Etruscan, pre-conquest, population).[14] The provenance of these representations of Aeneas from sanctuaries suggests that we are dealing with a cult of Aeneas, and not just representations of him. Veii was closely linked to Rome, so it is implausible that the cult was unknown there. In fact, Colonna has argued that the two cities were in some sort of dialogue or conflict over the cult.

The mythical connections of Aeneas with Lavinium also seem to reflect local beliefs from an early period. Lavinium is an important city in Latium, near the coast on the river Numicus. It had a sanctuary to Venus on the Tyrrhenian mouth of the river, perhaps acting as an *emporion*, called Troia according to Dionysius.[15] In the sixth century a sanctuary was created in the vicinity of the city with thirteen altars, from where an inscription attests the worship of Castor and Pollux; the sanctuary, perhaps dedicated to the Penates, and the inscription, show that contacts with Greek cities were intense. Lavinium is certainly associated with Aeneas by the third century, when Timaeus visited it and heard about its Trojan legends from locals in the third century BC (F59 = Dion. Hal. 1.67.4). But other evidence may suggest the cult was older than this. A tomb in Lavinium of the seventh century was used for cult in the sixth,[16] and then converted into a shrine in the fourth. The excavators have seen this as the Heroon of Aeneas referred to by Dionysius as visible in his own day (Dion. Hal. 1.46), although the identification is controversial.[17] Aeneas was said to have been worshipped as Jupiter Indiges (Livy, 1.2.6), or Pater

---

13. Colonna, 'Mito di Enea', 57, also reconstructs a large statue group, dating c.500–470 BC, of Aeneas carrying Anchises from the Campetti sanctuary in Veii on the basis of a fragment which may represent the sacred objects brought from Troy; cf. Maras, 'Dei, eroi', 21. This identification is questioned by Bernard, 'In search of Aeneas', 572.
14. Torelli, *Lavinio e Roma*, 227–8: fourth/third century; cf. Colonna, 'Mito di Enea'.
15. Torelli, *Lavinio e Roma*, terms it an 'Afrodision'.
16. Details in Carandini and Cappelli (eds), *Roma*, 213–15.
17. Castagnoli, *Enea nel Lazio*; doubts in Cornell, 'Aeneas and the twins'; Rodriguez-Mayorgas, 'Romulus, Aeneas', 102.

Indiges (Cassius Hemina, fr. 7 Peter).[18] Scholars have used this material to argue for the priority of the cult of Aeneas at Lavinium, or to the contrary to see the original point of origin as Rome or south Etruria. Further speculation along these lines is unproductive, given the ambiguity of the evidence, but an early reception of the myth in the highly interconnected cities of archaic central Italy is now difficult to dispute.[19]

In between Lavinium and Etruria, it seems likely that the myth of Aeneas was established at an early date at Rome, probably by the sixth century BC.[20] It was certainly evident before the late fourth century, given that some of the families that claimed Trojan descent had declined in importance by this period and must have invented this fictive genealogy much earlier. In the 270s Pyrrhus could appeal to the Greek cities in Italy by aiming to sack 'Trojan' Rome, just as his Greek forebears had done.[21] Quite how old the legend is, historians disagree, but an early adoption can be postulated for comparable myths. For instance, the literary tradition on the adoption of the cult of Hercules well before the foundation of the city is supported by archaeological evidence for the cult already in the Forum Boarium area by the sixth century BC. Similarly, the cult of Evander, linked to Carmenta, his mother according to some authors, also seems likely to be very ancient, given that Carmenta's festival is in the earliest stratum of the calendar, and she has her own *flamen* (an archaic priesthood).[22] More broadly, the terracotta decoration of the Regia and the Sant'Omobono temple show that 'Mediterranean' myths were already being adapted for local ends in the sixth century at Rome. Hellanicus' record of Aeneas as a founder of the city could reflect local Roman beliefs, as Fowler has recently postulated, and this tradition could go back to Stesichorus in the early sixth century.[23]

---

18. Cornell, 'Aeneas and the twins'; Momigliano, 'How to reconcile', 238; Rodriguez-Mayorgas, 'Romulus, Aeneas', with earlier references. An inscription from the nearby site of Tor Tignosa that seemed to attest a gift to a *Lare Aeneia* (the god Aeneas?) has now been reread as to the Lares alone (*ILLRP* 1271; La Regina, 'Lacus').
19. See also the links to Aeneas at Castrum Inui, near Ardea: Bernard, 'In search of Aeneas'.
20. Cornell, *Beginnings*, 66; Castagnoli, *Enea*, 111–12.
21. Pausanias 1.12.1; Momigliano, 'How to reconcile', 240–1. Fabius Pictor probably already has a detailed retelling in the late third century BC (Gruen, *Culture*, 32; *FRH* F1–3).
22. For Carmenta as Evander's mother, see e.g. Livy, 1.8; Dion. Hal. 1.32.2; Plutarch, *Mor.* 278 (with alternative explanations). Cf. Cornell, *Beginnings*, 68–9.
23. Fowler, *Early Greek Mythography*, II 567; Malkin, *Returns*, 191–4 for Stesichorus.

It is therefore evident that a wide range of myths circulated in central Italy that linked Rome and other cities into the wider mythological world of the Trojan War, and the travels afterwards of Greek and Trojan heroes. The origins of such myths are very difficult to establish, given that we have the merest fragments of the early writers that reported such stories. The fragments that survive to our day are likely to be part of a much greater body of myth that is now lost, and in any case do not provide a reliable indication of when the myths originated: the myth of Aeneas in Italy, for instance, is not necessarily older than that of Romulus and Remus, although it is first recorded over two centuries earlier.[24] As Grandazzi says,

> a legend has no author, no date either, insasmuch as it remains alive, that is, recounted, over the long term, and the fundamental elements that compose it lend themselves to every adaptation, every metamorphosis, and to the most diverse literary genres ... Just because moderns discover the first mention of a Latin legend in a Greek author does not compel us to conclude that its origin is Greek.[25]

Evidence in other media, such as 'Nestor's Cup', shows the diffusion of the Homeric epics in the Tyrrhenian west already by the late eighth century BC, and it is likely that such stories were part of the cultural background of the Euboean potters active in Veii in the mid eighth century. The sharing of these myths needs to be understood in the context of the wide interchange of shared technology and artisans (as evidenced by pottery and metalwork), active merchants, migration and intense interchange of eighth century BC onwards providing a fertile environment along the Tyrrhenian seaboard. In this context it becomes increasingly implausible to reject these early legends as abstract scholarly foreign projections onto central Italian societies, either invented by later authors or irrelevant to indigenous ('native') societies. It is increasingly evident that Greek knowledge of Rome has been underestimated in the early period, and it is also apparent that Greek and Phoenician connections were earlier and more precocious than has been assumed.[26]

It is unlikely in these circumstances that these myths are largely late and 'invented' in connection with specific Roman historical events;

---

24. Wiseman, *Remus*, 50: arguing that the myth of the twins is a later construction; Gruen, *Rethinking*, 233.
25. *Foundation*, 190.
26. Grandazzi, *Foundation*, 194.

rather, earlier myths are adapted for later means. Such myths could well be very ancient and paradoxically there is actually no reason why they should postdate 753 BC (a somewhat arbitrary date as we shall see), or the era of Homer (which merely marks the setting into writing of a long tradition of oral stories of Troy and *nostoi*). It is more likely that the myths first took form in the period when foreign interaction became regular, in the ninth and eighth centuries BC. We might also venture that Italy should not be seen as peripheral to some inventive hub in mainland Greece out of which these myths radiated. This is not how the myths work. Instead they probably arise out of the expansion of Greek (and Phoenician) settlement, the development of central Mediterranean trade, and the increase in migration that lead to characteristic encounters at the 'middle ground' of the Tyrrhenian coast of Italy.[27]

The significance of these legends for the Romans is a difficult question, and one that has exercised scholars for a considerable time. Scholars have tended to think in terms of the ethnic implications of the myths, seeing them as a sign that the Romans were identifying with Troy through Aeneas either to stress their sense of difference with the Greeks, or as a way of contrasting themselves with the Etruscans.[28] In addition, these 'Greek' myths of Evander, Hercules and Aeneas are normally contrasted by scholars with the 'indigenous' myth of Romulus and Remus, which we will come to shortly. But it may be more productive to see these myths as reflections of a very mixed Mediterranean milieu, perhaps without much awareness of 'national' allegiances, where myriad links to foreign peoples and cities could be overlaid in a type of palimpsest.[29] Taking these myths as 'Mediterranean' rather than 'Greek' also helps avoid the assumption that some legends are regarded in Rome as inherently local and others inherently foreign. If the Romans did want to be anti-Greek, as many think, then it is odd that the Evander myth is perpetuated in so many sources. Connections to the Trojan War are clearly part of it, and a prestigious element to promote. But the most distinctive feature is the belief in a mixture of stock and connections at Rome from across the Mediterranean, featuring waves of migration both from abroad (Pelasgian, Greek and Trojan) and from Italy (Sabines, Sicels).

27. Malkin, *Returns*; Debiasi, *Epica perduta*.
28. On the question of the Greekness of these myths, see Malkin, *Returns*, 29, who still regards them as essentially Greek, and Momigliano, *Alien Wisdom*, 239, taking them to be Roman rather than Greek.
29. For a similar approach, see Gruen, *Rethinking*, 243–9.

The Roman self-image would therefore seem to be one of a complex beginning before the foundation of the city, with additive accretions. It is not one of autochthony, or of racial conquest. These mixed origins were written into the topography of the city (e.g. through the settlement of particular hills by heroes and their followers, such as Evander on the Palatine, Caelius Vibenna on the Caelian and Hercules on the Capitolium). This is not to say that there was no clear sense of Roman identity expressed through these myths, or that they believed themselves no different from Greek cities. Despite the assertions of Heraclides of Pontus (fourth century BC) and Dionysius of Halicarnassus (first century BC) that Rome was actually Greek, there is a recognition of difference from Greek cities evident in the treatment of the ancient worship of Hercules (surely established by the late sixth century) conducted *graeco ritu*, by Greek rites, and in the insistence that the priestess of Ceres (established in the early fifth century BC) must be Greek.[30] But in mythical terms the assimilation of other 'foreign' elements is equally striking, such as the role of Aeneas as a founder, and the assimilation of the cults of Evander and Carmenta in the calendar.

The story of the foundation of Rome

The foundation of Rome by Romulus is one of the most famous myths in history, and it retains its power and popularity not only because of the importance of Rome, but also because of its strange and memorable details. It is a typically captivating tale shaped by centuries of retelling in oral tradition. The version of the story related by Livy, Dionysius and Plutarch that had become canonical by the first century BC goes as follows. Romulus and Remus were twins born to Ilia, the daughter of Numitor. Numitor was the rightful king of Alba Longa but had been deposed by his brother Amulius. Amulius had made Ilia a Vestal Virgin to ensure that she could not bear offspring, but she was raped by Mars, and gave birth to twin sons. When Amulius found out, he had her imprisoned and the twins set adrift on the Tiber in a basket to drown. They miraculously survived, and were washed up on the shores of the Palatine, at the site of the 'Lupercal'. There they were suckled by a she-wolf, and then picked up by the shepherd Faustulus and raised by him and his wife as his

---

30. Isayev, 'Just the right amount', 377–8.

own sons. As young men they lived in a band with runaways and outlaws, and raided neighbouring settlements. On coming of age, the twins killed Amulius, the illegitimate king of Alba, and set their grandfather Numitor back on throne. They determined to found a city on the site of their salvation. Romulus chose the Palatine, and Remus the Aventine. Different augural symbols occurred, and they disputed who was the rightful founder. Romulus fortified the Palatine, but Remus jumped over the half-built walls. In the ensuing melee, Remus was killed, and Rome came to be named after Romulus, its eponymous founder.

There were many different versions of how the city came to be founded besides this canonical story. Much was disputed and discussed, including who was responsible for the city gaining its name (Table 3.1). Even amongst Roman historians there were many alternative versions of the Romulus and Remus story, as Dionysius, for instance, records:[31]

> Some of these [Roman writers] say that Romulus and Remus, the founders of Rome, were the sons of Aeneas, others say that they were the sons of a daughter of Aeneas, without going on to determine who was their father; that they were delivered as hostages by Aeneas to Latinus, the king of the Aborigines, when the treaty was made between the inhabitants and the new-comers, and that Latinus, after giving them a kindly welcome, not only did them many other good offices, but, upon dying without male issue, left them his successors to some part of his kingdom. Others say that after the death of Aeneas, Ascanius, having succeeded to the entire sovereignty of the Latins, divided both the country and the forces of the Latins into three parts, two of which he gave to his brothers, Romulus and Remus. (Dion. Hal. 1.73.2–3)

Some authors speculated that the twins were suckled not by a wolf but by Faustulus' wife, who was a *lupa*, a prostitute, and that the story had developed from that. According to Livy, Remus was killed in the heat of a mass dispute, though he notes that a commoner version has him killed by Romulus. But in Dionysius and Ovid he was killed by a follower of Romulus called Celer.

These variants are typical of stories preserved in oral traditions, where disagreements arose through the fragmentation of a narrative

---

31. Cornell, *FRH* III 15–21 has a comparison of the versions in Plutarch and Dionysius in order to establish how far they go back to Fabius Pictor.

Table 3.1 Various founders of Rome in Festus, Plutarch and Dionysius[a]

Founder	Further details	Festus	Plutarch	Dionysius	Source of attribution
Rhomus/Roma	Son of Aeneas	✓		✓	Apollodorus, Cephalon of Gergis, Demagoras, Agathyllos
	Son of Ascanius			✓	Dionysius of Chalcis
	Son of Romulus	✓			Agathocles
	Son of Jupiter	✓			Antigonus
	Descendant of Aeneas	✓			Agathocles
	Follower of Aeneas	✓			Cephalon of Gergis
	Son of Emathion		✓	✓	
	Son of Italus			✓	
	Son of Odysseus and Circe			✓	Xenagoras
Rhome/Roma	Wife of Latinus	✓			Callias
	Wife of Aeneas		✓		
	Wife of Ascanius		✓		
Aborigines/ Pelasgians		✓	✓		Cumaean Chronicle
Aeneas and Odysseus			✓	✓	Hellanicus, Damastes of Sigeum
Achaeans/ Arcadians		✓		✓	Heraclides Lembus, Aristotle
Rhomis	King of the Latins		✓		
Romanus	Son of Odysseus and Circe		✓		
Romulus	Son of Latinus	✓	✓		
	Son of Telemachus and Circe	✓			Cleinias
	Grandson of Numitor	✓			Diocles of Peparethus
	Son of a Vestal Virgin and an unknown father	✓			
	Son of Aeneas		✓	✓	
	Grandson of Aeneas			✓	
	Son of Mars		✓		
	Son of a slave woman		✓		

[a] From Hall, *Artifact*, 125 – with modifications.

not committed to an authoritative text. This helps also to explain the power and drama of the narrative: the heroes rise up to take their rightful place; there is then a catastrophic conflict between the twins, and fratricide. The picture is not clearly favourable to Rome, and in fact gave its enemies useful ammunition to criticise the city. The dramatic element may have been enhanced by the retelling of the story through the medium of theatre: Naevius wrote plays entitled the *Upbringing of Romulus and Remus*, *Romulus*, and *Lupa* in the late third century BC, which may have influenced Fabius Pictor's account.[32] The oral character of the stories also explains the common elements that occur in them. There are the well-known motifs of a mother's tragedy, infant rescue, a totemic animal, and the redemption of the children when they grow up. All these features are commonly found elsewhere in stories in antiquity, even if not in this exact Roman combination.[33] For example, various heroes were said to have had mothers who were priestesses raped by gods, such as Auge the mother of Telephus, or Danae the mother of Perseus. Many heroes raised by animals, such as Enkidu in the *Epic of Gilgamesh* or Cyrus the Great of Persia in the Near East, and in Greek mythology the stories of Aegisthus (rescued by a goat), Phylacides and Philander (goat), Asclepius (goat), Aeolus and Boeotus (cow), Telephus (doe), Miletus (wolves), Atalanta (bear), Hippothous (mare), Antilochus (dog), Cydon (dog or wolf) and Iamus (snakes);[34] many were brought up by shepherds, such as Caeculus of Praeneste, or Paris of Troy; founders of cities or religious groups typically endured a period in the wilderness before they returned to society to fulfil their destiny. Such ideas are found from across Indo-European societies, and would seem to be either a very ancient stratum of shared myth, or a typical way that pre-literate societies mythologised their early heroes.[35]

Many of these ideas were common to other central Italian societies, as we can see from parallels in the foundation stories of cities like Praeneste, where Caeculus was a foundling with a divine father, who was raised by shepherds and lived with a band of young men as raiders before founding the city.[36] Tibur was founded by three brothers,

---

32. Cornell, *FRH* III 21, citing Wiseman, *Roman Drama*, 8–16.
33. Bremmer and Horsfall, *Roman Myth*, 25–48.
34. Rose, *Handbook*, 237–9.
35. Critical discussion of the Indo-European hypothesis in Cornell, *Beginnings*, 77–9. See also Cornell, 'Aeneas and the twins'.
36. Bremmer and Horsfall, *Roman Myth*, 49–59, arguing for considerable Roman contamination of the Praenestine myth; contra, Cornell, *FRH* III 114–16.

Tibertus, Catillus and Coras, and the city named after the eldest.[37] Particularly striking are the representations in Etruscan art of scenes of infants suckled by animals, including a grave stele from Bologna dating to the fifth or fourth century BC, with an infant suckled by an animal (wolf?) and a famous mirror from Bolsena in the second half of the fourth century (Fig. 3.1).[38] Despite some doubts, the mirror almost certainly shows the myth of Romulus and Remus. The mirror is of Praenestine artisanship and thus the myth must be current in central Italy, and perhaps Rome.[39] In fact, these representations suggest these elements of the myth where humans are raised by animals should not be considered uniquely Roman but rather central Italian, or perhaps even Mediterranean, in character.

Various scholars have argued that the apparent peculiarities of the myth can be explained as products of specific political milieux. In 1968, for instance, Strasburger claimed that the negative features of the Romulus myth, such as fratricide and rape, suggest that the myth was an invention of Rome's enemies. He suggested that this took place in the 270s BC, when Pyrrhus was attacking Rome, as part of a propaganda war against the city.[40] More recently, Wiseman has argued that Remus was added only in the third century BC to represent the plebs in their struggle with patricians. As both orders are eventually reconciled the awkward extra character of Remus must be eliminated at the end of the myth, and is therefore unlikely to predate the institution of the dual consulship in 367 BC. Wiseman argues that in fact there is no clear evidence for Remus before the setting up of a statue of the wolf and twins in 296 BC.[41]

---

37. Cato, *FRH* F61, with commentary at III 111.
38. Rodriguez-Mayorgas, 'Romulus, Aeneas'; Massa-Pairault, 'Romulus et Remus'; Momigliano, 'Origins', 59; Wiseman, *Remus*, 63–5. The coins of Cydonia in Crete (fourth century?) show an infant suckled by a dog or she-wolf in a very similar position to that of the twins in early Roman coinage (DeRose Evans, *Art of Persuasion*, 74).
39. For the identification of the twins see Carandini and Cappelli (eds), *Roma*, 233–4; Rodriguez-Mayorgas, 'Romulus, Aeneas', 92; Massa-Pairault, 'Romulus et Remus', 510. Dissenting view in Wiseman, *Remus*, 70–1, regarding them as Lares Praestites.
40. Strasburger, *Zur Sage*; for Pyrrhus' dream, see Pausanias 1.12.1 and the discussion above. Pausanias' report is rejected as weak evidence by Erskine, *Troy*, 158.
41. Livy, 10.23: 'The curule aediles, Cnaeus and Quintus Ogulnius, brought up several money-lenders for trial this year. The proportion of their fines which was paid into the treasury was devoted to various public objects ... They also placed near the Ficus Ruminalis a group representing the Founders of the City as infants being suckled by the she-wolf.'

Myths and legends of the foundation of Rome

Figure 3.1 Bronze mirror from Bolsena, Etruria, with scene of twins suckled by a wolf, late fourth century BC (from Roscher, *Ausführliches Lexikon*, I 1465)

Until ten years ago, the best evidence for the archaic existence of the myth of the twins was thought to be the so-called *lupa Capitolina*, the Capitoline wolf. This iconic statue has been preserved in Rome since 1471, and now occupies a prime position in the Capitoline

Figure 3.2 The lupa Capitolina (photo: Guy Bradley)

Museum (Fig. 3.2). The twins are known to be a Renaissance addition to the composition, but the statue of the wolf, with her full teats, suggests that the group originally portrayed the ancient legend. The wolf itself was thought on stylistic grounds to date to the late sixth or early fifth century BC, and to perhaps be a product of Veii in south Etruria.[42] But the conservation of the statue between 1997 and 2000 allowed a thorough review of the techniques involved and new scientific analyses. The chief conservator, Anna Maria Carruba, came to the conclusion that the piece was medieval rather than archaic Etruscan. This was because it was cast in one piece by the direct lost-wax method, which is normally regarded as having been used only for small items in antiquity, and was more typical of the medieval era. The scientific analyses initially seemed to produce further support, identifying the core around which the wax was sculpted as from the lower Tiber valley area, and dating it by thermoluminescence and radiocarbon methods to between AD 100 and 1155.

---

42. Wiseman, *Remus*, 63; Cornell, in Carandini and Cappelli (eds), *Roma*, 49.

However, this redating was disputed by many prominent archaeologists at a conference in 2007, and it was pointed out that the remnants of the core within the bronze were vulnerable to contamination, as the statue has a substantial fissure in it. Analysis of the bronze pointed in a different direction, showing a composition of alloys more typical of Etruscan than medieval bronzes, which were often made of recycled metal, unlike the wolf, and containing lead that originated from an ancient mine in Sardinia not known to be exploited in the medieval period.[43] Nevertheless, the most recent scientific dating by the University of Salento in 2012 of the organic material in the internal cavity (carbon, vegetable remains, seeds) puts its production at AD 1021–1153 with seemingly unquestionable scientific credentials, and it would appear that the wolf is definitively medieval. The issue has not, however, been entirely settled: Formigli has recently argued that this is a medieval recasting of an Etrusco-Italic original, thereby incorporating both the stylistic and scientific arguments.[44] It therefore remains possible that such a statue may have existed in archaic Rome, although this no longer offers a reliable means of dating the Romulus myth.

Despite these complex debates, there is still considerable evidence for the existence of a myth about Romulus by c.300 BC (a *terminus ante quem*). As we have seen, it features on the Bolsena mirror. The myth is also represented firmly in Rome in 296 BC, when a statue group of the twins being suckled by the wolf was set up by the Ogulnii, curule aediles of that year (Livy, 10.23.12).[45] Thirty years later, the image of the wolf and twins first appears on the earliest Roman coinage, of 269 BC. A different version of the myth is mentioned by the Sicilian historian Alcimus (probably mid to late fourth century), who describes Romulus as the son of Aeneas, and the grandfather of Rhomus (if that is the correct emendation of the text), the founder of the city. A little later, probably in the early third century BC, another Sicilian historian, Callias, says that 'Romê, one of the Trojan women who came into Italy with the other Trojans, married Latinus, the king of the Aborigines, by whom she had three sons, Romus, Romulus and Telegonus, . . . and having built a city, [they] gave it the name of their mother' (Dion. Hal. 1.72.5).

43. Bartoloni (ed.), *Lupa Capitolina*; Radnoti-Alföldi et al., *Römische Wölfin*, with review by Kinney, 'The Lupa Romana'.
44. Formigli, 'Storia della tecnologia'.
45. Oakley, *Commentary*, IV 264: the Latin can imply that the twins were added to a pre-existing statue of the wolf, but a full group is the more natural reading.

Scholars have seen these reports as telling us little about Roman views, and representing an ethnocentric Greek imposition on Roman mythography.[46] But the consistent mention of Romulus is striking, and such reports tie in with Sicilian interest in and contact with the city on the Tiber from the sixth century BC. We should remember that the first Rome–Carthage treaty already envisaged Romans trading in Sicily in the late sixth century BC, the era of Stesichorus, and Sicilian artists were active in Rome in the early fifth.[47] It is therefore likely that these historians reflect aspects of Roman stories about their foundation.

The canonical version of the story is first attested at Rome in Fabius Pictor, who clearly had a detailed account both of the mythical prehistoric heroes Evander, Hercules and Aeneas, and also a full version of the twins myth.[48] It is tempting to think that the canonical version was established by Fabius Pictor as the first Roman historian to record the story in the late third century,[49] perhaps motivated by the accusations of Rome's enemies to provide a 'tidied up', nationalistic account – we know that he wished to respond to pro-Carthaginian accounts of the Punic Wars, written in Greek. But strikingly Pictor is said by Plutarch to have followed a Greek author, Diocles of Peparethus (a small island in the western Aegean).[50] Diocles' date is uncertain, although the mid third century is likely. Plutarch is perhaps making a point about Greek primacy in such matters, but it is nevertheless extraordinarily striking that a Roman author retold his native history, containing many distinctively central Italian elements, following a Greek authority.[51] This implies that Diocles had a detailed knowledge of what the Romans themselves thought, and it implies that a properly detailed Greek discussion of Rome's origins had already been established before the Second Punic War. This should not be surprising in the context of a consistent Sicilian Greek interest in Rome, and in the aftermath of Rome's epoch-making defeat of Pyrrhus in 275 BC.[52]

46. Bickerman, 'Origines gentium'; Gruen, *Culture*, 15, 20.
47. See Chapter 5.
48. Gruen, *Rethinking*, 246 notes that Fabius credited the Phoenicians with the ultimate origin of the alphabet.
49. Hall, *Artifact*, 132; cf. Momigliano, 'Fabius Pictor', 101.
50. Plutarch, *Rom.* 3.1: 'But the story which has the widest credence and the greatest number of vouchers was first published among the Greeks, in its principal details, by Diocles of Peparethus, and Fabius Pictor follows him in most points.'
51. Central Italian elements: Bremmer and Horsfall, *Roman Myth*, 25–48.
52. Momigliano, 'Fabius Pictor', 100.

Overall, therefore, the Roman myths of their foundation seem to be an amalgam of different elements, influenced by contacts with other areas of central Italy and the wider Mediterranean. The current scholarly consensus takes the cult of Aeneas to be a Greek intellectual construct, at a late date welded artificially onto the 'indigenous' and more ancient cult of Romulus and Remus. But this hypothesis fits poorly with two pieces of evidence: that Aeneas' founding of Rome is attested earlier than Romulus', especially with the redating of the Capitoline wolf; and that the first Roman account, by Fabius Pictor, drew heavily on a pre-existing Greek tradition. Three points emerge from my earlier discussion. First, both myths are attested early in central Italy, and are, in my opinion, likely to be present in Rome in the monarchic period (that is, by the end of the sixth century BC). To assert the primacy of one or the other therefore seems somewhat arbitrary, given that it is highly likely that both myths substantially predate their first appearance in literary or iconographic form.[53] Secondly, the construction of both myths seems a process not exclusive to Greeks or Romans (or Etruscans), but rather a process of collaboration, the result of interaction between various Mediterranean peoples in the 'middle ground' of the central Tyrrhenian. To demonstrate how problematic earlier assumptions have been, it is even worth asking the admittedly provocative question of how 'Roman' Romulus was? Grandazzi notes that the Romulus legend is rooted in the city of Rome (especially the Palatine), and one might concur that this is unsurprising given that he is an eponymous founder of the city, just as many other Mediterranean cities had (such as Capys for Capua, or Amirus for Ameria).[54] On the other hand, we could assert that he has strong links to Alba Longa, seems to crop up elsewhere in central Italy in iconographic representations, and according to some scholars has, like his twin, an Etruscan name![55] But the games that scholars like to play about the (ethnic) origins of X are unproductive in such a situation of cultural fusion. In fact, the Roman self-image, as propagated through the myth, seems to stress their awareness of these early beginnings, with its emphasis on mixed ethnic origins, and contacts and connections at home and abroad with other cities, Greek and Trojan.[56]

---

53. Hall, *Artifact*, 132, rightly stressing that the Aeneas legend could not be ignored by Fabius' time.
54. Grandazzi, *Foundation*, 195.
55. Hall, *Artifact*, 132, for Romulus as Etruscan *Rumele* (from Orvieto). Bonfante, *Etruscan Language*, 32, for Remus as Etruscan.
56. Cf. Gruen, *Rethinking*, 244.

The foundation date and issues of chronology

The authoritative date of the foundation is usually thought of as 753 BC. But this chronological point was probably fixed only in a comparatively late period. A bewildering variety of dates exists in the historical record (Table 3.2). These wide variants raise questions about the authority of the canonical date of 753, which at some point was just one of various competing claims. How these dates were arrived at is generally unknown. Some general tendencies are apparent.[57] Earlier sources link the foundation of Rome closely to the fall of Troy, either deriving the name from a Trojan settler, or in some cases seeing Romulus and, more rarely, Remus, as close relations to Aeneas. Later accounts envisaged a much greater gap between Troy and the foundation of Rome, probably under the impact of the chronological investigations of Eratosthenes (third century BC), who placed the Trojan War in 1184, and the foundation of Rome in the second year of the seventh Olympiad (751/50) (Solinus 1.27). It is thought that this chronological vacuum presented a problem for historians of Rome such as Fabius Pictor, writing in the late third century. The solution they adopted was to invent a Trojan dynasty of kings of Alba Longa, beginning with Ascanius, son of Aeneas, and ending with Numitor, grandfather of Romulus and Remus.[58] This allowed scholars to link up the era of the Trojan War with that of Romulus and Remus, in the eighth century BC.

Table 3.2 Foundation dates of Rome[a]

Date BC	Source
c.1100 or 900	Ennius
814	Timaeus (synchronism with Carthage)
754/3	Varro
752	*Fasti Capitolini*[b]
751/50	Cato
750/49	Polybius
748/7	Fabius Pictor
729/8	Cincius Alimentus

[a]From Dion. Hal. 1.72, with Cornell, *Beginnings*, 72.
[b]*FRH* III 22.

57. Gruen, *Culture*, ch. 1.
58. Grandazzi, *Alba Longa*.

But how did this process of synchronisation of Rome and Troy come about? The reconstruction above presupposes that there was already agreement about the eighth century BC foundation of Rome. It is likely that the story of the foundation by Romulus was preserved through oral means. This means that it was unlikely to have included an accurate chronology, although it is possible that the time-depth of Romulus from the present was expressed in terms of generations.[59] The Republic, however, could be dated by the *Fasti* (and by the Capitoline era), to around 509 BC. Perhaps the foundation date was arrived at through later chronological calculations, such as assuming that there were seven kings, who reigned for around thirty-five years each.[60]

From Fabius Pictor onwards there is a general agreement amongst Roman historians that the city was founded in a period from the seventh to the twelfth Olympiad, that is in the middle eighth century BC by our reckoning. Even then, variant dates could be proposed. Various writers around the time of Fabius ignored his version, and placed Aeneas and Romulus close together, with no long intervening period. These include the historian Cassius Hemina (mid second century BC) and the poets Naevius (late third century) and Ennius (early second century).[61] Both Naevius and Ennius saw Romulus as Aeneas' grandson by his daughter (*Serv. Dan.* on *Aen.* 1.273). Ennius referred to an event 'seven hundred years, more or less, since renowned Rome was founded under prospering augury' (Varro, *Rust.* 3.1.2 = Ennius, *Ann.* 154–5 Skutsch), which would place the foundation of the city around 900 BC, if from his own time, or as early as the era of the Trojan War if from the time of Camillus' speech.[62]

The end result was a foundation date that was by the standards of contemporary Mediterranean cities,[63] and by comparison with the archaeological evidence, comparatively late. There are various possible explanations for this. Carandini has argued that the Romans preserved a memory of major urban developments dating from the mid eighth century, and therefore that this is a genuine reflection of historical developments: a foundational moment, but not the beginning of

---

59. Feeney, *Caesar's Calendar*, 88–91 for a critical assessment.
60. *FRH* III 21–3; De Cazanove 1988, 'Chronologie des Bacchiades'.
61. Gruen, *Culture*, 34ff.
62. Walbank, *Polybius*, 175; Elliott, *Ennius*, 65.
63. Later for example than Carthage, Capua or Interamna Nahars; much later than the Trojan War.

the settlement per se.[64] Other scholars have highlighted the artificiality and variability of the chronological estimates by ancient writers, and argue that alighting on one foundation date out of many is to privilege a point essentially picked out of thin air.[65] Many believe that Rome's foundation date was being manoeuvred to fit in with wider Mediterranean mythological and chronological schemes. Feeney in particular has argued that it was designed to fit in with historical time (as opposed to 'mythical time'), which was measured by the Olympiads. Whatever the actual reasons for the process (which seem largely irrecoverable by now), we again find Rome being connected to Mediterranean myths of foundation.

---

64. Carandini, *Nascita*, 494–5.
65. Feeney, *Caesar's Calendar*, 90. Discussion of the issue in *FRH* III 23.

CHAPTER 4

Kingship

The Reign of Romulus

The tradition on the reign of the first king has many interesting and curious features. First, we can note the youthful adventures that the tradition records the twins taking part in. Romulus and Remus belonged to a group of young shepherds, and the man who raised them, Faustulus, was the keeper of the king's flocks. Remus was seized by thieves at the Lupercalia, a pastoral festival involving animal products such as goatskin thongs and animal skins, which was thought to predate the foundation of Rome. It was linked to the Arcadian origins of Evander by ancient writers, who noted similarities with the Arcadian festival of Pan Lycaeus. This might appear to be an anachronistic, bucolic fantasy, conforming to the ancient evolutionary trope that societies went through a phase of pastoralism before graduating to the more civilised pursuit of agriculture. While it is possible that the story reflects a collective memory of the role of pastoralism in Roman prehistory (on which more later), it is striking that the story closely parallels many other foundation myths in the ancient world. Founders typically spend time outside their community, experience life as part of a band of young men, and often associate with shepherds on the fringes of society, occupying liminal spaces such as mountain pastures.[1]

Once established in power, Romulus organised the city like a typical ancient city founder. In order to populate it, he undertook two unusual measures. The first was to establish an asylum at a place between two groves on the lower saddle of the Capitoline hill. According to Dionysius, the idea was to provide an open house to refugees from neighbouring cities, and it succeeded in attracting an enlarged population from the local area. This was open to anyone of lowly origins, including runaway slaves. We can compare this to

---

1. For these themes see Bremmer and Horsfall, *Roman Myth*, 30–4.

the later custom, allegedly introduced by Servius Tullius, of enabling freed slaves to become citizens.[2] Outlaws often play an important role in the foundation myths of cities elsewhere in the ancient Mediterranean, such as in Greek foundation stories.[3] Whilst it is essentially impossible to discern whether the Roman myth of the asylum has any historical basis, it clearly represents an important element of the later Roman self-image, when the city had become a great demographic powerhouse.[4]

Similar themes occur in the famous myth of the Rape of the Sabine women. The myth further explains the ethnic mix of Roman origins in a mechanistic way: the asylum attracted males, and so women had to be added through seizure, Romulus' entreaties to neighbouring cities for brides having been unsuccessful. The story goes that Romulus invited people from neighbouring Sabine cities to a religious festival in Rome. This was a pretext for seizing their female visitors. The Romans used the myth to explain the origin of women as equal partners, persuaded by Romulus to stay at Rome and share citizenship and possessions. Hersilia, the wife of Romulus, requested citizen status for the rest of the Sabines. These women intervened in the battle of the Forum, reconciling Romulus with Titus Tatius, leader of the Sabines.

At the end of Romulus' reign, our sources agree that he disappeared. In some versions he achieved apotheosis, being taken up in a cloud. He was ultimately declared to be a god, Quirinus. In an extraordinary variant, Romulus was torn to pieces by senators, who concealed the parts of his body under their togas. Lack of agreement as to Romulus' end is a typical sign of the story's oral transmission. Such stories may also have had a political element in the late Republic. Romulus is said to have had a bodyguard (the so-called Celeres), but this made any analogy with Romulus uncomfortable for Augustus, who had reputedly toyed with adopting the name of the first king. The story of Romulus' violent end at the hands of the Senate was also probably used by supporters of radical tribunes like the Gracchi who had been lynched at the hands of the Senate.

---

2. Dion. Hal. 4.22.4.
3. McGlew, *Tyranny*, 168.
4. Bremmer and Horsfall, *Roman Myth*, 38–43; Ogilvie, *Commentary*, 62 argues that the concept of asylum is clearly 'very ancient', but see Rigsby, *Asylia*, arguing for the Hellenistic Greek derivation of the term, and Dench, *Romulus' Asylum*, 14–21.

The organisation of the Romulean city

In the Roman tradition Romulus is an archetypal founder, creating the elemental structures of the city. This is best set out in a passage of Dionysius (2.7.2–14.4) that Wiseman has traced back to Varro.[5] Romulus is said to have been responsible for the rapid building of the city, including two sets of fortifications, and the temple of Jupiter Feretrius, and to have established the basic structures of Roman society. Romulus divided the people into plebeians and patricians and linked them together through the invention of patronage. The citizen body and territory were divided into three *tribus* (tribes) and thirty *curiae*, with heads called *tribuni* and *curiones*. He created a Senate with one hundred members, and a bodyguard, known as the Celeres, with each *curia* supplying ten men. He established laws to govern the behaviour of the people, and set out the powers of king, Senate and people. Twelve lictors were appointed, according to Livy (1.8.3) adopted from an Etruscan model.

This represents something of a standard outcome of city foundation by a primordial founder. Romulus is attributed with the establishment of most of the major social and political structures of Rome. This package of measures seems to be a disparate group of the fundamentals of Roman society, bundled together and arbitrarily attributed to a hypothetical founder. It includes some features that were probably long-term evolutions, such as patronage, and others that probably emerged considerably later, such as the patrician–plebeian distinction, given that we do not hear about this again until the start of the Republic. But one aspect, the division into tribes and *curiae*, deserves more attention, and is more likely to be of historical value.

Both institutions are known from later sources, and the *curiae* seem to have continued to play a role in later society. As we have seen, Romulus divided the people into three tribes (*tribus*). Their names are known from later cavalry centuries: the Tities (or Titienses), Ramnes (or Ramnenses) and Luceres.[6] Their names are Etruscan according to an Etruscan playwright called Volnius (perhaps writing in the Gracchan period).[7] Tarquinius Priscus is said to have doubled the number of cavalry centuries, but retained their names on the insistence of the augur Attus Naevius. Each tribe is thought to have provided one of

---

5. Wiseman, *Remembering*, ch. 4. Livy is much briefer.
6. Livy, 1.13.7, not directly referring to tribes here.
7. Cited in Varro, *Ling.* 5.55; see Ogilvie, *Commentary*, 80.

these centuries, so the names presumably reflect the tribes.[8] These three tribes are therefore likely to have been a pre-existing organisation at the time of Tarquinius (nominally in the late seventh century, although this is uncertain, as we shall see). The tribes do not seem to have played much of a role later in the Republic, and seem to have been superseded by the new urban and rural tribes reportedly set up in the reforms of Servius Tullius.

The thirty *curiae* must be later than or contemporary with the tribes, as they were subdivisions of them.[9] According to Livy each was named after a Sabine woman (1.13). We know eight of their names.[10] The *curiae* were associations probably based on birth. The word *curia* may be derived from *co-viria* (meeting of men), as ancient writers suggested.[11] Each *curia* had its own meeting place (Dion. Hal. 2.7.4), and there were banqueting halls known as the *curiae veteres* on the slopes of the Palatine looking towards the Colosseum valley, which seem to have been in use from the archaic period to the late Republic.[12] Each *curia* had a leader called a *curio*. The *curio maximus* was the overall head (usually a patrician, but some were plebeian in the third century BC and probably earlier). In the Republic the *curiae* had a continuing role in religious festivals, celebrating the Fornacalia and Fordicidia. They also maintained a vestigial political function, forming the basis of an assembly called the *comitia curiata*, which lasted until the late Republic. It served as a kind of rubber stamp for the magistracies, passing a *lex curiata de imperio* to confer *imperium* (the right of command) on each magistrate prior to his term in office. The *comitia curiata* also confirmed the appointment of priests down to the late Republic. That it had once had a wider political role can be discerned from the loss of its powers to the *comitia centuriata* created by Servius Tullius, and from a reference in Cicero that it elected the early tribunes of the plebs, probably before 471 BC.[13] The curiate assembly probably also played a role in army recruitment.[14]

Modern scholars have made much of many elements of the foundation myth, particularly the symbolism of the numeric elements to the

---

8. Discussion in Smith, *Roman Clan*, 189.
9. Ogilvie, *Commentary*, 80.
10. Smith, *Roman Clan*, 202.
11. Cornell, *Beginnings*, 117.
12. Smith, *Roman Clan*, 204.
13. Cic. *Corn.*, cited in Asconius, *Corn.* 76 C.; Smith, *Roman Clan*, 225.
14. Cornell, *Beginnings*, 114; Smith, *Roman Clan*, 208–10.

story. Duality is certainly a common theme. Some have speculated that the dual kingship with Titus Tatius was invented to provide a precedent for the dual consulship, a relatively unusual form of government in antiquity.[15] We can think of the twins, and of the beginnings of the city on two different hills (the Aventine and Palatine). There is also the dual organisation of some archaic priesthoods (the Salii and Luperci), and the way that the early population was considered to have been formed of Latins and Sabines. But there are also several signs of tripartite organisation, such as with the three tribes and thirty *curiae*. For the influential French mythographer Georges Dumézil, the number three had great symbolism, being part of the primordial triadism of all ancient societies speaking Indo-European languages. Dumézil believed that he had uncovered such structures through comparisons between ancient Mediterranean societies and those of ancient India. But his hypotheses have not won many adherents among ancient historians.[16] Similarly unsuccessful have been racial interpretations of these two- or three-fold groups, with attempts in the early twentieth century to link them with archaeological evidence for Latins, Sabines and Etruscans.

Scholars are now inclined to think less in literal terms about the myth, and what hidden truths it might conceal, and focus more on what it says about the Romans' own image of themselves. Particularly striking is the lack of embarrassment about the lowly status of the original citizens, and about the subterfuge and Rape of the Sabines. This seems to be a sign of an early legend with melodramatic details, rather than a late one contrived to make Rome look good. The primordial three divisions of the *curiae* into tribes are not a reflection of separate racial groups making up the population. But the myths of the asylum and the Rape show awareness of the early ethnic diversity of the society of Rome, which is confirmed by archaeological and epigraphic evidence, and the importance of the Sabines and other 'outsiders' in early Roman history.[17]

A key feature of the legend is the rational city organisation that Romulus institutes. This does not require that we accept Romulus

---

15. Ogilvie, *Commentary*, 72.
16. E.g. Dumézil, *Archaic Roman Religion*. For critique of these theories, see Momigliano, 'Georges Dumézil'; Cornell, *Beginnings*, 77–9.
17. Ampolo, 'Roma ed i Sabini', for these as early but not primordial legends. Others have taken the Sabine element to reflect only the conquest of the region in the third century BC.

as a historical figure (although it is not entirely clear that this should be ruled out), or that we accept that such a founder should date to the middle of the eighth century.[18] But the institutions themselves would seem to have good grounds for being archaic. There are close parallels in similar Greek institutions in the archaic period, such as the *phyle* and *trittys* for the *tribus*, and the phratry and *lochos* for the *curiae* noted by Dionysius (2.7.3). The Roman tribes and *curiae* must be very ancient, as they were largely superseded by Servius' centuriate organisation in the mid sixth century. Scholars disagree on when they might have been formed, but tend to link their formation to the beginnings of an urban settlement. For instance, Cornell has argued that they cannot predate the mid seventh century, as that is when Rome becomes urban. By contrast, Carandini has proposed that the *curiae* date to the 'second Septimontium', before 775 BC, and moreover, that twenty-seven of the thirty *curiae* predate the Romulean foundation.[19]

It has been commonly held that this early urban organisation reflects Greek influence on early Rome.[20] The argument is that the division of the city into multiple tribes has parallels with Greek city states, but not with Greek territorial states (*ethne*), or with other Italic or Etruscan communities. In Italic states it is thought that the organisation was different, with the *tribus* being equivalent to the whole community, as at the Umbrian city of Iguvium, for instance, which had one tribe, called the *trifu*, which was equivalent to the *tota*, the whole community.[21] The distinction between *poleis* and *ethne* in Greece has been taken to indicate that only the *polis* had 'archaic rationality', as Murray puts it.[22] Thus Rome has been presented as the only Greek-style *polis* in central Italy, a

---

18. Cornell, *Beginnings*, 119: 'His name appears to be a crude eponym formed from the name of the city'; Hall, *Artifact*, 132 defends the historicity of the name, arguing it is perhaps Etruscan in origin and not a simple eponymn. Cf. De Simone in Carandini and Cappelli (eds), *Roma*, 31–2.
19. Cornell, *Beginnings*, 117; Carandini, *Nascita*, 382 (*curiae* correspond to districts the Argei), 432–3 (the three tribes also predate the foundation); Carandini, *Rome: Day One*, 24–5, 31–2; critique of this argument in Smith, *Roman Clan*, 361–2. Rieger, *Tribus*, argues that they are later than 650 BC, and probably were created under Tarquinius Priscus.
20. Ampolo, 'Nascita', 169–72; Cornell, *Beginnings*, 117–18. The historiography is traced by Bianchi, *Greci ed Etruschi*, 33–7.
21. Bradley, *Ancient Umbria*, 181–2.
22. Murray, 'Cities of reason'; Ampolo, 'Nascita', 169.

very significant claim. But this argument is fragile, dependent as it is on an absence of evidence for Italic and Etruscan constitutions, for which the sources are incredibly poor. The differences between Rome and its neighbours are overplayed, and it seems unlikely that similar subdivisions of the population did not occur elsewhere: in fact a very similar institution is attested in Umbria (even if only as a single entity) and in Etruscan Mantua (where there seem to have been multiple tribes and *curiae*), and according to Festus (358 L.) the Etruscans used ritual books for guidance on how to divide a city into tribes.[23] Furthermore, Greek studies have recently moved on from the older idea of an *ethnos* being a type of undeveloped *polis*. City divisions used for political and military purposes presuppose that they are of roughly equal size; they are therefore highly unlikely to have been inheritances from a pre-urban past, and must be artificial creations.[24]

A recent comprehensive survey of the issue by Rieger has linked the earliest Roman *tribus* to the *phylai* of Doric cities and identified Corinth as a possible source.[25] Rieger suggests that this might have been mediated via Etruria, but the hypothesis of an Etruscan imprint for the names of the Romulean tribes has been rejected by Rix, who instead believed them to be local toponyms of Latin origin.[26] Thus, in the current state of scholarly knowledge, the origin of the tribes seems to have local Latin, central Italian and broader Mediterranean elements, although attempts to emphasise one aspect at the expense of another have generally been unconvincing. This is a typical situation in early Roman history, given the intense interactions on many different levels that contributed to the emergence of Rome, and will be a repeated theme in subsequent chapters.

The list of Roman kings

The monarchy established by Romulus traditionally lasted from 753–509 BC.[27] The dates of the kings, according to the chronology

---

23. Virgil, *Aen.* 10.202, with Servius' commentary: *Mantua tres habuit populi tribus quae in quaternas curias dividebantur* ('Mantua had three tribes of people which were divided into four *curiae* each').
24. Hall, *History*, 88–91.
25. Rieger, *Tribus*.
26. Rix, 'Ramnes, Tites, Luceres'.
27. The reign lengths are given by Dion. Hal. at 1.75.

established by Varro in the first century BC, are as in Table 4.1. The canonical list of seven kings is found in all our major historical sources. Their average reign length is thirty-five years, which is extremely long by historical standards. It looks like an artificial construction, and has been questioned since Isaac Newton in the seventeenth century.[28] Varro's date might therefore be a product of speculation along the following lines: if the consuls go back to 509 BC, then 7 × 35 = 245 years, and 245 takes us back to 754, pretty much Varro's date BC. Variants could be the product of different ways of calculating. Thirty-five years per ruler is almost certainly too long; many of the kings are said to have been violently killed, with only Numa dying peacefully. Other historical comparisons such as the British monarchy are considerably

Table 4.1 The list of kings in the ancient sources[a]

King	Origin (and descent)	Wife	Traditional dates from Varro (BC)
Romulus (co-rule with Titus Tatius)	Latin from Alba Longa (of direct Trojan descent in some sources); Titus Tatius: Sabine from Cures	Hersilia	753–716
Numa Pompilius	Cures, Sabinum	Tatia (daughter of Titus Tatius) / Egeria / Lucretia	715–672
Tullus Hostilius	Latin from Medullia (grandfather)	Unknown	672–640
Ancus Marcius	Sabine; son of Marcius, friend of Numa, and Pompilia (Numa's daughter)	Unknown	640–616
Lucius Tarquinius Priscus ('The Elder')	Tarquinii, Etruria (Etrusco-Corinthian parentage)	Tanaquil	616–578
Servius Tullius (or Mastarna)	Latin (son of Ocresia, or a different slave), or Etruscan (Claudius)	Tarquinia (daughter of Tarquinius Priscus)	578–534
Lucius Tarquinius Superbus ('The Proud')	Rome (son or grandson of Tarquinius Priscus and Tanaquil)	Tullia (daughter of Servius Tullius)	534–509

[a] Sources: Forsythe, *Critical History*, 98; Glinister, *Roman Kingship*, 140.

28. Ampolo, 'Città riformata', 216.

shorter at twenty-one years per reign overall. Even the rather long-lived set of six monarchs from Queen Victoria to Queen Elizabeth II average only thirty years' reign.[29] There is the added problem of the awkward alignment with the Cypselids, who took power in Corinth in 657 BC, when the father of Tarquinius Priscus, Demaratus is said to have left for exile abroad. This leads to discernible problems in the sources, who are unsure about some points of the chronology. For instance, they disagree on whether Superbus was the son or grandson of Priscus; most say son, but as Dionysius (4.6–7) points out, Servius reigned for forty-four years, so this is highly unlikely. Note that the date of the creation of the Republic and the institution of the dual magistracy in 509 BC is also disputed by some scholars, but this is a separate issue that we will come to later.

If we accept that the reign dates are inauthentic, this poses major problems for understanding the nature of the monarchy.[30] The kings cannot be firmly linked to buildings chronologically, so bringing archaeological evidence which can be dated together with the literary tradition is perilous. Secondly, it shows that the tradition has been severely corrupted somewhere along the line, and that major aspects of the early Roman state could be misunderstood. Modern scholars have generally favoured two solutions. One is to argue that the monarchy began later, perhaps around the mid seventh century, when archaeological evidence suggests major urban developments took place. This hypothesis has the benefit of allowing the traditional king list to be retained, but it has now become complicated by the increasing quantity of archaeological evidence for the centre of Rome before the mid eighth century.[31] The second solution is to believe that there were other monarchs, who were written out of the canonical list. This seems more likely, as we shall see, and is accepted by many scholars – but it does not fully solve the problem.

This is because the nature of the tradition on the kings is very uneven. Although the reign of each king is treated properly in its own light by our major sources Livy and Dionysius, the value of their accounts varies greatly. The picture of the early kings is clearly much less reliable than that of the later ones. As we have seen, Romulus is presented as

---

29. The Spartan king list is not far off that of Rome, but this is also legendary, and so does not offer a useful parallel.
30. Cf. Smith, 'Thinking about kings', 35–6.
31. Cornell, *Beginnings*, 119–26; archaeological evidence: Carandini, *Nascita*; Carandini, *Rome: Day One*. The importance of the mid seventh century has recently been reasserted by Ampolo, 'Problema delle origini', and Hopkins, *Genesis*, 27–38.

something of an archetypal city founder, and may have a name that derives from that of the city. Eponymous founders such as this were common in ancient Mediterranean legend, such as Capys at Capua, and scholars have thus tended to regard them *en bloc* as later inventions. The next king, Numa, was a rather one-dimensional religious founder, the antithesis of Romulus as a peacemaker and someone predominantly concerned with rituals and the divine. Tullus Hostilius represents a contrast again; he is portrayed largely as a war leader, a characteristic embodied in his name. Unlike Numa he was impious and ultimately punished for his incorrect observance of religious practice, being struck by a thunderbolt from Jupiter and consumed in a fire in his palace. From Ancus Marcius onwards the question becomes more complex.[32] He is the first of the group of four last kings who could be said to be multi-dimensional and realistic figures. It is likely that these men existed, and are found in the right order, and that they have authentic names.

It is also generally accepted on various grounds that the Roman kingship is an authentically remembered institution.[33] It features in all the literary accounts, and there are historical records of kings elsewhere in central Italy in this era. These include independent historical records from other communities, such as the so-called Cumaean Chronicle preserved in Dionysius, referring to Lars Porsenna of Clusium, and the *Elogia Tarquiniensia*, referring to a king of Caere named Orgulnius.[34] We also have contemporary epigraphic evidence from the period from Rome itself, in the form of the inscription *rex* ('king') on the foot of a bucchero cup from the Regia (last quarter of the sixth century), and the form *recei* on an archaic inscription from the Lapis Niger (earlier sixth century) (Fig. 4.1).[35] A king is also referred to in various religious festivals carried out during the Republic, marked in the most ancient stratum of the calendar: the Regifugium ('Flight of the King') and the day marked *QRCF*, *Quando Rex Comitiavit Fas*, meaning that 'the day will be propitious when the king has held (or officiated in) the assembly'.[36] It is possible that some of this evidence

---

32. For biographies of this and subsequent kings, see Thomsen, *King Servius Tullius*; Camous, *Le roi et le fleuve* and *Tarquin le Superbe*.
33. Glinister, 'Kingship and tyranny'; Smith, 'Thinking about kings', 21.
34. Dion. Hal. 7.2–11; Zevi, 'Demaratus'; Torelli, *Elogia Tarquiniensia*, 39. For other examples, see Glinister, *Roman Kingship*.
35. *GRT* 22–3; Degrassi, *ILLRP* 3, with note.
36. Festus 348 L., 310 and 346 L. in Rüpke, *Roman Calendar*, 26–30.

Kingship

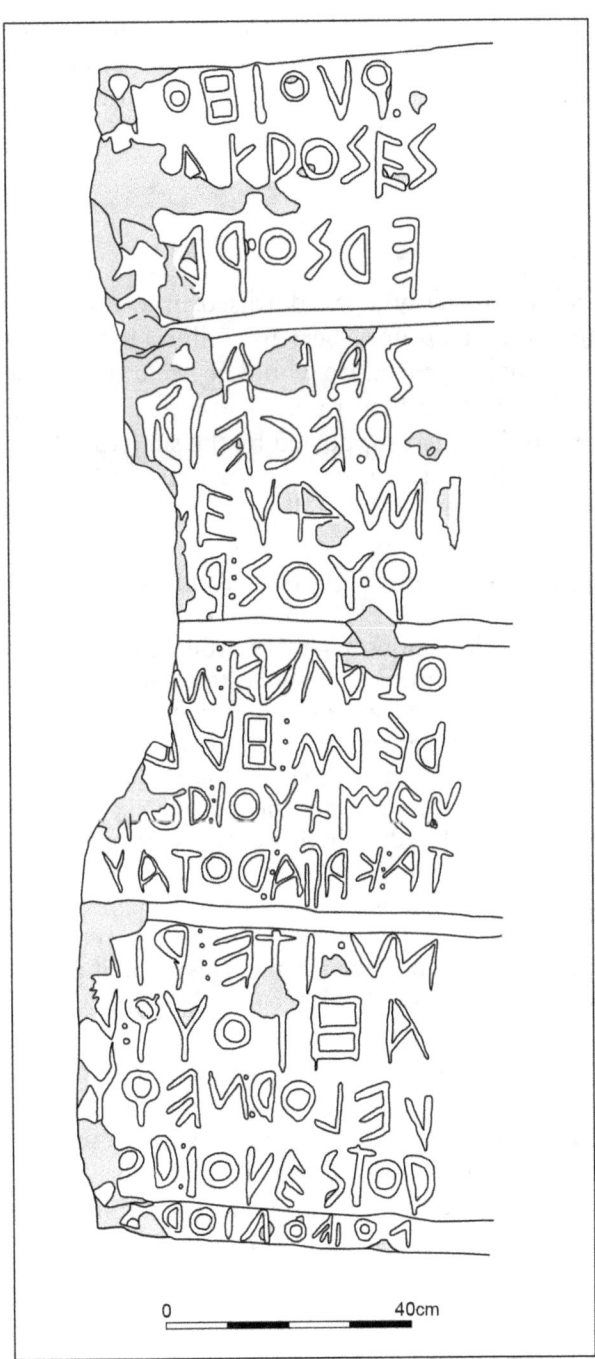

Figure 4.1 The four sides of the Lapis Niger inscription, with RECEI visible in line 5 (after *GRT*, fig. 3.1.39)

refers to the priest known as the *rex sacrorum*, but it is more likely to refer to the king per se. Finally, the institution of the *interregnum*, 'the period between reigns', used later during the Republic, provides further evidence, given that the term indicates an origin in a period of monarchy.[37]

The succession

The sources seem to follow a standardised procedure for appointing each king, at least up until Servius Tullius. It is not altogether implausible that such a procedure would be accurately remembered, given that it is generally a feature incidental to the narrative of the monarchic period. It is also supported by the survival of some of the institutions later. The first example is at the end of Romulus' reign, which was allegedly marked by a full year of *interregnum*, where no successor was found, which only ended when the plebs complained.

Plutarch describes the *interregnum* as follows:

> In order that their factions might not produce utter confusion from the absence of all authority, now that the administration of affairs was suspended, it was arranged by the senators, who were one hundred and fifty in number, that each of them in his turn should assume the insignia of royalty, make the customary sacrifices to the gods, and transact public business, for the space of six hours by day and six hours by night. The distribution of times seemed well adapted to secure equality between the two factions, and the transfer of power likely to remove all jealousy on the part of the people, when they saw the same man, in the course of a single day and night, become king and then a private citizen again. This form of government the Romans call 'interregnum'. (Plut. *Numa* 2.6–7)

The office of *interrex* was held by patricians only, and at the end of the *interregnum* the auspices were conferred by patrician senators on the new king. The *interregnum* process was presented as being under the Senate's control; the *patres* were required to ratify the choice of the next king. The new ruler was nominated by vote of people in the form of a vote of the *comitia curiata*,[38] the institution

---

37. See below.
38. Plut. *Num.* 7: 'When they had come down into the Forum, Spurius Vettius, whose lot it was to be "interrex" at that hour, called for a vote of the citizens, and all voted for Numa.'

that conveyed *imperium* on magistrates in the Republic. This may have involved acclamation instead of a vote, and it is likely that the people had little say in the process.³⁹ In fact, there was only ever one candidate for the kingship, and there is no case in which the *interrex* made a choice. The *interregnum* is also attested under the Republic, although there it operated somewhat differently. Rather than its regularised use in the early monarchy, under the Republic it was an emergency office, used only on the death or incapacity of a regular magistrate. This difference in practice makes it unlikely that it was back-projected into the monarchy on Republican lines, and it therefore has a good chance of being a genuine monarchic institution. Its name implies a gap between kings rather than magistrates, and it makes sense to envisage the continuity of use of the office in the Republic developing out of a regal tradition.⁴⁰

The king who succeeded Romulus was an outsider from Sabinum, named Numa Pompilius. Subsequent kings were also outsiders, either Sabine (Ancus), Latin (Tullus, Servius) or Etruscan (Tarquinius Priscus, who was technically Etrusco-Corinthian, or Servius according to Claudius). Typically, the future king would marry a daughter of the previous king, as attested with Numa, Ancus, Servius and Superbus. Numa set a pattern for outsider kings which is probably a structural feature of the Roman monarchy, with outsiders brought in to prevent infighting amongst the elite. Anthropological parallels provide examples of other societies where supreme rule was only conferred on outsiders.⁴¹

The tradition on the later monarchy

There is a watershed in our sources with the accession of the fifth king, Tarquinius Priscus. The reliability of our narratives seems to improve considerably from this point, although their historicity is still very problematic. The kings are no longer such obvious ciphers as Romulus, the founder of the city, Numa, the founder of religion, and Tullus Hostilius, the warlike king. In general, the last three kings are more plausible figures than the first four, and the major figures, events and institutions, more historical. Some major figures from this period are for the

---

39. Glinister, 'Kingship and tyranny', 19.
40. Glinister, 'Kingship and tyranny', 22–3.
41. For examples see Sahlins and Graeber, *On Kings*, a reference I owe to Christopher Smith.

first time attested in contemporary epigraphy (such as Aulus Vibenna and Publius Valerius Publicola). The developments in the later monarchy also seem to correlate more closely with contemporary trends evident elsewhere in Mediterranean history, such as the rise of tyranny, the importance of popular support, the use of divine power to reinforce legitimacy, and the prevalence of social and ethnic mobility.

Nevertheless, many issues remain with the tradition as it stands. Like the early monarchy, the tradition about the last three kings still remains strongly biographical, in contrast to the tradition on the Republic. The focus in Roman history remains on the royal household and biographies of the kings, and the transition to the city and community as the key focus is not yet realised.[42] There are fewer variants in the tradition than in that concerning the foundation, which might inspire faith in the reliability of the later narrative, but in fact the apparent coherence of the narrative may be misleading. A narrower range of sources is cited by our main accounts for this period, and perhaps early sources were more interested in the foundation. But it is also apparent that excerpters were more interested in that period. Some early sources did discuss this period in Roman history. It is clear, for instance, that there were Etruscan sources that related to Rome in this period, and that they were available to Roman historians in the early imperial period (as we shall see for the origins of Servius Tullius). A Greek source, perhaps even a near contemporary to events, may lie behind the account in Dionysius (7.2–11) of the saga of Aristodemus of Cumae, which impacts on Rome.[43] The influence of such alternative traditions seems to have been fairly limited on Roman historians, who had by the end of the first century BC refined a coherent account with few variants. This account is almost certainly too tidy, and probably omits some (perhaps many) major events and figures. A typical example is the rather implausible account of the events around the end of the monarchy and start of the Republic, which it is difficult to fit with archaeological evidence for considerable turmoil, and alternative traditions on Lars Porsenna capturing the city, rather than beating an honourable retreat.[44]

---

42. Wiseman, *Unwritten Rome*, 315: series of stories about individuals rather than continuous narrative.
43. Zevi, 'Demaratus' for the hypothesis that this Cumaean Chronicle was composed in the court of Aristodemus of Cumae in the early fifth century and covered the whole period of the Tarquins from Demaratus on. Criticised by Gallia, 'Reassessing', but for other reactions see Richardson and Santangelo (eds), *Roman Historical Tradition*, 81–2.
44. For some of the issues, see Wiseman, *Unwritten Rome*, 317.

In addition, there remains a mythical or fantastical flavour to many of the stories about all of the last kings. The myths associated with Servius Tullius are typical: he is said (in some versions) to have been fathered by Vulcan in the form of a phallus arising from the hearth; an eruption of fire around his head when he was a child symbolised his royal potential; as a ruler he is said to have consorted with the goddess Fortuna. Such stories were probably enlivened by repeated retelling in oral tradition.

The dramatic nature of many aspects of the narrative has struck many scholars. The saga of what has been dubbed 'the House of the Tarquins', with its prominent and colourful female characters, so rare in the historiography of the Republic, perhaps marks a transition to a different type of source. The potential transmission through the medium of drama is an attractive hypothesis.[45] Accius wrote a historical drama about Brutus, for instance, performed in 133 BC, which covered the fall of the Tarquins.[46] Poetry is another likely vehicle of transmission.[47] The historiographical shift from monarchy to Republic might reflect a changing audience or changing sources from oral to written. But we know little of the differing types of audiences for genres of Roman literature, and it is likely that the intricate web of oral and written means of memorialisation remains typical throughout the Republic. So we have to envisage that a mix of monuments, documents, and rituals preserve memory in collective consciousness, up to and beyond the written works of Timaeus, Fabius and others.

Speculation about our sources can only get us so far. Many aspects of the narrative, such as Servius' constitutional reforms, are unlikely to have featured in drama and/or poetry. We might imagine that they were straightforwardly invented by later sources, and scholars have not been slow to identify plausible later contexts where such inventions might make sense.[48] But in most cases it is not easy to make a compelling case, and many of the activities fit the archaic period as well or better than the third century or late Republic. For most episodes we simply do not know whether the report is true or not.

---

45. Wiseman, 'Roman legend', 133; *Unwritten Rome*, 313.
46. Cic. *Div.* 1.22.44; *Remains of Old Latin* II 560–5; Hall, *Artifact*, 149 with further references.
47. Zorzetti, 'Carmina convivalia'; see also above, Chapter 1.
48. E.g. Humm, 'Servius Tullius', on the centuriate reforms wrongly attributed to Servius rather than the fourth century.

In conclusion, the implications for the historical value of our sources are troubling but should not discourage us from making the attempt to recover what we can of archaic Roman history. As we shall see, recent developments in broader Mediterranean archaeology and history have provided reasons to be more optimistic, especially with elements that echo Greek history.

The origins of the later kings

The literary tradition is in agreement that Tarquinius Priscus was not originally from Rome, but came to the city from Tarquinii in Etruria and won the throne through skill, good fortune and inherited wealth. His origins are particularly interesting in the context of archaic Mediterranean connections. His father was said to have been Demaratus, a member of the ruling Bacchiad clan in Corinth. He became wealthy through trade with Etruria, and ultimately settled in Tarquinii when the Cypselid tyranny was established in Corinth. There he married an Etruscan woman and had two sons, one of whom was named Lucumo and inherited his fortune. Lucumo married the noble Etruscan woman Tanaquil and moved to Rome when he was thwarted in his social ambitions by the prejudice of the Tarquinians, Rome being more welcoming. There he befriended the king and ultimately succeeded to the throne, changing his name to Lucius Tarquinius Priscus.

Scholarly responses to this story have varied. Some have seen it as an independent Greek saga, artificially welded onto the story of the Roman monarchy by a spurious genealogy. It certainly has problematic chronological implications, as linking the movement of the father of Tarquinius Priscus (who traditionally reigned 616–578) with the rise of Cypselus (traditionally 657) makes Tarquin's son Superbus implausibly old.[49] Others have argued that it was a coherent story that encompassed not only Demaratus but also the whole of the 'Tarquin dynasty', the last three kings of Rome.[50] The Demaratus story undoubtedly preserves a memory of the strong

---

49. Dion. Hal. 4.6–7, 4.30; Cornell, *FRH* III 25–6. De Cazanove, 'Chronologie des Bacchiades'.
50. Zevi, 'Demaratus', claims this must be an early fifth-century account, before the 485 fall of Aristodemus, which covers the whole saga of Tarquin's property. Zevi convincingly argues that the Demaratus saga is not a separate element, added in at another time, and draws attention to the Corinthian elements in archaic Rome such as the festival of the Consualia; but the idea that the whole Tarquin saga comes from a Cumaean source is less convincing.

Greek penetration of Etruria that we saw in the last chapter. But the naïve culture-hero element, by which Demaratus was said to have further introduced the modelling of clay and the alphabet into Italy (Pliny, *HN* 35.152; Tacitus, *Ann.* 11.14), suggests that the story was reworked considerably over time, and introduces the suspicion that Demaratus may have been a figure invented to rationalise these links.[51] Doubts also arise over the (Augustan?) emphasis in some sources on Lucumo's exclusion from public life in Tarquinii due to Etruscan xenophobia, given that Demaratus was apparently welcomed as a resident (and in Strabo's version ruled the city), and like his son was able to marry a local woman.[52]

Nevertheless, the migrations described in the story fit well with the freedom of movement throughout the archaic Mediterranean evident from archaeological and epigraphic sources.[53] Etrusco-Corinthian pottery is the product of the same connections, created from the seventh century in Etruscan workshops under immigrant Corinthian potters. Lucumo's change of name in Rome to Lucius Tarquinius might appear like an awkward explanation to link the two traditions. But taking a new name to indicate origins is well attested in archaic Etruria and Latium: we can think here for example of the *Tite Latine* (Titus Latinus) buried in Etruscan Veii in the seventh century. The most striking parallel is that with Rutile Hipukrates, a wealthy figure of mixed Greek and Latin origins buried (or friendly with the deceased) in the prestigious Tumulus of the King in Tarquinii itself. Similarly, the Greeks apparently buried in Rome in the seventh century and Volsinii in the sixth attest the same movement.[54] The extraordinary closeness of these parallels with the story of Demaratus thus make the main elements of the saga very plausible, and reinforce the idea that Rome, Etruria and Greece were closely interconnected in the seventh century BC. The question of whether this leads to a predominantly Corinthian rather than Etruscan impact on sixth-century Rome, as some scholars postulate, is somewhat misleading. Whilst Tarquinius Priscus is an important figure, it is simplistic to see his personal origins as the decisive factor, given that this is merely one example of the myriad networks in which Rome acts as a hub.

---

51. Ridgway and Ridgway, 'Demaratus and the archaeologists'.
52. Dion. Hal. 3.47; Livy, 1.34.5; 4.3; Strabo, 8.6.20. Claudius (*ILS* 212) states that she must have been noble but poor to accept such a husband.
53. Ampolo, 'Demarato: osservazioni'; Ampolo, 'Demarato di Corinto'.
54. Bradley, 'Investigating aristocracy', with further references. Cf. Farney, 'Name-changes'.

The next king, Servius Tullius, also has complex and fascinating origins. There were many different versions of where he was from, although like all the previous kings he was portrayed as coming from outside the Roman elite. Roman sources make him the son of Ocresia, who was a noblewoman from the Latin city of Corniculum married to a royal figure from the city, captured in its siege. In a version reported by Dionysius and several other sources, Ocresia conceived Servius when Tanaquil instructed her to have intercourse with a phallus from the flames.[55] Other versions have him as a son of a client of Tarquinius Priscus and a slave woman in the court, or perhaps an Etruscan slave.[56] Tanaquil reputedly recognised Servius' royal potential through an omen, when flames surrounded his head without harming him. In most of these versions he rose from humble origins through miraculous events in the palace.

However, another version is given by Etruscan sources and reported by the emperor Claudius in a famous speech, preserved in bronze on the so-called Table of Lyons.[57] Claudius was a noted erudite, tutored by the historian Livy; the first of his four wives was an Etruscan noblewoman. In the speech, Claudius tried to persuade the Senate that it would be a good idea to accept Gauls into their ranks, and pointed to historical precedents such as the outsiders who were kings of Rome:

> Once kings ruled this city; however, they did not pass it on to successors within their families. Members of other families and even foreigners came to the throne, as Numa, coming from the Sabines, succeeded Romulus; he was a neighbour certainly, but at that time he was a foreigner, as Tarquinius Priscus succeeded Ancus Marcius. Tarquinius, prevented from holding office in his own land because of his impure blood – for he was the son of Demaratus of Corinth and his mother was from Tarquinii, a woman noble but poor, as she will have been if she needed to give her hand to such a husband – subsequently migrated to Rome and gained the throne. Between Tarquinius and his son or grandson (for even this is disputed among the sources), Servius Tullius intervened. If we follow Roman authorities, his mother was a prisoner of war, Ocresia; if we follow Etruscan authorities, he was once the most faithful companion of Caelius Vibenna and took part

---

55. Dion. Hal. 4.2; Ovid, *Fast.* 6.569–636; similar stories were told of Romulus (Plut. *Rom.* 2.4–8 from Promathion) and Caeculus of Praeneste (Cato, *FRH* F67; Servius, *Aen.* 7.678).
56. Cicero, *Rep.* 2.37–8; Justin, 38.6 – the meaning is not altogether certain.
57. *ILS* 212.

Kingship

in all his adventures; subsequently, driven out by a change of fortune, he left Etruria with all the remnants of the army of Caelius and occupied the Caelian hill, naming it thus after his leader Caelius; Servius changed his name (for his name in Etruscan was Mastarna) and was called by the name I have used and he obtained the throne, to the very great advantage of the state. (*ILS* 212, the Table of Lyons, trans. Cornell, *Beginnings*, 133–34)

This version implies an alternative history of the later monarchy from that in the Roman sources. It is not easily dismissed, given that it features plausible details such as Servius' migration to another city and a consequent change of name along the lines of the examples previously discussed from literature and epigraphy.

The particular interest of this version is that it is clearly very old and was not merely the result of later speculations at Rome. We know this because Mastarna features in a fresco from the François Tomb at Vulci of the third quarter of the fourth century BC, which seems to represent one of the adventures of Mastarna with Caelius Vibenna to which Claudius refers (Fig. 4.2). The scene is best interpreted as the rescue of prisoners held captive. Mastarna is shown freeing Caelius Vibenna,

Figure 4.2 The frescoes from the François Tomb, Vulci, *c.*350–325 BC Achilles sacrifices Trojan prisoners (above); scene with Mastarna and the Vibennae (below) (drawing: H. Mason)

echoing their close relationship in Claudius' speech; it also features Caelius' brother Aulus Vibenna. The others had been naked and bound as captives, but used weapons brought in to kill their captors.

The figures killed include a Cneve Tarchunies Rumach, 'Gnaeus Tarquinius of Rome'. Some scholars have speculated that the scene relates to the death of Tarquinius Priscus (killed in the Roman tradition by the sons of Ancus); perhaps here we have an Etruscan version with a group involving Servius killing him, and going on to occupy the Caelian hill at Rome and seize the throne by force. But it is important to note that this is a Gnaeus not a Lucius Tarquinius, and it is more probably an unknown episode involving another member of the dynasty rather than the Roman king himself. In fact, the position of the pair showing the killing of Tarquinius is around the corner from the main scene, which probably means that this does not form part of it. It is also bizarre that his killer is called Marce Camitlas. This is a very similar name to the Roman hero of the early fourth century Marcus Camilllus, but the scene bears no resemblance to stories of the Republican figure.[58]

Scholars have also drawn attention to the parallel scene from the Trojan War on the opposite wall, where Trojan prisoners are executed by Achilles at the funeral of Patroclus. The scenes would thus celebrate a set of heroes from Vulci, the city of the tomb, overcoming their captors, including a Roman, whereas the parallel shows a Greek hero (possibly identified with the Etruscans) killing Trojans (an easy parallel for the Romans).[59] This interpretation is seductive, making imaginative use of all the evidence. But it is uncertain whether this is the right reading. The war band defeated by Mastarna and his allies seem to come from various Etruscan cities as well as Rome judging from their names, and thus seem like the typical mixed-origin group that we might imagine emerging from archaic central Italy. There may be no intersection with a specific moment of Roman history. The symbolic identification of Romans with Trojans in the Trojan War scene is also debatable, given that we now have good evidence for Etruscan as well as Roman identification with Aeneas and Troy.[60]

58. Bruun, 'What every man in the street used to know'.
59. Coarelli, 'Pitture'.
60. See above, Chapter 4.

Other evidence helps to give these stories further historical weight. A figure with the name Aulus Vibenna is attested by an inscription on a bucchero cup dedicated in Veii around 580 BC. This could well be the same person as the brother of Caelius, given the coincidence between the date when the literary stories are set (just before reign of Servius in the mid sixth century) and the inscription.[61] Fabius Pictor probably mentions the same figure as *Aulus Vulcentanus* in a curious passage reported in the much later Christian source Arnobius, which tells of his death at the hands of a slave, and derives the name of the Capitolium from the burial of his head beneath the temple.[62] Aulus is linked to Romulus by Varro, but he is surely confused.[63] The Vibennae brothers also feature later on, in a mythical scene on an Etruscan mirror. The best way to understand this confusing mass of evidence seems to be that they were historical figures, from sixth-century Vulci, who along with Mastarna interacted with Rome, and that their adventures had become mythologised in the Etruscan tradition by the fourth century BC.

Thus, it is clear that Claudius' story is based on an Etruscan tradition going back at least to the late fourth century. This tradition is not necessarily right, but it does raise serious questions about the canonical Roman version of Servius' origins. If Claudius is correct, the Roman sources may simply be wrong, perhaps speculating about Servius' origins on the basis of the resemblance of his name to Latin *servus*, 'slave', to hypothesise humble 'servile' origins. This would mean that the second king of the Tarquin dynasty was also from Etruria. An alternative is that Claudius was mistaken in identifying Mastarna with Servius. Cornell thinks that he may have known that Mastarna was a king of Rome, and guessed that he was Servius, equating him with the (really very different) character of Servius in the Roman tradition.[64] We would thus have an extra king for the king list who perhaps forced a hostile takeover of Rome from the Caelian hill, making more sense of the chronology of the

---

61. *TLE* 35, 'mine muluv[an]ece Avile Vipiiennas', 'I was given by Aulus Vibenna' (Ampolo, 'Città riformata', 207, with picture). A later dedication has been interpreted as a sign of his cult (*TLE* 942: 'Avles Vpnas naplan').
62. Fabius Pictor, *FRH* F30 = Arnobius 6.7, with commentary in *FRH* III 45–7; Glinister, 'Sacred rubbish', 44–5, suggests that this story might have originated from the discovery of archaic architectural terracottas; on the myth see Thein, 'Capitoline Jupiter'.
63. Varro, *Ling.* 5.46; Festus 38 L.
64. Cornell, *Beginnings*, 141.

monarchy, but making the organisation of the Tarquin dynasty even more complex.

More certainly, these stories show the prevalence of groups of independent warrior–adventurers of variegated origins, and the role of powerful leaders such as the Vibennae (in activities that are too obscure to fully perceive). These complex events resulted from intense mobility between cities, and show that Rome and the Etruscan cities were very closely interlinked in the archaic period. Ampolo has suggested that the phrase coined in World War Two, 'Rome, open city', can apply to its earliest history. Movement between different cities was very easy and implies that a strong sense of ethnic difference had not yet emerged. Etruscan epigraphy attests Etruscans present in Rome, dedicating material at the sanctuary of Sant'Omobono and on the Capitol, and at sites in Latium such as Ardea, Satricum, Lavinium and Praeneste.[65] Greeks and Phoenicians were part of this ethnic mix, and were present in large numbers at *emporia* like Pyrgi and Gravisca as well as in Etruscan and perhaps Latin cities inland.

Both versions of the origins of Servius Tullius also fit this picture, whether he is a Latin slave from outside Rome, or an Etruscan adventurer. Momigliano coined the slightly unfortunate term 'horizontal social mobility' to encapsulate the idea of elite individuals moving from city to city, in a way comparable to that in which travellers and hosts in the Homeric period recognised each other's status through hospitality and gift exchange. Such strong parallels suggest that these stories of social mobility were not invented by our later sources, who found them strange and often tried to rationalise them. They provide one of the strongest arguments in favour of the authenticity of the principles behind the stories of the characters' origins (even if the precise details the sources relate remain debatable).

The assumption of monarchic power and the royal 'dynasty'

Both Tarquinius Priscus and Servius Tullius had interesting routes to power. Tarquinius Priscus became the right-hand man of king Ancus Marcius, and the tutor to his sons, who were ultimately excluded from

---

65. See below, Chapter 6; Pensabene et al., 'Ceramica graffita', 195 n. 6, for Etruscan inscriptions from Rome in the archaic period. For Latium see Naso, 'Etruscans in Lazio'; Bourdin, 'Ardée', 596–7. There are some uncertainties with the language and whether inscriptions on objects in tombs indicate the name of occupants, as with the Bernardini Tomb in Praeneste.

the succession. This is also the case with Servius, who became the chief lieutenant and successor of Tarquinius. Both figures eventually suffered at the hands of the heirs they had 'usurped': Tarquinius was killed by the sons of Ancus, Servius by the son or grandson of Tarquinius. It is striking that only Tarquinius Superbus actually succeeded a patrilineal relative. All other kings were outsiders in some sense, and did not inherit the crown: either they were invited in by the Senate (like Numa from Sabinum), or they gained the monarchy through their charisma. Typically the kings were the son-in-law rather than the son of the previous ruler: so Numa married the daughter of Titus Tatius, Servius the daughter of Tarquinius Priscus and Tarquinius Superbus the daughter of Servius. This appears to have been a structural feature of Roman kingship, and may imply a matrilineal custom of succession which has parallels in Greek myth and in some societies studied by anthropologists.[66] The role of women as kingmakers is also distinctive. Tanaquil encouraged Servius to seize the throne when Tarquinius was assassinated, and Tullia incited Superbus to overthrow Servius; both these influential women hailed the men publicly as king.

The last three kings are still called kings (*reges*) by the later tradition, but their reigns clearly had an irregular character. They show many similarities to contemporary Greek tyrants such as Pisistratus of Athens. All of their successions were problematic in some way, and they all obtained the throne by some sort of subterfuge. The *interregnum* procedure was used for Tarquinius Priscus, but not for Servius Tullius or Tarquinius Superbus.[67] It is also noticeable that the last three kings are said to have relied on their own supporters, filling the Senate with their own people, and making use of a retinue or bodyguard. Like their counterparts in archaic Greece, Servius and Tarquinius Superbus are presented as looking for support to the people rather than the aristocracy. Servius seems to have been more successful in this than Superbus, but even Superbus tried to win over the people with the booty of war. Superbus reputedly instituted violent attacks on the aristocracy, although it is difficult to say whether this picture was influenced by the actions of archaic Greek tyrants or late Republican figures like Sulla. The historicity of this picture is debatable, although it is now more plausible to defend it as a

---

66. Glinister, *Roman Kingship*, 146 n. 16 cites the examples of Bellerophon in the *Iliad* (6.155–95), and Cecrops and Amphictyon in Athens marrying the daughters of the king. Anthropological examples: Schneider and Gough (eds), *Matrilineal Kinship*.
67. Glinister, 'Kingship and tyranny', 20.

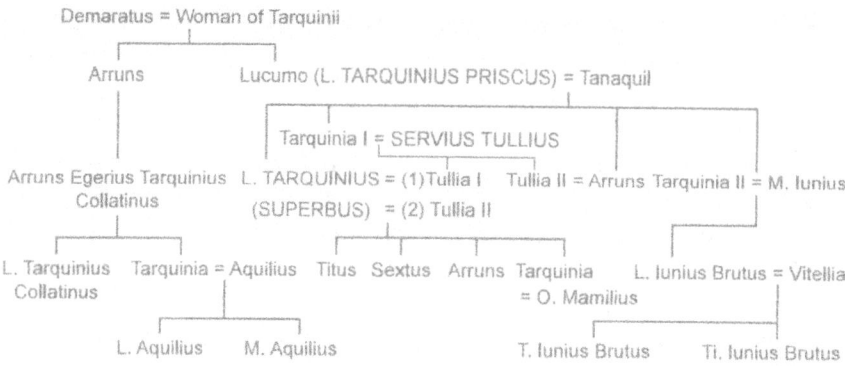

Figure 4.3 The Tarquin dynasty (after Cornell, *Beginnings*, fig. 14)

genuinely structural parallel with contemporary Greece, rather than a later reimagining along Greek historical lines, given the profound Greek links evident in sixth-century Rome.

Another important feature is the so-called 'Tarquin dynasty' that Tarquinius founded. This can be reconstructed from various sources, and implicitly lies behind the account in Livy, Dionysius and others (Fig. 4.3). Note that no one source has all this information, and the sources disagree on some details, such as whether Tarquinius Superbus was Priscus' son or grandson. It has a number of striking features. It included Servius Tullius as well as both the Tarquins, who joined the dynasty by marrying the king's daughter. Two of the major figures in the setting up of the Republic were themselves members of this dynasty: Tarquinius Collatinus and Junius Brutus. Brutus was a trusted lieutenant of Superbus in some versions, being Tribune of the Celeres and the king's nephew. This might suggest that the fall of the monarchy was something of a palace coup, but more on this later.

The dynasty should not be regarded as straightforwardly historical. The figures are probably mostly historical, and their relationships probably in the correct chronological order. But there are major chronological issues connected with the stretching of the sequence Demaratus – Tarquinius Priscus – Tarquinius Superbus to accommodate the Cypselid dynastic link. The sequence covers an implausibly long period and may exclude other figures. In fact, there are several potential interstitial figures, such as Aulus and Caelius Vibenna, and Mastarna.[68]

---

68. Ampolo, 'Città riformata', 217–18; Cornell, *Beginnings*, 121.

Institutional reforms and the creation of the Roman citizenship

Servius is said to have reformed the organisation of the state, and was regarded in the Roman tradition as the second founder of the city. The action for which he is most famous is the reorganisation of the citizen body and army of the Roman city state, the Servian reforms.

According to Livy and Dionysius, Servius divided the population into tribes based on place of residence, and into wealth classes.[69] There were five different classes, each of which had to equip themselves for military service according to their resources. Each of these classes was divided into groups known as centuries. The centuries voted as groups in the centuriate assembly. In this way Servius linked the voting rights of classes of Roman citizens, assembled as the centuries in the *comitia centuriata* (centuriate assembly), to their levels of wealth and role in the army. Each century voted individually, with the first class going first, and a majority of centuries was needed for an election. There were more centuries in the richest class (the first) than the others, and this class nearly had a majority by itself. As there were fewer people in each century of the first class, their votes counted for more. That the *comitia centuriata* is connected with the army from its origins is evident because it alone elected the offices such as the consulship which held *imperium*, the power of military command, and because it could only meet outside the *pomerium*, the sacred boundary of Rome. Livy (1.42–3) and Dionysius (4.13–21) provide detailed explanations of a complex system of five classes that Servius is said to have introduced, including the monetary qualifications for each class and the varying equipment that individuals from each class had to provide for themselves (Table 4.2).

Table 4.2 The arrangement of centuries in the centuriate assembly[a]

Class	Qualification in asses	Centuries
I (incl. Knights, *Sex Suffragia*, Engineers)	>100,000	98
II	75–100,000	20
III	50–75,000	20
IV	25–50,000	20
V (incl. horn-blowers)	12,500–25,000	32
Proletarii	<12,500	1

[a] From Forsythe, *Critical History*, 112, based on Livy 1.42–3.

69. For Roman tribes, see Chapter 10.

Scholars have long been dubious about the accuracy of this picture, and have identified various problems and anachronisms. Our main accounts (Livy, 1.42–3; Dion. Hal. 4.13–21; Cic. *Rep.* 2.20) are generally coherent, and agree on a surprising amount of detail, suggesting that at least the first two derive from a common source. There are, however, some differences, such as Cicero's attribution of seventy centuries to the first class rather than eighty, and in minor details of the weaponry.[70] The weaponry attributed to the separate classes has been considered an anachronistic amalgam; the first class start off with a full 'hoplite panoply', which is progressively reduced over the remaining four classes.[71] Scholars have also argued that the monetary equivalents given by Livy and Dionysius must be reconstructions, as there was no coinage before the 270s BC. In fact, such a highly complex system, with an apparently high qualification level for the first class, is usually considered anachronistic for Rome in the sixth century BC. There is a further problem of whether the cavalry voted before the first class, as would befit their elevated status in Roman society, or as some scholars maintain, afterwards, which would suggest that they were being disadvantaged. Finally, many scholars have seen suspiciously close parallels with the activities of reforming figures in Greece, suggesting that the activities of Servius Tullius may have been reconstructed on the model of Cleisthenes.[72]

The historical reality of the reforms is a problematic area, and despite scholarly effort expended over this critical issue, no neat answers have emerged. Something of a consensus does exist on the broad outlines: that the system must have become more complex over time; that it was attributed in its late Republican form to a single founder, Servius Tullius; and that various aspects such as military equipment and property qualification levels are presented by the annalistic sources in their later, rather than archaic form. But this scholarly consensus as it now exists is also problematic, given that the primitivising assumptions underlying it are insufficient for a straightforward rejection of the whole structure as monarchic.[73]

---

70. Cicero uses a system of seventy centuries for first class, but according to Livy and Dion. Hal. the first class were initially eighty; this is thought to have been reduced to seventy in the third century BC to correspond to the thirty-five tribes, instituted in 241 BC.
71. Judged 'artificial' by Poucet, *Rois*, 223–4.
72. Ridley, 'Enigma', 124; Scapini, *Temi greci*, 62–90; Scapini, 'Literary archetypes', 27. Solon was said to have introduced a similar timocratic constitution in Athens with four classes of property owners in the early sixth century.
73. D'Agostino, 'Military organization', 80; Viglietti, *Limite del bisogno*, 163–4; Bradley, 'Investigating aristocracy'.

Although the monetary figures are anachronistic reconstructions, the existence of property qualifications based on pounds of bronze in the archaic era is plausible and accepted by many scholars, and the monetary equivalents may have been adjusted at a later date to fit with the new system of coinage.[74] Most historians have argued that a five-class system is too complex for the state of the economy in archaic Rome, and, rejecting the version of Livy and Dionysius, instead use a passage of Cato to reconstruct Servius' system as one of two classes: on this reading he defined the group of heavy infantry for a phalanx, known as the *classis*, through a property qualification, and designated those below this level *infra classem*.[75] However, the Cato passage in Gellius (*NA* 6.13) used to support this idea is not clear evidence for a single (or two) class system, and there are sixth century precedents in the Greek world for more complex organisations (for example the Solonian four-class system of the early sixth century).

It is important to note that the antiquarian tradition supports the historicity of the major elements of the reforms under the monarchy, attesting multiple classes and centuries. This provides a different tradition to the narrative of Livy and Dionysius, for instance, where it is more likely that the picture of Servius has been distorted by historical parallels with Greek figures.[76] Festus seems to refer to a fifth class in the monarchy.[77] It is clear that antiquarian authors regarded centuries as forming part of the system from the start, even if a reduced number of centuries to begin with is likely.[78]

Despite the general thrust of modern interpretations to assign the reforms to the Republican period, they fit the monarchic period better. Arguments about the economic simplicity of archaic Rome have been undermined by the archaeological evidence. The reform presupposes a powerful original architect, which although possible

---

74. Ampolo, 'La città riformata', 227; Cornell, *Beginnings*, 181; Crawford, *Coinage*, 22–3.
75. Brunt, *Italian Manpower*, 27: 'so primitive a state would not have collected statistics of this kind'; Cornell, *Beginnings*, 187 dates the creation of a more elaborate voting system with five property classes to 406 BC; Humm, 'Servius Tullius', 222, with references to earlier work: late fourth century; cf. Forsythe, 'Army'.
76. Ridley, 'Enigma', points out that Servius' reign has many problematic constructs in the Roman annalistic tradition, attributing to him mythical and artificial features, and that in practice this was a period likely to have seen other interlopers as rulers at Rome.
77. 308 L. Also implied by Sempronius Tuditanus, *FRH* F7 (in Asconius, *Corn.* 60 St.).
78. Festus 184 L., 290 L., 452 L. Fraccaro, 'Storia dell'antichissimo esercito', reconstructs an original legion (and centuriate assembly) of sixty centuries and three classes; cf. Cornell, *Beginnings*, 181–3.

in the Republic seems more likely to belong in the monarchy.[79] The reforms also indicate a vision of the city as a political and military unity. This fits with the idea of a census and hoplite reforms, and ties in with the archaeological evidence of a walled circuit dating to the sixth century.[80] The introduction of such a timocratic system would have aroused plebeian opposition later on, and in fact there is no evidence at all in the narrative sources for a later date. These are somewhat fragile arguments, but they demonstrate that the scholarly reservations about the monarchic attribution of the full five-class system are unnecessary.

Ultimately the exact form of the centuriate organisation under the monarchy is uncertain, but the main elements seem monarchic. What then was the purpose of this new system? One key difference of the new system from that of the Romulean *curiae* was the periodic reinvention of the citizen body through the census, which allowed the inclusion of incomers.[81] The centuriate system was concerned with 'social and economic differentiation, but not hereditary privileges', according to Momigliano.[82] Fisher has shown that the function of parallel Greek reorganisations was to improve social cohesion, and he notes that they were undertaken by all sorts of regimes.[83] The key aim of the reforms is not, therefore, as many have thought, to undermine elite influence. It is more likely that they attempt to maximise Roman military potential. In fact, it is difficult to separate out the political and military roles of the reform. Both go together, with the burdens of military service rewarded by increased voting power, a sign of an archaic rationality.[84]

The reforms also promoted the absorption of outsiders. The value of the latter would not be lost on a king like Servius Tullius with his enigmatic outsider credentials, although Rome remained open to immigrants in the Republic. As Torelli notes, the reforms in origin must have resulted from a substantial expansion of the

---

79. Humm, 'Servius Tullius', envisages Appius Claudius Caecus in the late fourth century BC.
80. Cifani, *Architettura*, 264.
81. Last, 'Servian reforms'.
82. Momigliano, 'Origins', 106.
83. Fisher, '*Kharis*'.
84. Festus has Servius creating a century for those who were displaced, called *niquis scivit* (184 L.), implying that voting was an original part of the process.

Roman population in the sixth century BC.[85] The reforms therefore encompass a continuing fluidity and expansion of the Roman population and were forward-looking. The gradual regularisation of the census in the fifth century BC shows that not all the elements were in place to begin with, but that there was a continued need through the fifth century to renew the distribution of the changing population through the system of centuries and tribes, and to account for military losses and territorial fluctuations. Ampolo has interpreted the reforms as instituted in tension with mobility, but we can equally argue that the new system comes over time to accommodate mobility.[86]

Thus, it seems plausible to trace the outlines of a monarchy with a new organisational system of some complexity from this difficult picture. As we have seen, the arguments marshalled against the tradition by scholars, working from primitivising preconceptions, are all rather weak, even if many of the precise arrangements of the new institutions remain debatable.

The Republican revolution

A new era in Roman history begins in the late sixth century with the overthrow of Tarquinius Superbus. He was replaced by two yearly magistrates in (traditionally) 509 BC, thus inaugurating the Republic. But how real is the colourful picture in the tradition, and what is really happening?

A first point to note is that our ancient sources present the creation of the Republic as a straightforward change that happened in a short time frame. They write from the hindsight of nearly five hundred years of uninterrupted Republican rule, and so the setting up of the Republic, whilst important, is to them somewhat inevitable. Yet as Francis Oakley has argued, most ancient societies are ruled by sacred kings rather than Republics, and we should not naturally expect Republicanism to prevail.[87] The setting up and survival of the Roman Republic thus needs more explication than it is normally granted. Part of the answer must lie in the broader Mediterranean context

---

85. Torelli, 'Populazioni', 256. A huge number of citizens, numbering 80,000 or 83,000, is claimed to have been recorded in the first census (Livy, 1.44, Dion. Hal. 4.22.2, Eutropius 1.7); for discussion, see Chapter 6.
86. Ampolo, 'Città riformata'.
87. Oakley, *Kingship*, 6–8.

and in the influence of other, particularly Greek, political ideas circulating at the time. Another part must lie in the opening up of governmental power to a wider group of stakeholders. A third may be to follow Flower in thinking not of a monolithic single Republic, but rather of multiple, successive Republics over the course of the second half of the first millennium BC.[88]

The traditional account as conveyed by Livy and Dionysius of Halicarnassus has some interesting implications if we look at it closely. The immediate cause of the change was the rape of Lucretia, a Roman matron, by the tyrant's son Sextus Tarquinius. Lucretia was of such exemplary virtue that she killed herself because she could not live with the shame.[89] Lucretia's noble speech and actions inspired Brutus to swear to overturn Tarquinius and his 'criminal wife' Tullia (Livy, 1.59.1). He was joined by Lucretia's husband, Collatinus, and Publius Valerius Publicola. All three would become leaders in the new Republic. They inspired the people to declare the exile of the king. Brutus and Collatinus were elected as the first consuls, allegedly using rules drawn up by Servius Tullius (clearly portrayed in hindsight as a Republican figure).

The revolt is presented as the result of Tarquinius' overbearing personal character. He worked the population very hard in order to create monumental buildings and public works in the city, such as the Cloaca Maxima, which would enhance his own prestige. His regime is characterised as a very violent rule, beginning with the assassination of Servius Tullius, and also seeing the elimination of anyone who threatened his position. This has strong echoes of historical accounts of Greek tyrants, who commonly outrage decency by sexually abusing their subjects. The most famous example is the Pisistratid dynasty, whose fall was later connected by Athenians with the tyrant Hipparchus' desire for the young boy Harmodius. The Roman revolution looks in many ways like a palace coup – their family tree shows how those who led the overthrow of the regime were actually part of the Tarquin dynasty.[90] Tarquinius Collatinus was a cousin of Tarquinius Superbus; Junius Brutus was his nephew. No outside state was said to have been involved.

---

88. Flower, *Roman Republics*.
89. Livy 1.57–60; Dion. Hal. 4.64–85. The power of this famous story has frequently been reimagined by artists, as in Titian's *Tarquin and Lucretia*, 1571.
90. Cornell, *Beginnings*, 123.

Following the exile of Tarquinius Superbus, the Republic was effectively set up overnight by the appointment of the two consuls. They shared the power of the king, *imperium*, and their office was limited to a year. They immediately undertook various important steps. Junius Brutus enlarged the Senate with new recruits, called *conscripti*. The ancient tradition thus implies that the Senate already existed and was simply modified on the transition to the Republic. The king's religious duties were now assigned to a specially created priest, called the *rex sacrorum* or *sacrificolus*. Finally, the people demanded that no one bearing the hated name Tarquinius should be left in power. This meant that Tarquinius Collatinus was forced to go into exile, despite having had no part in the crimes of the regime, with all other members of the Tarquinian *gens*. In the traditional account most Roman institutions continued unaffected. This is particularly evident in religion, with virtually all the priesthoods believed to have been established under the monarchy. Most of the content of the calendar seems to date to the monarchic period. The Capitoline temple was dedicated by the first consuls and not destroyed, despite its royal associations. It is also the case for the major political institutions such as the *comitia tributa* and *comitia centuriata*, which apparently continue uninterruptedly in their monarchic form.

Some evidence supports this traditional account, particularly in terms of chronology. It is probably right to follow the tradition in locating this change in the late sixth century BC. Although there is still considerable controversy, the list of magistrates (the *Fasti*) seems to be in large part reliable and has enough names to take us back to just before 500 BC. This list is preserved in Livy and other historians (Livy provides names back to 502 BC), and also inscribed on stone in the Forum under Augustus, the so-called *Fasti Capitolini* (which provide names back to 509 BC). There are relatively few discrepancies in these separate sources, which reinforces the authentic nature of the lists. The names are also regarded as reliable as they include plebeian names down to around 450 BC, and also non-Roman names (including Etruscan ones).[91]

The fall of the monarchy is closely linked in time with the siege of Rome by Porsenna, an Etruscan king from Clusium. He tried to capture Rome to reinstall Tarquin (described in some sources as

---

91. For discussion, see Cornell, *Beginnings*, 218–23; Oakley, *Commentary*, I 39–41, concerning the period post 390 BC; for a more critical view, see Richardson, 'Roman nobility'.

a fellow Etruscan). The threat ends when his forces are defeated at Aricia in Latium, an event which Dionysius recounts. Dionysius later reports this episode from the perspective of the Cumaean ruler Aristodemus, who came to help Aricia in 504 BC. Scholars have generally agreed that this part of his history derives from a 'Cumaean Chronicle', a local history of Cumae now lost.[92] This Cumaean version is an independent account that places the start of the Republic in the last decade of the sixth century BC.

But there are also some major difficulties. Firstly, the literary tradition is obviously distorted by patriotism. It features a series of hugely idealised Roman heroes. Lucretia is a perfect vision of a Roman female victim: she barely featured in the story until she was raped, made an inspiring speech and killed herself. Brutus is the taciturn founder hero: he led the Romans to freedom; then, when his sons plotted against the new Republic, had them executed. Then a trio of Roman heroes helped keep Porsenna at bay. Horatius held off the Etruscan forces at the bridge, although dying in the attempt according to our oldest surviving source, Polybius. Mucius Scaevola tried to assassinate Porsenna, was captured, and burnt his hand off in the flames to demonstrate that he was not afraid of torture.[93] Finally, there is Cloelia, who escaped from Porsenna's camp along with the most vulnerable of the hostages (Livy, 2.13). Cloelia and Horatius were reportedly commemorated in statuary, and Horatius and Mucius given land to farm which came to bear their names. Clearly these stories of miraculous heroism have been shaped by oral tradition into powerful sagas emphasising the importance of self-sacrifice for the state, stories that must have coalesced, perhaps erroneously, around monuments and place names. Wiseman has suggested that much of the Porsenna story may have derived from stage performances of historical tragedy.

The second problem is confusion over the role of Porsenna and perhaps other unknown outside forces. In Livy and the main narrative tradition, Porsenna is repelled from the city, and leaves it on friendly terms. This rather implausible picture is undermined by two sources that imply a different story. According to Tacitus, the city capitulated to Porsenna (*Hist.* 3.72), and Pliny details a treaty 'granted by Porsenna to the Roman people after the expulsion of the kings that they should only use iron for purposes of agriculture' (*HN* 34.139). It is curious that this alternative version, with

---

92. Alföldi, *Early Rome*, 56ff.; Zevi, 'Demaratus', 82; contra, Gallia, 'Reassessing'. See p. 116 above.
93. Painted by Rubens and Van Dyck in 1620.

Porsenna capturing the city, only features in later sources. This could be a mistake, or it is possible that earlier Roman historians had tried to suppress this unflattering tradition.[94]

The third problem is whether the change was as quick as implied, or more evolutionary. There are some clear signs that the change from one type of regime to another was more gradual than the tradition portrays. One sign is the creation of the *rex sacrorum*, said by Livy to have been introduced at the start of the Republic to conduct the old king's religious duties. Many scholars have questioned this view, arguing that this office was the product of splitting off religious powers from the king rather earlier on.[95] Another is the shadowy indication of single powerful rulers with titles other than *rex*. From Livy we know that the consuls were originally called praetors; this later became the term for the next rank down below consuls (Livy, 3.55.12). At another point Livy refers to a *praetor maximus*, a chief magistrate, named in an ancient law, and states that this was a name for the dictator (in the Republic, a single ruler appointed in an emergency situation) (Livy, 7.3.5–9). Together this evidence implies that Rome was at one point ruled by a dictator, who had a less powerful colleague. This is reinforced by the presence elsewhere in neighbouring cities of magisterial single rulers. At Alba Longa in Latium, according to Licinius Macer, the kings were replaced by dictators. This was reported by Dionysius of Halicarnassus (5.73), who describes the dictatorship as an 'elective tyranny'. We can compare this with the ruler of Caere in Etruria, Thefarie Velianas. In the Pyrgi tablets of *c.*500–480 BC he seems to have occupied a position that seems to be equivalent to this half-magistrate/half-king: he is described as a king in the Phoenician text, yet is in the third year of his office according to the Etruscan text.

The last element to consider is the archaeological evidence. Very substantial atrium houses appear in Rome *c.*525 BC. They endure on this site on the slopes of the Palatine until the late third century BC, and would seem to be a sign of the growing wealth and assertion of the Roman elite. By contrast, a number of other monuments are destroyed and rebuilt in the years around 500 BC. These include the Regia, the building most strongly associated with the king, which was reconstructed several times in the sixth century, and finally established on a definitive plan around 500 BC.[96] A similar rebuilding took place at

---

94. Ridley, 'Lars Porsenna', for the historiography.
95. Cornell, *Beginnings*, 236; Glinister, 'Politics'.
96. Hopkins, *Genesis*, 84–6.

the Atrium Vestae at the same time. The rebuilding of the Regia has been associated with the shift to the Republic, but as Hopkins points out, there are comparable buildings in other neighbouring cities to the north and south of Rome, such as Acquarossa and Gabii, and the dating of the material from the Regia is not precisely aligned with the literary date of 509, instead pointing only to a period between c.520 and the early fifth century. Rebuilding also occurs at the Forum Boarium temples in the early fifth century BC, and at the Comitium, which was repaved in the late sixth century, with a large stepped platform being created.[97] This reconstruction and monumentalisation of the Comitium implies that the political function of assemblies had been well established under the monarchy, and that it was envisaged that assemblies such as the *comitia tributa* would continue to meet in the area. Lastly, we should note that the Capitoline temple is traditionally said to have been dedicated in the first year of the Republic. Whilst the archaeological evidence no longer supports the idea of a widespread burning of major monuments around the time of the end of the monarchy, it does indicate a considerable amount of monumental change at this time.

This evidence can be put together to argue for an alternative reconstruction along the following lines.[98] The king was replaced by a sole ruler, perhaps a dictator, at some point. The later monarchy was continually unstable and was probably seized periodically by adventurers such as Mastarna and Caelius Vibenna. Porsenna may simply be the last in a long line of such figures, who have been written out of the tidied-up canonical version in our sources. The role of monarch became more difficult to hold at Rome as the period went on, and the importance of consolidating the leader's prestige is evident in the extraordinary phase of sixth century monumental building, epitomised by the gigantic Capitoline temple.[99] The existence of the *rex sacrorum* suggests that the old king's powers were reduced and he adopted a ceremonial, ritual role at some point. He was perhaps replaced by a dictator who held consecutive periods of office (as with Thefarie Velianas in Caere), effectively making him a tyrant over the city. Servius Tullius and Tarquinius Superbus, and perhaps others like Mastarna, can be seen as tyrannical rulers (called dictators?) over Rome. In the late sixth century, in an obscure series of events that may be linked to Porsenna's capture of the city, the Republic was created. In c.504 BC Porsenna

---

97. Hopkins, *Genesis*, 89.
98. Cf. Cornell, *Beginnings*, 143–50; Forsythe, *Critical History*, 93–108.
99. Hopkins, *Genesis*, 163–71 argues that this building phase may be connected to other members of the elite besides the king, and continues well into the fifth century BC.

conquered Rome (a view concealed by the majority of annalists in the Roman tradition, but hinted at by antiquarian sources in terms of the impact that he had on the city, leaving both troops and goods behind). When he left, Rome came to be ruled by two consuls, and the dictatorship was reduced to a temporary role employed only in emergencies. Rome was ruled by two annual magistrates from then on. The *Fasti* go back to the last decade of the 500s, so the dual magistracy and the Republic must begin then.

Whilst this hypothesis is coherent, and a critical approach to the problematic ancient account is obviously sensible, it is impossible to verify. It is very different from the literary tradition, and very hard to fit with evidence such as the *Fasti* (if magistrates of some kind existed before 509 why are they not listed?). In fact, it is equally possible that the literary tradition is right that Porsenna did not capture the city. Nevertheless, the hypothesis of an unstable situation in the sixth century, out of which the Republic evolves at the end of the century, is quite plausible. Such a shift in regime must be linked to wider turmoil within central Italy in this period, and understanding the regional context is fundamental here. Modern scholars have suggested that Rome is merely one example of a broader shift to Republics throughout the Mediterranean at this time. A general period of political upheaval in the decades around 500 BC is thought to have made it difficult for previous regimes to continue untroubled. But this is not a clear pattern, as at this point tyrannies in fact become more common in Magna Graecia and Sicily, as at Syracuse. In addition, the seventh and sixth centuries see experimentation with different types of regime, law-giving and the creation of constitutions across Magna Graecia.[100] These trends are linked to Mediterranean-wide shifts that affect the economic and political networks established in the archaic era. In the west the most notable development is the rise of Carthage and the conflict with Greek cities on Sicily. In the east the rise of Persia placed new pressures on the Greek cities on the coast of Asia Minor and across the Aegean. Rome and other central Italian cities such as Caere and Tarquinii were dependent on an easily facilitated Tyrrhenian trade, which was disturbed by events such as the defeat of the Etruscan attack on Greek Cumae in 524, and the destruction of the great Greek city of Sybaris in 510. The impact of these trends is only beginning to be understood, and a new picture emerging of external forces playing both an indirect and direct role in the setting up of the new regime at Rome.

100. Pallottino, *History*, 88.

CHAPTER 5

Urbanism and city foundation

Introduction

In Chapter 2 we saw how central Italy was affected by processes of urbanisation around the end of the second and start of the first millennium BC. Rome was very much part of these trends, although given the difficult conditions of excavation it is hard to piece together a coherent picture. The archaeological evidence for the earliest settlement on the site of Rome consists of burials, habitation remains and fortifications. This material has expanded at an exciting pace in the last twenty years, although much remains controversial.

The focus in this chapter is on archaeological evidence for the beginnings and development of the city under the monarchy. On the whole I will not be trying to relate the archaeological evidence directly to the literary sources, because they throw very different types of light on the changes that occurred under the monarchy. But I will aim to highlight the general compatibility of the picture each type of evidence produces.

This chapter covers the beginning of settlement at Rome, around 1000 BC, the emergence of the city in the seventh century, and the major developments in urban building from c.625–480 BC. It should be noted that the chronology of the whole process remains very controversial. Debate has raged, for instance, around the archaeological date for the first gravel pavement of the assembly place, the Comitium, which has swung from the sixth century to as early as the eighth century.[1]

The geographical position

The geographical position of the city goes a long way to explaining its later pre-eminence. The site itself is characterised by higher ground in close proximity to a bend and island in the lower reaches

---

1. For the higher date see Carandini, *Nascita*, 500; Carafa, *Comizio di Roma*; 'Volcanal'; for a critique see Hopkins, *Genesis*, 26–35.

of the Tiber river. The Tiber is the most important river in central Italy, connecting Sabinum, Etruria and Umbria to the sea. It provided a ready link to the north and south, as well as a source of food. Its fundamental importance in Roman history has been somewhat downplayed, although reassessment has taken place in recent studies. There was a port in the bend of the river under the Capitoline hill, at the Forum Boarium (cattle market), where seaborne traders could alight. This corresponds to the zone where the flow of the river slowed as it passed around the Tiber island, and immediately downstream of the island was a fording point, the closest one there was to the coast. This crossing point was enhanced by the creation of the earliest bridge, the Pons Sublicius, reputedly during the reign of Ancus Marcius (Livy, 1.33; Plut. *Num.* 9).

The site of the city is unusual for central Italy in that it does not consist of a readily defensible plateau. Rather it is composed of a number of hills and spurs of higher ground made of volcanic tufa rock (Fig. 5.1). Famously Rome was supposed to have been built on seven hills, the most important of which are the Capitoline, the Quirinal, Viminal, Esquiline, Palatine, Caelian and Aventine. But ancient authors identify different hills, and in reality there are many more than the supposed seven, and most are in fact spurs of higher ground to the east. Even the distinctive hills of the Capitoline, Palatine and Aventine had complex topographies and were composed of multiple peaks, with separate names for each part, such as the Cermalus, the western peak of the Palatine. In addition, many of the hills are scarcely apparent today, as they have been built over, and large parts of them levelled.

In between the hills were water courses, running through low lying areas such as the Campus Martius, the Forum and the Velabrum, and a marshy area at the Lupercal on the southern foot of the Palatine. The Forum lay between the Capitoline, Velian and Palatine, and in consequence received the run-off from the surrounding hills and springs. The Velabrum was the valley between the Capitoline and the Palatine; it featured clay beds that were used to create tiles and pots, and there was cappellaccio stone in the slopes of the surrounding hills. The low-lying districts were regularly flooded as a result of the periodic inundation of the Tiber. In a normal year the river level rises to 9 m above sea level, which would have been enough to submerge the lower slopes of the Velabrum and the central part of the Forum. In an exceptional year the river could rise to 12 m above sea level. It was only with anthropogenic intervention,

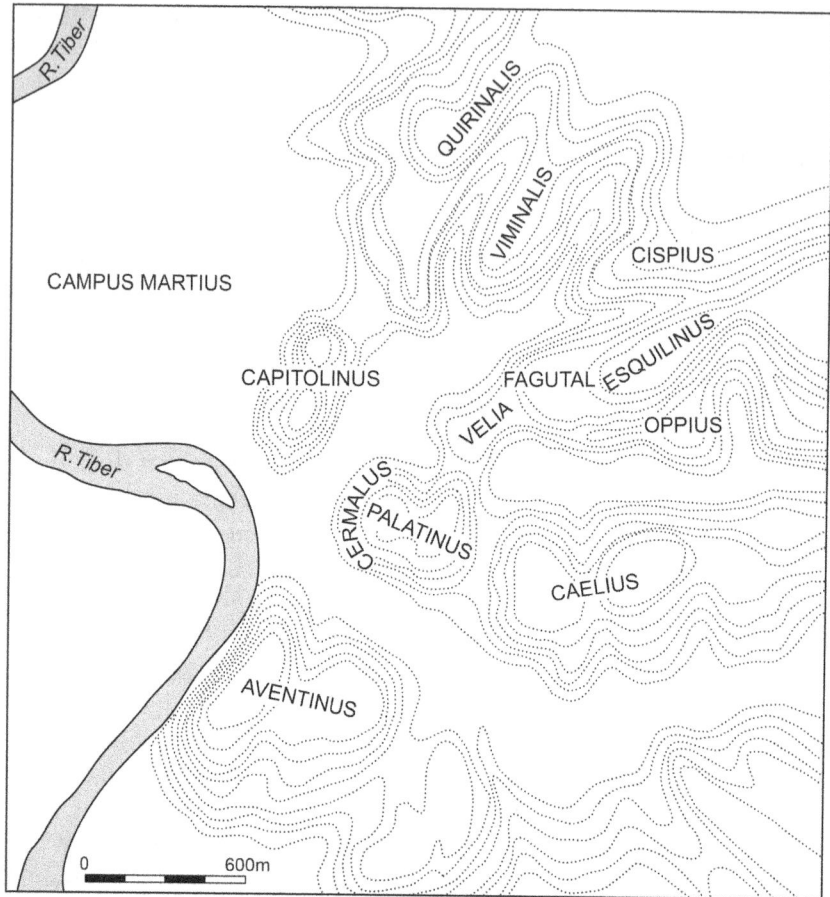

Figure 5.1 The topography of the site of Rome (after Momigliano and Schiavone (eds), *Storia di Roma*, I 577)

as we shall see, that the level of the Forum was raised above that of the regular winter flood.

Rome thus combined the typical upland positions favoured by late Bronze Age and early Iron Age settlers with the resources provided by the Tiber. Furthermore, the site occupied a central position within Italy in terms of communications. Rome was a vital crossroads of routes from the interior to the Tyrrhenian coast, and north–south, parallel to the coast. Some of this movement must have been environmentally determined and very ancient, and probably took place on a seasonal basis. As we saw above, Rome also controlled the point where the route along the Tyrrhenian coast of Italy could make the

Urbanism and city foundation

easiest crossing of the Tiber inland, some 19 miles upstream of the coast. Ancient authors emphasised that although the city was not on the coast, it still had many of the advantages of a coastal position.[2]

Rome was also the central hub of the route between the salt pans at the Tiber mouth and the mountainous interior of the peninsula. This was a very important route of great antiquity. The Via Campana led from the salt pans at the Tiber mouth to the Forum Boarium, following the northern bank of the river until the crossing at Rome.[3] The Via Salaria then led from Rome into Sabinum and the uplands. Salt is a product that is often difficult to trace archaeologically, but which was of fundamental importance to ancient societies, playing a key role in food preservation and stock-rearing.[4] The salt producing zones at the mouth of the Tiber, later called the *campus salinarum*, were on the right bank of the river and according to the literary tradition were originally Veientine before being captured by Romulus.[5] This was the primary source for much of central Italy, major salt-producing areas being rare along the Tyrrhenian coast.[6] The name 'Via Salaria' for the major route into Sabinum indicates the importance of this trade.

The earliest settlement on the site of Rome

Settlement evidence on the site of Rome can be traced back to the Middle and Recent Bronze Age, from when there are sherds of Apennine pottery from the Forum Boarium (in a redeposited context). There are also Recent Bronze Age sherds from the Tabularium (found in situ). Recent excavations in the Giardino Romano area of the Capitoline hill have provided clear evidence of a stable community here in the Late Bronze Age. This hill is separated from the Arx by a lower saddle of land, but is only approachable from the Forum side, and provides a readily defensible site near the river and its crossing point. There are redeposited fragments of pottery dating back to the Middle Bronze Age (seventeenth to fourteenth century BC). For the Late Bronze Age, stable occupation is attested by substantial deposits of faunal and ceramic material. Bronzeworking is in

---

2. See further, Chapter 6.
3. Coarelli, 'Santuari'; *Foro Boario*, 109–13.
4. Giovannini, 'Le sel'; Torelli, 'Gli aromi e il sale'.
5. Plut. *Rom*. 25.4; Dion. Hal. 2.55.5; 3.41.3; Livy, 1.15.5.
6. For smaller-scale manufacture in other areas along coastal Latium see Alessandri, *Latium Vetus*, 34–7.

evidence, there are remains of building structures, and there are signs of the remodelling of the slope of the hill leading into the saddle, for defensive or habitation purposes. In the early Iron Age there is further evidence of metalworking (this time iron), as well as burials of adults and babies.[7]

How far this settlement extended and whether it was restricted to the one hill is currently uncertain. Bronze Age material has now been recovered from a range of sites in the historical centre of Rome. Fragments of Recent Bronze Age pottery have been discovered in the Forum (in the area of the Arch of Augustus), which may be part of the same settlement as the Capitoline.[8] There are also traces of settlement on the Palatine from the early Iron Age, including a burial and evidence of habitation. A separate area of habitation is attested on the Quirinal in the early Iron Age. A recently discovered burial from the Forum of Caesar (Tomb 2) dates to the Final Bronze Age/early Iron Age transition (eleventh to tenth century BC); it is a particularly exciting find as along with miniaturised pottery it contained signs of high status in the form of miniaturised weaponry (a bronze spear and four double shields), a fibula with a serpentine bow, and a bronze knife (for ritual purposes). Terracing activity here in the Late Bronze Age, as on the Capitoline hill, provides further evidence of stable habitation. In addition, the first evidence of activity alongside the Tiber has been provided by recent coring works in the Forum Boarium, where the future harbour would come to be situated.[9] Thus, an increasing amount of evidence testifies to a stable settlement on the site of Rome from at least the Late Bronze Age. This may be more extensive than scholars have been prepared to envisage, encompassing the Capitoline hill, Forum and Forum Boarium. However, separate settlement areas are probably more likely in this period, given what we know of Villanovan settlement in Etruria.

The most important evidence for permanent settlement at Rome begins around 1000 BC with the cemetery known as the Sepulcretum, on the Sacra Via next to the later temple of Antoninus and Faustina. This was first excavated by Giacomo Boni in 1902. The burials here take a fairly standardised form in the first two Latial phases (1000–770 BC), with miniaturised pottery and bronzes,

---

7. Albertoni and Damiani, *Tempio di Giove*, 40–63.
8. Peroni, 'Comunità', 17.
9. Brock and Terrenato, 'Rome in the Bronze Age'.

sometimes with figurines and a hut urn containing the ashes, all placed in a large jar called a dolium which was buried in a pit.[10] Inhumation takes over from cremation in the eighth century BC, and after this the cemetery here seems to fall into disuse (the implications of this are discussed below). Peroni argued that this cemetery related to the Final Bronze Age/early Iron Age settlement (or settlements, as it is not clear that they are unified) on the Capitoline hill and the Palatine.[11]

Another cemetery, on the Esquiline, became the major necropolis for the city in the Orientalising period. The conditions of its discovery mean we know little about it.[12] It was identified earlier than the Forum cemetery, in the 1870s, when the modern city was expanding in this direction, and Roman archaeology was far less sophisticated. In consequence, most of the material was sold on the antiques market. A few pieces remaining, especially Greek imported pottery, give us the impression that this was becoming a wealthy centre, with an elite clearly distinguishing themselves through burial from those of lower social status.[13] There are some cremation tombs, although the cemetery mostly contains inhumation burials dating to the eighth and seventh centuries BC. Tomb group 98, with its distinctive military panoply, is particularly interesting (Fig. 5.2).

What is the significance of the two cemeteries? Different pottery styles show that the cemeteries have different eras of use, although there is some evidence that the Esquiline cemetery also began to be used from very early on.[14] The standard explanation of their sequence is that of Colonna, who noticed that child and infant burials seem to continue in the Forum in period IIB (830–770 BC), and argued that adult burials moved to the Esquiline cemetery. This could be because habitation was now moving into the Forum area from the hills, and only the burials of children, not yet considered full members of the community, remained possible amongst the huts. But the very existence of huts in the Forum is controversial because of the drainage of the area; in reality the burials seem to have been moved out at an early date, with the area remaining uninhabited until its first paving.[15]

10. Italian *pozzo*: hence often called burials *a pozzo*.
11. Peroni, 'Comunità', 18.
12. Ross Holloway, *Archaeology*, 21–2.
13. Ross Holloway, *Archaeology*, 22.
14. Alessandri, *Latium Vetus*, 387.
15. Ammerman, 'On the origins'; Hopkins, *Genesis*, 28.

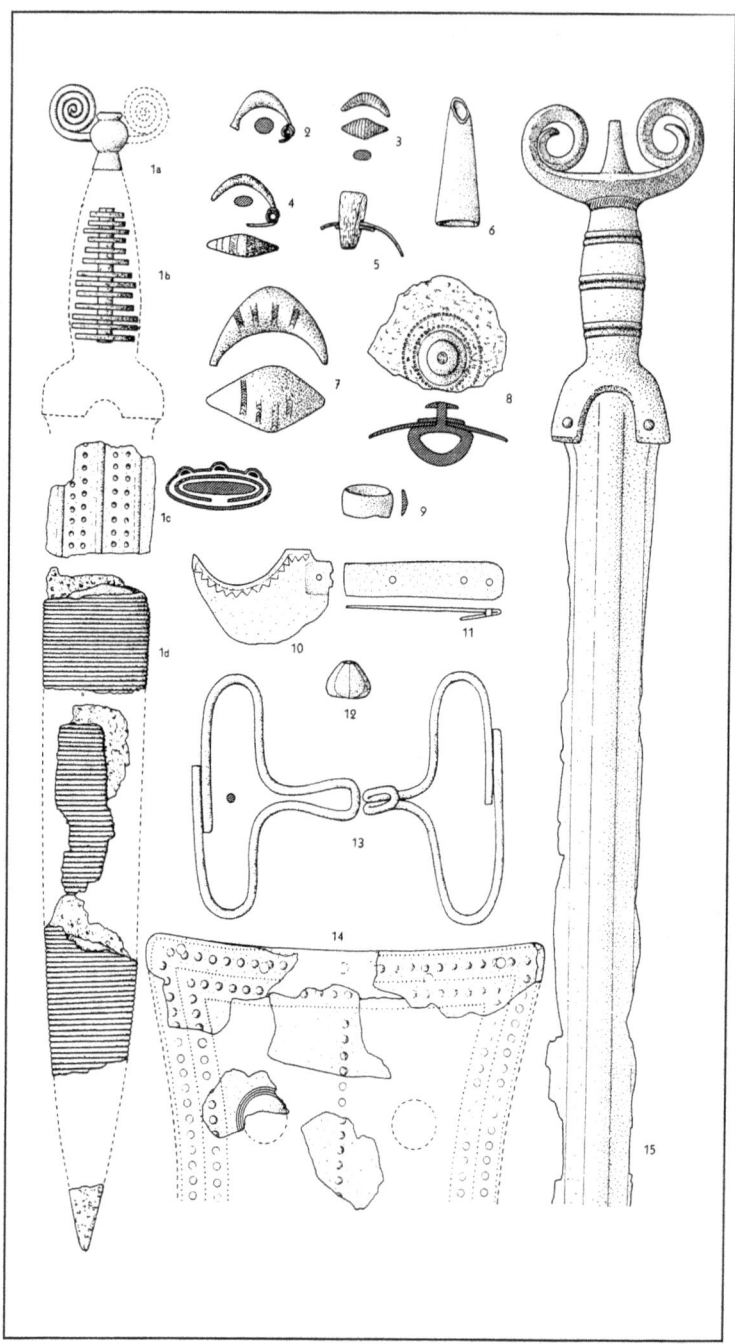

Figure 5.2 Funerary goods from Tomb 98, Esquiline cemetery, including a short iron sword with a wooden scabbard (1a–d), a spear butt (6), a bronze razor (10), a belt buckle (13) and a bronze pectoral (14) (drawing: R. Hook, for Sekunda and Northwood, *Early Roman Armies*, 7; reproduced with kind permission of the authors)

The earliest part of the Esquiline cemetery is the north-eastern portion. From the mid eighth century the tombs are generally found on the periphery of the hills, suggesting space on the higher ground near the centre was needed for habitation.[16] If unified, the settlement would have comprised a large proto-urban centre, measuring some 150–200 ha, encompassing the Capitoline, Palatine, Forum, Esquiline and Quirinal, beginning in the ninth century and expanding in the eighth century. This is comparable to the scale of the largest Villanovan centres.[17] It is identified by Carandini with the 'Septimontium', according to Varro (*Ling.* 5.41) the original name of the site of Rome.[18] Nevertheless, there are some difficulties in assuming that it was a single settlement. As we have seen, the extent of habitation in the Forum is controversial, with some scholars envisaging it as an annually flooded area that could not have been lived in before works of reclamation in the second half of the seventh century. In addition, comparisons with Villanovan centres show that settlement in the early Iron Age was rarely contiguous and completely unified.[19] It may be more realistic then to envisage a patchwork of habitation covering this wide area, with large gaps for hydrological features, and considerable caution is required in interpreting the evidence as attesting a coherent urban centre and/or state.

The developing settlement in the early Iron Age

The habitation structures contemporary with these cemeteries are typically called 'huts'. They can be traced archaeologically from the post-holes left by the wooden structure, a surrounding rain trench, door spaces, hearths, and traces of wattle and daub packing to the walls. Beyond this nothing much of the structure survives, but they can be reconstructed from the wooden frame and from representations of their form in cinerary hut urns. These show that they had doors, walls with geometric decoration, and elaborate roof finials. The term 'huts' is therefore potentially misleading, given that they are not flimsy, temporary structures; it is better instead to class them as 'habitation structures'.[20] They consist of wooden framed buildings, some with multiple

---

16. Carafa, 'Volcanal'.
17. Peroni, 'Comunità', 18–19.
18. Carandini, *Nascita*, especially 267–79.
19. Fulminante, *Urbanisation*, 79–80.
20. As we have seen in relation to Etruria, in Chapter 2. Note that the term 'huts' can cover a multitude of structures, from animal pens to elaborate houses. See Colantoni, 'Straw to stone'.

rooms, that can last more than a century, and are thus clear evidence of permanent habitation.

Groups of these habitation structures have been found in several areas in the centre of Rome. The most famous cluster is on the south-western part of the Palatine hill, which may be the settlement corresponding to the Forum cemetery. The foundations of habitation structures were discovered here in the 1930s, and dated to the ninth and eighth century BC. This is striking in the light of the literary tradition that made this area the primary nucleus of the ancient city founded by Romulus; a 'hut' said to have belonged to him was preserved well into the imperial period (Dion. Hal. 1.79.11). Traces of a very large wooden building of 900–750 BC have also been uncovered on the Cermalus, the westernmost part of the Palatine. Initially measuring 12 × 8 m, it was replaced by two wooden buildings around 750 BC, one of which was then expanded into a large, multi-roomed structure.

Habitation structures are also known from the Forum. There are around eleven on the site of the Regia, and various others on the site of the temple of Julius Caesar, the Arch of Augustus, the temple of Antoninus and Faustina, and the Atrium Vestae.[21] The structures below the temple of Antoninus and Faustina overlay the Sepulcretum, which fell out of use at the end of the eighth century, and may indicate that habitation was spreading down from the top of the hill.[22] Some structures may be remains of animal pens rather than dwellings, for example the smaller examples at the Regia, which were destroyed by a flood c.650 BC. Nearby, a rectilinear building, called the 'Domus Regia' by Carandini and his team, appeared in the second half of the eighth century BC.[23] Its full extent and exact floor plan are unclear, but the apparent multi-room arrangement and possible courtyard seem to signify increasing complexity (Fig. 5.3). All these habitation structures are normally dated from the ninth to seventh centuries BC, after which there was a shift towards the use of more labour-intensive materials, such as stone foundations, earthen walls, and terracotta tiled roofs. The social organisation related to the earlier structures is probably quite similar, however, with social spaces in the open air around hearths and shrines between huts likely to have performed the same function as the courtyards common in the later buildings.[24]

21. Colantoni, 'Straw to stone'; Hopkins, *Genesis*, 20–4. There are uncertain claims of structures on the Velian, Quirinal, and at Sant'Omobono.
22. Hopkins, *Genesis*, 39.
23. Filippi, 'Domus Regia'.
24. Colantoni, 'Straw to stone'; Prayon, 'Architecture'.

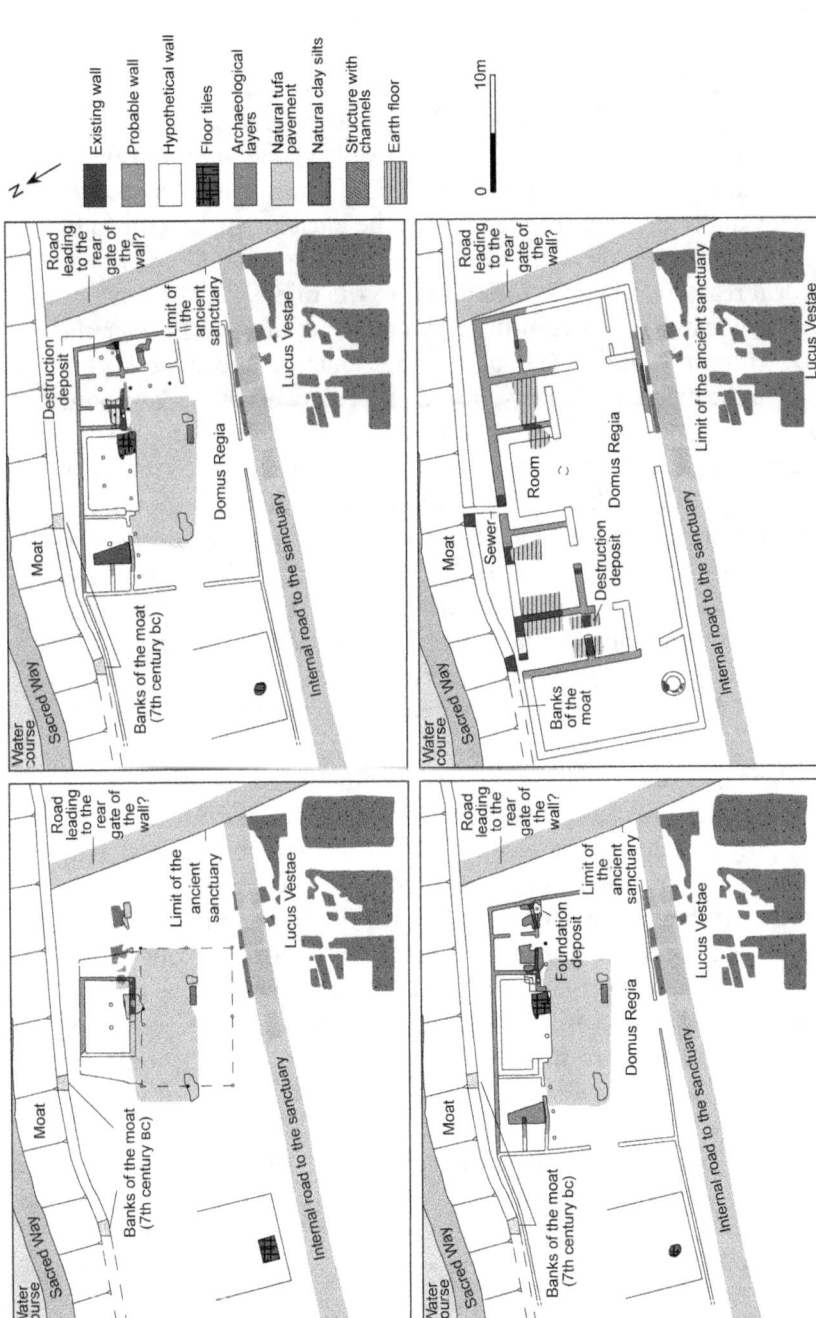

Figure 5.3 The Domus Regia, *c.*770–750 BC (top left), *c.*750–700 BC (top right), *c.*700–650 BC (bottom left), *c.*650–600 BC (bottom right) (after Filippi, 'Domus Regia', 101–21)

Together with the cemeteries, this reinforces a picture of separate settlements that later unify. Habitation structures are found, as we might expect, on higher areas around the Forum. The lowest lying areas were probably unoccupied, as the zone below, 9 m above sea level, was inundated regularly by the Tiber in flood. But as the settlements on the hills grew larger, some habitation structures probably spread down from the higher ground to the lower slopes of the Palatine and Velian, encroaching towards the cemeteries. Cemeteries in the ancient world tend to be near rather than within the settlements to which they relate, for hygiene and cultural reasons. The presence down to the mid eighth century BC of the cemeteries in the Forum district, at the Sepulcretum under the temple of Antoninus and Faustina, and the cemetery under the Forum of Caesar, indicate that the low-lying district between the Capitoline hill and the Palatine was not yet regarded as habitable. More broadly we can say that the settlement as yet lacked a full urbanistic character. The ending of burial in these areas in period IIA, and the beginning of the cemeteries at a considerable remove on the Esquiline and Quirinal hills, marks an important stage of unification.[25] These two new cemeteries may directly replace the earlier two in the Forum of Caesar and the Sepulcretum, although there may also be some overlap in their use. Nevertheless, they signify the emergence of a large unified centre in periods IIB and IIIA. If this centre extended from the Forum to the cemeteries, it would have a hypothetical area of around 202 ha.[26]

How far this indicates that the settlement in the eighth century should be seen as a proto-urban centre, even a state, is controversial. Some support for this picture has come from the extensive excavations undertaken on the Palatine slopes, where Carandini and his team have identified a range of structures of political and ritual function and potentially civic status. This is a very important zone at the centre of Rome, encompassing the area of elite private housing and the temple of Vesta and its associated structures. The presence of so many layers of important historical structures right through the Roman period and beyond means that the difficult circumstances of the excavations have only been able to provide a severely limited picture of the oldest levels. The interpretations of the early structures represented by the very fragmentary remains, backed up by optimistic reconstruction drawings, have proved controversial. This has made reaching a global picture of what is going on very difficult,

---

25. Note also the Viminal: Fulminante, *Urbanisation*, 80.
26. Alessandri, *Latium Vetus*, 387–90; Fulminante, *Urbanisation*, 79.

and caution remains necessary at what in effect is a very preliminary stage of our understanding of this period.

The most striking discovery is a wall 12.1 m long on the lower northern slopes of the Palatine, which went through three phases from the mid eighth to the mid sixth century BC (Fig. 5.4).[27] The earliest wall is dated to c.730–720 BC, on the basis of a votive deposit or a burial under the threshold of the wall.[28] It seems to have been constructed with wooden posts within a mud wall, considerably thicker than the walls of contemporary habitation structures. There was a gap in the wall, interpreted as a gate, the Porta Mugonia, and an associated wooden structure, interpreted as a guard post or sacred building. The wall was then destroyed and reconstructed in the early seventh century on wider scale around the Palatine. Burials of a child and four adults were found in association with this phase of the wall, dating to the early seventh century BC, which have

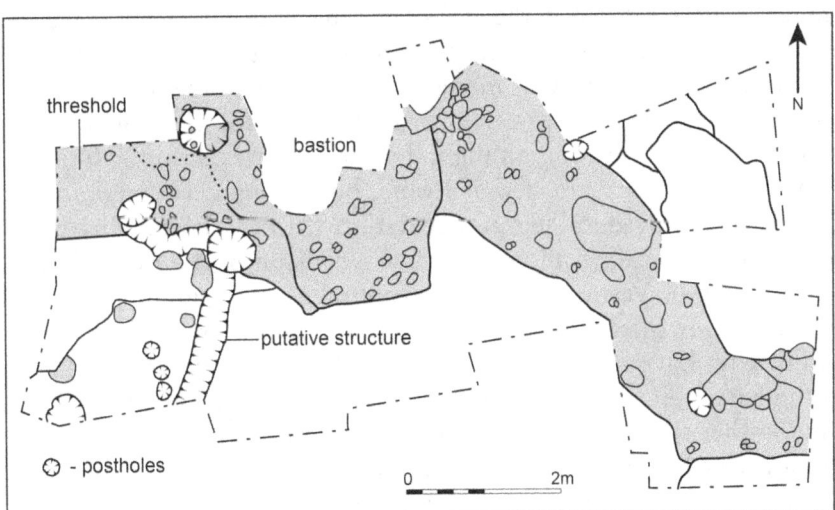

Figure 5.4 Sector 9 of the first phase of the Palatine wall, c.730–720 BC, showing the threshold identified as the Porta Mugonia and an associated wooden structure (after Carandini and Carafa, *Palatium e Sacra Via*, fig. 106)

27. Carandini, 'Mura'; Carandini and Carafa (eds), *Palatium*, 139–214; Carandini, *Nascita*, 491–520. For useful summaries, see Fulminante, *Urbanisation*, 82–7; Hall, *Artifact*, 132–3.
28. Carandini and Carafa (eds), *Palatium*, 194; Ampolo, 'Problema delle origini', 253–4 interprets this as a burial.

been interpreted as foundation rites. The wall was reconstructed in ashlar masonry around 560 BC, after which it was removed to make way for elite housing around 530 BC. A further stretch has also been identified from the Cures Veteres near the Colosseum, on the north-east slopes of the Palatine.[29] The excavators interpreted the first phase of this wall in the light of the Roman literary tradition that Romulus first fortified the Palatine. In the dating that had become canonical by the late first century BC, Romulus reigned from 753–716 BC. This tradition thus would not signify the actual beginning of the settlement, as this had existed on the Capitoline hill and in nearby areas since the Late Bronze Age. Instead, the foundation story preserved a memory of the political organisation of the community into a city state by a guiding figure.

Other developments indicate the importance of the eighth century BC. A very significant discovery is the large structure, referred to above, that has been called the Domus Regia (Fig. 5.3). This was a multi-roomed building built around a courtyard. It went through a number of phases down to the late sixth century BC. Its precise structure is uncertain, given the extent of the reconstruction on the plans of the remains (consisting of many 'likely' and 'hypothetical' walls). The eighth century also sees an early cult site on the Capitoline hill, dating to 750–725 BC, containing miniaturised vases. From 750–700 BC the first roads are attested at Rome, built using clay conglomerate. One has been identified in association with the Porta Mugonia and wall complex, and another with the division of the Regia from the sanctuary of Vesta.[30] This is interpreted as the beginning of the urban structure of early Rome, marking out public space. Carandini and his team have therefore made a case that the second half of the eighth century BC is the key period for the formation of the city at Rome, rather than the second half of the seventh century BC as has commonly been maintained. This period sees the creation of the first public hearth on the site of the temple of Vesta, fortifications and a shared meeting place. The second half of the seventh century BC is not then the birth of the city, but a new era of monumentalism.

This combined archaeological and literary reconstruction, however, remains controversial on a number of points. The presence of burials in association with the first two phases of the wall contradicts the idea of a clear urban space being marked out by the walls.

---

29. Carandini, *Nascita*, 662; Zeggio, in Carandini and Cappelli (eds), *Roma*, 301–2.
30. Gjerstad, *Early Rome*, III 322–58; Carafa, *Officine*, 10–12.

Ampolo has argued that the interpretation of the burials as human sacrifices is far less likely than that these are typical burials in a zone with no clear sense of an urban area until the later seventh century.[31] Furthermore, the idea that the central public hearth of the city was established outside the city boundaries, as marked by the supposed wall of Romulus, is problematic. There are also difficulties with interpreting the wall as a fortification. It has a highly unusual construction technique, with wooden posts inside the earth construction, where they are likely to decay. The wall is thicker than that of a normal habitation structure, but its defensive character is debatable, given that it was at the foot of the hill, and its foundation was only a metre across. In fact some regard it as more likely to be a symbolic wall, connected with the foundation of the city in a deliberate way.[32] Many scholars have also drawn attention to the hypothetical nature of the reconstruction plans and superstructures of the identified buildings.[33] Lastly, it may be problematic to seek a close equivalence between the archaeological and the literary evidence, given the highly artificial nature of the tradition on the foundation of Rome and the essentially arbitrary date assigned to the Romulean foundation.

All these issues remain to be resolved and considerable uncertainty reigns concerning the proposed interpretations, particularly in terms of city foundation. But this should not detract from the importance of the archaeological remains discovered. The Palatine wall and the large rectilinear building called the Domus Regia seem to be important public structures that required planning and a substantial workforce, even if they are not clear confirmation of the urban character of the settlement in the eighth century BC, or proof that the literary tradition accurately remembered an individual founder of Rome called Romulus at that date.

The beginnings of the Forum

Our best archaeological evidence for the increasing political organisation of the city comes from the paving of the Forum, the huge rectangular space between the hills that formed the civic and commercial centre of the city. Particularly significant is the Comitium, the assembly place of the later city, and hence a highly symbolic

---

31. Ampolo, 'Problema delle origini', 256.
32. Fontaine, 'Des "remparts de Romulus"'; Fulminante, *Urbanisation*, 89.
33. E.g. Wiseman, 'House of Tarquin'; Moormann, 'Carandini's royal houses'.

political space. It is striking that this assembly place, later associated with the democratic element in the Republic, was first laid out during a period of monarchic rule. This suggests that the assembly was a vital component of the community from its earliest formation, which contradicts our modern western tradition of absolutist monarchies where the palace and court were the centre of politics, and assemblies of the people largely irrelevant. But in the city states of the Homeric Mediterranean, kings such as Agamemnon in the *Iliad* and Alcinous in the *Odyssey* seem to have interacted with assemblies. They were not necessarily needed for voting to elect the king or his officials, but provided an arena for the king to test opinion, gain counsel and receive acclamations, as Agamemnon does in the four great assemblies held before Troy in the *Iliad*.

Our understanding of the origins of the Forum has been significantly advanced in recent decades, as alongside the key stratigraphic data obtained from excavations by Boni in 1902 and Gjerstad in the 1950s, we now have the scientific evidence of coring samples taken in the 1980s.[34] These coring activities identified the hydrography of the Forum as a crucial issue. The Forum is in origin a low-lying district between the Capitoline, Palatine and other hills, where rainfall and natural springs drained down to the Tiber through the valley known as the Velabrum. The earlier excavations showed that the level of the Forum had risen tens of metres from the earliest levels to the paving level of the imperial period, and that a series of twenty-eight fills and pavements were laid down during the monarchic and Republican period (Fig. 5.5).

The key contribution of the coring was to show that the original level of the Forum was only a few metres above the bed of the Tiber. The lowest-lying areas of the valley were only 6 m above sea level, and had to be raised by some 3 m or so to prevent them being inundated by the river, which in spring and winter regularly rose to around 9 m above sea level. This meant that much of the future Forum district was too damp for permanent habitation structures. Ammerman therefore argued that the remains of wattle and daub in thick layers beneath the first Forum paving (gravel pavement 2 in Fig. 5.5) were not, as Gjerstad had assumed, the remnants of habitation structures created before the Forum's first paving. Instead, the layers were formed from material brought in as fill from an inhabited area elsewhere, most likely on the surrounding hilltops. The layers in which

---

34. Ammerman, 'Comitium'.

Urbanism and city foundation 153

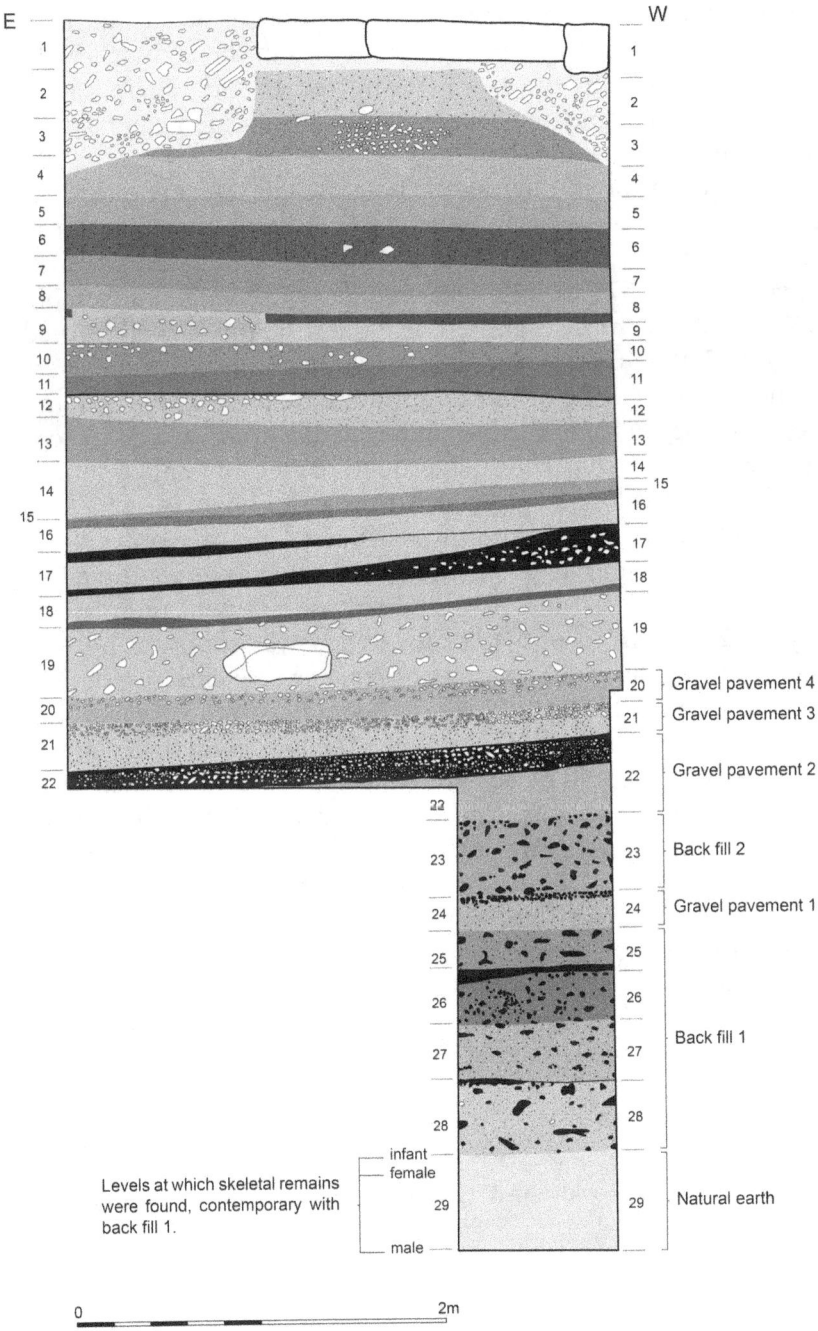

Figure 5.5 The stratigraphy of the Roman Forum (after Filippi, 'Velabro', fig. 5)

they occur must have been laid down in order to artificially raise the level of the Forum, to protect the area from the regular floods. With at least 23,000 m³ of earth being moved, this represents a huge amount of labour, and must have required considerable political organisation and planning.[35]

The identification and dating of the gravel pavements on top of these fills is not without dispute. Broadly speaking, there have been three stages of interpretation. In the 1950s Gjerstad dated the earliest pavement to c.575 BC; this was revised by Colonna and Ampolo to c.625–600 BC; most recently, Carafa and Filippi have proposed a dating to 700–650 BC.[36] Carafa has argued that two beaten layers and a hearth on the site of the Comitium date to 750–700 BC, and that cult activity of same period can be dated by pottery and a loom weight. He argues that the first proper paving of the Comitium should be identified with the uppermost part of layer 24, which he dates to 700–650 BC, and that it was followed by three others (layers 22, 21 and 20 in Fig. 5.5).[37] Other scholars have continued to hold to the traditional view that the first true paving is represented by layer 22, dating to 650–600 BC, which was followed by two further layers in the monarchic period.[38] There are various possible reasons for the landfill operations in the mid seventh century. This was the period when the Velabrum clay beds were first exploited, and so the landfill could be connected to the removal of thick sediments lying above them. It is also a period when trade increased, and so there was a need to provide a trading space for merchants coming up the Tiber.[39] Torelli has noted that the large rectangular space that resulted from these works is paralleled by similar spaces in Greek cities, which tended to have a large central agora for commerce.[40] Assuming then that the landfill operation was a deliberate procedure, and not an accidental by-product of other activity such

---

35. Figure from Hopkins, *Genesis*, 34; other estimates range from 3,500 m³ (Filippi, 'Velabro', 112, under the first pavement) to 10,000 m³ (Ammerman, 'On the origins', 642). Cf. Dion. Hal. 2.50.2, who says that Romulus and his co-king Titus Tatius created the Forum by cutting down a wood and using the material from it to fill in the lake in the hollow below the Capitoline.
36. Filippi, 'Velabro', 105–13.
37. Carafa, 'Volcanal'.
38. Ammerman et al., 'Clay beds', 27, for a defence of the traditional view; cf. Hopkins, *Genesis*, 189 nn. 40–1.
39. Ammerman et al., 'Clay beds', 27; Hopkins, *Genesis*, 34 for trade.
40. Torelli, 'Topography', 84.

as the exploitation of the clay beds, we can envisage a central political authority, surely the king, organising the labour for this vast architectural project.

The wider significance of these measures, whatever their exact date, should be properly appreciated. In the 1950s and 1960s two major models were proposed to explain the importance of these events, which we can call the synoecism and the city development models. Gjerstad argued that the archaeological record showed a number of small villages united by the paving of the Forum, a unilateral political act. Müller-Karpe by contrast saw slow development as the key, with the Palatine nucleus expanding to take in other hills.[41] But these arguments about state formation are rather artificial, and cities generally take shape through a number of different processes, both gradual and immediate. In fact, the physical 'synoecism' of the community is less important than the political implications of this act, as the essence of a Greco-Roman city state is its people and their interactions, not the buildings they used (Sparta was famously lacking in a developed urban centre well into its classical history). The important thing to note is that the process begins by the end of the eighth century BC, and is clearly manifested by the late seventh century BC. Arguments identifying a particularly critical formation point overemphasise political intervention. We should still retain some element of the city foundation model, although recognising that Rome must have already reached a certain level of political sophistication around 650 BC (to be able to organise preparatory work). The late eighth and first half of the seventh century BC thus emerges as the critical background to the major developments of the mid seventh century, even without (yet) accepting the new higher dating. This is the phase in which we should look for the foundation of Rome in political and perhaps physical terms. Following on from this preparatory work comes the architectural transformation of the city with new public spaces and buildings, to which we now turn.

The changing cityscape of Rome: the great building projects of 650–480 BC

The city of Rome was undoubtedly transformed by building work from the late seventh century BC. Our archaeological evidence

---

41. Müller-Karpe, *Zur Stadtwerdung*; cf. Grandazzi, *Foundation*, 145.

improves in quality and quantity from this point on, as buildings began to be created using new monumental techniques involving stone foundations, terracotta tile roofs, and heavy wooden superstructures to support the weight of the roof. These techniques leave much more visible archaeological remains, particularly foundations, tiles and architectural terracotta decorations.

Though the less mythical nature of the literary evidence makes cross correlations more possible, the evidence does not remain without problems. Some structures are attested by both types of evidence, although close correlations are rare (the example of the Capitoline temple is perhaps the best, and is examined below). Most structures are attested either by archaeological or by literary evidence alone. This poses considerable problems of identification, interpretation and reliability, but the global picture of a huge and highly developed city cannot be disputed.

The major archaeological phases from the seventh to the sixth century BC are summarised in Table 5.1. The monumentalisation process affected most areas of the centre of Rome. Much of the evidence comes from the Forum, where the reclamation project enhanced the viability of the area as a communal space. The earliest structures on the site of the Comitium (Fig. 5.6) are attested by tiles and architectural terracottas, including a Gorgon antefix, and revetment plaques

Table 5.1 Archaeological phases, late seventh to sixth century BC[a]

Approximate date BC	Archaeological evidence
700–650?	Gravel paving of the Forum over massive infill
650–625	Renewed paving of the Forum after another infill operation
625–600	Third paving renewal and extension to cover Comitium area; first Regia built
600–575	Curia Hostilia (Senate house) built next to Comitium Third phase of Regia (with architectural terracottas); first temple of Forum Boarium replaces open-air cult site
570–550	Comitium reconstructed with Volcanal cult site on southern side; temple of Vesta built
530	Fourth phase of Regia; Forum Boarium temple rebuilt with architectural terracottas
500	Regia rebuilt on its definitive Republican plan; Forum Boarium temple destroyed and rebuilt with twin temples in early fifth century; fourth paving of Comitium

[a] Following Smith, 'Beginnings of urbanization', and Carafa, 'Volcanal', 135–49.

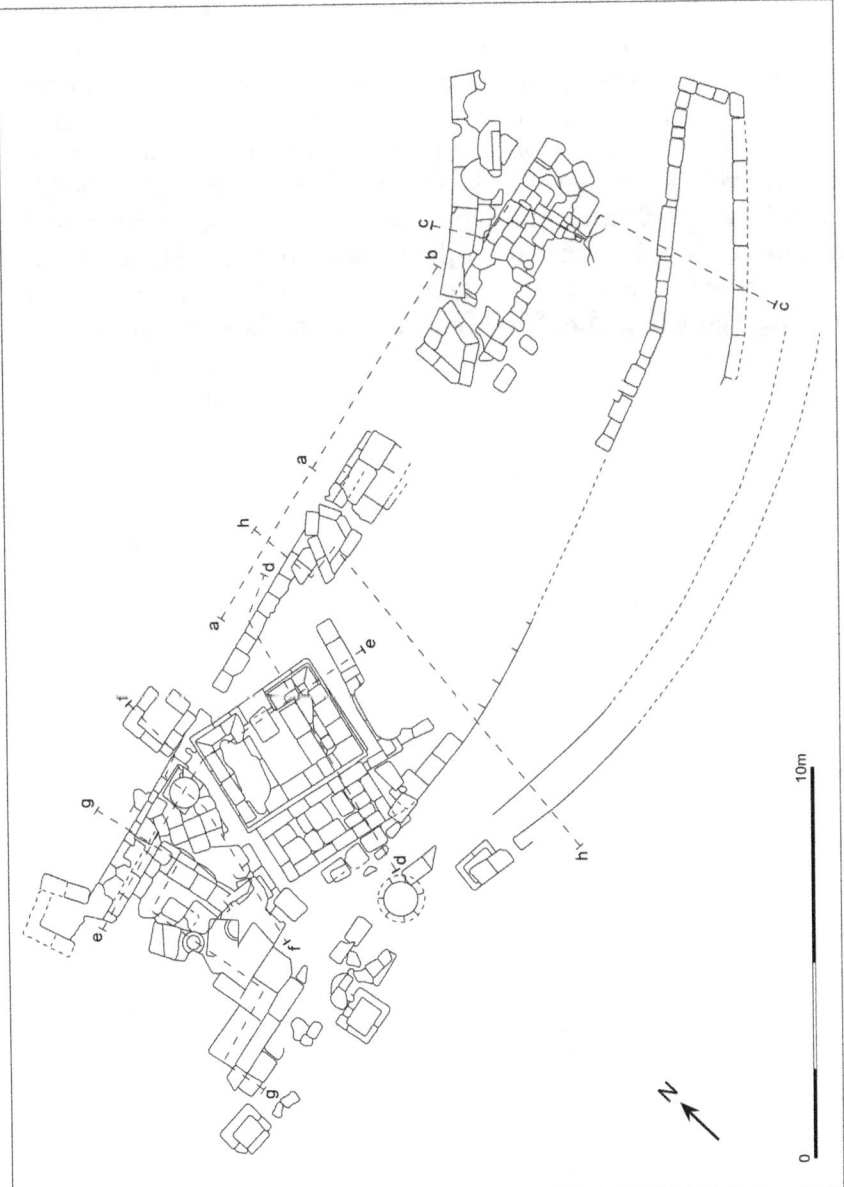

Figure 5.6 Comitium, general plan of the excavated remains (after Cifani, *Architettura*, fig. 94)

with a feline, and with a horse and rider. These date to c.590–580,[42] and may relate to the first Senate house, the Curia Hostilia, named after its legendary founder king Tullus Hostilius.

At the south-eastern end of the Forum, the first phase of the Regia was erected around 620 BC (Fig. 5.7). It was a multi-roomed structure with stone foundations, and had a tiled roof decorated with horn acroteria. A second phase has been identified in the early sixth century, and a third phase of construction dates to 590–580 BC, with a courtyard-type arrangement similar to monumental palace buildings in Etruria at Murlo and Acquarossa.[43] It had a set of terracotta decorations similar to that from the Comitium, with disc acroteria, Gorgon antefixes and plaques decorated with birds, felines and a minotaur figure (Figs 5.8, 5.9). These terracottas belong to a series of very similar examples from elsewhere in Rome on the Capitoline, as well as from Latium (Gabii) and Campania (Cumae and Pithecusae).

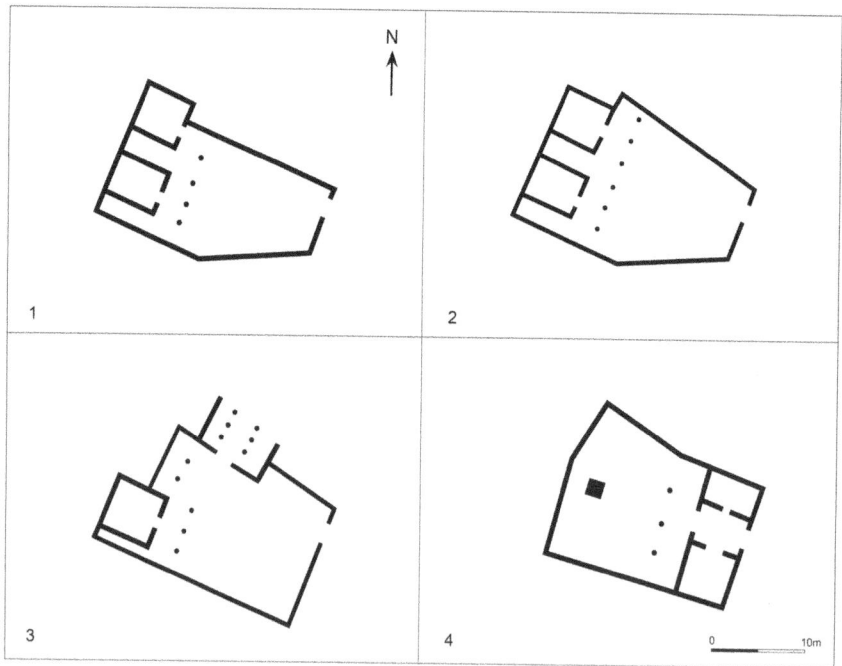

Figure 5.7 The four phases of the monarchic Regia according to F. Brown (after GRT, 59)

42. Winter, *Symbols*, 144; Hopkins, *Genesis*, 49.
43. Cifani, *Architettura*, 126–30; Hopkins, *Genesis*, 41–6, 84–7.

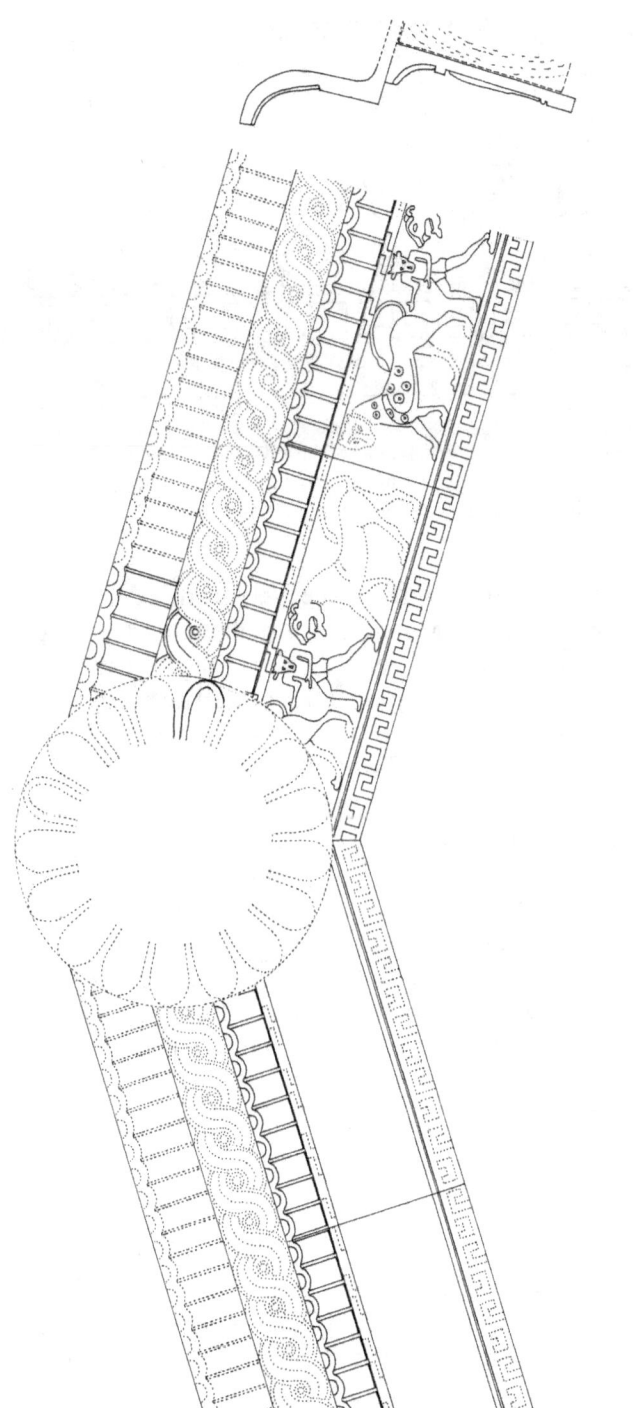

Figure 5.8 Terracotta roof of the third phase of the Regia with disc acroteria (drawing: R. Sponer Za, for Winter, *Symbols*, 144–7, Roof 3–2)

Figure 5.9 Architectural terracotta plaque from the third phase of the Regia with felines and minotaur (drawing: R. Sponer Za, for Winter, *Symbols*, Ill. 3.5.1)

The examples from Rome use clay from the Velabrum beds. They indicate that the artistic initiative probably comes from craftworkers at Rome, and that Rome was in this period an exporter of expertise (and perhaps artisans) in the working of terracotta. The close links with Campania are echoed many times in Roman history, perhaps most notably with the withdrawal of Tarquinius Superbus to Cumae in his exile. Rome was thus in this period well connected with other major polities along the Tyrrhenian coast.

Remains of more permanent and costly dwellings begin to appear in the seventh century BC at other sites in Rome and elsewhere in central Italy. A seventh-century roof terracotta discovered by Boni was similar to those of Acquarossa; and at the Sepulcretum a substantial seventh-century building was excavated by Boni in the early twentieth century.[44] It was some 10 m across, had walls built with square tufa blocks and covered in plaster, and will have required a heavy timber structure to carry the weight of its roof tiles.

The Forum Boarium

Apart from the Forum, there were significant developments in the early sixth century BC in the Forum Boarium, the zone next to the Tiber and between the Capitoline and Aventine. It is an extremely important site in the development of the city, but is very difficult to excavate

44. Cifani, *Architettura*, 130–5; Hopkins, *Genesis*, 40–1, 90.

due to the very deep stratigraphic sequence, and the high water table. This was the landing place of the city, on a bend in the river. It was a cosmopolitan zone, and seems to have been visited by foreign traders from the eighth century BC, judging by the presence of Greek geometric pottery, mostly of Euboean production with some Tyrrhenian imitations.[45] The Forum Boarium is the site of a very ancient cult of Hercules at the Ara Maxima. Although no archaeological remains of the altar are known from the archaic period, the cult's Phoenician characteristics and its mythical associations with the Arcadian hero Evander suggest an early establishment. Filippi has recently described the Hercules cult as having an 'emporic character'.[46]

Sacrificial remains attesting to the religious use of the site date from the mid to late seventh century BC, and tiles indicate that there was probably a building here from the late seventh or early sixth century BC. Then, around 580 BC, the first temple was erected (Fig. 5.10). This

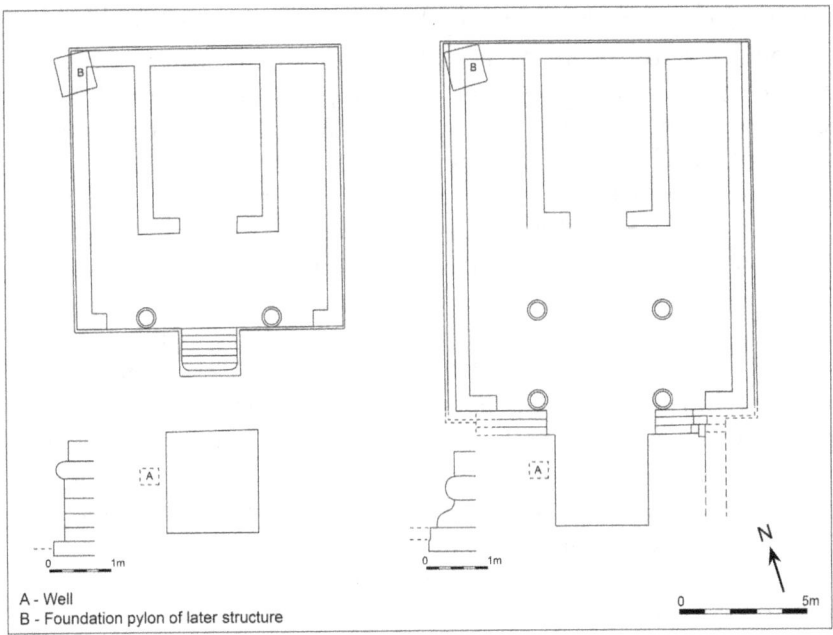

Figure 5.10 The two phases of the temple at Sant'Omobono (after Cifani, *Architettura*, 168, fig. 164)

45. La Rocca, 'Ceramica'.
46. Filippi, 'Velabro'. On the Ara Maxima, see Van Berchem, 'Hercule–Melqart à l'Ara Maxima'; Torelli, '*Ara Maxima Herculis*'.

building was the earliest temple not just in Rome but in central Italy as a whole. The first phase was raised above flood levels by a podium 1.7 m high. It probably had a square plan with a single *cella*, steps leading up to a frontal entrance with two columns, and an altar at the front. The roof had terracotta decoration, with a pediment, unusually, closed by terracotta plaques. The pedimental sculpture has been reconstructed to show two felines facing a central Gorgon. This replicates similar sculptural groups at Corcyra, also of the early sixth century BC but carved in limestone, and at the temple of Athena from Syracuse, in terracotta.[47] This displays Rome's international contacts at a prominent site for foreign visitors, and has been connected by some scholars with a political programme by the Bacchiads of Corinth, a dynasty linked to the overthrow of the Cypselids in their home city in 583 BC. By tradition, the Tarquin kings of Rome traced their roots back to the Bacchiads via the Corinthian immigrant Demaratus, and Bacchiads were also reputedly responsible for the foundation of Syracuse.[48] Judging by the parallels, the relief from the temple at Rome must refer to the Greek myth of Medusa and her offspring Pegasus, which clearly features in the surviving parts of the Syracusan version of this composition. It therefore provides one of the earliest examples of the assimilation of Greek mythology at Rome. Whilst it might refer to Roman links with Corinth (a city which used Pegasus as a motif on its coins and was considered the birthplace of Bellerophon, who rode Pegasus to destroy the monstrous Chimera), its full symbolism in archaic Rome is obscure.[49]

We also have the terracotta decoration of a second phase of this temple, now on a slightly larger footprint, and with a more sophisticated double moulding, dated to around 530 BC. This consists of plaques of the so-called Rome-Veii-Velitrae series, featuring 'antefixes with female heads between lion-head spouts, and reliefs depicting departing warriors in semi-divine processions with female charioteers, armed horsemen, and chariot races', as well as banquet scenes and images of seated deities.[50] Plaques belonging to this series have also been found in the Forum, on the Palatine, Esquiline and Capitoline, as well as at Veii in Etruria and at Velitrae in Latium, and were probably made from moulds created in Rome.

---

47. Hopkins, 'Creation', 39 adds Athens and Aegina.
48. Mertens-Horn, 'Corinto'; Potts, *Religious Architecture*, 59.
49. Zevi, 'Demaratus', 77, mentions the Corfu pediment in the context of identifying Poseidon Hippius as the Corinthian patron of the Ludi Romani, but does not make the connection with the Forum Boarium temple.
50. Lulof, 'Reconstructing', 115.

The most striking feature of the terracotta roof decoration is an acroterial statue group of Hercules and Minerva, about 1.4 m high (Fig. 5.11). The statue group most probably represents the apotheosis of Hercules, led into Olympus by Minerva. Both statues are high-quality products with distinctive Greek characteristics, recalling examples from Attica, Ionia and Cyprus.[51] Lulof argues that they must have been created by Eastern Greek artisans (or their offspring) resident in Rome. This pair was attached to a decorative base and was probably flanked by large volutes, with sphinxes decorating the corners of the roof (Fig. 5.12). The presence of further fragments of another base and statue group, along with four volutes, suggests that there was originally a pair of temples here in the archaic period, as the literary tradition attests.[52]

Linking this archaeological evidence to the literary sources is problematic. Servius Tullius is said to have founded temples of Mater Matuta and Fortuna in the Forum Boarium.[53] The first archaic temple is often taken to be that of Mater Matuta, founded by Servius, and the second a reconstruction by Tarquinius Superbus. Yet as we have seen, the archaeological evidence of the temple decoration can be linked with the Bacchiad background of Servius' predecessor, king Tarquinius Priscus. For the second temple, much previous scholarship has been concerned with demonstrating the specific relevance of the Hercules–Minerva group to the 'tyrannical' regime of Tarquinius Superbus at Rome.[54] But there are considerable issues here. The dates of both temple phases may be too early for the traditional dates of each king (Servius from 578–534 BC, and Tarquinius Superbus 534–509 BC; these are in any case highly artificial dates). In addition, it is now apparent that large numbers of sites both at Rome and elsewhere employed this same roof pattern, including places such as Veii which were outside Roman political control.[55] In fact, temples at Caere, Veii and Satricum (Fig. 5.13) had already featured this iconography of Hercules and Minerva for earlier roofs (dated 540–530 BC).[56] This complicates any symbolic messages we

---

51. Hopkins, *Genesis*, 72–8.
52. Lulof, 'Reconstructing', 114–15; Livy, 24.14.17; 25.7.6; 33.27.4.
53. Dion. Hal. 4.27.7 (Fortuna); Livy, 5.19 (Mater Matuta); Ovid, *Fast.* 6.480 (both founded by Servius).
54. Discussed in Chapter 4.
55. Around ten are known in Rome and ten from outside the city.
56. Lulof, 'Reconstructing', 118.

Figure 5.11 Temple acroterion with Heracles and Athena, second phase of the temple at Sant'Omobono (drawing: R. Sponer Za, for Winter, *Symbols*, Ill. 5.16.2)

Urbanism and city foundation

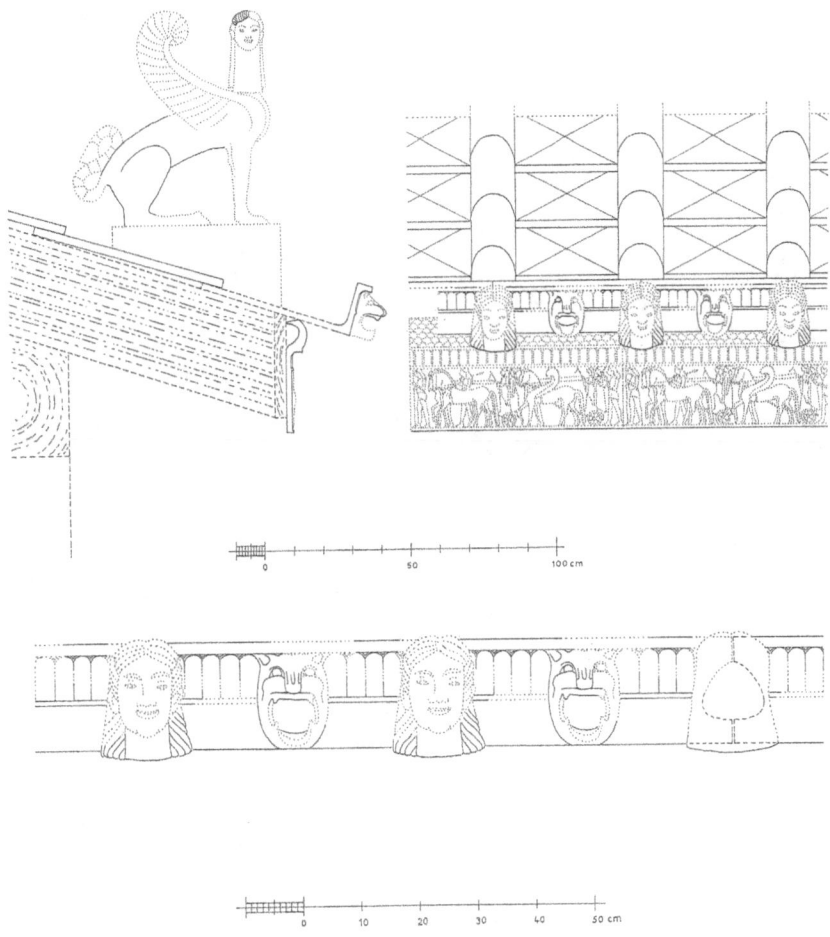

Figure 5.12 Architectural terracotta decoration of the second phase of the temple at Sant'Omobono (drawing: R. Sponer Za, for Winter, *Symbols*, 316–18, Roof 5-4, Plan 12.2)

might like to draw from the iconography, which is unlikely to refer solely to Rome. Nevertheless, it is another clear example of the thorough assimilation of Greek myth in archaic Rome and surrounding areas.

The archaic temple site was cleared at the end of the sixth century BC when it was destroyed by fire. Two new temples were set up on a huge new platform, created by raising the level by some 6 m. The fill incorporated rich materials from the previous occupation of the site, including Bronze Age and Greek geometric pottery. None of the sherds is later

Figure 5.13 Satricum, roof of sacellum or temple of Mater Matuta (drawing: R. Sponer Za, for Winter, *Symbols*, 398–400, Roof 6-1, Plan 15)

than the fifth century BC, and a revetment plaque was found in association with the twin temples that dates to around 480 BC. This indicates that the rebuilding took place in the early fifth century BC. The temples dominated the approach to the Forum Boarium and formed one of the largest temple complexes in central Italy at that time.[57]

57. Hopkins, 'Creation', 42.

The Capitolium

Yet while the Forum Boarium temple helps reveal the precocious nature of Rome's international links, it was not the most impressive building project in the archaic period. That was the Capitolium, the temple of Jupiter Optimus Maximus, Juno and Minerva, on the Capitoline hill. This temple was a major monument throughout Roman history, existing on the same site with the same dimensions from the late sixth century BC to the end of antiquity, with three reconstructions after fires in 83 BC, AD 69 and AD 80. The temple is described in some detail by Dionysius of Halicarnassus (4.61.3–4), and other authors discuss its construction and features.

The literary sources portray it as an enormous project, requiring massive labour resources. According to Dionysius and Livy it was vowed during the course of a war against the Sabines by Tarquinius Priscus, who began the work by levelling the Capitoline area (Livy, 1.38.7; Dion. Hal. 3.69.1). It was brought to near completion by Tarquinius Superbus (Livy, 1.55.2; Dion. Hal. 4.59.1) and then dedicated in the first years of the Republic (Livy, 2.8.6; 7.3.8; Dion. Hal. 5.35.3).[58] Dionysius provides quite precise dimensions, describing it as almost square, with three rows of columns to the front, and one row to the sides, and having three *cellae*, housing Jupiter in the middle, Minerva to the right and Juno to the left (Dion. Hal. 4.61.3–4). The central roof ridge was decorated with a terracotta statue of a quadriga (four-horse chariot) driven by Jupiter. According to Varro, Tarquinius Priscus commissioned this group, the cult statue of Jupiter and a statue of Hercules from the renowned coroplast Vulca of Veii (Pliny, *HN* 35.157, Plut. *Pub.* 13). The quadriga was replaced, perhaps in bronze, by the Ogulnii in 296 BC. There was also a statue of Summanus (a god of nocturnal lightning related to Jupiter), which was struck by lightning in 278 BC during the Pyrrhic Wars (Cic. *Div.* 1.10.6, Livy, *Per.* 14.2).

Our knowledge of the temple remains has been transformed by excavations undertaken in the last few decades.[59] The temple foundation built from local cappellacio stone has been known since the sixteenth century. After excavation and re-study, it has now been incorporated, magnificently, into the Capitoline Museum (Fig. 5.14). It is noteworthy that while substantial segments of the foundations remain, hardly any trace of the superstructure had been recovered.

---

58. Cifani, *Architettura*, 80 for full references to the sources.
59. Mura Sommella et al., 'Primi risultati'; Mura Sommella, 'Tempio di Giove'.

Figure 5.14 The foundations of the Capitoline temple visible in the Capitoline Museum (photo: G. Bradley)

However, that changed in 2014 with the excavation in the Giardini della Rupe Tarpea of a large deposit of around 1000 fragments of tiles and architectural terracottas that may pertain to the temple site.[60] They date to the late sixth, early fourth and third centuries BC. Although study of these terracottas is ongoing, we are now able to date the first phase of the building both archaeologically and stylistically to the late sixth century BC, which accords with its attribution in the literary tradition to Tarquinius Superbus.[61]

The excavation of the platform for the temple has revealed its enormous extent, with a width of 54 m and a length of 62 or 74 m (Fig. 5.15). It is built out of very thick intersecting ashlar masonry walls, measured in

---

60. Parisi Presicce and Danti (eds), *Campidoglio*.
61. Mura Sommella, 'Grande Roma', 21: bucchero in the foundation trench provided a *terminus ante quem* of the second half of the sixth century BC. Some material is late sixth or early fifth century BC (Mura Sommella et al., 'Primi risultati', 342–5; Cifani, *Architettura*, 99), which suggests that construction should not be pushed into the mid sixth century (a point I owe to E. Colantoni's forthcoming *Archaeology of Early Roman Religion*).

units of the Attic foot (29.6 cm), with voids in areas not supporting the superstructure of the temple. Mura Sommella's analysis of the podium interior shows that the superstructure rested on stone walls and must have covered the whole front of the podium; anything smaller would involve resting columns and the walls of the *cellae* on the earth infill.

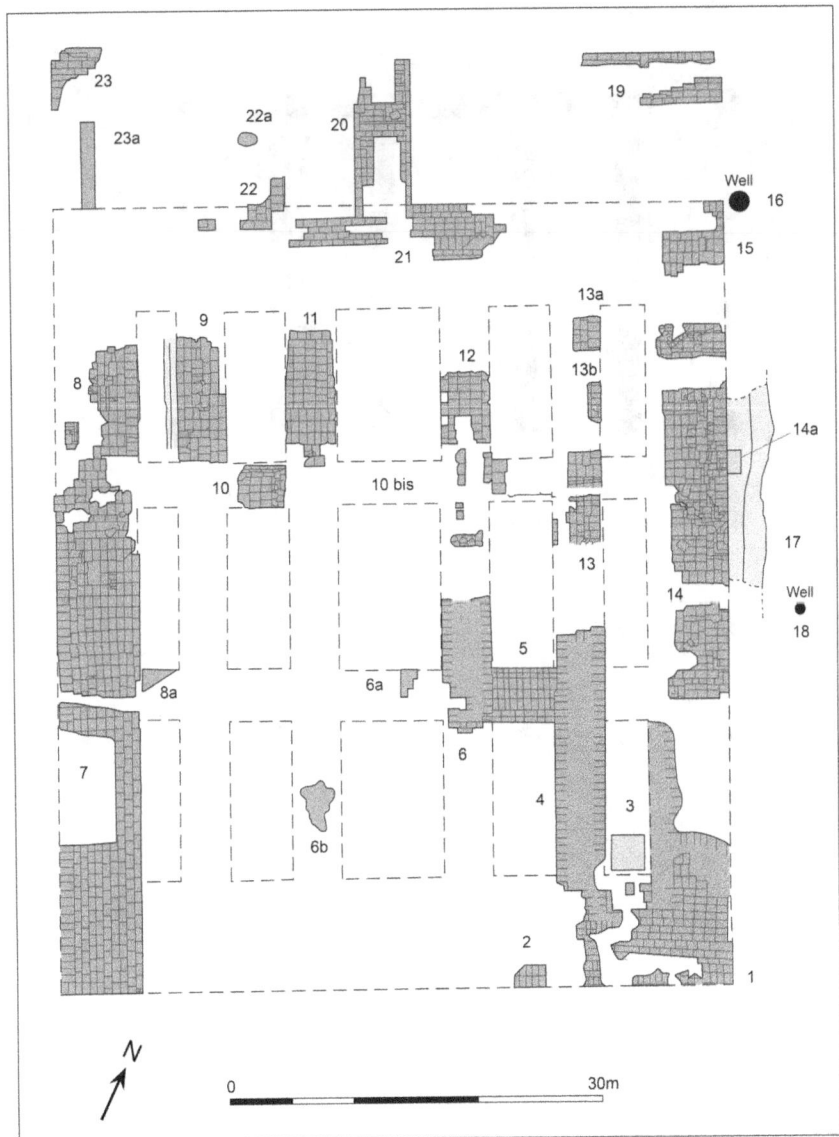

Figure 5.15 The foundations of the Capitoline temple (after Cifani, *Architettura*, fig. 70)

We can therefore reconstruct the overall plan of the temple, which had *cella* walls and column rows resting on the walls of the substructure (Fig. 5.16).[62] The temple was a major feat of engineering, some 54 m wide, with a massive inter-columnar span. This had often been considered

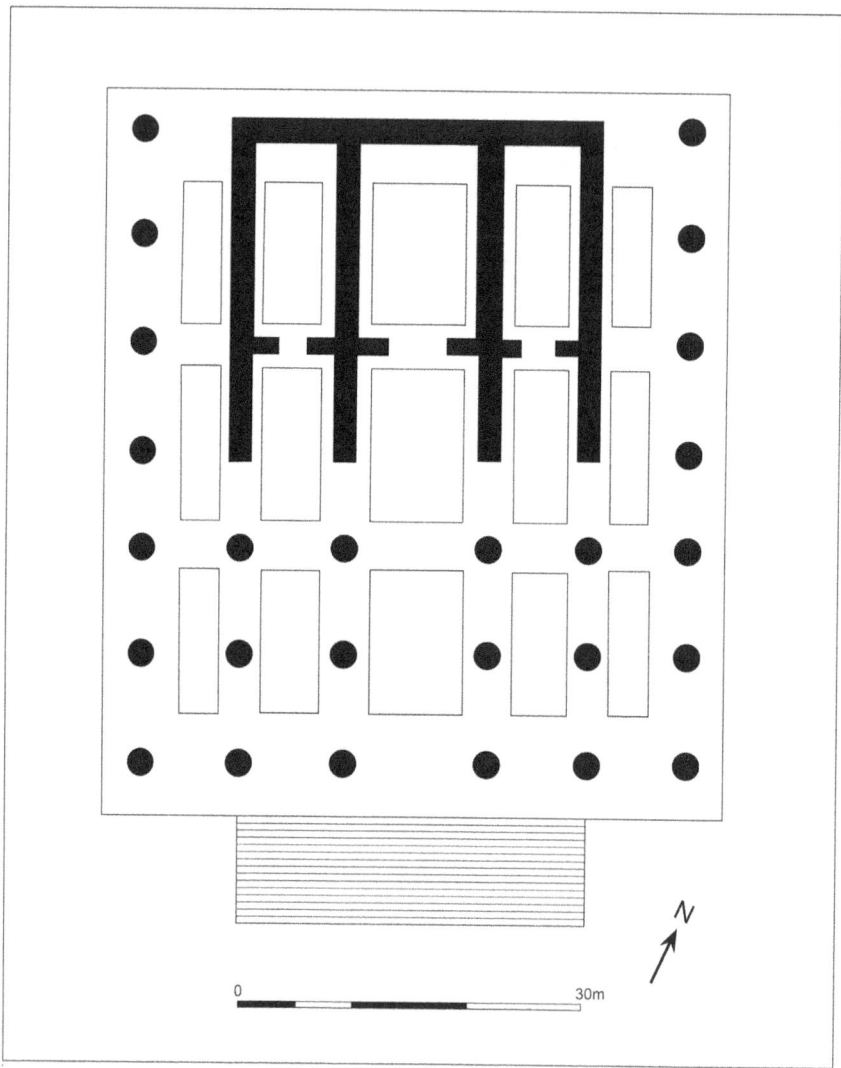

Figure 5.16 The Capitoline temple: a reconstruction of the plan (after Cifani, *Architettura*, fig. 85)

62. Potts, *Religious Architecture*, 123, expresses reservations about the relationship between substructure and superstructure.

impossible with the building technology of the time, but recent studies have argued that wooden truss construction, capable of spanning the 10.5 m gap between the middle two columns, was used in central Italy at the time.[63]

Less clear is how long the building was. Dionysius implies it was about 60 m (200 Roman feet), and almost square. Cifani has reconstructed the temple in this manner (see his 2008 plan, Figs 5.16, 5.17), with a length of 62 m. In contrast, Mura Sommella has argued that the podium is 74 m long, based on the archaeological materials on the north side, and reconstructs the temple as peripteral (as in the larger reconstruction in the comparison of plans, Fig. 5.17). The issue is whether or not the remains extending for 12 m beyond the perimeter of Cifani's plan form part of the superstructure. At present this problem is unresolved, and it is uncertain if these remains relate to the temple, in which case they pose some challenges in terms of the roofing structure. If the well along the eastern side of the temple collected water from the roof, as Mura Sommella envisaged, it is more likely that the rear roof terminated here rather than continuing for another 12 m.[64]

Even with the more restricted plan, it dwarfs all other temples in central Italy. More appropriate comparanda are the massive Ionian temples set up in Athens, Samos and Ephesus in the sixth century BC, and at Agrigentum and Selinus in Sicily from the late sixth century BC onwards. These have a similar scale, although they tend to be longer and less wide, a constraint that was perhaps imposed on the Capitolium by the topography of the hilltop. Various details point to a direct model in the Greek east. Like the Greek examples, the Capitoline employs a triple colonnade at the front of the temple, creating a visually striking 'forest of columns'.[65] The substructure of the Capitoline temple, with a transverse wall supporting the third row of columns, is replicated in the Heraion of Samos (Heraion IV).

A variety of terracotta decorative features have been found in the area of the podium, although it is difficult to be certain if they pertain to the temple. One element that may is a terracotta frieze decorated with an *anthemion* motif, whose exceptional dimensions would fit

---

63. Turfa and Steinmayer, 'Interpreting'; Hopkins, 'Colossal temple', 23.
64. For discussion, see Hopkins, *Genesis*, 108–9; Cifani, 'Small, medium or extra-long?'. Albertoni and Damiani, *Tempio di Giove*, 59, note that the depth of the well suggests it was for collecting water rather than gathering it from the roof (a point I owe to E. Colantoni's forthcoming publication, *The Archaeology of Early Roman Religion*).
65. Cifani, *Architettura*, 292; Hopkins, *Genesis*, 115.

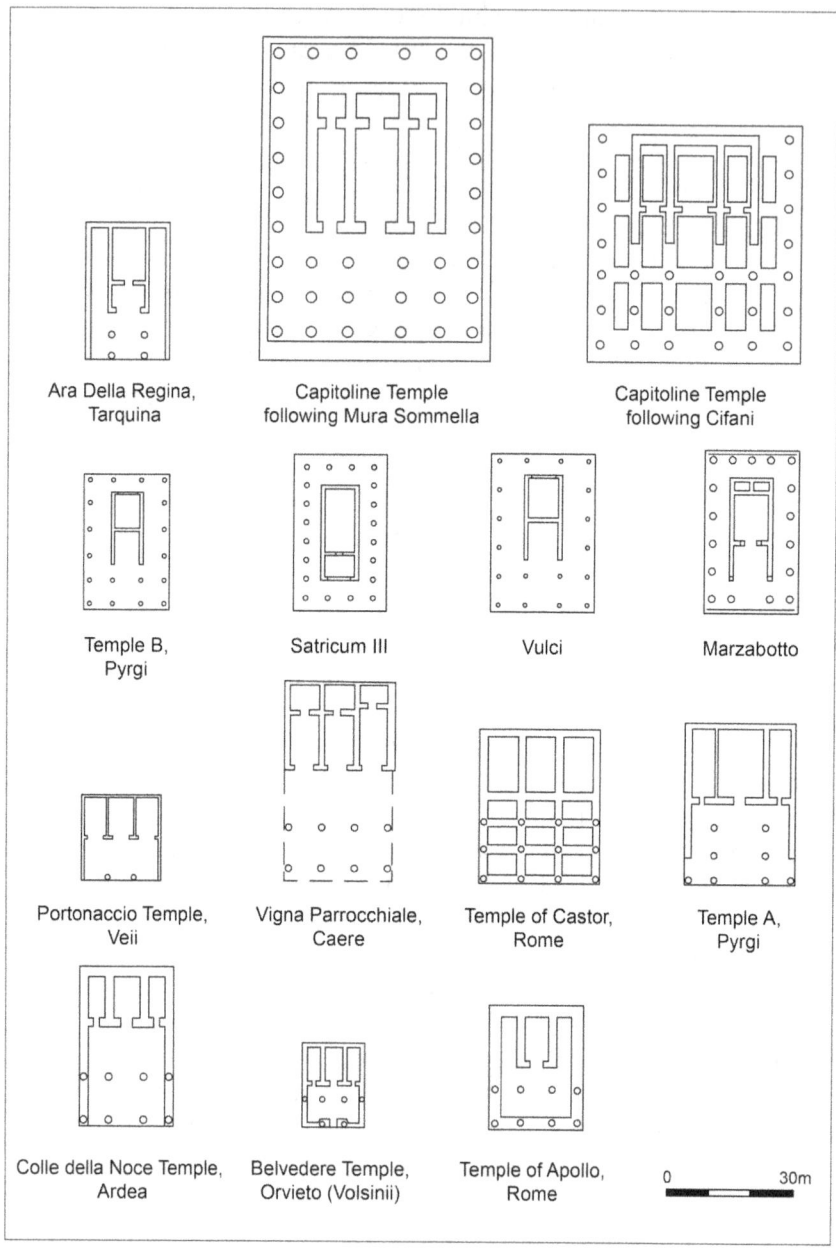

Figure 5.17 A comparison of the Capitoline temple with other temples in central Italy (after Mura Sommella, 'Tempio di Giove', fig. 26)

the scale of the reconstructed temple.⁶⁶ This was a motif that developed in Ionia, and had spread to central Italy by the mid sixth century, coming to dominate temple eaves decoration by the end of the century in both areas.⁶⁷ These details, along with the unprecedented scale and complexity of the construction project, have led scholars to propose, plausibly, that Ionian architects worked on the Capitoline.⁶⁸

Recent discoveries and studies have therefore begun to reveal the complexity of this extraordinary project, and the way that it metaphorically faces both outwards and inwards. The three-*cella* arrangement and terracotta decoration are typically central Italian, produced by Latial and Etruscan artisans, while the scale and constructional expertise belongs in the top tier of archaic Mediterranean architecture. The choice of cults for the temple also shows both local and international features. It may be competing with the great Latin cult of Jupiter Latiaris on the Alban Mount. It includes tutelary deities that oversaw nearby Etruscan cities, such as Uni (Juno) at Veii. It may also allude to the Greek cults of Zeus and Hera at Olympia, and of Olympian Zeus at Athens, introduced under the Pisistratids in the sixth century. Varro, by contrast, saw the triad as based on the cults of Samothrace.⁶⁹

The huge scale of the project expresses Rome's dominant position in central Italy and the protection of Jupiter for the city in very visible terms to all who passed through the city or who came up the Tiber. It is also unthinkable without the close links of Rome to the wider Mediterranean world, and particularly the Greek cities both in southern Italy and Sicily, and in the Aegean. The temple is linked to the person of the king, and would seem to express kingly pretensions of unimaginable grandeur; but it is also a product of the Roman community, and of 'peer polity interaction' on a Mediterranean stage.⁷⁰

---

66. Mura Sommella, 'Grande Roma', 22; Hopkins, *Genesis*, 102–3. Cifani, *Architettura*, 107 expresses caution about attribution to the temple.
67. Hopkins, *Genesis*, 116–18.
68. Cifani, 'Problemi', 391; Hopkins, *Genesis*, 114–19. Hopkins argues that the same team may have moved from Samos to work at Rome, but the uncertainty about the dates of the Samian construction, which remained unfinished, and the differences in construction (e.g. the much greater use of stone at Samos) and decoration (the extensive use of terracotta in Rome), on which see Whitley, *Archaeology*, 223–8, render such proposals speculative at the moment. Full study of the newly discovered Capitoline terracottas may help clarify the buildings' parallels.
69. Greek parallels: Purcell, 'Becoming historical', 30–2. Varro, *Ant. Div.* fr. 205 (quoted in Serv. *Aen.* 2.296, Macrob. *Sat.* 3.4.7) is discussed by Van Nuffelen, 'Varro's Divine Antiquities'.
70. Cifani, *Architettura*, 294 n. 946.

Walls

Another fundamental aspect of the city recently illuminated by archaeological research is its fortifications. The literary tradition attributes to many of the kings wall-building of some kind, with the incorporation of different parts of the city occurring in a gradual fashion. According to Livy, Romulus fortified the Palatine; then Ancus Marcius added the Aventine and Janiculum to the pre-existing settlement of the Palatine, Capitoline and Caelian; Tarquinius Priscus built a wall in stone around the full settlement; and Servius Tullius enlarged the wall to include the Quirinal, Viminal and Esquiline. According to Dionysius, Romulus fortified the Palatine, Aventine and Capitoline; Tullus Hostilius extended the wall to the Caelian; Ancus included the Aventine in the city; Tarquinius Priscus built the first stone wall; Servius Tullius added the Viminal and the Esquiline; and Tarquinius Superbus strengthened the fortifications previously established.

The tradition is not without problems. Often the hills are thought to have been added to the city after they were settled by individual peoples from immigrant or conquered communities, as with Ancus moving the populations of Tellenae and Politorium to the Aventine (Dion. Hal. 3.43.2). This seems a rather artificial and late construction. There are also some discrepancies in the hills assigned to certain kings, notably the Caelian (Tullus, Ancus and possibly others) and Aventine (Romulus or Ancus). But the tradition is strikingly coherent on several key features. There is a consistent view that the ancient heart of the city was the Palatine and Capitoline; that the Aventine and higher areas of the Viminal, Quirinal and Esquiline were added later on; and that the city reached its largest extent for several centuries under Servius Tullius. All the sources assume that Rome had a full fortification circuit from the beginning of the Republic, and that this wall protected the city on many occasions (e.g. Livy, 2.39.9; 3.66.5; 4.21.8; 6.27–8; Dion. Hal. 5.44.1; 8.22.2; 8.38.3; 9.68). Scholars have tended to dismiss these reports as anachronistic and resulting from the sources' expectations that the city must always have been walled. They note that the Gauls were able to capture the city in 390 BC. They focus instead on two passing mentions by Livy of wall-building and repair for 378 and 353 BC, which are claimed to have been the first occasion on which the city was fully walled. But the problems with the literary tradition have been exaggerated, and recent archaeological surveys show that it is more plausible than most scholars admit.

The remains of the fortifications are very difficult to understand, given their frequent refurbishment, complete rebuilding in the Republican period, and subsequent absorption into the urban fabric. Nevertheless most scholars think that there were two major phases of walling, the older of which was archaic.[71] The oldest is in smaller blocks of cappellaccio tufa (a local volcanic stone), cut in modules of the Italic foot of 27.5 cm; it is found in substantial stretches around the 11 km extent of the 'Servian' city, including the Aventine (Figs 5.18, 5.19, 5.20). This type of stone was the primary building material of the archaic period, widely (if not exclusively) used for a range of structures in the seventh and sixth centuries BC, such as the podium of the Capitoline temple. It was readily available on site, for instance from the Palatine hill, and was an easily workable if friable stone. It came to be replaced with harder tufa stone from quarries outside the urban area of Rome which could be cut in larger sizes, most notably Grotta Oscura from quarries near Veii. This stone forms the most visible sections

Figure 5.18 The cappellaccio wall underneath Termini station (photo: G. Bradley)

71. *Roma medio repubblicana*, 7–31; Cifani, *Architettura*, 45–73; Coarelli, *Collis*, 43–4; Nijboer, 'Fortifications'; Ziółkowski, 'Servian enceinte'. Bernard, 'Continuing the debate' and Hopkins, *Genesis*, 92–7 both express caution about the existence of a full circuit.

Figure 5.19 The Servian Walls outside Termini station (photo: G. Bradley)

of the 'Servian Walls', such as the long surviving section outside Termini railway station (Fig. 5.19). The use of stone from the territory of Veii implies that it postdates the conquest of that city, in 390 BC, and this is presumed by most scholars to represent the wall to which Livy refers in 378 and 353 BC.

There are several reasons for believing that the cappellaccio phase is archaic, and probably belongs to the sixth century BC. In places (such as on the Aventine hill near Santa Sabina) it survives under the 378 walls, so it is generally considered the older stone. The development of the Esquiline cemetery shows a clear horizontal stratigraphy. Whereas the tombs of the eighth and seventh centuries are found on both sides of the later wall circuit, those from the fifth and fourth centuries are clearly moved to outside the walled circuit (Figs 5.21, 5.22). This would be odd if the circuit was not finished before the Republican era. Furthermore, the most recent discussions of the stratigraphy of the wall and associated *agger* (ditch) date it clearly to the sixth century BC.[72]

---

72. Cifani, *Architettura*, 257–60; Bonghi Jovino, 'Affinità', 36–40.

Urbanism and city foundation

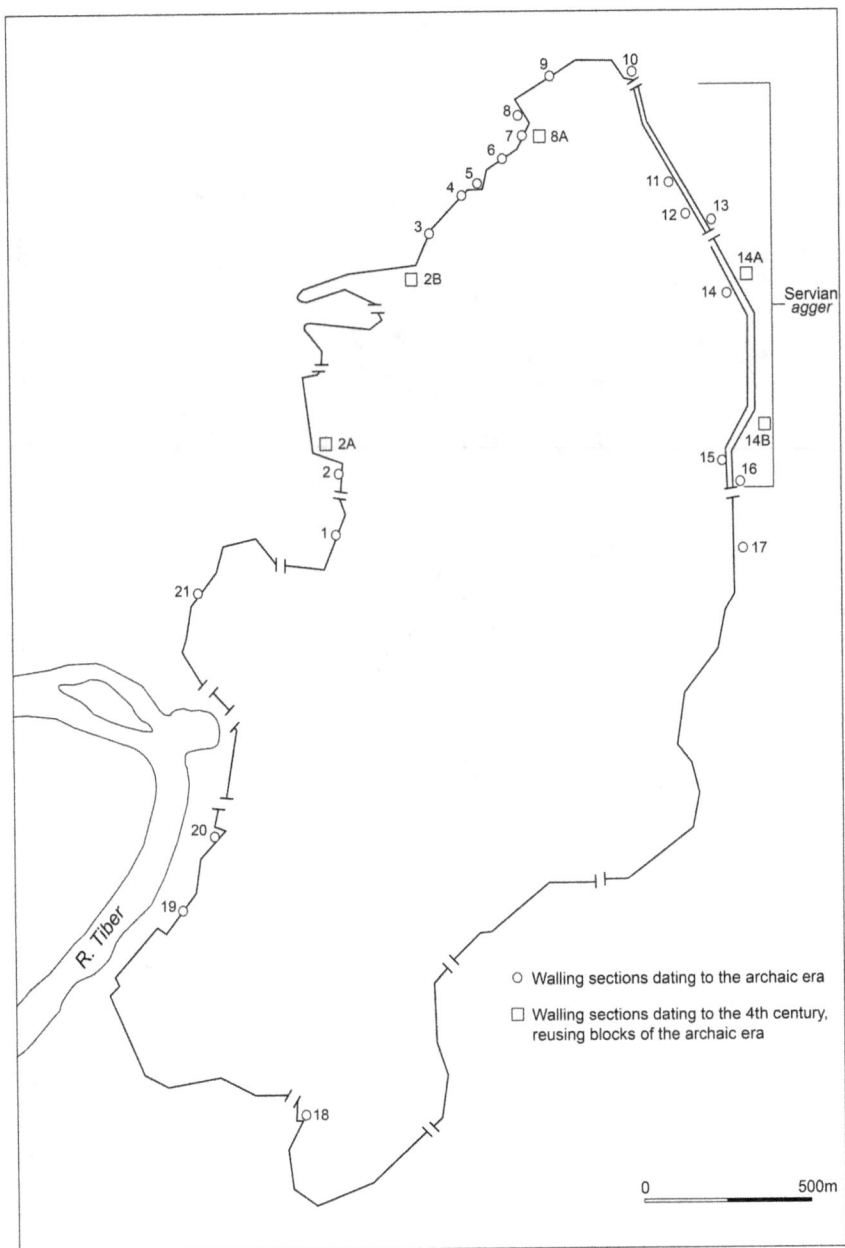

Figure 5.20 Surviving and reused sections of cappellaccio walling in the Servian Walls (after Carandini, *Nascita*, pl. 33)

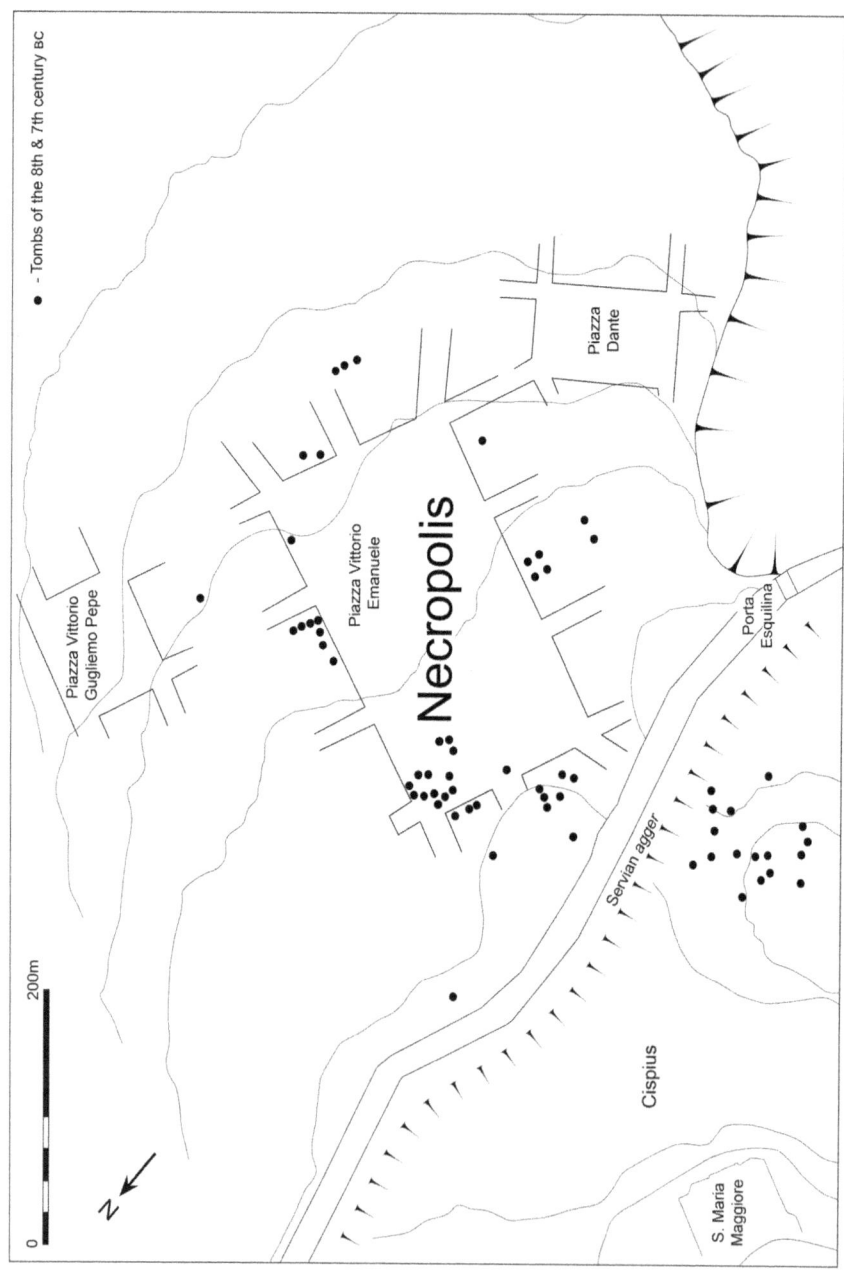

Figure 5.21 The distribution of tombs in the Esquiline cemetery, eighth and seventh centuries BC (after Cifani, *Architettura*, fig. 235)

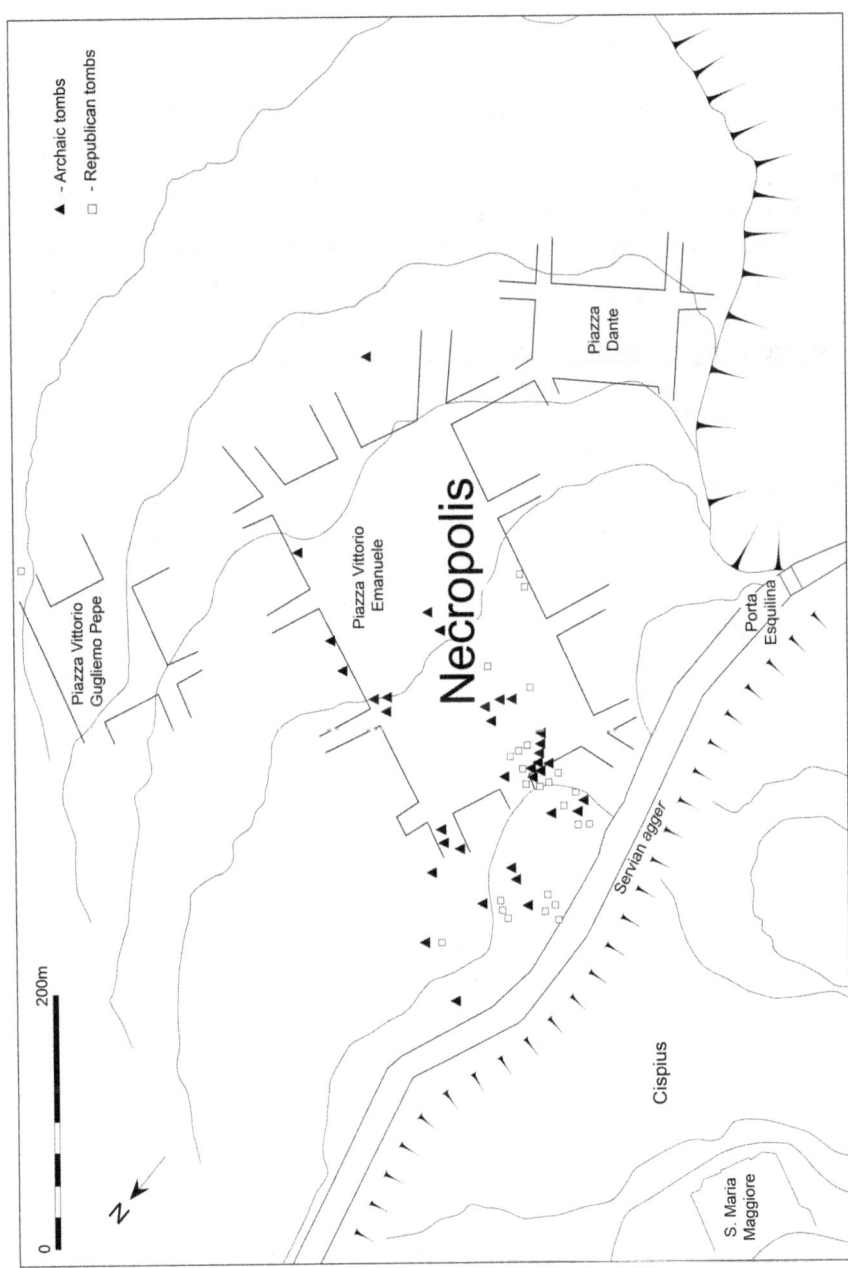

Figure 5.22 The distribution of archaic and Republican tombs in the Esquiline cemetery (after Cifani, *Architettura*, fig. 236)

Comparative evidence from central Italy supports a sixth-century date. The walls of Tarquinii offer a close parallel, as Bonghi Jovino has recently shown that they date to the first half of the sixth century BC. Given that they are 8 km long, if covering a much smaller area (around 150 ha), the project for their construction must have been comparable to the walls of Rome (11 km long). Many Latin cities are now known to have had unified circuits in the sixth century BC, such as Ardea, Antium, Castel di Decima, Ficana and Lavinium, although they were much smaller in scale than the southern Etruscan cities (Fig. 5.23).[73] We now know, too, of unified circuit walls from the sixth century in Campania, at Capua and Pompeii. All this makes a large unified circuit at Rome in the sixth century BC quite feasible, and suggests that counter-hypotheses are less likely.[74]

The total area enclosed is 427 ha, well beyond the size of other cities in central Italy at this time, and close to some of the largest cities of Magna Grecia and mainland Greece (Fig. 5.24). This therefore paints a similar picture to the Capitoline temple, of a Rome without local parallel, and on a par with the greatest centres in the archaic Mediterranean. The area within the walls is unlikely to have been completely filled with residential areas. Comparative studies suggest that most large ancient cities had substantial open spaces for cultivation and stock-rearing, sacred groves and such like. In fact, unoccupied space was probably 'designed in' when the walls were created, to allow for future urban growth, and to enable the walls to follow the best defensive line.[75]

The extent of the fortification is also significant for what it implies about conceptions of the city in the archaic period. The provision of a wall circuit shows that the community needed a collective defence, and was in itself an important manifestation of Roman civic and collective identity. We might also link the wall to the Servian reforms, which created a collective defensive organisation for the citizen body (the centuriate system) and which organised the city into four separate districts, urban tribes for voting and probably for levying troops.[76] We do need to be cautious about linking the archaeological evidence

73. Such as Lavinium, where the walls enclosed 30 ha.
74. For other comparisons see Cifani, *Architettura*, 262–4; Bonghi Jovino, 'Affinità'; Nijboer, 'Fortifications'. Bernard, 'Continuing the debate' argues that only the hills were fortified, pointing out the absence of evidence in the valleys, although this is now disputed by Ziółkowski, 'Servian enceinte'.
75. Further discussed in Bradley, 'Rome of Tarquinius Superbus'.
76. Cf. Cifani, 'Fortifications', 89.

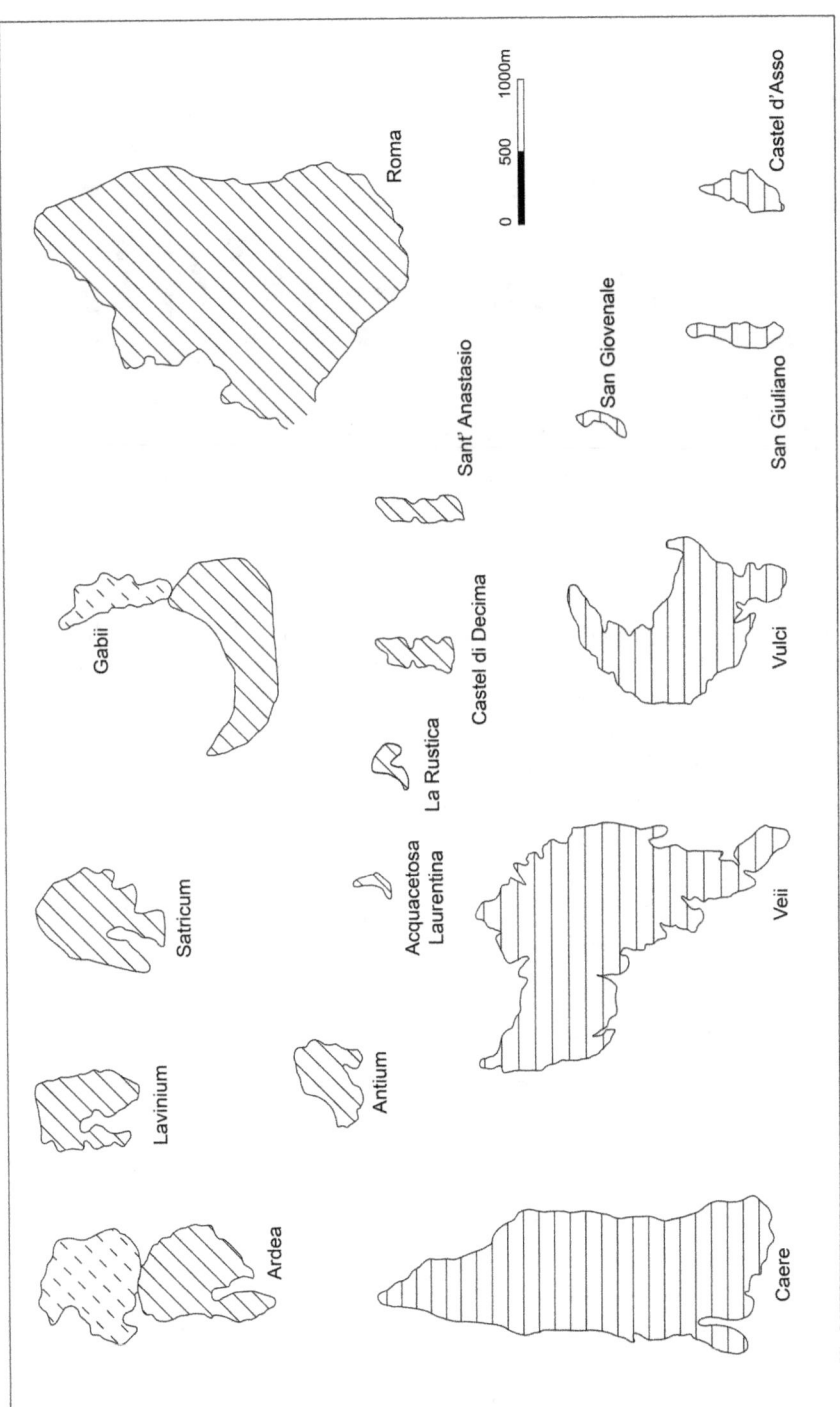

Figure 5.23 The comparative sizes of central Italian cities (drawing: H. Mason, after Momigliano and Schiavone (eds), *Storia di Roma*, I 586)

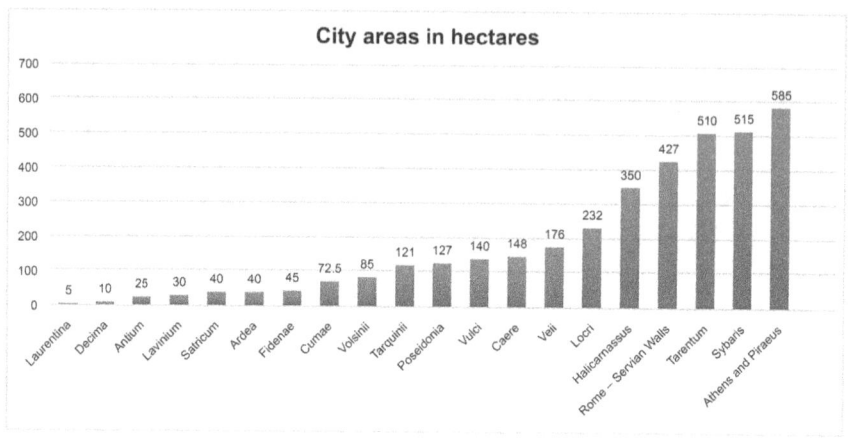

Figure 5.24 City areas in hectares (figures from Cifani, *Architettura*, 257; Cornell, *Beginnings*, 204; Ampolo, 'Città riformata', 168)

of a sixth-century wall to the traditional dates of Servius Tullius in the mid sixth century. The dating evidence for the wall is imprecise, and the monarchic dates are almost certainly highly artificial, as well as probably oversimplifying the picture of the sixth-century rulers of Rome. Nevertheless, it is striking that the literary sources attribute the wall to the same figure as the socio-political reforms, even given the tendency of the tradition to require 'founder figures' for all such innovations, and that two independent types of evidence, literary and archaeological, point towards similar conclusions about the organisation of the community in the sixth century BC.

Other urbanistic projects

A huge range of other urban projects in this period reinforce this picture of a powerful and vibrant Mediterranean city. In the period from the late seventh to the first quarter of the fifth century BC we can truly talk of the transformation of the city, though our understanding of this process is still at an early stage, given the challenges of the evidence. The archaeological remains of most archaic buildings are very fragmentary, and are far less clearly attested than the buildings discussed above, such as the Regia, and the Capitoline and Forum Boarium temples. Many sacred (and perhaps also profane) buildings are attested by isolated architectural terracottas, which are found in very large numbers at many sites in

Rome. Some buildings are attested only through literary evidence, which by itself is uncertain. The foundation of temples has a good case to be trusted, as they were normally included in priestly records. Some have archaeological correlation of their foundation dates, as in the case of the Capitoline (although the 'fit' is not by any means without issues, as we have seen). Where major structures are attributed to the last three kings without archaeological correlation, such as seating at the Circus Maximus to Tarquinius Superbus, there is a danger that the sources are retrojecting major monuments onto more recognisable founders. Nevertheless, while certainty is mostly elusive, scholars are increasingly inclined to accept such notices, particularly where monuments can be linked to archaic institutions, such as the Circus, linked to the festival of the Ludi Romani and to the Triumph.

A substantial number of temple foundations are attested for the monarchy and early Republic. Various temples are said to have been founded in the 'mythical' era of the early kingship, such as those of Janus and Jupiter Feretrius by Romulus, and that of Vesta by Numa (or Romulus according to some sources). Although archaeological remains of sacred activity from the eighth century BC have been found on the site later associated with the temple of Vesta and on the Capitoline hill (where the temple of Jupiter Feretrius was supposedly founded), there is very little certainty about these foundations.[77]

Much more significant are the developments in the sixth century BC, following the innovative precedent set by the first Sant'Omobono temple around 580.[78] Besides multiple shrines to Fortuna, Servius Tullius is said to have founded the temple of Diana on the Aventine as a federal centre for the Latin peoples, based on the model of the temple of Artemis at Ephesus.[79] Founded around 550 BC, this was one of the greatest Ionic temples of the archaic Mediterranean. It measured 115 × 46 m, and provides a possible model for the structure of the Capitolium. Virtually no archaeological traces have been found of the Aventine temple, but Strabo (4.5.180) records that the cult statue of the Roman temple was very similar to that of Massilia,

---

77. Edlund Berry, 'Early Rome', 415. Note also Plut. *De fort. Rom.* 10: 'The temple of Fortuna Virilis (Manly Fortune) was said to have been built by Ancus Marcius, the fourth king.'
78. Potts, *Religious Architecture*, 40–5.
79. Livy, 1.45.2; Dion. Hal. 4.26.3.

a Greek colony founded by Phocaeans from Asia Minor, who had close relations of friendship with archaic Rome.[80]

Some buildings are attested archaeologically by the discovery of architectural terracottas. In some cases these can be related to building foundations, or to buildings attested by literary evidence, as in the case of the Sant'Omobono temple. For many sites no such correlation exists. Architectural terracottas were not originally used exclusively for sacred buildings; they appear on structures with mixed sacred and residential purposes, such as the palaces at Murlo and Acquarossa in Etruria, and the Regia in the Forum at Rome. However, in the course of the sixth century BC architectural terracottas came to be confined to buildings of civic and religious significance.[81] This means that architectural terracottas, particularly from the later sixth century onwards, are likely to represent the remains of temples. Significantly, large numbers of such buildings are attested in this way. According to Lulof, there are ten attestations of the Rome–Veii–Velitrae roof series in Rome, and some sixteen to twenty in total, including sites in Etruria and Latium (see for example Fig. 5.25). Such roofs must have related to small temples such as that found at Sant'Omobono.[82] Important findspots of other architectural terracottas in Rome include the western corner of the Palatine, under the future site of the temple of Victory, the Porta Esquilina, the Capitoline, the Comitium, the Regia, the temple of Castor and temple of Divus Julius in the Forum, the Velian, Tiber and the Esquiline.[83] Overall, Nancy Winter has catalogued eighty-three separate findspots of architectural terracottas from Rome prior to the imperial period, the majority of them archaic.[84]

It is also striking to note that this huge process of temple-building continues in the first few decades of the Republic. We have archaeological and literary evidence for the temple of Saturn, perhaps dedicated in 497 BC, the temple of Mercury in 493 BC, the temple of Ceres, Liber and Libera on the Aventine in 493 BC, the temple of Fortuna Muliebris in 493 or 488 BC,[85] the temple of Castor in 484 BC

---

80. Ampolo, 'Artemide'.
81. Potts, *Religious Architecture*, 51–61.
82. Lulof, 'Reconstructing', 114–17.
83. Included by Lulof in the Rome–Veii–Velitrae series.
84. Ampolo, 'Città riformata', 235, citing Colonna, 'Templi del Lazio'. For Winter's catalogue, see the Etruscan and Central Italian Architectural Terracottas Online Database: www.beazley.ox.ac.uk/databases/terracottas.htm.
85. Dion. Hal. 8.55–6; defended by Schultz, *Women's Religious Activity*, 37–44.

Figure 5.25 Architectural terracotta decoration of the temple of SS. Stimmate, Velitrae (drawing: R. Sponer Za, for Winter, *Symbols*, 320–3, Roof 5–7, Plan 18)

and the temple of Dius Fidius in 466 BC. The huge number of these projects is striking, and their continuation into the Republic suggests that broader forces were at work than simply the personal political manifestos of the kings.[86]

86. Hopkins, *Genesis*, 153–71.

The later kings are also said to have adorned the city in terms of its collective spaces and infrastructure. One of the most important structures is the Circus Maximus, attributed to Tarquinius Priscus (Livy, 1.35.8; 1.56; Dion. Hal. 3.68). Although it is not attested archaeologically until the mid Republic, a monarchic date would fit in with the use of the space for the Triumph, which was probably elaborated by Tarquinius Priscus, and the Ludi Romani, which probably date to the sixth century. Zevi argued that the Corinthian associations of the cult of Poseidon Hippius, associated with the central structure of the Circus, links the structure and its use to the (Bacchiad) Tarquins.[87] Games in the Circus were interrupted by a flood in 363 BC (Livy, 7.3.2), reports of which must have come from priestly records, attesting its existence by that date.

Both Tarquin monarchs are said to have taken an interest in the drainage of the Forum. Priscus is said to have created conduits for water from the hills to run down to the Tiber, which was probably essential for stabilising the artificial fill of the Forum.[88] Then Superbus is credited with transforming this open drainage system into the great underground drain, the Cloaca Maxima.[89] Livy describes this as an enormous construction, and the structure is still evident today. The oldest surviving tracts are probably archaic, although we lack an up-to-date archaeological survey to date it precisely and it was probably repaired and reconstructed throughout the Roman period. There is another example of such drainage work, covered by a stone vault of archaic date, in the Colosseum valley.[90]

A range of other public amenities are attributed to the kings by our sources, including the first bridge (the Pons Sublicius: Livy, 1.33.6), the Carcer or Tullianum (prison) (Livy, 1.33.8; Festus 490 L.), and the Forum Tabernae (shops) (Livy, 1.35.10; Dion. Hal. 3.67). Also under the monarchy, the road network of the city was first established. Traces of roads created from hard packed clay agglomerate have been dated to as early as the eighth century BC on the Palatine slopes (particularly in the vicinity of the Porta Mugonia) and in the area of the Meta Sudans.[91] The gates into the city are evident from

---

87. Zevi, 'Demaratus', 75–6.
88. Livy, 1.38.6–7; Dion. Hal. 3.67; Hopkins, *Genesis*, 23–33.
89. Livy, 1.56; Dion. Hal. 4.44; Pliny, *HN* 36.24 attributes the work to Priscus; Hopkins, 'Sacred sewer'.
90. Cifani, *Architettura*, 308–11.
91. Carandini, *Nascita*, 662.

their later position on the Servian Wall. Coarelli points out that we can distinguish two types of ancient route: prehistoric routes named from their function or position (the Via Salaria or Via Tiberina) which probably predate the site of Rome, and later routes named after their destination city (Via Labicana, Tibertina, Praenestina), which must postdate the urbanisation of Latium.[92] The alignment of rectangular stone houses along recognisable streets is one of the key signs of an urban layout.[93] It is apparent in Rome from the seventh-century BC house with a tiled roof found along the Sacra Via above the Sepulcretum, and the sixth-century BC atrium houses created along a street at the foot of the Palatine (Fig. 5.26). It is tempting to connect these great houses in an area of the Palatine that remained the most desirable place to live in the late Republic with the emergence of the elite families that formed the Republic. Nevertheless, it remains highly likely that such families were already in existence, given the appearance of wealthy tombs in the Esquiline cemetery in the seventh century BC.

Conclusion

We are thus able to track the rapid development of Rome from small settlements on several hills at the start of the first millennium BC through to the extraordinary urban monuments of the seventh and sixth centuries BC. This latter period is one of huge significance for the political and cultural development of Rome, and it can be documented increasingly clearly through the evidence of architecture.[94] This development does not straightforwardly correlate with the literary evidence. The foundation of the city seems considerably earlier than the traditional date of 753 BC, even if a case can now be made for important developments, whose full extent is yet unclear, in the second half of the eighth century BC. The late seventh and sixth centuries BC saw multiple building phases of major monuments in the Forum and the surrounding hills, particularly at the Comitium (Fig. 5.27), the Regia and in the Forum Boarium. Many of these sites were destroyed and rebuilt multiple times, which may suggest that the regimes in control of Rome had a much more complex history than is evident in the sketchy literary accounts.

---

92. Coarelli, *Origini*, 19.
93. Drews, 'Coming of the city'.
94. Cifani, *Architettura*, 298–305; Hopkins, *Genesis*.

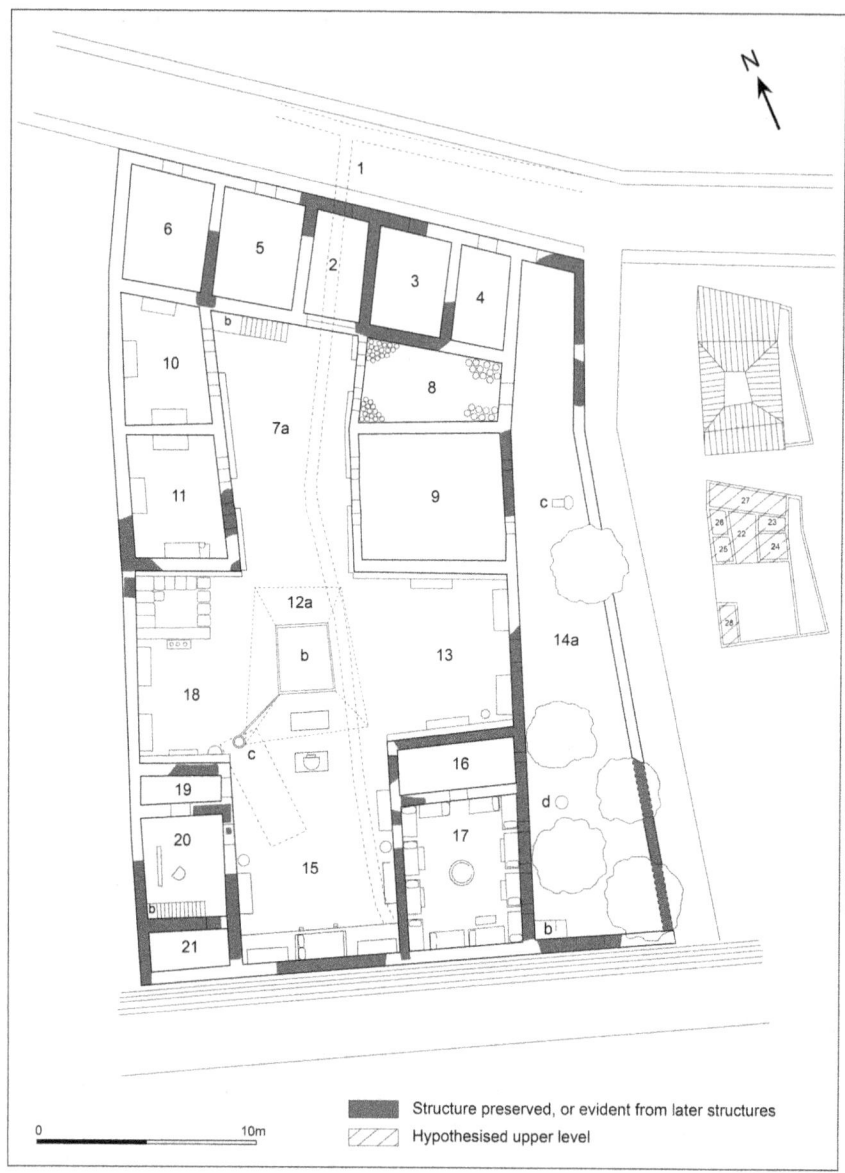

Figure 5.26 Plan of atrium house (Domus 3) on the slopes of the Palatine (after *GRT*, fig. 4.2)

The urbanisation of the city is a critical process and one that remains controversial. We see this taking place through various key points. The establishment of new cemeteries on the edge of the settlement area; the creation of a large number of monumental sacred

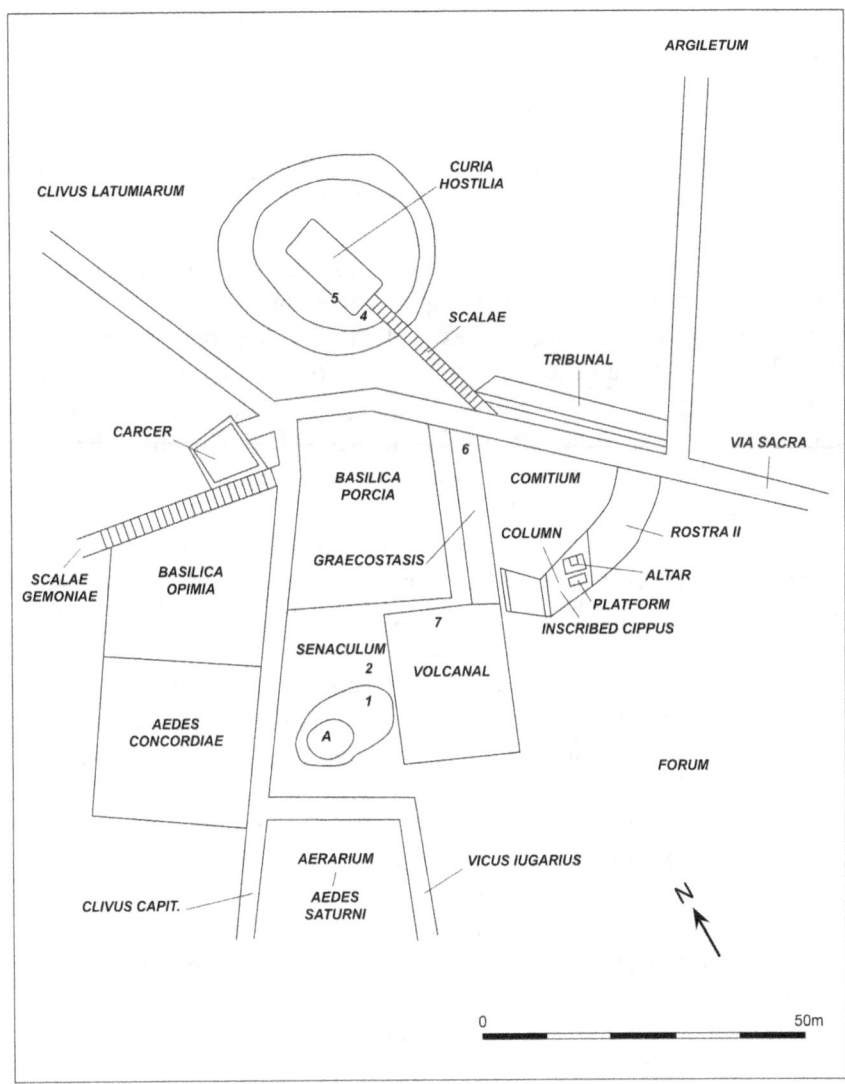

Figure 5.27 The Comitium and associated monuments in the Archaic and Republican period (after Carafa, *Comizio*, 152, fig. 95)

buildings on sites of open-air sanctuaries such as the temple of Vesta and the Forum Boarium; the provision of stone houses aligned along streets; the creation of fortifications enclosing the city; the provision of a central meeting space through landfill work to counteract flood risk; and the development of a harbour just below the Tiber island. Scholars have connected these changes with the adoption of new building and roofing technologies. The ultimate origins of these technologies seem to lie in the Greek East and the Levant, with the widescale employment of terracotta tiles and ashlar masonry foundations. These foreign links combine with local innovations and traditions, for instance in the use of terracotta decorative roofs and temple podia, to create a distinctively central Italian type of architecture and urbanism.[95]

Intense debates are currently taking place about the beginnings of the urbanisation of Rome. Some scholars have argued that the excavations on the Palatine slopes and the re-examination of older material demonstrate that the city shifted from a proto-urban to an urban state already in the mid eighth century BC, thus to a large extent validating the ancient tradition on the foundation of Rome by Romulus. Others have strongly rejected these claims, arguing that it is only the developments of the second half of the seventh century BC onwards in which urbanisation took place. These debates concern not only the contested interpretation of fragmentary evidence, but also conceptual problems about state formation, which normally precedes urbanisation by many decades if not centuries.[96]

These changes have important social implications. Buildings were becoming more permanent (although we should not exaggerate the temporary nature of earlier wooden structures), suggesting that society was becoming less fluid. Stone architecture requires more resources and artisanship, and provides a way to demonstrate the accumulation of elite wealth and power. The elite now adopted an iconography partially borrowed from Greece, but also adapted locally to express this power in their own distinctive terms. Generally, however, it is important to note that urbanisation and the creation of stone architecture to lay down the physical presence of a city is really just a manifestation of political organisation. This is what actually marks the most important stage in the creation of the city, which it is easy to lose sight of when our evidence is primarily archaeological.

The monumental development of the city in the late seventh and sixth centuries is less controversial, and a broad consensus is currently developing on the strong Hellenic influence on Rome and on the parallels between Rome and other Mediterranean societies. But the significance of monumentalism and its connection with the

---

95. Cf. Turfa and Steinmayer, 'Interpreting' for similar points about the independent development of wooden roofs.
96. Bradley, *Ancient Umbria*, 30–41; cf. Carandini, *Nascita*, 498.

political situation is still disputed. Vigorous debates are ongoing, stressing different factors such as the link between urbanism and autocracy, the 'thermodynamic' theory of monumentalism, and the unreal 'despotic' scale of sixth-century architecture at Rome. Who was responsible for the commissioning, and does the diversity of building projects reflect more than just a king at work? How far should the archaeological evidence be linked up to the character of the regime in Rome? Much debate also remains over the nature of the *Grande Roma dei Tarquini*, the 'Great Rome of the Tarquins' a phrase coined by Pasquali in the 1930s. Whilst it is now accepted that this represents a much more valid characterisation of the archaic city than sceptics such as Alföldi have argued, scholars still point out the difficulties in the appropriateness of the term. There remain considerable problems in combining the archaeological with the literary evidence. Nevertheless, the question of the influences on Rome in this era is a very stimulating one, encompassing the link with the Etruscans through the origin of Tarquinius Priscus, and ultimately the Corinthian origins of the 'dynasty' through Demaratus.[97]

Scholars have also pointed out the ready comparisons with other contemporary Mediterranean cities. In particular, the remodelling of city institutions and creation of public infrastructure are closely paralleled by the projects of Greek tyrants. The hydraulic projects attributed to the Tarquins echo the aqueducts of Samos and Athens, built by Polycrates and Pisistratus. The Cypselids of Corinth were responsible for fortifications, temples, a harbour at Lechaeon, and the great engineering work of the *diolkos* (trackway) across the Isthmus.[98] There are also close parallels with the building projects of Polycrates in Samos, such as the great temple of the Heraion of Samos (perhaps the closest model yet found for the Capitoline), the 6 km long fortification walls, the creation of a famous water tunnel, and a new harbour. Nevertheless, it is not just autocratic rulers in the Greek world who created monumental buildings, which were undertaken by all sorts of regimes, just as all types of governments undertook institutional reforms in the name of civic harmony. For example, democratic Athens undertook the Great Drain which made the agora more usable (just like the Cloaca Maxima at Rome) in the early fifth century BC.[99]

---

97. Zevi, 'Demaratus'.
98. Nielsen and Roy, 'Peloponnese', 265; Hall, *History*, 141.
99. Whitley, *Archaeology*, 225–8 warns against a moralising picture of the association of autocracy and monumentalism.

CHAPTER 6

Economy and society in archaic Rome and central Italy

Approaching the archaic economy

It is something of a paradox that the current scholarly consensus holds Rome to be a large and powerful urban state, yet one with an economy dominated by subsistence agriculture. From the religious structures of the city it is clear that agriculture and pastoralism played a very important role in the Roman community, especially in its early phases. Nevertheless, it is also unarguable that by the late archaic period (and perhaps even a long time before that) Rome was a large city supporting a population of tens of thousands. The weight of evidence makes it unlikely that the majority of the urban population were subsistence farmers. Instead, this chapter will argue that the economy of early Rome was fundamentally diversified by the sixth century BC, with important roles being played by manufacture, commerce, agriculture and pastoralism. Rome was tied into wider commercial, social and intellectual exchanges as part of a Mediterranean 'world system' encompassing the Mediterranean basin and the ancient Near East that had emerged by the sixth century BC.[1] In addition, an increasingly important role in the Roman economy during the late monarchy and early Republic was played by imperialism (which gradually came under firmer state control). This brought land, slaves and moveable booty into the city state in ultimately huge quantities.

The archaic economy, as it developed under the Roman monarchy, had many distinctive and dynamic features that would determine the development of Rome for centuries to come. This dynamism ran alongside features that Karl Polanyi argued were fundamental in pre-industrial economies: that the 'economy' was not a distinct or separate area of life, but embedded in existing social structures; that

---

1. Sherratt and Sherratt, 'Growth'; Vlassopolous, *Unthinking*. The term 'world system' comes from the work of Immanuel Wallerstein.

land and labour were crucial factors in economic relations, and that they were heavily influenced by social relations.²

Agriculture and pastoralism

Agriculture and pastoralism had a fundamental importance in the Roman economy as a source of wealth. Land ownership was the essential requirement for army service. Those who qualified were termed *assidui* (occupiers), and the colonists who were sent out to conquered land, frequently army veterans, were termed *coloni* (cultivators).³ Agriculture was part of a wider diversified economy with market characteristics by the sixth century BC; and like other elements in that economy, such as commerce, it was dynamic and changed over time.⁴ Although traditionally scholars have tended to stress the predominant place of agriculture over commerce and trade in the ancient economy, more recent studies have emphasised the intimate connection of these spheres, and their reciprocal development in the archaic Mediterranean.⁵

Perhaps the most important innovation in Roman agriculture in the archaic period is the development of vine and olive cultivation, the central elements of typical Mediterranean polyculture. Pliny expresses the view that neither crop was as old as the foundation of the city (*HN* 14.14; 15.1; 18.5). However, the cultivated vine was certainly present in central Italy from the ninth century BC, and active cultivation developed in the seventh century BC, probably in connection with Greek practices.⁶ Local cultivation of the vine is evident at Rome from the end of the eighth or first half of the seventh century BC, through palaeobotanical evidence, the use of specialised vessels for wine and the presence in the oldest stratum of the calendar of festivals associated with wine, the Vinalia and the Meditrinalia.⁷ Olive production seems more recent, and does not appear in the Roman botanical record until the first half of the sixth century BC. Fenestella claimed that in the reign of Tarquinius Priscus (traditionally 616–578 BC) olive cultivation was unknown in Spain, Africa and Italy.⁸

---

2. See Morris, 'Foreword' and M. Nafissi, *Ancient Athens* for a critical discussion of Polanyi's ideas.
3. XII Tables 1.4 for *assidui*; Drummond, 'Rome', 119.
4. Smith, *Early Rome and Latium*, 114–22; Nijboer, *From Household Production*, 29–45.
5. Van Wees, 'The economy', for this approach to the archaic Greek economy.
6. Bartoloni, *Cultura villanoviana*, 211.
7. Ampolo, 'Condizioni', 31–2. Bartoloni, *Cultura villanoviana*, 211, dates the wide distribution of drinking vessels to the early eighth century BC in Etruria.

But this is certainly not the case in Italy, where there is evidence from eighth-century BC Etruria. If the production of the numerous aryballoi (small jars used for oil and perfume) found in Latium in period IVB (c.630–580 BC) was local, this would provide further evidence that oliviculture probably reached back into the seventh century BC here too.[9] By the early fifth century BC, large-scale production of oil was becoming a standard feature of rural establishments, as shown by the inclusion of an olive press in the second phase of the Auditorium building (discussed below). These developments have a broader social significance, as both types of farming require considerable investment and stability of tenure. Newly planted vineyards and olive groves take at least five years to produce fruit, and harvesting requires considerable labour resources.

The eighth to the sixth centuries BC saw other, related, innovations such as the production of metal ploughs, and more efficient practices of crop rotation. The importance of agriculture to the Roman economy comes through clearly from the XII Tables of c.450 BC: the law code sets out penalties for damaging crops, the use of items like vine-props and plough oxen, and regulations for field boundaries.[10] Its importance is also evident in the religious calendar. Eighteen of the fifty festivals in the oldest stratum of the Roman calendar relate to fertility and crops (such as the Robigalia on 25 April, for the avoidance of wheat rust).[11] That many Roman deities were multi-valent, having fertility/agricultural concerns as well as other associations, suggests that the Romans did not conceive of agriculture as a distinct specialism as we tend to do (and later Romans did).

The raising of livestock was also a significant part of the archaic economy. The remains of funerary banquets from the Forum cemetery and the evidence of the XII Tables show that pigs were the most commonly raised animal, and sheep and goats were also readily available. Cattle were rarely used for meat, and probably largely reserved for the plough.[12] Varro (in Gell. *NA* 11.1) claims that fines were originally assessed in terms of livestock, and only converted into a monetary equivalent (*asses*, bronze pounds) by the Aternian

---

8. Fenestella was an Augustan historian with antiquarian interests who is cited by Pliny, *HN* 15.1.
9. Ampolo, 'Condizioni', 32; 'Periodo IVB', 179.
10. Drummond, 'Rome', 199. See Chapter 7.
11. See Scheid, *Introduction*, 48–53 for a list.
12. Ampolo, 'Condizioni', 35; Cifani, *Architettura*, 286; pigs are mentioned in the XII Tables at 7.10; 7.9; 8.11.

law of 454 BC.[13] However, the monetary unit of the *as* is standardly employed in the XII Tables, implying that they were entirely familiar by the mid fifth century BC.[14] Excellent summer pastures in the nearby mountainous areas of the Sabine and Aequian Apennines to the north-east of Latium must have been important for provisioning sheep and goats. The name of the Forum Boarium, the 'cattle market', on the Via Salaria which led from Sabinum, may hint at Rome's role in this movement and trade of livestock, but archaeological evidence is currently limited. Only two or three archaic festivals seem directly concerned with stock-raising and herding (the Fordicidia of 15 April, the Parilia of 21 April and perhaps the Lupercalia of 15 February).

Archaeological evidence also reveals the intensification in the archaic period of rural settlement in the hinterland of Rome, notably in the lower Tiber valley and south Etruria. Site numbers expand steadily from the seventh century BC to the archaic period.[15] Our best example of a rural establishment is the Auditorium site, a little outside the northern periphery of the city of Rome. In its first phase of c.550–500 BC a large courtyard building was constructed with tiled roofs and separate rooms for the processing and production of food. When it was replaced by a more elaborate structure of 700 m^2 in its second phase (c.500–300 BC), two differentiated zones were set up, one with more prestigious accommodation for a presumably elite owner to the north, and the other for productive activities to the south. There was also a substantial annex, which took the form of multiple small rooms around courtyard spaces (Fig. 6.1). The presence of an olive press raises interesting questions about the relative lack of amphora evidence from Rome: did the market at Rome consume all local production to such an extent that export was unnecessary?[16]

We have little information on the scale of land holdings in this period. Antiquarian sources such as Varro (*Rust.* 1.10.2) imply that tiny plots of two *iugera* in early colonies replicated the land holdings of the earliest Roman farmers in Romulean times. But this seems an anachronistic reconstruction based on learned speculation.[17] By 367

---

13. Drummond, 'Rome', 123, argues that this came later, given the confusion in our sources.
14. Crawford, *Coinage*, 19–20, arguing that the designation of the *as* goes back to Servius Tullius in the mid sixth century BC.
15. Di Giuseppe, 'Villae', 6.
16. Cifani, *Architettura*, 287.
17. Drummond, 'Rome', 121.

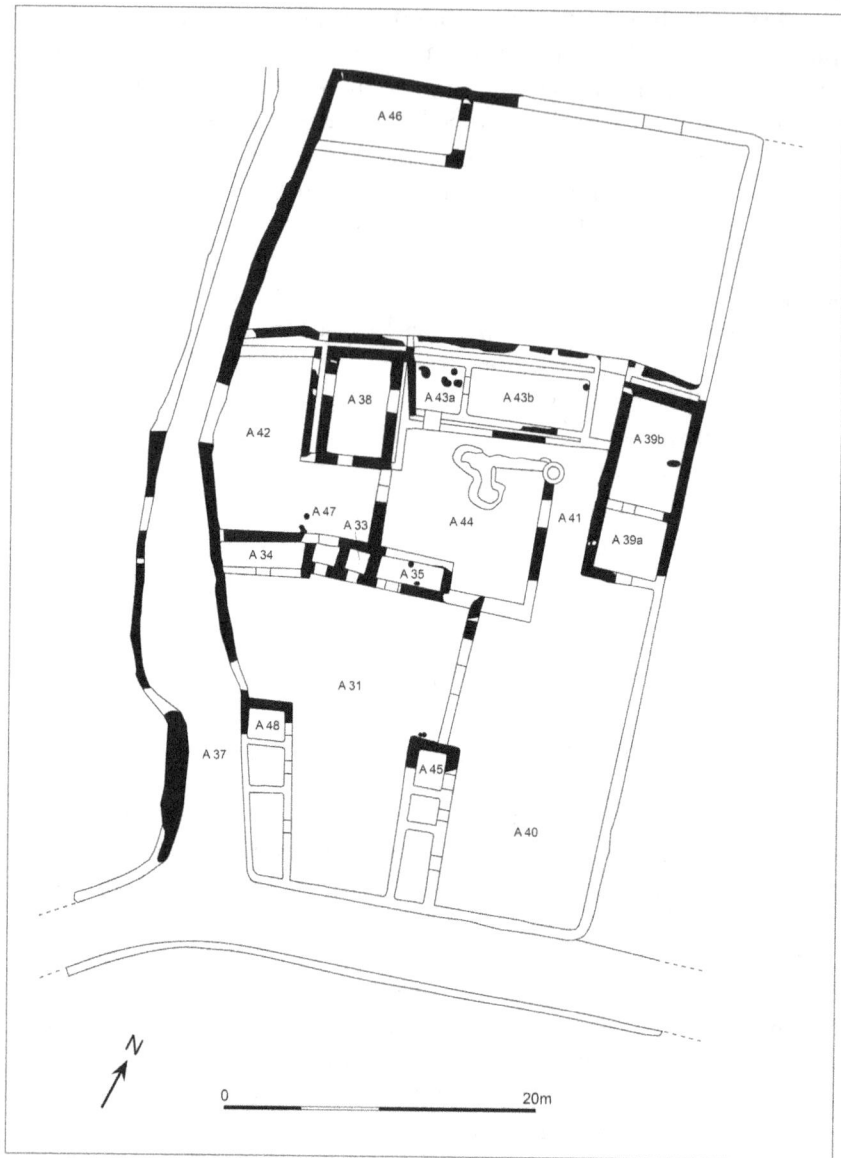

Figure 6.1 Plan of the Auditorium villa annex, c.500–350 BC (after Cifani, *Architettura*, fig. 191)

BC elite land holdings could clearly be sizeable: the Licinian-Sextian rogations of this year attempted to restrict holdings of all land (not just public land as modern historians had conservatively tended to assert) to 500 *iugera* (125 ha).[18] Even 500 *iugera* was far more than a family could work itself, and this clearly implies that the elite had dependent labour readily available: a conclusion that correlates with our literary evidence, as we shall see.

Production

Evidence for artisanship and industry at Rome is patchy and, in many ways, limited compared to Etruria: at Rome we find little equivalent of the copious testimony of high-quality pottery production in Etruria, for instance. The familiar problems surface, of recovering archaeological artefacts from the seriously compromised record, although recent excavations and reassessments of earlier material are improving the situation.[19] There is also the uncertainty with the literary evidence: Pliny, for instance, provides interesting information on the earliest Roman productive activities, trade guilds (Pliny, *HN* 35.46), and the migration to Etruria of Demaratus of Corinth in 657 BC with the first modellers of clay (35.43). Much of the sources' information is unproveable either way, and has the stamp of antiquarian speculation: immigrant potters can be dated archaeologically to earlier than 657 BC, and 'founder figures' with emblematic natures, such as Demaratus' potter Euchir (whose name means 'good-handed'), give rise to suspicion. But new archaeological knowledge has displayed some intriguing synergies with the literary evidence, suggesting that it contains some information of value.[20]

The origins of Roman production can be traced back to the ninth century BC, with pottery and metallurgy. Coarseware made from local impasto clay with large inclusions is characteristic of early Roman production, with large quantities produced in unsophisticated, small-scale settings. The pottery was handmade on a slow-turned wheel.[21] The presence in burials on the Esquiline hill at Rome from the seventh

---

18. Rich, 'Lex Licinia'; see further, Chapter 7.
19. See Ampolo, 'Periodo IVB'; Colonna, 'Produzione'; *GRT*, especially 129–30; Carafa, *Officine*.
20. E.g. Ampolo, 'Periodo IVB', 173–8; Ridgway and Ridgway, 'Demaratus and the archaeologists'.
21. Carafa, *Officine*, examined 29,000 sherds of locally produced pottery; Nijboer, *From Household Production*, 101.

century BC of Greek Protocorinthian wares, Etruscan bucchero and Etrusco-Corinthian wares (see further below), produced 'en masse' in Etruria from the seventh century BC, demonstrates the local demand for finer-quality pottery products. This demand seems to have been met by imports rather than by local production. Similarly, there is as yet no evidence for a Roman equivalent to the Etruscan transport amphorae widely exported around the western Mediterranean from c.625–c.500 BC, and perhaps produced in Vulci. However, the limited quantity of the Roman evidence may be misleading here. What is apparent is that Rome provided a very sophisticated market, and that it probably had its own urban pottery workshops from the sixth century BC.[22] Roman production includes bucchero, loom weights, and miniaturised objects discovered in the Forum Boarium deposit. This deposit also contains evidence of local metalworking in the form of sixth-century BC bronze statuettes of offerants, and probably also ivory/bone figures, found at Sant'Omobono and elsewhere in Latium.[23] The name of one such craftsman may appear in an archaic Latin inscription on the so-called 'Duenos vase' of c.575 BC, found in a votive deposit on the slopes of the Quirinal: it includes the phrase *duenos med feced*, 'Duenos made me'.[24]

According to our sources, Numa established separate trade guilds (*collegia*), which included musicians, goldsmiths, carpenters, dyers, leatherworkers, curriers, braziers and potters (Plut. *Num.* 17.2; Pliny, *HN* 34.1; 35.46). Numa's ahistorical characterisation makes this report suspicious, and an alternative tradition attributes them to Servius Tullius (Florus 1.6.3).[25] *Collegia* are attested more firmly in association with the foundation of the temple of Mercury in 495 BC, and are documented in the XII Tables of 450 BC.[26] It is thus reasonable to assume that they existed in the sixth century BC.[27] The main area of pottery production seems to have been the potters' quarter on the

---

22. Nijboer, *From Household Production*, 185. See now Biella et al. (eds), *Artigiani*. See also below.
23. Colonna, 'Produzione', 315.
24. Ampolo, 'Periodo IVB', 173; *GRT* 20–1; Colonna, 'Duenos', arguing that it was a note of donation not a potter's signature, and arguing that *duenos* meant 'a good man' rather than being a proper name. The inscription was incised after firing. See also Forsythe, *Critical History*, 88–9.
25. Sceptical: Ampolo, 'Grande Roma', 82–3; Nijboer, *From Household Production*, 183; more optimistic: Torelli, 'Dalle aristocrazie', 259.
26. Livy, 2.21.7; Gaius, *Dig.* 47.22.4.
27. Cf. Ampolo, 'Periodo IVB', 176–8 argues that the types of expertise in Plutarch's list best fit a sixth-century context.

Esquiline (Varro, *Ling.* 5.50; Fest. 344 L.), which like the Ceramicus at Athens was also adjacent to the main cemetery area.

The most spectacular evidence for production at Rome relates to the great building projects of the late seventh and sixth centuries BC. These required large-scale production of tiles and decorative architectural terracottas, the result of a technology that was created in Corinth in the first half of the seventh century BC, and rapidly shared across Etruria and the rest of central Italy. Production was often near to the place of extraction in dedicated workshops, and shows that Rome had an increasing specialisation of labour. Beds in the Velabrum, the low-lying zone between the Palatine, Tiber and Forum Boarium, provided a ready source of clay.[28] Tiled roofs are first attested at Rome on a house on the Sacra Via of 650–625 BC.[29] More elaborate roofs for public buildings were created in two great phases of building, around 580 and around 530 BC. These building phases involved important structures on a range of sites in the city: a temple, perhaps of Jupiter Feretrius, on the Capitoline hill; the so-called Curia Hostilia; the Regia (Figs 5.8 and 5.9); and the temple at Sant'Omobono in the Forum Boarium. Winter has recently argued that, judging by the similarities between moulds, the workshops in Rome were also responsible for commissions in Campania in 590–580 BC (Pithecusae and Cumae), northern Etruria in 580–575 BC, Veii (south Etruria) and Velitrae (Latium) in *c.*530 BC and Caprifico (Latium) in *c.*520 BC (Fig. 6.2).[30] The Greek motifs in the architectural decoration, and the rapidity of its spread from Greece, suggests that these workshops included, or were strongly influenced by, emigrant artisans from Greece.[31]

The Greek models of the seventh and sixth centuries BC were Ionian. In the fifth century these were replaced by Sicilian Greek influences.[32] Pliny (*HN* 35.45) records that the temple of Ceres, Liber and Libera on the Aventine, dedicated in 493 BC, was decorated by the Greek artists Damophilus and Gorgasus, who signed their work in Greek. This is contemporary with the famous sixth- and early

---

28. Ammerman and Filippi, 'Dal Tevere'; Ammerman et al., 'Clay beds'.
29. Hopkins, *Genesis*, 40.
30. Winter, *Symbols*, 556. Other architectural terracottas were imported from Caere for the fourth phase of the Regia *c.*530 BC (Winter, *Symbols*, 55) and the temple of Castor *c.*490–470 BC (Torelli, 'Topography', 83).
31. Winter, *Symbols*, 577–81, linking this to the emigration of Demaratus and associates from Corinth in 657 BC and (less perilously) to the Ionian emigration following the Persian capture of Sardis in 546 BC.
32. Torelli, 'Topography', 83.

Figure 6.2 Architectural terracotta decoration of the temple at Caprifico di Torrecchia (Cisterna di Latina) (drawing: R. Sponer Za, for Winter, *Symbols*, 323–4, Roof 5–8)

fifth-century BC painted chamber tombs of nearby Tarquinii, also the work of Greek artists. The significant Greek presence in this part of central Italy is reinforced by the find on the Esquiline of the torso of a wounded warrior, whose exquisite terracotta artisanship has also been linked to the presence of Sicilian artists.[33]

There is a considerable hiatus in the archaeological evidence from the second half of the fifth century to the fourth century BC. This is in part a result of cessation in Latium of the practice of burying grave goods with the deceased from the sixth century BC, but it also reflects a considerable slowdown in the construction of public buildings, perhaps linked to the straightened economic circumstances of fifth-century BC Rome. After the disappearance of Attic pottery, the most prestigious import of the archaic period, by the end of the fifth century BC, Campania and Etruria emerge as local producers of fine pottery in the fourth century BC. The most typical products are red-figure pottery, used in funerary contexts, and black-gloss pottery, used for tableware, with Falerii Veteres emerging as the most significant producer until it was superseded by Rome in the late fourth century BC. Roman production seems to have picked up from the second half of the fourth century BC. The widely distributed Genucilia plates (Fig. 6.3) (whose Roman origin is disputed) and 'atelier des petites estampilles' black-gloss bowls were produced in large quantities.[34] Metalworking also seems to be significant at Rome around 300 BC, to judge by the spectacular Ficoroni cista (decorated bronze container). Cistae, dating between the late fifth and early third century BC, are found only at Praeneste in Latium; the Ficoroni cista, one of the most sophisticated examples of the genre, is inscribed 'Novius Plautius made me at Rome' (*Novios Plautios med Romai fecid*: CIL I² 561 = ILLRP 1197). Although this is the only example that can be directly linked to Rome, it is a clear indication of the quality of Roman bronzeworking at the time of its production around 315 BC.[35]

Trade, seafaring and piracy

Trade and commerce are usually afforded little attention in studies of early Rome. The city's oldest surviving law code, the XII Tables,

---

33. Coarelli, *Foro Boario*, 283; Lulof, 'Amazzone' for an alternative view that the torso should be connected with the temple of Ceres on the Aventine.
34. Torelli, 'Topography', 88; see Bilde and Poulsen, *Temple*, 49 for the origin of the Genucilia plates.
35. Cornell, *Beginnings*, 390; Haumesser, 'Hellenism', 652.

Figure 6.3 Genucilia plates, Ashmolean Museum (photo: G. Bradley)

emphasises agriculture rather than trade; in the calendar, agricultural rather than commercial concerns predominate; and the Romans are often regarded as having a disdain for trade, especially of the seaborne variety. According to Cicero (*Rep.* 2.9–10), Romulus deliberately founded the city some 19 miles inland to prevent it suffering the corrupt lifestyle typical of full-blown ports. The same author claimed that commercial trade was less respectable than agriculture, an attitude echoed elsewhere in many sources. There is little sign of an organised Roman navy in the era before the third century BC, and control over the Tyrrhenian sea was disputed by Etruscans, Carthaginians and Greeks rather than Romans. Polybius believed them ignorant of the sea until they were forced into naval warfare by the Carthaginians.[36] In consequence, Etruria is often assigned a mediating role between Greece and Rome, and is frequently presented as the source of prestigious Greek imports to the city.

But despite these anachronistic stereotypes, part of the 'Roman mirage' propagated by our sources, there is good reason for treating maritime trade and the link to the sea as a critical feature in early Roman history. A primary indication is the size and position of Rome, one of a series of large coastal or near-coastal centres like Athens, Corinth and Carthage that emerged within a Mediterranean-wide 'world system' in the sixth century BC.[37] These cities had surpassed the carrying capacity of their agricultural hinterlands, and for the first time were dependent on imported grain. This was probably the case with Rome in the sixth century BC, given the emergency procurements reportedly sought from Cumae, Sicily and Etruria from the start of the fifth century BC.[38] Maritime and commercial interests in Rome are also reflected by the dedication of a temple to Mercury in 495 BC and the establishment of a guild of traders (*collegium mercatorum*), and by the worship of Neptune, god of water and the sea, as part of the oldest phase of the calendar.[39]

Although it experienced considerable seasonal variation in flow, the Tiber was navigable as far as Rome by boats up to 200 tonnes.[40] Even large ocean-going ships could sail up the river to the city, as happened later on with the introduction of the Magna Mater from

---

36. See, for instance, 1.20.12.
37. Sherratt and Sherratt, 'Growth'. Note that the centre of Athens is 12 km from its port at Piraeus.
38. In 492 BC Roman ships seeking grain were repelled from Cumae (Livy, 2.34.3) but successful in Sicily and Etruria (Dion. Hal. 7.1–2); there were also grain expeditions to Sicily in 432 and 412/11 (Livy, 4.52.19–21). Discussed in Drummond, 'Rome', 134; Garnsey, *Famine*, 167ff.; Oakley, *Commentary*, I 58; Coarelli, 'Demografia', 321.
39. Livy, 2.27.
40. Coarelli, 'Santuari', 123, citing Casson, 'Harbour and river boats', 32.

Asia Minor in 204 BC and with Perseus' royal ship in 167 BC.[41] A typical oared Greek merchant ship of the sixth century BC would have been capable of making its way against the current upstream to the city. That some did is suggested by literary sources attesting the presence of Phocaean Greek ships at the mouth of the Tiber (Justin, 43.3.4), and the preservation of an archaic pentecontor (a fifty-oared galley) in the Navalia.[42] Thus, while ancient sources stressed that the city benefited from being set back from the coast, it still had many of the advantages of a coastal position.[43]

Contemporary ships are unknown from Rome, but are attested in evidence from neighbouring Etruria which ranges from tomb paintings (such as the mid fifth-century BC vessel represented in the Tomb of the Ship at Tarquinii, Fig. 6.4) to shipwrecks. It is often impossible to ascertain the ownership of cargo vessels wrecked off the coast of modern Italy and France, but very broad trading links including with the eastern Mediterranean are revealed by their cargoes, for example the Corinthian helmet and Greek pottery on the Giglio wreck of *c.*580 BC.[44] Etruscan products are also prominent in these ships. For example, the wreck of Grand Ribaud F (*c.*500 BC) contained around a thousand Etruscan amphorae, and was commanded by an Etruscan merchant of Latin extraction, to judge by the names inscribed on some of the ceramic vessels.[45]

The Navalia was the Roman military port on the left bank of the river next to the Campus Martius.[46] It already existed by 338 BC, when part of the captured fleet of Antium was confiscated to here; other Antiate ships were broken up, and their beaks used to decorate the tribunal in the Comitium, which led to it acquiring the name *Rostra* ('beaks'). Commercial ships used the *portus Tiberinus*, next to the Forum Boarium ('cattle market'), the riverbank between the Capitoline and the Aventine hills.[47] This was also the location of the first bridge over the river, the Pons Sublicius, ascribed by Livy (1.33.6) to the reign of Ancus Marcius. Although controversial, Coarelli's interpretation of the Forum Boarium as the *emporion*

---

41. Livy, 29.10; 45.35.3; Plut. *Aem.* 30.1–3; Tuck, 'Tiber', 237. The larger grain ships of 200 tons plus had to unload at Ostia in the imperial period.
42. Procopius, *Goth.* 4.22.7–16; Coarelli, 'Santuari', 123–6.
43. As recognised by Cicero, *Rep.* 2.9–10 and Dion. Hal. 3.44.
44. Discussed in Chapter 2.
45. Colonna, 'Commercio', 678; Bruni, 'Seafaring', 767; see also p. 79 above.
46. For the navy see Steinby, *Roman Republican Navy*.
47. Doubts about the existence of the port are combatted by Coarelli, 'Santuari', 113–27.

Figure 6.4 Trading vessel from the Tomb of the Ship at Tarquinii, mid 5th century BC (after Minetti, *Pittura*, 74)

(mercantile trading place) of the city is convincing. He compares it to other *emporia* dotted along the Tyrrhenian coast at Minturnae, Pyrgi, Gravisca, Punicum and Regisvilla, several of which (Pyrgi and Gravisca in particular) have evidence of intense foreign frequentation. The regular spacing of such sites reflected the pattern of *cabotage* (trading along a coast port to port, with overnight stops) practised by most ancient Mediterranean seaborne traders. Several had sanctuaries with Greek- or Eastern-inspired terracotta statuary, like the Hercules and Athena group at Sant'Omobono, and have substantial assemblages of imported Greek and Eastern products, especially pottery.

Ostia, the port of Rome, was said by the literary tradition to have been founded by Ancus Marcius, when he conquered the lower stretches of the Tiber and set up salt works on the northern side (Livy, 1.33.9). The main archaeological evidence for the colonial *castrum* on the south bank of the Tiber dates to 380–350 BC. The foundation of the colony in the early fourth century BC cemented Roman control over the mouth of the river. But there are earlier archaeological traces of a settlement here from the late seventh and sixth century BC, in the form of roof tiles, hut foundations and architectural terracottas.[48]

Roman involvement in overseas trade is already apparent from the first Rome–Carthage treaty, formed in 509 BC.[49] Polybius (3.23.4) says, 'To Carthage itself and all parts of Libya on this side of the Fair Promontory, to Sardinia and the Carthaginian province of Sicily the Romans may come for trading purposes, and the Carthaginian state engages to secure payment of their just debts.' Rome was similarly bound to Massilia by treaties, the first apparently formed c.600 BC with the arrival of Phocaean Greeks (see above), and the second an equal treaty formed after Massilia had helped Rome during the Gallic sack (389 BC). We know nothing of their clauses, although it is likely they had similar purposes to the Carthage treaties.[50]

Rome was also connected to the world of Mediterranean seafaring through the less benign mechanism of piracy. According to Strabo (5.3.5), 'In earlier times the people of Antium used to possess ships and take part with the Tyrrheni in their acts of piracy, although at that time they were already subjects of the Romans.' These activities brought objections from Alexander and Demetrius Poliorcetes direct to Rome, the sovereign power over the colony of Antium: the city had been a Latin colony from 467 BC, but was renewed as a Roman colony in 338 BC. Their embassies suggest that they knew about Roman dominance in central Italy, and that Antiate piracy reached even to the eastern Mediterranean.[51] These activities were not officially condoned by Rome, but Rome did not closely supervise the day-to-day activities of colonies.[52] A similar case in 339 BC saw the Sicilian tyrant Timoleon put to death a certain Postomion (Postumius), accused of piracy. He is called a Tyrrhenian by Diodorus; his name suggests he is Latin, either Roman or Antiate.[53] *Tyrrhenos* is normally understood to mean Etruscan; but as Dionysius recalls, there was little precision in the use of this term by older Greek writers, who used it to designate all the inhabitants of the Tyrrhenian coast. All the Latin coast

---

48. Bartoloni, 'Latini', 110; Zevi, 'Roma arcaica'.
49. See Chapter 8, p. 277 for the text of the treaty and a discussion of its authenticity.
50. Second treaty: Pompeius, 43.5.8; cf. Strabo, 5.4; Ebel, *Transalpine Gaul*, 8; Cornell, *Beginnings*, 321.
51. Bispham, 'Rome and Antium', 236, 240; De Souza, *Piracy*, 51–2. Dion. Hal. 7.37.3–4: Rome recovers Sicilian crews taken prisoner by the Antiates in 491 BC.
52. Bispham, 'Rome and Antium', 240–1.
53. Diod. Sic. 16.82; Harris, 'Roman warfare', 500.

might be described as Tyrrhenia, and Rome as a Tyrrhenian city.[54] This raises the intriguing possibility that the copious Greek references to Tyrrhenian pirates may include Romans and Latins.

Thus, there is a fair amount of evidence that early Rome was well connected to the sea, and its inhabitants were not at all the reluctant seafarers presented by Polybius and others. Some contemporary Greeks had a more realistic idea. Already in the early third century BC Lycophron (1226ff.) was able to prophesy that the Romans would enjoy hegemony not just across the earth but also the sea.[55]

Rome's connections with the Mediterranean probably made it a pivotal point for the Sabines and other peoples of the mountainous hinterland of the central Apennines. Rome was a source of staples like grain and salt, as well as luxury goods such as imported pottery and metalwork. In return, Rome could provide products of the interior for Mediterranean traders, such as salt (essential for preserving fish), leather, textiles, wood, meat and perhaps slaves. Little of this trade can be traced archaeologically, due to the perishable nature of the materials. But imported materials in Rome itself show the process at work. For instance, Tomb 193 from the Esquiline cemetery contained an urn of marble from Paros in the Aegean, where it was probably produced c.500 BC and from where it was imported to Italy, along with other examples that ended up in Spina, Tarentum and Caere. The Esquiline cemetery has also turned up substantial quantities of Protocorinthian pottery, now in the Capitoline Museum vaults, and dating to c.650–600 BC. Most comes from one tomb, including an olpe of the late seventh century BC with a Greek inscription, *Kleikos*, perhaps indicating the owner.[56] The votive deposit at Sant'Omobono in the Forum Boarium, as yet only partially excavated, is the most striking source of imported material.[57] The quantity of material here implies a strong Greek and Phoenician presence. There are fifteen fragments of eighth-century BC Greek-style pottery (perhaps Veientine imitations), and important sixth-century BC material including amber, ivories, Etruscan bucchero and Greek pottery.[58] The latter includes

---

54. Dionysius 1.29.1–2; Ps.-Scylax, *Peripl.* 5, 'the Latins hold Tyrrhenia down to Circeum'; Bispham, 'Rome and Antium', 236–8; Fulminante, 'Latins', 489.
55. Momigliano, 'Terra marique' argued that Lycophron must be early third century BC; cf. Erskine, *Troy*, 154–6.
56. Cornell, 'Rome and Latium Vetus', 88; Ampolo, 'Periodo IVB', 184; Ross Holloway, *Archaeology*, 22; Mura Sommella, *GRT* 249.
57. Estimated at 10 per cent of deposit, *GRT* 129–30.
58. Earlier material: Smith, *Early Rome and Latium*, 80.

over 100 items of Attic, Laconian and Eastern Greek pottery from the second quarter of the sixth century BC onwards. There are Corinthian aryballoi (perfume holders), and three alabastra from Naucratis in Egypt. Pottery from Attica is the most striking of the imported ceramics, with a good range of high-quality material from the Lapis Niger, Forum and Palatine, as well as Sant'Omobono.[59] Importation of Attic pottery continues into the fifth century BC, but largely ends by the middle of that century.

The topographic position of Rome meant that it was well placed for overland communications. As we have seen, the ancient route of the Via Salaria ran from the Forum Boarium to the central Italian mountains; Rome was linked to the mouth of the Tiber (and the salt works there) by the Via Campana, following the northern bank of the river, and to the south by the Via Latina. The purpose of this very ancient network was to provide salt for the Sabine hinterland, hence the name Salaria.[60] This route, with its prolongation to the coast, ran north–south. The city was also well placed on the route north to south along the Tyrrhenian coast: the easiest crossing of the Tiber was at Rome. Overland trade with Etruria is widely attested through the archaeological evidence. For instance, the Etruscan pottery par excellence, bucchero, is found widely in archaic Rome during the last quarter of the seventh and the sixth century BC, such as in the Sant'Omobono, Quirinal, Capitoline and Forum votive deposits.[61] Trade to the south with Latium is more difficult to trace, given the inherently Latial character of most Roman material culture, but was undoubtedly pervasive.

While trade was unlikely to be as important in Rome as at cities such as Corinth on the Greek mainland, Rome was well connected to the active maritime commerce along the Tyrrhenian coast from at least the seventh to the middle of the fifth century. The archaeological evidence then evaporates, which is at least in part a product of the drying up of the pottery supply, as trading routes along the Tyrrhenian coast were interrupted by Greek and Etruscan inter-state rivalries. But in the fourth century BC, the increasingly detailed literary evidence reveals continued connections with the part of the

---

59. Gilotta, *GRT* 140–1. Smith, *Early Rome and Latium*, 184 notes that there is much more Greek pottery from Rome than from other Latin sites, on a level with the largest Etruscan sites. Cf. Meyer, *Pre-Republican Rome*, 160–1.
60. Fest. 436 L., Pliny, *HN* 31.89, with Coarelli, 'Santuari'.
61. *GRT* 130.

Greek world around the Aegean, as well as intense exchange with Magna Graecia.

The economy of the archaic period differs from the economy of the middle and late Republic in various important features. Firstly, there was the lack of a developed slave system, and greater reliance on unfree labour from debt-bondage within Roman society. It was probably from the fourth century BC that substantial use of slaves developed in the Roman economy. The economy of the archaic period also relied on less advanced ship technology. The size of ships found in wrecks increases considerably from the fourth century BC onwards, and dedicated harbour facilities begin to appear to accommodate them; the Navalia in Rome existed by the mid fourth century BC, although purpose-built harbours are considerably later. In the archaic period, few states had organised navies, and piracy is likely to have been endemic. There was also probably less state control over the economy, with a less developed tax-raising system; *tributum* is first attested in Rome in the late fifth century BC. State interest in profiting from economic activity grows from the fourth century BC, when we see innovations such as a tax introduced on manumissions (357 BC). Piracy formed an important element of earlier economic activity for communities on the Latin coast and Roman interest in naval activity considerably expands in the third century BC.

This picture of an economy transforming around 300 BC is also supported by the evidence of coinage.[62] It is striking that full-scale production of Roman coinage is not needed before the 270s. This could suggest a retardation of the economy, but it is not quite so straightforward. Coinage in the ancient world is typically generated by the needs of the state, particularly the requirement to pay for military forces and large-scale public works, rather than responding to the needs of the economy. Thus, the lack of an earlier coinage at Rome may chiefly reflect the lack of a need to pay for mercenary troops, and the effective organisation of the citizen levy.[63] Nevertheless, money in a sense had existed for some time at Rome, with a recognised system of weights and measures from the sixth century BC. The Servian classes, which were assessed by the value of their property, must by all accounts predate the introduction of coinage. Weight equivalents in bronze were presumably used for the Servian

---

62. Crawford, *Coinage*, ch. 3; Bernard, 'Social history'.
63. Cornell, *Beginnings*, 288; Armstrong, *War and Society*, 99–100.

classes, as the sources indicate. Weights and measures were perhaps set by Servius Tullius in connection with this system.[64]

In addition, coinage from other societies circulated in Rome. There were already *argentarii*, who may be handlers of silver coinage (that is, bankers) in the Forum in 309 BC (Livy, 9.40.15).[65] This implies that by this date there was already enough coinage in circulation to enable bankers to make a living. Roman bronze coinage first appeared around this date, with production initially undertaken by Naples, and then in connection with the building of the Via Appia of 312 BC.[66] These issues closely followed a Greek model, with a Greek weight standard and appearance, but using Roman legends. The phrase *Romano(rum)*, 'of the Romans', implies that Roman identity was clearly manifested, but viewed from an outsiders' perspective. More standardised production only appeared in the context of the Pyrrhic War of the 270s.[67] This corresponds to the large-scale use of armies abroad, particularly in the First Punic War, from 264 BC, and Italian coinages also appear as allies become more systematically employed in contingents for the Roman army, paid for by their own states. Thus, coinage is not so much a sign of a developing economy as of the continuing Hellenisation of the city state. It does of course also enable a new type of economy, in which wealth could be transferred more fluidly, but does not necessarily signify that the earlier Roman economy was particularly unsophisticated.

Demography

The demography of Rome has recently received a great deal of renewed attention. The recent debate has mainly focused on the period from the late third century BC to the Augustan era. Relatively little attention has been paid to early Rome.[68] As can be seen from Table 6.1, census figures survive from various sources, primarily Livy, dating back through the early Republic to the first census undertaken by Servius Tullius. The reliability of the figures is uncertain. The figures from the third century BC have been widely accepted as trustworthy, but earlier figures have been dismissed by Beloch and Brunt. Nevertheless, there

---

64. Ampolo, 'Servius'.
65. Andreau, *Banking*, 30.
66. Crawford, *Coinage*, 29.
67. See Rosenstein, *Rome and the Mediterranean* in this series.
68. Fulminante, *Urbanisation* is a notable exception; Bradley, 'Rome of Tarquinius Superbus', with previous bibliography.

Table 6.1 Roman census figures[a]

Date (BC)	Census figure	Reference
Servius Tullius	80,000	Livy 1.44
	84,700	Dion. Hal. 4.22.2
	83,000	Eutropius 1.7
508	130,000	Dion. Hal. 5.20; Plut. *Pub.* 12
503	120,000	Hieron. *Ol.* 69.1
498	150,700	Dion. Hal. 5.75.4
493	110,000	Dion. Hal. 6.96
474	103,000	Dion. Hal. 9.36
465	104,714	Livy 3.3.9
459	117,319	Livy 3.24; Eutropius 1.16
393/2	152,573	Pliny, *HN* 33.16
340/39	166,000	Eusebius, *Ol.* 110.1
c.336	130,000	Plut. *Mor.* 326C
	150,000	Oros. 5.22.2; Eutropius 5.9
	250,000	Livy 9.19
294/3	262,321	Livy 10.47

[a] Source: Brunt, *Italian Manpower*, 13; Coarelli, 'Demografia', 319, 338.

have been attempts to rehabilitate the earliest figures by Momigliano and Coarelli.[69] The aim here is to explain the nature of the evidence and its problems rather than finding a solution.

There are several difficulties with accepting the figures as they stand. Scholars have questioned how the census figures could have been preserved without the office of the censorship, which was not instituted until 443 BC. Dionysius (1.74.5) tells us that from this point on the records were kept by the families of the censors. But we know that archaic Rome was capable of keeping detailed literary records, such as the calendar, before this time and the organisation of the centuriate assembly, which many accept to be sixth century, presupposes such records. A further challenge is what the figures record. In giving the figure under Servius Tullius, Livy (1.44.2) quotes 'Fabius Pictor, the oldest of our historians, [who] states that this was the number of those who could bear arms'. The main difficulty this poses is that women and children would have to be added to the total that Livy

---

69. Beloch, *Bevölkerung*; Brunt, *Italian Manpower*; Momigliano, 'Timeo'; Coarelli, 'Demografia'; Bradley, 'Rome of Tarquinius Superbus' for further references.

gives of 80,000 at a ratio of 7:2, which would imply a total population of around 280,000 people. This is unsustainably high for the size of Rome's territory at the time. Momigliano argued that Fabius was in polemic with Timaeus, who must have taken the figures as all the population. This would be more plausible, and in fact we do have some reason to think that early censuses may have included all citizens, not just adult males.[70]

Scholars have generally followed Beloch and Brunt in rejecting the early figures, and have looked to other means to calculate a likely Roman population. The most authoritative estimate was provided by Ampolo, who argued that the carrying capacity of Roman territory was in the order of 20–30,000 people. He compared this to Heurgon's estimate for the Etruscan city of Caere, based on the dead in its cemetery, which put the population at around 25,000.[71]

In fact, there are some positive factors in favour of a larger Roman population in the monarchy. As several scholars have pointed out, the carrying capacity of a city's territory is not necessarily the best way to calculate ancient city populations.[72] The use of imported grain throughout the fifth century at times of crisis in Rome suggests that the carrying capacity of the territory should be a minimum rather than a maximum of the Roman population, which is likely to be much larger. In practice, equating the population with territory is very difficult for Rome, as we have no certain way of knowing the full extent of Roman territory in this period, and in any case, it is likely to have ebbed and flowed during the wars of the fifth century BC. In considering a similar question for the population of ancient Greek cities enumerated by the Copenhagen Polis Project, Hansen argued that the extent of the intramural area of the urban centre is a more reliable basis for calculating their populations than the carrying capacity of the territory. He noted that the percentage of large cities occupied by

---

70. Pliny, *HN* 33.16 states that the census in 390 BC covers *capita libera*, which may mean all citizens. Dion. Hal. 4.15.6 says that women and children were recorded, even if their numbers were not published.
71. Ampolo, 'Periodo IVB' envisaged 35,000 maximum for a territory of Rome in 509 BC of 822 km². This figure for the territory was calculated by Beloch, *Bevölkerung*, although Coarelli, 'Demografia' argued it is an underestimate. For Caere, see Heurgon, *Daily Life*, 145–8. See further, Bradley, 'Rome of Tarquinius Superbus.'
72. Coarelli, 'Demografia', 322; Fulminante, *Urbanisation*, 130 argues that Rome had already exceeded the carrying capacity of its territory by the early Iron Age.

habitation was low, and estimated only 33 per cent of the area on average was used.[73]

Even if the city population of Rome did not fill the urban area within the walls, the huge expanse of the urban area that is enclosed by the fortifications has important implications for the city population. Caere, at 150 ha, should be considerably smaller rather than comparable to Rome, which at 427 ha should have a population several times larger.[74] Working from Hansen's figures for Greek cities, I have argued that the city of Rome is likely to have had a population range of 21,100–28,200 in the sixth century, and that the total Roman population was 64,050–85,400.[75] Although hypothetical, this estimate is based on the implications of the latest archaeological evidence, and on the picture in the sources of a rapidly expanding population under the monarchy. There is a clear line in the sources that immigrants moved to Rome throughout the monarchic period, often with large numbers of followers, such as Mastarna with the army of Caelius Vibenna, and Attus Clausus with a large body of clients. This is consonant with rapid population growth, and with Torelli's argument that the movement of people into the city during the Tarquin dynasty gave rise to the plebeian order.[76] Archaeological evidence from the territory of Rome suggests a rising population in the sixth century.[77] In addition, the centuriate organisation presupposes a large body of potential recruits and a sizeable army, especially if Fraccaro is correct to believe that there are two legions of 3,000 men each in 509 BC.

However, this should not necessarily lead us to rehabilitate the early census figures, despite their correlation with my estimate for the total population of Rome in the late sixth century. There remains the problem of who exactly is being counted, whether total population or adult males, and there is insufficient evidence to explain why and when the nature of the census might have changed from counting all people to just adult males, as was the case from 200 BC onwards. We still cannot clearly identify a point when the figures suddenly become plausible. The figure of 150,700 for 498 BC is generally discounted as excessive.

---

73. Hansen, *Shotgun Method*, ch. 1.
74. Cf. Richard, *Origines*, 308.
75. Bradley, 'Rome of Tarquinius Superbus', 130.
76. Torelli, 'Dalle aristocrazie', 24ff.
77. Di Giuseppe, 'Villae', 6 n. 22.

It is true that the other figures generally correspond to what we know of the ebb and flow of Roman territory in the fifth and fourth century BC, with a decline in the first half of the fifth century followed by a long rise to 340 BC. Coarelli has plausibly argued that we should accept Livy's figure of 250,000 in 336 BC, as Rome has now absorbed part of Latium and Campania. These figures also seem to reflect the extension of voting tribes, which slowly increase from twenty-one in 495 BC.[78] It is widely agreed that the tribal figures were genuinely recorded and transmitted to Livy, and the fact that there are no further additions from 495 for the whole of the fifth century is striking. The next major increase is not until 387, when four new tribes were created in the territory of Veii, and from this point on the increase in tribal numbers reflects the increasing census figures. Nevertheless, the issues with the figures before 400 BC mean that they remain deeply problematic.

Society and social institutions

It is also worth examining the society of archaic Rome as a distinct phenomenon, although few studies of Roman social relations incorporate this period. This is understandable given the challenges of approaching the subject with the evidence at our disposal, but it should not lead us to substitute assumption for proper analysis. Interpretations of early Roman society have often been based on institutional 'fossils', such as the *gens* (clan) and *clientela* (patronage), which scholars have seen as pre-dating the city. This approach is perfectly logical but relies on notions of long-lasting Roman conservatism and faces a number of challenges. For instance, recent specialist studies of the *gens* and related institutions have seen them as associated strongly with urban societies and almost impossible to trace earlier. Scholars have turned to archaeological evidence to do this, but serious uncertainties remain about the nature of the social groups attested, and the length of time that they can be attested archaeologically.[79] Other studies show that ancient claims of immemorial traditions in these fields are unsubstantiated, and that Romans both overestimated and misrepresented the level of conservatism in

---

78. See the discussion in Chapter 9, p. 312–14.
79. Riva, *Urbanisation*, 4–12, for the contested nature of the *gens* and critique of the use of archaeological evidence to trace such groups; cf. Bietti Sestieri, 'Role of archaeological and historical data'.

their city, in support of traditional elite power structures.[80] Comparative anthropological studies of pre-industrial societies have tended to highlight their dynamism, and show that change is often obscured for present advantage. It is therefore important to avoid assuming or creating a static picture, and our end result should be a much more dynamic picture of Roman society, as scholars have recently proposed for archaic Greece.[81] There is a further problem in relying on our literary picture of Roman society, in that it overemphasises archaic habits of 'austerity'. This may correspond to a brief period of economic retrenchment in the fifth century BC, which has then been generalised by the literary sources into a wider image. But it is certainly illusory for the seventh and sixth centuries BC, and probably later on too. Nevertheless, it remains clear that many important features of Roman society are of archaic date, and can be identified through critical use of the source material.

One clear feature of Roman society from an early date is the presence of stratified hierarchies. The literary sources attest various elements of the elite, the plebs and slaves under the monarchy. Our narrative histories are not likely to be particularly trustworthy on this, as they tend to assume early social conditions are identical to the later period, but more substantial evidence is available. The elite in Rome is characterised as being formed by a wide range of groups, including the patriciate, the senators (or *patres*), the equestrians (the *equites*), the first class of the centuriate system (which allegedly required a property qualification of 100,000 *asses*), and the leaders of the various clans, the *gentes*. An elite is evident both in Rome and in neighbouring cities of Latium and south Etruria through archaeology from the beginning of the Orientalising period, in the late eighth century BC. We have the remains of prestigious burials, houses, and votive dedications in sanctuaries. This of course contradicts the self-image of the Roman elite as austere and disdainful of wealth. It is true that ostentatious burials came to an end in Rome and Latium in the early sixth century BC, but this is probably a sign not of impoverishment but rather of the formalisation of the elite in urban settlements. By contrast, the frantic display of wealth in the central Italian burials of the Orientalising period is perhaps best seen as a sign of elite insecurity in the fluid conditions of that period. The growth of the city provided new ways to contain elite competition. Rather

---

80. Smith, *Roman Clan*; Bradley, 'Investigating aristocracy'.
81. cf. Vlassopoulos, *Unthinking*, on Greece.

than being manifested in the deposition of grave goods, ostentation amongst the elite was redirected, including into elaborate funeral processions. Our sources date only to around 200 BC and later, but it is likely that such rituals go back early into the Republic, and that these elaborate rituals compensate for changes in burial practice and the diminution of funerary goods.[82]

The existence of an elite implies a differentiated society, with social mobility between it and the plebs. Within the hierarchy of Roman society the plebeians were a group that (at least initially) seems to have been set apart from the elite. By the fourth century BC the plebeians would include families who must have been as wealthy as the established elite, given that they could aspire to share high office with the patricians. The term seems related to Greek *plethos* – multitude.[83] Their status is unclear before the early fifth century BC, when they organise the First Secession (see Chapter 7). They must have been citizens, but in this period citizenship probably offered very limited protection, given that citizens might be subject to debt-bondage (effectively serfdom in the service of a creditor). There is a strong sense in the sources of the plebeian grievance against the cruelty and torture to which they were often subjected. This is briefly mentioned under the monarchy, with Tarquinius Superbus forcing the plebs to labour on public construction works (Livy, 1.56; Dion. Hal. 4.44; Pliny, *HN* 36.24), and then escalates, to become one of the more prolific themes of Roman history in the fifth and fourth century BC. These disputes are likely to be connected to political upheavals in other contemporary Mediterranean societies, notably in Greece and Magna Graecia. Such complaints were typical of the underclass in Mediterranean society according to Finley, with the developing ideologies of *isonomia*, equality before the law, and citizenship in the sixth century BC.[84] The emergence of the plebs must be linked to openness and mobility in the seventh and sixth century, which allowed a massive enlargement of the population. This new population was be integrated into the Roman institutional system through the flexibility of the census, tribes and centuries.[85] That some sort of

---

82. For elite funerals see Plaut. *Amph.* 458–9; Polybius, 6.53; Cic. *Mil.* 33, 86, with Flower, *Ancestor Masks*, 97.
83. Cornell, *Beginnings*, 257.
84. Finley, 'Debt-bondage'.
85. Torelli, 'Dalle aristocrazie'; Ampolo, 'Città riformata'; Bradley, 'Investigating aristocracy'. See further, Chapter 5.

hierarchy and subaltern class existed is also attested by the classes and *infra-classem* of the centuriate system under the monarchy mentioned by antiquarian sources.

A central institution in early Roman society was debt-bondage. This was not the same as chattel slavery, which we know from legal sources also existed from an early period, but was a situation where the debtor came almost totally under the power of the person who gave them a loan. Roman sources called it *nexum* and the debt-bondspeople *nexi*, and state that it was abolished in 326 BC. It was a central issue in the Struggle of the Orders in the fifth and fourth centuries BC (see Chapter 7). Our sources paint a picture of general plebeian indebtedness to the rich, and of them being 'enslaved to the rich'. The *nexi* complained that they were being enslaved by the rich on account of their debts; Livy provides a lurid picture of a worthy ex-centurion, who also suffered this fate:

> But not only was war with the Volsci imminent; the citizens were at loggerheads among themselves, and internal dissensions between the Fathers and the plebs had burst into a blaze of hatred, chiefly on account of those who had been bound over (*nexos*) to service their debts. These men complained loudly that while they were abroad fighting for liberty and dominion they had been enslaved and oppressed at home by fellow-citizens.
>
> [An ex-centurion complained that] during his service in the Sabine war ... he had contracted debts. When these had swelled by usury, they had first stripped him of the farm ... the rest of his property and finally like an infection they had attacked his person, and he had been carried off by his creditor, not to slavery, but to the prison and the torture-chamber. (Livy, 2.23.1–12, 495 BC)

In an innovative study of debt-bondage Moses Finley drew attention to similar types of this institution across the archaic Mediterranean, in Greek societies as well as in Rome. He argued that debt-bondage was the product of the harshness of the ancient law of debt. In return for a loan, so that they could avoid the penalty for debt, the poor would come under the complete control of the creditor, who took possession of their person, and benefited from their labour.[86] Debt was probably aggravated by the lack of Roman military success in the fifth century BC, but in the fourth century BC more successful warfare meant that more land and slaves became available

---

86. Finley, 'Debt-bondage'; Cornell, *Beginnings*, 266–7, 281–2, 330–3.

at the same time as the plebeians became more powerful in political terms. In 326 BC *nexum* was ostensibly outlawed by the Lex Poetelia-Papiria,[87] although continuing references to debtors being held as slaves suggest that the practice continued in some form.

Slavery is assumed to exist under the monarchy by our sources, although the value of these reports is questionable. It is mentioned on several occasions, such as in the case of Servius Tullius, who was the son of a slave woman (a prisoner of war), and a slave himself according to some authors.[88] There are also casual references in the fifth century BC to slaves. In 499 BC the mistreatment of a slave before the Ludi Magni led to divine mispleasure (Cic. *Div.* 1.55). Livy reports that a slave was first freed by *vindicta* (the touch of a staff) in the very first year of the Republic, leading to the custom of enfranchising slaves in this way (Livy, 2.5.9–10). In 460 BC the Sabine Appius Herdonius captured the Capitoline hill with an army of exiles and slaves, and called for Roman slaves to join him (Livy, 3.15). In 420 BC a slave rebellion was averted by informants, who were rewarded by the Senate.[89] The king of Veii used slave actors for a dramatic performance at the Etruscan festival at the Fanum Voltumnae (Livy, 5.1.5). None of these mentions is compelling by itself, given the much later date of our sources. But they correlate with contemporary evidence, such as the references to slaves in the XII Tables (1.14; 1.19; 12.2). Slaves also feature in Etruscan wall paintings of this era (such as the Golini Tomb in Volsinii), and in epigraphy in the form of *lautni*.

Rome is also likely to have had resident foreigners on the lines of Athenian metics. Examples include the Greek Kleikos attested in the Esquiline cemetery, the Etruscan Spurinna known from the Sant'Omobono *tessera hospitalis*, the Etruscan sculptor Vulca, and other craftspeople. Whether such immigrants had a recognised status in archaic Rome, as they did in the exceptionally cosmopolitan Greek city of Athens, is uncertain: they may have been *incolae*, the later legal term for residents in colonies, although the XII Tables uses the term *hostis* (see Chapter 7).

We can also reconstruct some basic features of Roman social relations. One fundamental part of social life is the institution of *clientela*

---

87. Livy, 8.28; Dion. Hal. 16.
88. Stories referred to but doubted by Livy, 1.39.5; cf. 1.40.3. Stories about the slave status of Servius probably derive from the similarity of his name to the Latin for 'slave', *servus*.
89. Livy, 4.45.1–2; see Stewart, *Plautus*, ch. 1 for a discussion of early Roman slavery.

(patronage), attested widely in our narrative texts for the fifth and fourth centuries BC. The ancients regarded the institution as having been founded by Romulus, as part of his primordial organisation of the citizen body (Dion. Hal. 2.9–11; Plut. *Rom.* 13). Unsurprisingly, scholars have been sceptical of this 'foundation' event, and have pointed out various dubious elements: Dionysius' picture of clients obliged to support the costs of their patrons in magistracies and to vote for them in elections is anachronistic, and cannot predate the Republic; Plutarch simplistically reports that Romulus divided the population in two, on one side the senators (*patres*) as patrons, and on the other the multitude as their clients. Both sources regard the institution as a fundamental reason for Rome's social stability (at least relative to ancient Mediterranean standards) in the period before the problems of their own day, and thus use it to construct an idealised picture of early Rome.[90]

But to recognise these issues does not mean that the institution of patronage itself has no archaic currency. This would be implausible given that it is a typical feature of sharply hierarchical societies like Rome.[91] In fact, our sources' emphasis on the power of patron–client relationships, and on their continuation over long periods of time through inheritance, is probably well grounded. It is more likely that *clientela* was a custom that grew up over time, rather than being created by a single founder. It was slowly formalised by legal regulations, such as the provision in the XII Tables that a patron should be *sacer*, condemned to the gods of the underworld, if they harmed their client.[92] This shows that *clientela* must be older than the mid fifth century BC, and supports the historicity of the picture in Livy and other sources of clients playing an important part in the social struggles of the fifth and fourth centuries, in support of their patrician patrons (Livy, 2.35.4; 2.56.3; 2.64.2; 3.14.4 etc.). We also find 'a large body of clients' accompanying Attus Clausus on his migration to Rome in 504 BC, and clients providing an army several thousand strong for the Fabii to fight Veii in 477 (Livy, 2.49.5). It is further evident that clients could include plebeians (Livy, 5.32.8 on the followers of Camillus), and that Roman clients might be found abroad, such as in Etruria (Livy, 4.13.2).

---

90. Brunt, *Italian Manpower*, ch. 8; Drummond, 'Rome', 157–63.
91. Cornell, *Beginnings*, 289–90, with references.
92. See Forsythe, *Critical History*, 217; Burton, *Friendship and Empire*, 31 n. 19 for discussion of the historicity of this notice.

The power of the bond was clearly very strong, reinforced by stories of punishment of wrongdoers, the oaths taken by patron and client, and the sacred aura that surrounded the relationship (clear from the divine punishment for harming clients). There are some hints in our sources that clients owed their position to land provided by the patron (Festus 288 L.; 289 L.), which suggests that the relationship might shade into debt-bondage, with the client being reduced to the patron's serf, if abused by the patron.[93] But it is unlikely to have been an all-encompassing force for elite control: the plebs are said to have opposed the clients of the patricians, implying that they had freedom of action, and could attach themselves as clients to those whom they favoured, such as Camillus; the networks created are likely to have been very complex, with wealthier clients having clients of their own.

We also hear of other followers, called by the archaic term *sodales* (companions). These are attested in the entourage of various elite Romans, such as the group of young princely followers of the Tarquins in 509 BC, the followers of the Fabii when they set out to do battle at Veii, and the youths around Caeso Quinctius in his battle against the plebeians in 461 BC. The archaic character of this term is reinforced by its occurrence in the Lapis Satricanus, a dedication to Mars made at Satricum by the *sodales* of *Poplios Valesios* around 500 BC (Fig. 8.2).[94] The 'companion' seems to be a distinct type of follower of an elite figure, fighting alongside his leader in battle, as part of an entourage with sacred overtones.

Women in early Rome and central Italy

Appian reports that in 278 BC, Cineas, the ambassador of Pyrrhus, brought gifts to win over the Roman side, 'knowing that the people were fond of money and gifts, and that the women had had large influence among the Romans from the earliest times'. The gifts were refused, although an armistice was agreed (App. *Sam*.3.27). Although the story is a typical morality tale about Roman incorruptibility, the remark contradicts two archetypal features of the Roman self-image, that their archaic forebears were austere and that they were strictly patriarchal. Whose view this is (Cineas, Appian, Appian's source, or the Byzantine excerpter of Appian?), is irrecoverable,[95] but the

---

93. Cornell, *Beginnings*, 291.
94. It also crops up in the XII Tables (8.27).
95. The story is mentioned in Livy, *Per*. 13.5 and Plut. *Pyrrh*. 18 without this qualification.

position of women in early Rome is a fascinating topic that ought to have more of a mainstream role in Roman history.[96] There is copious evidence, but there are also many methodological challenges.

A key aim if we are to advance our state of knowledge is to compare the literary material to the archaeological evidence of the Orientalising and archaic periods, particularly in the form of female burials from neighbouring sites in Etruria and Latium. We have important epigraphic evidence from Etruscan and some Latin female tombs. We also have iconographic evidence in the form of tomb paintings and architectural plaques, which show scenes of banqueting and processions with insignia of power. This material is particularly valuable because it is contemporary, but there are some challenges. The most critical issue is the limited state of the burial evidence from Rome, although the presence of near-identical architectural terracottas in Rome and nearby cities shows that Rome must have been very similar to its neighbours.

Various interesting themes emerge from the archaeological evidence for female burials in Etruria and Latium.[97] The most visible tomb groups are those of the Orientalising period, when the richest tombs are often attributed by archaeologists to 'princesses'. Female burials are characterised by jewellery and woolworking equipment such as spindle whorls and spools, spindles and distaffs. They do not generally display weaponry, although there are some exceptions, such as the three shields in the Castellani Tomb at Praeneste.[98] The princely tombs are characterised by collectionism, for example the huge number of items in the Tomb of the Greek Vases, which reflects their acquisition and display in life, and the display of silver plate as wealth. Typically they also contain distinctive symbols of authority. Chariots are present only in the wealthiest graves,[99] but there are other emblems of power such as diadems, pectorals, fans, thrones and various types of transport. These reflect the enthusiastic adoption of a Near Eastern ideology of power, present in Assyria and the Levant, and also include items such as Egyptian-style scarabs, pectorals and faience, and Levantine silver and gilt tableware. The most famous of these are the Regolini-Galassi Tomb at Caere (675–650 BC), perhaps belonging to a woman

---

96. Cf. Osborne, *Greece in the Making*, 226–32, on archaic Greece.
97. Lulof and Van Kampen (eds), *Etruscans* for a clear discussion.
98. Nielsen, 'Etruscan women', 70 on woolworking equipment in female graves at Villanova.
99. Twelve out of 250 chariot burials are female.

called Larthia, and the Bernardini Tomb at Praeneste (675–650 BC), which may be the tomb of a certain Vetusia.[100]

The presence in female tombs of inscribed names on the tableware implies that these women were literate, an impression reinforced by writing equipment such as styluses and tablets, which appear from the seventh century BC, and also many thousands of inscribed mirrors, generally in burials of a later date, with detailed labelling of mythical figures. Other prominent examples include the Bocchoris Tomb at Tarquinii, and the Isis Tomb at Vulci, both containing much Egyptian-influenced material that was probably mediated via Phoenician traders (Fig. 6.5). Female burials in both Etruria and Latium also display much banqueting equipment, designed for use in a symposium style setting. This includes wine containers such as amphorae, wine serving items such as bowls for mixing wine and large decorative stands. In fact, some bowls for mixing wine are attested *only* in female burials. One even has an inscription of greeting to the hostess.[101] Women are also commonly represented at banquet in Etruscan tomb paintings, as seen in the reclining couples of the Tomb of the Leopards, Tarquinii, c.470 BC, or in monuments such as the splendid Sarcophagus of the Married Couple from Caere, c.500 BC (now in the Louvre). Overall, the general impression is of the enthusiastic display of wealth, status and power, with central Italian elite women enjoying a privileged status, and a particularly key role at the feast.

Foreign links seem particularly evident in female graves, possibly as a result of intermarriage and the mixed origins of many wives. Intermarriage between ethnic groups, and between migrants and indigenous populations, is widely attested in archaic central Italy. It has been identified in archaeological evidence, as with the Etruscan wives hypothesised at Pithecusae on the basis of their fibulae, which echo Veientine types, or the Latin women possibly attested through the use of 'suspended rings' decoration in Etruria, Sabinum and Umbria.[102] Intermarriage is also attested in literary sources, notably in the story of Demaratus and his sons marrying local women in

---

100. For the debate about the gender of the tomb occupants, see Sannibale, 'Ori', 344 with earlier references.
101. *GRT* 100: *salvetod tita* on an olla (vase) from Tomb 113, Osteria dell'Osa; cf. *GRT* 101: the inscription in Latin 'I am the urn of Tita Vendia', on an olla from Etruscan Caere, c.630–600 BC.
102. Ridgway, *First Western Greeks*, 67; Coldstream, 'Mixed marriages'.

Economy and society

Figure 6.5 Faience vase with cartouche naming the Pharoah Bocchoris, from a tomb in Tarquinii, late eighth century BC (photo: G. Bradley by concession of the Polo Museale del Lazio – Tarquinia (VT). Museo Archeologico Nazionale)

Tarquinii, the widespread Roman–Latin intermarriage attested by Dionysius (6.1.2), and the marriage of the last of the Fabii with the daughter of Otacilius from Beneventum in 470 (Festus 174 L.). Intermarriage is important, as it offered immigrants a chance to rapidly assimilate within new communities, particularly when it involved elite locals, such as Tanaquil at Tarquinii.

Archaeological evidence is considerably more scarce from Rome itself. This has been regarded as highly significant by some scholars who draw a sharp contrast between Etruscan and Roman women.[103] But the proliferation of wealthy female burials discovered in the neighbourhood of Rome, such as the chariot burials in Latium at Laurentina (Tomb 70, c.675–650 BC) and at Castel di Decima, show that this contrast is quite unwarranted. In fact, a few wealthy female burials have been found in the Forum and Esquiline cemeteries (including one with thirteen fibulae, and another with luxurious imports). In addition, the shared iconography of the Rome–Veii–Velitrae plaque series also suggests a situation of archaic 'cultural koine' (as Ampolo has suggested), rather than sharp ethnic contrast.[104] As we have seen, these are identical revetment plaques dating to around 530 BC from buildings in Rome, Veii (Etruria) and Velitrae (Latium), amongst other sites, showing scenes of women participating in banqueting (including wine-drinking), gatherings of important figures, and processions (Fig. 6.6). These plaques were very probably designed and produced in Rome. All this material undermines later Roman (and Greek) conceptions of women in the archaic city, as well as casting doubt on Roman notions of the ingrained austerity of their archaic ancestors. We should certainly not consider Rome a poorer centre than neighbouring Latin cities.

In terms of the literary evidence, it is notable that female characters are prominent in the tradition on pre-foundation and monarchic Rome, in contrast to the early and middle Republic. We can identify specific roles attributed to women in the tradition. Some are said to act as facilitators, figures who by marriage connect rival groups, such as Lavinia, daughter of Latinus, whose marriage unites Aeneas' Trojans with the indigenous Latins, and Hersilia, wife of Romulus and leader of Sabine women, whose mediation helps unite Romans and Sabines into a single community. The importance of

---

103. E.g. Bonfante, 'Etruscan women'; critique in Glinister, 'Women and power'.
104. Ampolo, 'Presenze etrusche'; Coldstream, 'Mixed marriages'; Iaia, 'Elements of female jewellery'.

Figure 6.6 Illustration of banqueting on an architectural terracotta plaque from the temple of SS. Stimmate, Velitrae, produced in Rome, c.530 BC (drawing: R. Sponer Za, for Winter, *Symbols*, Ill. 5.14.1)

female facilitators continues in the early Republic, as in 491 BC when Veturia and Volumnia lead out the Roman women to prevent Coriolanus and the Volsci from attacking Rome.[105] Women also play a significant role in the foundation story as mothers (such as Rhea Silvia, mother of Romulus and Remus) or surrogate mothers (Larentia, wife of the shepherd Faustulus, who found the wolf suckling the twins and took them back to her to rear). In fact some even argued that the story of the wolf originated from the fact that Larentia was a prostitute (a play on the word *lupa*, which means both wolf and prostitute). Some women are role models, used by later writers to provide moral *exempla* for behaviour. Some are ambivalent and negative models, like Tarpeia (possibly a Vestal priestess), who betrayed Rome to the Sabines in return for gold; she got her just punishment when crushed to death by the Sabines under the weight of their shields. Or Horatia, killed by her brother for daring to weep at the death of an enemy, her betrothed Curiatius, after the duel of the Horatii and Curiatii. The most famous example is Lucretia, whose death triggers constitutional reform and represents the newly born state unsullied by the past. The strangest positive female role model is the virago Cloelia, one of the heroes whose brave acts discourage Lars Porsenna from conquering Rome at the

---

105. Livy, 2.40.1–12.

start of the Republic. She is a girl (*virgo*) who displays 'manliness' (*virtus*) greater than that of men, celebrated, extraordinarily, with an equestrian statue on the Sacra Via.[106]

A few women are depicted in roles of power and influence, for example the mythical Lavinia, who is said to have ruled Lavinium after the death of Aeneas. More historical examples are the queens Tanaquil, the Etruscan wife of Tarquinius Priscus, and her granddaughter Tullia, the daughter of Servius Tullius. They are said to have played a significant role in the monarchic succession, influencing events behind the scenes. Tanaquil persuaded her husband to emigrate to Rome, disliking the loss of status she experienced as the wife of the son of a Greek refugee. En route for Rome, she interpreted an eagle swooping down to lift off and replace Tarquinius Priscus' cap as an omen of his rise to power (the Etruscan skill at interpreting omens was widely recognised in Rome). She also had a major role in the career of Servius Tullius, predicting his future kingship when flames appeared around his head. Following the prodigy, she had him adopted by the king and brought up in the palace, eventually marrying the king's daughter. But Tanaquil had a public role only once, when Priscus is murdered. In a striking scene, she appeared at the palace window asking the people to accept Servius as his deputy until the king recovered, giving Servius the opportunity to consolidate his position and take the throne (Livy, 1.41.4; Plut. *Quaest. Rom.* 36). Since the motif of the 'woman at the window' has Near Eastern origins, some scholars claim that the story reflects the matriarchal function of the queen as a source of royal power.[107]

The second figure shown in a powerful 'kingmaking' role is Tullia, daughter of Servius Tullius. Later writers used her as a classic *exemplum* of the evils of female ambition, inspiring the murders of her husband and sister, in order to marry her brother-in-law Tarquinius Superbus. Tullia pushed him to kill Servius and usurp the throne. After saluting her husband as king at the Senate house, Tullia drove a chariot over her father's corpse at the place later known as the *Vicus Sceleratus* (Wicked Street). Her negative characterisation was connected with the Roman hatred of the tyranny of her husband, and

---

106. Livy, 2.13.11, 'at the top of the Sacra Via was placed [a statue] of the maiden on horseback'; Dion. Hal. 5.35.2; Seneca, *Consolatio ad Marciam* 16.2; Plut. *Pub.* 19.5, *Mor.* 250F; Serv. *Aen.* 8.646; Pliny, *HN* 34.28.
107. Discussed in Cornell, *Beginnings*, 146; Glinister, 'Women and power'.

may have been elaborated in the form of historical dramas on the House of the Tarquins.

In a surprising aspect of a tradition on the kingship that is otherwise male-dominated, Tanaquil and Tullia seem to control the succession through their personal power or influence: the former inspires Servius to take on the king's robes; the latter incites Superbus to murder his way to the top. Both women contrast strongly with the heavily idealised figure of Lucretia, who kills herself when raped by Sextus Tarquinius (the son of Tarquinius Superbus). Her story also reflects later Roman views of proper womanly behaviour, with Lucretia declaring that she must die in order not to provide a precedent for unchaste women (Livy, 1.58.10).

The stories involving royal women are problematic to take at face value, even leaving aside the miraculous elements such as omens and prophecies. They act as hinges for the transition between the rulers of the 'Tarquin dynasty', but as we have seen there is reason to suspect the neatness of the king list was a later construct. For example, there are signs of more violent transitions involving the destruction and reconstruction of monuments such as the Regia and the Forum Boarium; there are also variant traditions on where the kings came from, as well as potential alternative rulers at Rome, such as Caelius Vibenna and Lars Porsenna. Lucretia is a critical figure in the traditional narrative of the setting up of the Republic, but her brief appearance largely provides a plot device to justify Brutus' palace coup. Her tale is also suspiciously similar to moralising stories of other sacrificial maidens whose purity contrasted with the corruption of aspiring autocrats: the classic example is Verginia, whose death led to the overthrow of the tyrannical Decemvirs in 450 BC (Livy, 3.44–8).

Nevertheless, there are also substantial reasons for identifying an element of truth in these stories, and accepting that powerful women played an important role in the later Roman monarchy. The archaeological evidence shows that such figures are to be expected in early Roman society, judging by its immediate neighbours. Royal women are much more prominent in the narrative of the later stages of the monarchy than the earlier, suggesting that the stories were not simply fabricated by later authors. In fact, historically, women tend to have been particularly influential in monarchies because of their role in the palace, which is the centre of political power. In Rome, the critical role they are said to have played in the succession, with candidates typically marrying the daughter of the previous king, seems unlikely to be invented. A balanced assessment therefore suggests that Tanaquil and Tullia are mythologised historical figures, rather than pure myths of later invention.[108] Although our written sources are generally late, the stories themselves predate the examples of Livia and other late Republican women, who are therefore unlikely to provide models. Furthermore, they are probably not an artefact of the profound Hellenisation of Rome in the second century BC, as we know that Fabius Pictor had already provided an account of the Tarquin dynasty in the late third century BC. Rather, they are most likely the product of oral sagas, which were commonly attached to monuments such as the Vicus Sceleratus or the statue of Servius Tullius in the temple of Mater Matuta.[109]

There is also discussion of early Roman women in legal sources and in moralising anecdotes. These sources generally stress the importance of female sobriety, virtue and piety. Thus, Dionysius notes approvingly that Romulus allowed families to punish female drinking of wine, like adultery, by death (Dion. Hal. 2.24). Romulus is said to have absolved Egnatius Mecenius from the murder of his wife as she had drunk wine from the household vat. Fabius Pictor records another instance where a woman was starved to death by her family for 'having opened a purse in which the keys of the wine-cellar were kept'.[110] Punishments for women who drank wine should match those for adultery according to Cato, who adds that a female could legitimately be put to death by the *paterfamilias*.[111] In traditional marital unions, symbolised by the sharing of spelt (*confarreatio*, from *far*), or by fictitious sale (*coemptio*), women were unable to divorce their husbands, and were under 'marital subordination', the *manus* of their husband (Gaius, *Inst.* 1.111). This clear delineation of marital powers was thought to have enhanced the stability of marriage in Rome, and the rarity of divorce before the late Republic. In addition, in the aftermath of the Rape of the Sabines, when the Sabine women agreed to remain in Rome, women were allegedly accorded various honours and recognised as the mistresses of their

---

108. For contrasting positions on this question, see Glinister, 'Women and power', which I follow here; Rathje, 'Princesses'; Wiseman, *Myths of Rome*, 131–2.
109. Livy, 2.13.11; Pollitt, *Art of Rome*, 21, with further references; Ovid, *Fast.* 6.571.
110. Pliny 14.14; Val. Max. 6.3.9; Cornell, *FRH* III 41 for other sources.
111. Cato as cited by Gellius, NA 10.23.1: 'Those who have written about the life and civilization of the Roman people say that the women of Rome and Latium "lived an abstemious life"; that is, that they abstained altogether from wine.'

households, 'exempt from all labour and all drudgery except spinning' (Plut. *Rom.* 19).[112]

This type of evidence is heavily idealised. Our sources, mostly dating as they do to the late Republic or later, are looking back nostalgically, and express ideals of morality, austerity, duty and patriotism. It is clear why these ideals were relevant to late Republican authors and readers, as many scholars have highlighted,[113] but they also have an older history. Roman anxieties about women and the family, and moralising on female behaviour, date to at least the late third century BC: these types of ideas feature in Fabius Pictor, Plautus and Cato. Ritual attention paid to priestly marriage, and stress on the uncorrupted nature of young Vestal candidates, suggests that such ideas probably predate this era too. Of course, institutional fossils such as *confarreatio* and *manus* are significant and are unlikely to be a later fantasy. However, it is difficult to be certain how extensively they were employed. They should probably not be generalised to include all archaic Romans, as ancient sources tend to imply, and they were clearly obsolete by the time that our sources such as Cato were writing.[114]

We need to be cautious in contrasting this evidence for restrictions on Roman women with contemporary archaeological material for the apparent freedoms of Etruscan women, as some scholars have done. A more productive approach is to use the archaeological evidence for central Italian women as a foil for literary idealisations. With the help of archaeology we can reconstruct a rather different picture of high-status women in Etruria, Rome and Latium who were involved in many of the social activities of their male peers, including wine-drinking and networking at banquets.

Finally, women occupied a diverse range of religious roles in archaic Rome and Latium. These included senior female priesthoods such as the Vestal Virgins, the Salian Virgins and the *flaminicae* (wives of the *flamines*, priests of specific deities such as Mars). All these priesthoods probably existed by the later monarchy. This can be supported if not proven by their central role in festivals of archaic character such as the October Horse, which belong to the oldest stratum of the calendar. Active ritual roles are also attested by the archaeological

---

112. Hersch, *Roman Wedding*.
113. Jaeger, *Livy's Written Rome*; Vasaly, *Livy's Political Philosophy*; Fox, *Roman Historical Myths* for examples.
114. Linderski, 'Religious aspects'; Dixon, 'From ceremonial to sexualities'.

evidence of items such as bronze knives from wealthy female tombs in Osteria dell'Osa in the Orientalising period.[115] Recent scholarship has cast doubt on the hypothesis that women were generally prohibited from involvement in sacrifice, or from drinking wine, and have shown that such prohibitions were generally confined to specific contexts or circumstances (such as the ban on sacrifice to Hercules at the Ara Maxima, or drinking wine to excess), rather than acting as a general rule.[116]

Overall, this aspect of Roman society needs to be studied using the contemporary evidence of its near neighbours as much as the later 'mirage' of the literary sources. The increasing archaeological material allows us to document female roles in central Italy more clearly than ever, although it is mute on key questions such as the legal status of women, and marriage. From a critical reading of both types of evidence, women in Rome and central Italy emerge as playing key roles in the mobility and elite networks of these societies. They wield power and authority in terms of influence over the succession and through involvement in religious rites.

In this context, some features of the literary stories about Tanaquil and Tullia as powerful figures seem likely to be historical, although earlier characters such as Hersilia and Tarpeia seem entirely mythical. Some opportunities for power must have been related to structural features of Roman society in this era. Monarchies empower elite women in the ruling family through their role in the palace and court, and it is not by chance that Livia is the next truly significant Roman female powerbroker after Tullia. On the other hand, from the archaeological evidence female roles seem largely domestic.[117] This includes an emphasis on woolworking (attested not only through woolworking equipment in contemporary burials but also in stories about Tanaquil and Lucretia), banqueting and personal adornment. The evidence indicates that while women had important religious roles and could enjoy political influence, they did not hold official political power, instead playing a key role within the household, controlling aspects such as the wealth and lineage of the family.

---

115. Bietti Sestieri, *Iron Age Community*, 131.
116. See further p. 358. Flemming, 'Festus'; Hemelrijk, 'Women and sacrifice', 255. On the link to female social habits like the prohibition from drinking wine: Val. Max. 2.1.5. But see Serv. *Aen.* 1.737.
117. cf. Homeric women, and Izzet, *Archaeology*, on Etruscan women.

Ethnicity

This section collects together the evidence for Roman identity in the period before 290 BC and examines how it relates to the broader context of central Italy and the Mediterranean. These issues have started to be systematically addressed only recently, which is unsurprising given how complex they are.[118] The extent to which Roman identity is likely to have changed in the years from 300–50 BC, as Rome was transformed from a regional power with hundreds of thousands of inhabitants into a Mediterranean superpower governing many millions, is huge. Recovering a sense of Roman identity in 700 BC would be even more challenging. The perspectives of our sources need particular care, given that they were either written by outsiders or date from the late Republic onwards, when Roman identity was bound up with issues of citizenship. The very different situation of the sources' own period may explain their interpretation of the archaic Roman monarchy on ethnic lines, such as the stories of Tarquinius Priscus being ostracised in Tarquinii as the son of an immigrant, or Tarquinius Superbus appealing to Etruscan monarchs on the grounds of shared ethnic background.[119] But there are also other types of literary evidence, such as early Greek sources and antiquarian evidence, and we can also draw on the contemporary evidence of archaeology and epigraphy.

The modern study of the topic really began in 1970 with Carmine Ampolo's pioneering work on Demaratus of Corinth, the Greek father of king Tarquinius Priscus, in which he suggested that ethnic boundaries were little barrier to mobility in archaic central Italy, and that a strong sense of ethnic difference may have been absent in this early period. This offered an interesting contrast with the widely accepted consensus in Italian prehistory that the major central Italian ethnic groups such as the Latins, Etruscans and Sabines and their specific territories are already visible in the material culture of the early Iron Age and epigraphic evidence from the eighth century BC. Scholars are now more alert to the problems of the visibility of evidence (epigraphy is contingent on adopting the habit of inscribing on stone, for instance), and to the problematic legacy in classical archaeology of

---

118. For examples, see Bourdin, *Peuples*, 715–20; Dench, *Romulus' Asylum*; MacMullen, *Earliest Romans*.
119. On ethnic identity in Augustan Rome, influenced by the desirability of Roman citizenship, see Suet. *Aug.* 40, with Dench, *Romulus' Asylum* 257–8. This also affects Virgil's *Aeneid*: see Syed, *Vergil's Aeneid*.

'culture history'.[120] It is no longer assumed that the major Italian ethnic groups emerged fully fledged in the early Iron Age. Nevertheless, other approaches have shown some reason for optimism, such as Blake's study of artefact circulation networks in the late Bronze Age, which seem to contribute to the formation of some central Italian identities.[121] It is also increasingly clear that the interchange between central Italy and other Mediterranean societies had already begun in the Bronze Age, as attested by the presence in Italy of Mycenaean materials, and became more active in the early and later Iron Age.[122] So the pre-existing conditions for a sense of ethnic difference are apparent well before the archaic era, and many Italian ethnicities are likely to have had deep roots.

The most critical era for the development of ethnic identities is probably the Orientalising and archaic periods. The mobility and intense exchange characteristic of this era undoubtedly accelerates the manifestation of ethnic identity.[123] The elite accumulate huge quantities of foreign goods, developing a fascination in particular with Near Eastern symbols of power and prestige. The period also sees the first substantial immigration of foreign artisans and merchants, such as the 'Aristonothos' who created the krater that bears his name at Caere.[124] The circulation of foreigners is widely attested in coastal *emporia* such as Gravisca, Pyrgi and (although of a different type) the sanctuary of Sant'Omobono in the Forum Boarium at Rome. These visitors and residents include Sostratos (a famous Greek trader) and someone identified as Ombrikos ('Umbrian') at Gravisca, Phoenicians at Pyrgi (attested by the Pyrgi tablets), Carthaginians at Rome (the Rome–Carthage treaty) and Etruscans in Carthage (note the name Puniel Karthazie on a *tessera hospitalis*).[125] Demetriou has recently argued that *emporia* played a crucial role in the development of Greek identities through stimulating contact and a sense of difference, and the same must hold for local identities in the places such as coastal Etruria and Rome which they frequented.[126]

---

120. As pioneered by Kosinna and other early twentieth-century archaeologists; for discussion, see Bradley, 'Tribes, states and cities'; Fulminante, 'Ethnicity'.
121. Blake, *Social Networks*; see further the discussion in Chapter 2.
122. Blake, 'Mycenaeans'; Iacono, 'Westernizing'.
123. Isayev, *Migration*, ch. 3.
124. See Chapter 2.
125. For references, see Bradley, 'Investigating aristocracy'.
126. Demetriou, *Negotiating Identity*.

Emerging senses of ethnic identity amongst the peoples of central Italy can also be traced in other ways. Communal sanctuaries and festivals played a powerful role in fostering identities. The origins of most cannot be precisely dated, but some are very ancient, such as the Latin Festival (*Feriae Latinae*) on the Alban Mount, which many scholars have seen as pre-urban and so at least eighth century BC.[127] Others may date to the archaic era (sixth and fifth centuries BC), such as the Etruscan festival at the Fanum Voltumnae, probably the site identified just outside Volsinii that was in use from the late sixth century BC onwards. Others are attested around the same time, such as the Umbrian sanctuary at Hispellum (perhaps dedicated to Jupiter), and the Latin sanctuary of Diana on the Aventine hill at Rome, whose foundation is attributed to Servius Tullius.[128] The impression from these sites is of considerable investment in sanctuaries important to group identities from the sixth century BC. They show that the Latin identity which Rome and its neighbours shared was well established by the seventh and sixth centuries, and reinforced by participation in annual festivals at cult sites.

Early Greek literary sources also provide information about ethnicity in central Italy. The ethnic groups of the Latins and Tyrrhenians are first mentioned by Hesiod in the eighth century BC. In the sixth century BC, Greek sources such as Stesichorus mention Aeneas' voyage to the west (although they may not have connected him with the Latins), and may have discussed Evander's presence at Rome; early Greek awareness of the Etruscans is also evident from the Homeric Hymn to Dionysus (perhaps sixth century BC).[129] However, the imprecise use of 'Tyrrhenians' in these early sources betrays some confusion, and it is very difficult to say how far they reflect local or Greek conceptions.

In ethnic terms Rome seems best characterised as an open and adaptive city. Its accessibility to migrants and visitors was expressed in myth, such as the Rape of the Sabine Women, and also in history, as with the immigration of Etruscans in the late monarchy. Rome had a long history of assimilating 'foreign' ideas, whether Greek, Italic or Etruscan, and the Romans later reflected on this as a source of strength. This tradition of openness is likely to be an unconscious product of a highly mobile archaic environment, rather than the

---

127. Fulminante, *Urbanisation*, 44.
128. Bourdin, *Peuples*, 335–40.
129. See Chapter 3.

result of conscious decision-making by a Romulus-type figure. Fluidity and openness was typical of all central Italian societies, such as south Etruscan cities like Caere and Veii, and Latin cities such as Praeneste and Satricum.[130] Rome seems to have made a particular virtue of these characteristics through its early history, and seems to have been a type of 'frontier city' (in Torelli's illuminating model) along the lines of Etruscan Volsinii, where the complex origins of its citizens are clearly revealed by funerary epigraphy. Romans were, for instance, able to move into exile in neighbouring cities with comparative ease, as in the cases in Table 6.2.[131]

In this context it might be argued that 'Roman identity' is very difficult to pin down. There is little direct evidence from before the second century BC, and most attestations come from literary sources written after the Hannibalic War, when to be 'Roman' meant belonging to something much broader than just the inhabitants of the city, and could apply to a wide range of Italians. Evidence such as the legend *Romano* on coinage dates only from the 270s BC, and there is little trace of a distinctly Roman language or culture at this stage. Nevertheless, it is clear enough that a definite, and perhaps powerful, sense of Roman identity already existed in the archaic period. The Roman myths of origin concerning Evander, Aeneas and Romulus must be at least sixth century BC, if not earlier.[132] These myths stress the connections of Rome with elsewhere, and the mixed character

Table 6.2 Roman exiles in the early Republic

Date BC	Exiles	Reference
After expulsion of Tarquins	Roman exiles in Pomptine plain and Cumae	Dion. Hal. 7.2
509	L. Tarquinius Collatinus at Lavinium	Livy 2.2.10; Dion. Hal. 8.49.6
491	Coriolanus amongst Volscians	Livy 2.35.6; Gell. NA 17.21.11; Dion. Hal. 8.1.6
461	Caeso Quinctius amongst Etruscans	Livy 3.13.8; Dion. Hal. 10.8.4
458	M. Volscius in Lanuvium	Livy 3.29.7
449	M. Claudius at Tibur	Livy 3.58.11; Dion. Hal. 11.46.5
390	M. Furius Camillus at Ardea	Livy 5.32.9; 44.1; Dion. Hal. 14.5.3

130. Bourdin, *Peuples*, 551–89; cf. Bradley, 'Mobility and secession'.
131. Kelly, *History of Exile*, 70.
132. See Chapter 3.

of the population. The terms 'Roman' and 'Latin' are also attested by this period on contemporary epigraphy from Etruria and Sicily, although not from Rome.[133] Further evidence comes from archaic cults and festivals, of likely monarchic date, which celebrate a unified Roman community made up of different elements of the city. Many were linked to the city's topography (such as the cults of the Septimontium, Lupercalia and Argei), to the fortunes of Rome (Vesta, the Triumph), and to the myths of Roman origins (cults of the Ara Maxima, Carmentalia, Penates and the Parilia).

There is also evidence of other ethnicities present in early Rome, notably Sabines and Etruscans. The myths of the Rape of the Sabines, the dual kingship of the Sabine Titus Tatius and Romulus, and the Sabine origins of the kings Numa and Ancus Marcius provide a powerful vision of a mixed community. But the historical significance of such legends is uncertain. More usefully, certain *gentes* amongst the Roman elite claimed Sabine descent, such as the Valerii and the Claudii, who famously migrated from Inregillum in Sabinum in 504.[134] The Sabines were also linked to Veii in the early fifth century BC, and some triumphs in this period were celebrated dually over the Sabines and Veii.

An Etruscan presence in the city is well attested from the late seventh century BC, most obviously in the form of the Tarquin dynasty.[135] It is worth noting that this dynasty had mixed Etrusco-Corinthian origins. Etruscans of the lower orders were also settled in the city as artisans (alongside Latins and probably some Greeks), and were said to have given their name to the quarter of the city known as the Vicus Tuscus. Etruscan influence on early Rome was widely recognised in the ancient sources in terms of the regal insignia, the Triumph, and the organisation of the city, although such borrowings are perhaps overstated by late Republican writers. This literary evidence is supported by a small number of archaic Etruscan inscriptions found in Rome, attesting the presence of Etruscan speakers. De Simone has argued that these show a distinctive Roman dialect of Etruscan, and bilingualism is likely to have been common.[136] Modern scholars have long argued over the nature of this undoubted presence, with Alföldi

---

133. Colonna, 'Quali Etruschi', on Etruscan evidence for 'Roman'; Malkin, *Returns*, 184 on 'Latinus'. See also p. 293.
134. Bradley, 'Mobility and secession'.
135. See discussion in Chapter 4.
136. De Simone, 'Etruschi a Roma'; Adams, *Bilingualism*, 160–3.

claiming that archaic Rome was an insignificant centre controlled by successive Etruscan powers. More recent scholarship has preferred to emphasise the independent position of Rome within a situation of cultural koine along the Tyrrhenian coast.[137] Nevertheless, it remains likely that there was substantial Etruscan influence on monarchic and early Republican Rome.

Overall, therefore, Rome was probably from its earliest origins a multi-ethnic frontier city, and as a result, a clear sense of unified ethnicity in archaic Rome is difficult to recover. Nevertheless, we have established three main points. First, the intense interactions and mobility of the Orientalising and archaic period form a vital background to discussions of ethnicity. Rome was part of a network including the Etruscan cities, Latium and Campania in central Italy, and Sicily, Sardinia, Massilia, Carthage and the Aegean in the wider Mediterranean world. We have evidence for Latins on the island of Sicily in the seventh century BC, and Romans travelling throughout the Tyrrhenian sea are mentioned in the Rome–Carthage treaty at the end of the sixth century BC. Secondly, this situation is difficult to describe in terms of ethnic blocks, such as Latins, Sabines, Greeks and Etruscans, which oversimplify the complexities of the archaic era. For instance, the common idea of an 'Etruscan Rome' under the Tarquins neglects the mixed Corinthian–Tarquinian background ascribed to Tarquinius Priscus, and the Latin or Etruscan background of Servius Tullius. More helpful are modern notions of 'entangled histories', which recognise that ancient societies such as Athens and Rome are rarely monoethnic, and that trying to sift out original, primary identities in these cities is unhelpful. A third point is that the openness of the archaic era was slowly transformed as states grew in the seventh to fifth centuries BC, and citizenship structures made the place of residence more critical. In the fifth and fourth century BC mobility was also slowly drawn under Roman state control as it was channelled into colonisation schemes, although it remained a continual feature of the wider environment.[138] The archaic era thus bequeathed a complex situation of mobility and emerging ethnicities to the later era, which remembered it through stories, myths, institutions and customs.

---

137. Alföldi, *Early Rome*, with the review by Momigliano in *JRS* 57 (1967), 211–16. Cornell, *Beginnings*, ch. 6; 'Ethnicity'.
138. Bradley, 'Colonization and identity'; Isayev, *Migration*, chh. 4–5; Horden and Purcell, *Corrupting Sea*, 342–400.

CHAPTER 7

Rome in the early Republic

The new Republic

The new form of Republican government was traditionally set up in 509 BC, when the king was shut out of the city. Although in hindsight the transition from monarchy to Republic is regarded as an epochal change, very little constitutional reform seems to have taken place. According to the literary sources, *imperium*, the pre-existing power of the king, was shared between two consuls (perhaps originally called praetors),[1] whose term of office was limited to one year. *Imperium* was required to lead the army, and conveyed the power of life and death over subordinates both in military and in civilian contexts. These magistrates were elected by the *comitia centuriata*, the centuriate assembly, which had reportedly been set up by Servius Tullius. Subsequently, in the later fifth and early fourth century BC, there was a phase in which there were more than two supreme magistrates, known as military tribunes. These magistrates, like the king and the *custos urbis* before them, had the right to convoke the Senate.[2]

Later Romans believed that most institutions continued as before. The major Roman assemblies were all thought to predate 509 BC. The centuriate assembly was very likely a monarchic institution, although the level of its complexity in regal Rome is disputed (see Chapter 4). As we have seen, most modern scholars have claimed that it becomes more elaborate in the fifth or fourth century BC, but the evidence for this is largely based on inference. The other main assembly, the *comitia tributa* (tribal assembly), is also credited to Servius Tullius.[3] These assemblies seem to have superseded the *comitia curiata* (curiate assembly), whose foundation was attributed to Romulus. All the major priesthoods, such as the *pontifices* (pontiffs), augurs, Vestals

---

1. See Chapter 4.
2. *Custos urbis* was the original term for the *praefectus urbi*: Lydus, *Mag.* 1.34, 38; cf. Tac. *Ann.* 6.11.
3. Doubts in Mouritsen, *Politics*, 38.

and *duumviri sacris faciundis* ('board of two for sacred affairs') are said to have continued unchanged from the monarchy. Only the *rex sacrorum*, the 'king of sacred things', is allegedly instituted at the start of the Republic, although as we have seen, there are considerable doubts about this chronology. In addition, the sources present the Senate as continuing in its previous form as a board of advisors. According to Festus (290 L.) the Senate was first made up of the friends of the king, and then with the Republic became a group of advisors of the consuls. There remains considerable uncertainty over whether membership was ad hoc and changed yearly (so Festus), or semi-permanent (as sources such as Livy imply, possibly anachronistically).[4] The composition of the Senate was clearly altered by the Lex Ovinia, one of a series of radical tribunician bills in the later fourth century BC.

Thus, the sources record surprisingly little change in the structure of the state, given that we might have expected the patriotic Roman version of the story to exaggerate the role of the founders of the Republic. Whether this picture is reliable is open to question given that our earliest written sources are at least three hundred years later than these events and there are major problems with the traditional account of the late sixth century BC.[5] The prevalent Roman conception of the incremental foundation of the city by multiple kings also may mean that more institutions were attributed to the monarchy than should have been. Nevertheless, we might expect more innovation attributed to the heroic Republican founders. In fact, we find in many other archaic Mediterranean cities such as Athens, Corinth and the cities of Magna Graecia that single rulers played as important a role in constructing and modifying state institutions as later, more democratic regimes.

Two sources offer support to the picture of continuity in our historical tradition. Antiquarian authors such as Festus record details about early institutions independently of the historical tradition. They also support a regal date for many institutions, such as the Servian constitution and most of the priesthoods.[6] This picture is also to some extent supported by the archaeology of the physical infrastructure of the city. Admittedly, archaeology often does not neatly

---

4. Festus 290 L. with Cornell, 'Lex Ovinia'; accepted by Jehne, 'Rise of the consular', 218; doubts in Forsythe, *Critical History*, 168; Mouritsen, *Politics*, 37.
5. See Chapter 4; cf. Wiseman, 'Roman Republic'.
6. See the discussion above in Chapter 4.

map onto institutional structures, as Jonathan Hall has pointed out.[7] For instance, there is only one assembly place apparent archaeologically inside the city, and the *comitia centuriata* met outside the walls, without a physically bounded space. In addition, magistrates were not allocated dedicated offices, but used temples for public business. Nevertheless, the general continuity across this period in the main urban spaces and their buildings is very striking. This includes the Senate house, assembly place, the temple of Jupiter, and the temples of Castor and Saturn, and perhaps the Circus.[8]

The patriciate

The new magistracies of the Republic came to be dominated by 'patricians', members of favoured *gentes* (clans). They enjoyed various privileges that originated in the monarchy and continued into the Republic. The origins of the patricians are unclear and controversial. They occupied a privileged position under the monarchy and early Republic. According to our sources, Romulus created a Senate of 100 members, whose descendants were known as patricians (e.g. Livy, 1.8.1; Dion. Hal. 2.8.3; Cic. *Rep*. 2.23; Plut. *Rom*. 13). According to Dionysius (2.8.1) he 'distinguished those who were eminent through their birth, approved for their virtue and wealthy for those times, provided they already had children, from the obscure, the lowly and the poor'. The latter were the plebeians. The term *patricii* probably comes from *patres* ('fathers'), commonly used to refer to senators. Patrician status was inherited (hence the careful cultivation of ancestral lineage amongst elite Republican families), and was ultimately thought to derive from the original Romulean Senate. In scholarship of the late nineteenth and early twentieth centuries the primordial distinction between patricians and plebeians was explained in terms of racial conquest (e.g. of Sabines over Ligurians, or Aryans over Mediterranean peoples). But there is no basis for this interpretation in the ancient evidence, and it is clearly influenced by contemporary ideas of 'more civilised' nations conquering and controlling the 'racially inferior' peoples of their colonies.[9] It is also problematic to see the patricians as descendants of the original Romulean senators, as our

---

7. Hall, *Artifact*, ch. 8.
8. See Hall, *Artifact*, 158–62 and Hopkins, *Genesis*, 163–71, on this continuity in archaeology.
9. Critique of these ideas in Cornell, *Beginnings*, 243 and Cornell, 'Ethnicity'.

sources assert them to be. The Senate was not exclusively patrician at any stage of its history, as far as we can tell, and was not evidently a stable entity until the mid Republic.[10] Patrician privileges seem in fact to be independent of the Senate's nature as an institution.

The origins of the patricians are more likely to be the product of the slow emergence from the late Bronze Age to the fifth century BC of this dominant social group, claiming primordial ancestry, and consolidating their hold over various sources of power in the monarchy.[11] The emergence of individuals with a claim to an inherited position of superiority within the social hierarchy is recognisable in the funerary archaeology of central Italy from the late Bronze Age.[12] Funerary display particularly develops in the Orientalising period, from c.720–580 BC. Burial goods manifest aspirations of a princely lifestyle, based on Near Eastern ideals of luxury and monarchic rule, amongst these new social elites. Many of the grave goods, such as sacrificial knives, sceptres, thrones, footstools, parasols and chariots, manifest the claim of the family of the deceased to political and religious dominance. These items extend to burials of women and children, indicating that high status was not just enjoyed by adult males but extended to entire families. Over the course of the seventh century BC the structure of high elite burials became more elaborate, with multiple burial chambers set within enormous tumuli, apparently representing elite claims to the multi-generational inheritance of position. Often an element of ancestor worship was included.[13] By the end of the seventh century BC this myth of aristocratic power had been bolstered by the creation of great palaces such as those at Murlo and Acquarossa.[14] We know from epigraphy that these elites were mobile, well connected across the Mediterranean world, and permeated by wealthy outsiders. But the archaeological evidence suggests that already by the middle of the seventh century BC the elites in central Italy were making claims of a primordial right to power of the type recognisable from the portrayal in the literary sources of the patriciate in the Struggle of the Orders.[15]

Recent scholarship has taken two contrary positions on the extent of aristocratic power in early Rome. Some have argued that the state

---

10. Cornell, *Beginnings*, 245–50.
11. Torelli, 'Dalle aristocrazie'; Bradley, 'Investigating aristocracy'.
12. Fulminante, *Sepolture*.
13. Riva, *Urbanisation*, 124–31.
14. Torelli, *Storia*, 248–9.
15. For further discussion see Bradley, 'Investigating aristocracy'.

was really a vehicle largely controlled for their own interest by powerful clans (*gentes*) that endured over huge spans of time from the Bronze Age to the late Republic. This view is in part inspired by a comparative approach, based on the copious archaeological evidence for the extraordinary accrual of wealth by Orientalising elites, and on the literary evidence for the power of the patriciate and other comparable elites in other central Italian cities (particularly those in Etruria). One example might be the naming, in the monarchy and early Republic, of various rustic tribes apparently after particular *gentes* (such as the Claudii and Fabii), which may reflect the domination of landholding in these districts by particular families or clans.[16] This has led some scholars to envisage an almost mafia-style state, run to perpetuate elite dominance over the masses, rather than for any notion of the public good. Others have emphasised the extent to which the existence and flourishing of the *gentes* is connected with state formation, and that these *gentes* cannot be assumed to be primordial in origin. Indeed a more critical approach to elite claims of ancestral heritage and rights, characterised as 'aristocratic myths' in comparative work, emphasises that elite power was always in tension with other institutions, and always contested by other groups in Roman society.[17] As Richardson has recently pointed out, a state requires the consent of its population to work effectively and expand successfully in the way that Rome did.[18]

Modern scholars do not agree on a list of patrician families, and no recent work of scholarship has attempted a definitive list. According to Dionysius (1.85) there were fewer than fifty families by the late Republic. The high level of mortality in antiquity took a heavy toll on family continuity, and some patrician families seem to have died out by the middle Republic. The patriciate is likely to have been more numerous originally, and perhaps numbered as many as one hundred and thirty families. It is clear that the patriciate had groups added to them over time. This included a group of *minores gentes* ('minor clans'), whom Tarquinius Priscus is said to have added to the Senate as a result of the expansion of the Roman population (Livy, 1.35),

---

16. Torelli, *Storia*, 247. For this general approach see Torelli, 'Popolazioni'; Terrenato, 'Versatile clans'; Armstrong, *War and Society*, 129–82; and now Terrenato, *Early Roman Expansion*.
17. Smith, *Roman Clan*, 299; Bradley, 'Investigating aristocracy'. For 'aristocratic myths' see Doyle, *Aristocracy*, 22–39.
18. Richardson, 'The people and the state'.

although the *maiores gentes* ('greater clans') retained the prerogative of speaking first in the Senate. The *minores gentes*, however, were not exclusively patrician, but included plebeian families as well.[19] Another group was added to the Senate at the start of the Republic, known as the *conscripti* ('enrolled'), from which the typical address of the Senate as *patres (et) conscripti* came (Livy, 2.1.10–11; Dion. Hal. 5.13.2). There is also the late case recorded by Livy of the clan of the Claudii being added to the patriciate after its leader Attus Clausus emigrated to Rome from the neighbouring region of Sabinum with his relatives and followers, traditionally in 504 BC.[20]

The power of the patricians was based on their exercise of various privileges.[21] They had *auctoritas patrum*, the right of approving decisions made by the assemblies. This included lawmaking and elections of the *comitia centuriata* and *comitia curiata*. This privilege was removed by the Lex Publilia (339 BC) and the Lex Maenia (287 BC), which required the *patres* to approve the action of the assembly before a vote took place, rather than potentially veto it afterwards. The patricians also claimed exclusive rights to hold the *interregnum* (see Chapter 4 above). This implies that they were able to play a role in choosing a king. In addition, the patricians monopolised the major priesthoods and claimed the sole right of interpreting the will of the gods through 'holding the auspices' (*auspicia*). Livy provides a revealing response to plebeian demands to hold the consulship in 445 BC:

> When the consuls had come forth to the people and set speeches had given place to wrangling, the tribune demanded what reason there was why a plebeian should not be chosen consul; Curtius replied to him, with truth perhaps, yet, in the circumstances, to little purpose, 'because no plebeian has the auspices, and that is the reason the decemvirs have forbidden intermarriages [between plebeians and patricians], so that the auspices should not be confounded by the uncertain standing of those born of them'. At this the plebeians fairly blazed with anger, because it was declared that they could not take the auspices, as though they were hated by the immortal gods. (Livy, 4.6, 445 BC)

---

19. This is clear from Suetonius, *Aug.* 1.2, which shows that the kings such as Servius Tullius could create new patrician families.
20. Livy, 2.16.4–5; Dion. Hal. 5.40.3–5. This migration is presented by our sources as the result of a purely internal dispute, but it is evident that the patriciate is part of an internationally connected mobile elite.
21. Smith, *Roman Clan*, 256.

Whilst it is reported speech, it does represent what Livy thought was at the root of the problem. This should be treated as a reflection of disputed patrician claims rather than a constitutional principle, and may illuminate early Republican elite ideology.

This is no longer an issue after the middle Republic, when new laws allowed the plebeians to hold the major priesthoods. In the monarchical period and the early Republic the most important priestly colleges (the pontiffs, the augurs, the board of two for sacred affairs) and the major individual priesthoods (the *flamines* of particular gods and the *rex sacrorum*) were all required to be patrician. The archaic nature of many of these offices, particularly the *flamines*, helps reinforce the perception that the religious foundation of patrician power is likely to be a genuine early feature.[22] This has a number of interesting implications. In the monarchical period, the patricians clearly operated as an alternative source of religious authority to the king, despite his political and judicial power. They may have had the right to approve the appointment of the king. When the king was replaced by the consuls, his political and judicial powers were divided into two yearly appointments and opened up for competition, and could be held by non-patricians, at least in the early days of the Republic. But the religious power of the patricians, which surely predated the Republic, remained undiminished, and could be used to lever control over the assemblies and magistrates of the new Republic.[23]

The emergence of the plebeian movement

Political and social opposition to the patricians came from the plebeian movement. Social strife developed in the early Republic hand in hand with a deterioration in economic conditions. Rome suffered a series of military setbacks at the hands of its enemies, particularly the Volsci and Aequi, and lost control of territory that had been gained by the end of the monarchy. Hence, it is not surprising that according to our sources the major concerns of the plebeians included the burden of debt, the lack of land and the distribution of food. All these demands are plausible in an early fifth-century context. Much of this must be connected to the expansion of the city in the seventh and sixth centuries BC, as immigrants were attracted into the city by the

---

22. Cornell, *Beginnings*, 251–2; Smith, *Roman Clan*, 258–68. The Vestals are said to have included plebeians in the monarchy.
23. Cornell, *Beginnings*, 252.

employment prospects on building projects and other economically rewarding activities. Many of the families who went on to hold plebeian offices seem to have been of non-Roman origin.[24] However, the plebeians were not purely or even mostly made up of urban dwellers, and it would be a mistake to see them simply as newcomers against the older-established patricians. In the Roman tradition, both orders go back to Romulus. The elite claim to a primordial origin in the city is in any case likely to be a myth, and it is impossible to understand the Struggle of the Orders without hypothesising that many plebeians were farmers who owned property and served in the army.[25]

Other factors gave impetus to the plebeian movement. First, the masses had probably become more important in the latter stages of the monarchy, as the last kings are said to have sought popular support for their rule against the senatorial (and perhaps wider) elite. Servius Tullius is clearly presented in this light, and a similar case can be made for Tarquinius Priscus, who energetically sought the plebs' support, and Tarquinius Superbus, who attacked the established aristocracy.[26] The magistrates of the new Republic must have relied for legitimation on the curiate and centuriate assemblies, which already existed under the monarchy. The centuriate assembly was weighted prejudicially against the poor (and excluded the poorest), through the unequal distribution of voting groups (centuries). But the very mechanism of electing magistrates, introduced with the Republic, must have encouraged aspirations towards more representative government.[27] Secondly, the Romans were well acquainted with contemporary Greek states, such as those in south Italy and Sicily. Connections are attested both in the literary evidence and through contemporary archaeological material.[28] Democratic movements were common here, even if they often failed in the long term. Thirdly, the nature of the army had changed in the

---

24. Lanfranchi, *Tribuns*, 92–8, with table 2, 679–95.
25. Torelli, 'Dalle aristocrazie'; Smith, *Roman Clan*, 275; Bradley, 'Mobility and secession'. Lanfranchi, *Tribuns*, 92 notes that consular and patrician families were as commonly of non-Roman origin as tribunes' families.
26. Tarquinius Priscus: Livy, 1.35.2. Servius: Cic. *Rep.* 2.37–8; Livy, 1.46.1; Plut. *De fort. Rom.* 10; see in general Cornell, *Beginnings*, 145–50.
27. Smith, *Roman Clan*, 276. Some magistrates may have been elected under the monarchy, such as *interreges*.
28. Architectural terracottas produced in Rome in the sixth century BC turn up at Pithecusae and Cumae, and the artists who worked on the temple of Diana on the Aventine were probably Sicilian (see Chapters 5 and 6).

sixth and fifth centuries BC.[29] Heavily armed infantry, with hoplite armour, had taken over as the dominant constituent of military forces in the sixth centuries BC. The role of the cavalry (dominated by the elite) was diminished, and ordinary landowners who could self-equip as hoplites became more important to the state.

The peak of patrician power in Rome is probably in the second half of the fifth century BC. The evidence of the *Fasti Consulares* is critically important here. The *Fasti* show that some non-patricians gained the top magistracy in the first half of the fifth century BC. This proportion declined as the fifth century went on, reducing from 21 per cent in the first quarter, to 7 and 8 per cent in the second and third, and finally to 1 per cent in the last.[30] Many of the holders seem to have been of foreign origin, to judge by their names, which are attested epigraphically elsewhere in central Italy (Table 7.1).[31] Others are of uncertain plebeian status, as there is a significant gap before others of the same name come to hold plebeian magistracies. The *Fasti* have been doubted by many scholars, but there is a clear pattern visible in them, unlikely to be invented. Non-patrician names do not increase (as we might otherwise expect given that they later came to share government with the patricians), but rather decrease dramatically. Hardly any plebeians feature in the *Fasti* in the second half of the century. This process has been called the 'Closure of the Patriciate', as they came to dominate the newly created offices of the Republic. It was ultimately challenged in the fourth century BC by the plebeian movement, which had probably formed as an alliance of the oppressed poor and the richer non-patricians in the late sixth and early fifth century BC.[32]

The plebeian secessions and mobility

The first organised action of the plebeian movement was the 'secession' of 494 BC.[33] A secession was an organised withdrawal from the city. Three are attested in the canonical version of early Roman history in Livy and Dionysius of Halicarnassus, and they led to the patricians conceding a range of measures in favour of the plebeian organisation.

---

29. See Chapter 9.
30. Cornell, *Beginnings*, 254.
31. Bourdin, *Peuples*, 543–4.
32. Momigliano, 'Rise of the plebs'; Cornell, 'Failure of the *plebs*'; Raaflaub, 'Conflict of the orders'; for a different view, see Drummond, 'Rome'.
33. This section represents a reworking of my argument in Bradley, 'Mobility and secession'.

Table 7.1 Patricians of presumed foreign origin[a]

Gens	Date of accession to the consulship (BC)	Presumed origin
Tarquinii	509	Etruscan
Horatii	509	Etruscan
Valerii	508	Sabine
Lucretii	508	Etruscan
Larcii	506	Etruscan
Herminii	506	Etruscan
Postumii	505	Sabine
Menenii	503	Etruscan?
Verginii	502	Etruscan
Cominii	501	Etruscan
Aebutii	499	Etruscan
Veturii	499	Etruscan, Sabine?
Claudii	495	Sabine
Nautii	488	Etruscan, Latin?
Siccii	487	Etruscan
Aquilii	487	Etruscan
Manlii	480	Etruscan
Volumnii	461	Etruscan
Romilii	455	Etruscan?
Tarpeii	454	Etruscan?
Aternii	454	Etruscan?
Folii	433	Sabine, Volscian?

[a] From Bourdin, *Peuples*, table 28, 543–4, based on Ranouil, *Recherches*.

The First Secession is said to have taken place in 494 BC to the Sacred Mount (Mons Sacer), a hill north of the Tiber and some 5 km from the city (Fig. 7.1). The story of the First Secession in Livy and Dionysius begins with a debt crisis, which led to a large portion of the plebs becoming indebted, and subject to creditors' abuses. An army was enlisted to fight against the Volsci, Aequi and Sabines, but then refused to go to war, diverting instead to the Sacred Mount. There the plebeians under military service were joined by the mass of the plebeian city dwellers. Various discussions took place, and eventually peace was restored between the Senate and the plebeians, with

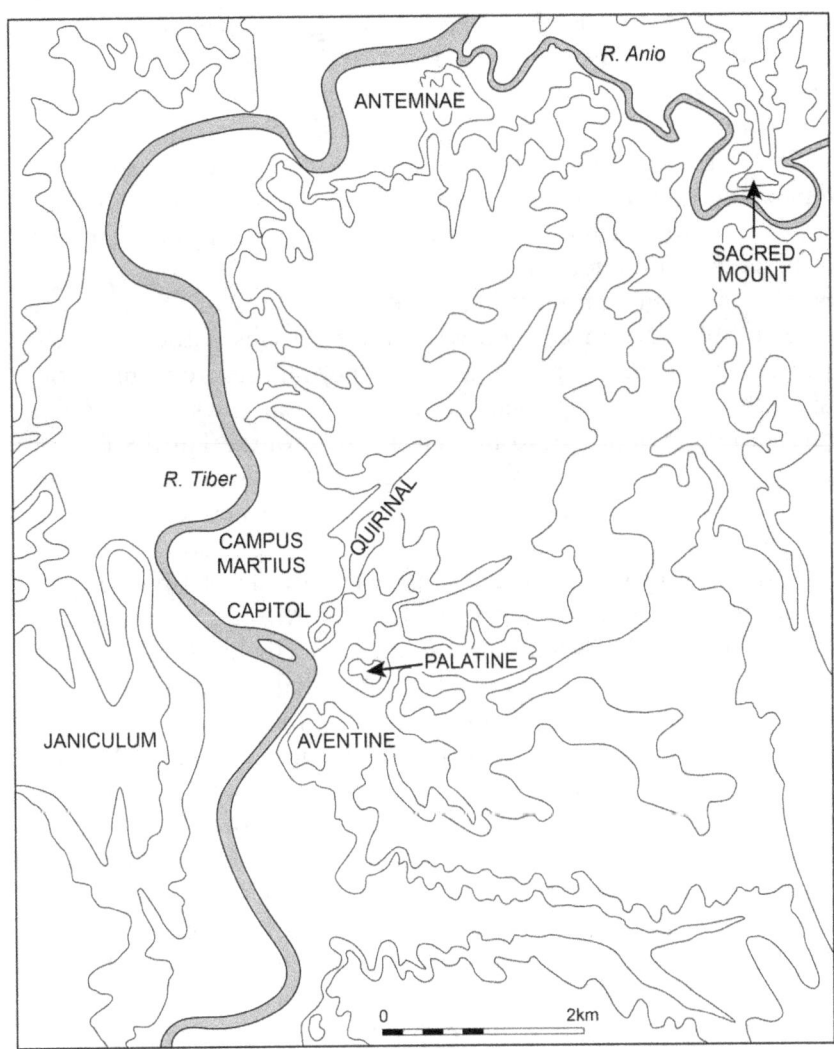

Figure 7.1 The sites of the plebeian secessions (after Wiseman, *Remus*, 115)

the latter being allowed to elect representatives, known as tribunes of the plebs, for the first time.[34]

The Second Secession is dated by our sources to 450 BC, and was associated with the ending of the Decemvirate. This was a board of ten men appointed to replace the existing magistrates and draw up a

---

34. Livy, 2.21–33; Dion. Hal. 6.41–89.

law code for Rome. When the Decemvirs began to behave in a tyrannical fashion, the plebs sought to overturn the regime. Those serving in the army at first assembled on the Aventine hill in the south of the city, and then ultimately withdrew to the Sacred Mount again (Fig. 7.1). The Second Secession in particular comes down to us in a complex and dubious narrative tradition. It is a story woven around exemplary figures such as the tyrannical Decemvir Appius Claudius, and the sacrificial maiden Verginia.[35]

Finally, in the most poorly attested episode, the Third Secession of the plebs took place in 287 BC, when the plebeians withdrew to the Janiculum hill. They returned only when they had secured a final concession, the right of the plebeian assembly to pass laws fully binding on the entire population of Rome. The sources for the Third Secession suffer less from obvious problems, in part as there is so little information on it, and we have lost Livy's narrative for this period.[36]

The sources provide variant traditions on the destination, date and number of the secessions. The main tradition identifies the destination of the First Secession as the Sacred Mount, in the district of Crustumerium, between the Anio and the Tiber.[37] A variant version, less common according to Livy, identified the Aventine as the destination.[38] The Livian tradition indicates that there were two further secessions, in 450 BC to the Aventine and Sacred Mount, and in 287 BC to the Janiculum, but other sources give different numbers; it is not clear that they represent more authoritative traditions.[39] Some authors have argued that a notice in Diodorus (11.68.8) indicates that the First Secession really took place in 471 BC; but Diodorus merely reports that this was the first time four, rather than two, tribunes were elected. Our sources also differ on the names of the first elected tribunes, and Livy notes that some versions have only two tribunes elected in the first instance.[40]

Some of the details of these accounts may be problematic because of later distortions. The parallels between the secessions and the withdrawal of C. Gracchus to the Aventine in 121 BC raise questions about

---

35. Livy, 3.50–4; Wiseman, *Clio's Cosmetics*, 77–84.
36. Livy, *Epit.* 11; Pliny, *HN* 16.37; *Dig.* 1.2.2.8.
37. Livy, 2.32.4, Dion. Hal. 6.45, Varro, *Ling.* 5.81; see Richard, *Origines*, 547–9, and Mignone, *Republican Aventine*, 17–23, with further references, who defend the tradition.
38. Piso (late second century BC) in Livy, 2.32.4 and perhaps Sallust, *Iug.* 31.17.
39. Sallust, *Iug.* 31.17: two; Ampelius 25: four.
40. Ogilvie, *Commentary*, 309–12; Richard, *Origines*, 541; Livy, 2.33.3.

whether the latter provided the model for the former.[41] The parable of the parts of the body told by Menenius Agrippa to convince the plebs to return to Rome and resolve the crisis drew on early Greek stories, as Dionysius recognised (6.83.2); the role of the Claudii as archetypal villains in both the First and Second Secessions, in contrast with the very positive role attributed to the Valerii, has generated legitimate suspicions that the annalist Valerius Antias has had a distorting effect on the history of his ancestors.[42]

In contrast, details such as the role of debt in the Struggle of the Orders seem more plausible.[43] The *Lex sacrata* passed by the plebeians, a sacred law (of protection for the tribunes) that probably originated as an oath, also seems plausible. This is a typically Italic phenomenon with military overtones, being used by other Italic peoples such as the Samnites to levy troops, and in the context of the Sacred Spring rite.[44] According to Dionysius (6.89.3), the oath sworn by the plebeians included the dedication to Ceres of the goods of anyone who violated sacrosanctity. Ceres is a cult with Campanian links, and in 493 BC, soon after the First Secession, was honoured by a temple on the Aventine. It was dedicated to the triad of Ceres, Liber and Libera, an innovative Roman mix of Italic deities. Thus, rather than being a later invention, the oath to Ceres fits well in an early Republican context.[45] The plebs could be understood as a group akin to the mobile armed bands of the archaic period, devoted to a particular tutelary deity, and potential founders of a new community on land that they conquered.

The historical issues with the secessions are discussed at some length in modern scholarship. Most authors accept the historicity of the last secession in 287 BC, which is likely to be historical given that it is within a few generations of the first Roman historian, Fabius Pictor (writing in the late third century BC).[46] Modern authors have particularly questioned the authenticity of the early secessions. Some have regarded the repetition of secessions as suspicious, and doubt that the social struggle would have been ongoing for over two centuries, with

---

41. E.g. Ogilvie, *Commentary*, 311; Mignone, *Republican Aventine*, 17–47.
42. Ogilvie, *Commentary*, 311; Wiseman, *Clio's Cosmetics*, 65–76, who sees a contradictorily mixed tradition on the Claudii.
43. Cornell, *Beginnings*, 265–8; Gabrielli, 'Debiti'.
44. Ogilvie, *Commentary*, 313–14; Cornell, *Beginnings*, 259.
45. Ogilvie, *Commentary*, 314; Spaeth, *Roman Goddess Ceres*, 86.
46. Raaflaub, 'Conflict of the orders', 209.

the plebeians seemingly taking an extraordinarily long time to achieve their ends. On this interpretation the earlier examples were modelled on the secession of 287 BC. Others have argued that the narrative is unbelievable and modelled on Greek stories.[47]

In fact, the unique nature of the early secessions is more striking, and should be understood in the context of the widespread inter-community mobility of the first half of the fifth century BC.[48] The Third Secession is quite different: it occurs considerably later, involves a different venue much closer to the city, and represents an apparent military threat to the city. It therefore makes an unlikely model for the first two secessions. The unprecedented nature of the story of the First and Second Secessions, and the general unanimity of the traditions on the broad lines of events, supports their historical nature.[49] As Lintott has noted, the presentation of the plebeian secessions as intense political strife but not leading to violence makes it unlikely that they were modelled on stories of stasis in Greek states. The uniqueness of the events is in fact a powerful argument in favour of their authenticity rather than a sign of their invention.[50]

Modern views of what a secession signified vary widely.[51] For Mommsen, the First Secession 'threatened to establish in this most fertile part of the Roman territory a new plebeian city'.[52] For others, this was potentially a rival state that might join Rome's enemies, given that many of the plebeians originated elsewhere. The secession is defined in standard reference works as 'technically a withdrawal from the state' and an 'extreme form of civil disobedience' which 'implies detachment from public life as well as emigration from Rome'.[53] Other authors have been more cautious, arguing that it was clearly distinct from a defection, and the plebs were keen to ensure that they remained part of the Roman state.[54]

---

47. Forsythe, *Critical History*, 174, claims it was likely to have been modelled on the Herodotean story of Telines, ancestor of Gelon (Hdt. 7.153). However, this story is very sketchily outlined in Herodotus and provides only a weak parallel with the Roman story.
48. Bradley, 'Mobility and secession'.
49. Richard, *Origines*, 541–7; Cornell, *Beginnings*, 258, is more cautious.
50. Lintott, *Constitution*, 32.
51. Discussed in Poma, 'Secessioni'.
52. Mommsen, *History of Rome*, 280.
53. Gagarin and Fantham (eds), *Oxford Encyclopedia of the Ancient World*; Hornblower et al. (eds), *Oxford Classical Dictionary*.
54. E.g. Daube, *Civil Disobedience*, 143, noting that the sources deliberately use the term *secessio* rather than *deficere* or *defectio*.

The contrary nature of these views is in part determined by disagreements over who the plebeians were, which in turn reflects the complexity of the picture in the sources. So Ogilvie argues that the plebs were for the most part craftspeople and businesspeople, recent émigrés, lacking a patron's protection (which contradicts the image in the sources of impoverished farmers). For Momigliano, the plebs largely belonged to the *infra classem* (or *proletarii*), the group lacking the property qualification for the army. This would explain why plebeian demands were not immediately met, and why Appius Claudius disparages the commitment of the plebs to war.[55] But this interpretation also meets the difficulty that the sources unanimously link secession with a military strike, which was provoked by the debt crisis. Richard argued that the secession must have been primarily the work of citizen soldiers, who allied with the *infra classem* and *nexi* (those enslaved for debt). He argued that the *assidui* (those meeting the property qualification for the Servian classes) were the key group affected by the agrarian crisis, and the issues of the *proletarii* were secondary.[56] Along similar lines, Raaflaub argued that the secession must have mainly been made up of the hoplites, infantry soldiers equipped with heavy armour. He considered that the power of the Roman elite, visible in the tombs of their central Italian peers, and manifested in their rigid sacred control, explains the slowness of the reform process that resulted. He also asserted that the institution of the tribunate was a very dramatic concession, implying that the plebeian power of extortion was considerable. In fact, the secession is best explained if the plebs are seen as a mixed group, with a substantial military element, reflecting Rome's complex society and economy.[57]

The secessions are often seen in terms of a military strike, but a more substantial threat of leaving the community completely is implicit.[58] In the context of a mobile environment, the act of secession implies the potential of regular and easy migration to another city. Secession was therefore not simply a military strike, but also a kind of paused migration. In fact, the sources clearly refer to it in these terms on several occasions. In the First Secession Dionysius (6.47.1) describes

---

55. Momigliano, 'Rise of the plebs', 173–7; Dion. Hal. 6.63.3.
56. Richard, *Origines*, 512, 549.
57. Cornell, *Beginnings*, 257; Richard, *Origines*, 512–19; Raaflaub, 'Conflict of the orders'.
58. Cf. Poma, 'Secessioni', section 3.

patrician fear that the plebs might defect to the enemy. Once the secession has been established on the Sacred Mount, the plebs remaining in the city begin to slip away one by one, both openly and secretly, to join the movement (Dion. Hal. 6.48). Most strikingly, Dionysius has the plebeian leader Junius Brutus (not related to the consul of the same name) suggest in a speech that they should leave Rome and found a colony elsewhere (Dion. Hal. 6.80.3).[59] On another occasion, when further civil strife had broken out in 471 BC, Livy describes the Volsci as aiming to encourage a secession of the plebs to their side.[60]

How far these annalistic views reflect fifth-century conditions is uncertain.[61] Given that these are speeches or attributed feelings, it would be unwise to take them as firm evidence of historical reality. Nevertheless, they show that both Livy and Dionysius thought that secessions could lead to permanent migration to an enemy of Rome, which is an idea in striking opposition to their general construct of Roman history in the fifth century BC. This period is portrayed in our sources as one of a veritable struggle for survival between Rome and its enemies such as the Volsci and Aequi; the potential defection of the plebs would be a strange spectre to raise in this context.

Other evidence suggests that the idea of withdrawing from one community and transferring to another did exist in the archaic period. The idea that secession can shade into migration or colonisation is preserved in later sources: the late Roman commentator on Virgil, Servius, distinguishes colonies founded by public agreement from those founded through secession.[62] An example of the latter is the plan by a Roman garrison to seize control of Capua in 342 BC, a curious episode that almost develops into a secession. Although Livy (7.38–42) does not present it as a formalised secession like the others, nevertheless the plebs won various concessions from the Senate. In another episode Livy records the violent secession of plebeians at

---

59. From Brutus' speech: 'We, who are abandoning the life which had for us no city and no hearth, are going forth as a colony (*apoikia*) that will be neither hateful to the gods nor troublesome to men nor grievous to any country.' This feature of the First Secession is only in Dionysius.
60. Livy, 2.58.3: *Uolscum Aequicumque inter seditionem Romanam est bellum coortum. uastauerant agros ut si qua secessio plebis fieret ad se receptum haberet.* 'During the Roman disturbance the Volsci and Aequi began war. They laid waste the fields in order that if the plebs should secede, they might find a refuge with them.'
61. Poma, 'Secessioni', section 3.
62. Serv. *Aen.* 1.12: *hae autem coloniae sunt quae ex consensu publico, non ex secessione sunt conditae.* 'So these colonies are those which have been founded by public agreement, not as a result of a succession.'

Ardea, following social conflict connected to a marriage proposal dispute there:

> The plebs were routed, but, unlike the Roman plebs, having armed and withdrawn from their city and encamped upon a certain hill, they sallied forth, sword and torch in hand, to sack the farms of the nobles. (Livy, 4.9.8–13)

In an article on early colonisation, J. Bayet called these movements 'armed secessions'.[63] Some were successful in establishing what we might term a 'colony', such as the Mamertini at Messana in the 280s, or the *Legio Campana* at Rhegium in 281 BC. In one version of the Mamertines' story, they left their homeland and came to Messana in a Sacred Spring, echoing the sacred oath of the plebeians.[64] Secession as an option or tactic was thus linked to the broader context of general mobility, and could amount to a real threat to withdraw from the community on a permanent basis and take up residence elsewhere.

Our understanding of these movements is hampered by the anachronistic approach of our much later sources. As many commentators have shown, they tend to reinterpret the early Republic in terms of their own day. They classify episodes of mobility in the terminology of the late Republic, using concepts such as *colonia* and *secessio*. But we should be alert to the idea that such classifications are misleading, and that types of mobility, unofficial and official, merge into one another.[65] This is particularly evident in the sphere of colonisation, where the term *colonia* is applied to a wide variety of different communities that come under Roman control in the early Republic, and receive varying numbers of settlers or garrisoning soldiers.[66]

Ultimately, therefore, even if we consider it impossible to recover plebeian intentions in the secessions, the act of moving out of Rome within the highly mobile environment of fifth-century Italy has dramatic implications. Although understanding the nature of the threat is hindered by the successful resolution of the disputes, and by the extreme hindsight of the sources, one implication must have been that the plebs could move off and found a 'colony', which might be in 'enemy' territory.

63. Bayet, 'Tite-Live'.
64. Festus 150 L.; Dench, *From Barbarians*, 211.
65. Isayev, *Migration* for an overview of types of mobilty.
66. Crawford, 'Roman history'; Bradley, 'Colonization and identity'.

Almost an alternative state in Rome, the plebs created their own assembly (the *concilium plebis*, formalised in 471 BC) and magistrates (the tribunes and plebeian aediles). What is striking is the complexity of the plebeian movement, creating parallel structures to the patrician-dominated state.[67] The tribunes were protected by their sacrosanctity, the result of an oath sworn by all plebeians to protect them, and came to exercise a power of *veto* (literally, 'I forbid') against magistrates and the Senate, the body of elders that advised the consuls.[68] The plebeians adopted the temple of Ceres on the Aventine as the focus for their movement. They had a guardian cult there consisting of a triad of deities (Ceres, Liber and Libera), which echoed the Capitoline triad (Jupiter, Juno and Minerva), the most important state cult. The plebeian group derived from the Greek gods Demeter, Kore and Dionysus, the former two for instance worshipped at Eleusis near Athens; nevertheless, the combination was Italic.[69] The temple was decorated by Sicilian artists: further evidence of links to southern Italy. It became a great plebeian centre, acting as an archive for documents and a treasury for their finances. Religious, cultural and political ideas travelled together, and the origins of the plebeians' presiding deities suggests that their political inspiration owed much to the Greek cities of southern Italy.

The Decemvirate and the Second Secession

The plebeian movement pursued its aims of a share in political opportunity and the alleviation of oppression for poor citizens through further secessions (450 BC, 287 BC) and political agitation. It was reputedly the plebs which demanded the establishment of the *decemviri* (board of ten) to publish a code of laws, in 451 BC. The Board created ten laws, which it published in the form of bronze tablets (Livy, 3.34.1; Diod. Sic. 12.26). Although the Board was initially envisaged as requiring only one year in office, supplements to the laws were thought to be required, and another Decemvirate was elected. However, in its second year of office the leader of the Decemvirate, Appius Claudius, is said to have become tyrannical. All other magistracies had been suspended, and there was no right of appeal against the judgement of

---

67. Smith, *Roman Clan*, 277.
68. Livy, 3.55, Dion. Hal. 6.89.2–4, on sacrosanctity, which echoes patrician claims of religious aura (Smith, *Roman Clan*, 277 with prior references).
69. Spaeth, *Roman Goddess Ceres*, 86, and see above p. 249.

the Decemvirs. The Decemvirs published just two further tables, one of which famously prohibited intermarriage between members of the patrician and plebeian orders. Together these laws formed the famous XII Tables, which became key founding elements of Roman law. The Decemvirate was deposed in 450 BC, after the plebs undertook the Second Secession.

This is a very confusing period in Roman history, and there are a number of issues with the traditional narrative over which modern scholars have long puzzled. Despite the integral role of the Struggle of the Orders in the setting up of the Tables, the laws barely refer to social conflict, beyond the prohibition on intermarriage in Table XII. The narrative of the Decemvirate, first appointed at the instigation of the plebs, but then turning against them in tyrannical fashion, is somewhat implausible. The tradition includes a number of very colourful sagas, such as that of Appius Claudius and Verginia, that must have been dramatised through retelling in oral tradition, or indeed through their performance on stage. The maiden Verginia was claimed as his slave by an agent of Appius, who was inflamed with lust for her, and she was only saved from sexual slavery by death at the hands of her father. This story shows similarities with the downfall of Tarquinius Superbus and stories of Greek tyrants abusing their subjects. There are also problems with the names of the Decemvirs, given in full in some of our sources. The second set of magistrates includes a considerable number of plebeians, yet it is that group which passes the controversial intermarriage legislation, detrimental to plebeians. The other laws of the XII Tables do not clearly favour the plebeians, and on the contrary include some very harsh punishments.[70]

Nevertheless, there are a number of reasons why the basic story of the Decemvirate and the establishment of the XII Tables is plausible. The text of the laws survives in fragments quoted by later authors. According to Cicero (*Leg.* 2.59), the full text was learnt by young Romans off by heart as part of their education. As our sources claim, the Tables must have drawn on a variety of sources for inspiration: the *leges regiae* ('Laws of the Kings', Livy, 6.1), custom (Dion. Hal. 10.55; 10.57) and law codes that were already well developed in other Mediterranean societies. Many Mediterranean communities had drawn up law codes in the seventh and sixth centuries BC. These were not usually political in aim, but rather designed to minimise civil

---

70. Discussed below.

strife.[71] This aim would also seem applicable to the XII Tables. Some parallels are evident with Near Eastern codes, but archaic Greek examples were probably more influential.[72] Our sources report Greek influence on the XII Tables through various channels: three commissioners were allegedly sent to Athens for inspiration in 452 BC, returning with copies of the laws of Solon (Livy, 3.31-3), and a famous Greek lawgiver, Hermodorus of Ephesus, in exile at Rome, is said to have aided in the composition of the Tables (*Dig.* 1-1.2-4; Pliny, *HN* 34.11; Strabo, 14.25). Although the precise details of these stories have been questioned, the consistent and strong story of Greek influence fits well with what we know about early Rome. Rome was a Hellenised society that regularly drew on the cultural experiences of neighbours, particularly the Greek cities of southern Italy.

The surviving fragments of the Tables provide an extraordinary level of insight into Rome of the mid fifth century BC.[73] They reveal a hierarchical society, composed of different classes of citizens, freed-persons, slaves, debt-bondspeople, and foreigners. Citizens were classified according to whether they were property owners (*assidui*) or landless (*proletarii*) (1.4). Such divisions required a census, which reinforces the Roman tradition that this institution had existed since the sixth century BC (Festus 47, 5 L.). The laws prohibited illegal gatherings (*coetus*) (8.14-15) and punished treason by execution (9.5). This was a harsh society, with cruel penalties that included being hanged 'for Ceres' (goddess of grain), burnt, cut into parts (if unable to pay a debt), sold into slavery, and hurled from the rock (the spur of the Capitoline hill known as the Tarpeian rock). Nevertheless, the Tables also provided some protection for individuals, who were not to be the subject of specific laws (9.2), nor executed unless condemned.

Life was particularly tough for the lower classes. The Tables carefully regulated the status of *nexi*, debt-bondspeople, who could be given to mysterious groups called *forctes* and *sanates* (1.5). Debtors could be sold abroad beyond the Tiber (3.7; this must mean into the territory of Veii), and fathers could sell their sons. Disputes over slave status were recognised as a possibility (1.11), just as had happened

---

71. Hölkeskamp, 'Arbitrators'; Eder, 'Political Significance'.
72. Near Eastern influence: Yaron, 'Semitic influence'; Westbrook, 'Nature and origins'; unconvincing according to Crawford (ed.), *Roman Statutes*, 561.
73. Warmington, *Remains of Old Latin* III; Crawford (ed.), *Roman Statutes*, 555-721 for text and commentary. Cornell, *Beginnings*, 280-92.

with Verginia. Injury to slaves was punished less harshly than that to free persons (1.14). Damage caused by slaves was to be recompensed (12.2). Other economic measures show the importance of agriculture and the protection of crops. There were to be minimum standards in road building (7.6–7), and farmland was to be protected against magic spells and hostile songs (8.1). The issue of debt features heavily; the code here was not particularly favourable to plebeians, even if its publication reflects the plebeians' claim of full citizen rights. Some complexity of economic life is revealed through the presence of guarantors (1.4), sureties (1.10), debt (3.1–7), interest (possibly, 8.7), and deposits (8.8, also uncertain). Foreigners (*hostes*) might be present, who could not gain *usucapio*, possession through use (2.2; 6.4). Penalties were enacted in *asses*, pounds of bronze, which acted as a pre-monetary measure of wealth (1.13; 1.14; 1.15).[74]

Measures on the household and social relations reveal a heavily patriarchal outlook, with familial and supra-familial groups envisaged. Women were subject to guardianship, unless a Vestal Virgin (5.1; 5.2), and marital subordination, although the latter could be avoided (6.5). But women could also divorce (4.3), and inherit estates (5.4). Estates passed to the *gens* (clan) in the absence of heirs (5.5). Strong paternal power within the family was mandated: the father could kill disabled children, and sell his offspring into slavery, presumably to other Romans (4.1; 4.2 on selling sons). The Tables aimed to reinforce patronage: freedmen could be transferred as clients from *familia* to *familia* (5.8), and patrons were to be accursed if they wronged their clients (8.10).

There were also measures reflecting religious beliefs, and regulating funerary expenditure. The Tables mention the priesthood of the Vestal Virgins and the goddess Ceres, and cover sacred oaths, and votive objects left in sanctuaries. Causing harm by magic was prohibited (see above). One regulation may have dealt with intercalation of the calendar (11.2).[75] Other regulations restricted funerary luxuries such as perfume, wine, gold, purple or musicians (10).

The most controversial measure was the law prohibiting intermarriage between patricians and plebeians (11.1), which demonstrates that social conflict between the two groups was a genuine feature of fifth-century Rome. If we follow our sources, intermarriage had occurred previously within Rome, such as with the Tarquinii and

---

74. Ampolo, 'Città riformata', 227–8; Cornell, *Beginnings*, 288.
75. Crawford, *Roman Statutes*, 713 is sceptical.

Coriolanus, and in Etruria, such as with Demaratus.[76] This measure seems to have been an unsuccessful effort to accentuate divisions evident in pre-existing custom. The ban on intermarriage may be a response to the creation of the plebeian order and the rise of a successful plebeian movement. The measure was repealed only five years later by the Lex Canuleia (445 BC – see below), but still remained an issue in the fourth century BC. The story of the founding of the Shrine of Plebeian Chastity on the Quirinal in 296 BC by a wife who had lost her patrician status through marriage to a plebeian shows that even in later eras such tensions continued to exist (Livy, 10.23.1–10).

According to our sources the novel experiment of government marked by the Decemvirate was brought to an end by the Second Secession. In the Roman tradition, the initial spark came from the killing of Verginia by her father. The army, then in camp at two places (Mount Vecilius and Sabinum), was inspired to rebel by the anguished appeal of Verginius. Both armies went first to the Aventine. This area of the city was already important to the plebeians both as a place of residence and as a centre of their movement, as we saw above.[77] However, the plebeians then withdrew to the Sacred Mount, outside the *pomerium* and used in the First Secession, as the more remote point of withdrawal would apply more pressure on the Senate. The plebs were persuaded to return to the city only by the resignation of the Decemvirate. Appius Claudius was prosecuted by Verginius and committed suicide. The most pro-plebeian leaders in the Senate, Valerius and Horatius, were made consuls for the next year, 449 BC. They passed the Valerio-Horatian laws, which met various plebeian demands: the right of appeal was restored; the resolutions of plebeian assemblies were to be binding on all; tribunician power was restored, and the inviolability of the tribunes was reinstated and reinforced.

These laws have been doubted by modern historians. There were repeated instances of laws on appeal (509 and 300 BC, both enacted by other Valerii), and laws on plebeian resolutions (339 and 287 BC). This has encouraged scholars to argue that they were only passed in 300 and 287 BC, and the earlier instances of such laws were unhistorical.[78] But at least thirty-five plebiscites were passed between 449

---

76. Cornell, *Beginnings*, 292. Compare Rutile Hipukrates, for whom see Chapter 4.
77. Mignone, *Republican Aventine*, doubts the historicity of the Second Secession.
78. E.g. Forsythe, *Critical History*, 230–3 rejects all the Valerio-Horatian laws and the Second Secession.

and 287 BC,[79] and it is likely that the later iterations of the same laws modified and reinforced earlier measures which had fallen into abeyance (just as the Gracchi later reworked archaic laws on landownership). Overall, the importance of these events lies not in the details of the reign of the Decemvirate and the composition of the XII Tables, which remain problematic, but in the laws which resulted and the renewed social compromise between the orders.

The remainder of the fifth century BC was marked by continued social agitation and further military pressure. The offices of state remained firmly under the control of the patricians. In 445 BC the Lex Canuleia repealed the intermarriage law that formed part of the XII Tables. Its author, Canuleius, also proposed allowing one consul to be plebeian. This was rejected in favour of an alternative proposal from the Senate, of electing three supreme magistrates (and subsequently more: four from 426 BC, six from 405 BC). They were called military tribunes with consular power. But this provided no aid for the plebeians, who were not elected until 400 BC, and then only again in 396, 383 and 379 BC. Military tribunes were abolished after the consulship was reinstated in 367 BC by the Licinio-Sextian laws.

The plebeian movement in the fourth century BC

The most important achievements of the plebeian movement came in the fourth century BC. Another pivotal point in the Struggle of the Orders came in 367 BC, once more motivated by a debt crisis, and exacerbated by the ambition of the plebeian leaders. A long period of plebeian agitation was followed by radical laws. The tribunes Licinius and Sextius were allegedly re-elected nine times from 377 BC. In office they prevented the election of patrician magistrates from 375–370 BC (until consular tribunes were elected 370–367 BC). The theatrical treatment of the episode provided by Livy – the tribunes were spurred on by the ambition of Licinius' wife, slighted by her patrician-wedded sister – and the extraordinary length of time when magistracies were prohibited has generally been questioned by modern scholars. But the outcome is reasonably certain.

In 368 BC they are said to have succeeded in passing two laws, limiting landholding (via a *Lex agraria*) and restricting the rate of interest. The *Lex agraria* is often assumed to apply only to *ager publicus*

---

79. Figure from Cornell, *Beginnings*, 276–8; Lanfranchi, *Tribuns*, 254 identifies sixty-eight from 509–287 BC, including fifty-six between 439 and 287 BC.

(public land), as that is how the reactivation of the law was framed by Tiberius Gracchus, which concerned holdings of *ager publicus* above 500 *iugera*. But the sources do not specify public land, and it probably applied to all land holdings.[80] This radical law therefore shows the scale of elite landownership, and the concern it provoked. This is a sign that Rome too was affected by wider political currents, particularly evident in fourth-century Athens and Magna Graecia, promoting the democratisation of city constitutions, and *isonomia*, equality before the law. In 367 BC the two tribunes were able to pass further laws on the consulship, which Livy says instructed that one consul should be plebeian, and on adding plebeians to the priesthood of the *duumviri sacris faciundis*. A new college of *decemviri*, a board of ten, was created, with the plebeians and patricians holding five priesthoods each. As recompense, the patricians were given new magistracies – the praetorship and two curule aedileships – to hold each year, the latter soon opened to plebeians as well.

In reality, the Licinio-Sextian rogations do not seem to have been decisive in opening up the consulship, as from 355–343 BC both consuls were often patrician.[81] In 342 BC the Lex Genucia is said by Livy to have returned to these same issues, prohibiting the charging of interest on loans, and allowing both consuls to be plebeian (Livy, 7.42). In the *Fasti* one of the two consuls was always plebeian from this point on. It was not until 172 BC that both consuls were plebeian. This has encouraged modern scholars to argue that Livy was mistaken, and that the law of 367 BC merely made plebeians eligible, while it was only in 342 BC that one consul had to be plebeian.[82] This seems reasonable, although it presupposes, perhaps implausibly, that such laws were diligently obeyed.

Thus, the Struggle of the Orders took in religious as well as magisterial offices, as they were key sources of patrician authority. The final stage in the process of the opening up of religious power came in 300 BC, when the Lex Ogulnia added plebeian pontiffs and augurs to the existing patrician ones. This allowed plebeians to hold all the major collegiate priesthoods, even if other archaic priesthoods such as the *flamines* remained restricted to patricians alone. Finally, in 287 BC, after the plebeians had held the Third Secession, this time to the Janiculum, the poorly attested Hortensian law gave plebiscites

---

80. Rich, 'Lex Licinia'.
81. In 355, 353, 351, 349, 345 and 343 BC.
82. Cornell, *Beginnings*, 337–8; Forsythe, *Critical History*, 274.

(decrees of the plebeian assembly) the force of law over the whole population.[83] Hitherto their decrees had applied only to plebeians; this law effectively made the plebeian assembly a regular institution of state. Such a measure had been passed before, in 445 BC, but this repeated attempt implies that it had been disregarded.

The result of all these measures was the formation of a new mixed patrician–plebeian nobility. This is visible through the appearance of plebeian names in the *Fasti* as the wealthiest plebeian families came to hold magistracies and join the Senate. To some extent the poor lost their political champions, but the movement had been successful to a degree in alleviating poverty and exploitation. In 326 BC *nexum*, the debt-bondage of Roman citizens, was outlawed (Livy, 8.28 provides an overly dramatised picture of the law's promulgation). Such a measure might suggest that the rich already had an alternative labour source in slaves, although the law cemented the rights of Roman citizens by preventing any return to *nexum*.[84] Distribution of conquered land, especially through the foundation of Latin colonies, had become extensive from 334 BC (see next chapter). This is another manifestation of the outlook embodied in the Licinio-Sextian laws, which aspired to create an ideal Roman community of relatively equal citizen farmer–soldiers. As we know from the account in Appian of the background to Tiberius Gracchus' reinstatement of the agrarian law in 133 BC (*B. Civ.* 1.8), many of the elite remained resistant to this vision, and exceeded 500 *iugera* in their holdings of public, let alone private land.

The social conflicts and associated secessions of the plebs could be taken to imply that communal civic identity was underdeveloped in Rome's early history. If so, it must have been strengthened by the partial resolution of the early social struggles. One way this may be apparent is in the changing focus of Rome's historical tradition, evident in the first ten books of Livy. His history of the monarchy and early Republic is dominated by stories of great individuals: kings and generals such as Servius Tullius, Coriolanus and Camillus. By the middle Republic, Livy's focus has shifted noticeably to the community as a whole, the city and the state, with a far less prominent role accorded to major figures. This probably in part reflects changes in Roman governance. Prominent individuals were restrained by the Republican ideology of power-sharing, and had greater difficulty

---

83. Millar, 'Political power', 143.
84. Finley, 'Debt-bondage'; Bernard, 'Debt, land, and labor', 322–3; see further, Chapter 6.

dominating politics from the time of the sack of Rome in 390 BC until Scipio Africanus' great victory over Carthage in 202 BC. But it must also reflect a shift in Roman collective memory and the nature of record-keeping, which was operating at a more communal than individualised level, as it had for the archaic period. And finally, the resolution of these issues shows a redefinition of the Roman sense of community, and, as Christopher Smith has argued, the coherency of the early Roman state, whose strength in this period has been questioned.[85]

---

85. Smith, *Roman Clan*, 280. More questioning: Terrenato, 'Versatile clans'; Armstrong, *War and Society*.

CHAPTER 8

Roman foreign relations in the sixth, fifth and fourth centuries BC

Introduction

Rome's foreign relations in the period c.600 BC–338 BC are critical in understanding the rise and development of the city, although the situation was very different to that after 338 BC. Rome at this time was an embryonic imperial power, building up a small empire in Latium by the end of the sixth century, but then suffering a number of setbacks that prevented it from dominating its neighbours. Our knowledge of Rome before 338 BC suggests that it was superior in resources to all its near neighbours. It had a larger city site than any rival central Italian city, one that was several times greater than any of the other Latin centres. Its territory was at the centre of one of the most fertile plains in central Italy, and on the banks of central Italy's most important river. Judging from the extent of the city and its walling in the sixth century BC, it must have had substantial manpower resources. Monumental buildings such as the temple of Jupiter Optimus Maximus suggest that it had greater economic reserves than its neighbours, at least in the sixth century BC. Yet the political crises of the early Republic seem to have prevented the efficient marshalling of these resources, as plebeians and patricians struggled over issues such as debt and the right to raise and lead military forces. It was only when the plebeians succeeded in gaining concessions that Rome's potential superiority could be brought into play. In addition, the complex shifting league organisations and city-state alliances operating in central Italy in this period made asserting control very difficult even for the most powerful city state. Only when Rome organised its alliances to its own benefit was it able to expand more quickly and keep hold of its conquests.

As ever, we face difficulty in gaining an unbiased perspective, given that our key evidence is literary, and all the major literary sources come from within the Greco-Roman tradition. Renewed interest in these authors and their sources as literary works has illuminated both strengths and weaknesses. There is an increasingly detailed narrative of Roman expansion from the start of the Republic, particularly in Livy (down to 292 BC) and Dionysius (down to 445 BC), supplemented by the writings of Diodorus, Polybius and others. The material becomes increasingly reliable over the fifth and fourth centuries, a trend which must be linked to the growing use of documentary records.[1] Although there are disparities, our sources largely agree in outline on the main events of the period. Their information covers not only Rome but also the foreign cities and peoples of Italy as they come into contact with Rome, and there are valuable digressions on the Etruscans, Samnites and Gauls in particular.

Many weaknesses in our literary sources are also readily apparent. Most notoriously, all of our major sources were written at least a century and a half after the events they covered, and the ultimate source material is clearly regarded with some suspicion by them. Invention and distortion of events has clearly taken place within the tradition. Obvious factors in this regard include the influence of family histories (both Cicero and Livy express reservations about their reliability), and the constant refashioning of material transmitted orally. Livy refers to disputes over victories, and provides some face-saving and implausible reverses of enemy triumphs which even he finds unlikely.[2] More insidiously, all our sources (even Greek ones) write with a largely Roman perspective: foreign cities such as Veii are on the whole only mentioned in connection with Roman expansion; peaceful interaction in terms of trade, migration and religious practices is generally ignored. In addition, this Romanocentricity obscures the role of broader historical developments, such as the expansion of the Etruscan cities beyond Etruria, in the rise of Rome. Our sources are inevitably conditioned by the hindsight of writing at the peak of Roman power, and therefore portray Rome's progressive conquests as ever expanding in an inexorable fashion.

It is therefore very important that, within the constraints of the sources, historians try to locate Rome within Italy-wide developments.[3] More extensive use of archaeology and epigraphy, which lack the biases of our literary sources, helps considerably where this

---

1. See Chapter 1. Cf. Oakley, *Commentary*, I 39.
2. Examples collected in Oakley, *Commentary*, I 96–7.
3. For a similar approach see studies such as Pallottino, *History*; Torelli, 'Dalle aristocrazie', and 'Popolazioni'; Lomas, *Rise of Rome*; Terrenato, *Early Roman Expansion*.

material is available and pertinent. It is also essential to appreciate the very complex origins of the Greco-Roman historical tradition on the rise of Rome. At least in part, this tradition depends on contemporary written records or earlier Greek sources that lack the hindsight of the post-Augustan era. Many of the Greek sources are preserved in later histories such as those of Dionysius and Diodorus, although they are prone to their own distortions. Overall, therefore, we must be mindful of our dependence on the peculiar framing of the narrative by the literary sources. The aim of this chapter is to consider the situation in Etruria and Latium, and then examine the expansion of Rome within that broader context.

The Etruscans and the Etruscan League

The cities of Etruria played an important role in the rise of Rome. Their unity has been the subject of much scholarly discussion. There is a consistent literary tradition that the Etruscans were organised into twelve cities, as in the following statement by Strabo:

> When Tyrrhenus came, he not only called the country Tyrrhenia after himself, but also put Tarco in charge as 'coloniser', and founded twelve cities; Tarco, I say, after whom the city of Tarquinii is named, who, on account of his sagacity from boyhood, is said by the myth-tellers to have been born with grey hair. Now at first the Tyrrheni, since they were subject to the orders of only one ruler, were very strong, but later on, it is reasonable to suppose, their united government was dissolved, and the Tyrrheni, yielding to the violence of their neighbours, were broken up into separate cities. (Strabo, 5.2.2)

Livy (5.33) claims by contrast that there were originally twelve cities in Etruria itself; he adds that this organisation was then replicated in northern Italy when the Etruscans expanded there. The Etruscans were also said to have founded another twelve cities in Campania. This tradition is likely to be based on some sort of collective organisation, and such stories may originate from Etruscans. But it is suspiciously formulaic, and Strabo admits that the transition from united government under a mythical leader to the situation of separate cities is only supposition. The number twelve may be speculation by Roman antiquarian authors, and there was never a canonical list of the cities (or 'peoples'), while later on we hear of an organisation into fifteen cities. As far as our sources allow us to say, Rome was never a member of this collective.

The literary sources record Etruscan leaders meeting in council as part of a League at the Fanum Voltumnae, the Shrine of Voltumna. Voltumna was a key political deity for the Etruscans. All our sources agree that this meeting place was in the territory of Volsinii (Orvieto), a convenient central meeting point for most Etruscans. It was the site of an annual festival and fair involving all the cities of Etruria. Sacred games are also attested in inscriptions mentioning an Etruscan League of fifteen peoples established in the early empire, perhaps by the Etruscophile Claudius. The festival was still celebrated in the fourth century AD, when an annual cult was performed at Volsinii and Hispellum by the *sacerdos* of the Etruscans and the Umbrians (who joined this celebration at some unknown point), and games were organised.[4]

It was often assumed that the League was disbanded after the Roman conquest, to be revived in the imperial period at Roman whim. But recent excavations at a site outside Orvieto which has a reasonable claim to be considered the Fanum Voltumnae have raised questions about this idea. The excavations uncovered an imposing sanctuary which matches the scale and importance attributed to the Fanum Voltumnae by our written sources.[5] It is 30 ha in extent, with altars, basements of large buildings and two ceremonial roads (6 m wide and uncovered for a length of 60 m). There is pottery from as early as the eighth century BC, and high-quality black- and red-figure Attic pottery fragments from the sixth and fifth centuries BC. There are fragments of statuary in Greek marble, and architectural terracottas from the sixth to the third century BC; these are of high quality and must have belonged to various sacred buildings. Other finds include Umbrian, Greek and Sicilo-Punic coinage. The locale continued in use down to late antiquity and eventually the church of San Pietro in Vetere (the name suggests a connection with ancient remains) was built on the site in the twelfth century AD. All the evidence corresponds to the likely wealth and international links that we would expect of such events, and suggests that the festival continued with little interruption from early in Etruscan history until well beyond the Roman conquest.

---

4. *CIL* XI 5265 (AD 333–7): 'You state that you [Umbrians] are linked with Tuscia, and that by ancient established custom you and the aforementioned Tuscians take turns in alternate years to appoint the priests who present the theatrical shows and gladiatorial games at Vulsinii, a municipality of Tuscia.'
5. Stopponi, 'Orvieto'.

Writing about the events of 403 BC, Livy mentions that a priest (*sacerdos*) was elected as head of the league by the Twelve Peoples:

> The Veientes, weary of the annual canvassing [for magistrates], which was sometimes the cause of disagreements, chose a king. This offended the feelings of the Etruscan peoples, who hated monarchy as much as the king himself. He had for some time been hateful to the Etruscans by reason of his wealth and arrogance, since he had violently disrupted the solemn games, which it is impious to interrupt, in his resentment of a political rebuff; and because the votes of the Twelve Peoples had returned another man as priest in preference to him, he had suddenly removed the actors, most of whom were his own slaves, in the middle of the games. So the people which was devoted beyond all others to religious rites (all the more because it excelled in the art of observing them) voted to refuse its help to the men of Veii, so long as they should obey a king. This vote the Veientes would not allow to be mentioned, in fear of their king, who had a way of treating the man by whom any such saying was reported as a leader in sedition, not as the bearer of an idle tale. (Livy, 5.1.3–7)

Thus the cities did not automatically act in collective defence of one of their members. Some sources encourage the idea of a powerful league with common political aims. Some scholars have suggested that the figure called the *zilath meχl rasnal* should be translated as the *praetor Etruriae populorum* ('magistrate of the Etruscan people').[6] Whilst this is a magisterial rather than priestly title, it now seems more likely that it refers to a leader of an individual Etruscan community, rather than the whole League. It has also sometimes been thought that the League undertook military action under a common leader, partly based on Dionysius' comment that the *fasces* (symbols of power) of each Etruscan king were handed over to single leader with absolute power during joint military expeditions (3.61.2).

But the real extent of the League is questionable, and its actual existence has been doubted by some scholars.[7] Evidence for any joint military activities is sparse, and mostly refers to the mythical era of Etruscan history. By contrast, there are frequent references to the *refusal* of military aid, such as to Veii in 403 and 397 BC. The sources also attest joint Etruscan military activities not connected to a league.

---

6. E.g. *Tabula Cortonensis* 2.1. See discussion in Turfa, *Etruscan World*, 355.
7. E.g. Harris, *Rome in Etruria and Umbria*, 101; Cornell, 'Principes of Tarquinia', 171.

Some cities cooperated in the face of a threat, although this typically involved pairs of states rather than any mass alliance. Contrary to Strabo's claim, it is unlikely that Etruria was ever a united entity in political terms. Indeed, in spite of their ethnic commonality, various Etruscan cities had a history of aggression towards one another. This is attested for example in the *Elogia Tarquiniensia*, a series of inscriptions from Tarquinii of the first century AD, which contain information probably stemming from a local historical source, independent of Roman history (the reading and date referred to is uncertain, but is likely to be the fifth century BC). One *elogium* records:

> Aulus Spurinna ... twice praetor [?, =*zilath* on the original Etruscan document] ... exp[elled] the king of Caere Orgolnius from power ... [and ended a slave?] war at Arretium.[8]

Thus, the Etruscans are best understood as a group of independent city states that periodically came together for common purposes. Religious festivals and military cooperation generated a sense of collective Etruscan identity amongst separate cities that shared the same language, rather than emerging from a situation of primordial unity.

Some sources make extravagant claims about Etruscan power. Cato in his *Origines* asserts that 'almost all of Italy was under the dominion of the Etruscans' (*FRH* F72, quoted by Serv. *Aen.* 11.567–8), but it is clear that this is referring to a very early period of Etruscan history, probably to a mythical prehistory. More realistically, Livy (5.33) says that 'before the Roman supremacy, the power of the Etruscans was widely extended both by sea and land'. Whilst this suggests a simplistic concept of ethnic substitution, with the Etruscans being replaced by the Romans, there is good evidence that two areas of Italy outside of Etruria proper, Campania and northern Italy, were indeed under Etruscan control.

Etruscans outside Etruria

Several sites in Campania (such as Capua, Pontecagnano and Vallo di Diano) have an archaeological history similar to that of the great Iron Age centres in Etruria, with Proto-Villanovan and Villanovan phases going back to the ninth century BC (Fig. 2.2). These Campanian cemeteries exhibit what has become known as Southern

---

8. Torelli, *Elogia Tarquiniensia*; Cornell, 'Principes of Tarquinia', 171.

Villanovan culture. There are considerable likenesses in funerary practices, cemetery typologies and settlement patterns with Etruria itself. Later on, epigraphy shows the Etruscan language in use in Campania, for example at Pompeii, as well as at Pontecagnano, where links to Veii and Caere are apparent.

There is also literary evidence for this presence. Strabo reports that there were twelve Etruscan cities in Campania, including Pompeii and Herculaneum:

> Again, others say that, although it [Campania] was first inhabited by the Opici, and also by the Ausones, later on it was taken by the Sidicini, an Oscan tribe, but the Sidicini were ejected by the people of Cumae, and in turn the Cumaeans by the Tyrrheni. For on account of its fertility, they continue, the plain became an object of contention; and the Tyrrheni founded twelve cities in the country and named their capital city 'Capua'; but on account of their luxurious living they became soft, and consequently, just as they had been made to get out of the country around the Padus [Po river], so they had to yield this country to the Samnites . . . Next after Neapolis comes the Heracleian Fortress [Herculaneum], with a promontory which runs out into the sea and so admirably catches the breezes of the southwest wind that it makes the settlement a healthy place to live. Both this settlement and the next one after it, Pompaia [Pompeii], past which flows the River Sarnus, were once held by the Osci; then, by the Tyrrheni and the Pelasgi; and after that by the Samnites. (Strabo, 5.4–8)

The nature of the Etruscan settlements varied. Some were perhaps established by Etruscan cities, such as Capua. Others such as Pontecagnano are more likely to have been *emporia* that grew with trade and were connected to Etruscan sea power. The connections between south Etruria and Campania were in part seaborne, making use of the Tyrrhenian coast. But there must also have been links via land, which involved travel through Rome and Latium. The Etruscan naval defeat at Cumae in 474 BC must have made the sea links with Etruria much more precarious, and thus jeopardised Etruscan control over these southern settlements; they were ultimately lost in the late fifth century BC, according to our sources.

Capua was the largest and most powerful Etruscan city in Campania, and the most northerly of this group. Its importance was connected to its position at a natural crossroads on the Volturnus river, controlling the land and river routes between north and south Italy. In its early history Capua would have been linked to Rome by the overland routes later followed by roads such as the Via Latina and Via Appia. Velleius Paterculus maintained that it was founded around 800 BC (1.7); he also records the date given by Cato of 472 BC, but that seems too late for the archaeological remains. Capua had a grid plan of the late seventh century BC, similar to that of Pompeii, probably sixth century BC, which may also be Etruscan in origin. Strabo describes Capua as the capital of this area. One of the longest Etruscan inscriptions, the Capua tile, comes from here. The city was eventually captured by the Samnites, which Livy records in a highly dramatised picture dating to 423 BC. The reality is probably less striking, but Etruscan influence was eroded and epigraphy declined. The Samnites had come to control all Campania by the end of the fifth century BC, and Oscan had become the dominant language in epigraphy.

There is a similar wealth of evidence for an Etruscan presence in the Po valley (Map 2), including epigraphy and literary attestations. Polybius (2.17) thought that control of this fertile zone formed the basis of Etruscan wealth, though the major cities seem to postdate the earliest phases of Etruscan civilization. Perhaps drawing on lost parts of Polybius, Strabo (5.1.7) presented Etruscan colonisation here as the result of competition with Umbrians. The region supposedly consisted of yet another twelve Etruscan cities, founded as colonies from Etruria:

> They first settled on this side of the Apennines by the western sea in twelve cities. Afterwards they founded twelve colonies beyond the Apennines, corresponding to the number of the mother cities. These colonies occupied the entire area beyond the Po as far as the Alps, with the exception of the corner inhabited by the Veneti, who dwelt round an arm of the sea. (Livy, 5.33)

Felsina, modern Bologna, was probably the most important settlement: it is recorded as *princeps Etruriae* ('leader of Etruria') by Pliny (*HN* 3.115). Servius, in his commentary on Virgil's *Aeneid*, suggests that Felsina was founded by a mythical relative of the founder of Perusia (10.198). It had wealthy cemeteries, such as at Villanova and Certosa with its famous situla (bucket-shaped ritual vessels).[9]

The settlement best known in archaeological terms is Marzabotto, which was positioned to control trans-Apennine trade. Early sixth-century huts on the site were replaced by a planned layout around

---

9. This is also the origin for the name of the Villanovan culture.

500 BC; the regular nature of settlement would suggest that this was an instance of colonisation. The site was probably conquered around 350 BC by the Gauls, and thereafter occupied in a residual fashion. One of the most prestigious finds is a marble *kouros* statue, probably imported from Spina, the most important northern Etruscan port, at the mouth of the Po. Spina had a grid plan laid out c.530–520 BC, and the massive amounts of Attic pottery found here point to its important role as a node for Adriatic trade. Grain may have been the primary export. Its wealth was attested by the treasury it maintained at the great Greek sanctuary of Delphi (Strabo, 5.1.7). By the time the Romans conquered the area in the early second century BC, Felsina was under Gallic control (Livy, 33.37.4), although Strabo (5.1.11) believed that even then there was a residual Etruscan and Umbrian presence in cities such as Ariminum and Ravenna.

Overall, therefore, the league of the Twelve Peoples was probably more a religious than military or political organisation, and there was never really an Etruscan empire in Italy. Nevertheless, the Etruscan presence in Campania and northern Italy can be verified archaeologically. Whether these were really 'colonies' from mother cities in Etruria is difficult to tell. That is an ancient *topos* (stereotype), but it is true that some settlements seem to have been newly founded on grid plans, reinforcing the literary picture. More clearly, the cities here were closely linked culturally to Etruria and, like the cities of Etruria proper, they were independent of and competitive with one another. This situation attests both the mobility of individual Etruscans outside their area of origin, and the networks formed between their cities and settlements elsewhere. These networks were apparent through Latium and Campania, and played an important role in the development of Rome.

Latins and the Latin League

The region of Latium has only a limited geographical basis (Map 4). The core area occupied by the Latins was the relatively restricted plain bounded by the Tiber and Anio rivers, and the mountains to the north-east. The region's definition is more obvious to the east and north, but it lacks natural geographical borders to the south-west. Latium Vetus (Old Latium) is really the area in the shadow of the central Alban Hills and lake, the remains of volcanic activity. This is typical of Italian regions, which were defined more by the ethnic identity of their inhabitants than by natural topographical features.

The individual cities and towns that made up the Latins perceived themselves as part of this wider community because they shared certain features in common. All spoke a common language, Latin. All had a common myth of origin as the descendants of the aboriginal king Latinus, father-in-law of the Trojan Aeneas. They shared a common material culture. And, perhaps most importantly, they all took part in a number of common cults. The most important of these was the *Feriae Latinae*, held on the Alban Mount. The participants are listed by Pliny:

> In the first region [created by Augustus] there were before the following celebrated towns of Latium besides those mentioned: Satricum, Pometia . . .; and with these the Alban peoples who were accustomed to receive meat [i.e. take part in sacrifices] on the Alban mount, that is the Albani, Aesolani, Accienses, Abolani, Bubetani, Bolani, Cusuetani, Coriolani, Fidenates, Foreti, Hortenses, Latinienses, Longulani, Manates, Macrales, Munienses, Numinienses, Olliculani, Octulani, Pedani, Polluscini, Querquetulani, Sicani, Sisolenses, Tolerienses, Tutienses, Vimitellari, Velienses, Venetulani, Vitellenses. And so 53 peoples from old Latium have disappeared without a trace. (*HN* 3.5.68–70)

Scholars have long tried to identify these peoples, pointing out that several appear to be peoples named after individual hills of Rome, and therefore perhaps remnants of villages on the site of Rome that predated the unification of the city.[10] The Velienses are normally connected to the Velian, and the Querquetulani to the Caelian hill.[11] Grandazzi argued that this list probably originates from a fifth-century BC inscription, suggesting that this custom was already archaic by then. These indications suggest that the cult on the Alban Mount is of huge antiquity, stretching back into the Bronze Age.

The Alban Mount was not the only cult site shared by the Latins. They also met at Lavinium to celebrate the cult of Venus at the sanctuary of the Thirteen Altars. This sanctuary is known from archaeological excavations in the 1960s, which identified a series of building phases from the early sixth to the end of the fourth century BC with the gradual accumulation of monumental altars, now thought to number fourteen or fifteen.[12] Another common Latin sanctuary was

---

10. Grandazzi, *Alba Longa*, 517–729; Fulminante, *Urbanisation*, 42–4.
11. Tacitus, *Ann.* 4.65.1, notes that the Caelian hill was originally called the Mons Querquetulanus.
12. Moser, *Altars*, 115.

located at Lake Nemi, where the grove of Diana was ruled by a priest known as the *rex nemorensis* (Virgil, *Aen.* 6.137; Ovid, *Fast.* 3.271). Another was the temple of Diana, built on the Aventine hill at Rome by Servius Tullius in the sixth century BC. According to our sources this was an attempt by Servius to unify the Latins under Roman control, following the model of the Artemision of Ephesus (Livy, 1.45). It is striking that all the common Latin sanctuaries are outside cities, which must have made it easy for individuals from other communities to come and use them. Servius followed the same policy when he set up the temple of Diana by placing it on the Aventine. This hill lay outside Rome's sacred boundary (*pomerium*), although it was within the 'Servian' sixth-century walled circuit.

The common identity of the Latins was also reinforced by their sharing of various common rights.[13] These rights were ratified by a treaty organised by Rome in the early Republic, but had probably been customary before. There is no real way of telling whether this is an attempt to formalise earlier arrangements, or impose greater unity on Latium. Latins had *conubium*, the right to legally marry someone from another Latin community, *commercium*, the right to form legally binding contracts with another Latin (for example, to own land elsewhere), and the *ius migrationis*, the right to move to another Latin city and gain its citizenship.[14]

Rome was both part of this wider community, and at the same time different from the other Latin peoples in ways that reflect its peripheral position. Rome shared most of the important elements of Latin identity; Romans took part in common Latin cults, shared in the common culture, and spoke the language.[15] But the Romans had a more complicated vision of themselves than simply being descended from indigenous early Latins or the immigrant Aeneas. The defining factor of Roman identity was that they believed themselves to be a people of ethnically mixed origins.[16] As we have seen, the sources present Rome as an open city in the legends of the asylum established by Romulus, open to anyone who wanted to join the city, and the Rape of the Sabine women, where the founding female element

---

13. Cornell, *Beginnings*, 295–7; Broadhead, 'Rome's migration policy'; Roselaar, 'Concept of *commercium*'.
14. Note that Roselaar and Broadhead question the legal basis of *commercium* and migration.
15. The earliest public document found at Rome, the Lapis Niger inscription, is in Latin.
16. Cornell, 'Ethnicity'; Dench, *Romulus' Asylum*.

of the population was abducted from the neighbouring Sabines. As well as these myths, the Romans also preserved stories of more plausibly historical migrations into Rome, such as that of Lucumo from Tarquinii (to become Tarquinius Priscus), and Attus Clausus and his followers migrating from Sabinum to Rome in the late sixth century, to form the nucleus of the great Claudian tribe.

This sense of difference from Latins is also clear in the Roman tradition on the expansion of the city's territory under the kings, most of which was at the expense of other Latin towns.

Roman expansion under the kings

Estimating the early extent of Rome's territory, before the sixth century BC, is very difficult.[17] Strabo suggests that some of Rome's festivals preserved a record of the boundaries of Roman territory at a stage when they were extremely close to the city:

> Between the fifth and the sixth of those stones which indicate the miles from Rome there is a place called 'Festi', and this, it is said, is a boundary of what was then Roman territory; and in addition the priests celebrate sacrificial festivals called 'Ambarvalia' on the same day, both there and at several other places, as being boundaries. (Strabo, 5.3.2)

Whether this is a reliable indication of Rome's early territory is questionable, however, as sacred relics such as this are notoriously prone to reinvention.

The first big accretion of Latin territory to the Roman state is reputed to have occurred under Tullus Hostilius. This was the conquest of Alba Longa, whose population was bodily moved to Rome. The traditional site of this city was on the Alban Hills, close to Rome. But only signs of scattered villages have been found archaeologically, and these generally fall into decline in the late ninth century.[18] We are obviously dealing with myth here, although it is clear that this massif was a part of Roman territory from an early period. Expansion in this direction makes sense, as it was not blocked by the great city

---

17. For the historical tradition on the *ager Romanus antiquus* see Fulminante, *Urbanisation*, 105–9; Capanna, 'Dall'"ager antiquus"'; Smith, 'Ager Romanus antiquus'.
18. Fulminante, *Urbanisation*, 210–12.

states that arose with Rome to the north in Etruria. Latin city states were all much smaller.[19] Under Ancus Marcius various towns in the Tiber valley were conquered and Ostia was founded at the mouth of the Tiber; he reputedly brought the defeated populations into Rome to increase its size, just as Tullus Hostilius had done. It is interesting to note that this is very different from later colonisation practice, which was to send out Roman settlers to conquered territory, and so seems unlikely to have been invented in imitation of it.[20]

To the two Tarquins is attributed the policy of conquering the areas of Sabinum and Latium adjacent to Rome. Livy (1.52–3) reports that Tarquinius Superbus reorganised the Latin League and captured Suessa Pometia from the Volsci. The tradition on their conquests seems confused and exaggerated; for example, Priscus is said to have conquered all of the Latins, and Superbus to have gained control of the Latin League, but the latter still has to attack Gabii and Ardea. Nevertheless, the general picture of expansion is entirely plausible. It is notable that Priscus' conquests are all said to have been close to home, and Superbus' further afield. Fulminante has mapped the expansion of Roman territory in the monarchic period according to the Roman literary tradition, using Thiessen polygons for neighbouring city territories (Fig. 8.1). As she points out, this reveals the geographical logic of the accounts, even if they are likely to oversimplify a much more complex process. We cannot be certain about the historicity of the tradition. Whilst its internal logic is reassuring, such logic may also be the result of later artificial invention.[21]

Nevertheless, from the end of the sixth century we have more reliable, independent evidence to confirm that Rome had built up a substantial empire within Latium. Firstly, a report in Livy records the creation of new tribes bringing the number up to twenty-one in 495 BC. As this was the way that the Romans organised new citizens' voting rights, it suggests that Rome had gained territory in the preceding period.[22] The unelaborated nature of Livy's notice, and its connection to a report of the foundation day of the temple of Mercury,

---

19. Nijboer, 'Fortifications'.
20. Bayet, 'Tite-Live'; Bradley, 'Colonization and identity'.
21. Fulminante, *Urbanisation*, 113.
22. Livy, 2.21: 'The same year (495 BC) a fresh batch of colonists was sent to complete the number at Signia, a colony founded by King Tarquin. The number of tribes at Rome was increased to twenty-one. The temple of Mercury was dedicated on May 15.' The authenticity of this notice is discussed by Cornell, *Beginnings*, 174; Smith, *Roman Clan*, 236.

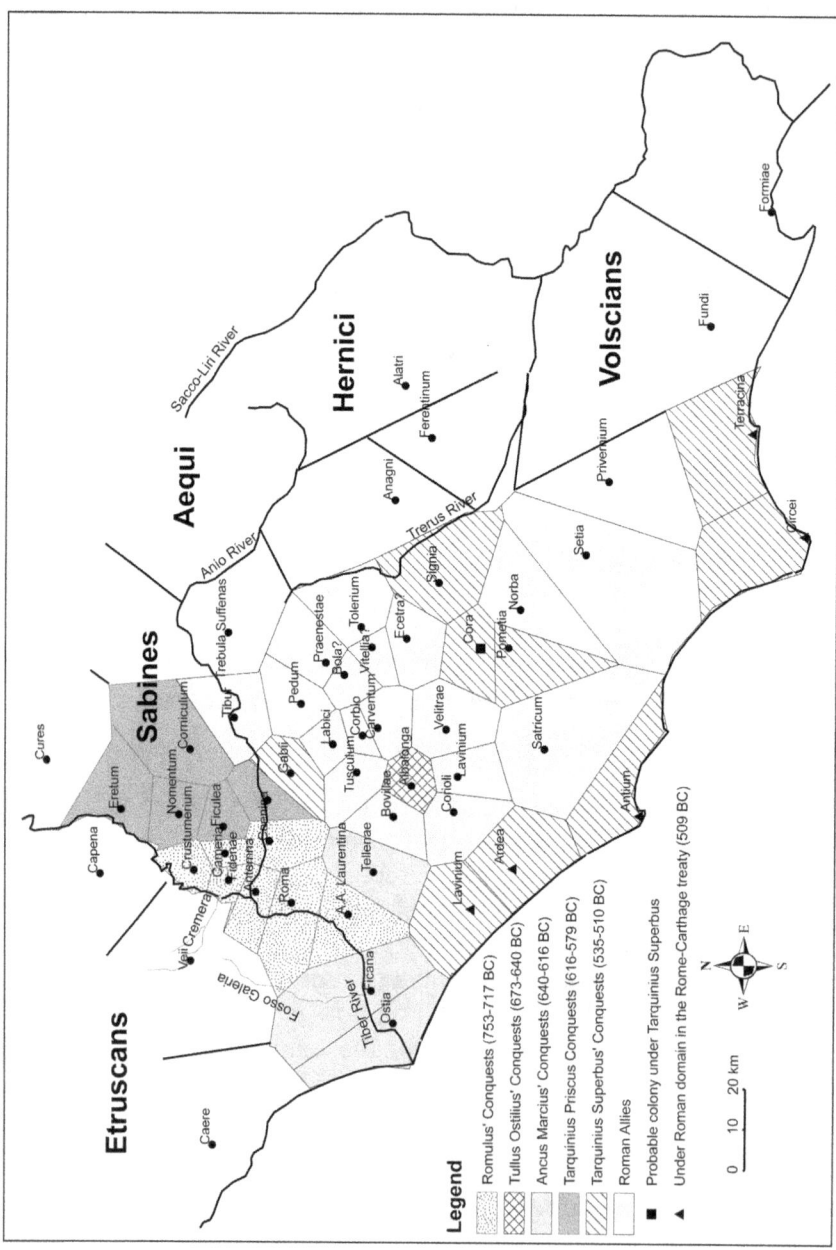

Figure 8.1 Map of Roman monarchic conquests, based on the literary sources, using Thiessen polygons for hypothetical city territories (reproduced with kind permission of the author from Fulminante, *Urbanisation*, fig. 33)

enhances its reliability: such records are very likely to be preserved in priestly records.

Further confirmation comes from the first Carthage treaty, which Polybius dates to 509 BC. He reports its text as follows:

> The first treaty between Rome and Carthage dates from the consulship of Lucius Junius Brutus and Marcus Horatius, the first Consuls after the expulsion of the kings, and the founders of the Temple of Jupiter Capitolinus. This is twenty-eight years before the crossing of Xerxes to Greece. I give below as accurate a rendering as I can of this treaty, but the ancient Roman language differs so much from the modern that it can only be partially made out, and that after much application, by the most intelligent men. The treaty is more or less as follows: 'There is to be friendship between the Romans and their allies and the Carthaginians and their allies on these terms: The Romans and their allies are not to sail beyond the Fair Promontory unless forced by storm or by enemies: it is forbidden to anyone carried beyond it by force to buy or carry away anything beyond what is required for the repair of his ship or for sacrifice, and he must depart within five days. Men coming to trade may conclude no business except in the presence of a herald or town-clerk, and the price of whatever is sold in the presence of such shall be secured to the vendor by the state, if the sale takes place in Libya or Sardinia. If any Roman comes to the Carthaginian province in Sicily, he shall enjoy equal rights with the others. The Carthaginians shall do no wrong to the peoples of Ardea, Antium, Laurentium, Circeii, Tarracina, or any other city of the Latins who are subject to Rome. Concerning the Latins who are not subjects, they shall keep their hands off their cities, and if they take any city shall deliver it up to the Romans undamaged. They shall build no fort in the Latin territory. If they enter the land in arms, they shall not pass a night therein.' (Polybius, 3.22)

There has been considerable debate about the chronology and authenticity of the treaty. Polybius claims that he read the original treaties in person, and most scholars consider them unlikely to be an annalistic invention.[23] The discovery in the 1960s of the Pyrgi tablets, which are bilingual in Phoenician and Etruscan, helped to confirm that Phoenician-speakers were present along this coast just

---

23. Polybius, 3.26: 'Such treaties exist and are preserved on bronze tablets to this day in the treasury of the Aediles beside the temple of Jupiter Capitolinus.' Richardson, 'Rome's treaties' points out that the Polybian and Livian traditions on the Rome–Carthage treaties are not easily assimilated.

after 500 BC. This reinforced the chronology of the first treaty in Polybius.[24] Carthage must have been concerned to secure the friendship of the new Republican regime at Rome, and perhaps to replace a treaty that they already had with one of the kings. At any rate, the new treaty recognised that the Romans controlled virtually the whole of the coast of Latium (as far down as Antium and Circeii), but also that there were some Latin peoples who were independent from Rome. This corresponds quite closely to the situation described in Livy, according to whom Tarquinius Superbus colonised Circeii, succeeded in capturing Gabii, and was exiled in the process of besieging Ardea. The authenticity of the information Polybius preserved therefore helps confirm the general lines of the tradition at least on the latter stages of monarchic expansion.

The Latin revolt and the battle of Lake Regillus

The reaction to this gradual takeover of Latium was for the Latins to organise themselves into a federation which we call the Latin League. Like the Etruscan League, this structure must have been based on pre-existing religious cooperation, which was extended to political and military ends. Livy says that some such federation had already opposed Ancus Marcius, and Tarquinius Superbus is presented as taking over an existing Latin organisation based at the grove of Ferentina. Superbus made them contribute troops to a joint Roman and Latin army, which was under his supreme control (Livy, 1.52). But the powerbase that he is said to have built up seems to have been lost with the overthrow of the monarchy around 509 BC, and a more unstable situation developed.

The Latins fought together against Lars Porsenna at Aricia in 504 BC; Roman involvement is uncertain. Around this time the Latins orientated themselves against Rome. The existence of the alliance is attested by a fragment of Cato, which was probably transcribed from an inscription of c.500 BC (the date is unlikely to be later as Pometia was captured by the Volsci from the Latins in the early fifth century BC):

> Egerius Baebius of Tusculum, the Latin dictator, dedicated the grove of Diana in the wood at Aricia. The following peoples took part jointly: Tusculum, Aricia, Lanuvium, Laurentum (i.e. Lavinium), Cora, Tibur, Pometia, Rutilian Ardea ... (Cato, *Orig.* 2.28 C. = *FRH* F36)

---

24. Ampolo, 'Grande Roma', 82–4; Serrati, 'Neptune's altars'. See p. 77 above.

The grove at Aricia is thought to be identical with the ancient Latin cult site at Nemi. The list makes no mention of Rome as a participant (although it is not complete), and the leadership of the group by a Tusculan dictator suggests that this is a record of a group opposed to Rome.[25]

This Latin League was defeated by Rome at the battle of Lake Regillus in 499 or 496 BC (Livy, 2.21.3–4 expresses confusion), which was heavily elaborated in the literary tradition. The Latins had been attempting to re-establish Tarquinius Superbus as king in Rome. In the aftermath of the Roman victory the two sides contracted the Cassian Treaty, named after the consul Spurius Cassius, in 493 BC. Cicero and Livy record that the text of the treaty survived until the late Republic on a bronze column next to the Rostra.[26] The inscription preserved the memory of the treaty and the name of the consul responsible. Dionysius gives us a text of this treaty, although presumably he used an antiquarian source that recorded the text, rather than observing it himself:

> These were the terms of the treaty: 'Let there be peace between Rome and all the cities of the Latins for as long as the sky and earth shall remain in their places. And let them not make war on each other, or bring in enemies or grant right of passage to the enemies of either. Let them help each other, when at war, with all their strength, and let the spoils and plunder from wars fought in common be divided into equal shares for each of them. Let disputes about private contracts be decided within ten days and in the state where the contract was made. And do not let anything be added or subtracted from this treaty except by consent of Rome and all the Latins.' These terms were agreed by the Romans and the Latins and ratified by oaths and sacrifices. (Dion. Hal. 6.95)

Thus the treaty seems to have been a pact of mutual aid between Rome and the Latins. Its most important function was probably common defence against the encroaching Volsci and Aequi. Dionysius says that the participants were to receive equal shares of any spoils, which seems rather unlikely given that Rome was by far the largest state. Command of the joint armies is uncertain. A treaty formed after a Roman victory is likely to have favoured the Romans, and joint armies were always commanded by Romans in our sources. A

---

25. Cornell, *FRH* III 82–5.
26. Livy, 2.33.9; Cicero, *Balb.* 53.

passage of Festus discusses this, on the face of it implying a joint decision concerning the commander. But the key phrase is ambiguous: 'in a year when it was the responsibility of the Romans to send commanders to the army by order of the Latin name' (Festus 276 L.). This could imply that there were years in which the Latins provided commanders, but it is more likely that only Rome could provide commanders.[27] In other years, no army would be formed.

The League gradually expanded over time. New colonies were created which became members. In 486 BC the Hernici joined the alliance after a Roman defeat, and on similar terms to the Latins according to Dionysius (8.69.2). The Cassian Treaty established the bilateral relationship between the Latins and Romans that lasted until the late fourth century BC. It probably also formalised the rights that existed between them (discussed above). In summary, the Latins and Romans were brought together by the new, weaker nature of the Rome state, and also by an external threat, the hill tribes of the Volsci and Aequi who were attempting to capture the fertile plains of Latium in the fifth century BC. This was part of a wider Italian trend in which peoples of the central Apennines were successful in taking over low-lying cities (as at Poseidonia and Capua), but in this case they failed to capture the heartland of Latium. Nevertheless, it is quite clear that, as with the Samnites in Campania, the Volsci succeeded in infiltrating many cities in Latium, including Satricum, Antium and Velitrae, and were ultimately enfranchised by Rome when these cities became part of the Roman state.

Volsci and Aequi

The history of Rome in the fifth century BC was dominated by wars with two peoples, the Volsci and Aequi. They had ceased to exist by the time most of our sources were writing, in the late Republic, and so they remain rather obscure groups. The Aequi occupied the upper Anio valley, in the hills behind Praeneste and Tibur; we have remains of hillforts from these areas but little else.[28] We are slightly better informed about the Volsci, for whom there is some useful archaeological and epigraphic evidence. Two inscriptions have been identified as Volscian, one on a miniature axe head from the cemetery at

---

27. Cornell, *Beginnings*, 299; Sanchez, 'Fragment'. Armstrong, *War and Society*, 71 argues that this passage refers to the later fourth century.
28. Benelli, 'Aequi'.

Satricum, and another on a bronze tablet from Velitrae (the *Tabula Veliterna*). If correctly identified, the language was closer to Umbrian than Oscan, which is surprising given the historical position of the Volsci in southern Latium.[29] This could suggest that the Volsci had links to Umbria, but the complexity of the linguistic situation in central Italy makes this far from certain. In the historical era they are firmly attested as occupying the Monti Lepini and Pomptine plain (Map 4), where there has been a detailed investigation of the cemetery and settlement at Satricum, and around Sora in the Liris valley, considered by some to be their core area.[30]

The First Rome–Carthage treaty shows that in 509 BC Rome controlled the Latin coast down to Tarracina. The Volsci were probably already present in Latin towns such as Antium and Pometia. The conquest of Suessa Pometia by Tarquinius Superbus in the late sixth century BC is often identified as the point at which Roman–Volscian relations became hostile. Volscian pressure on Latium can be mapped by the literary sources and also by the archaeology of the settlements taken over by the Volsci, particularly Satricum. The impression we gain from the literary sources is that the Volsci and Aequi rapidly posed a very serious threat to Rome in the early fifth century BC. Livy tells us that Cora and Pometia were in Volscian hands by 495 BC (2.22.2). Antium on the coast is described as Volscian in 493 BC (2.33.4). Velitrae on the southern slopes of the Alban massif was Volscian in the early fifth century, although it was supposedly recaptured by the Romans in 493 BC. Velitrae is also reputedly the findspot of the *Tabula Veliterna*, one of the Volscian inscriptions mentioned above, which dates to the fourth or third century BC; this date would imply a continued Volscian presence in Latium. However, it is worth noting that modern scholars have questioned whether the Volsci were truly an expansionist force in southern Latium, or were instead victims of Roman aggression.[31]

The Pomptine plain was an area of particular interest to the Romans. Coarelli has connected the archaic drainage tunnels in this area (of the sixth and fifth century BC) to the reported use of corvée

---

29. For discussion of the identification see Crawford, *Imagines Italicae*, Satricum 1; Benelli, 'Problems', 97–8; Zair, 'Languages',132.
30. Gnade, 'Volscians'.
31. The idea of a Volscian advance is questioned by Rich, 'Warfare', 12; see also Gnade, 'Volscians'.

labour by the Tarquins for the Cloaca Maxima at Rome.[32] The richness of the surrounding land is suggested by the wealth of the votive deposit found at Satricum in association with the temple (in fact the richest in Latium), and by the references to its splendour in the literary sources. The spoils from Pometia funded the building of the Capitoline temple, although there was disagreement in the earliest sources about the exact quantity of metal that was obtained. Pomptine land was also regularly sought by the plebs in their agitation for land distribution. The Romans came here for grain during an early fifth-century shortage, and the loss of this land to the Volsci is also one of the factors behind the economic problems in Rome of the early fifth century BC, manifested in stories about debt and in the gap in the record of temple-building.

The height of the Volscian advance is probably represented in the legend of Coriolanus (the subject of Shakespeare's play).[33] Coriolanus is portrayed by Livy, Dionysius and Plutarch as a haughty Roman aristocrat who, despite his heroism in battle, was unfairly condemned by the plebeians and forced into exile. He went over to the Volsci and became their best general. He then led his troops on an unstoppable march right up to the gates of Rome. This is divided by the sources into two advances, one in the area of Praeneste, and the other through the Pomptine plain.[34] He was only finally stopped when his mother, wife and children left the city and came out to his camp to plead with him (with Livy and Plutarch making much of the triumph of family values and loyalty towards Rome over personal revenge and anger). The historicity of the episode remains very problematic. The oral character of the tale is clear from the lists of obscure places he captured and the dramatic nature of the story (suggesting that it was subject of epic song or another type of saga). Coriolanus did not feature in the consular *Fasti*, which also raises doubts about his identity. But the movement of Coriolanus from one community to another is typical of elite social mobility in the archaic period, and correlates closely with other evidence for this, both literary and epigraphic.[35] Irrespective of the historicity of Coriolanus himself, the story is indicative of the serious threat posed around that

---

32. Coarelli, 'Roma, i Volsci'.
33. Cornell, 'Coriolanus', for a full discussion of this legend.
34. Livy, 2.39.
35. See the discussion of the plebeian secessions in Chapter 7, for instance.

time by the Volscian advance. The Volsci continued as bitter enemies of Rome in the fifth and fourth centuries, although the emphasis in the sources shifts from them to other enemies after 431 BC, when they and the Aequi were crushingly defeated by Rome at the battle of Mount Algidus near Praeneste.

Archaeology adds another interesting dimension. The city known as Pometia or Satricum provides a useful case study in this context of the way in which we can connect archaeology with the literary tradition. Positioned in the centre of the rich Pomptine plain, according to the literary sources it was captured by Tarquinius Superbus, but was in the hands of the Volsci soon after 500 BC. The site has been extensively excavated, revealing large elite houses and a temple dedicated to Mater Matuta on the acropolis.[36] The temple had several main building phases, the first in the mid sixth century BC, and the second after a fire in the early fifth century. This subsequent phase was built on a different alignment, along with substantial aristocratic houses. New burials were laid down inside the confines of the old settlement, a sign of cultural practices different from those of the earlier Latin inhabitants. It suggests that the occupiers had a non-urban mentality, which fits with the literary picture of the Volsci. Satricum is probably the Volscian name for this site. This was one of their capitals along with Ecetra. Its other name, Suessa Pometia, is an amalgam of Latin and Auruncian. The Aurunci occupied the area south of the Pomptine plain. They were probably the first settlers here, followed by Roman colonists in the time of Tarquinius Superbus, and then Volsci. We can compare this to (Latin) Tarracina, which was given the Volscian name Anxur.[37] Ultimately, all these cities and peoples would become part of the Roman state, but the process would take centuries.

Nature of archaic warfare

Warfare in this period was linked to the nature of society in archaic central Italy. States were less powerful than in later eras and, in the unstable conditions in central Italy at the time of the fall of the Roman monarchy, saw regular migrations and secessions from groups joining or leaving their place of origin. Private groups or *gentes* (clans)

---

36. Gnade, 'Volscians'.
37. Festus 16 L.: 'What is now called Tarracina used to be known as Anxur by the Volscian people; as Ennius said, "the Volscians lost Anxur".'

moving about in central Italy engaged in warfare alongside the forces of the state.[38]

The most famous example is attested by an inscription of *c*.500 BC found in the temple of Mater Matuta at Satricum in 1977 (Fig. 8.2).[39] In the rebuilding of the sixth-century temple, an ancient block with a slightly earlier Latin inscription was reused, built with its face turned towards the inside of the building. This may be a sign that the language used, which is Latin, was not understood by the new Volscian inhabitants of the site. On the most likely reading it records a dedication to Mars by the *sodales* (companions) of *Poplios Valesios*. The two most important features of the text are that, firstly, it is a dedication by a group that describes itself in terms of its elite leader rather than through membership of a state; and secondly, *Poplios Valesios* is the archaic version of the name Publius Valerius. This may be the figure of the same name (Publius Valerius Publicola) who according to the literary sources held the consulship at Rome multiple times in the first years of the Republic, holding office in 509, 508, 507 and 504 BC. The most common scholarly interpretation is that the dedication to Mars, the god of war, was made by a private war band

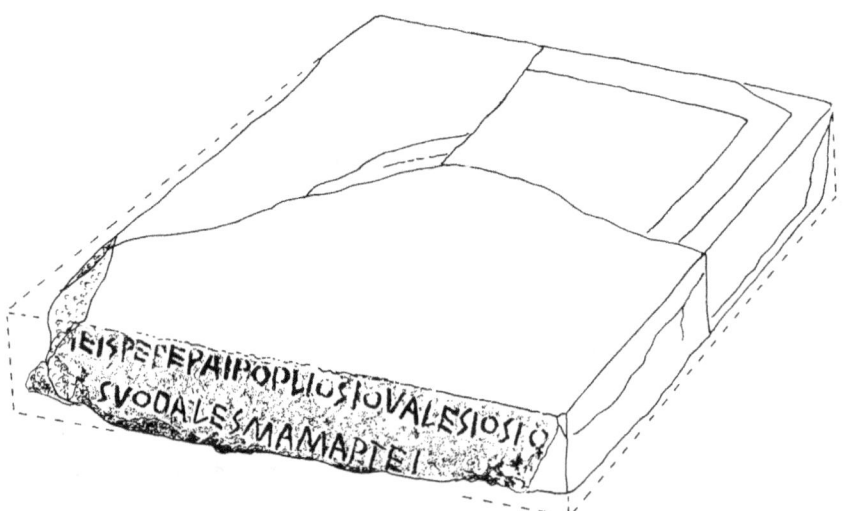

Figure 8.2 The Lapis Satricanus (after *GRT*, fig. 1.10)

38. Rawlings, 'Condottieri'; Rich, 'Warfare'; Cornell, *Beginnings*, 130–45; Armstrong, *War and Society*, ch. 4.
39. Stibbe, *Lapis Satricanus*.

undertaking an expedition outside of any state control. However, we cannot rule out the possibility that it could also be a private dedication set up by companions who had fought under Roman command, or a dedication without specific military overtones by a purely religious group.[40]

A similar case of a personal group adhering to a leader rather than a state is found in the migration of Attus Clausus 504 BC with an entourage of 'clients'. These clients were his followers, and their movement to Rome could well have had military connotations.[41] Another example is the capture of the Capitoline hill by Appius Herdonius in 460 BC. Accompanied by an armed band (of 4000 men in some sources), Herdonius was aiming to seize control of Rome, perhaps as powerful figures may have done in the sixth century BC (notably Servius Tullius, if he truly was the Etruscan adventurer Mastarna). Herdonius failed, but it is striking that the attempt involved another movement to Rome from the Sabine area, a zone where many communities saw emigration to the Tyrrhenian coastal districts.[42]

These movements seem typical of archaic warfare, with independent armed groups (perhaps clients) following elite leaders with their own agenda. The obvious parallel is with the kings of Homeric Greece, as in the *Iliad*, where leadership seems to have been based partly on descent, partly on charisma, and partly on martial ability. These movements were a sign of the migration and personal networks that we have met frequently in previous chapters. We have seen other examples of powerful figures leading followers on expeditions, such as Caelius Vibenna and Mastarna in Etruria and then Rome. Here Publius Valerius seems to be an example of movement in the other direction, since a major figure from Rome is found operating in an environment well away from the city.

This phenomenon is recorded in the sources, but not fully understood, given that ancient writers generally saw things in terms of their own day, that is, organised armies under the strict control of the state. The clearest manifestation of this is the action of the Fabii at the Cremera in 479 BC. Livy (2.48–9) records how the entire Fabian clan left Rome with their followers and clients to fight Veii, but were almost totally wiped out at the Cremera river. The event is presented

---

40. Rich, 'Warlords', 273.
41. Bradley, 'Mobility and secession', 161–5. For a 'huge [metaphorical] army of clients' defending the patrician cause after the exile of Caeso Quinctius, see Livy, 3.14.4.
42. Ampolo, 'Roma ed i Sabini'.

by Livy as the Fabii heroically taking on the duties of the state. The Fabian rural (Roman) tribe was located in this district, which suggests that they were probably defending the centre of their clan lands. They may therefore have been fighting for their own interests and not under the full control of the government at Rome (although Livy does believe that the action of the Fabii was undertaken with the approval of the Senate).

We know that other Roman clans had territorial associations: the Valerii for instance were linked with the Pomptine region. Another example comes from Suetonius (*Vit.* 1.3), although the date is unstated. In discussing the family origins of the emperor Vitellius, he records that:

> Traces of this lineage endured long afterwards in the Vitellian Road, running from the Janiculum all the way to the sea, as well as in a colony of the same name, which in ancient days the family had asked the privilege of defending against the Aequicoli with troops raised from their own line.

If we follow the details of the source (which we have no guarantee are trustworthy), this again seems to have been a type of warfare undertaken by a private group but with the consent of the Roman authorities, given that the group had, like the Fabii, requested the right to undertake this war. This picture of clan-based warfare is also supported by contemporary evidence from Etruria, which probably experienced similar conditions. A stash of 125 bronze helmets dating to the fifth century BC from Vetulonia, all inscribed with *hapnas*, may be a relic of a similar type of clan-based army. What looks like a typical clan raid – the return in triumph with captives and cattle – is depicted on the Sperandio sarcophagus from Perusia (*c.*500 BC).[43]

Scholars have therefore generally concluded that this seems to be a period which is characterised by elite adventurers and clan-based groups engaging in private war, and one in which the state lacks a monopoly on the use of violent force. Private and clan bands seem to have been formidable military agents in this period, and types of warfare must have extended well beyond the heavy infantry phalanx set up by the Servian reforms to encompass frequent raiding, ambushes and skirmishing more commonly than the clash of city-based armies.

---

43. Haynes, *Etruscan Civilization*, 186–7, 265; Smith, *Roman Clan*, 161 and 290–5 (for the Fabii).

Whilst this new consensus makes good sense of a wide range of evidence, some of it contemporary, and ties in well with what we know of archaic social mobility, its hypothetical nature should not be obscured. It depends on the sources conveying genuine information that they do not fully understand and attempt to rework in anachronistic terms to fit their own preconceptions. In addition, the precise significance of the contemporary iconographic and epigraphic source material, such as the Lapis Satricanus, is often disputed. In fact, the many signs of the growing power of city states in this era means that we should not necessarily exaggerate the weaknesses of central Italian states in the sixth and fifth century BC.[44] It is uncertain how far many of these 'private' war bands operated under state control, and whether for example the sanction of the state that Livy and Suetonius imply for the wars of the Fabii and the Vitellii were merely anachronistic embellishments. It is particularly interesting in this light to consider the role of the Fetial priests in Rome. The rituals of this priesthood may represent an attempt to rein in such privately based warmaking, as they required the enemies of Rome to give up individuals who had raided Roman territory, and created a formalised system, under community control, for the declaration of war.[45]

Colonisation in Latium

The clan colony of Vitellia takes us on to colonisation, which, like the war of the sixth and fifth century BC, resembled a primitive land-grabbing exercise as much as the organised city-state foundations of the mid Republican period.[46] For example, the possible dedicatee of the Lapis Satricanus, Publius Valerius Publicola, is presented as having founded colonies alone:

> Publicola was chosen consul for the second time, in his absence, and Titus Lucretius as his colleague. Returning, therefore, to Rome, and wishing, in the first place, to surpass Porsenna in the loftiness of his spirit, he built the city of Sigliuria, although his adversary was already near at hand. After he had fortified it at great expense, he sent to it a colony of seven hundred men, indicating that he had no concern or

---

44. This is a major theme of Hall, *Tyrrhenian Way of War*, 111–70. See also Chapter 2 above.
45. Rawlings, 'Condottieri'; Rich, 'Warfare', 15.
46. Crawford, 'Roman colonization'; Bradley, 'Colonization and identity'; Armstrong, *War and Society*, 215–31.

fear about the war. However, a sharp assault was made upon its wall by Porsenna, and its garrison was driven out. (Plut. *Pub.* 16.2-3)[47]

Further indications are provided elsewhere. Livy and Dionysius thought that generals and their soldiers had a right to keep land that they had won militarily (Livy, 2.48.2-3; 4.49.11). Generals who were responsible for the most decisive victory that won Rome new territory had the right to control its distribution (Dion. Hal. 8.30.2). They were given the most important place on the triumvirate that organised the setting up of a colony.[48]

The colonies founded in Latium before the Latin War were known as *priscae coloniae Latinae*.[49] According to Livy they were founded first by the kings and then by the Senate. This remained the same after the Latin War in 340 BC. But modern scholars have taken a different tack, suggesting that the colonies were founded collectively by the Latin League. According to Salmon, this practice had its origins in the problem of how to share out land that was conquered by the League. He argued that conquered land abutting Roman territory, such as the territory of Veii, was absorbed into the Roman state and settled 'viritane' (i.e. given to individual Roman settlers). But land to the south and east could not be divided between Rome and all the small Latin states. The solution was to create a new city on conquered land to the south where it abutted Latin territory, and have it join the League as another Latin state.[50] The colonies listed in Table 8.1 are recorded in our sources. These colonies are normally assumed to have had a military purpose. They had regular fortifications, as at Signia and Norba, and seem to have been independent cities. Their positions roughly mark the line of the Roman and Latin advance, and they presumably helped to cement Latin control of conquered districts.

However, this neat picture has been criticised in recent years, as scholars have begun to appreciate some of the problems with our sources and the wide variety of motives for colonisation. Colonies were often founded for explicitly socio-economic reasons, and many were on preexisting sites. These were colonies added to cities, rather than created from scratch, and they often seem more akin to garrisons, as in the case

---

47. Torelli, *Tota Italia*, 17, identifying the otherwise unknown site of Sigliuria with Signia.
48. Crawford, 'Roman colonization'.
49. Salmon, *Roman Colonization*, 40-54; Chiabà, *Roma e le priscae Latinae coloniae*; Termeer, 'Early colonies'; Armstrong, *War and Society*, 215-31.
50. Salmon, *Roman Colonization*, 41-2.

Table 8.1 Latin colonies in the early Republic

Date BC	Colony
498	Fidenae
495	Signia
494	Velitrae
492	Norba
467	Antium
442	Ardea
418	Labici
404	Velitrae (second colonisation)
395	Vitellia
393	Circeii
385	Satricum
383	Nepet
383	Sutrium
379	Setia

of Sigliuria mentioned above. All Latins had the right to participate in colonisation through the *ius migrationis* ('right of migration'). The largest contingents of colonists were probably Roman, given that the Roman population was much more numerous than the populations of the other Latin cities, and this acted as a vital way of increasing the Roman and Latin population.[51] But it is also clear that surviving local inhabitants were also sometimes enrolled, as at Antium in 467 BC when Livy (3.1.7) says that 'Volscian colonists were added to fill out the numbers'. This is also a feature of colonisation at Ardea (Livy, 4.11.3–7), at Circeii (Dion. Hal. 8.14.1) and at Velitrae (Dion. Hal. 7.12–13).[52]

51. Cornell, *Beginnings*, 367.
52. Bradley, 'Colonization and identity', 167–8; Armstrong, *War and Society*, 224. For example, the Roman garrison in Anxur admit Volsci and trade with the neighbouring area (Livy, 5.8.2–4); Velitrae was in the late fourth century a Roman colony with *meddices* and Volscian-language epigraphy (Bourdin, *Peuples*, 247).

It may explain the frequency of colonial revolts against the League or against Rome, with some joining the Volsci. It is a clear factor in the Latin League's revolt against Rome in the 340s BC, before its dissolution, in alliance with the Volsci, and most colonies joined the Latins rather than Rome, as we shall see.[53]

Colonisation should be seen in the broader context of individual and group mobility in central Italy from the archaic period to the middle Republic. In many ways this represents the state formalising movement which was already taking place, and might often be up to individual initiative. Colonisation should also be seen in the context of land hunger. There were frequent plebeian complaints of famine in the early fifth century BC (for instance, Livy, 2.34), and colonisation may have developed as a strategy when the international links of the sixth century BC, and the economic prosperity they brought, were lost in the difficult conditions of the fifth century BC. In this context it is instructive to note that Cleisthenes sought to resolve social conflicts in Athens in the late sixth century BC by creating cleruchies in Euboea and Salamis.[54]

The wider context: crisis in Italy?

The challenges faced by Rome in the fifth century BC, with social crises and pressure from external enemies, can be paralleled elsewhere in Italy in this era. There are plenty of signs that this was not just a Roman crisis, but rather that major changes were taking place to the archaic balance of power in Etruria, Campania and southern Italy. In fact, scholars have identified the fifth century BC as an era of 'crisis' across central Italy.[55] In part this is related to changes in international networks in the central Mediterranean, as the trade routes between central Italy and mainland Greece were severely disrupted. This is evident from the decline in Attic imports in Rome and Etruria from the mid fifth century BC.[56] It is also partly connected to the rise of Syracuse as a major seaborne power, and the defeat of an Etruscan naval force by the Syracusans and Cumaeans at the battle of Cumae in 474 BC.

This sense of crisis is particularly manifested in the setbacks experienced by the Etruscan and Greek-dominated cities in Campania. The sources report the violent takeover of Cumae, Capua

---

53. Livy, 8.3.9.
54. Rose, *Class*, 360.
55. E.g. Massa-Pairault, 'Introduction'.
56. Meyer, *Pre-Republican Rome*, 161; Gilotta, 'Ceramica'.

and Poseidonia by Oscan-speakers, Samnites in Campania and Lucanians in Poseidonia, in the fifth century BC.[57] In a lurid passage Livy portrays Oscan-speakers gradually infiltrating the cities, and then turning on the old elite and butchering them in 423 BC:

> During this year an incident is said to have taken place, which, though not connected with Roman history, is nevertheless of interest. The Etruscan town of Volturnum was seized by the Samnites, who gave it its modern name of Capua. The name is supposed to have been derived from their leader, Capys; but it is more likely to have been descriptive of the region in which it lies – campus, or 'plain' country. The seizure of the town took place in peculiarly horrible circumstances. The Samnites had been allowed by the Etruscans, whose strength had been drained by war, to share the amenities of the town and in the working of the land belonging to it, and one night, after a public holiday, when the native Etruscans were sleeping off the effects, they set upon them and butchered them. (Livy, 4.37)

The process itself is likely to have been more long-term, although it does seem to have led to a change in the nature of the elite (whether by violent takeover we are unable to confirm). The elite of these towns in the sixth and fifth centuries BC seems to have been a mix of Etruscans and local Campanians.[58] Etruscan epigraphy is plentiful in Capua and Pompeii in the sixth and fifth centuries BC, but then declines. Similarly, Greek epigraphy in Cumae and Paestum disappears in the fourth century BC. In all of these cities the chief magistrates became the Oscan *meddices*. Aristoxenus writes of the near-total barbarisation of the Greeks in Paestum in the early third century, although it is clear that they maintained some of their customs.[59]

The movement of Samnites and Lucanians from their traditional areas of habitation in the Apennines down into the wealthy cities of the plains may parallel the expansion of the Volsci and Aequi into Latium in the fifth century BC. A similar development can be seen in southern Italy, where the Samnites, Lucanians and Iapygians began to exert considerable military pressure on the Greek cities of the south. This type of movement was linked to population increase and the attraction of the wealth of the lowland cities,

---

57. Strabo, 5.4.3.
58. Lomas, *Rise of Rome*, 165.
59. Fr. 124 Wehrli, in Ath. 14.632a.

and affected Apulia as well.[60] But the process is probably misrepresented by our sources as military conquest.[61] The reality, judging by the archaeological remains, seems more like infiltration followed by political coups or transformations. We know that this period saw regime change elsewhere: the prominent tyrant Aristodemus was overthrown in Cumae in 490 BC, and republican regimes were established in Magna Graecia and Campania.[62]

But it is clear that this is not the whole picture. Characterising this period as one of crisis for the Etruscans as a whole, for instance, is clearly misleading. As southern Etruscan cities with strong links to Campania such as Tarquinii, Caere and Veii experienced setbacks, so the northern and inland centres in this period prospered. Wealth in Etruria was becoming more widely distributed and new forms of classical art emerged. There was a shift away from ostentatious burials, and new customs emerged for votive depositions. The end result of these changes in the fifth century was the dominant presence of new groups of Oscan-speakers in areas of Campania and some cities of southern Italy where previously Greeks and Etruscans had been prominent. But in Latium and Etruria groups like the Sabines, the Volsci and the Aequi were less successful in establishing a permanent presence, and the ultimate beneficiary of change was the newly resurgent power of Rome.

The conquest of Veii

By the end of the fifth century BC, Rome had strengthened its position against the Volsci and the Aequi, and in 396 BC, after a series of wars, Roman forces captured the nearest Etruscan city, Veii. This was a very significant milestone in Roman imperialism as it eliminated a key rival city state and opened up south Etruria to Roman expansion.

Veii was only 9 miles away from Rome, in a highly defensible position on the Cremera, a tributary of the Tiber (Fig. 8.1). The city site lay on a natural tufa plateau, protected on most sides by steep cliffs. Dionysius (2.54.3) reports that 'it is situated on a high and craggy rock and is as large as Athens'. Whilst this is an exaggeration, it was certainly the largest city by area in Etruria, at 194 ha (although not

---

60. Livy, 9.13.6–8.
61. Terrenato, *Early Roman Expansion*, 126–7.
62. Dion. Hal. 7.2–11 for Aristodemus.

necessarily all of it was occupied). It had a rich agricultural territory, whose potential was increased by drainage tunnels and roads. The city became extremely prosperous in the seventh and sixth centuries BC, probably on the basis of agriculture and its control over Tiberine trade.[63] Artefacts attest trading connections already from the eighth century BC with Greece (Euboean cups with semi-circular pendants of the mid eighth century BC) and the Near East (ribbed bowls from Assyria and Uratu of the late eighth century BC). In the seventh century BC the burgeoning wealth of the elite is attested by princely tombs such as Tomb V of the Monte Michele cemetery (second quarter of the seventh century BC) and some of the earliest tomb paintings in Etruria (such as the Tomb of the Roaring Lions, 700–680 BC, and the Tomb of the Ducks, 680–660 BC). Funerary custom favoured an austere restriction on grave goods from the early sixth century, showing how the city shared close cultural connections with Latium. From epigraphy we know that Veii was also linked to Latium by the migration of individuals, such as the *Tite Latine* (Titus Latinius) who is attested at Veii in the seventh century BC. (This is the earliest mention of 'Latin' as an ethnic.) Whilst the burial evidence declines in the sixth century BC, this period also sees the creation of great sanctuary buildings such as the Portonaccio temple, and very wealthy votive deposits attest the frequentation of its sanctuaries by elite individuals, including members of the Vibennae and Tolumnii families.[64] In the late sixth century BC the famous Veientine sculptor Vulca was said to have been employed by Tarquinius Superbus in Rome.[65]

As Rome and Veii emerged as the two most important centres in the lower Tiber valley in the eighth and seventh centuries BC, it was probably inevitable that they would come into conflict. Particularly important were the routes north–south along the Tiber and into the hills, such as the Via Salaria, and the routes east–west from Etruria to Latium and Campania (Map 4). Both cities clashed early on over control of the salt pans at the mouth of the Tiber, supposedly captured by Romulus

---

63. Livy, 5.22.8: Veii was *urbis opulentissimae Etrusci nominis*, 'the wealthiest city of the Etruscan name'.
64. Ampolo, 'Città riformata', 207. Aulus Vibenna, perhaps the same figure named as a companion of Mastarna by Claudius, dedicated a bucchero vase in the sanctuary of Menrva, c.580 BC, quoted above on p. 123. The sanctuary also includes a dedication by two members of the Tolumnii (the family of the fifth-century king of Veii), and *Avile Acvilnas* (whose family was probably connected to the Roman consul of 487 BC Aquilius Tuscus (*TLE* 942).
65. Pliny, *HN* 35.157; see also Chapter 5 above.

from Veii (Plut. *Rom.* 25.4), and over control of the small fortified centre of Fidenae, which lay in a dominating position overlooking the Tiber. In the fifth century BC there were repeated wars between Rome and Veii, which particularly centred on Fidenae, and also encompassed the famous defeat of the Fabii at the Cremera river in 479 BC (discussed above). Veii was supported in these wars by their neighbours the Faliscans, who were culturally and linguistically close to the Latins, Capenates and Fidenates. As an isolated Etruscan site on the left, Latin bank of the river, Fidenae came under repeated attack by Rome until it was definitively captured in 435 BC. Veii had already in the mid sixth century BC built (or refurbished) 8 km of walls around the city plateau on a similar scale to the Servian Walls of Rome.[66]

The narrative in our sources of the capture of Veii is heavily mythologised, organised as it is around the legendary figure of Camillus. According to Livy, the Romans laid siege to the city for ten years, ending in 396 BC when certain prophecies were fulfilled, and the city was captured with the blessing of the gods. This account seems modelled in part on the similar span of the Trojan war, so it should probably not be taken literally.[67] But the siege was clearly a massive operation for Rome, given the difficulty of taking the site by assault. Livy (4.59.11) records that preparations for the siege involved the establishment of *stipendium* (military pay) for the Roman army for the first time. Connected to this was the imposition of *tributum* (taxation) on Roman citizens and indemnities on enemies, both of which are mentioned regularly from now on in Livy's text.[68] The Veientines appealed for help to the council of the twelve Etruscan cities, but according to Livy they were refused because they had recently appointed a king, whose impious behaviour had alienated other members of the League.[69]

The territory of the defeated city was added to that of Rome. This increased Roman territory by about 50 per cent in the estimate of the German historian Beloch, and opened up control of the lower Tiber valley and the route north.[70] Many colonists were sent to Veii from Rome (and presumably Latium), with families settled individually

66. Tabolli and Cerasuolo, *Veii*, 147–8.
67. Ogilvie, *Commentary on Livy*, 628.
68. Crawford, *Coinage*, 22; Erdkamp, 'War and state formation', 105.
69. Livy, 5.1.3–7, quoted above, p. 267.
70. Beloch, *Römische Geschichte*, 620: adding 562 km^2 to bring it up to 1,510 km^2; cf. Rich, 'Warfare', 13. Beloch's figures are criticised as an underestimate by Coarelli, 'Demografia', 321.

on plots of land ('viritane' colonisation). Most but not all of the conquered population was treated harshly. Livy (5.22) says that all the freeborn survivors were enslaved. This would indicate a considerable demand for slaves already in the Roman economy, although slaves could also have been sold to other communities. Later Livy (6.3–5) says that many of the locals who had come over to Rome were given citizenship and an allotment of land. Out of the new settlers and these surviving Etruscans four new tribes were created in 387 BC. The precise impact of the sack is difficult to follow in the reappraisal of the survey results from the area, published by the Tiber Valley team. These show a substantial decline in sites from the archaic period (sixth and early fifth century BC) to the early Republic (later fifth and early fourth century BC). There is little trace of new foundations relating to viritane settlers after the sack, but a substantial number of sites that survive from the archaic period go on to become villas.[71] Just as they may have absorbed part of the local population, so the Romans took on the cult of Juno, the goddess who had protected the city. The cult was transferred to the Aventine by the *evocatio* ('calling out') of the deity (Livy, 5.22). This assimilation of some survivors and gods of the city is a sign of Roman openness, an archaic outlook that prioritised the fullness of the Roman citizen body and divine pantheon over and above concerns about the ethnicity of the new additions.

Rome's victory over Veii had almost immediate social and religious consequences. The attraction of the site to subsequent Romans was notorious, and soon after the conquest the tribunes of the plebs are said to have brought forward two proposals for part of the plebs to migrate there. Both were rejected through the influence of Camillus, who was later celebrated for his patriotism.[72] These proposals have largely been rejected as unhistorical by modern historians, but the close parallels with the plebeian secessions mean that they should be taken seriously as historically plausible episodes.[73] Camillus himself was allegedly exiled on the basis of misappropriating spoils from the wealthy city, including bronze doors or gates.[74] He had apparently attracted the ire of the plebeians due to neglecting until some

---

71. Di Giuseppe, 'Villae', 8–9, 13.
72. Livy, 5.24.5–11; 5.49.8–55; for this quality see especially his *elogium* from the Forum of Augustus: Dessau, *ILS* 52 = Degrassi, *Inscriptiones Italicae, Elogia*, 61.
73. The story is doubted by Ogilvie, *Commentary*, 741–2, but for the positive case see Bradley, 'Mobility and secession', with further references.
74. Livy, 5.32.8, Plut. *Cam.* 12.1.

time after the event to dedicate part of the spoils to the gods. When this was remedied, having consulted the Delphic oracle for advice on capturing the city, the Romans subsequently dedicated a golden bowl there in the treasury they shared with Massilia (Appian, *Italian Wars* 8). In commemorating this brutal victory, Rome was claiming to enjoy the support of Apollo, the presiding deity of this famous international centre where the Etruscans had long had a presence. This may reveal some Roman disquiet with the huge scale of the carnage, but it also shows Rome's concern to advertise itself positively in the diplomatic language of Mediterranean city states.[75]

The Gallic sack

Shortly after this major victory which gave Rome a dominant position in the lower Tiber basin, the city suffered a catastrophic defeat. In 390 BC, a large Gallic army utterly routed the Romans at the Allia river just north of the city and plundered an unguarded Rome. Later Romans considered this the most serious blow Rome ever received. It was, after all, the only documented time when the city was captured by a hostile power before the Goth Alaric in AD 410. For Livy this was the most calamitous episode in Roman history prior to the Punic Wars; it forms a key centrepiece in his first ten books. He claimed that the city was burnt and hurriedly rebuilt, resulting in a disorganised street pattern. He also believed that all earlier documents were lost in the conflagration, and this was why Roman history was so poorly known beforehand.[76] In fact, both suppositions are probably misguided. There is good evidence for the survival of earlier documents from before 390 BC, and the unplanned street layout is more likely to be the result of organic growth than of a one-time rebuilding. Nevertheless, the sources are probably correct in seeing this event as a catastrophic disaster.[77]

Although there are differences in the story, the sources generally concur that the Gallic army was comprised of a core of Senones, from the Adriatic coast, joined by groups of other Gauls. Livy in particular relates this to the general advance of the Gauls from north

---

75. Consultation of the Delphic oracle in the time of the siege of Veii: Livy, 5.14.5 and 5.16.8–11; Plut. *Cam*. 4.4.
76. Livy, 5.55; 6.1. Cf. Edwards, *Writing Rome*, 51.
77. So Eckstein, *Mediterranean Anarchy*, 132; cf. Santoro, *Galli*; Cornell, *Beginnings*, 313–17; Oakley, *Commentary*, I 344–7.

of the Alps into Italy, lured by the wealthy Etruscan cities. The Gauls had initially attacked Etruscan Clusium when they were diverted to Rome, supposedly because some of the Roman ambassadors to the Gallic army joined with the Clusines and killed a prominent Gallic chieftain. The tradition reported that the huge Gallic army immediately marched towards Rome, where a hastily raised force was defeated at the Allia, a tributary of the Tiber. Some remnants of the army retreated to Veii, and others to Rome. The slowness of the Gauls to realise their huge victory meant that Rome could prepare to defend the less accessible hill, the Capitoline, with its best fighting men. The Gauls then sacked the main part of the city, which, although it was walled (Livy, 5.38–9), could not be defended given the absence of the main fighting force. The gates were said to have been left open as there were insufficient troops to defend the walls.

The priests buried some of the most sacred artefacts, and carried the others to neighbouring Caere, a sign of Rome's special relationship with that Etruscan centre. Much of the plebeian segment of the population abandoned the city and fled into the territory or to neighbouring towns (Dion. Hal. 13.6 1; Livy, 5.40.5–6). This detail is also reminiscent of the earlier plebeian secessions, and another sign of the ready mobility of plebs as well as elites. The Gauls sacked and burnt the city, and according to some sources occupied it for some seven months.[78] Meanwhile the defenders heroically held onto the Capitoline right through the siege. At one point Manlius Capitolinus is said to have been alerted to a Gallic assault by the sacred geese of Juno; a few years later he would be executed by being thrown off the same rock from which he heroically ejected the Gauls. Some accounts imply that the Capitoline itself eventually fell.[79] The Gauls only left when paid a massive ransom. In a series of variant reports, this ransom was recovered when the Gauls were defeated either by the Romans in the neighbourhood of Rome (implausibly), or by the Caeretans as they passed that city.[80] Rome was said to have been

---

78. Polybius, 2.22; Plut. *Cam.* 30.1: 'So strangely was Rome taken, and more strangely still delivered, after the Barbarians had held it seven months in all. They entered it a few days after the Ides of July, and were driven out about the Ides of February.'
79. Tacitus, *Hist.* 3.72: 'a temple which neither Porsenna on the capitulation of the city nor the Gauls when they captured it had been able to desecrate'.
80. Polybius, 2.18 simply has the Gauls having to return to northern Italy as a result of an attack by the Veneti; Diod. Sic. 14.117.

supported in paying the extortionate cost by Massilia, its longtime ally in southern Gaul.[81]

The sources, particularly the very elaborate version in Livy, present us with a patriotically uplifting version that has clearly been manipulated for its moral lessons. The whole saga is linked to that of the historically exaggerated figure of Camillus, who was exiled during the sack, but returned to save Rome and inflict revenge on the Gauls. The Romans were punished for the reckless actions of their ambassador, and for the impiety and haste with which the army was prepared at the Allia. But the basic outline of events is plausible and should be taken at face value: the defeat at the Allia, the abandoning of the city by the plebeians, and the ransom paid to the Gauls. The event was noted by fourth-century Greek writers such as Heraclides of Pontus, a philosopher at Athens (who calls Rome a 'Greek city'), Aristotle, who has a version of the story (also in Livy) of a plebeian who rescues the sacred relics, and Theopompus, a historian from Chios.[82] This was thus an event with Mediterranean-wide ramifications, even if the details are rather hazy to early Greek sources.

The Roman tradition remembered the occasion very clearly, documenting the psychological impact through the later designation of the *Dies Alliensis* (Day of the Allia) on 18 July as one of the most inauspicious days in the Roman calendar. They later had a special term for a levy in case of a Gallic invasion, a *tumultus gallicus*, when even priests could be called to army service, and all the allies were obliged to send their full forces to the aid of Rome.[83] This is known to have happened in 225 BC (Polybius, 2.24), when another huge Gallic force invaded central Italy with the claimed intention of destroying Rome (Polybius, 2.35), although this time to be defeated. The impact is also clear from very harsh Roman treatment of the

---

81. Justin, 43.5.8: 'After peace was thus obtained, and security established, some deputies from Marseilles, as they were returning from Delphi, whither they had been sent to carry presents to Apollo, heard that the city of Rome had been taken and burned by the Gauls. This calamity, when the news of it was brought home to them, the Massilians lamented with a public mourning, and contributed gold and silver, both public and private, to make up the sum to be given to the Gauls, from whom they knew that peace was bought. For this service an exemption from taxes was decreed them, a place in the theatre assigned them among the senators, and a treaty made with them upon equal terms (*foedus aequo iure*).'
82. Quoted in Plut. *Cam.* 22.3 and Pliny, *HN* 3.57: 'for Theopompus, before whom nobody had mentioned them, merely states that Rome was taken by the Gauls'.
83. Williams, *Beyond the Rubicon*, 171.

Gauls of northern Italy, which began with the expulsion of the Senones from the Ager Gallicus in 284 BC.[84]

The impact on Rome remains controversial. Although the archaeological destruction layer thought to relate to this event has now been redated to the late sixth century, there is now new evidence for a widespread fire from excavations in the Forum of Julius Caesar, and at the foot of the Capitolium.[85] The sources were certainly convinced that the city was severely burnt, and a seven-month occupation implies a devastating situation. The longer-term impact is more uncertain. In the traditional picture, the main body of the population was not besieged in the city, but was able to escape the city, and take refuge in the surrounding area. The Gauls themselves seem to have been a very mobile mercenary band, who were probably only interested in capturing booty.[86] That they could be bought off shows that they were not aiming to settle Roman territory, and according to Justin they then moved on to ally with Dionysius of Syracuse after the sack (Justin, 20.4). Quite how Rome was able to reconstitute itself after the capture of the city and the dispersal of the population is intriguing, especially if the occupation lasted for as long as the sources allege. The mobility of the population seems to be part of its strength, and the re-establishment of the city a testament to the natural attraction of the site.

The aftermath of the Gallic sack

The twin sackings of Veii and Rome, the two major cities of the lower Tiber valley, show the unsettled and violent conditions of the early fourth century BC. Eckstein rightly points out that the unpredictable nature of the inter-state environment and fear of extinction haunted all actors on the ancient Mediterranean stage, and in many ways these were critical events in shaping the Roman psyche. Even in the late Republic the idea that the Gauls were an ever-present danger remained.[87] But the impact on Veii was much more devastating and longer-lasting than that on Rome: the former never recovered,

---

84. Polybius, 2.19, with a very interesting digression on Roman relations with the Gauls; see Williams, *Beyond the Rubicon*, 207–18.
85. Bernard, 'Continuing the debate', 7, with further references.
86. Cornell, *Beginnings*, 318.
87. Eckstein, *Mediterranean Anarchy*, 131–8; Cic. *Cat.* 3 and 4; *Fam.* 10.4.4; *Att.* 14.4.1, with Williams, *Beyond the Rubicon*, 177–8.

becoming an insignificant settlement by the late Republic; the latter rose within a century to dominate the whole Italian peninsula.

Rome seems to have still been able to call on substantial forces in the aftermath of the sack, suggesting that the population had not been completely devastated.[88] Control over Latium was loosened, and the next few years had to be spent in reasserting Roman power in the region. The Gauls returned to Latium some thirty years later, establishing a base in the Alban Hills which they held for a few years, and using it to raid the surrounding countryside.

The gradual Roman recovery after the Gallic sack was symbolised by various factors. There was renewed urban building, most notably with the so-called 'Servian Wall', initiated about a decade later in 378 BC (Livy, 6.32.1). This was built with stone from the territory of the newly captured Veii. The use of a new type of stone strongly suggests that this was a renovation of the earlier circuit, rather than the first building of the circuit that many modern scholars have suggested.[89] Following the existing course of the wall was nevertheless a massive undertaking, as at 11 km long it was still the largest in central Italy. An area of around 427 ha was enclosed, still considerably larger than any comparable neighbouring city some two centuries after it was built.[90]

Rome also embarked on a renewed colonial programme in the aftermath of the sack. New colonies were founded in the north of the territory of captured Veii, at Sutrium and Nepet in 383 BC, and at Ostia between 380 and 350 BC. Rome also displayed various foreign ambitions in the western Mediterranean. The city renewed the archaic treaty it had with Massilia in 389 BC (Justin, 43.5.10) as a result of the city's help with the Gallic ransom. Rome also sent colonies to the nearest islands. Diodorus relates that in 378 BC 'the Romans sent out five hundred colonists with immunity from taxes to Sardinia'. From Theophrastus, *Hist. pl.* 5.8.2 we hear the story that 'the Romans, wishing to establish a city, once sailed to the island [Corsica] with twenty-five ships'. Theophrastus says that the expedition failed, and does not date it. Various periods have been suggested, but it seems most likely that it should be placed in the fourth century BC, alongside the expedition to Sardinia.[91]

---

88. We lack census records from the period immediately after the sack to document the losses.
89. See Chapter 5 for details; cf. Cifani, *Architettura*, 260–1.
90. Bernard, *Building*, ch. 4.
91. Torelli, 'Colonizzazioni'; Coarelli, 'Santuari'; Cornell, *Beginnings*, 321; Bispham, 'Rome and Antium'.

Roman interests in the western Mediterranean are confirmed by the second treaty between Rome and Carthage, for which Polybius again provides the text (3.24). Although the date is not certain, it is likely to be the treaty which Livy (7.27) tells us was formed in 348 BC. The text suggests that Rome had not expanded its power significantly since the previous treaty in 509 BC.[92] Rome had a subject area within Latium, and interest over the rest of it. Romans could trade in the western Mediterranean islands, except for Sardinia. Rome was also now treated as a potential founder of colonies. Carthage was concerned to prevent too much Roman contact with Sardinia or Africa, but trade with Carthage and Sicily was enabled. The signing of this treaty is in itself a confirmation that the Carthaginians believed that Roman power had recovered, and shows that Rome remained a Mediterranean-focused city, something actively obscured by our sources. Certainly, a renewed phase of expansion from here on led its armies to enter new spheres of activity and to come into contact with new opponents, beginning with intervention in Campania.

Campania and the Latin War

Roman power increased dramatically from the late 340s BC. In the 350s and 340s BC Rome fought defensive actions, fending off attacks from the Gauls, Latins, Etruscans and even Greek seaborne raiders. This period saw a number of hard-fought Roman victories in the immediate vicinity of Rome, such as the defeat of the Gauls and Tibertines at the Colline Gate in 360 BC. It also saw several reported instances of Romans, such as Manlius Torquatus and Valerius Corvus, fighting single combats with Gallic adversaries. The heroic victories of these figures over larger Gallic opponents was commemorated by the adoption of cognomina (Torquatus after the torque taken from his opponent and Corvus after the raven that supposedly aided Valerius in battle). The ultimate source of such stories must be family histories.

In the late 340s BC the Romans took several momentous steps. They fought a short war with the Samnites, which ended up having major implications. They took control of Capua, the most important city in Campania, and the surrounding area of the Campanian plain. They also dissolved the Latin League and reorganised the whole of Latium and adjoining parts of Campania under their control.

---

92. Eckstein, *Mediterranean Anarchy*, 133.

Hostility between the Romans and their great enemies the Samnites arose because both expanded into Campania in the mid fourth century BC. This region has some of the best agricultural land in Italy, whose wealth was naturally attractive to outsiders. The first conflict came about because the Samnites defeated the people of Teanum Sidicinum, who appealed to Capua, the most important city in the region, for help in 343 BC. The Campanians (as the people of Capua were called) were then defeated themselves twice by the Samnites, and the Samnites began to besiege their city. Its inhabitants appealed to Rome for help, looking to the powerful city state to the north for protection, and not wishing to fall under the control of the upland Samnites. Ironically, the Campanians themselves were of Samnite origin, judging by Livy's story of the infiltration and capture of the city eighty years or so earlier in 423 BC. Our sources claim that the Roman Senate was wary of coming to the aid of Capua, as it would have violated the treaty formed with the Samnites in 354 BC, but they were persuaded by the Campanians undertaking a *deditio*, a surrender of themselves to Rome's power. Eckstein regards this situation as characteristic of international anarchies, where larger powers were drawn into conflict by the supplications of minor states, and of Rome's aggressive diplomacy, pursued despite the likelihood of war.[93] The resulting short conflict was the first of many major battles between Rome and the Samnites, but in this case it was soon interrupted by internal turmoil and external rebellion for Rome, and the two powers resumed their alliance.

This war led to a chain of connected events. In 342 BC a mutiny broke out in the Roman garrison at Capua, which led to major political changes at Rome.[94] This political discord encouraged the Latins to organise against Rome in 341 BC, and the next few years for Rome were taken up with dealing with these forces. The Latins were joined by the Volsci, whose members included the people of Antium, which had been a Roman colony in 467 BC. Similarly, the leaders of the Latins were 'L. Annius of Setia and L. Numisius of Circeii, both belonging to the Roman colonists' (Livy, 8.3.9). They were joined by the colonies of Signia and Velitrae, indicating that the colonies founded in this period, with their mixed populations of Romans, Latins and sometimes Volsci, identified more with the Latins than with Rome. They were joined by the Campanians too.

---

93. Eckstein, *Mediterranean Anarchy*, 142.
94. See Chapter 7.

The eventual Roman victory in what came to be called the Latin War between 341 and 338 BC led to an epoch-making change. After several attempts the Roman Senate came to a definitive reorganisation of the area between itself and Capua (Fig. 9.1). The complex settlement was partly based on earlier arrangements, and partly on the principle of divide and rule, with three different status groups created. The Latin League was dissolved, and all its cities were defined not by their communal organisation but by their relationship to Rome. Some cities were directly incorporated into the Roman state: Nomentum, Pedum, Tusculum, Lavinium, Aricia, Lanuvium, Lavinium, Antium and Velitrae. Some of the more distant communities, including Capua and Cumae in Campania, and Privernum, Fundi and Formiae in southern Latium, were given citizenship without the vote (an innovative status). Other cities continued to have the status of Latin allies of Rome, such as Cora, Praeneste, Tibur, Ardea, Signia Norba, Setia and Circeii. They kept the traditional Latin rights of *conubium*, *commercium* and *migratio*.

This innovative and flexible arrangement gave Rome firm and lasting control over two of the richest agricultural areas of Italy, Latium and Campania. These areas were densely populated, and provided huge manpower resources for the Roman state. Rome's territory increased from 1,902 to 5,525 km^2, according to Beloch.[95] This gave the Romans the largest supply of military manpower in the peninsula and allowed them to expand out of this powerbase along the Tyrrhenian coast to control the entire Italian peninsula. What was symbolically important in this settlement was that Roman citizenship was imposed on communities well away from Rome itself. The members of incorporated city states (*municipia*) now had citizenship of Rome as well as their own city – a very flexible concept of citizenship in comparison with Greek notions.[96] The settlement that the Romans imposed after their victory was the most important stage in the formation of the system by which land conquered by the Romans would be organised, first in Italy, then in the Mediterranean and ultimately in the rest of the empire.

Conclusion

Rome and the Latins were intimately linked throughout their history, even though at times their relationship was a hostile one. Both came

---

95. Beloch, *Römische Geschichte*, 620.
96. Humbert, *Municipium*.

together primarily for collective defence against their enemies, and the pattern of colony foundation that was set in motion by the Romans and Latins together would continue and reinforce conquests later on. Rome retained a bitter memory of the difficulty of the struggle in the fifth century BC, which ultimately led to punitive treatment of the Volsci and Aequi, of whom little is heard after this period. The Aequi were virtually wiped out in a rapid campaign in 304 BC according to Livy (9.45), and the battles that these peoples fought with Rome set the tone for later wars such as those against the Samnites and Carthaginians. The Roman state was also critically shaped in this period by the siege of Veii and by the Gallic sack. Whereas Rome was able to recover to reassert its control over its neighbours after its population largely escaped the destruction, the population of Veii, trapped in the city for a long siege, was less fortunate, even if some survived to be incorporated into the Roman citizen body.

CHAPTER 9

Rome and Italy 338–290 BC: conquest and accommodation

Introduction

The period from the end of the Latin War in 338 BC to the conquest of Sabinum and defeat of the Samnites in 290 BC saw epoch-making changes in the fortunes of Rome. The conquest proceeded swiftly and most of Italy was brought under Roman control, a process ultimately completed by 264 BC.[1] Large numbers of new colonies were founded by Rome, and the huge increase in Roman territory and manpower would transform the state in the third century BC. Italy went from a disunified peninsula of competing city and ethnic states to the heartland of a Mediterranean-wide Roman empire, which it would remain for another six centuries.

There has been considerable recent debate as to why the Roman conquest of Italy was so rapid and whether the triumph of Rome was inevitable. Ancient explanations centred on the superiority of Roman character, emphasising Roman morality, discipline, determination and a propensity for self-sacrifice, such as in single combat. These self-glorifying claims have been deconstructed by modern authors, and more critical approaches to ancient stereotypes and ethnocentricity have allowed new perspectives on the conquest to emerge.[2]

Decades of research focused on the peoples of Italy mean that we now have a much better knowledge of the enemies of Rome in this period.[3] The fragmented and highly competitive inter-state environment of Italy during the period of conquest meant that Rome faced many different opponents. We have begun to appreciate the state-level complexity of most central Italian communities, and the expansionist ambitions of other states in Italy besides Rome. Scholars have also

---

1. For the period from 290–264 BC, see Rosenstein, *Rome and the Mediterranean*.
2. See for instance, on the Samnites, Dench, *From Barbarians*; Scopacasa, *Ancient Samnium*; Tagliamonte, 'Samnites'.
3. Farney and Bradley (eds), *Peoples of Ancient Italy*.

begun to explore parallels that Rome had with Athens, Persia and other empires. Recent work has also stressed the importance of networks in Italy, which created the conditions for the rapid spread of information and the sharing of military technology. Rome developed a highly organised military by the late fourth century, although many Italian forces were the match of Rome's in quality if not quantity. Romans were often linked to the peoples they came to control, through marriage and other forms of social interaction. Much of the expansion we call the Roman conquest came about by the projection of power rather than straightforward battlefield defeat and resultant subjection.[4] We have also come to appreciate how far the expansion of Rome in this period is linked to contemporary political changes in Rome itself. The creation of a new mixed aristocracy led to more intense competition for glory within Rome and added impetus to the urge to conquer.[5]

The Samnites

In the fifty years after the Latin War (341–338 BC) the Samnites grew to become Rome's most significant enemies. Livy portrays them as rivals for hegemony in Italy. They fought a series of wars with Rome which are conventionally divided into three phases: 343–341 BC, 327–303 BC and 301–290 BC. These phases are conventionally called the First, Second and Third Samnite Wars, although this is a modern designation which does not appear in our sources.[6] In fact, our sources regard Rome and Samnium as almost continually at war until the late 270s, when the Samnites joined with the Epirote king Pyrrhus.

Samnium was a large area organised into an effective political unity. There were probably four main tribes that fought together in this period, later divided by separate Roman alliances. By the mid fourth century they were threatening Campania, which inevitably brought them up against the growing power of Rome. The Samnites are vividly described in Greco-Roman sources as hardy uplanders. Livy describes their relations with the Apulians in the following terms:

> The Samnites, who at that time lived in villages in the mountains, ravaged the places on the plain and along the coast, whose cultivators they despised as softer and, as often happens, similar to their place of origin, just as they themselves were rough mountain men. (Livy, 9.13.7)

4. See Terrenato, *Early Roman Expansion* on the importance of this aspect.
5. Hölkeskamp, *Reconstructing*.
6. Cornell, 'Deconstructing'.

They were certainly powerful. Polybius' breakdown of Roman manpower when they were fighting the Gauls in 225 BC (2.24) shows that the Samnites provided the largest allied contingent (some 77,000 men) to the Roman army, which, given that this is some fifty years after the end of the conquest, suggests that the Samnites had been even more powerful before the wars with Rome. Like the Romans, they built up a wide network of alliances and expanded against the peoples of the lowlands throughout the fourth century BC. On multiple occasions they invaded Latium, and while they were never in a position to capture Rome, they were at times a genuine threat to Roman supremacy.[7] Archaeological research has both supported and undercut the ancient view, and a more complex reality is slowly emerging.[8] The Samnites shared many features of a Hellenised culture and their Oscan language with their neighbours. Like many peoples of the Apennines, they had adopted a dispersed settlement pattern of villages, fortifications and sanctuaries, although some of the major centres were moving towards urban status in the fourth and third centuries BC. Rather than being seen as a more primitive form of settlement organisation than city states like Rome, the Samnites are better compared to states of a non-*polis* type, common throughout the Mediterranean, like the *ethne* of mainland Greece such as Aetolia, or the Gauls of northern Italy.

Campania and Second Samnite War

After the brief battles before the Latin War, the second phase of Roman conflict with the Samnites erupted for a range of reasons. The gradual assertion of Roman control over southern Latium in the 330s BC had threatened the fringes of Samnium, as well as Samnite links to Campania. In 328 BC Rome founded the colony of Fregellae on the site of an earlier Volscian settlement on the Samnite-controlled left bank of the Liris. By this action Rome must have broken the treaty formed with the Samnites in 354 BC and renewed after their conflict in 343–341 BC. A year later, in 327 BC, a Roman army was sent to Campania to deal with Samnites in Paleopolis and Neapolis who had allegedly been attacking Romans in Campania. This marked an escalation of Roman intervention in the area, and led to Rome gaining control over Neapolis.

---

7. Eckstein, *Mediterranean Anarchy*, 138–47; this is doubted by Cornell, 'Deconstructing'.
8. Tagliamonte, *Sanniti*, 'Samnites'; Bispham, 'Samnites'; Scopacasa, *Ancient Samnium*.

The war saw consistent Roman aggression, from the foundation of Fregellae to attacks on Samnite allies and neighbours such as the Vestini in 325 BC. Battles took place across central Italy, in southern Latium, Campania and Samnium. Towards the end of the war most battles occurred on Samnite territory, and Roman forces seem to have been able to roam at will by the later stages. However, the Samnites, whose expansionism had brought them into contact with Rome, were also aggressive, and as we have seen invaded Latium on multiple occasions. The only lull in the fighting came after the battle of the Caudine Forks in 321 BC, a great victory for the Samnites. The Samnites trapped a double consular Roman army in a narrow valley in Samnium and humiliated the captive legionaries by forcing them to pass under a yoke made of spears as a symbol of their submission. The consuls were forced into an agreement dictated by the Samnites (Livy, 9.1–11). This curious diplomatic decision was explained in the Roman tradition as the result of a typically riddling legend. The Samnite commander Gaius Pontius, unsure what to do given his unprecedented luck, called on his father Herennius for advice. Herennius advised the total destruction of the army, and then, when this was rejected as unpalatable, suggested the complete opposite, joining with Rome as an ally. The puzzled Pontius unwisely rejected both courses of action and imposed a treaty on Rome. This was then conveniently ignored by Rome, citing spurious excuses, and Rome was able to recover and dominate Samnium by 306 BC. The story emphasised to later Romans the precarious nature of Rome's rise to power, and the divinely ordained chance that led to its supremacy. Although it is highly elaborated, the outcome, which is probably genuine, shows that the Samnites were familiar with the precepts of international diplomacy, in contrast to their uncivilised portrayal in the Roman tradition.[9]

The end of this war in 306 BC marked an important stage in the establishment of Roman control over Italy, which was recognised by various foreign powers. Already during their struggle with the Samnites the Romans had been in contact with Alexander the Great. He had warned them not to allow pirates to plunder Greek ships. Rome formed a treaty with his brother-in-law Alexander of Epirus in 332 BC, and in 323 BC they were among the Italian states which sent

---

9. Oakley, *Commentary*, III 31–4: the treaty that was probably imposed on the Romans was transformed in the Roman account into a less binding *sponsio*, a promise.

embassies congratulating him on his conquests.[10] Carthage renewed its treaty with Rome in 306 BC, and if the pro-Carthaginian historian Philinus is to be believed, it recognised Roman control over the whole of Italy.[11] It is also probably at this point that the Rhodians initiated a long friendship with Rome.[12]

Rome and the Etruscans and Umbrians

Rome was also involved in hostilities against the Etruscans and Umbrians. These hostilities lasted a very long time, beginning in the monarchical period and ending with the destruction of Volsinii in 264 BC, although the story is complex, as it includes long periods of peace and many alliances, such as with Caere in the fourth century BC. Rome had fought against Veii and the Faliscans in the fifth and fourth centuries BC, and against Tarquinii and other southern Etruscan states including Vulci from the mid fourth century BC. From the 310s BC they began to move against the northern Etruscan cities of Perusia and Arretium and were also drawn into conflict in Umbria. The assembled peoples of Umbria were defeated in the plain before Mevania in 308 BC. Other Roman interventions included the conquest of Nequinum and the establishment of the colony of Narnia on a defensible site above the Nar river in 299 BC, and the critical Roman victory over an alliance of Samnites, Gauls, Etruscans and Umbrians at Sentinum in 295 BC.[13]

Roman expansion northwards into Etruria was slower than southwards into Latium and Campania, for the large Etruscan city states were more formidable opponents. Etruscan warfare was advanced (it had heavily influenced the Roman army). Most cities had elaborate fortifications supplementing often inaccessible sites. The Etruscan cities mostly acted alone, although they also conducted alliances a few cities wide. From the early third century the increased threat of Rome induced wider alliances, which included the Gauls and Samnites by the time of Sentinum.

During the war between Rome and the Samnites between 303 and 290 BC, the Etruscans and Umbrians took part in an unprecedented central Italian alliance. According to Livy it was engineered by the

10. For piracy, see Chapter 6; for the embassies, see Chapter 10.
11. Polybius, 3.26.3–4; Forsythe, *Critical History*, 312.
12. Polybius, 30.6.5; Harris, 'Quando e come', 313–18.
13. Bradley, *Ancient Umbria*, 115–16.

Samnite general Gellius Egnatius, and involved the Samnites with the Gauls, Umbrians and Etruscans. This seems an attempt to match the level of manpower on which the Romans could call, and which since 338 BC had probably far surpassed that of any other central Italian state. The high point of the conflict came in 295 BC with the battle of Sentinum in the Umbrian Apennines, probably the greatest battle fought in Italy up to this date. Both armies were huge by the standards of the day. There were four legions (about 18,000 men) and at least an equivalent number of allies on the Roman side (perhaps 36,000 in all). Livy presents the opposing forces as heavily outnumbering the Romans, claiming that 25,000 were eventually killed. A less plausible figure of 100,000 enemy dead comes from the contemporary Greek historian Duris of Samos, preserved by Diodorus (21.6.1–2). Leaving aside this hyperbole, it is striking that the fame of this battle was noted near the time by a writer in Greece.

Sentinum was later celebrated on the temple frieze at nearby Civitalba, dating to the second century BC, with a scene of Gauls being defeated by the gods. The intended parallel is perhaps with the repulse of the Gauls from Delphi by Apollo, although it could also refer to other defeats of Gauls in Italy, such as by Caere in the 380s BC.[14] Whatever the precise allusion, this seems to be a Roman attempt to mark the battle as an Italian defeat of the Gauls, rather than that of a Roman-led coalition over a Samnite-led coalition. The battle was decisive for the destiny of Italy. In the subsequent years Rome defeated the Samnites at the battle of Aquilonia in 293 BC, and in 290 BC the Samnites sued for peace (Livy, *Epit.* 11).

The loss of the main narratives of Roman history in the 280s and 270s BC means that the latter stages of the conquest are much more obscure. The concentration of triumphs between the 310s and 280s BC show that this was a critical period for Etruria. It was also probably the decisive period for the formation of the Roman alliance system. The major players in central Italy were never again able to create a similar level of opposition to Rome, although there were substantial battles in Etruria between Rome and the northern Etruscan states in alliance with the Gauls, as at Vadimon in 280 BC. The final stages of the conquest of Etruria were marked by the destruction of further Etruscan cities besides Veii, including Doganella and Volsinii. Umbria became heavily colonised, Etruria less so in the immediate aftermath. Rome perhaps here relied more on the domination of Etruscan cities by pro-Roman

---

14. Santoro (ed.), *Galli*, 196–203.

elites.[15] Control over Etruria was ultimately consolidated by the 270s BC, with colonies on the Etruscan coast such as Cosa, Pyrgi and Alsium, and roads such as the Via Aurelia through Etruria in 241 BC and the Via Flaminia through southern Etruria and Umbria in 220 BC.

Rome and the Adriatic coast

The defeat of the anti-Roman alliance at Sentinum opened up the wider Adriatic coast to Rome (though Rome had already moved into northern Apulia in 320 BC as part of the Samnite Wars, and founded a colony at Luceria, some distance from the coast, in 314 BC). Control over this coast was important, as until this period foreign states had the potential to found colonies of their own on the coast of Italy – Syracuse had founded the colony of Ancona on the Adriatic around 387 BC, for example. The west coast was different: in the Rome–Carthage treaty of 348 BC Carthage was prohibited from founding colonies on the Tyrrhenian coast of central Italy, just as Rome was on the islands of Sicily and Sardinia.

In 290 BC, victory over the Samnites allowed Manius Curius Dentatus to conquer the Sabines and Praetuttii in a rapid campaign. A large swathe of land across the centre of Italy was confiscated and incorporated into the Roman state, placing a block of Roman territory in the way of any further attempts to create another Samnite–Etruscan coalition. It was a major addition to Roman territory, but we are poorly informed about this episode, having lost the full text of Livy by this stage. It is likely that much of the local Sabine and Praetuttian population remained in place, with individual Roman settlers sent out to much of the country.

Roman territory now stretched from the Tyrrhenian to the Adriatic coast. In the 280s BC Rome attacked and expelled the Senones from the territory known as the Ager Gallicus, in between Novilara and Firmum further up the Adriatic coast (Map 1). The Roman presence on the Adriatic was strengthened through further colonisation. Individual settler families were sent to the Ager Gallicus, while citizen colonies with Roman status were founded at Castrum Novum (290–286 BC) and Sena Gallica (283 BC). Their duty was probably to garrison the coast and watch for seaborne attacks. A Latin colony was founded at Hadria in the same period (290–286 BC), which will have had a more substantial colonial presence. In 266 BC the northerly Umbrian Sassinates were

---

15. Harris, *Rome in Etruria and Umbria*.

defeated, along with the Picentes. Rome's grip on the Adriatic coast was strengthened by the foundation of colonies at Ariminum in 268 BC, Firmum Picenum in 264 BC and Brundisium in 244 BC. The latter were port cities and included many members of the local population in their foundation.[16]

The expansion of Roman territory

If one part of the story is the rapidity with which Rome brought the other peoples of Italy under its direct domination, the other is the way in which it set up a stable system for controlling these conquests. The success of Roman consolidation can be seen in the lack of serious opposition Rome faced from other Italian peoples before the Social War, apart from the Second Punic War (218–202 BC), when there was a powerful alternative force, Hannibal's Carthaginian army, at large within Italy. There were three main ways in which Rome consolidated the conquests that it made during the late fourth and early third century BC: incorporation of conquered land, colonisation and alliances.

During the conquest, large areas of land were confiscated from the defeated and made Roman territory. We can follow the spread of the Roman state across Italy through the creation of voting tribes, the means by which Rome organised its territory (marked with dates of creation on the map, Fig. 9.1; Table 9.1). These were recorded in Roman documentary records and can be relied on as genuine reflections of the expansion of the Roman state.[17] The earliest tribes were created in the immediate confines of the city, and by 495 BC there were twenty-one (four urban and seventeen rural).[18] No further tribes were created in the fifth century BC, which is a striking indicator of there being little new land to assign at this time. The creation of tribes resumed again after the conquest of Veii, when four were created in the territory of the defeated city in 387 BC (Fig. 9.1). The next tribes were created in southern Latium and Campania in the decades either side of the Latin War of 341–338 BC. In 299 BC

---

16. Cass. Dio 10.7; Bradley, 'Colonization and identity', 174; Yntema, 'Material culture'.
17. Taylor, *Voting Districts*; Oakley, *Commentary*, I 440.
18. Livy (2.21.7) records that the 'number of tribes at Rome was increased to twenty-one' in 495 BC; cf. Dion. Hal. 4.15.1 and 7.64.6, 490 BC: 'For out of the twenty-one tribes that were then in existence and gave their votes Marcius [Coriolanus] had nine in favour of his acquittal.'

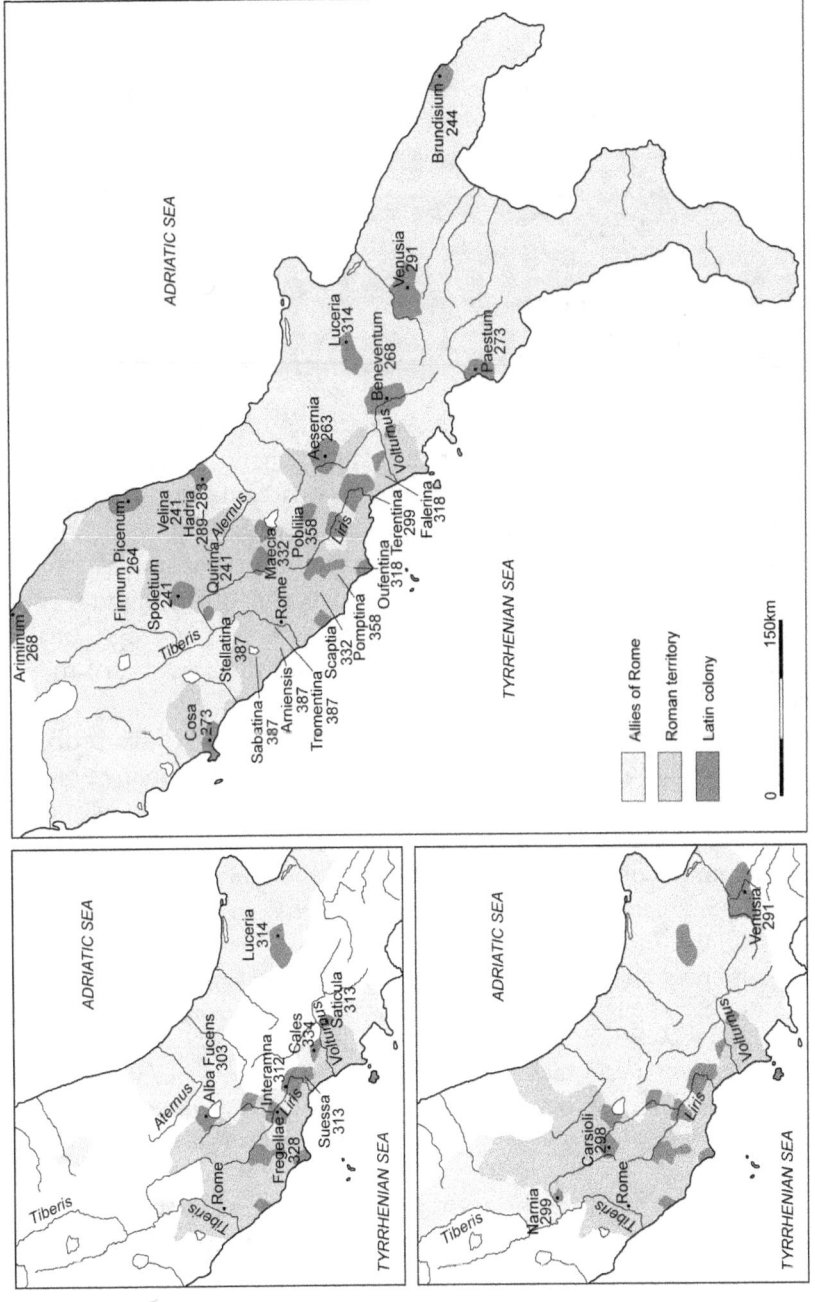

Figure 9.1 Roman territory and colonies in Italy, 302, 290 and 241 BC (after Cornell and Matthews, *Atlas*, 40–1)

Table 9.1 Roman voting tribes

Date BC	Tribes
Pre-495	Urban: Palatina, Collina, Esquilina, Suburana Rural: Aemilia, Camilia, Claudia, Clustumina, Cornelia, Fabia, Galeria, Horatia, Lemonia, Menenia, Papiria, Pollia, Pupinia, Romilia, Sergia, Voltinia, Voturia
387	Arnensis, Sabatina, Stellatina, Tromentina
358	Poblilia, Pomptina
332	Maecia, Scaptia
318	Falerina, Oufentina
299	Aniensis, Teretina
241	Quirina, Velina

the Teretina was created on the Via Appia in southern Latium, and the Aniensis in the upper valley of the Anio, where the Aequi had been defeated. The most sweeping confiscations came in the Sabine area (stretching from Rome across to Hadria), where a large swathe of land from coast to coast became Roman with the conquests of Manius Curius Dentatus in 290 BC. The existing Sabine inhabitants were probably given citizenship without the vote at this stage, but were elevated to full citizen rights in 241 BC with the creation of the Quirina and Velina tribes.

Our sources on the Roman extension of the citizenship have problems fully understanding this Roman practice. In particular, many non-Roman writers regarded it as extraordinary, as in the Greek world citizenship was traditionally much more restricted. Philip V of Macedon, an ally of Hannibal during the Second Punic War, commends it as a successful policy in a letter to the inhabitants of Larissa in 215 BC:

> It is also possible to look at others who make use of similar enrolments of citizens, among whom are the Romans, who receive into the state even slaves, when they have freed them, giving them a share in the magistracies, and in such a way not only have they augmented their own fatherland, but they have also sent out colonies to almost seventy places. (*Sylloge Inscriptionum Graecarum*[3] 543, trans. Bagnall)

In the late Republic and beyond, authors often interpreted the spread of citizenship as a sign of Roman generosity, because they were writing at a time when Roman citizenship was prestigious and sought-after. This is clear with Dionysius of Halicarnassus (writing in the Augustan era), who comments on the benevolent liberality of Rome in this context:

> And in the course of time the Romans contrived to raise themselves from the smallest nation to the greatest and from the most obscure to the most illustrious, not only by their humane reception of those who sought a home among them, but also by sharing the rights of citizenship with all who had been conquered by them in war after a brave resistance. (Dion. Hal. 1.9.4)

In fact, the ancient sources misrepresent the situation, because Roman citizenship was probably much less desirable in the earlier period.[19] Several passages in Livy suggest that the incorporation of Roman enemies in the fourth and third centuries BC was a hostile move and followed a defeat. This occurred, for instance, with the Hernici of Anagnia in 306 BC, who were made citizens after a revolt (Livy, 9.43). In 304 BC, Livy says that the Aequi complained to Rome that

> the Romans were trying, by threat of war, to intimidate them into becoming Roman citizens; how little this was desirable was demonstrated by the Hernici, since those who had been allowed to had opted for their own laws rather than Roman citizenship: those who had not been allowed to choose were to have citizenship forced upon them as a punishment. (Livy, 9.45)

This makes sense since Roman citizenship made newly incorporated peoples liable for burdens such as legionary service and the payment of *tributum*. But it did not provide the benefits of political power if they were made citizens without the vote, as happened with the Sabines (from 290 BC) and the Caeretans (from 273 BC), amongst others. It also often involved confiscation of land, which became Roman *ager publicus* and was distributed to Roman settlers, as at Veii in 387 BC and in Sabinum in 290 BC. Thus, the expansion of Roman territory should probably be seen as punitive in many scenarios. It was a means to swallow up conquered states and benefit from the extra manpower they provided, an advantage clearly recognised by Philip V.

Colonisation

The other key way of holding down conquered territory was to found colonies on it, which Rome continued to do after the Latin War even though the Latin League had been disbanded. There were two types of colony founded by Rome: citizen and Latin. These were distinctly

---

19. Sherwin-White, *Roman Citizenship*; Humbert, *Municipium*.

different institutions by the late fourth century BC, although the distinction may not have been so clear in the fifth century BC.[20] Citizen colonies were small fortresses founded mainly on the coast, like Ostia, Antium, Pyrgi and Alsium. Their role was primarily maritime, defending the ports in Roman territory and preventing the landing of seaborne raiders such as the Carthaginians and Syracusans. They normally comprised a few hundred settlers, who retained Roman citizenship.

Latin colonies were more important than Roman colonies in the period from 338–264 BC. They were significantly different from the colonies of the early Republic, being major independent cities. They were large fortified settlements, either founded afresh or existing communities supplemented by Rome, in which the settlers were given Latin status. From 338 BC the Romans began to found Latin colonies outside Latium – previously such colonies had been founded in Latium by Rome and the Latin League. The first was Cales in northern Campania, in 334 BC (Fig. 9.1). Two decades later came Luceria, probably the first colony to be founded on a site set apart from Roman territory, and surrounded by allied or enemy land. It is striking that Livy records a debate over whether it ought to be founded (Livy, 9.26.1–5). From this point on many colonies were established beyond Roman territory at some distance from Rome, such as Paestum (273 BC), Venusia (291 BC) and Brundisium (244 BC). The foundation of colonies is recorded by Livy, normally in unadorned records giving the year, territory and number of colonists, which must reproduce documentary records. For example:

> In the consulship of Lucius Genucius and Servius Cornelius there was in general a respite from foreign wars. Colonies were established at Sora and Alba. Six thousand settlers were enrolled for Alba, in Aequian territory. Sora had belonged to the territory of the Volsci, but the Samnites had gained possession of it; four thousand men were sent here. (Livy, 10.1.1–6, 303 BC)[21]

Latin colonies became important strongholds for the Roman state. They always had impressive fortifications, most of which were created using the typical Latial polygonal masonry building technique,

---

20. Salmon, *Roman Colonization*; for a discussion of the ambiguous nature of the distinction earlier in Roman history see Bispham, 'Coloniam deducere', 'Rome and Antium'.
21. Cf. the digression on colonies by Velleius Paterculus 1.14–15.

although some walls were probably refurbishments of earlier defences. Their role in the defence of Rome is emphasised by later sources. Cicero (*Leg. agr.* 73) describes ancient colonies as set up 'in such suitable places to guard against all suspicion of danger, that they appeared to be not so much towns of Italy as bulwarks of the empire'. Appian, drawing on a source of the late Republican period, says:

> The Romans, as they subdued the Italian peoples successively in war, used to seize a part of their lands and build towns there, or choose settlers from their own people to go to the existing towns – this being the alternative they devised to garrisons. In the case of the land they acquired by war they assigned the cultivated part directly to colonists, or sold or leased it. (Appian, *B. Civ.* 1.7)

Some colonies were linked to Rome by roads, which permitted quicker and easier travel between them. Rome had created roads prior to 338 BC, but from the late fourth century these became more ambitious affairs that took the name of the commissioning censor. The first of these new roads was the Via Appia, built in 312 BC by the censor Appius Claudius Caecus. It linked Rome to colonies on the Latin coast and ultimately to Capua in Campania. The Via Appia was followed by a series of roads in the late fourth and third century BC connecting Rome to its central Italian colonies (Fig. 10.1). The Via Valeria (probably 306 BC) joined Carseoli (founded 298 BC) and Alba Fucens (founded 303 BC) to Rome. The Via Aurelia (241 BC) linked Cosa (273 BC) along the Etruscan coast. The Via Flaminia (222 BC) joined Spoletium (241 BC) and Ariminum (268 BC) to Rome. Although roads generally linked colonies to Rome, they sometimes terminated in allied cities; the Via Amelia for example ends at Amelia in Umbria, while the Via Aurelia ends at Pisa. They might also join up with Roman cities such as Capua. This suggests that roads were designed as much to allow armies to reach potential problem points quickly (such as Campania and the Ager Gallicus south of Ariminum) as to 'connect up' colonies. It is notable that the Via Appia did not prevent Capua's defection to Hannibal in 216 BC.

Many scholars have read strategic purpose into the placement of Latin colonies, particularly in connection with the creation of the road network. Already in the nineteenth century, Mommsen emphasised this role, stating that by 311 BC 'the designs of the Romans were more and more fully developed; their object was the subjugation of Italy, which was enveloped more closely from year to year in a network of Roman fortresses and roads'.[22] More recently some scholars have questioned the extent to which this view overstates the inevitability of Roman expansion and is dependent on modern colonial tropes.[23] Long-term strategy in colony foundation is not clearly referred to by ancient authors, who instead emphasise control over local populations.[24] We certainly see colonies acting as important refuges for the Roman army, but colonists are rarely attested playing an active 'garrison' role. Colonies certainly could end up being strategically important, like Spoletium and Venusia in the Hannibalic War in the late third century BC, and Alba Fucens and Aesernia in the Social War in the early first century BC. But it is a stretch to see this as part of the original plan of their Roman founders, rather than the view in hindsight of sources writing under the quite different conditions of the late Republic and early imperial period. Roads in particular have been seen as a sign of some kind of senatorial master plan, but the sources on their foundation suggest instead a more straightforward popular intent.[25] Road-building was 'a political act', and their commissioners used these projects to enhance their popularity with the plebeians in Rome.[26]

This is not the only area where modern scholarship on the Roman colonisation has come to be revised. Recent studies have revealed the complexity of influences on Roman colonies. In the second century AD the emperor Hadrian claimed that colonies were 'miniatures and copies' of 'the greatness and majesty of the Roman people' (reported by Gellius, NA 16.13.9). Salmon used this phrase to interpret colonies such as Cosa in Etruria (founded in 273 BC) as ideal types of mini-Romes.[27] But the origins of colony layouts were probably ecletic, drawing on Mediterranean-wide models such as the assembly places of southern Greek cities for buildings like the Comitium, and the rectilinear grid plans of colonies of Massilia for their layouts.[28] In a similar way we should probably see Roman road-building activity

---

22. *History*, 486; cf. Salmon, *Roman Colonization*; Coarelli, 'Colonizzazione'; de Cazanove, 'Colonies'.
23. Mouritsen, *Italian Unification*; Pelgrom and Stek 'Roman colonization'; Bradley, 'Nature of Roman strategy'; Terrenato, *Early Roman Expansion*.
24. E.g. Asconius on Placentia, *Pis.* 3 C.; Livy, 10.10.5 on Narnia in Umbria, founded in 299 BC 'against the Umbrians'.
25. Laurence, *Roads*, 12–33; Bradley, 'Nature of Roman strategy'.
26. See for instance Diod. Sic. 20.36 on the Via Appia; cf. Laurence, *Roads*, 39.
27. Salmon, *Roman Colonization*.
28. Sewell, 'Gellius, Philip II'.

as less uniquely Roman, and more of a widespread Mediterranean practice that Rome refines. Major roads had already been created by other Mediterranean and Near Eastern states such as Persia and Macedon. In fact, the peculiar Roman practice of naming Roman roads after consuls or censors probably reflects the royal patronage of roads in the eastern Mediterranean. As Michel Humm has pointed out, the naming of the Via Appia after the praenomen of Appius Claudius in the manner of a Hellenistic monarch reinforced the impression of his almost regal beneficence.[29]

It is now becoming increasingly evident how closely colonies were linked to their local environment. Land is thought to have been confiscated from defeated enemies and reassigned to the colonists. The locals who were not killed might be enslaved or evicted and replaced by Roman colonists. But the situation was often more complex than the simple replacement of an existing population with a Roman one.[30] Colonists were frequently added to long-established cities, as at Paestum and Brundisium, or developed out of garrisons sent to control pre-existing populations, as at Sora or Fregellae. At Cosa the local population seems to have been eliminated, but in many places they must have remained on the land and even physically within the walls, even if they initially lacked full Latin status. It is unlikely that these status divisions persisted very long, as no later Latin colonies have evidence of double communities living alongside one another. Latin colonies such as Ariminum are described by the Augustan author Strabo (5.1.10–11) as mixed Roman and Umbrian settlements which had received Roman settlers in the past. We also know of Samnites living in the Latin colony at Aesernia: an inscription from the colony refers to *Samnites inquolae*, 'resident Samnites'.[31] Allies too were in some cases eligible to join colonies.[32]

It is also clear that Latin colonies were socio-economic in purpose as well as military. This may even be their primary purpose in this period. The sources record that they had 2,500, 4,000 or 6,000 male settlers, who, if the traditional picture is to be believed, were sent to the colony from Rome. They would farm the land allocated to them, and thus become eligible for military service. This is often cited by

---

29. Humm, 'Appius Claudius Caecus et la construction de la via Appia'; *Appius Claudius Caecus*, ch. 10.
30. Bradley, 'Colonization and identity'; Roselaar, 'Colonies'.
31. La Regina, 'Contributo'; cf. Roncaglia, *Northern Italy*, ch. 2.
32. E.g. Livy, 33.24.8; 34.42.5–6.

the sources as a reason for colony foundation, and presented by them as popular with the plebs.[33] Colonisation might be undertaken as a political move, as it would bring favour to the proposer and could be used by generals to reward their soldiers.[34] The Romans were also perpetually concerned about the vigour and size of their population and undertook colonisation to increase it.[35]

Colonisation and road-building were thus promoted in this period for a complex variety of reasons. All these measures were linked to Roman success in capturing land, to the intensifying political competition in the late fourth century BC, and to the demands of the plebs. These measures began to restructure Italy in a way that benefited Rome as the centre, although the unified and networked peninsula that formed the heartland of the Roman empire was some way off.

Treaties and allies

The other main means by which Rome controlled Italy was through alliances. By 264 BC all the cities and peoples of Italy south of the Po valley that had not been colonised or incorporated into Roman territory were allies of Rome. Rome had used treaties as early as the sixth century BC, when alliances were contracted with Massilia and Carthage. Dionysius even claimed that the text of the treaty made with Gabii by Tarquinius Superbus survived in the temple of Dius Fidius.[36] Seeking allies had long been habitual to Rome, a characteristic behaviour of states in an international anarchy according to Eckstein, and had certainly become regularised by the early fifth century BC with the organisation of the Cassian Treaty between Rome and the Latins. This propensity to seek new allies wherever possible and to fight alongside them in composite forces continued into the fourth century BC as Roman warfare became more successful. With the expectation in the unstable inter-state environment of Italy that Rome would need to fight continual wars, it made sense to seek manpower contributions to

---

33. It was, for instance, the reason why Cales was founded according to Livy (8.16.10–14). For colonies founded for the plebs, see Ardea: Livy, 4.11.3–7; Velitrae: Dion. Hal. 7.12–13.
34. Plut. *Flam.* 1.4–2.1 for political benefit; Diod. Sic. 19.101 on Q. Fabius allotting land gained in a successful campaign to his soldiers in 313 BC, which pleased the people.
35. Livy, 27.9.11: a consul's speech to rebel colonies in the Hannibalic War, stating that 'they were not Capuans or Tarentines, but Romans, sprung from Rome and sent from there into colonies and on land captured in war, to increase their stock (*stirpis augendae causa*)'. See also the letter of Philip V of Macedon to Larissa, cited above, which connects colonisation with the increasing Roman population.
36. Dion. Hal. 4.58.4.

Rome and Italy: conquest and accommodation

the Roman army rather than ask for monetary tribute. Unlike Athens, Rome never shifted over to demanding a financial contribution from its allies.

Table 9.2, listing treaties attested during the period of conquest, shows how wide the range of peoples was with whom Rome formed treaties. It includes peoples spread right over Italy, as well as foreign powers such as the Carthaginians. Even some Gauls are included,

Table 9.2 Roman treaties 390–264 BC[a]

State with whom treaty formed	Date treaty formed (BC)	Reference
Samnites	354	Livy 7.19.4
Carthage	348	Livy 7.27.2; ?Polybius 2.24
Latins, Hernici	338	Livy 8.14
Gauls	334	Polybius 2.18
Neapolis (equal)	326	Livy 8.26.6
Lucani and Apuli (*societas*)	326	Livy 8.27.2
Apulian Teates	317	Livy 9.20.7–8
Camerinum (equal)	310	Livy 9.36.8; Cic. *Balb.* 46
Carthage (third renewal according to Livy)	307	Livy 9.43.26
Sora, Arpinum, Cesennia (described as allied)	305	Diod. Sic. 20.90.4
Samnites (renewal)	304	Livy 9.45.4; cf. Diod. Sic. 20.101.5
Marsi, Paeligni, Marrucini and Frentani	304	Livy 9.45.18; Diod. Sic. 20.101.5
Vestini	302	Livy 10.3.1
Marsi (renewal)	302	Livy 10.3.5
Picentes	298	Livy 10.10.12
Lucani	298	Livy 10.11.11–12.2
Iguvium	?295–266	Cic. *Balb.* 47
Samnites (renewal)	?290	Livy, *Epit.* 11
Boii	284	Polybius 2.20
Heraclea (equal)	278	Cic. *Arch.* 6 Cic. *Balb.* 50
Carthage (fourth renewal according to Livy)	278	Livy, *Epit.* 13
Tarquinii	?	NSc (1948) 267

[a]From Bradley, *Ancient Umbria*, 301. See Salmon, *Making of Roman Italy*, 66 for a list of allies for whom there is *some* evidence.

whose treaties remained in force until the first century BC.[37] Nevertheless, many of the Italian peoples are missing, notably most of the numerous Umbrian and Etruscan city states. In the early stages of the conquest in the late fourth century BC, it seems that only states which welcomed Rome in peace were given full treaties, such as Camerinum in Umbria in 310 BC. This included groups such as the Marsi, Marrucini, Paeligni and Frentani, who were frightened by the massacre of the Aequi in 304 BC into seeking Roman aid.[38] States defeated in war could be granted a truce or be asked to pay an indemnity, like Tarquinii, or given a *sponsio* (promise), like Ocriculum.[39]

The typicality of treaties as a way to control the large part of Italy that remained unoccupied or uncolonised has proved controversial. Since the nineteenth century many scholars have assumed that the lack of explicit evidence for these alliances is a product of the fragmentary nature of the source material, particularly for the period after 292 BC, and probably also because our sources were not systematic in reporting treaty formation.[40] This consensus has recently been challenged by Rich, who argued instead that formal treaties were likely to be untypical of most Italian states defeated by Rome, and that the majority were subject to less formal arrangements that resulted from the *deditio* (surrender) of the state into Rome's power.[41] While this would help to explain why some allies such as Tarquinii and Camerinum later on celebrated their treaties with Rome as if they were something exceptional that brought them prestige, the best policy is probably agnosticism. In fact, even if some states had treaties with Rome while others had less formal arrangements, the practical implications were largely the same.

We know very little about what treaties contained, lacking a text of any of them, but a few principles can be discerned. Although some treaties were described as *aequum* ('equal'), most probably contained clauses benefiting Rome more than the contracting Italian party. All treaties had as an essential requirement that allies levy their own contingents to the Roman army, pay for them, and send them to

---

37. Roncaglia, *Northern Italy*, 41.
38. Livy, 9.45.16 (304 BC).
39. Livy, 9.41.5–7; 9.41.20 (308 BC).
40. E.g. Harris, *Rome in Etruria and Umbria*, 98–113; Bradley, *Ancient Umbria*, 118–28; Fronda, *Between Carthage and Rome*, 21 n. 51.
41. Rich, 'Treaties', estimating that there were at least 150 states in Italy that were subject to or allies of Rome.

Rome on demand. Polybius shows that the organisation of the allied peoples centred on Rome:

> The consuls send instructions to the cities of the allies in Italy which they wish to contribute troops, saying how many they want, and the day and the place at which they must be present. The magistrates dispatch them, having levied them in the manner described, sworn them in and appointed a commander and a treasurer. (Polybius, 6.21.4)[42]

There are some similarities to the early organisation of the Athenian empire, where contributions of troops in the Delian League were coordinated by Athens. But in the Delian League this slid into an annual monetary tribute. In Italy it operated like a tax on the allies, but in a distinctly less humiliating form. For most allies, Rome probably had the power to call out all their manpower if it so wished. In practice Rome only needed to ask for a part of their total forces each year. It was important to distribute the burden in a balanced way amongst the allies, who were very different in size; it would have been unfair to ask the same number of soldiers from a tiny Umbrian city as from the whole of the Samnites. This is probably the function of the *formula togatorum* ('the list of those who wear the toga') mentioned in the *Lex agraria* in 111 BC.[43] Possessing a list of each ally's forces, Rome could then work out what fraction of each might be required.

On the face of it, it is quite surprising that the Romans used alliances when it was theoretically possible to incorporate all Italy into the Roman state, as in fact happened after the Social War of 91–88 BC. In general, the pattern is likely to be the result of the fragmentation of Roman command on the ground, and the preferences of individual generals. Some generals took this option because allied areas did not have to be directly controlled from Rome. It was also a more practical solution in many ways than creating more Roman citizens, and it made efficient use of allied forces. The allied contingents to the Roman army were substantial, although proportionally less of their manpower than that provided by Rome itself for the legions. According to Polybius (6.26), the allies' total infantry was normally

---

42. Cf. Polybius, 6.26.5–6 on the appointment of leaders of these contingents.
43. *Lex agraria*, section 21 [111 BC]: '... whichever Roman citizen or ally or member of the Latin name, from whom they are accustomed to demand troops in the land of Italy according to the list of those who wear the toga (*ex formula togatorum*)'.

equal to the Roman forces, with three times as many cavalry. They were under the command of officers of the consuls called *praefecti sociorum*, and organised as ethnic groups, probably using their own language. This preserved their sense of identity and provided effective fighters on behalf of Rome. They gained a share of the booty and benefited from Roman success indirectly.

The advantages of remaining in the Roman alliance system are evident from the Second Punic War, where the major defections of allies from Rome came only after the third and most catastrophic Roman defeat, at Cannae in 216 BC (Livy, 22.61). Many allies remained loyal to Rome and fought enthusiastically for it, such as the Paelignian cohort that led the capture of a Carthaginian camp near Beneventum (Livy, 25.14). In 205 BC an impressive list of allies contributed voluntarily to Scipio's invasion of Africa (Livy, 28.45). It is therefore implausible to think that the allies were cowed by fear of Rome alone: self-interest and identification with Rome were important forces in retaining their loyalty too.[44] In fact, the local autonomy allowed to allied states, run by elites with shared interests and links with the Roman nobility, was a defining feature of the Roman system of control: *municipia*, colonies and allied states were all run like this.[45] The system is probably the result of expediency rather than any Roman 'generosity' of spirit or calculation, as it was later seen. The Roman state at this time was simply not able to govern all its conquests directly, although as the state became more powerful, so the Senate interfered more in Italian affairs. The system held up well under the severe military pressure of the Pyrrhic and Hannibalic Wars, and the ultimate triumph of Rome in both, despite the devastating losses inflicted on Rome, shows the resilience of the system.

Patterns of war and imperialism

In order to understand the conquest, we also need to look at the Roman army and imperialism, and explore why Rome was so successful in warfare and what motivated Romans to go to war. The rise of Rome has some interesting parallels elsewhere. Scheidel points out that Rome and Athens are both typical of the way Republican empires could develop from city states. Both were initially leaders of defensive

---

44. Fronda, *Between Carthage and Rome*.
45. Terrenato, *Early Roman Expansion*.

leagues occasioned by external threats. This consensual leadership was then converted into hegemony which 'permitted them to coordinate and eventually dominate consensual interstate institutions of collective defence and predation'.[46] Nevertheless, there were also some peculiarities of the Roman Republican military system that derive from the Italian context: it never used mercenaries, being heavily reliant on citizens, and was predominantly infantry-focused (rather than relying on cavalry or naval forces). Whereas occupation of enemy land was rare in archaic Greek warfare, such as the Spartan seizure of Messene, Rome had captured and incorporated an Etruscan city and enslaved or absorbed its Etruscan population by 396 BC.

The structure of the Roman army underwent significant changes in this period. The Servian reforms had set up a military structure in the sixth century BC that was based around a large force of heavily armoured infantry. They were self-equipped with hoplite-style arms and armour, typically a round shield, body armour such as greaves, and a spear. Whether they fought in a broad phalanx is uncertain, given that type of military organisation has been questioned in recent work on archaic Greek armies.[47] At some point in the fourth century BC a new formation was introduced, either in the early part of the century in connection with the introduction of military pay (Livy, 8.8), or in the late fourth century during the Second Samnite War (Diod. Sic. 23.2). This new force consisted of three lines of infantry, the *hastati, principes* and *triarii*, each of which was divided into smaller groups (maniples) of 120 men. This gave the army a great deal of flexibility in its deployment, and allowed part of the force, the *triarii*, to be held in reserve for the critical point of the battle. This reform must be related to a change in armour. The anonymous author of the *Ineditum Vaticanum* claims that the phalanx had been copied from the Etruscans, and the oblong shield and javelins typical of the manipular army from the Samnites.[48] While this is an overly formulaic idea, the highly interconnected world of early Italy enabled very rapid transfer of military technology, and manipular weaponry was probably cheaper than what had gone before. In reality, as with so many other features of early Rome, a heterogenous range of western and eastern Mediterranean influences was drawn on

---

46. Scheidel, 'Republics', 7.
47. Rosenstein, 'Phalanges in Rome?'; on Greek warfare, see Van Wees, *Greek Warfare*; Rawlings, *Ancient Greeks at War*.
48. For the *Ineditum Vaticanum*, see the translation in Cornell, *Beginnings*, 170; cf. Diod. Sic. 23.2.1; Ath. 6.273–4.

for Roman military tactics and armour. Probably the standard Roman equipment in this period saw oblong Samnite-style shields replace circular shields, spears adapted from thrusting to throwing, short swords, and perhaps mail replacing bronze armour. In addition, cavalrymen were provided with a horse by the state.

This allowed an increase in the size of the army. It had probably been standardly two legions strong from the start of the monarchy, and was increased to four in 311 BC.[49] Each legion was probably around 3,700 men, rising to around 4,200 by the time of Polybius in the mid second century BC. Allied contingents were also critical, and generally provided the same number of men for each army as the legions. This was key to Rome's strength and success, which must have relied more commonly on superiority of numbers than our sources care to admit. The Roman army was large by ancient standards. At the battle of Platea in 479 BC the Spartan force consisted of only 5,000 Spartiates, fighting alongside 5,000 less heavily armed *perioikoi* and 35,000 helots, and the Athenian force consisted of 8,000 hoplites (Hdt. 9.28). In comparison, the Roman and allied force at Sentinum is likely to have been around 36,000 strong.[50]

Roman economic power was another essential factor in Rome's military success. We know from Polybius that finances were as important as manpower in the First Punic War, so it is probably much the same for this period. Historically, war has always been a costly and risky enterprise. In eighteenth-century Britain, the demands of war led to the creation of income tax and the Bank of England, which provided the apparatus for financing long-term military expenditure.[51] Similarly, reforms to the economic system allowed Rome to finance increasing warfare in the fourth century BC. From 443 BC the censors were able to assess all citizens' property, providing the state with the data to distribute taxation equitably. Pay had been introduced in the Veientine War in 406 BC (Livy, 4.59.11) and through the Republic Rome continued to pay for larger armies than its neighbours. The basic Roman tax, *tributum*, is thought to have been instituted around 400 BC to finance army pay. Indemnities began to be

---

49. Livy, 9.30.3; cf. 7.23, which implies that four legions had been raised on occasion earlier; Cornell, *Beginnings*, 254.
50. Cf. Eckstein, *Mediterranean Anarchy*, 151: Tarentum at its peak could reputedly field 30,000 infantry and 4,000 cavalry. Alexander's army for the invasion of Persia was around 47,000 strong.
51. Brauer and Van Tuyll, *Castles*.

used in the fourth century BC to supplement the costs of war, and this enabled some generals to make campaigns self-financing, such as that against Troilum and the Faliscans in 293 BC, when the Faliscans had to pay 100,000 bronze coins and finance the army for a year in order to secure peace.[52]

Successful warfare was very rewarding for Rome and the allies. A wide variety of forms of booty could be captured: prisoners (to be sold as slaves), silver and bronze, and even valuable elements from the townscape of the defeated city, such as the bronze doors from Veii allegedly appropriated by Camillus.[53] Huge wealth is said to have accrued to Rome in this period from the conquest of the Sabines (Strabo, 5.228), the Gauls (Polybius, 2.29), the Samnites and the Etruscans (Livy, 10.46).[54] Metrodorus of Scepsis claims that Rome plundered 2,000 statues from the Etruscan city of Volsinii alone in 264 BC. The numbers of captives began to be recorded for the first time from the early 290s, which suggests that the state kept official records of the sale of slaves.

Modern studies have shown that the risks that commanders were prepared to take depended on the investment in training of troops and the availability of replacements. Little training and plentiful soldiers enabled Roman commanders, like their modern equivalents, to take more risks in battle.[55] Rome went further than many states in its willingness to lose troops in great wars, perhaps a sign of the plebs' lack of real political power: democracies like Athens were more constrained by the dangers of popular discontent. Furthermore, unlike monarchies such as Macedon, the Roman system provided interchangeable generals, who might equally be sacrificed along with their troops, replaced, or prolonged in office dependent on their fortunes. One of the keys to Roman success, as Rosenstein has demonstrated, is the elastic way in which Rome handled defeats, which were more frequent than Rome's reputation might suggest.[56]

The reasons for Rome's eventual success are still hotly debated. Since the 1970s it has generally been accepted that Rome was an

---

52. Livy, 10.46; Erdkamp, 'War and state formation', 105.
53. Plut. *Cam.* 12; Bastien, *Triomphe*, 324–44.
54. Cf. Harris, *War and Imperialism*, 67 n. 4.
55. Brauer and Van Tuyll, *Castles*, ch. 1. Note that Rosenstein, *Rome at War*, 31, thinks that Roman training improved during the fourth century BC.
56. Rosenstein, *Imperatores Victi*.

intensely militaristic society.⁵⁷ The elite and the plebs viewed war positively. Roman greed was proverbial amongst its enemies. Imperialism was built into many of its institutions and customs. It could appoint an emergency dictator in times of extreme peril. The triumphal ritual joined the general, army, people and gods in a celebration of Roman victory. The Roman alliance system implies a perpetual need for troops. Rome had a highly competitive oligarchy that remained focused on military glory despite its changing composition in the late fourth century BC. For ordinary soldiers, too, valour was important, and commemorated by a whole series of military awards, epitomised by the story of Lucius Sicinius Dentatus:

> We read in the annals that Lucius Sicinius Dentatus, tribune of the plebs in the consulship of Spurius Tarpeius and Aulus Aternius [454 BC], was a warrior of incredible energy; that he won a name for his exceedingly great valour, and was called the Roman Achilles. It is said that he fought with the enemy in one hundred and twenty battles, and had not a scar on his back, but forty-five in front; that he was awarded golden crowns eight times, the siege crown once, mural crowns three times, and civic crowns fourteen times; that eighty-three neck chains were bestowed on him, more than one hundred and sixty armlets, and eighteen spears; he was presented besides with twenty-five decorations; he had a number of spoils of war, many of which were won in single combat; and he took part with his generals in nine triumphal processions. (Gellius, *NA* 2.11.1–4)⁵⁸

The striking record of Sicinius Dentatus may have been elaborated as a type of folk hero (the 'bravest Roman') who featured in popular stories if he was, as our sources report, killed during the Second Decemvirate. Nevertheless, it implies that single combat could be a common experience for some Roman soldiers. The Roman tradition had many stories of renowned victors in such combats. Particularly famous examples include Titus Manlius Torquatus in 361 BC and Valerius Corvus in 349 BC. The narratives of their victories are problematic, given the formulaic nature of the stories and the mythological aspects evident in the retelling. Despite being at a disadvantage, the Roman is always the victor in these tales, and ends by stripping the spoils from the enemy body as a symbol of victory. These stories often involve divine intervention

---

57. Hopkins, *Conquerors and Slaves*; Harris, *War and Imperialism*; North, 'Development'.
58. Cf. Pliny, *HN* 7.101–3; Dion. Hal. 10.36–49. He is called Siccius Dentatus in some sources.

on the Roman side, such as the *corvus* (raven) which helped Valerius by attacking his Gallic opponent in 349 BC. Both figures receive commemorative *cognomina*, Torquatus from the torque he removed from his enemy, and Corvus from the raven. These motifs probably stem from the retelling of the stories in family histories. Nevertheless, anecdotal evidence such as that of Sicinius Dentatus reinforces the likely historicity of these events, as do the edicts by commanders prohibiting the practice of single combat, which implies that its frequency was actually rather significant.[59]

War was intimately connected to the Roman sense of community from its origins. The opening and closing of the campaigning season was built into the Roman calendar with festivals such as the Armilustrium and October Horse.[60] From the later fourth century BC armies began to campaign further afield, and for several years at a time.[61] Legions began to be kept in the field over the winter for the new consuls to take over from 335 BC, and are attested on multiple occasions during the Samnite wars as serving for more than one year.[62] Commanders began to be appointed to further years of continuous command from 327 BC, and it would make sense for them to retain their soldiers. More extensive training was required for the manipular system, and disbanding a trained army in an offensive position made little military sense.[63]

There were social pressures in Rome to go to war. According to Dionysius (10.33), foreign war was used during the Struggle of the Orders as a means of quietening the lower classes and lessening civil strife. When none existed, Rome tended to create wars to fight, as in 303 BC when Livy (10.1.1–5) reports that 'in order that the Romans might not pass a whole year without any military operations, a small expeditionary force was sent into Umbria'. The allied system, where Rome used contingents of troops from the states under its power rather than financial tribute, meant that no benefit could accrue

---

59. Oakley, 'Single combat'; examples of generals said to have prohibited single combat include the very same Torquatus (340 BC), and Titus at Jerusalem (AD 70).
60. Quinquatrus, 19 March; Tubilustrium, 23 March, 23 May; Armilustrium, 19 October; Equus October (October Horse), 15 October. Rich, 'Warfare', 10 expresses some doubts about this.
61. E.g. Livy, 10.39.1: veteran legions assigned to Carvilius to fight Samnites, which had been in the field in the year before too.
62. Rosenstein, *Rome at War*, 31, identifying 316, 315, 314, 313, 310, 296, 295 and 293 BC as years when this occurred.
63. Rosenstein, *Rome at War*, 31.

unless war was fought.[64] According to Polybius, in the mid second century BC the Roman Senate grew anxious that the Italians might 'become effeminate owing to the long peace'.[65] This culture of perpetual war was shared by the other states of central Italy, who were enthusiastic raiders of their neighbours, and generally expressed their bellicose ideals through militaristic iconography.[66] The Roman alliance system provided a regular outlet for the militaristic cultures of allied states even after their subjection in the conquest.

Roman brutality towards the defeated is candidly recorded in sources like Livy. Small tribes such as the Ausones and Aequi were said to have been almost wiped out.[67] Thousands of 'rebels' were punished by flogging and execution in the Roman Forum, including 'traitorous' colonists at Satricum. Atrocities are recorded on both sides. The Tarquinians executed Roman prisoners in their forum in 357 BC, and the Romans returned the favour with increased violence in 354 BC (Livy, 7.19).[68] Curiously, Roman claims of genocide in some cases prove to be exaggerated (the ancient world lacked the weapons and ideology of modern ethnic cleansers).[69] Part of the population at Veii survived the sack and was later given Roman citizenship, although we are initially told that the entire population was sold into slavery; there is a similar case with Tarquinii, where all were supposedly killed in 354 BC. The reason for Roman exaggeration must be generals claiming a more complete victory than they had in fact achieved, in order to qualify for a triumph (which from the second century BC reportedly required 5,000 of the enemy killed). Roman sources seem to take an unashamed pride in describing crushing victories over peoples who later formed an integral and valued part of the empire. While such rhetoric is clearly exaggerated, this violent ethos is equally apparent in other ancient Italian peoples, who as we have seen also glorified military conflict and the execution of enemies. In addition, Roman massacres had a psychological impact on the other Italian peoples: the Samnites sued for a treaty after seeing the outcome of the Tarquinian campaign in 354 BC, and the Marsi, Paeligni, Marrucini and Vestini after the Aequian campaign in 303 BC.

64. Momigliano, *Alien Wisdom*, 44.
65. Polybius, 36.13.6–7 (156 BC); Cornell, 'End of Roman imperial expansion', 157; Champion, *Roman Imperialism*, 82.
66. Note for instance the military scenes in Etruscan funerary urns and Campanian and Lucanian tomb painting from Nola and Paestum.
67. Aequi: Livy, 9.45.16 (304 BC); Ausones: Livy, 9.25 (314 BC).
68. Cf. Livy, 9.12: the Samnites burn the inhabitants of Fregellae alive.
69. Colwill, *Genocide*.

Some scholars have recently argued that this is typical of an anarchic inter-state system where only the strongest survive, drawing on a 'Realist' perspective from modern international relations.[70] In this view, fear of opponents in such a system was genuine and pervasive, and was as important a factor as the positive drives towards war. The pivotal position of Rome relatively near to aggressive and comparatively unstructured states such as the Senonian Gauls had a formative influence on their early development, and arguably made their international environment even more challenging than that of Carthage and the cities of mainland Greece. Rome was shaped by its enemies, providing some basis to the flattering Roman self-image of learning from and ultimately surpassing all those whom they fought. The impact of the Gallic sack in 390 BC must have been particularly determinative in encouraging a more aggressive Roman stance towards its potential enemies.[71] Rome is very similar to its neighbours in terms of its military practices: the extensive use of heavy infantry, the glorification of military prowess in single combat, the setting up of trophies, and the love of booty are widely paralleled by other states in Italy. They too habitually sought allies and treaties, and make much use of religion and ritual in war. Furthermore, many Italian states had republican forms of government where the limited term of magistrates in office must have encouraged the seeking of opportunities and profit through warfare.[72]

Nevertheless, a Realist perspective on the conquest of Italy can be misleading.[73] Realism as a theory is a product of the particular conditions of the Cold War, and neglects the non-military elements of hegemony. Realism emphasises the consensus for war among the dominant classes, but the plebs in both Rome and the Italian cities were also essential to imperialism. In Rome they had a new interest in the affairs of the state after the reforms of the fourth century BC. The Realist argument probably works best when analysing the imperialism of large, multi-ethnic empires, such as Rome and Carthage in the

---

70. Eckstein, *Mediterranean Anarchy*; cf. Rich, 'Fear'.
71. Williams, *Beyond the Rubicon*; Eckstein, *Mediterranean Anarchy*.
72. See Eckstein, *Mediterranean Anarchy* for an overview; further research is needed on the Italian peoples from this point of view; see for instance Farney and Bradley (eds), *Peoples of Ancient Italy*, for an overview.
73. Laurence, *Roads*, 12ff.; Smith and Yarrow, 'Introduction'; as reviewers of Eckstein have pointed out, ironically the theory depends heavily on the proto-Realist views of Thucydides and Polybius, and thus represents a rather circular argument when reapplied to the ancient world.

Punic Wars, and the Hellenistic kingdoms in the east. Applying it to Rome in the fifth or fourth centuries BC is rather more problematic.[74] In emphasising the genuine threat posed by rivals to Roman power, Realist approaches could be been seen as insufficiently critical of Livy and other sources who exaggerated enemy strength and thus Roman heroism.[75] In fact, diplomacy was used widely even if it often failed. The situation during the conquest is one of a web of networked city states interacting, rather than a clash of great empires. The elites of these states were mobile and interconnected, such as Vitruvius Vaccus from Fundi in southern Latium, who owned a house on the Palatine at Rome, yet led the people of Privernum in revolt in 330 BC (Livy, 8.19.4, Cic. *Dom.* 101); or the Samnite recuperating in an elite Roman house in 264 BC (Cass. Dio, fr. 10.42). Thus, the conquest needs to be understood in part as the product of elite interrelations. Italian city states often did not behave like unified Realist actors, and independent (non-state) elite interaction was as important as eliminationist war.[76]

Conclusion

Wars are a critical focus of historical study, serving as crisis points where long-running, pre-existing tensions are played out. For instance, the defection of many allies to Hannibal in the Second Punic War reveals key aspects about their relationship with Rome. The Roman conquest was the product of several complex historical processes that involved both Rome and the peoples of Italy. This included the expansion of various Italian powers including Rome and Samnium, and the competition for wealth and resources that this brought up between them in trying to control rich regions such as the Campanian plain. The conquest was also a product of Rome's incremental wealth and manpower advantages, and its gradual accumulation of powerful, militaristic allies. Plebeian enthusiasm for military service also played a part, linked to the way in which Roman generals shared the profits of war. The conquest was also facilitated by the division and weaknesses of many of Rome's enemies, who were often loose leagues of small city states (such as the Umbrians), or who came together too

---

74. This criticism could also be extended to other attempts to interpret the early phases of the conquest of Italy in terms of 'imperialism', given that no Roman Empire yet exists.
75. Cf. Cornell, 'Deconstructing'.
76. Cf. Kent, 'Reconsidering'; Isayev, *Migration*; Terrenato, *Early Roman Expansion*.

sporadically and too late to reverse the Roman advance, as with the alliances between the Samnites and Gauls in the 290s BC, and the Greek cities and the Samnites from the 270s BC. A further key factor is the transformation of the Roman nobility into a broader and hyper-competitive ruling class in the late fourth century, as we shall see in the next chapter.

CHAPTER 10

Rome around 300 BC

Introduction

The period from 338–290 BC saw dramatic changes in the Roman state in terms of politics, economy, culture, demography and religion. Political competition intensified as a result of the widening of access to the topmost magisterial positions. Hellenisation advanced, as Rome became more closely connected not only to the Greek cities of southern Italy but to the cities of mainland Greece. Rome's outlook grew more internationalised as it began to take a greater interest in Mediterranean affairs. These themes can be seen in each of the sections that follow.

Mid Republican politics: the Senate and elite

The late fourth century and early third century BC was a formative period for Roman politics, as the reforms enacted during the Struggle of the Orders began to take effect, and the conquest of Italy massively expanded the territory of the Roman state. The position of many Roman political institutions was formalised in this period, with the regularisation of the magistracies and the establishment of the dominance of the Senate. These changes created a state that would have felt familiar to late Republican writers such as Cicero and Livy, but because of this transformation, it is often difficult to work out what form Roman customs and institutions took before this period. As a result, establishing the exact nature of the changes is challenging.

Most of our sources preserve a distorted idea of early institutions, given that few of the surviving Roman writers had experience of a functioning Republican system. Our main sources are often confused and contradictory when it comes to the political struggles of the period, because earlier disputes and the laws that resulted were important precedents for politicians such as Cicero in the late Republic. For example, there was enormous controversy over the land reforms of 367 BC, as they provided the Gracchi with precedents for their agrarian reforms in the 130s and 120s BC, which were disputed by their opponents. As a result, the sources tend to be influenced by unrealistic nostalgia and a moralising perspective on what was going wrong with politics in their own day. Our earliest surviving source is Polybius, who wrote in the mid second century BC. Book 6 of his history provides a very valuable account of the mixed constitution of mid Republican Rome, although Polybius tends to overstate its balanced nature and underestimate the level of elite control. Antiquarian authors such as Varro (mid first century BC) and Festus (probably second century AD, but transmitting the work of the Augustan scholar Verrius Flaccus) also provide precious information about the forms of early institutions.

In spite of the issues with our sources, some major political developments are discernible in this period. The first significant development is that the Senate gained a dominant position in Roman politics from the late fourth century BC. It is clear from an important passage of Festus that the Senate was originally a more informal advisory body, a *consilium*, picked by the consuls themselves, and that there was no disgrace in being omitted. Then at some point between 318 and 312 BC enrolment was entrusted to the censors by the Ovinian law:[1]

> There was once a time when it was not considered disgraceful for senators to be passed over, because, just as the kings by themselves used to choose (or to choose as replacements) men who would serve them as public advisers (*in publico consilio*), so under the Republic the consuls or military tribunes with consular power used to choose for themselves their closest friends from among the patricians and then from among the plebeians. This practice continued until the law of the tribune Ovinius put an end to it. Ovinius' law bound the censors by oath to enrol in the Senate the best men from all ranks. The enforcement of this law had the consequence that senators who were passed over, and thus lost their place, were held in dishonour. (Festus, 290 L.)

Thus, the appointment of ex-magistrates was probably formalised at this point. The censors could add others, and exclude people for immoral conduct. But, effectively, membership of the Senate was now for life, given good behaviour. This gave that body a new permanence, and a standard membership of around three hundred. Exclusion became a cause of disgrace according to Festus, which must

---

1. See Cornell, 'Lex Ovinia' (his translation); Lanfranchi, *Tribuns*, 331–5 for the date.

have raised the stakes in political competition. This law also helped formalise the situation in which membership of the Senate came to define the Roman *nobilitas* (nobility). From this point on, being a member of the *nobilitas* came to mean being someone with ancestors who had served in the Senate, and this is the sense in which the term is used in the late Republic by Cicero and others.[2]

By Polybius' day, in the mid second century BC, the Senate was in control of finances and foreign relations, including the administration of Italy, as well as the security of the state:

> In the first place it has the control of the treasury, all revenue and expenditure being regulated by it . . . Similarly crimes committed in Italy which require a public investigation . . . if any private person or community in Italy is in need of arbitration . . . It also occupies itself with the dispatch of all embassies sent to countries outside of Italy for the purpose either of settling differences, or of offering friendly advice, or indeed of imposing demands, or of receiving submission, or of declaring war; and in like manner with respect to embassies arriving in Rome it decides what reception and what answer should be given to them. (Polybius, 6.13)

Senatorial power also resided in the prerogative to advise on the suitability or otherwise of legislation (which had, however, to be proposed by a serving magistrate). The Senate also decided where to send the consuls, and it received delegations, although magistrates in the field often had to act quickly and so could not always consult it on matters requiring a rapid response.

The Senate had few formal powers, but its recommendations were difficult to refuse and were rarely ignored. There are some interesting cases, for example in 264 BC when the consul incited a popular vote for intervening in Sicily to aid the Mamertini of Messana, but these were exceptional. The reason for the Senate's power over the chief magistrates was that while most Roman nobles would only hold the consulship for a year, they would always be members of the Senate. They were thus loath to ignore its immense authority, as this might limit their own influence later on in their career. Nevertheless, it is notable that the debates it held over questions such as whether to seek peace with Pyrrhus in 279 BC were real, and it was often divided. It is thus unhelpful to conceive of the Senate as a unified actor in the

---

2. Brunt, 'Nobilitas'.

politics of the Republic, when there was often a range of opinions within it.

The second major development in this period was the rise of a new nobility. As we saw in Chapter 7, the patricians came to monopolise power in the early Republic. The plebeian movement sought access to the magistracies of the state, which were controlled by patricians, and relief from the poverty and debt that oppressed the poorest members of Roman society. The fourth century BC saw various measures that opened up state offices to plebeians. The patricians had tried to prohibit any plebeians who had been tribunes of the plebs from becoming magistrates of the state. The plebeians fought against this and passed a series of laws that opened up the consulship to plebeians (367 BC), and then made it compulsory to have one plebeian consul (342 BC). The struggle also extended to the state priesthoods, some of which were also politically powerful positions, and which were opened to plebeians in 367 and 300 BC. This satisfied the wealthier members of the plebeian movement, who joined the patricians in the Senate. The result was the formation of a mixed plebeian–patrician nobility. The Struggle of the Orders is conventionally thought to come to an end, effectively, with these laws in the fourth century, from which point the new nobility is manifested in the *Fasti*.

By the end of the fourth century other important changes had been made to the institutions of state. In 447 BC quaestors, who had hitherto been chosen by the consuls, became subject to election (Tacitus, *Ann.* 11.22). In 366 BC the praetorship and curule aedileship (matching the plebeian aedileship) were established. These new offices contributed towards the emergence by the end of the fourth century of a *cursus honorum*, a career ladder which led from the quaestorship, aedileship or tribunate and praetorship to the consulship, and ultimately the censorship (if only in a few exceptional cases, given that censors were only appointed every five years).

The success of the plebeians and the widening of eligibility for the top offices of state aggravated competition. Now, as well as patricians, all the wealthy plebeians could stand for high office. As the main way that a Roman magistrate could achieve glory was through military victory, securing this at all costs became more important. This was also accelerated by the disappearance of iteration (repeat periods of officeholding). Before 300 BC consuls were often able to obtain re-election: Quintus Fabius Maximus was elected five times down to 295 BC. But iteration was phased out from around 290 BC, from which point on a consul could standardly expect to hold this office only once in his lifetime. Repeated consulships became rare, if not unheard of. Instead, the Senate extended the *imperium* (command) of the magistrate, a process known as prorogation. This turned ex-magistrates into proconsuls or propraetors, with control over a *provincia* (not a province, but a 'sphere of action'). The first proconsul was Quintus Publilius Philo in 326 BC. This development enhanced the Senate's control over the careers of magistrates, and made the Senate's advice doubly difficult to ignore.

These changes also help to explain the massive thirst for conquest from this point on, and why competitive instincts came to be built into Roman culture. Roman nobles commemorated their achievements in funeral orations, public monuments and (later on) through legends and iconography on coinage.[3] A series of *novi homines* ('new men'), plebeian consuls without a senatorial background, came to power in this period and promoted an aggressive Roman policy of expansion within Italy. These included Manius Curius Dentatus (as consul in 290 and 275 BC, against the Sabines and Pyrrhus), Titus Coruncanius (consul in 280 BC, against Vulci and Volsinii, and censor in 270 BC) and Gaius Fabricius (consul in 282 and 278 BC, against Pyrrhus). This new elite shared an increasingly well-defined set of ideological attitudes centred around military glory, self-promotion and the sharing out of office. The principle that no one man should become too successful was made plain in highly elaborated tales of early Republican figures like Spurius Maelius, Spurius Cassius and Manlius Capitolinus, who, it was claimed, aimed at kingship, and who met deserved punishment as a result. Such stories, retold in Livy and other sources, emphasised the dangers posed by radical popularist measures, the potential for the revival of kingship and the justness of their eventual execution.[4] Through such stories, developed in oral tradition, the idea of kingship at Rome came to be built up into a great evil, which the elite ought to resist at all costs. Their type of *libertas* came to mean not the right of all citizens to power, but rather the right of the elite to share office.[5]

Ultimately, a small group of families within this new nobility, such as the Claudii, Valerii, Fabii, Decii and Cornelii, came to dominate the uppermost offices, the praetorship and consulship. Beyond the

---

3. Hölkeskamp, 'Conquest'.
4. E.g. Livy, 2.41 on the would-be tyrant Spurius Cassius in 486 BC; cf. Smith, *Roman Clan*, 311–12.
5. Arena, *Libertas*, 88.

upper echelons of this elite, however, the much broader ranks of senators who never reached the highest curule offices display very considerable fluidity, and saw a continual turnover.[6]

The workings of the political system

This period is usually seen as one of consensus amongst the aristocracy, and a time when the Roman constitution is meant to have been at its most stable. This is certainly the vision of Polybius, when he outlines what he sees as the balanced nature of the Roman government. In many ways the Republican system could be seen to function at its best from the late fourth to the early second century BC. The plebeians were able to benefit from imperialism through colonisation and the influx of wealth into Rome from conquests. Elite competition was heavily regulated for most of the period, and no individuals achieved a truly dominant position before Scipio Africanus in the late third century BC. But this rather benign view neglects signs of continuing social conflict, and the very different nature of our source material from the mid to the late Republic.[7]

In particular, the tribunes of the plebs passed a series of laws in the fourth and third centuries that addressed a wide range of issues of interest to the plebeians, on land use, debt and constitutional matters. The last included efforts to define the role of the censors (the Lex Ovinia, 318–312 BC), the introduction of elections for the sixteen *tribuni militum* (military tribunes: the Lex Atilia-Marcia, 311 BC) and the opening up of priesthoods to the plebeians (the Lex Ogulnia, 300 BC). These laws expressed the principle of popular sovereignty, ultimately the right of the people to control their elected leaders, and so represent an extension of the ideas of the Struggle of the Orders.[8] In addition, we find figures behaving like demagogues or populists, appealing to the people, especially in the famous career of Appius Claudius Caecus. As censor in 312 BC he commissioned substantial public infrastructure projects (the Via Appia and Aqua Appia) and overhauled the Senate. He is also said to have attempted to distribute the *humiles*, probably the city residents, throughout all voting tribes,

---

6. Hölkeskamp, *Reconstructing*; Bradley, 'Investigating aristocracy'.
7. Millar, 'Political power' stresses the importance of the principle of 'popular sovereignty' in this period. For reactions to Millar see Cornell's review, 352 and Hölkeskamp, *Reconstructing*.
8. Lanfranchi, *Tribuns*, 655–78, with a list of tribunician laws.

rather than just the four city tribes to which they were restricted. This measure would have made their votes far more valuable, but it was soon reversed.[9]

Appius' secretary, Gnaeus Flavius, the son of a freedman, was elected as curule aedile in 304 BC. He published legal procedures and the calendar indicating *dies fasti* (days for legal business), which previously had been secret and had probably given patricians considerable power over legal procedure. This stirred up contemporary hostility, reflected in the very negative picture of Flavius and Claudius in the sources, perhaps as a result of their conflict with Quintus Fabius Maximus (for which see below): it is likely that the role of Fabius was presented positively by his descendant Fabius Pictor, the first Roman historian.

> In the same year a government clerk, Gnaeus Flavius, son of Gnaeus, was curule aedile. He had been born in humble circumstances, his father being a freedman, but was an able man and a good speaker... There is no doubting the stubborn determination with which he battled against the nobles, who looked down on his humble birth. He published the forms of civil law which had been hidden away amongst the secret archives of the pontiffs, and posted the official calendar on white noticeboards around the Forum, for the dates to be generally known when a legal action could be brought... Flavius had been elected aedile by a faction of the Forum, which had gained power from the censorship of Appius Claudius. Claudius had been the first to lower the standard of the Senate by filling up its list of members from the sons of freedmen, and when no one accepted his selection and he failed to obtain the political influence he sought in the Senate house, he distributed the *humiles* amongst all the voting tribes, with damaging effect on the Forum and Campus. And so great was the indignation roused by the election of Flavius that the majority of the nobles discarded their gold rings and military decorations. From then on the citizens were divided into two parties; the honest men who supported and upheld right principles took one view, and the faction of the Forum another, until Quintus Fabius and Publius Decius were elected censors [304 BC] and Fabius, partly to establish harmony and partly to prevent the elections being in the hands of the lowest of the low, weeded out all the Forum mob and deposited them in four tribes, to which he gave the name Urban tribes. This is said to have been so gratefully received that, for his settlement of the orders, Fabius won the surname of Maximus which all his many victories

---

9. Livy, 9.46, quoted below.

had not brought him. It is said too that it was Fabius who instituted the annual parade of the equestrians every 15th July. (Livy, 9.46)[10]

That this was not the end of popular agitation is shown by the Third Secession of the Plebs in 287 BC.[11] This ensured that the decrees of the plebeian assembly, plebiscites, became regular laws.

Thus, by the early third century BC the main political institutions of the Roman state had become settled in their classic form. The elite that dominated the magistracies had changed in composition. Whilst plebeians were now eligible, in practice only the rich could stand, and the voting assemblies that elected the magistrates remained dominated by the wealthy. The poor lost their dedicated plebeian leaders, who now began to identify with the Senate, an institution that attained a powerful position in Roman government from this time. But alongside this development, the power of the magistracies was curtailed by a series of tribunician laws, and some figures among the elite proved willing to act on the grievances of the poor.

Mid Republican society and culture

These dramatic changes in Roman politics from 367 BC were closely linked to developments in Roman society and culture. Rome profited heavily from its successes in the conquest of Italy. Revenue from booty was spent on temples, infrastructure and other major building projects in Rome and its environs. The new nobility was highly competitive, and sought new ways to advertise its successes. Their wealth could also be spent on luxury items, so new crafts developed to service this demand. New markets were also opened up by the conquest of Italy, and the creation of Roman roads helped the economies of the Italian regions to become more integrated. This period saw renewed and reinvigorated Mediterranean links, and a new self-confidence in Roman identity.

Beginning with the building projects in the city in this period, the most striking development is the large number of new temples attested in the literary sources.[12] Their foundations correlate to some extent with Roman successes in warfare. A distinctive pattern is visible. A

---

10. Trans. Radice. Cf. Pliny, *HN* 33.6.
11. Livy, *Epit.* book 11; see Chapter 7.
12. Ampolo, 'Città riformata', 237; Cornell, *Beginnings*, 384; Orlin, *Foreign Cults*, app. 1; Bastien, *Triomphe*, 333–5; Harris, *War and Imperialism*, 182 no. 1; Forsythe, *Critical History*, 341ff. For archaeologically attested temples, see Coarelli, *Origini*, 120.

good number were built in the early years of the Republic, continuing on from the sixth-century building boom, but this was followed by a lull in the main part of the fifth century BC. Building then revived in the early fourth century BC, to be followed by another lull until 304 BC, when an extraordinary burst of temple-building began that did not let up until the start of the Punic Wars in 264 BC (Table 10.1).

Table 10.1 Temple foundations attested by literary sources, 509–264 BC

Date (BC)	Temple
509	Jupiter Optimus Maximus, Juno, Minerva
501–493	Saturn
495	Mercury
493	Ceres, Liber and Libera
493 or 488	Fortuna Muliebris
484	Castor
466	Dius Fidius
431	Apollo
396	Mater Matuta
392	Juno Regina (II)
388	Mars
375	Juno Lucina
344	Juno Moneta
304	Concordia (I)
302	Salus
296	Bellona Victrix
295	Venus Obsequens
295	Jupiter Victor
294	Victoria
294	Jupiter Stator
293	Quirinus
293	Fors Fortuna
291	Aesculapius
278	Summanus
272	Consus
268	Tellus
267	Pales
264	Vertumnus

Temples were normally built to fulfil vows made in battle. They were a thank-offering for divine support against the enemies of Rome, but also celebrated the achievements of the victorious general himself. Thus, many of the new cults celebrated military victory, for example in the form of gods with epithets such as Victor and Victrix, in the cult of Victoria, 'victory' personified, and via other deities such as Fors Fortuna that commemorated the divine favour granted to Rome. These personified cults or 'divine qualities' are a sign of connections to the Greek world, where such cults had spread widely from the time of Alexander the Great. Greek influence is also apparent in cults such as that of Salus (Safety) and the Greek healing god Aesculapius. Other cults such as Consus (associated with granaries) and Tellus (an earth goddess) relate to Italic conceptions, whilst Juno Regina and Vertumnus are Etruscan deities, rehoused at Rome after the *evocatio* ('calling out') of the tutelary deities of the defeated cities of Veii and Volsinii respectively.

Another important area of building activity in this period was the construction of public works such as roads and aqueducts. The provision of this type of infrastructure has parallels elsewhere in Greece and the wider Mediterranean, and implies the need to cater for a rapidly growing city population. The censor Appius Claudius was a great innovator in this regard, constructing the Via Appia which linked Rome to Capua in Campania (Fig. 10.1).[13] Initially it was a gravel road, only later paved, and according to Diodorus (20.36) an extremely expensive undertaking, as 'he dug through elevated places and levelled with noteworthy fills the ravines and valleys'. It provided what Diodorus called a 'deathless monument' to its creator. During his censorship Appius also built an aqueduct, the Aqua Appia, to bring water into the city from a source around 16 km away along the Via Praenestina.

In designating the road and aqueduct by his own *praenomen* (forename), Appius set a new precedent for self-advertisement in Rome. He was soon followed by others. The censor Marcus Valerius Maximus together with his colleague Gaius Junius Bubulcus built the Via Valeria in 307 BC, linking Rome to Alba Fucens in the central Apennines. A further aqueduct, the Anio Vetus, was built in 272 BC by M'. Curius Dentatus. At least 60 km in length, this was a much more expensive project than the Appia. It was financed by booty from the sack of

---

13. Livy, 9.29.5–9.

Figure 10.1 Republican roads and colonies near Rome (after Salmon, *Roman Colonization*, fig. 5)

Tarentum in 272 BC, which was exceptionally rich (Florus 1.13.16–27; Frontinus, *Aq.* 6.1–4). These ambitious projects benefited the plebs both in terms of their living conditions and in employment opportunities, and brought (one might also say bought) their creators popularity in the wider populace.

This period also saw the Forum improved and adorned. The speaker's platform at the edge of the Comitium was decorated with the beaks of ships captured from Antium in 338 BC, and gained the name Rostra from them. The Comitium–Curia complex (assembly and Senate house) may have been reworked in 318 BC, along the lines of the assembly places of Greek cities in southern Italy.[14] Shops

---

14. Coarelli, *Foro Romano*, 138–60; Carafa, *Comizio*, argues that the space was not altered in the mid Republic, and instead triangular.

were built along the north side from 310 BC.[15] These were decorated with golden shields by L. Papirius Cursor, after his triumph over the Samnites in 309 BC (Livy, 9.40.16). Such a display of captured weaponry echoes both Greek and Italic practice: for instance, Athens displayed Spartan shields from a victory during the Peloponnesian War in the Stoa Poikile (Pausanias 1.15.4), while captured Greek armour from the fifth and fourth centuries BC was displayed at the great Samnite sanctuary of Pietrabbondante.[16]

The Comitium was also decorated in the late fourth century BC. It was already crowded with statuary, including depictions of the early Republican hero Horatius Cocles, the ambassadors slain by the Fidenates in 438 BC, and Hermodorus of Ephesus, the Greek philosopher who allegedly advised on the composition of the XII Tables in the mid fifth century BC.[17] In the late fourth century BC other statues were added, notably Marsyas, a figure said to be symbolic of liberty (Fig. 10.2). In Greek myth, Marsyas was an attendant of Dionysus whose hubris displeased Apollo, leading him to be flayed alive by the god after losing a musical contest. At Rome he was linked to Liber (equivalent to Dionysus), one of the Aventine triad, a cult with strong plebeian associations.[18]

Figure 10.2 Denarius of L. Marcius Censorinus, 82 BC, with the head of Apollo, and the statue of Marsyas with a wineskin from the Comitium (from Classical Numismatic Group, LLC, www.cngcoins.com)

15. Varro, ap. Non. 853 L. s.v. *Tabernas*.
16. See Forsythe, *Critical History*, 341 for earlier dedications made from booty.
17. Gellius, NA 4.5.1–6; Pliny, *HN* 34.11.
18. Wiseman, *Unwritten Rome*, 99.

The Comitium also had statues of two Greek figures, Alcibiades and Pythagoras (Pliny, *HN* 34.26; Plut. *Num.* 8.20). According to Pliny they were dedicated in response to the Delphic oracle, 'when during one of our Samnite Wars Pythian Apollo had commanded the erection in some conspicuous position of an effigy of the bravest man of the Greek race, and likewise, one of the wisest men'. Probably dating to the second half of the fourth century BC, this was a slightly eccentric and revealing choice. It shows a certain western bias, choosing the Athenian responsible for the expedition to Sicily, and the Greek philosopher who founded a school in Croton in southern Italy *c*.530 BC, rather than one of the more famous figures of the Greek mainland like Socrates. Pythagoras' teachings had become widely disseminated in southern Italy in the fourth century BC, particularly through Tarentum. That this influence spread to Rome during this period is evident from the contemporary source Aristoxenus of Tarentum (fr. 17 Wehrli), who describes the Romans as followers of Pythagoras, along with the 'Leucanians, Messapians, Peucetians' (Italic peoples of southern Italy).[19] The reception of Pythagorean ideas may explain the increasing measures to establish a more egalitarian system, as well as the reforms to the calendar at this time.[20]

Other important monuments were renewed or created across Rome in this period. A statue to Hercules was erected on the Capitoline hill in 305 BC (Livy, 9.44.16), while a few years later in 296 BC the aediles were able to finance several projects through the prosecution of moneylenders:

> The wooden thresholds of the Capitol were replaced by bronze, silver vessels were made for the three tables in the shrine of Jupiter, and a statue of the god himself, seated in a four-horse chariot, was set up on the roof. They also placed near the Ficus Ruminalis a group representing the founders of the city as babies being suckled by the she-wolf. The street leading from the Porta Capena to the temple of Mars was paved, under their instructions, with stone slabs. (Livy, 10.23)

Livy may mean that the original terracotta statue of Jupiter on the roof of the Capitolium was replaced in bronze. If so, this shows the city being brought up to contemporary Hellenistic standards. His men-

---

19. Cic. *Tusc.* 4.1–2.
20. Humm, 'Numa'.

tion of the setting up a statue of the wolf and twins is the first securely dated reference to the myth in Rome, and shows a new interest in Roman origins, and perhaps a new sense of Roman identity in connection with Rome's expansion into the Greek world of southern Italy.

Changes are also visible in terms of private culture. A Roman tradition of bronze sculpture appeared for the first time in this period. The most famous is the Capitoline Brutus, a rare surviving personal portrait from the second half of the fourth century BC. Although its subject is unknown and the attribution to Rome not altogether certain, the sophisticated Greek-style rendering probably shows the willingness of the elite to be represented in new ways. The first monuments to commemorate individual achievements were set up in this period. In 338 BC the consuls C. Maenius and Camillus were celebrated with the so-called *columna maenia* in the Comitium.[21] An equestrian statue of the consul of 306 BC, C. Marcius Tremulus, was set up in front of the temple of Castor.[22] A statue of the consul of 293 BC, Carvilius, was placed at the foot of his new statue of Jupiter, both made from the Samnite arms he had captured.[23] In the 280s statues were set up in Rome of the tribune of the plebs Aelius and the general C. Fabricius, paid for by the people of Thurii, the first instance of a commission in Rome by a foreign city.[24] All these were a sign of intensifying elite competition.

Funerary culture

This competitive ethos is also evident in funerary culture. Funerary evidence largely disappears in Rome from the early sixth century BC. There are a few isolated examples of fifth-century burials using plain stone sarcophagi, with one example in marble from the Greek island of Paros.[25] It was then renewed in the late fourth century under the influence of Hellenistic practices in the Greek East, and from engagement with Greek cities of the south of Italy where chamber tombs,

---

21. Pliny, *HN* 34.20, Livy, 8.13.9, Pliny, *HN* 7.212, Eutr. 2.7.3; Forsythe, *Critical History*, 341.
22. Livy, 9.43.22; Cic. *Phil.* 6.13, Pliny, *HN* 34.23: 'before the temple of Castor, there was an equestrian statue of Q. Marcius Tremulus, dressed in a toga. He had twice defeated the Samnites, had captured Anagnia, and had freed the people from paying the tax for army pay'.
23. Livy, 9.40.16; cf. 10.39.13f.; Pliny, *HN* 34.43.
24. Pliny, *HN* 34.32.
25. See Chapter 5 above; Colonna, 'Aspetto oscuro'.

sometimes painted, were employed. The renewed funerary custom was unlike the old practice, where ostentatious tomb furnishings would be interred with the deceased. Polybius provides a detailed description of Roman funerary practices in his own day, the middle second century BC, which is probably applicable to an earlier period too. He refers to the funerary speech (called in Latin an *elogium*) given by a close relative 'on the virtues and successful achievements of the dead'.

> By this constant renewal of the good report of brave men, the celebrity of those who performed noble deeds is rendered immortal, while at the same time the fame of those who did good service to their country becomes known to the people and a heritage for future generations. (Polybius, 6.54.2)

This characteristic combination of memory, state service and family honour is common to many facets of mid Republican culture, and is likely to date back to the emergence of a new elite ideology associated with the new mixed nobility from around 300 BC.

These funerary speeches and their written commemoration in family records undoubtedly had an important influence on Roman history.[26] Livy and Cicero complain about the exaggerations and distortions that they often contain, and the nature of the genre can be gauged by the very few remaining examples of funerary *elogia* that survive from the mid Republic. The most famous example is the epitaph of L. Cornelius Scipio Barbatus, consul in 298 BC and censor in 290 BC, inscribed on his monumental sarcophagus (Fig. 10.3). The form of the sarcophagus, with its Doric frieze and volutes, was drawn from Sicilian Greek models.[27]

> Lucius Cornelius Scipio, son of Gnaeus
> Lucius Cornelius Scipio Barbatus, Gnaeus' begotten son, a brave and wise man, whose appearance perfectly matched his bravery, he was aedile, consul, and censor among you; he took Taurasia and Cisauna in Samnium; he overcame all Lucania and brought hostages back. (*CIL* I² 6; Warmington, *Remains of Old Latin* 4: 2–9)

Recording his offices, personal virtues and famous victories, this shows us how Hellenistic standards of appearance and wisdom were

---

26. See Chapter 1.
27. Coarelli, *Roma*, 379.

Figure 10.3 Francesco Piranesi, 'Prospetto del Sarcofago di Scipione Barbato, e del Monumento d'Aula Cornelia' (View of the sarcophagus of Scipio Barbatus and the Monument of Aula Cornelia). The top line of inscription belongs to a separate monument to another member of the family, Paulla Cornelia (from Monumenti degli Scipioni (1785), Tav. 3, via Wikimedia Commons)

valued amongst the Roman elite. In a direct address to the audience, his offices are described as being held *apud vos* 'among you', emphasising how it was the Roman people which had elected Scipio to these positions. The places he conquered were recorded, including two otherwise obscure places in Samnium, and the exaggerated claim made that he had subdued *omne loucana*, 'all Lucania'.[28]

Equally instructive is the oration given by Quintus Metellus for his father Lucius Metellus, consul in 251 and 247 BC, recorded by Pliny:

> Quintus Metellus, in the oration which he gave at the final eulogy of his father the pontiff Lucius Metellus, twice consul, dictator, Master of Horse, and land-commissioner, who was the first to lead elephants in his triumph from the First Punic War, left it in writing that his father achieved the ten greatest and most glorious objects in the pursuit of which wise men pass their lives. For he had aimed at being the foremost warrior, an outstanding speaker, a brave general, at achieving great things under his own command, obtaining the highest offices,

---

28. Hölkeskamp, 'Conquest', 30.

enjoying the greatest honour, possessing exceptional wisdom, being considered the leading senator, gaining great wealth in a respectable way, leaving many children and being the most distinguished member of his community; and these fell to his father and no one else since the foundation of Rome. (Pliny, *HN* 7.139–40)

Like the Barbatus inscription, this records the capture of faraway places (and in this case exotic animals too). It also emphasises the elite values of wisdom, looks, wealth, *virtus* (manliness) and family. There is the expected detailing of political success and military glory, but also some other, more surprising values: political oratory is represented as a useful skill in this electorally governed political system, and 'great wealth' is to be sought rather than disdained. This contrasts with the nostalgic image of austere mid Republican leaders propagated by later sources.

This period also saw development of elaborate chamber tombs such as the Tomb of the Scipios on the Via Appia (where the monumental sarcophagus of Scipio Barbatus was found), and the use of frescoes. Probably once common, the tradition of mid Republican painting survives through the odd example and literary reference. The most famous survival is a fragment of a tomb fresco from the Esquiline, of the early third century BC (Fig. 10.4).[29] Several scenes of warfare and treaty formation between Rome and Samnium are recorded in different rows. An inscription on the third row lists the name *Q. Fabio(s)*, which may relate to Q. Fabius Rullianus, a commander in the third Samnite war. This fresco provides key contemporary evidence for the importance of foreign relations to elite prestige at this time, and accords with the emphasis on foreign interventions in the *elogia* cited above.

Greek political and cultural links

Links with Greek cities were re-invigorated in the late fourth century BC, although there was never a total break. Rome had become more orientated towards the Tyrrhenian sea in the early fourth century BC, and gained control over Greek cities in Campania, such as Naples, from the 320s BC. Rome had come into contact with Tarentum already in 326 BC, when Tarentum had offered rival help to Naples, and in 320 BC, when Tarentine ambassadors warned Rome against

---

29. Coarelli, *Origini*, 156–9.

Figure 10.4 Fresco from the Tomb of the Fabii, Esquiline, of *c*.300–280 BC (drawing: R. Hook, for Sekunda and Northwood, *Early Roman Armies*, 44; reproduced with kind permission of the authors)

fighting the Samnites at Luceria in Apulia. Rome had friendly relations with Rhodes from around 306 BC. But it was not until the 280s BC that Rome had significant direct interaction with the Greek cities of the south, forming an alliance with Thurii, and gaining direct control over Paestum in 273 BC (where a Latin colony was founded), and Tarentum, which was sacked in 270 BC. The intensification of cultural links with Greek cities in this period helps to explain why ambitious tribunes using popular pressure carried legislation controlling the actions of magistrates at Rome, just as in the earlier fifth century BC the plebeian movement had drawn on Greek democratic ideas of the equal rights of all citizens.

Rome also developed its contacts with mainland Greece and with the Hellenistic East in the late fourth century. The Romans are said to have sent an embassy to Alexander after the conquest of Persia in 323 BC (Arrian, *Anab.* 7.15.4–6). Arrian doubts this, but the presence of comparable embassies from other western states such as the Bruttians, Lucanians, Etruscans and Carthage reinforces the historicity of the mission, which is confirmed by its mention in the contemporary historian Cleitarchus (Pliny, *HN* 3.57).[30] Rome in turn received embassies from Alexander and Demetrius Poliorcetes concerning the problem of piracy.[31] At the end of the Pyrrhic War, Rome also exchanged embassies with the Ptolemies, in the late 270s (Cassius Dio, fragment of book 41). Simultaneously in the fourth century BC, Greek knowledge of Rome was expanding. For instance, the philosopher Aristotle, who happened to be Alexander's tutor, took note of the new power in the west, discussing the foundation of Rome and its sack by the Gauls. In the third century BC the Sicilian Timaeus covered the beginnings of Rome in his history of the Western Greeks, and in a work on the Pyrrhic War.[32]

Another manifestation of this interaction is coinage, first issued on Rome's behalf in Naples, in connection with the building of the Via Appia.[33] When Rome came to mint regular issues itself, its moneyers used motifs of Greek gods such as Heracles and Apollo (perhaps an allusion to his role as the saviour of Delphi from the Gauls) to show how Rome formed part of this civilised, pan-Mediterranean world.

30. Bosworth, *Conquest*, 167; Bispham, 'Rome and Antium', 239.
31. See Chapter 6.
32. Timaeus was insufficiently detailed according to Dionysius (1.5.6), but Gellius (*NA* 11.1.1) describes his history as broadly concerning the 'affairs of the Roman people'; see Baron, *Timaeus*, 45.
33. See Chapter 6.

It is not surprising in this context to see the Greek writer Heraclides of Pontus call Rome a Greek city, just as others characterised Caere, an Etruscan city with its own treasury at Delphi.[34]

The growth of slavery

The growth of slavery was probably related to the decline in debt-bondage (*nexum*) at Rome. As we have seen, the XII Tables make it clear that slavery already existed at Rome by the fifth century BC, although it seems to have been less important at this point than debt-bondage. The XII Tables have much more to say about debt than slavery, and the plebeian struggle was mostly concerned with debt-bondage. From this it can be suggested that until the fourth century BC debt-bondage probably provided the main labour force for the large land holdings of the elite, the extent of which the Licinio-Sextian laws aimed to restrict in 367 BC.

In the fourth century the balance between debt-bondage and slavery altered. The evidence for early slavery is problematic, as it is essentially made up of casual references in Livy, but various episodes indicate that a substantial demand for slaves arose in the fourth century BC.[35] In 396 BC the Romans captured the huge Etruscan city of Veii after a long siege, and Livy reports that the population was sold into slavery. The exact number is unclear, and it is unlikely to have included everybody, given that some survivors loyal to Rome were later enfranchised. But there must have been tens of thousands enslaved, representing a severe act of vengeance against a long feared and hated enemy. That the Roman market itself was substantial enough to absorb these slaves is clear from the imposition of a 5 per cent tax on the freeing of slaves in 357 BC: this presupposes that slaves were numerous enough to make it worth taxing their manumission. In 326 BC, as we have seen, *nexum* was formally abolished. It was now imperative that the elite find alternative labour sources, but slavery had probably already become the most important source of dependent labour by this time. As a result, Finley argued, mass slavery at Rome was in some senses a product of the freedom of the plebs, as was also the case for the *demos* (the masses) in Greece.

---

34. Plut. *Cam.* 22.3 for Heraclides; at 21.1, Plutarch describes Caere as a Greek city. Cf. Dion. Hal. 1.89 on the Greek nature of Rome.
35. See Chapter 6: Society and social institutions.

There were enough freedmen by 312 BC for it to be controversial for the censor in this year, Appius Claudius, to enrol descendants of slaves in the Senate. As noted above, he also aimed to distribute all the *humiles*, presumably including the freedmen in the four urban tribes, across all the Roman tribes, to increase the value of their vote. Both measures were soon overturned, but they show the scale of the freed slave presence in Roman society, something also suggested by the recruitment of freedmen into the army in 296 BC during an emergency. All this presupposes a considerable presence of slaves even in the fourth century BC. In short, by 300 BC Rome was well on the way towards being a 'slave society'. This is one of the consequences of new conquests. It allowed the development of a new, more intensive type of agriculture, and the large-scale production of ceramics at Rome, both based around extensive use of slave labour.

Religion

Significant changes are also evident in Roman religion during the fifth and fourth centuries BC. With the source material available to us, studying the development of Roman religion chronologically is problematic. The late sources tend to obscure the origins of religious institutions. Whilst there are reliable indications of religious changes in the Republic, the establishment of religious institutions and practices is mostly attributed to the early monarchy. Few dates can be accepted before the Tarquin dynasty, yet our sources maintain that the Tarquins were responsible for relatively few religious innovations. Nevertheless, various important themes are discernible in religion by the middle Republic: the connection of religion with the growing complexity of the state; the influence of other cultures on Roman religion, and particularly Hellenisation; the link between religion, politics and society; and the role of religion in ethnic and community identity. Many of these topics have been touched on before, but it is worthwhile having a consolidated analysis of Roman religious life in the era around 300 BC, as this marks an important stage in the evolution of the Roman religious system.

The first thing to note is the complexity of early religion and its implications for Roman state formation. The system of religious institutions is one of the most complex aspects of early Rome evident from the sources. This is not by chance, as religion is closely associated with record-keeping. Detailed written documents such as the calendar, priestly records and ritual instructions, alongside oral tradition, enabled the 'correct' performance of rituals on long-term cycles (often annual but sometimes longer). Punctiliousness and record-keeping were closely associated with worship and propitiation through blood (animal) sacrifice, a cycle of festivals and ceremonies, and regularly repeated rituals (in temples and shrines or in the open air). These records underlay much of Roman collective memory, and thus preserved a great deal of information about religion.[36] Many sacred institutions were attributed to the second king of Rome, Numa Pompilius, whose one-dimensionality marks him out as something of a stereotypical religious founder. Although these attributions are probably spurious, it was one way in which our sources were able to express their belief in the antiquity of Rome's religious institutions.

Our sources believed that a very wide range of priesthoods had been established before the end of the monarchy.[37] These included the *pontifices*, who were responsible for religious law and rituals; the augurs, who were in charge of interpreting the auspices, the signs sent by the gods, particularly in terms of the flight of birds; the *duumviri sacris faciundis*, a board of two men responsible for performing sacred rites, who looked after the Sibylline oracles and thereby sanctioned the importation of foreign cults;[38] the Vestal Virgins, who tended the sacred flame in the temple of Vesta; and the *flamines*, who were devoted to certain individual deities such as Jupiter and Mars. These priesthoods played a key role in the archaic festivals of Rome attested in the oldest stratum of the calendar, and in some cases were subject to a series of archaic taboos and social requirements (such as marriage by *confarreatio*) that only make sense in a very early context.

The ritual calendar is important in this context. The sole surviving Republican example, the *Fasti Antiates maiores* discovered in Antium (84–55 BC), has festivals and annotations marking out the religious character of the days in larger and smaller letters. These traditionally have been seen as indicating different strata of composition. The 'large letter festivals' exclude cults said to have been introduced under the Tarquins (such as the Capitoline triad) or in the early Republic (such as the cult of Apollo, introduced in 431 BC).

---

36. See Chapter 1.
37. Beard, 'Priesthood' provides a convenient, simplified list.
38. They became a board of ten (*decemviri*) in 367 BC (Livy, 6.37, 42), and later a board of fifteen (*quindecemviri*).

They are thus regarded as earlier than the Tarquin dynasty.[39] This is significant, as this very complex written document contained a huge amount of information about the arrangement of festivals and the pattern of days around which the citizen community organised itself: days devoted to religious activities, markets or the pursuit of legal business. Rome also celebrated complex festivals involving sacred games (for example, the Ludi Romani) from an early era.[40] The origins of this festival are uncertain, whether emerging under Tarquinius Priscus (as Livy thought, describing it as a development of earlier practice), or after Lake Regillus in 499/496 BC. Dionysius describes the festivities as wholly Greek-inspired, involving a procession, a chariot race, athletic competitions and dramatic performances (lasting several days by the late third century BC). It was celebrated on an annual basis from the fourth century BC.[41]

Roman religion is also a sensitive index of the networks to which Rome belonged. Greek, Etruscan and Italic influences are all evident from the monarchic period, and grow stronger over time.[42] This is symptomatic of the openness of Rome in other areas such as citizenship. The Roman view as expressed in Varro and other sources was that Rome did not worship images of the gods in the first 170 years of the city, that is, before 583 BC.[43] This is pretty implausible given that there was already imagery of Greek deities at Rome around 575 BC, and was probably a typical ancient evolutionary schema. In fact, Rome seems to have had a mixture of anthropomorphic and aniconic gods throughout its history.[44] Roman state religion was superficially conservative, but in practice flexible and eclectic. Rome readily adopted new gods, during the monarchy as well as during the Republic. The Sibylline oracles are attested as sanctioning importations in the third century BC and very probably did so earlier too.

This openness to outside influence is characteristic of Mediterranean polytheistic systems of belief, and led at Rome to a diverse pantheon of hundreds of gods, many of them quite obscure. There are clear parallels with the closely related religious systems of Greek

---

39. Beard et al., *Religions*, I 6; for a contrary view dating the calendar to c.300 BC, see Rüpke, *Roman Calendar*.
40. Livy, 1.35.7–9; Dion. Hal. 3.68.1; Cic. *Rep.* 2.20.36; Manuwald, *Roman Republican Theatre*, 42.
41. Livy, 8.40.2 on the Ludi as a regular annual festival in 322 BC.
42. Bianchi, *Greci ed Etruschi*, 89–110, for a survey of the historiography.
43. Varro, cited in Augustine, *De civ. D.* 4.31; cf. Plut. *Num.* 8; Tertullian, *Apol.* 25.12.
44. Beard et al., *Religions of Rome*, II 1.1a.

and Etruscan cities. Divine names show a complex pattern of sharing and borrowing across the three cultures: some are very closely related and have identical names, such as Apollo (Etruscan Apulu, Greek Apollon); some are shared between Rome and Etruria but not Greece, such as Minerva (Etruscan Menrva but Greek Athena) and Juno (Etruscan Uni but Greek Hera). Some gods have different names in each of the three cultures, such as Venus, (Etruscan) Turan and (Greek) Aphrodite. This suggests an origin as three different deities, who became assimilated in the Roman mind.

One of the most characteristic features of Roman religion is its use of triads. Purcell has argued that the Capitoline cult of Jupiter Optimus Maximus, Juno and Minerva must be linked to Greek ideas of an all-powerful Zeus and to Greek city cults of Athena and Hera. As at Olympia and Athens, the cult of Saturn (Greek Cronus) was linked to that of Jupiter (Greek Zeus) by the proximity of their temples in Rome, perhaps marking the mythological defeat of Cronus by Zeus.[45] Rome also had a range of Italic cults such as Feronia and Mefitis, and housed various Etruscan deities, most famously those attracted to Rome from their home cities by *evocatio*: Juno Regina from Veii, and Vertumnus from Volsinii.

The ancient cults in the emporic centre of the Forum Boarium had a clear Hellenic imprint, notably the pair of Minerva and Hercules and the separate cult of Hercules at the Ara Maxima. But there were also Greek-influenced cults in the Forum, such as Hephaestus, attested in the area of the Lapis Niger, and the Dioscuri, worshipped in the temple of Castor.[46] While there was less emphasis on myth than in the Greek world, Roman religion is not at all myth-less. The Romans were intimately familiar with Greek myth from the archaic period, as is evident from temple terracottas in the Forum Boarium, Regia and other central sites.[47] This interest is also evident in the late fourth century BC in items such as the Ficoroni *cista* (*c*.330 BC), incised with the myth of the Argonauts. There is also a reasonable case to be made for Phoenician influence on cults in Rome at the Ara Maxima, and for Near Eastern influence on the practice of haruspicy, for which Rome relied on Etruscan priestly experts.[48]

---

45. Purcell, 'Becoming historical'.
46. See Chapter 5.
47. See Chapter 5. Cf. Wiseman, *Myths of Rome*.
48. Van Berchem, 'Hercule–Melqart à l'Ara Maxima'; 'Sanctuaires d'Hercule–Melqart'. Compare the Phoenician items in nearby Orientalising burials at Praeneste and Caere.

Religion also reveals much about political power. At least from the early Republic, politics and religion were closely intertwined. Religion was embedded in city life, and an important element of elite and state power. In the monarchic and early Republican period, patrician priests were able to guard religious and legal procedures as arcane knowledge that only they could know. This was undermined by the publication of the calendar and the revelation of the dedicatory formula for temples associated with Cn. Flavius' aedileship in 304 BC, discussed above. The patricians also preserved power through the domination and political use of priesthoods, and through claimed ownership of the auspices. The augurs, for instance, were able to control when assemblies could and could not be legitimately held (Cicero, *Leg.* 2.12.31). Religion also reinforced the hierarchical patriarchy of Roman society through the male domination of (most) priesthoods and the prohibition of women from certain cults, notably that of Hercules at the Ara Maxima. However, recent scholarship has demonstrated that women were involved in many aspects of ritual, and could for the most part take part in the regular religious activities of sacrifice and offerings. This work has also clarified the importance of the role played by priestesses such as the Vestals, *flaminicae* and Salian Virgins in state cults.[49]

Political power was also manifested through the profusion of new religious building in the late monarchic and Republican periods, particularly in the late fourth and early third century BC.[50] The vowing of temples acted as political advertisements for their founders as well as ways of introducing new cults. The Capitolium was the ultimate statement of the monumental power of monarchy, which came after 509 BC to symbolise the new Republican regime. Capitoline Jupiter was designated the most powerful Republican deity, Jupiter *Optimus Maximus* ('Jupiter Greatest and Best'). This was particularly demonstrated in the Triumph, a festival which acted as the ultimate manifestation of a general's power and his connection with divine favour, as well as celebrating the role of the gods in Roman victory. Although the subject of much recent debate, strong Near Eastern and

---

49. For the debate over women and sacrifice see Schultz, *Women's Religious Activity*; Flemming, 'Festus and the role of women'; Hemelrijk, 'Women and sacrifice'; Glinister, 'Bring on the dancing girls'.
50. See Table 10.1 and the discussion above, pp. 341–343.

Etruscan influences on the Triumph remain plausible.⁵¹ The changing nature of the festival through the Republic is important, particularly in terms of its elaboration with Hellenistic ideas.⁵²

Finally, religion in this era played a key role in identity and senses of community. It has often been observed that Roman religion was a 'locative religion', based on the city and its society, as opposed to a 'utopian religion', focused away from the present world. Roman religion was a communal religion, concerned with participation in groups, whether ethnic, city, collegial, gendered or life-stage focused. It did not require individual commitment or belief. This is clear from the way that prodigies were interpreted as significant for the collective fate of the population. Many festivals were associated with particular places within Rome and its territory, such as the Lupercalia with the Palatine and Lupercal, or the Ambarvalia with the boundaries of the city. Religion also mediated links with Rome's neighbours, through Roman participation in Latin federal cults and through the use by foreign visitors and residents alike of the cults of *emporia* such as the Forum Boarium. Participation in festivals was crucial to Roman identity, and many cults and festivals were shared with Rome's neighbours, particularly the Latins, for example Diana on the Aventine, and Jupiter in the *Feriae Latinae* on the Alban Mount. The antiquity of these shared cults helps us to understand the ancient roots of these ethnic identities. Rome also participated in cult centres of Mediterranean-wide significance, notably Delphi, where periodic offerings were made and a treasury kept, shared with Massilia. This cosmopolitan mix helped to make up the distinctive character of Roman religion, with its combination of gods, priesthoods and festivals drawn and elaborated from a wide variety of sources.

---

51. Versnel, *Triumphus*. Versnel, 'Red (herring?)' rejects Rüpke's thesis that the Triumph was only introduced in the fourth century BC, and reasserts its Etruscan and Near Eastern influences.
52. Beard, *Roman Triumph*, ch. 5 Armstrong, 'Coming in from the cold'.

CHAPTER 11

Conclusion

Pulling together some of the key themes of the work, one of the first points to stress is the great depth of history in Rome and central Italy. Settlement goes back to the late Bronze and early Iron Age in Rome (well before the traditional foundation date of 753 BC), just as in the other major centres of south Etruria and Latium. The early settlement at Rome shows many close parallels with contemporary Villanovan communities on the sites of the great Etruscan cities. The mid seventh century BC seems more likely now to be end of the first phase of state formation rather than its start, judging by the new archaeological evidence for developments at Rome in the late eighth and early seventh century BC, and the beginnings of monumental building, which presupposes complex political organisation, already by the last quarter of the seventh century BC. This matches what we know from Etruscan sites like Murlo and Acquarossa, even if the exact significance of the fragmentary finds from Rome remains controversial.

The development of Rome should be seen within the context of the wider Italian and Mediterranean environment. This has been obscured by our sources, who emphasise the internal struggles and self-determination of the Roman community. They tended to write out of their histories the contribution of other cultures such as the Etruscans, treating Rome as a land-based power that was unfamiliar with the sea before the opening of the First Punic War in 264 BC. Yet Roman links with other cultures are clearly attested in various types of evidence. For example, the evidence of Mediterranean-wide myths shows that they circulated in the Tyrrhenian region from a very early date and, as scholars such as Fowler and Malkin have shown, probably date back at least to the eighth century BC. This shared body of mythical stories about central Italy, heavily influenced by Greek connections, was something that Rome participated in from at least the sixth century BC, judging by representations of aspects of these stories in architectural terracottas from the Regia and Forum Boarium temple. Literary manifestations of these stories appear in Greek sources from the eighth century BC, and involve Rome from at least the fifth century BC.

In archaeological terms, the Forum Boarium sanctuary deposit reveals connections with Greek traders through imported pottery already from the eighth century BC, and shows that Rome was embedded in wider cosmopolitan trading networks in the sixth century BC encompassing Etruria, Sardinia, Carthage and Greek cities across the Mediterranean. This should not be surprising within the context of a vibrant trade along the Tyrrhenian coast in this period that also gave rise to similarly cosmopolitan sites at places like Pyrgi and Gravisca. It is reinforced by the evidence for Greeks and Etruscans resident and even buried in Rome, such as the Greek Kleikos in the Esquiline cemetery. The architectural developments in the late seventh and sixth centuries BC, such as the Regia, the Forum Boarium temple and the Capitoline temple, show the influence of sites as distant as Corcyra, Samos and Athens. The recent realisation of the extent of Roman production of architectural terracottas has also revealed the close connections between Rome and cities in Etruria, Latium and Campania in the sixth and early fifth centuries BC.

In the seventh and sixth centuries Rome formed part of a central Italian network that was closely linked to the Eastern Mediterranean. This is evident from the Near Eastern style ideology expressed in Latin and Etruscan princely burials. Burial goods such as fans, footstools and dining equipment, familiar from Near Eastern iconography, expressed a shared ideology of banqueting which included powerful women as well as men, probably indicating a direct link to the Near East via Phoenician traders rather than transmission through Greek intermediaries, where the practice was different. These connections are also expressed by the similarities in statuary and tombs between the cemeteries of south Etruria and sites in areas such as Anatolia and Syria. Furthermore, the profound influence of Greek contacts is evident through the presence of eighth- and seventh-century items such as semi-pendant skyphoi found in Veii in the eighth century BC, which are precociously copied in local workshops.

These Mediterranean-wide trade links show that the sporadic literary evidence of early contacts between Rome and foreign powers are plausible, such as the treaties with Massilia and Carthage, Roman dedications at Delphi in the late monarchy and early Republic, and Greek influence on politics and law in the early Republic. This type of material does not help to resolve the complex question of whether the emergence of city states in central Italy was due to links with Greeks and Phoenicians or was a largely internally driven development. But this is probably too crude a question, given our increasing appreciation of the highly interconnected nature of the Mediterranean in the first half of the first millennium BC.

Another important point is the size and primacy of Rome compared to its neighbours in central Italy by the archaic period (c.580–480 BC). Archaeology has shown how many cities were protected by full walled circuits from at least the sixth century BC. The key evidence at Rome, the remains of archaic walling in local cappellaccio stone, although still disputed, should probably be interpreted as evidence of a full circuit of fortifications in the sixth century BC. The full extent of the walls, 11 km long, may not have directly reflected habitation expansion, as they were in part a propagandist statement, and most large archaic cities had less than half of their space within their walls occupied by housing. Nevertheless, the scale of the fortifications is inconceivable without one of the largest city populations in central Italy. Comparable evidence is provided by the huge foundations of the Capitoline temple and other large-scale projects attributed to the monarchy in the sixth century BC such as the Cloaca Maxima and Circus Maximus. There still remains the enigma of the early census figures, which imply a very large sixth-century population, but which cannot be accepted at face value. Rome's primacy is supported by the construction here of the first known temple within central Italy, the Forum Boarium temple of around 580 BC, and the innovative nature of the substructure and decoration of the Capitoline temple. Finally, the dominant position of Rome within Latium by the end of the monarchy is also attested by the first Carthage treaty of 509 BC.

Mobility and ethnicity also play a key role in early Roman history. The size of Rome was undoubtedly connected to its openness in the archaic era. Rome experienced population growth through the migration of individuals, such as the Greek Kleikos and the Etrusco-Corinthian Tarquinius Priscus from Tarquinii, and groups, such as the Claudian clan from Sabinum. The peak evidence for this mobility comes in the seventh to fifth centuries BC. Nevertheless, it is notable that Roman legends stress the continual openness of the city from its foundation through stories such as Romulus' asylum and the abduction of the Sabine women, which may dimly reflect genuine early practices. Rome also remains a highly mobile society after the fifth century BC, through colonisation, piracy, and military service shading into mercenary activity such as the 'secession' of the army at Capua in 342 BC. Rome also regularly faced the potential loss of parts of the population in the early Republic through plebeian secessions and (probably) the proposed migration to Veii, but these movements were averted by the pragmatic flexibility of the Roman elite and (perhaps) an emerging sense of collective Roman community. Nevertheless, controlling the fission of the citizen body was only managed through important concessions, such as the establishment of the tribunate, which changed the nature of the Roman political system.

The fluidity of the population must relate to the 'liminal' position of Rome, which although predominantly a Latin city experienced strong Etruscan influence. Rome in many ways is the mirror image of Etruscan Volsinii, another frontier city, which experienced very strong Italic influence. Roman identity encompassed a strong sense of hybridity, probably also common to other central Italian cities. Although our sources envisage openness as a deliberate policy from the time of Romulus, it may have only become such under the later kings, an archaic attitude continued by the Republican elite. Continual mobility was linked to the very dynamic nature of Roman society.

The expansion of Rome takes place within the 'anarchic' environment of inter-state relations in ancient Italy. For instance, Rome and Veii, the two greatest cities in central Italy, were both sacked in the early fourth century BC. Rome recovered, whereas Veii did not. The outcome could easily have been different. Recent research has shown how Rome was shaped by the highly competitive environment of central Italy. The Roman conquest of other states in Italy should be understood within the context of a long history of interaction within the peninsula. The conquest was merely one episode in a relationship that starts in the Orientalising period, and continues beyond Augustus, mediated at a personal and family as well as a state level. Rome was characterised by the eclectic, opportunistic nature of its alliance-building in Italy. Like its opponents, Rome continually sought support from friendly groups, and fought in coalition wherever possible, making use of diplomatic relations within elite networks which enmeshed all of the peoples and cities of Italy. Roman success was not inevitable, but its latent power and advantage over other central Italian states has become clearer as archaeological investigation continues.

Republican Rome inherited a large population, a pivotal geographical position, and complex social, religious and economic structures from the monarchy. It experienced many setbacks in the fifth century BC, and was engulfed in bitter social conflict. The classical form of the Roman

Republic took a long time to emerge, the result of progressive and innovative state-building that created powerful offices such as the consulship, tribunate and dictatorship. A very important part was played by the Servian reforms, which seem linked to the mobility of the sixth century BC, and were probably modified at some point in the early Republic. The system of government was the product not of a single architect but of contributions by kings, the Republican elite and forces like the plebeian movement. The Roman elite emerged in the early Republic as a powerful force equal to the splendour and wealth of their Orientalising predecessors (and perhaps ancestors). They undertook a continual struggle for prestige amongst themselves and as a collective body against the plebs. But the archaic state that survived for the first century and a half of the Republic was modified by important reforms in the fourth century BC. These created the classic form of mid Republican regime that we know from Polybius' description in the mid second century BC. The result of these reforms was the emergence of a militaristic elite, a politically stable government, and an army founded on citizen farmers. The reorganisation of the army and regularisation of colonisation in the late fourth century BC also helped create a state equipped to conquer the Mediterranean. In the years around 300 BC Rome expanded within Italy and developed its connections overseas, all the while experiencing a transformation of Roman identity in social and religious terms. Rome was no longer a city state in the traditional political and religious sense, but the hub of an expanding empire.

The late fourth and early third century BC saw the emergence of a competitive elite culture which led to the redevelopment of the urban image of Rome and a new culture of self-celebration. New cults were adopted, many Greek but others from Italic sources. Rome engaged more profoundly with the wider Hellenistic Mediterranean from this point on, and began to benefit economically from the broader integration of the Italian regions, and international exchange. This marked the growing Hellenisation of the city, but alongside the development of a distinctly Roman culture and artistic forms. The stage was now set for the rapid expansion of Rome into a world empire, a story addressed in the successive volumes of this series.

Chronology

Many of the early dates deriving from the Roman tradition are uncertain. The dates given for the Republic are those from the traditional Roman consular chronology, which is problematic before c.300.

Political/Military	Religious/Cultural	Events elsewhere
	c.1600–1000 Middle and Late Bronze Age material from site of Rome	1194–1184 date of Trojan War (Eratosthenes); diaspora of Aeneas and other heroes
		814 Foundation of Carthage (Timaeus)
753 Foundation of Rome (Varro)	c.720–580 Orientalising phase in Tyrrhenian Italy	c.775 Euboean foundation of Pithecusae
c.700–650 Infilling and creation of Roman Forum	715–672 Numa establishes key religious institutions	c.725 Euboean foundation of Cumae (followed by many other settlements)
		c.656 Expulsion of the Bacchiads from Corinth; migration of Demaratus
616–509 Tarquin dynasty; Servius Tullius enacts centuriate and tribal reforms	Servius Tullius founds Temple of Diana on Aventine and twin temples in Forum Boarium	c.600 Gauls infiltrate northern Italy c.600 Treaty of Rome with Massilia c.540 Carthaginian and Etruscan fleet defeated at Alalia, Corsica 541–514 Pisistratids rule Athens 510 Democratic reforms of Cleisthenes in Athens
509 Fall of the monarchy and beginning of the Republic	509 or 507 Foundation of Capitoline temple	509 Carthage forms first treaty with Rome (Polybius)
504 Migration of Attus Clausus to Rome		
499 or 496 Battle of Lake Regillus		

Political/Military	Religious/Cultural	Events elsewhere
494 First Secession of the plebs 493 Cassian Treaty between Rome and Latins	493 Temple of Ceres, Liber and Libera dedicated	489–488 Volscian advance on Rome under Coriolanus
458 Cincinnatus defeats the Aequi at Algidus	484 Temple of Castor dedicated	474 Hiero and Cumaeans defeat Etruscan fleet near Cumae
451–450 First and Second Decemvirate 450 Second Secession of the plebs 444 Consular tribunes appointed for first time	431 Temple of Apollo founded	421/20 Samnites seize Capua 414/13 Athenian expedition against Syracuse defeated c.400 Lucanians capture Poseidonia
396 Roman capture of Veii 390 Gallic sack of Rome		389 Roman alliance with Massilia
367 Licinio-Sextian laws 366 Consulship re-established; institution of praetorship	367 College of *decemviri sacris faciundis* opened to plebeians	384 Dionysius of Syracuse sacks Pyrgi
354 Roman treaty with the Samnites		348 Carthage renews treaty with Rome
343–341 First Roman war with Samnites, over Capua		
338 Roman control established over Latium		
327–304 Second Roman war with Samnites 310 Roman victory over Etruscan cities 308 Roman victory over Umbrians	312 Via Appia created 307 Via Valeria created	323 Embassies from Etruria, Rome and other Italians to Alexander at Babylon 306 Carthage renews treaty with Rome
298–290 Third Roman war with Samnites 295 Roman defeat of Gallic–Samnite alliance at Sentinum 290 Conquest of Sabines and Praetuttii by M'. Curius Dentatus	302–264 Regular foundation of temples at Rome 300 Colleges of augurs and *pontifices* opened to plebeians	
287 Third Secession of the plebs 280–275 Roman war against Pyrrhus		264 Appeal of Messana to Rome; beginning of First Punic War

Guide to further reading

This is intended to act as a general introduction to the material for readers looking for further guidance, primarily in the English language. The proliferation of work on early Rome in many different scholarly traditions makes an exhaustive survey impossible. However, for some idea of the range of work available, see the bibliography on Romulus and the kings compiled by A. Meurant on the Lupa Capitolina Electronica site at https://sites.uclouvain.be/lupacap/lce.sit.louve.accueil.htm. For full details of items, see the bibliography in this volume.

The most authoritative general study of early Rome is T. J. Cornell, *The Beginnings of Rome*. Excellent overviews can also be found in G. Forsythe, *A Critical History of Early Rome*, which as its title suggests is less optimistic in its reading of the sources, and K. Lomas, *The Rise of Rome*, which contextualises Roman history through more use of up-to-date Italian archaeological material. R. MacMullen, *The Earliest Romans* provides an interesting thematic outline. There is also comprehensive coverage of the period in F. W. Walbank et al. (eds), *The Cambridge Ancient History* 7.2, and A. Momigliano and A. Schiavone (eds), *Storia di Roma* I. Although now somewhat long in the tooth, they contain many valuable chapters, particularly those by Cornell, Drummond, Momigliano and Torelli in the *CAH* and by Ampolo, Coarelli and Torelli in the *Storia di Roma*. A. Grandazzi, *The Foundation of Rome* remains useful on the beginnings of the city, and P. Lulof and C. Smith (eds), *The Age of Tarquinius Superbus* provides in-depth studies of the later monarchic era.

The reliability of the literary sources remains heavily debated and there are a wide range of scholarly positions. Key examples of the more optimistic approach include Cornell, *The Beginnings of Rome*, chapter 1 and the various articles by Momigliano and Ampolo cited in the bibliography. For more pessimistic approaches, see for instance T. P. Wiseman, *Clio's Cosmetics* and *Unwritten Rome*, and J. H. Richardson, *The Fabii and the Gauls*. There are important chapters on these issues in A. Feldherr (ed.), *The Cambridge Companion to the Roman Historians*; J. H. Richardson and F. Santangelo (eds), *The Roman Historical Tradition*; and C. J. Smith and K. Sandberg (eds), *Omnium annalium monumenta*.

Livy is the best served of the literary sources, with the first ten books covered by two outstanding commentaries: R. M. Ogilvie, *A Commentary on Livy: Books 1–5*, now outdated in some respects, and S. P. Oakley, *A Commentary on Livy Books VI–X*, 4 vols, the first volume of which is the best overview of Livy's value as a historian. There are also many valuable studies in B. Mineo (ed.), *A Companion to Livy*. On Dionysius of Halicarnassus, see E. Gabba, *Dionysius and the History of Archaic Rome*. T. J. Cornell (ed.), *The Fragments of the Roman Historians*, 3 vols, has transformed our understanding of the lost historians on which our major surviving sources drew.

For early epigraphic sources in Latin see the texts in A. Degrassi (ed.), *Inscriptiones Latinae liberae rei publicae*, and for translations E. H. Warmington (ed.), *Remains of Old Latin IV: Archaic Inscriptions*. Etruscan inscriptions are collected by M. Pallottino, *Testimonia linguae Etruscae*, 2nd edn, and Italic inscriptions by M. H. Crawford (ed.), *Imagines Italicae*, 3 vols. The best text and commentary on the XII Tables is M. H. Crawford (ed.), *Roman Statutes*.

On myth in early Italy see J. N. Bremmer and N. M. Horsfall, *Roman Myth and Mythography*; T. P. Wiseman, *Remus* and *The Myths of Rome*. For myth in the wider Mediterranean, see I. Malkin, *The Returns of Odysseus* and R. L. Fowler, *Early Greek Mythography*, 2 vols.

Excellent studies of the recent archaeology of Rome and central Italy can be found in F. Fulminante, *The Urbanisation of Rome and Latium vetus*; J. N. Hopkins, *The Genesis of Roman Architecture*; and C. R. Potts, *Religious Architecture in Latium and Etruria*. G. Cifani, *Architettura romana arcaica* is the most comprehensive survey of archaic building in Rome. Older but still useful are R. Ross Holloway, *The Archaeology of Early Rome and Latium*, and C. J. Smith, *Early Rome and Latium*. A. M. Bietti Sestieri, *The Iron Age Community of Osteria dell'Osa* is an in-depth analysis of one of the best excavated Latin cemeteries, at ancient Gabii, with reflections on its broader implications. J. M. Hall, *Artifact and Artifice* is a stimulating discussion of the challenges in joining archaeological and literary evidence.

Many of the archaeological discoveries in recent years have appeared in important museum catalogues, such as M. Cristofani (ed.), *La grande Roma dei Tarquini*, and A. Carandini and R. Cappelli (eds), *Roma:*

Romolo, Remo e la fondazione della città. The broader implications of the excavations on the north-west slopes of the Palatine are discussed in a series of publications by Carandini and his collaborators, such as A. Carandini, *La nascita di Roma* and A. Carandini, *Remo e Romolo*. There is an English summary in A. Carandini, *Rome: Day One*. Extensive responses have come from C. Ampolo, 'Il problema delle origini di Roma rivisitato', and in reviews by T. P. Wiseman (e.g. in the *Journal of Roman Studies* 2000, 210–12 and 2001, 182–93).

A number of important studies of the early Republic have recently appeared. On politics and society see K. A. Raaflaub (ed.), *Social Struggles in Archaic Rome*, 2nd edn, and C. J. Smith, *The Roman Clan*. J. Armstrong and J. H. Richardson (eds), *Politics and Power in Early Rome 509–264 BC* has a range of chapters on this period. Useful discussions of Roman militarism include J. Armstrong, *War and Society in Early Rome*; W. V. Harris, *War and Imperialism in Republican Rome 327–70 BC*; and A. M. Eckstein, *Mediterranean Anarchy, Interstate War and the Rise of Rome*. For early Roman religion, see M. Beard, J. North and S. Price, *Religions of Rome*, 2 vols, and C. Schultz, *Women's Religious Activity in the Roman Republic*.

Overviews of recent research into the peoples of Italy are provided by G. Bradley, E. Isayev and C. Riva (eds), *Ancient Italy*; S. Bourdin, *Les peuples de l'Italie préromaine*; and G. D. Farney and G. Bradley (eds), *The Peoples of Ancient Italy*. For more detailed studies of individual regions and peoples see E. Dench, *From Barbarians to New Men*; G. Bradley, *Ancient Umbria*; E. Isayev, *Inside Ancient Lucania*; and R. Scopacasa, *Ancient Samnium*. Notable overviews of the Etruscans include S. Haynes, *Etruscan Civilization*; A. Naso, *Etruscology*, 2 vols; C. J. Smith, *The Etruscans*; M. Torelli (ed.), *The Etruscans*; and J. M. Turfa (ed.), *The Etruscan World*. There are reliable studies of the Greek cities in Italy in D. Ridgway, *The First Western Greeks*, and K. Lomas, *Rome and the Western Greeks, 350 BC–AD 200*. Finally, an Italy-wide perspective is provided by M. Pallottino, *A History of Earliest Italy*.

For wider Mediterranean developments, see M. E. Aubet, *The Phoenicians and the West*, 2nd edn; J. M. Hall, *A History of the Archaic Greek World ca. 1200–479 BCE*, and R. Osborne, *Greece in the Making, 1200–479 BC*, 2nd edn. On connectivity across the ancient Mediterranean see P. Horden and N. Purcell, *The Corrupting Sea*; E. Isayev, *Migration, Mobility and Place in Ancient Italy*; and I. Malkin, *A Small Greek World*.

Bibliography

Adams, J. N., *Bilingualism and the Latin Language*, Cambridge: Cambridge University Press, 2003.
Agostiniani, L., 'The Etruscan language', in Turfa, J. M., *The Etruscan World*, 457–77. London; New York: Routledge, 2013.
Albertoni, M. and I. Damiani, *Il tempio di Giove e le origini del colle capitolino*, Milan: Electa, 2008.
Alessandri, L., *Latium Vetus in the Bronze Age and Early Iron Age / Il Latium vetus nell'età del Bronzo e nella prima età del Ferro*. British Archaeological Reports International Series 2565, Oxford: BAR Publishing, 2013.
Alföldi, A., *Early Rome and the Latins*, Ann Arbor: University of Michigan Press, 1965.
Ammerman, A. J., 'The Comitium in Rome from the beginning', *American Journal of Archaeology* 100.1 (1996), 121–36.
Ammerman, A. J., 'On the origins of the Forum Romanum', *American Journal of Archaeology* 94 (1990), 627–45.
Ammerman, A. J. and D. Filippi, 'Dal Tevere all'Argileto: nuovi osservazioni', *BCAR* 105 (2004), 7–28.
Ammerman, A. J., I. Iliopoulos, F. Bondiolo, D. Filippi, J. Hilditch, A. Manfredini, L. Pennisi and N. Winter, 'The clay beds in the Velabrum and the earliest tiles in Rome', *Journal of Roman Archaeology* 21 (2008), 7–30.
Ampolo, C., 'L'Artemide di Marsiglia e la Diana dell'Aventino', *La Parola del Passato* 25 (1970), 200–10.
Ampolo, C., 'Aspetti dell'economia e della società', in *Italia omnium terrarum parens*, 549–80. Milan: Scheiwiller, 1989.
Ampolo C., 'La città riformata e l'organizzazione centuriata: lo spazio, il tempo, il sacro nella nuova realtà urbana', in A. Momigliano and A. Schiavone (eds), *Storia di Roma* I: *Roma in Italia*, 203–39. Turin: Einaudi, 1988.
Ampolo, C., 'Le condizioni materiali della produzione: agricoltura e paesaggio agrario', in *La formazione della città nel Lazio. Dialoghi di Archaeologia*, n.s. 2 (1980), 15–46.
Ampolo, C., 'Demarato: osservazioni sulla mobilità sociale arcaica', *Dialoghi di Archeologia* 9–10 (1976), 333–45.
Ampolo, C., 'Demarato di Corinto "bacchiade" tra Grecia, Etruria e Roma: rappresentazione e realtà fonti, funzione dei racconti, integrazione di genti e culture, mobilità sociale arcaica', *Aristonothos* 13.2 (2017), 25–118.
Ampolo, C., 'La "grande Roma dei Tarquini" revisitata', in E. Campanile (ed.), *Alle origini di Roma*, 77–87. Pisa: Giardini, 1988.

Bibliography

Ampolo, C., 'La nascita della città', in A. Momigliano and A. Schiavone (eds), *Storia di Roma* I: *Roma in Italia*, 153–80. Turin: Einaudi, 1988.

Ampolo, C., 'Periodo IVB', in *La formazione della città nel Lazio. Dialoghi di Archeologia* n.s. 2 (1980), 165–93.

Ampolo, C. 'Presenze etrusche, koiné culturale o dominio etrusco a Roma e nel Latium vetus in età arcaica', in G. M. Della Fina (ed.), *Gli Etruschi e Roma*, 9–41. Rome: Quasar, 2009.

Ampolo, C., 'Il problema delle origini di Roma rivisitato: concordismo, ipertradizionalismo acritico, contesti. I.', *Annali della Scuola Normale Superiore di Pisa, Classe di lettere e filosofia* ser. 5.1 (2013), 217–84.

Ampolo, C., 'Roma arcaica fra Latini ed Etruschi: aspetti politici e sociali', in M. Cristofani (ed.), *Etruria e Lazio arcaico*, 75–87. Rome: Consiglio Nazionale delle Ricerche, 2013.

Ampolo, C., 'Roma ed i Sabini nel V a.C. secolo', in G. Maetzke (ed.), *Identità e civiltà dei Sabini: atti del XVIII Convegno di studi Etruschi ed Italici. Rieti-Magliano Sabina: 30 maggio–3 giugno 1993*, 87–103. Florence: Olschki, 1996.

Ampolo, C., 'Servius rex primus signavit aes', *La Parola del Passato* 29 (1974), 382–8.

Ampolo, C., 'La storiografia su Roma arcaica e i documenti', in *Tria corda: studi in onore di Arnaldo Momigliano*, 9–26. Como: New Press, 1983.

Ampolo C., 'Su alcuni mutamenti sociali nel Lazio tra l'VIII e il V secolo', *Dialoghi di Archeologia* 4–5 (1970–1), 37–68.

Andreau, J., *Banking and Business in the Roman World* (trans. J. Lloyd), Cambridge: Cambridge University Press, 1992.

Arena, V., *Libertas and the Practice of Politics in the Late Roman Republic*, Cambridge; New York: Cambridge University Press, 2012.

Armstrong, J., 'Coming in from the cold: triumphs in early Rome', in J. Armstrong and A. Spalinger (eds), *Rituals of Triumph in the Mediterranean World*, 7–21. Leiden: Brill, 2013.

Armstrong, J., *War and Society in Early Rome: From Warlords to Generals*, Cambridge: Cambridge University Press, 2016.

Armstrong, J. and J. H. Richardson (eds), *Politics and Power in Early Rome 509–264 BC. Antichthon* special issue 51, Cambridge: Cambridge University Press, 2017.

Aubet, M. E., *The Phoenicians and the West: Politics, Colonies and Trade*, 2nd edn, Cambridge: Cambridge University Press, 2001.

Baglione, M. P., B. Belelli Marchesini, C. Carlucci, M. D. Gentili and L. M. Michetti, 'Pyrgi: a sanctuary in the middle of the Mediterranean Sea', in E. Kistler, B. Öhlinger, M. Mohr and M. Hoernes (eds), *Sanctuaries and the Power of Consumption*, 221–37. Wiesbaden: Harrassowitz Verlag, 2015.

Baglione, M. P., 'The sanctuary of Pyrgi', in J. M. Turfa (ed.), *The Etruscan World*, 613–31. London; New York: Routledge, 2013.

Barker, G., R. Hodges and G. Clark, *A Mediterranean Valley: Landscape Archaeology and Annales History in the Biferno Valley*, London: Leicester University Press, 1995.

Barker, G. and T. Rasmussen, *The Etruscans*, Oxford: Blackwell, 1998.

Baron, C. A., *Timaeus of Tauromenium and Hellenistic Historiography*, Cambridge: Cambridge University Press, 2013.

Bartoloni, G., *La cultura villanoviana: all'inizio della storia etrusca*, 2nd edn, Rome: Carocci, 2002.

Bartoloni, G., 'I Latini e il Tevere', *Archeologia Laziale* 7.2 (1986), 98–110.

Bartoloni, G. (ed.), *La lupa Capitolina: nuove prospettive di studio*, Rome: 'L'Erma' di Bretschneider, 2010.
Bartoloni, G., 'Le necropoli', in A. M. Moretti Sgubini (ed.), *Veio, Cerveteri, Vulci: Città d'Etruria a confronto*, 89–120. Rome: 'L'Erma' di Bretschneider, 2001.
Bartoloni, G., ed., *Principi etruschi: tra Mediterraneo ed Europa*, Venice: Marsilio, 2000.
Bartoloni, G., 'La tomba', in G. Bartoloni (ed.), *Principi etruschi: tra Mediterraneo ed Europa*, 163–71. Venice: Marsilio, 2000.
Bastien, J.-L., *Le triomphe romain et son utilisation politique à Rome aux trois derniers siècles de la République*, Rome: École française de Rome, 2006.
Bayet, J., 'Tite-Live et la précolonisation romaine', *Revue de Philologie* 12 (1938), 97–119.
Beard, M., 'Priesthood in the Roman Republic', in M. Beard and J. North (eds), *Pagan Priests: Religion and Power in the Ancient World*, 17–48. London: Duckworth, 1990.
Beard, M., *The Roman Triumph*, Cambridge, MA: Harvard University Press, 2007.
Beard, M., J. North and S. Price, *Religions of Rome*, 2 vols, Cambridge: Cambridge University Press, 1998.
Beloch, J., *Die Bevölkerung der griechisch-römischen Welt*, Leipzig: Duncker & Humblot, 1886.
Beloch, J., *Römische Geschichte bis zum Beginn der punischen Kriege*, Berlin; Leipzig: De Gruyter, 1926.
Benelli, E., 'The Aequi', in G. D. Farney and G. Bradley (eds), *The Peoples of Ancient Italy*, 499–507. Boston: De Gruyter, 2017.
Benelli, E., 'Problems in identifying central Italic ethnic groups', in G. D. Farney and G. Bradley (eds), *The Peoples of Ancient Italy*, 89–103. Boston: De Gruyter, 2017.
Bernard, S., *Building Mid-Republican Rome: Labor, Architecture, and the Urban Economy*, Oxford: Oxford University Press, 2018.
Bernard, S., 'Continuing the debate on Rome's earliest circuit walls', *Papers of the British School at Rome* 80 (2012), 1–44.
Bernard, S., 'Debt, land, and labor in the early Republican economy', *Phoenix* 70.3/4 (2016), 317–38.
Bernard, S., 'In search of Aeneas at the sanctuary of Castrum Inui (Ardea)', Review of M. Torelli and E. Marroni (eds), *Castrum Inui: il santuario di Inuus alla foce del Fosso Dell'Incastro*, Rome: 'L'Erma' di Bretschneider, 2018. *Journal of Roman Archaeology* 32 (2019), 561–73.
Bernard, S., 'The social history of early Roman coinage', *Journal of Roman Studies* 108 (2018), 1–26.
Bettelli, M., *Roma: la città prima della città. I tempi di una nascita: la cronologia delle sepolture ad inumazione di Roma e del Lazio nella prima età del ferro*, Rome: Bretschneider, 1997.
Bianchi, E., *Greci ed Etruschi in Roma arcaica nella storiografia moderna del secondo dopoguerra*, Catania; Rome: Edizioni del Prisma, 2013.
Bickerman, E. J., 'Origines gentium', *Classical Philology* 47.2 (1952), 65–81.
Biella, M. C., A. F. Ferrandes, M. Revello Lami and R. Cascino (eds), *Gli artigiani e la città: officine ceramiche e aree produttive tra VIII e III sec. a.C. nell'Italia centrale tirrenica. Scienze dell'Antichità* 23.2, Rome: Quasar, 2017.
Bietti Sestieri, A. M., *The Iron Age Community of Osteria dell'Osa: A Study of Socio-political Development in Central Tyrrhenian Italy*, Cambridge: Cambridge University Press, 1992.

Bietti Sestieri, A. M., 'The role of archaeological and historical data in the reconstruction of Italian protohistory', in D. Ridgway, F. R. Serra Ridgway, M. Pearce, E. Herring, R. D. Whitehouse and J. B. Wilkins (eds), *Ancient Italy in its Mediterranean Setting: Studies in Honour of Ellen Macnamara*, 371–402. London: Accordia, 2000.

Bilde, P. G. and B. Poulsen, *The Temple of Castor and Pollux: The Finds II.1*. Occasional Papers of the Nordic Institutes in Rome, Rome: 'L'Erma' di Bretschneider, 2008.

Bispham, E., 'Coloniam deducere: how Roman was Roman colonization during the middle Republic?', in G. Bradley and J. P. Wilson (eds), *Greek and Roman Colonization: Origins, Ideologies and Interactions*, 73–160. Swansea: Classical Press of Wales, 2006.

Bispham, E., 'Rome and Antium: pirates, polities and identity in the middle Republic', in S. Roselaar (ed.), *Processes of Integration and Identity Formation in the Roman Republic*, 227–45. Leiden: Brill, 2012.

Bispham, E., 'The Samnites', in G. J. Bradley, E. Isayev and C. Riva (eds), *Ancient Italy: Regions without Boundaries*, 179–223. Exeter: University of Exeter Press, 2007.

Bispham, E. and T. J. Cornell, 'Q. Fabius Pictor', in T. J. Cornell (ed.), *The Fragments of the Roman Historians*, vol. 1, 160–78. Oxford: Oxford University Press, 2013.

Blake, E., 'The Mycenaeans in Italy: a minimalist position', *Papers of the British School at Rome* 76 (2008), 1–34.

Blake, E., *Social Networks and Regional Identity in Bronze Age Italy*, Cambridge: Cambridge University Press, 2014.

Blösel, W., 'Die Geschichte des Begriffes mos maiorum von den Anfängen bis zu Cicero', in B. Linke and M. Stemmler (eds), *Mos maiorum: Untersuchungen zu den Formen der Identitätsstiftung und Stabilisierung in der römischen Republik*, 25–97. Stuttgart: Franz Steiner, 2000.

Bonfante, G. and L. Bonfante, *The Etruscan Language: An Introduction*, rev. edn, Manchester: Manchester University Press/Palgrave, 2002.

Bonfante, L. (ed.), *Etruscan Life and Afterlife: A Handbook of Etruscan Studies*, Warminster: Aris and Phillips, 1986.

Bonfante, L., 'Etruscan women', in E. Fantham, H. Peet Foley, N. Boymel Kampen, S. B. Pomeroy and H. A. Shapiro (eds), *Women in the Classical World*, 243–59. Oxford: Oxford University Press, 1994.

Bonfante Warren, L., 'Roman triumphs and Etruscan kings: the changing face of the triumph', *Journal of Roman Studies* 60 (1970), 49–66.

Bonghi Jovino, M., 'Affinità e differenze nelle esperienze architettoniche tra Roma e Tarquinia: qualche riflessione', in G. M. Della Fina (ed.), *La grande Roma dei Tarquini*, 31–65. Orvieto: Quasar, 2010.

Bosworth, A. B., *Conquest and Empire: The Reign of Alexander the Great*. Cambridge: Cambridge University Press, 1988.

Botto, M., 'Considerazioni sul periodo orientalizzante nella penisola italica: la documentazione del Latium vetus', in J. Jiménez Ávila and S. Celestino Pérez (eds), *El periodo orientalizante*, 47–74. Anejos de Archivo Español de Arqueología 35, Merida: SCIC, 2005.

Botto, M., 'I primi contatti fra i Fenici e le popolazioni dell'Italia peninsulare', in S. Celestino, N. Rafel Fontanals and X.-L. Armada (eds), *Contacto cultural entre el Mediterráneo y el Atlántico (siglos XII–VIII ane)*, 123–48. Madrid: CSIC, 2008.

Bourdieu, P., *Outline of a Theory of Practice*, Cambridge: Cambridge University Press, 1977.

Bourdin, S., 'Ardée et les Rutules: réflexions sur l'émergence et le maintien des identités ethniques des populations du Latium préromain', *Mélanges de l'École française de Rome – Antiquité* 117.2 (2005), 585–631.

Bourdin, S., *Les peuples de l'Italie préromaine: identités, territoires et relations interethniques en Italie centrale et septentrionale*, Rome: École française de Rome, 2012.

Bradley, G., *Ancient Umbria: State, Culture and Identity from the Iron Age to the Augustan Era*, Oxford: Oxford University Press, 2000.

Bradley, G., 'Colonization and identity in Republican Italy', in G. J. Bradley and J.-P. Wilson (eds), *Greek and Roman Colonization: Origins, Ideologies and Interactions*, 161–87. Swansea: Classical Press of Wales, 2006.

Bradley, G., 'Investigating aristocracy in archaic Rome and central Italy: social mobility, ideology and cultural influences', in N. Fisher and H. van Wees (eds), *'Aristocracy' in Antiquity: Redefining Greek and Roman Elites*, 85–124. Swansea: Classical Press of Wales, 2015.

Bradley, G., 'Mobility and secession in the early Roman Republic', in J. Armstrong and J. H. Richardson (eds), *Politics and Power in Early Rome 509–264 BC. Antichthon* special issue 51, 149–71. Cambridge: Cambridge University Press, 2017.

Bradley, G., 'The nature of Roman strategy in mid-Republican colonization and road building', in T. Stek and J. Pelgrom (eds), *Roman Republican Colonization: New Perspectives from Archaeology and Ancient History*, 60–72. Papers of the Royal Netherlands Institute in Rome 62, Rome: Palombi, 2014.

Bradley, G., 'Romanization: the end of the peoples of Italy?', in G. J. Bradley, E. Isayev and C. Riva (eds), *Ancient Italy: Regions without Boundaries*, 295–322. Exeter: University of Exeter Press, 2007.

Bradley, G., 'The Rome of Tarquinius Superbus: issues of demography and economy', in P. Lulof and C. Smith (eds), *The Age of Tarquinius Superbus: Ancient History, Archaeology, and Methodology*, 123–33. Leuven: Peeters, 2017.

Bradley, G., 'Tribes, states and cities in central Italy', in E. Herring and K. Lomas (eds), *The Emergence of State Identities in Italy in the First Millennium BC*, 109–29. London: Accordia, 2000.

Bradley, G. J., E. Isayev and C. Riva (eds), *Ancient Italy: Regions without Boundaries*, Exeter: University of Exeter Press, 2007.

Brauer, J. and H. Van Tuyll, *Castles, Battles, and Bombs: How Economics Explains Military History*, Chicago: University of Chicago Press, 2008.

Bremmer, J. N., 'Caeculus and the foundation of Praeneste', in Bremmer, J. N. and N. M. Horsfall, *Roman Myth and Mythography*, 49–59. BICS Supplement 52, London: Institute of Classical Studies, 1987.

Bremmer, J. N. and N. M. Horsfall, *Roman Myth and Mythography*. BICS Supplement 52, London: Institute of Classical Studies, 1987.

Broadhead, W., 'Rome's migration policy and the so-called ius migrandi', *Cahiers Glotz* 12 (2001), 69–89.

Brocato, P. and N. Terrenato (eds), *Nuovi studi sulla Regia di Roma*, Paesaggi Antichi 2, Cosenza: Pellegrini, 2016.

Brock, A. L. and N. Terrenato, 'Rome in the Bronze Age: late second-millennium BC radiocarbon dates from the Forum Boarium', *Antiquity* 90 (2016), 654–64.

Bruni, S., 'Seafaring: ship building, harbors, the issue of piracy', in J. M. Turfa (ed.), *The Etruscan World*, 759–77. London; New York: Routledge, 2013.

Brunt, P. A., *Italian Manpower*, Oxford: Oxford University Press, 1971.

Brunt, P. A., '*Nobilitas* and *novitas*', *Journal of Roman Studies* 72 (1982), 1–17.

Bruun C., '"What every man in the street used to know": M. Furius Camillus, Italic legends and Roman historiography', in C. Bruun (ed.), *The Roman Middle Republic: Politics, Religion, and Historiography c.400–133 B.C.*, 41–68. Rome: Institutum Romanum Finlandiae, 2000.

Budin, S., *The Myth of Sacred Prostitution in Antiquity*. New York: Cambridge University Press, 2008.

Burton, P. J., *Friendship and Empire: Roman Diplomacy and Imperialism in the Middle Republic (353–146 BC)*. Cambridge; New York: Cambridge University Press, 2011.

Burton, P. J., 'The last Republican historian: a new date for the composition of Livy's first pentad', *Historia: Zeitschrift für Alte Geschichte* 49.4 (2000), 429–46.

Camous, T., *Le roi et le fleuve: Ancus Marcius Rex aux origines de la puissance romaine*, Paris: Les Belles Lettres, 2004.

Camous, T., *Tarquin le superbe*, Paris: Payot, 2014.

Capanna, M. C., 'Dall'"ager antiquus" alle espansioni di Roma in età regia', *Workshop di archeologia classica: paesaggi, costruzioni, reperti* 2 (2005), 173–88.

Carafa, P., *Il comizio di Roma dalle origine all'età di Augusto*, Rome: 'L'Erma' di Bretschneider, 1998.

Carafa, P., *Officine ceramiche di età regia: produzione di ceramica di impasto a Roma dalla fine dell'VIII alla fine del VI secolo a.C.*, Rome: 'L'Erma' di Bretschneider, 1995.

Carafa, P., 'Il progetto della Prima Roma: il Palatino e il Santuario di Vesta. Parte prima – L'"aedes" e il "vicus" di Vesta: i reperti', *Workshop di archeologia classica: paesaggi, costruzioni, reperti* 1 (2004), 135–43.

Carafa, P., 'Il Volcanal e il Comizio', *Workshop di archeologia classica: paesaggi, costruzioni, reperti* 2 (2005), 135–49.

Carandini, A., 'Le mura del Palatino, nuova fonte sulla Roma di età regia', *Bollettino di Archeologia* 16–18 (1992), 1–18.

Carandini, A., *La nascita di Roma: dei, Lari, eroi e uomini all'alba di una civiltà*, Turin: Einaudi, 1997.

Carandini, A., 'La nascita di Roma: Palatino, santuario di Vesta e Foro', in E. Greco (ed.), *Teseo e Romolo: le origini di Atene e Roma a confronto*, 13–28. Athens: Scuola archeologica italiana di Atene, 2005.

Carandini, A., *Palatino, Velia e Sacra Via: paesaggi urbani attraverso il tempo*. Workshop di archeologia classica Quaderni 1, Rome: Ateneo, 2004.

Carandini, A., *Remo e Romolo: dai rioni dei Quiriti alla città dei Romani (775/750–700/675 a. C.)*, Turin: Einaudi, 2006.

Carandini, A., *Rome: Day One*, Princeton: Princeton University Press, 2011. Trans. of *Roma: il primo giorno*, Bari: Laterza, 2007.

Carandini, A. and P. Carafa (eds), *Palatium e Sacra Via* I. Bollettino di Archeologia 31–4. Rome: Istituto Poligrafico e Zecca dello Stato, 2000.

Carandini, A. and R. Cappelli (eds), *Roma: Romolo, Remo e la fondazione della città*, Milan: Electa, 2000.

Carruba, A. M. and L. De Masi, *La lupa capitolina: un bronzo medievale*, Rome: Luca editori d'arte, 2006.

Càssola, F., 'Problemi di tradizione orale', *Index* 28 (2000), 1–34.
Casson, L., 'Harbour and river boats of ancient Rome', *Journal of Roman Studies* 55 (1965), 31–9.
Castagnoli, F., *Enea nel Lazio: archeologia e mito*, exhibition catalogue, Rome: Palombi, 1976.
Champion, C. B., *Roman Imperialism: Readings and Sources*, Oxford: Blackwell, 2003.
Chaplin, J. D. and C. S. Kraus (eds), *Livy*. Oxford Readings in Classical Studies, Oxford: Oxford University Press, 2009.
Chassignet, M., *L'annalistique romaine* I: *Les annales des Pontifes et l'annalistique ancienne*, Paris: Budé, 1996.
Chassignet, M., *L'annalistique romaine* II: *L'annalistique moyenne (fragments)*, Paris: Budé, 1999.
Chassignet, M., *Caton: Les Origines (fragments)*, Paris: Budé, 1986.
Chiabà, M., *Roma e le priscae Latinae coloniae: ricerche sulla colonizzazione del Lazio dalla costituzione della repubblica alla guerra latina*, Trieste: EUT, 2011.
Childe, V., 'The urban revolution', *The Town Planning Review* 21.1 (1950), 3–17.
Cifani, G., *Architettura romana arcaica: edilizia e società tra Monarchia e Repubblica*, Rome: 'L'Erma' di Bretschneider, 2008.
Cifani, G., 'Aspects of urbanism and political ideology in archaic Rome', in E. Robinson (ed.), *Papers on Italian Urbanism in the First Millennium* BC, 15–28. Journal of Roman Archaeology Supplement 97, Portsmouth, RI: Journal of Roman Archaeology, 2014.
Cifani, G., 'The fortifications of archaic Rome: social and political significance', in R. Frederiksen, M. Schnelle, S. Muth and P. Schneider (eds), *Focus on Fortifications: New Research on Fortifications in the Ancient Mediterranean and the Near East*, 82–93. Fokus Fortifikation Studies 2 / Monographs of the Danish Insitute at Athens, Oxford: Oxbow, 2016.
Cifani, G., 'Problemi e prospettive di ricerca sull'architettura romana tra VI e V sec. a.C.', in G. M. Della Fina (ed.), *Gli Etruschi e Roma: fasi monarchica e altorepubblicana*, 383–423. Rome, 2009.
Cifani, G., 'Small, medium or extra-long? Prolegomena to any future metaphysics on the reconstructions of the Temple of Jupiter Optimus Maximus Capitolinus', in P. Lulof and C. Smith (eds), *The Age of Tarquinius Superbus: Ancient History, Archaeology, and Methodology*, 113–22. Peeters: Leuven, 2017.
Clackson, J. and G. Horrocks, *The Blackwell History of the Latin Language*, Malden, MA; Oxford: Wiley-Blackwell, 2007.
Coarelli, F., *Collis: il Quirinale e il Viminale nell'antichità*, Rome: Quasar, 2014.
Coarelli, F., 'Colonizzazione romana e viabilità', *Dialoghi di Archaeologia* 6 (1988), 35–48.
Coarelli, F., 'Demografia e territorio', in A. Momigliano and A. Schiavone (eds), *Storia di Roma* I: *Roma in Italia*, 317–39. Turin: Einaudi, 1988.
Coarelli, F., *Il Foro Boario dalle origini fino alla fine della repubblica*, Rome: Quasar, 1988.
Coarelli, F., *Il foro romano* I: *Periodo arcaico*, Rome: Quasar, 1983.
Coarelli, F., *Le origini di Roma: la cultura artistica dalle origini al III sec. a.C.*, Milan: Jaca Book, 2012.

Coarelli, F., 'Le pitture della Tomba François a Vulci: una proposta di lettura', *Dialoghi di Archaeologia* 1, ser. 3, 1.2 (1983), 43–69.

Coarelli, F., *Roma: guida archeologica Laterza*, Rome; Bari: Laterza, 2009.

Coarelli, F., 'Roma, i Volsci e il Lazio antico', in F.-H. Massa Pairault (ed.), *Crise et transformation des sociétés archaïques de l'Italie antique au Ve siècle av. J.C. Actes de la table ronde, Rome, 19–21 novembre 1987*, Rome: CEFR, 135–54, 1990.

Coarelli, F., 'I santuari, il fiume, gli empori', in A. Momigliano and A. Schiavone (eds), *Storia di Roma* I: *Roma in Italia*, 127–51. Turin: Einaudi, 1988.

Colantoni, E. *The Archaeology of Early Roman Religion*, New York: Routledge (forthcoming).

Colantoni, E., 'Straw to stone, huts to houses: transitions in building practices and society in protohistoric Latium', in M. L. Thomas and G. E. Meyers (eds), *Monumentality in Etruscan and Early Roman Architecture: Ideology and Innovation*, 21–40. Austin: University of Texas Press, 2012.

Coldstream, J. N., 'Mixed marriages at the frontiers of the early Greek world', *Oxford Journal of Archaeology* 12.1 (1993), 89–107.

Colonna, G., 'Un aspetto oscuro del Lazio antico: le tombe del VI–V secolo a.C.', in C. Ampolo and G. Sassatelli (eds), *Italia ante romanum imperium: scritti di antichità etrusche, italiche e romane (1958–1998)* 1.2, 493–518. Pisa; Rome: Istituti Editoriali e Poligrafici Internazionale, 2005.

Colonna, G., 'Il commercio etrusco arcaico vent'anni dopo (e la sua estensione fino a tartesso)', *Annali della Fondazione per il Museo "Claudio Faina"* 13 (2006), 9–28.

Colonna, G., 'Duenos', *Studi Etruschi* 47 (1979), 163–72.

Colonna, G., 'Il mito di Enea tra Veio e Roma', in G. M. Della Fina (ed.), *Gli etruschi e Roma: fasi monarchica e alto-repubblicana*, 51–92. Rome: Quasar, 2009.

Colonna, G., 'La produzione artigianale', in A. Momigliano and A. Schiavone (eds), *Storia di Roma* I: *Roma in Italia*, 291–316. Turin: Einaudi, 1988.

Colonna, G., 'Quali Etruschi a Roma', in *Gli Etruschi e Roma: atti dell'incontro di studio in onore di Massimo Pallottino, Roma 11–13 dicembre 1979*, 159–72. Rome: Bretschneider, 1981.

Colonna, G., 'I templi del Lazio fino al V secolo compreso', *Archeologia Laziale* 6 (1984), 396–411.

Colwill, D., 'Genocide' and Rome, 343–146 BCE: State Expansion and the Social Dynamics of Annihilation. Unpublished PhD thesis, Cardiff University, 2017.

Cornell, T. J., 'Aeneas and the twins: the development of the Roman foundation legend', *Proceedings of the Cambridge Philological Society* n.s. 21 (1975), 1–32.

Cornell, T. J., *The Beginnings of Rome: Italy and Rome from the Bronze Age to the Punic Wars (c.1000–264 BC)*, London: Routledge, 1995.

Cornell, T. J., 'Cicero on the origins of Rome', in J. G. F. Powell and J. A. North (eds), *Cicero's Republic*, 41–56. BICS Supplement 76, London: Institute of Classical Studies, 2001.

Cornell, T. J., 'Coriolanus: myth, history and performance', in D. Braund and C. Gill (eds), *Myth, History and Culture in Republican Rome: Studies in Honour of T. P. Wiseman*, 73–97. Exeter: University of Exeter Press, 2003.

Cornell, T. J., 'Deconstructing the Samnite Wars', in *Samnium: Settlement and Cultural Change. Proceedings of the Third E. Togo Salmon Conference on Roman Studies*, 35–50. Hamilton, Ontario: McMaster University, 2004.

Cornell, T. J., 'The end of Roman imperial expansion', in J. Rich and G. Shipley (eds), *War and Society in the Roman World*, 139–70. London: Routledge, 1993.

Cornell, T. J., 'Ethnicity as a factor in early Roman history', in T. J. Cornell and K. Lomas (eds), *Gender and Ethnicity in Ancient Italy*, 9–21. London: Accordia, 1997.

Cornell, T. J., 'The failure of the *plebs*', in E. Gabba (ed.), *Tria corda: scritti in onore di A. Momigliano*, 101–20. Como: Edizione New Press, 1983.

Cornell, T. J., 'The formation of the historical tradition of early Rome', in I. S. Moxon, J. D. Smart and A. J. Woodman (eds), *Past Perspectives: Studies in Greek and Roman Historical Writing*, 67–86. Cambridge: Cambridge University Press, 1986.

Cornell, T. J., 'The foundation of Rome in the ancient literary tradition', in H. McK. Blake, T. W. Potter and D. B. Whitehouse (eds), *Papers in Italian Archaeology* I, 131–40. British Archaeological Reports International Series 41, Oxford: BAR Publishing, 1978.

Cornell, T. J. (ed.), *The Fragments of the Roman Historians*, 3 vols, Oxford: Oxford University Press, 2013.

Cornell, T. J., 'The lex Ovinia and the emancipation of the Senate', in C. Bruun (ed.), *The Roman Middle Republic: Politics, Religion, and Historiography c.400–133 B.C.*, 69–89. Rome: Institutum Romanum Finlandiae, 2000.

Cornell, T. J., 'Livy's narrative of the Regal period and historical and archaeological facts', in B. Mineo (ed.), *A Companion to Livy*, 245–58. Oxford: Blackwell, 2014.

Cornell, T. J., 'Principes of Tarquinia', review of M. Torelli, *Elogia Tarquiniensia*, Florence: Sansoni, 1975. *Journal of Roman Studies* 68 (1978), 167–73.

Cornell, T. J., Review of F. Millar, *Rome, the Greek World and the East*, vol. 1: *The Roman Republic and the Augustan Revolution*, H. Cotton and G. Rogers (eds), Chapel Hill; London: University of North Carolina Press, 2002, *Journal of Roman Studies* 93 (2003), 351–4.

Cornell, T. J., 'Rome: the history of an anachronism', in A. Molho, K. Raaflaub and J. Emlen (eds), *City States in Classical Antiquity and Medieval Italy*, 53–69. Ann Arbor: University of Michigan Press, 1991.

Cornell, T. J. 'Rome and Latium Vetus, 1974–79', *Archaeological Reports* 26 (1979), 71–89.

Cornell, T. J., 'The tyranny of the evidence: a discussion of the possible uses of literacy in Etruria and Latium in the archaic age', in J. H. Humphrey (ed.), *Literacy in the Roman World*, 7–34. *Journal of Roman Archaeology* Supplement 3, Portsmouth, RI: Journal of Roman Archaeology, 1991.

Cornell, T. J., 'The value of the literary tradition concerning archaic Rome', in K. A. Raaflaub (ed.), *Social Struggles in Archaic Rome*, 2nd edn, 47–74. Malden, MA; Oxford: Blackwell, 2005.

Cornell, T. J. and J. Matthews, *Atlas of the Roman World*, Oxford: Phaidon, 1982.

Crawford, M. H., *Coinage and Money under the Roman Republic*, London: Methuen, 1985.

Crawford, M. H. (ed.), *Imagines Italicae: A Corpus of Italic inscriptions*, 3 vols. BICS Supplement 110, London: Institute of Classical Studies, 2011.

Crawford, M. H., 'The Roman history of Roman colonization', in J. H. Richardson and F. Santangelo (eds), *The Roman Historical Tradition: Regal and Republican Rome*, 201–6. Oxford Readings in Classical Studies, Oxford: Oxford University Press, 2014.

Crawford, M. H. (ed.), *Roman Statutes*. BICS Supplement 64, London: Institute of Classical Studies, 1996.

Cristofani, M., *Gli etruschi del mare*, Milan: Longanesi, 1983.

Cristofani, M. (ed.), *La grande Roma dei Tarquini*, Rome: 'L'Erma' di Bretschneider, 1990.

D'Agostino, B., 'Euboean colonisation in the Gulf of Naples', in G. R. Tsetskhladze (ed.), *Ancient Greeks West and East*, 207–27. Leiden: Brill, 1999.

D'Agostino, B., 'Military organization and social structure in archaic Etruria', in O. Murray and S. Price (eds), *The Greek City from Homer to Alexander*, 59–84. Oxford: Oxford University Press, 1990.

Daube, D., *Civil Disobedience in Antiquity*, Edinburgh: Edinburgh University Press, 1972.

de Cazanove, O. 'La chronologie des Bacchiades et celle des rois étrusques de Rome', *Mélanges de l'École française de Rome – Antiquité* 100 (1988), 615–48.

de Cazanove, O., 'Les colonies latines et les frontières régionales de l'Italie: Venusia et Horace entre Apulie et Lucanie: Satires, II, 1, 34', *Mélanges de la Casa de Velázquez* 35-2 (2005), 107–24.

De Simone, C., 'Gli Etruschi a Roma: evidenza linguistica e problemi metodologici', in *Gli Etruschi e Roma: Atti dell'incontro di studio in onore di Massimo Pallottino, Roma 11–13 dicembre 1979*, 93–103. Rome: Bretschneider, 1981.

De Souza, P., *Piracy in the Graeco-Roman World*, Cambridge: Cambridge University Press, 1999.

Debiasi, A., *L'epica perduta: Eumelo, il Ciclo, l'occidente*. Rome: 'L'Erma' di Bretschneider, 2004.

Degrassi, A. (ed.), *Inscriptiones Italiae*, vol. 13, *Fasti et Elogia* (fasc. 3: *Elogia*), Rome: Libreria dello stato, 1937.

Della Fina, G. M. (ed.), *Gli etruschi e il Mediterraneo: commerci e politica*, Fondazione per il Musco Claudio Faina, Rome: Quasar, 2006.

Della Fina, G. M. (ed.), *Gli Etruschi e Roma: Fasi monarchica e alto-repubblicana*, Fondazione per il Museo Claudio Faina, Rome: Quasar, 2009.

Della Fina, G. M. (ed.), *Etruschi, greci, fenici e cartaginesi nel Mediterraneo centrale*, Fondazione per il Museo Claudio Faina, Rome: Quasar, 2007.

Della Fina, G. M. (ed.), *La grande Roma dei Tarquini*, Fondazione per il Museo Claudio Faina, Rome: Quasar, 2010.

Demand, N. H., *The Mediterranean Context of Early Greek History*, Malden, MA; Oxford: Wiley-Blackwell, 2011.

Demetriou, D., *Negotiating Identity in the Ancient Mediterranean: The Archaic and Classical Greek Multiethnic Emporia*, Cambridge: Cambridge University Press, 2012.

Dench, E., *From Barbarians to New Men: Greek, Roman, and Modern Perceptions of Peoples of the Central Apennines*, Oxford: Oxford University Press, 1995.

Dench, E., *Romulus' Asylum: Roman Identities from the Age of Alexander to the Age of Hadrian*, Oxford: Oxford University Press, 2005.

DeRose Evans, J., *The Art of Persuasion: Political Propaganda from Aeneas to Brutus*, Ann Arbor: University of Michigan Press, 1992.

Di Giuseppe, H., 'Villae, villulae e fattorie nella Media Valle del Tevere', in B. Santillo Frizell and A. Klynne (eds), *Roman Villas around the Urbs: Interaction with Landscape and Environment*, 7–25. Rome: Swedish Institute at Rome, 2005.

Dixon, S., 'From ceremonial to sexualities: a survey of scholarship on Roman Marriage', in B. Rawson (ed.), *A Companion to Families in the Greek and Roman Worlds*, 245–61. Oxford: Blackwell, 2011.

Doyle, W., *Aristocracy: A Very Short Introduction*, Oxford: Oxford University Press, 2011.

Drews, R., 'The coming of the city to Central Italy', *American Journal of Ancient History* 6 (1981), 133–65.

Drummond, A., 'Rome in the fifth century, I: the social and economic framework', in F. W. Walbank, A. E. Astin, M. W. Frederiksen, R. M. Ogilvie and A. Drummond (eds), *The Cambridge Ancient History 7.2: The Rise of Rome to 220 BC*, 2nd edn, 113–71. Cambridge: Cambridge University Press, 1989.

Dumézil, G., *Archaic Roman Religion*, 2 vols, Chicago: University of Chicago Press, 1970.

Duplouy, A., *Le prestige des élites: recherches sur les modes de reconnaissance sociale en Grèce entre les Xe et Ve siècles avant J.-C.*, Paris: Les Belles Lettres, 2006.

Ebel, C., *Transalpine Gaul: The Emergence of a Roman Province*, Leiden: Brill, 1976.

Eckstein, A. M., *Mediterranean Anarchy, Interstate War and the Rise of Rome*, Berkeley: University of California Press, 2006.

Eder, W., 'The political significance of the codification of law in archaic societies: an unconventional hypothesis', in K. A. Raaflaub (ed.), *Social Struggles in Archaic Rome: New Perspectives on the Conflict of the Orders*, 262–300. Oxford: Blackwell, 2005.

Edlund Berry, I., 'Early Rome and the making of "Roman" identity through architecture and city planning', in J. DeRose Evans (ed.), *A Companion to the Archaeology of the Roman Republic*, 406–25. Oxford: Blackwell, 2013.

Edwards, C., *Writing Rome: Textual Approaches to the City*, Cambridge: Cambridge University Press, 1996.

Elliott, J., *Ennius and the Architecture of the Annales*, Cambridge: Cambridge University Press, 2013.

Erdkamp, P., 'War and state formation', in P. Erdkamp (ed.), *A Companion to the Roman Army*, 96–113. Oxford: Blackwell, 2007.

Erskine, A., *Troy between Greece and Rome: Local Tradition and Imperial Power*, Oxford; New York: Oxford University Press, 2001.

Etruscan and Central Italian Architectural Terracottas Online Database: www.beazley.ox.ac.uk/databases/terracottas.htm.

Farney, G., *Ethnic Identity and Aristocratic Competition in Republican Rome*, Cambridge: Cambridge University Press, 2007.

Farney, G. D., 'The name-changes of legendary Romans and the Etruscan–Latin bilingual inscriptions: strategies for Romanization', *Etruscan Studies* 13 (2010), 149–57.

Farney, G. D. and Bradley, G. (eds), *The Peoples of Ancient Italy*, Berlin: De Gruyter, 2017.

Feeney, D., 'The beginnings of a literature in Latin', *Journal of Roman Studies* 95 (2005), 226–40.

Feeney, D., *Caesar's Calendar: Ancient Time and the Beginnings of History*, Berkeley: University of California Press, 2007.

Feldherr, A. (ed.), *The Cambridge Companion to the Roman Historians*, Cambridge: Cambridge University Press, 2009.

Filippi, D., 'Dal Palatino al Foro Orientale: le mura e il santuario di Vesta', *Workshop di archeologia classica: paesaggi, costruzioni, reperti* 1 (2004), 89–100.

Filippi, D., 'La Domus Regia', *Workshop di Archeologia classica: paesaggi, costruzioni, reperti* 1 (2004), 101–21.

Filippi, D., 'Il Velabro e le origini del Foro', *Workshop di archeologia classica: paesaggi, costruzioni, reperti* 2 (2005), 93–115.

Finley, M. I., 'Debt-bondage and the problem of slavery', in *Economy and Society in Ancient Greece*, 150–66. London: Chatto & Windus, 1981.

Fisher, N. R. E., *'Kharis, Kharites*, festivals, and social peace in the classical Greek City', in R. Rosen and I. Sluiter (eds), *Valuing Others in Classical Antiquity*, 71–112. Leiden: Brill, 2010.

Flemming, R., 'Festus and the role of women in Roman religion', in F. Glinister and C. Woods (eds), *Verrius, Festus, and Paul: Lexicography, Scholarship, and Society*, 87–108. London: Institute of Classical Studies, 2007.

Flower, H. I., 'Alternatives to written history in Republican Rome', in A. Feldherr (ed.), *The Cambridge Companion to the Roman Historians*, 65–76. Cambridge: Cambridge University Press, 2009.

Flower, H. I., *Ancestor Masks and Aristocratic Power in Roman Culture*, Oxford: Oxford University Press, 1996.

Flower, H. I., '*Fabulae praetextae* in context: when were plays on contemporary subjects performed in Republican Rome?', *Classical Quarterly* 45 (1995), 170–90.

Flower, H. I., *Roman Republics*, Princeton: Princeton University Press, 2010.

Fontaine, P., 'Des "remparts de Romulus" aux murs du Palatin: du mythe à l'archéologie', in P. A. Deproost and A. Meurant (eds), *Images d'origines, origines d'une image: hommages à Jacques Poucet*, 35–54. Louvain-la-neuve: Academia Bruylant, 2004.

Formigli, E., 'La storia della tecnologia dei grandi bronzi', in G. Bartoloni (ed.), *La Lupa Capitolina: Nuove Prospettive di Studio*, 15–24. Rome: 'L'Erma' di Bretschneider, 2010.

Forsythe, G., 'The army and centuriate organization in early Rome', in P. Erdkamp (ed.), *A Companion to the Roman Army*, 24–41. Oxford: Blackwell, 2007.

Forsythe, G., *A Critical History of Early Rome: From Prehistory to the First Punic War*, Berkeley: University of California Press, 2005.

Fowler, R. L., *Early Greek Mythography*, vol. 2: *Commentary*, Oxford: Oxford University Press, 2013.

Fox, M., *Roman Historical Myths*, Oxford: Oxford University Press, 1996.

Fraccaro, P., 'La storia dell'antichissimo esercito romano e l'età dell'ordinamento centuriato', in *Atti del II Congresso Nazionale di Studi Romani*, vol. 3, 91–7. Rome: Cremonese, 1931. Reprinted in *Opuscula*, vol. 2, 287–92. Pavia: Presso la rivista 'Athenaeum', 1957.

Frier, B. W., *Libri Annales Pontificum Maximorum: The Origins of the Annalistic Tradition*, Rome: American Academy in Rome, 1979.

Fronda, M., *Between Carthage and Rome*, Cambridge: Cambridge University Press, 2010.

Fulminante, F., 'Ethnicity, identity and state formation in the Latin landscape: problems and approaches', in S. Stoddart and G. Cifani (eds), *Landscape, Identity and Ethnicity in the Archaic Mediterranean Area*, 89–107. Oxford: Oxbow, 2012.

Fulminante, F., 'The Latins', in G. D. Farney and G. Bradley (eds), *The Peoples of Ancient Italy*, 473–97. Boston: De Gruyter, 2017.

Fulminante, F., *Le sepolture principesche nel Latium Vetus fra la fine della prima età del Ferro e l'inizio dell'età Orientalizzante*, Rome: 'L'Erma' di Bretschneider, 2003.

Fulminante, F., *The Urbanisation of Rome and Latium Vetus from the Bronze Age to the Archaic Era*, Cambridge: Cambridge University Press, 2014.

Gabba, E., *Dionysius and the History of Archaic Rome*, Berkeley: University of California Press, 1991.

Gabrielli, C., 'Debiti e secessione della plebe al monte sacro', *Diritto@storia* 7.1–8 (2008): www.dirittoestoria.it/7/Memorie/Gabrielli-Debito-secessione-plebe-Monte-Sacro.htm.

Gagarin, M. and E. Fantham (eds), *The Oxford Encyclopedia of Ancient Greece and Rome*, Oxford: Oxford University Press, 2010.

Gallia, A., 'Reassessing the "Cumaean Chronicle": Greek chronology and Roman history in Dionysius of Halicarnassus', *Journal of Roman Studies* 97 (2007), 50–67.

Gallia, A. B., *Remembering the Roman Republic: Culture, Politics and History under the Principate*, Cambridge; New York: Cambridge University Press, 2012.

Garnsey, P., *Famine and Food Supply in the Graeco-Roman World: Responses to Risk and Crisis*, Cambridge: Cambridge University Press, 1988.

Gilotta, F., 'La ceramica di importazione', in M. Cristofani (ed.), *La grande Roma dei Tarquini*, 140–1. Rome: 'L'Erma' di Bretschneider, 1990.

Giovannini, A., 'Le sel et la fortune de Rome', *Athenaeum* 63 (1985), 373–86.

Gjerstad, E., *Early Rome*, vol. 3. Lund: C. W. K. Gleerup, 1960.

Gjerstad, E., *Early Rome*, vol. 4.1. Lund: C. W. K. Gleerup, 1966.

Glinister, F., '"Bring on the dancing girls": some thoughts on the Salian priesthood', in J. H. Richardson and F. Santangelo (eds), *Priests and State in the Roman World*, 107–36. Stuttgart: Franz Steiner, 2011.

Glinister F., 'Constructing the past', in F. Glinister and C. Woods (eds), *Verrius, Festus, and Paul: Lexicography, Scholarship, and Society*, 11–32. London: Institute of Classical Studies, 2007.

Glinister, F., 'Kingship and tyranny in archaic Rome', in S. Lewis (ed.), *Ancient Tyranny*, 17–32. Edinburgh: Edinburgh University Press, 2006.

Glinister, F., 'Politics, power, and the divine: the *rex sacrorum* and the transition from monarchy to Republic at Rome', in J. Armstrong and J. H. Richardson (eds), *Politics and Power in Early Rome 509–264 BC*, 59–76. *Antichthon* special issue 51, Cambridge: Cambridge University Press, 2017.

Glinister, F., 'The Rapino bronze, the *touta marouca*, and sacred prostitution in early central Italy', in A. Cooley (ed.), *The Epigraphic Landscape of Roman Italy*, 18–38. BICS Supplement 73, London: Institute of Classical Studies, 2000.

Glinister, F., The Roman Kingship in the Sixth Century BC. Unpublished PhD thesis, University College London, 1995.

Glinister, F., 'Sacred rubbish', in E. Bispham and C. Smith (eds), *Religion in Archaic and Republican Rome and Italy*, 54–70. Edinburgh University Press: Edinburgh, 2000.

Glinister, F., 'Women and power in archaic Rome', in T. J. Cornell and K. Lomas (eds), *Gender and Ethnicity in Ancient Italy*, 115–27. London: Accordia, 1997.

Glinister, F. and C. Woods (eds), *Verrius, Festus, and Paul: Lexicography, Scholarship, and Society*, London: Institute of Classical Studies, 2007.

Gnade, M., 'The Volscians and Hernicians', in G. D. Farney and G. Bradley (eds), *The Peoples of Ancient Italy*, 461–72. Boston: De Gruyter, 2017.

Grandazzi, A., *Alba Longa, histoire d'une légende: recherches sur l'archéologie, la religion, les traditions de l'ancien Latium*, 2 vols, Rome: École française de Rome, 2008.

Grandazzi, A., *The Foundation of Rome: Myth and History*, Ithaca: Cornell University Press, 1997.

Gras, M., *La Méditerranée archaïque*, Paris: Armand Colin, 1995.

Grifi, L., *Monumenti di Cere antica spiegati colle osservanze del culto di Mitra*, Rome: Monaldi, 1841.

Gruen, E. S., *Culture and National Identity in Republican Rome*, Ithaca: Cornell University Press, 1992.

Gruen, E. S., *Rethinking the Other in Antiquity*. Martin Classical Lectures, Princeton; Oxford: Princeton University Press, 2011.

Guidi, A., P. Pascucci and A. Zarattini, 'Confini geografici e confini culturali: le facies della Preistoria e della Protostoria nel Lazio meridionale', *Latium* 19 (2002), 5–21.

Gunter, A. C., 'The Etruscans, Greek art and the Near East', in S. Bell and A. A. Carpino (eds), *A Companion to the Etruscans*, 339–52. Blackwell Companions to the Ancient World, Malden, MA; Oxford: Blackwell, 2016.

Habinek, T., *The Politics of Latin Literature: Writing, Identity, and Empire in Ancient Rome*, Princeton: Princeton University Press, 1998.

Habinek, T., *The World of Roman Song: From Ritualized Speech to Social Order*, Baltimore: Johns Hopkins University Press, 2005.

Hall, J. M., *Artifact and Artifice: Classical Archaeology and the Ancient Historian*, Chicago; London: University of Chicago Press, 2014.

Hall, J. M., *A History of the Archaic Greek World ca. 1200–479 BCE*, Malden, MA: Blackwell, 2007.

Hall, J. R. (2016), The Tyrrhenian Way of War: War, Social Power, and the State in Central Italy (c.900–343 BC). Unpublished PhD thesis, Cardiff University.

Hansen, M. H., *The Shotgun Method: The Demography of the Ancient Greek City-State Culture*, Columbia: University of Missouri Press, 2006.

Harris, W. V., *Ancient Literacy*, Cambridge, MA: Harvard University Press, 1989.

Harris, W. V., 'Quando e come l'Italia divenne per la prima volta Italia?', *Studi Storici* 48 (2007), 301–22.

Harris, W. V., 'Roman warfare in the economic and social context of the fourth century BC', in W. Eder (ed.), *Staat und Staatlichkeit in der frühen römischen Republik*, 494–510. Stuttgart: Franz Steiner, 1990.

Harris, W. V., *Rome in Etruria and Umbria*, Oxford: Clarendon Press, 1971.

Harris, W. V., *War and Imperialism in Republican Rome 327–70 BC*, Oxford: Clarendon Press, 1979.

Haumesser, L., 'Hellenism in Central Italy', Naso, A. (ed.), *Etruscology* (2 vols.), 645–64. Berlin/Boston: De Gruyter, 2017.

Haynes, S., *Etruscan Civilization: A Cultural History*, Los Angeles: J. Paul Getty Museum, 2000.

Hemelrijk, E. A., 'Women and sacrifice in the Roman empire', in O. Hekster, S. Schmidt-Hofner and C. Witschel (eds), *Ritual Dynamics and Religious Change in the Roman Empire*, 253–67. Leiden; Boston: Brill, 2009.

Hersch, K. K., *The Roman Wedding: Ritual and Meaning in Antiquity*, Cambridge; New York: Cambridge University Press, 2010.

Heurgon, J., *Daily Life of the Etruscans*, London: Weidenfeld and Nicolson, 1964.

Hickson Hahn, F., 'Livy's liturgical order: systematization in the History', in B. Mineo (ed.), *A Companion to Livy*, 90–101. Oxford: Blackwell, 2014.

Hobsbawm, E. and T. Ranger (eds), *The Invention of Tradition*, Cambridge: Cambridge University Press, 1983.

Hodkinson, S. and I. Macgregor Morris, 'Introduction', in S. Hodkinson and I. Macgregor Morris (eds), *Sparta in Modern Thought*, vii–xxvi. Swansea: Classical Press of Wales, 2012.

Hölkeskamp, K.-J., 'Arbitrators, lawgivers and the "Codification of Law" in Archaic Greece: problems and perspectives', *Metis* 7 (1992): 49–81.

Hölkeskamp, K.-J., 'Conquest, competition and consensus: Roman expansion in Italy and the rise of the *nobilitas*', *Historia* 42 (1993), 12–39.

Hölkeskamp, K.-J., 'History and collective memory in the Middle Republic', in N. Rosenstein and R. Morstein-Marx (eds), *A Companion to the Roman Republic*, 478–95. Oxford: Blackwell, 2006.

Hölkeskamp, K.-J., *Reconstructing the Roman Republic: An Ancient Political Culture and Modern Research*, Princeton: Princeton University Press, 2010. Trans. of *Rekonstruktionen einer Republik: die politische Kultur des antiken Rom und die Forschung der letzten Jahrzehnte*. Historische Zeitschrift Beiheft 38, Munich: R. Oldenbourg, 2004.

Hopkins, J., 'The Capitoline temple and the effects of monumentality on Roman temple design', in M. L. Thomas and G. E. Meyers (eds), *Monumentality in Etruscan and Early Roman Architecture: Ideology and Innovation*, 111–27. Austin: University of Texas Press, 2012.

Hopkins, J., 'The colossal temple of Jupiter Optimus Maximus in archaic Rome', in S. Camporeale, H. Dessales and A. Pizzo (eds), *I cantieri edili dell'Italia e delle province romane 2: Italia e province occidentali. Workshop di Siena, Certosa di Pontignano*, 15–33. Merida: Instituto de Arqueología de Mérida, 2010.

Hopkins, J. N., 'The creation of the Forum and the making of monumental Rome', in E. C. Robinson (ed.), *Papers on Italian Urbanism in the First Millennium B.C.*, 29–61. *Journal of Roman Archaeology* Supplement 97, Portsmouth, RI: Journal of Roman Archaeology, 2014.

Hopkins, J. N., *The Genesis of Roman Architecture*, New Haven; London: Yale University Press, 2016.

Hopkins, J., 'The sacred sewer: tradition and religion in Rome's Cloaca Maxima', in M. Bradley (ed.), *Pollution and Propriety: Dirt, Disease and Hygiene in Rome from Antiquity to Modernity*, 81–102. Cambridge: Cambridge University Press, 2011.

Hopkins, K., *Conquerors and Slaves*, Cambridge: Cambridge University Press, 1978.

Horden, P. and N. Purcell, *The Corrupting Sea: A Study of Mediterranean History*, Oxford: Blackwell, 2000.

Hornblower, S., A. Spawforth and E. Eidinow (eds), *The Oxford Classical Dictionary*, 4th edn, Oxford: Oxford University Press, 2012.

Horsfall, N., 'Stesichorus at Bovillae?', *Journal of Hellenic Studies* 99 (1979), 26–48.

Humbert, M., *Municipium et civitas sine suffragio: L'organisation de la conquête jusqu'à la Guerre Sociale*, Rome: École Française de Rome, 1978.

Humm, M., 'Appius Claudius Caecus et la construction de la via Appia', *Mélanges de l'École française de Rome – Antiquité* 108 (1996), 693–749.

Humm, M., *Appius Claudius Caecus: La République accomplie*, Rome: École française de Rome, 2005.

Humm, M., 'Numa and Pythagoras: the life and death of a myth', in J. H. Richardson and F. Santangelo (eds), *The Roman Historical Tradition: Regal and Republican Rome*, 35–51. Oxford Readings in Classical Studies, Oxford: Oxford University Press, 2014.

Humm, M., 'Servius Tullius et la censure: élaboration d'un modèle institutionnel', in M. Coudry and T. Späth (eds), *L'invention des grands hommes de la Rome antique*, 221–47. Paris: De Boccard, 2001.

Iacono, F., 'Westernizing Aegean of LH IIIC', in M. E. Alberti and S. Sabatini (eds), *Exchange Networks and Local Transformations*, 60–79. Oxford: Oxbow, 2013.

Iaia, C., 'Elements of female jewellery in Iron Age Latium and southern Etruria: identity and cultural communication in a boundary zone', in *Scripta praehistorica in honorem Biba Teržan*, 519–31. Ljubljana: Nardoni musej Slovenije, 2007.

Isayev, E., *Inside Ancient Lucania: Dialogues in History and Archaeology*. BICS Supplement 90, London: Institute of Classical Studies, 2007.

Isayev, E., 'Just the right amount of priestly foreignness: Roman citizenship for the Greek priestess of Ceres', in F. Santangelo and J. H. Richardson (eds), *Priests and State in the Roman World*, 373–90. Stuttgart: Franz Steiner, 2011.

Isayev, E., *Migration, Mobility and Place in Ancient Italy*, Cambridge: Cambridge University Press: 2017.

Izzet, V., *The Archaeology of Etruscan Society*. Cambridge; New York: Cambridge University Press, 2007.

Jaeger, M., *Livy's Written Rome*. Ann Arbor: University of Michigan Press, 1997.

Janko, R., 'From Gabii and Gordion to Eretria and Methone: the rise of the Greek alphabet', *Bulletin of the Institute of Classical Studies* 58 (2015), 1–32.

Jannot, J.-R., *Religion in Ancient Etruria*, Madison: University of Wisconsin Press, 2005.

Jehne, M., 'Methods, models, and historiography', in N. Rosenstein and R. Morstein-Marx (eds), *A Companion to the Roman Republic*, 3–28. Oxford: Blackwell, 2006.

Jehne, M., 'The rise of the consular as a social type in the third and second centuries BC', in H. Beck, A. Duplá, M. Jehne and F. Pina Polo (eds), *Consuls and Res Publica: Holding High Office in the Roman Republic*, 211–31. Cambridge: Cambridge University Press, 2011.

Keaney, A., 'Three Sabine nomina: Clausus, Cōnsus, *Fisus', *Glotta* 69.3/4 (1991), 202–14.

Kelly, G. P., *A History of Exile in the Roman Republic*, Cambridge: Cambridge University Press, 2006.

Kent, P., 'Reconsidering socii in Roman armies before the Punic Wars', in S. Roselaar (ed.), *Processes of Integration and Identity Formation in the Roman Republic*, 71–84. Brill: Leiden, 2012.

Kinney, 'The Lupa Romana: an antique monument falls from her pedestal', *Speculum* 88.4 (2013): 1063–5.

Kraus, C., '"No second Troy": topoi and refoundation in Livy, Book V', *Transactions of the American Philological Association* 124 (1994), 267–89.

La Regina, A., 'Contributo dell'archeologia alla storia sociale: territori sabellici e sannitici', *Dialoghi di Archaeologia* 4–5 (1970–1), 443–59.

La Regina, A., 'Lacus ad sacellum Larum', in A. Capoferro, L. D'Amelio and S. Renzetti (eds), *Dall'Italia: omaggio a Barbro Santillo Frizell*, 133–50. Florence: Polistampa, 2013.

La Rocca, E., 'Ceramica d'importazione greca dell'VIII secolo a.C. a Sant'Omobono: un aspetto delle origini di Roma', in *La céramique grecque ou de tradition grecque au VIIIᵉ siècle en Italie centrale et méridionale*, 45–54. Naples: Publications du Centre Jean Bérard, 1982.

Lanfranchi, T., *Les tribuns de la plèbe et la formation de la République romaine, 494–287 avant J.-C.*, Rome: École française de Rome, 2015.

Last, H., 'The Servian reforms', *Journal of Roman Studies* 35 (1945), 30–48.

Laurence, R., *The Roads of Roman Italy: Mobility and Cultural Change*, London: Routledge, 1999.

Lendon, J. E., 'Historians without history: against Roman historiography', in A. Feldherr (ed.), *The Cambridge Companion to the Roman Historians*, 41–61. Cambridge: Cambridge University Press, 2009.

Levene, D., *Livy on the Hannibalic War*, Oxford, Oxford University Press, 2010.

Linderski, J., 'Religious aspects of the Conflict of the Orders: the case of *confarreatio*', in K. A. Raaflaub (ed.), *Social Struggles in Archaic Rome: New Perspectives on the Conflict of the Orders*, 223–38. Malden, MA; Oxford: Blackwell, 2005.

Lintott, A., *The Constitution of the Roman Republic*, Oxford: Clarendon Press, 1999.

Lo Schiavo, F. and M. Milletti, 'The Nuragic heritage in Etruria', in J. M. Turfa (ed.), *The Etruscan World*, 216–30. London; New York: Routledge, 2013.

Lomas, K., *The Rise of Rome: From the Iron Age to the Punic Wars (1000 BC–264 BC)*, London: Profile, 2017.

Lowenthal, D., *The Past is a Foreign Country*, Cambridge: Cambridge University Press, 1985.

Luce, T. J., 'The dating of Livy's first decade', in J. D. Chaplin, C. S. Kraus (eds), *Livy*, 17–48. Oxford Readings in Classical Studies, Oxford: Oxford University Press, 2009.

Lulof, P., 'L'Amazzone dell'Esquilino: una nuova riconstruzione', *BCAR* 108 (2007), 7–31.

Lulof, P. S., 'Reconstructing a golden age in temple construction: temples and roofs from the last Tarquin to the Roman Republic (*c*.530–480 B.C.)', in E. C. Robinson (ed.), *Papers on Italian Urbanism in the First Millennium B.C.*, 113–25. *Journal of Roman Archaeology* Supplement 97, Portsmouth, RI: Journal of Roman Archaeology, 2014.

Lulof, P. and C. Smith (eds), *The Age of Tarquinius Superbus: Ancient History, Archaeology, and Methodology*. Peeters: Leuven, 2017.

Lulof, P. and I. van Kampen (eds), *The Etruscans: Eminent Women, Powerful Men*, Amsterdam: Zwolle, 2011.

McGlew, J., *Tyranny and Political Culture in Ancient Greece*, Ithaca: Cornell University Press, 1993.

MacMullen, R., *The Earliest Romans: A Character Sketch*, Ann Arbor: University of Michigan Press, 2011.

Malkin, I., *The Returns of Odysseus: Colonization and Ethnicity*, Berkeley: University of California Press, 1998.

Malkin, I., *A Small Greek World. Networks in the Ancient Mediterranean: Greeks Overseas*, Oxford; New York: Oxford University Press, 2011.

Manuwald, G., *Roman Republican Theatre*, Cambridge: Cambridge University Press, 2011.

Maras, D. F., 'Dei, eroi e fondatori nel Lazio antico', in *Anzio: dei, eroi e fondatori dal Lazio antico*, exhibition catalogue, 17–26. Anzio: Marina, 2011.

Martínez Pinna, J., *La monarquía romana arcaica*, Barcelona: Publicacions i Edicions de la Universitat de Barcelona, 2009.

Martínez Pinna, J., *Tarquinio Prisco: ensayo histórico sobre Roma arcaica*, Madrid: Ediciones Clásicas, 1996.

Massa-Pairault, F.-H., 'Introduction', in *Crise et transformation des sociétés archaïques de l'Italie antique au Ve siècle av. JC*, 1–5. Publications de l'École française de Rome 137, Rome: École Française de Rome, 1990.

Massa-Pairault, F.-H., 'Romulus et Remus: réexamen du miroir de l'Antiquarium Communal', *Mélanges de l'École française de Rome – Antiquité* 123 (2011), 505–25.

Mertens-Horn, M., 'Corinto e l'Occidente nelle immagini: la nascita di Pegaso e la nascita di Afrodite', in *Corinto e l'Occidente: Atti del trentaquattresimo convegno di studi sulla Magna Grecia*, 257–89. Taranto: Istituto per la storia e l'archeologia della Magna Grecia, 1995.

Meyer, J. C., 'Roman history in the light of the import of Attic vases to Rome and Etruria in the 6th and 5th centuries BC', *Analecta Romana Instituti Danici* 9 (1980), 47–68.

Meyer, J. C., *Pre-Republican Rome: An Analysis of the Cultural and Chronological Relations, 1000–500 BC*, Odense: Odense University Press, 1983.

Meyers, G. E., 'The experience of monumentality in Etruscan and early Roman architecture', in M. L. Thomas and G. E. Meyers (eds), *Monumentality in Etruscan and Early Roman Architecture: Ideology and Innovation*, 1–20. Austin: University of Texas Press, 2012.

Michetti, L. M. and M. P. Baglione (eds), *Le lamine d'oro a cinquant'anni dalla scoperta: dati archeologici su Pyrgi nell'epoca di Thefarie Velinas e rapporti con altre realtà del Mediterraneo. Scienze dell'Antichità* 21.2, Rome: Quasar, 2015.

Mignone, L., *The Republican Aventine and Rome's Social Order*. Ann Arbor: University of Michigan Press, 2016.

Miles, G. B., *Livy: Reconstructing Early Rome*, Ithaca: Cornell University Press, 1995.

Millar, F., 'Political power in mid-Republican Rome: Curia or Comitium?', *Journal of Roman Studies* 79 (1989), 138–50.

Mineo, B. (ed.), *A Companion to Livy*, Oxford: Blackwell, 2014.

Minetti, A. (ed.), *Pittura etrusca: Problemi e prospettive*, Siena: Protagon Editori Toscani, 2003.

Momigliano, A., *Alien Wisdom: The Limits of Hellenization*, Cambridge: Cambridge University Press, 1976.

Momigliano, A., 'Fabius Pictor and the origins of national history', in A. Momigliano, *The Classical Foundations of Modern Historiography*, 80–108. Berkeley: University of California Press, 1990.

Momigliano, A. 'Georges Dumézil and the trifunctional approach to Roman civilization', *History and Theory* 23.3 (1984): 312–30.

Momigliano, A., 'How to reconcile Greeks and Trojans', in *Settimo contributo alla storia degli studi classici e del mondo antico*, 437–62. Rome: Edizioni di storia e letteratura, 1984.
Momigliano, A., 'An interim report on the origins of Rome', *Journal of Roman Studies* 53.1–2 (1963), 95–121.
Momigliano, A., 'The origins of Rome', in F. W. Walbank, A. E. Astin, M. W. Frederiksen, R. M. Ogilvie and A. Drummond (eds), *The Cambridge Ancient History 7.2: The Rise of Rome to 220 BC*, 2nd edn, 52–112. Cambridge: Cambridge University Press, 1989.
Momigliano, A., 'Perizonius, Niebuhr and the character of early Roman tradition', *Journal of Roman Studies* 47 (1957), 104–14.
Momigliano, A., Review of A. Alföldi, *Early Rome and the Latins*, Ann Arbor: University of Michigan Press, 1965. *Journal of Roman Studies* 57.1/2 (1967), 211–16.
Momigliano, A., 'The rise of the plebs in the Archaic Age of Rome', in K. Raaflaub (ed.), *Social Struggles in Archaic Rome: New Perspectives on the Conflict of the Orders*, 168–84. Malden, MA; Oxford: Blackwell, 2005.
Momigliano, A., 'Terra marique', *Journal of Roman Studies* 32 (1942), 53–64.
Momigliano, A., 'Timeo, Fabio Pittore e il primo censimento di Servio Tullio', in *Miscellanea di studi alessandrini in memoria di Augusta Rostagni*, 180–7. Turin: Bottega d'Erasmo, 1963 = *Terzo Contributo*, Edizioni di Storia e Letteratura, 649–56. Rome, 1966.
Momigliano, A. and A. Schiavone (eds), *Storia di Roma I: Roma in Italia*, Turin: Einaudi, 1988.
Mommsen, T., *The History of Rome* (trans. W. P. Dickson), London: Macmillan, 1862.
Moormann, E. M., 'Carandini's royal houses at the foot of the Palatine: fact or fiction?', *BABesch* 76 (2001), 209–12.
Moretti Sgubini, A. M. (ed.), *Veio, Cerveteri, Vulci: città d'Etruria a confronto*, Rome: 'L'Erma' di Bretschneider, 2001.
Morris, I., 'Foreword', in M. I. Finley, *The Ancient Economy*, updated edn, ix–xxxvi. Berkeley: University of California Press, 1999.
Moser, C., *The Altars of Republican Rome and Latium: Sacrifice and the Materiality of Roman Religion*, Cambridge: Cambridge University Press, 2019.
Mouritsen, H., *Italian Unification: A Study in Ancient and Modern Historiography*. BICS Supplement 70, London: Institute of Classical Studies, 1998.
Mouritsen, H., *Politics in the Roman Republic*, Cambridge; New York: Cambridge University Press, 2017.
Müller-Karpe, H., *Vom Anfang Roms*, Heidelberg: Kerle Verlag, 1959.
Müller-Karpe, H., *Zur Stadtwerdung Roms*, Heidelberg: Kerle Verlag, 1962.
Mura Sommella, A., '"La grande Roma dei Tarquini": alterne vicende di una felice intuizione', *BCAR* 101 (2000), 7–26.
Mura Sommella, A. 'Il tempio di Giove Capitolino: una nuova proposta di lettura', in G. M. Della Fina (ed.), *Gli Etruschi e Roma: fasi monarchica e alto-repubblicana*, 333–72. Rome: Quasar, 2009.
Mura Sommella, A., A. Cazzella, A. De Santis, F. Lugli, C. Rosa, I. Baroni, P. Boccuccia, F. Micarelli, S. Brincatt, C. Giardino, A. Danti and M. Albertoni, 'Primi risultati delle indagini archeologiche in Campidoglio nell'area del Giardino Romano e del Palazzo Caffarelli', *BCAR* 102 (2001), 261–364.

Murray, O., 'Cities of reason', in O. Murray and S. Price (eds), *The Greek City from Homer to Alexander*, 1–25. Oxford: Oxford University Press, 1990.

Nafissi, M., *Ancient Athens and Modern Ideology: Value, Theory and Evidence in Historical Sciences. Max Weber, Karl Polanyi and Moses Finley*, London: Institute of Classical Studies, 2005.

Naso A., 'The Etruscans in Lazio', in G. Camporeale (ed.), *The Etruscans outside Etruria*, 220–35. Los Angeles: J. Paul Getty Museum, 2004.

Naso, A. (ed.), *Etruscology*, 2 vols, Berlin; Boston: De Gruyter, 2017.

Naso, A., 'Gli influssi del Vicino Oriente sull'Etruria nell'VIII–VII sec. a.C.: un bilancio', in V. Bellelli (ed.), *Origine degli Etruschi: storia archeologia antropologia*, 433–53. Rome: 'L'Erma' di Bretschneider, 2012.

Nielsen, M., 'Etruscan women: a cross-cultural perspective', in L. Larsson Lovén and A. Strömberg (eds), *Aspects of Women in Antiquity*, 69–84. Göteborg: Jonsered, 1998.

Nielsen, T. H., and J. Roy,, 'The Peloponnese', in K. Raaflaub and H. van Wees (eds), *A Companion to Archaic Greece*, 255–72. Oxford: Wiley-Blackwell, 2009.

Nijboer, A. J., 'Fortifications in and around Rome, 950–300 BC', in A. Ballmer, M. Fernández-Götz and D. P. Mielke (eds), *Understanding Ancient Fortifications: Between Regionality and Connectivity*, 111–22. Oxford; Philadelphia: Oxbow Books, 2018.

Nijboer, A. J., *From Household Production to Workshops: Archaeological Evidence for Economic Transformations, Pre-monetary Exchange and Urbanisation in Central Italy from 800 to 400 BC*, Groningen: University of Groningen, 1998.

North, J., 'The development of Roman imperialism', *Journal of Roman Studies* 71 (1981), 1–9.

Oakley, F., *Kingship: The Politics of Enchantment*, Oxford: Blackwell, 2006.

Oakley, S. P., *A Commentary on Livy books VI–X*, vols 1–4, Oxford: Oxford University Press, 1997–2005.

Oakley, S. P., 'Livy and his sources', in J. D. Chaplin and C. S. Kraus (eds), *Livy*, 439–60. Oxford Readings in Classical Studies, Oxford: Oxford University Press, 2009.

Oakley, S. P., 'The Roman conquest of Italy', in J. Rich and G. Shipley (eds), *War and Society in the Roman World*, 9–37. London: Routledge, 1993.

Oakley, S. P., 'Single combat in the Roman Republic', *Classical Quarterly* 35.2 (1985), 392–410.

Ogilvie R. M., *A Commentary on Livy: Books 1–5*. Oxford: Clarendon Press, 1965.

Orlin, E., *Foreign Cults in Rome: Creating a Roman Empire*, Oxford: Oxford University Press, 2010.

Osborne, R., 'Urban sprawl: what is urbanization and why does it matter?', in R. J. Osborne and B. Cunliffe (eds), *Mediterranean Urbanization 800–600 B.C.*, 1–16. Oxford: Oxford University Press, 2005.

Osborne, R., *Greece in the Making, 1200–479 BC*, 2nd edn, London; New York: Routledge, 2009.

Pacciarelli, M., *Dal villaggio alla città: la svolta proto-urbana del 1000 a.C. nell'Italia tirrenica*, Florence: All'insegna del Giglio, 2001.

Pacciarelli, M., 'Forme di complessità sociale nelle comunità protourbane dell'Etruria meridionale', in P. Fontaine (ed.), *L'Étrurie et l'Ombrie avant Rome: cité et territoire. Actes du colloque international, Louvain-la-Neuve*, 17–33. Brussels; Rome: Institut historique belge, 2010.

Pallottino, M., *A History of Earliest Italy* (trans. M. Ryle and K. Soper), London: Routledge, 1991.

Pallottino, M., *Origini e storia primitiva di Roma*, Milan: Rusconi, 1993.

Parisi Presicce, C. and A. Danti (eds), *Campidoglio: mito, memoria, archeologia*, Rome: Campisano, 2016.

Patterson, H. (ed.), *Bridging the Tiber: Approaches to Regional Archaeology in the Middle Tiber Valley*. London: British School at Rome, 2004.

Pelgrom, J. and T. Stek, 'Roman colonization under the Republic: historiographical contextualisation of a paradigm', in T. Stek and J. Pelgrom (eds), *Roman Republican Colonization: New Perspectives from Archaeology and Ancient History*, 11–41. Rome: Palombi, 2014.

Pensabene, P. and S. Falzone, *Scavi Del Palatino*, Rome: 'L'Erma' di Bretschneider, 2001.

Pensabene, P., S. Falzone, F. M. Rossi, S. Valerio, O. Colazingari, 'Ceramica graffita di età arcaica e repubblicana dall'area sud-ovest del Palatino', *Scienze dell'Antichità* 10 (2000), 163–247.

Peroni, R., 'Comunità e insediamento in Italia fra età del bronzo e prima età del ferro', in A. Momigliano and A. Schiavone (eds), *Storia di Roma* I: *Roma in Italia*, 7–37. Turin: Einaudi, 1988.

Peroni, R., 'Formazione e sviluppi dei centri protourbani medio-tirrenci', in A. Carandini and R. Cappelli (eds), *Roma: Romolo, Remo e la fondazione della città*, 26–30. Milan: Electa, 2000.

Petrain, D., *Homer in Stone: The 'Tabulae Iliacae' in their Roman Context. Greek Culture in the Roman World*, Cambridge; New York: Cambridge University Press, 2014.

Polignac F. de, 'Forms and processes: some thoughts on the meaning of urbanization in early archaic Greece', in R. J. Osborne and B. Cunliffe (eds), *Mediterranean Urbanization 800–600 B.C.*, 45–69. Oxford: Oxford University Press, 2005.

Pollitt, J. J., *The Art of Rome, c.753 B.C.–A.D. 337: Sources and Documents*, Cambridge: Cambridge University Press, 1983.

Poma, G., 'Le secessioni della plebe (in particolare quella del 494–493 a.c.) nella storiografia', *Diritto@storia* 7.1–16 (2008): www.dirittoestoria.it/7/Memorie/Poma-Secessioni-plebe-storiografia.htm.

Potts, C. R., *Religious Architecture in Latium and Etruria, c.900–500 BC*, Oxford: Oxford University Press, 2015.

Poucet, J., 'Les grands travaux d'urbanisme dans la Rome "étrusque": libres propos sur la notion de confirmation du récit annalistique par l'archéologie', in *La Rome des premiers siècles: légende et histoire. Actes de la table ronde en l'honneur de Massimo Pallottino (Paris, 3–4 mai 1990)*, 215–34. Florence: Olschki, Istituto Nazionale di Studi etruschi e italici, 1992.

Poucet, J., *Les origines de Rome: tradition et histoire*, Brussels: Facultés universitaires Saint-Louis, 1985.

Poucet, J., *Les rois de Rome: tradition et histoire*, Brussels: Académie royale de Belgique, 2000.

Prayon, F., 'Architecture', in L. Bonfante (ed.), *Etruscan Life and Afterlife: A Handbook of Etruscan Studies*, 174–201. Warminster: Aris and Phillips, 1986.

Purcell, N., 'Becoming historical: the Roman case', in D. Braund and C. Gill (eds), *Myth, History and Culture in Republican Rome: Studies in Honour of T. P. Wiseman*, 12–40. Exeter: University of Exeter Press, 2003.

Raaflaub, K. A., 'The conflict of the orders in archaic Rome: a comprehensive and comparative approach', in K. A. Raaflaub (ed.), *Social Struggles in Archaic Rome*, 2nd edn, 1–46. Malden, MA; Oxford: Blackwell, 2005.

Raaflaub, K. A. (ed.), *Social Struggles in Archaic Rome*, 2nd edn, Malden, MA; Oxford: Blackwell, 2005.

Radnoti-Alföldi, M., E. Formigli and J. Fried, *Die römische Wölfin: ein antikes Monument stürzt von seinem Sockel*, Stuttgart: Franz Steiner, 2011.

Ranouil, P. C., *Recherches sur le patriciat: 509–366 avant J.-C.*, Paris: Les Belles Lettres, 1975.

Rathje, A., '"Princesses" in Etruria and Latium Vetus?', in D. Ridgway, F. R. Serra Ridgway, M. Pearce, E. Herring, R. D. Whitehouse and J. B. Wilkins (eds), *Ancient Italy in its Mediterranean Setting: Studies in Honour of Ellen Macnamara*, 295–300. London: Accordia, 2000.

Rawlings, L., *The Ancient Greeks at War*, Manchester: Manchester University Press, 2007.

Rawlings, L., 'Condottieri and clansmen: early Italian raiding, warfare and the state', in K. Hopwood (ed.), *Organised Crime in Antiquity*, 97–127. Swansea: Classical Press of Wales, 1999.

Rich, J., 'Annales Maximi', in T. J. Cornell (ed.), *The Fragments of the Roman Historians*, vol. 1, 141–59. Oxford: Oxford University Press, 2013.

Rich, J., 'Fear, greed and glory: the causes of Roman war-making in the middle Republic', in J. Rich and G. Shipley (eds), *War and Society in the Roman World*, 38–68. London: Routledge, 1993.

Rich, J., 'Lex Licinia, lex Sempronia: B. G. Niebuhr and the limitation of landholding in the Roman Republic', in L. de Ligt and S. J. Northwood (eds), *People, Land, and Politics: Demographic Developments and the Transformation of Roman Italy 300 BC–AD 14*, 519–72. Leiden: Brill, 2007.

Rich, J., 'Treaties, allies and the Roman conquest of Italy', in P. de Souza and J. France (eds), *War and Peace in Ancient and Medieval History*, 51–75. Cambridge: Cambridge University Press, 2008.

Rich, J., 'Warfare and the army in early Rome', in P. Erdkamp (ed.), *A Companion to the Roman Army*, 7–23. Oxford: Wiley-Blackwell, 2007.

Rich, J., 'Warlords and the Roman Republic', in T. Ñaco del Hoyo and F. López Sánchez (eds), *War, Warlords and Interstate Relations in the Ancient Mediterranean*, 266–94. Leiden; Boston: Brill, 2017.

Richard J.-C., *Les origines de la plèbe romaine: essai sur la formation du dualisme patricio-plébéien*, 2nd edn, Rome: École française de Rome, 2015.

Richard, J.-C., 'Patricians and plebeians: the origins of a social dichotomy', in K. A. Raaflaub (ed.), *Social Struggles in Archaic Rome*, 2nd edn, 107–27. Malden, MA; Oxford: Blackwell, 2005.

Richardson, J. H., *The Fabii and the Gauls: Studies in Historical Thought and Historiography in Republican Rome*, Stuttgart: Franz Steiner, 2012.

Richardson, J. H., 'The people and the state in early Rome', in A. Brown and J. Griffiths (eds), *The Citizen: Past and Present*, 63–91. Auckland: Massey University Press, 2017.

Richardson, J. H., 'The Roman nobility, the early consular Fasti, and the consular tribunate', in J. Armstrong and J. H. Richardson (eds), *Politics and Power in Early Rome 509–264 BC*, 77–100. *Antichthon* special issue 51, Cambridge: Cambridge University Press, 2017.

Richardson, J. H., 'Rome's treaties with Carthage: jigsaw or variant traditions?', in C. Deroux (ed.), *Studies in Latin Literature and Roman History XIV*, 84–94. Brussels: Latomus, 2008.

Richardson, J. H. and F. Santangelo (eds), *The Roman Historical Tradition: Regal and Republican Rome*, Oxford: Oxford University Press, 2014.

Ridgway, D., 'Demaratus and his predecessors', in G. Kopcke and I. Tokumaru (eds), *Greece between East and West: 10th–8th Centuries* BC, 85–92. Mainz: Philipp von Zabern, 1992.

Ridgway, D. and F. R. Ridgway, 'Demaratus and the archaeologists', in R. D. De Puma and J. P. Small (eds), 6–15. *Murlo and the Etruscans*, Madison: University of Wisconsin Press, 1994.

Ridgway, D., *The First Western Greeks*, Cambridge: Cambridge University Press, 1992.

Ridgway, D., F. R. Serra Ridgway, M. Pearce, E. Herring, R. D. Whitehouse, J. B. Wilkins (eds), *Ancient Italy in its Mediterranean Setting: Studies in Honour of Ellen Macnamara*. Accordia Specialist Studies on the Mediterranean 4, London: Accordia, 2000.

Ridley, R., 'The enigma of Servius Tullius', in J. H. Richardson and F. Santangelo (eds), *The Roman Historical Tradition: Regal and Republican Rome*, 83–128. Oxford: Oxford University Press, 2014. Reprint of Ridley, R., 'The enigma of Servius Tullius', *Klio* 57 (1975), 147–77.

Ridley, R., 'Lars Porsenna and the early Roman Republic', in J. Armstrong and J. H. Richardson (eds), *Politics and Power in Early Rome 509–264* BC, 33–58. *Antichthon* special issue 51, Cambridge: Cambridge University Press, 2017.

Rieger, M., *Tribus und Stadt: die Entstehung der römischen Wahlbezirke im urbanen und mediterranen Kontext (ca. 750–450 v.Chr.)*, Göttingen: Ruprecht, 2007.

Rigsby, K. J., *Asylia: Territorial Inviolability in the Hellenistic World*, Berkeley: University of California Press, 1996.

Riva, C., *The Urbanisation of Etruria: Funerary Practices and Social Change, 700–600* BC, Cambridge: Cambridge University Press, 2010.

Rix, H., 'Ramnes, Tites, Luceres: noms étrusques ou latins?', *Mélanges de l'École française de Rome – Antiquité* 118.1 (2006), 167–75.

Rodriguez-Mayorgas, A., 'Romulus, Aeneas and the cultural memory of the Roman Republic', *Athenaeum* 98 (2010), 89–109.

Roller, M., *Models from the Past in Roman Culture: A World of Exempla*, Cambridge: Cambridge University Press, 2018.

Roma medio repubblicana: aspetti culturali di Roma e del Lazio nei secoli IV e III a.C., exhibition catalogue, Rome: 'L'Erma' di Bretschneider, 1973.

Roncaglia, C., *Northern Italy in the Roman World*, Baltimore: Johns Hopkins University Press, 2018.

Roscher, W. H., *Ausführliches Lexikon der griechischen und römischen Mythologie*, vol. 1, Leipzig: Teubner, 1881–90.

Rose, H. J., *Handbook of Greek Mythology*, London; New York: Routledge, 2004.

Rose, P. W., *Class in Archaic Greece*, Cambridge: Cambridge University Press, 2012.

Roselaar, S. T., 'Colonies and processes of integration in the Roman Republic', *Mélanges de l'École française de Rome – Antiquité* 123.2 (2011), 527–55.

Roselaar, S. T., 'The concept of *commercium* in the Roman Republic', *Phoenix* 66.3/4 (2012), 381–413.

Rosenstein, N. S., 'Aristocrats and agriculture in the middle and late Republic', *Journal of Roman Studies* 98 (2008), 1–26.

Rosenstein, N. S., *Imperatores Victi: Military Defeat and Aristocratic Competition in the Middle and Late Republic*, Berkeley; Los Angeles: University of California Press, 1990.

Rosenstein, N. S., 'Phalanges in Rome?', in G. Fagan and M. Trundle (eds), *New Perspectives on Ancient Warfare*, 289–303. Leiden; Boston: Brill, 2010.

Rosenstein, N. S., *Rome and the Mediterranean 290 to 146 BC: The Imperial Republic*, Edinburgh: Edinburgh University Press, 2012.

Rosenstein, N. S., *Rome at War: Farms, Families, and Death in the Middle Republic*, Chapel Hill: University of North Carolina Press, 2004.

Ross Holloway, R. *The Archaeology of Early Rome and Latium*, London; New York: Routledge, 1994.

Ross Taylor, L., *Roman Voting Assemblies from the Hannibalic War to the Dictatorship of Caesar*, Ann Arbor: University of Michigan Press, 1966.

Rüpke, J., *Fasti Sacerdotum: A Prosopography of Pagan, Jewish, and Christian Religious Officials in the City of Rome, 300 BC to AD 499*, Oxford: Oxford University Press, 2008.

Rüpke, J., *Pantheon: A New History of Roman Religion*, Princeton: Princeton University Press, 2018.

Rüpke, J., *The Roman Calendar from Numa to Constantine* (trans. D. M. B. Richardson), Boston: Wiley-Blackwell, 2011.

Rüpke, J., 'Triumphator and ancestor rituals: between symbolic anthropology and magic', *Numen* 53 (2006), 251–89.

Rutledge, S., *Ancient Rome as a Museum: Power, Identity, and the Culture of Collecting*, Oxford: Oxford University Press, 2012.

Sahlins, M. and D. Graeber, *On Kings*, London: Hau Press, 2017.

Salmon, E. T., *The Making of Roman Italy*, London: Thames and Hudson, 1981.

Salmon, E. T., *Roman Colonization under the Republic*, London: Thames and Hudson, 1969.

Salmon, E. T., *Samnium and the Samnites*, Cambridge: Cambridge University Press, 1967.

Sanchez, P., 'Le fragment de L. Cincius (Festus p. 276 L) et le commandement des armées du Latium', *Cahiers Glotz* 25 (2014), 7–48.

Sannibale, M. 'Gli ori della Tomba Regolini-Galassi: tra tecnologie e simbolo. Nuove proposte di lettura nel quadro del fenomeno orientalizzante in Etruria', *Mélanges de l'École française de Rome – Antiquité* 120.2 (2008), 337–67.

Sannibale, M., 'Orientalizing Etruria', in J. M. Turfa (ed.), *The Etruscan World*, 99–133. London: Routledge, 2013.

Santoro, P. (ed.), *I Galli e l'Italia*, exhibition catalogue, Rome: Soprintendenza archeologica di Roma, 1978.

Scapini, M., 'Literary archetypes for the regal period', in B. Mineo (ed.), *A Companion to Livy*, 274–85. Oxford: Blackwell, 2014.

Scapini, M., *Temi greci e citazioni da Erodoto nelle storie di Roma arcaica*. Studia Classica et Mediaevalia 4, Nordhausen: Verlag Traugott Bautz, 2011.

Scheid, J., *An Introduction to Roman Religion*, Edinburgh: Edinburgh University Press, 2003. Trans. of *La religion des Romains*, Paris: Armand Colin, Coll. Cursus, 1998.

Scheidel, W., 'Republics between hegemony and empire: how ancient city-states built empires and the USA doesn't (anymore)', *Princeton/Stanford Working Papers in Classics* (2006), 1–16.

Schiappelli, A., 'Veii in the protohistoric period: a topographical and territorial analysis', in R. Cascino, H. Di Giuseppe and H. L. Patterson (eds), *Veii: The Historical Topography of the Ancient City. A Restudy of John Ward-Perkins's Survey*, 327–36. Archaeological Monographs of the British School at Rome 19, London: British School at Rome, 2012.

Schmitz, P., 'The Phoenician text from the Etruscan sanctuary at Pyrgi', *Journal of the American Oriental Society* 115.4 (1995), 559–75.

Schneider, D. M. and K. Gough (eds), *Matrilineal Kinship*, Berkeley: University of California Press, 1961.

Schultz, C., *Women's Religious Activity in the Roman Republic*, Chapel Hill: University of North Carolina Press, 2006.

Schultze, C., 'Authority, originality and competence in the Roman Archaeology of Dionysius of Halicarnassus', *Histos* 4 (2000): https://research.ncl.ac.uk/histos/Histos_BackIssues2000.html.

Sciacca, F., 'La circolazione dei doni nell'aristocrazia tirrenica: esempi dall'archeologia', *Revista d'Arqueologia de Ponent* 16–17 (2006–7), 281–92.

Sciacca, F., *Patere baccellate in bronzo: Oriente, Grecia ed Italia in età orientalizzante*, Rome: 'L'Erma' di Bretschneider, 2005.

Scopacasa, R., *Ancient Samnium: Settlement, Culture and Identity between History and Archaeology*, Oxford: Oxford University Press, 2015.

Sekunda, N. and S. Northwood, *Early Roman Armies*, London: Osprey, 1995.

Serrati, J., 'Neptune's altars: the treaties between Rome and Carthage (509–226 B.C.)', *Classical Quarterly* 56 (2006), 113–34.

Sewell, J., 'Gellius, Philip II and a proposed end to the "model-replica" debate', in T. D. Stek and J. Pelgrom (eds), *Roman Republican Colonization: New Perspectives from Archaeology and Ancient History*, 125–39. Rome: Palombi, 2014.

Shepherd, G., 'Fibulae and females: intermarriage in the Western Greek colonies and the evidence from cemeteries', in G. R. Tsetskhladze (ed.), 267–300. *Ancient Greeks West and East*, Leiden: Brill, 1999.

Sherratt, S. and A. Sherratt, 'The growth of the Mediterranean economy in the early first millennium BC', *World Archaeology* 24.3 (1993), 361–78.

Sherwin-White, A. N., *The Roman Citizenship*, 2nd edn, Oxford: Clarendon Press, 1973.

Skutsch, O., *The Annals of Quintus Ennius*, Oxford: Oxford University Press, 1985.

Smith, C. J., 'Ager Romanus antiquus', *Archeologia Classica* 68, n.s. II.7 (2017), 1–26.

Smith, C. J., 'The beginnings of urbanization in Rome', in R. J. Osborne and B. Cunliffe (eds), *Mediterranean Urbanization 800-600 B.C.*, 91–111. Oxford: Oxford University Press, 2005.

Smith, C. J., *Early Rome and Latium: Economy and Society, c.1000 to 500 BC*, Oxford: Oxford University Press, 1996.

Smith, C. J., *The Etruscans: A Very Short Introduction*, Oxford: Oxford University Press, 2014.

Smith, C. J., 'The Latins: historical perspective', in M. Aberson, M. C. Biella, M. Di Fazio and M. Wullschleger (eds), *Entre Archeologie et histoire: dialogues sur divers peuples de L'Italie préromaine*, 21–31. Bern: Peter Lang, 2014.

Smith, C. J., 'Latium and the Latins: the hinterland of Rome', in G. Bradley, E. Isayev and C. Riva (eds), *Ancient Italy: Regions without Boundaries*, 161–78. Exeter: University of Exeter Press, 2007.

Smith, C. J., 'The magistrates of the early Roman Republic', in H. Beck, A. Duplá, M. Jehne and F. Pina Polo (eds), *Consuls and Res Publica: Holding High Office in the Roman Republic*, 19–40. Cambridge: Cambridge University Press, 2011.

Smith, C. J., 'Pliny the Elder on early Rome', in E. Bispham and G. Rowe (eds), *Vita vigilia est: Essays in Honour of Barbara Levick*, 147–70. London: Institute of Classical Studies, 2007.

Smith, C. J., *The Roman Clan: The Gens from Ancient Ideology to Modern Anthropology*, Cambridge: Cambridge University Press, 2006.

Smith, C. J., 'Thinking about kings', *Bulletin of the Institute of Classical Studies* 54.2 (2011), 21–42.

Smith, C. J. and K. Sandberg (eds), *Omnium annalium monumenta: Historical Writing and Historical Evidence in Republican Rome*. Leiden; Boston: Brill, 2017.

Smith, C. J. and L. M. Yarrow, 'Introduction', in C. J. Smith and L. M. Yarrow (eds), *Imperialism, Cultural Politics, and Polybius*, 1–14. Oxford: Oxford University Press, 2012.

Smith, M., 'V. Gordon Childe and the urban revolution: a historical perspective on a revolution in urban studies', *Town Planning Review* 80 (2009), 3–29.

Snodgrass, A. M., 'The hoplite reform and history', *Journal of Hellenic Studies* 85 (1965), 110–22.

Spaeth, B. S., *The Roman Goddess Ceres*, Austin: University of Texas Press, 1996.

Spivey, N., *Etruscan Art*, London: Thames and Hudson, 1997.

Squire, M., *The Iliad in a Nutshell: Visualizing Epic on the Tabulae Iliacae*, Oxford: Oxford University Press, 2011.

Stadter, P. A., *Plutarch and his Roman Readers*, Oxford: Oxford University Press, 2015.

Stamper, J. W., *The Architecture of Roman Temples: The Republic to the Middle Empire*, Cambridge: Cambridge University Press, 2005.

Stamper, J. W., 'The temple of Capitoline Jupiter in Rome: a new reconstruction', *Hephaestos* 16–17 (1998–9), 107–38.

Stary, P., 'Early Iron Age armament and warfare', in D. Ridgway, F. R. Serra Ridgway, M. Pearce, E. Herring, R. D. Whitehouse and J. B. Wilkins (eds), *Ancient Italy in its Mediterranean Setting: Studies in Honour of Ellen Macnamara*, 209–20. London: Accordia, 2000.

Steinby, C., *The Roman Republican Navy: From the Sixth Century to 167 B.C.* Helsinki: Societas Scientiarum Fennica, 2007.

Steingraber, S., *Abundance of Life: Etruscan Wall Painting*, Los Angeles: J. Paul Getty Museum, 2006.

Stek, T., 'The impact of Roman expansion and colonization on ancient Italy in the Republican period: from diffusionism to networks of opportunity', in G. D. Farney and G. Bradley (eds), *The Peoples of Ancient Italy*, 269–94. Berlin: De Gruyter, 2017.

Stewart, R., *Plautus and Roman Slavery*, Malden, MA; Oxford: Wiley-Blackwell, 2012.

Stibbe, C. M., *Lapis Satricanus: Archaeological, Epigraphical, Linguistic and Historical Aspects of the New Inscription from Satricum*, Rome: Staatsuitgeverij, 1980.

Stoddart, S. and J. Whitley, 'The social context of literacy in Archaic Greece and Etruria', *Antiquity* 62 (1988), 761–72.

Stopponi, S., 'Orvieto, Campo della Fiera', in J. M. Turfa (ed.), *The Etruscan World*, 632–54. London; New York: Routledge, 2013.

Strasburger, H., *Zur Sage von der Gründung Roms*. Sitzungsberichte der Heidelberger Akademie der Wissenschaften, phil.-hist. Kl. 1968.5, Heidelberg.

Syed, Y., *Vergil's Aeneid and the Roman Self*, Ann Arbor: University of Michigan Press, 2005.

Tabolli, J. and O. Cerasuolo (eds), *Veii. Cities of the Etruscans*, Austin: University of Texas Press, 2019.

Tagliamonte, G., 'The Samnites', in G. D. Farney and G. Bradley (eds), *The Peoples of Ancient Italy*, 419–46. Berlin; Boston: De Gruyter, 2017.

Tagliamonte, G., *I Sanniti: Caudini, Irpini, Pentri, Carricini, Frentani*, Milan: Longanesi, 1997.

Tandy, D. W., *Warriors into Traders: The Power of the Market in Early Greece*, Berkeley; London: University of California Press, 1997.

Taylor, L. R., *The Voting Districts of the Roman Republic: The Thirty-five Urban and Rural Tribes*, Rome: American Academy in Rome, 1960.

Termeer, M. K., 'Early colonies in Latium (ca 534–338 BC): a reconsideration of current images and the archaeological evidence', *Bulletin Antieke Beschaving* 85 (2010), 43–58.

Terrenato, N., 'The clans and the peasants: reflections on social structure and change in Hellenistic central Italy', in P. Van Dommelen and N. Terrenato (eds), *Articulating Local Cultures: Power and Identity under the Expanding Roman Republic*, 13–22. Journal of Roman Archaeology Supplement 63, Portsmouth, RI: Journal of Roman Archaeology, 2007.

Terrenato, N., *The Early Roman Expansion into Italy: Elite Negotiation and Family Agendas*, Cambridge: Cambridge University Press, 2019.

Terrenato, N., 'The versatile clans: archaic Rome and the nature of early city states in central Italy', in N. Terrenato and D. C. Haggis (eds), *State Formation in Italy and Greece: Questioning the Neoevolutionist Paradigm*, 231–44. Oxford: Oxbow, 2011.

Thein, A., 'Capitoline Jupiter and the historiography of Roman world rule', *Histos* 8 (2014), 284–319.

Thomas, R., *Oral Tradition and Written Record in Classical Athens*, Cambridge: Cambridge University Press, 1989.

Thomsen, R., *King Servius Tullius: A Historical Synthesis*, Copenhagen: Gyldendal, 1980.

Torelli, M., '*Ara Maxima Herculis*: storia di un monumento', *Mélanges de l'École française de Rome – Antiquité* 118.2 (2006), 573–620.

Torelli, M., 'Gli aromi e il sale: Afrodite ed Eracle nell'emporia arcaica dell'Italia', in A. Mastrocinque (ed.), *Ercole in occidente*, 91–117. Trento: Dipartimento di Scienze Filologiche e Storiche, Universita degli Studi di Trento, 1993.

Torelli, M., 'Colonizazzioni etrusche e latine di eta arcaica', in *Gli Etruschi e Roma: Atti dell'incontro di studio in onore di Massimo Pallottino, Roma 11–13 dicembre 1979*, 71–82. Rome: Bretschneider, 1981.

Torelli, M., 'Dalle aristocrazie gentilizie alla nascita della plebe', in A. Momigliano and A. Schiavone (eds), *Storia di Roma* I: *Roma in Italia*, 241–61. Turin: Einaudi,1988.

Torelli, M., *Elogia Tarquiniensia,* Florence: Sansoni, 1975.
Torelli, M. (ed), *The Etruscans,* London: Thames and Hudson, 2001.
Torelli, M., *Lavinio e Roma: riti iniziatrici e matrimonio tra archeologia e storia,* Rome: Quasar, 1984.
Torelli, M., 'Le popolazioni dell'Italia antica: società e forme del potere', in A. Momigliano and A. Schiavone (eds) *Storia di Roma* I: *Roma in Italia,* 53–74. Turin: Einaudi, 1988.
Torelli, M., *Storia degli Etruschi,* Rome; Bari: Laterza, 1981.
Torelli, M., 'The topography and archaeology of Republican Rome', in N. Rosenstein and R. Morstein-Marx (eds), *A Companion to the Roman Republic,* 81–101. Oxford: Blackwell, 2006.
Torelli, M., *Tota Italia: Essays in the Cultural Formation of Roman Italy,* Oxford: Clarendon Press, 1999.
Tuck, S., 'The Tiber and river transport', in P. Erdkamp (ed.), *The Cambridge Companion to Ancient Rome,* 229–45. Cambridge: Cambridge University Press, 2013.
Turfa, J. M. (ed.), *The Etruscan World,* London; New York: Routledge, 2013.
Turfa, J. M. and A. G. Steinmayer Jr, 'Interpreting early Etruscan structures: the question of Murlo', *Papers of the British School at Rome* 70 (2002), 1–28.
Vaahtera, J., 'Livy and the priestly records: à propos ILS 9338', *Hermes* 130 (2002), 100–8.
Van Berchem, D., 'Hercule–Melqart à l'Ara Maxima', *Rendiconti della Pontificia Accademia Romana di Archeologia,* series 3, 32 (1959–60), 61–8.
Van Berchem, D., 'Sanctuaires d'Hercule–Melqart. III, Rome', *Syria* 44 (1967), 307–38.
Van Nuffelen, P., 'Varro's Divine Antiquities', *Classical Philology* 105 (2010), 162–88.
Van Wees, H., *Greek Warfare: Myths and Realities,* London: Bloomsbury, 2004.
Van Wees, H., 'The economy', in K. Raaflaub and H. van Wees (eds), *A Companion to Archaic Greece,* 444–67. Oxford: Wiley-Blackwell, 2009.
Vasaly, A., *Livy's Political Philosophy: Power and Personality in Early Rome,* Cambridge: Cambridge University Press, 2015.
Versnel, H. S., 'Red (herring?): Comments on a new theory concerning the origin of the triumph', *Numen* 53 (2006), 290–326.
Versnel, H. S., *Triumphus: An Inquiry into the Origin, Development and Meaning of the Roman Triumph,* Leiden: Brill, 1970.
Viglietti, C., *Il limite del bisogno: antropologia economica di Roma arcaica,* Bologna: Il Mulino, 2011.
Vlassopoulos, K., *Unthinking the Greek Polis: Ancient Greek History beyond Eurocentrism,* Cambridge; New York: Cambridge University Press, 2007.
Walbank, F. W., *Polybius, Rome and the Hellenistic World: Essays and Reflections,* Cambridge: Cambridge University Press, 2002.
Walbank, F. W., A. E. Astin, M. W. Frederiksen and R. M. Ogilvie (eds), *The Cambridge Ancient History* 7.2: *The Rise of Rome to 220 BC,* 2nd edn, Cambridge: Cambridge University Press, 1989.
Wallace-Hadrill, A., '*Mutatas formas*: the Augustan transformation of Roman knowledge', in K. Galinsky (ed.), *The Cambridge Companion to the Age of Augustus,* 55–84. Cambridge: Cambridge University Press, 2005.
Warmington E. H., *Remains of Old Latin,* vol. 2: *Livius Andronicus, Naevius, Pacuvius, Accius.* Loeb Classical Library, Cambridge, MA: Harvard University Press, 1936.

Warmington E. H., *Remains of Old Latin*, vol. 3: *Lucilius, the Twelve Tables*. Loeb Classical Library, Cambridge, MA: Harvard University Press, 1938.

Warmington, E. H., *Remains of Old Latin*, vol. 4: *Archaic Inscriptions*. Loeb Classical Library, Cambridge, MA: Harvard University Press, 1940.

West, M. L., *The East Face of Helicon: West Asiatic Elements in Greek Poetry*, Oxford: Oxford University Press, 1997.

Westbrook, R., 'The nature and origins of the Twelve Tables', *Zeitschrift der Savigny-Stiftung für Rechtsgeschichte: Romanistische Abteilung*, 105 (1988), 74–121.

Whitley, J., *The Archaeology of Ancient Greece*, Cambridge: Cambridge University Press, 2001.

Williams, J. H. C., *Beyond the Rubicon: Romans and Gauls in Republican Italy*, Oxford: Oxford University Press, 2001.

Winter, N., *Symbols of Wealth and Power: Architectural Terracotta Decoration in Etruria and Central Italy, 640–510 B.C.*, Ann Arbor: University of Michigan Press, 2009.

Winther, H. C., 'Princely tombs of the Orientalizing period in Etruria and Latium Vetus', in H. Damgaard Andersen, H. W. Horsnæs, S. Houby-Nielsen and A. Rathje (eds), *Urbanization in the Mediterranean in the Ninth to Sixth Centuries BC*, 423–46. Copenhagen: Museum Tusculanum Press, 1997.

Wiseman T. P., *Clio's Cosmetics: Three Studies in Greco-Roman Literature*, Leicester: Leicester University Press, 1979.

Wiseman, T. P., 'The house of Tarquin', in *Unwritten Rome*, 271–92. Exeter: University of Exeter Press, 2008.

Wiseman, T. P., *The House of Augustus: A Historical Detective Story*, Princeton: Princeton University Press, 2019.

Wiseman, T. P., *The Myths of Rome*, Exeter: University of Exeter Press, 2004.

Wiseman, T. P., 'The prehistory of Roman historiography', in J. Marincola (ed.), *The Blackwell Companion to Greek and Roman Historiography*, 67–75. Oxford: Blackwell, 2007. Reprinted in T. P. Wiseman, *Unwritten Rome*, 231–42. Exeter: University of Exeter Press, 2008.

Wiseman, T. P., *Remembering the Roman People: Essays on Late-Republican Politics and Literature*, Oxford; New York: Oxford University Press, 2009.

Wiseman, T. P., *Remus: A Roman Myth*, Cambridge: Cambridge University Press, 1995.

Wiseman, T. P., *Roman Drama and Roman History*, Exeter: University of Exeter Press, 1998.

Wiseman, T. P., 'Roman legend and oral tradition', *Journal of Roman Studies* 79 (1989), 129–37.

Wiseman, T. P., 'Roman Republic, year one', *Greece and Rome* 45 (1998), 19–26.

Wiseman, T. P., *Unwritten Rome*, Exeter: University of Exeter Press, 2008.

Woolf, G., 'Moving peoples in the early Roman Empire', in L. de Ligt and L. E. Tacoma (eds), *Migration and Mobility in the Early Roman Empire*, 438–62. Leiden: Brill, 2016.

Xella, P. and V. Bellelli (eds), *Le lamine di Pyrgi: nuovi studi sulle iscrizioni in etrusco e in fenicio nel cinquantenario della scoperta*. Studi epigrafici e lingustici sul Vicino Oriente antico 32–3, Verona: Essedue, 2016.

Yaron, R., 'Semitic influence in early Rome', in A. Watson (ed.) *Daube noster: Essays in Legal History for David Daube*, 343–57. Edinburgh: Scottish Academic Press, 1974.

Yntema, D., 'Material culture and plural identity in early Roman southern Italy', in T. Derks and N. Roymans (eds), *Ethnic Constructs in Antiquity: The Role of Power and Tradition*, 144–66. Amsterdam Archaeological Studies 13, Amsterdam: Amsterdam University Press, 2009.

Zair, N., 'The languages of ancient Italy', in G. D. Farney and G. Bradley (eds), *The Peoples of Ancient Italy*, 127–48. Boston: De Gruyter, 2017.

Zevi, F., 'Demaratus and the "Corinthian" kings of Rome', in J. H. Richardson and F. Santangelo (eds), *The Roman Historical Tradition: Regal and Republican Rome*, 53–82. Oxford: Oxford University Press, 2014. Trans. of 'Demarato e i re "corinzi" di Roma', in A. Storchi Marino (ed.), *L'incidenza dell'antico: studi in memoria di Ettore Lepore*, vol. 1, 291–314. Naples: Luciano, 1995.

Zevi, F., 'Roma arcaica e Ostia: una riconsiderazione del problema', in *Damarato: Studi di antichià classica offerti a Paola Pelagatti*, 233–43. Milan: Electa, 2000.

Ziółkowski, A., 'The Servian enceinte: should the debate continue?', *Palamedes* 11 (2016), 151–70.

Zorzetti, N., 'The Carmina Convivalia', in O. Murray (ed.), *Sympotica: A Symposium on the Symposion*, 289–307. Oxford: Oxford University Press, 1990.

Index

Individual Romans are listed under their *gens*, except for writers, who are listed under the form normally used in English. Dates of offices are given only where necessary to distinguish homonyms.

Acquarossa, 66, 158, 160, 184, 240
Adriatic coast, 40, 83, 271, 296, 311–12
aediles, 13, 97, 254, 260, 337, 340, 346, 358
Aeneas, 82–90, 97, 98, 99, 100, 101, 233
Aequi, 252, 280–3, 291, 292, 304, 314, 315, 330
Ager Gallicus, 299, 311, 317
agriculture, 192–7, 202, 257, 293, 354
Alba Fucens, 317, 318, 343
Alba Longa, 83, 99, 100, 135, 274
Alban Hills, 33, 43, 300
Alban kings, 12, 100
Alban Mount, 39, 173, 233, 272, 359
Alcibiades, 346
Alcimus of Sicily, 16, 85, 97
Alexander of Epirus, 308
Alexander the Great, 206, 308, 352
Allia, 296, 297, 298
alphabet, 61–3, 78, 119
Ambarvalia, 274, 359
Ampolo, Carmine, 131, 151, 154, 224

Ancus Marcius, 112, 120, 139, 174, 205, 235, 275, 278
Annales Maximi, 8, 10–13, 31
antiquarian sources, 4, 22, 23–4, 46, 129, 137, 195, 197, 217, 238, 265, 279
Antium, 77, 180, 204, 206, 277, 278, 280, 281, 289, 302, 303, 316, 344, 355
Aqua Appia, 339, 343
Aquilonia, 310
Ara Maxima, 83, 161, 230, 235, 357, 358
architectural terracottas, 25, 53, 81, 123, 156–60, 162–6, 168, 182, 184–5, 199, 200, 206, 221, 224–5, 244, 266, 360–1
  Rome-Veii-Velitrae series, 162, 184–5, 199, 224, 225
Ardea, 38, 39, 46, 47, 77, 124, 180, 252–3, 275, 277, 278, 289, 303
Aristodemus of Cumae, 116, 134, 292
Aristonothos krater, 232
Aristotle, 16, 85, 298, 352
army, Roman, 106, 127, 193, 210, 213, 237, 244–5, 251, 278, 280, 294, 298, 307, 308, 310, 318, 320–1, 324–9, 354, 364

Artemis, temple at Ephesus, 183, 273
asylum, 104, 107, 273
Athens, 72, 125, 171, 173, 191, 199, 203, 218, 238, 254, 256, 260, 290, 321, 323, 327, 345, 357, 361
Atrium Vestae, 136, 146
Attus Clausus *see* Claudius, Appius
Attus Naevius, 105
auctoritas patrum, 242
Auditorium villa, 25, 194, 195–6
Augustus, emperor, 20, 85, 104
Aurunci, 283
auspices (*auspicia*), 114, 242, 355, 358
Aventine, archaic laws, 8, 9
Aventine hill, 9, 91, 107, 139, 174, 175, 176, 183, 184, 248, 258, 273, 295

banquet songs, 4–5, 31, 32
banqueting, 43, 53, 54, 57, 69, 106, 162, 194, 221, 222, 224–5, 229, 230, 361
Beloch, Karl Julius, 210, 212, 303
Bologna (Felsina), 36, 40, 94, 270
Bonghi Jovino, Maria, 180
Boni, Giacomo, 24–5, 26, 142, 152, 160
Brutus *see* Junius Brutus
burials *see* funerary culture

cabotage, 77, 205
Caere (Cerveteri), 43, 44, 55, 56–7, 67, 69, 72, 76, 77, 85, 112, 135, 136, 163, 207, 212, 213, 221–2, 268, 269, 297, 309, 310, 315, 353
calendar, 8, 9, 13, 87, 90, 112, 133, 193, 194, 203, 229, 257, 298, 329, 340, 346, 354, 355–6, 358

Camillus *see* Furius Camillus
Campania, Campanians, 26, 39, 40, 43, 51, 53, 55, 63, 70, 77, 79n, 158, 160, 180, 199, 201, 236, 265, 268–70, 271, 280, 290–2, 301–3, 306, 307–8, 312, 316, 317, 332, 343, 350
Capitoline hill, 141, 150, 183
Capitoline temple *see* temples
Capitoline triad, 154, 167, 254, 355, 357
Capua, 40, 43, 55, 84, 99, 112, 180, 252, 268–70, 280, 290–1, 301–3, 317, 343, 362–3
Capys (founder of Capua), 84, 99, 112, 291
Carafa, Paolo, 25, 26, 154
Carandini, Andrea, 101–2, 108, 145, 146, 148, 150
Carmenta, Carmentalia, 87, 90, 235
Carthage, 9, 10, 16, 27, 29, 32, 49, 51, 77, 83, 203, 206, 232, 236, 277–8, 301, 309
Cassius Dio, 22
Cassius, Spurius, 9, 279, 338
Cato, M. Porcius (the Elder), 11, 18, 31, 129, 228, 229, 268, 270, 278–9
Caudine Forks, 308
cavalry, 105–6, 128, 245, 326
  allied, 323–4
censors, 13, 14, 18, 211, 317, 319, 326, 335, 337, 339, 343, 348, 354
census, 13, 130–1, 210–14, 256, 362
centuriate assembly *see comitia centuriata*
centuriate system, 108, 127–31, 133, 180, 211, 213, 215, 217, 237, 239, 242, 244

Ceres, 249, 256, 257; *see also* temples
Ceres, priestess of, 90
chronology, 25, 100–2, 109–12, 123–4, 133–4, 138, 238, 277–8, 365–6
Cifani, Gabriele, 171
Circeii, 77, 83, 85, 277, 278, 289, 302, 303
Circus Maximus, 183, 186, 239, 362
cities, comparative sizes, 180–2; *see also* urbanisation
city walls, 149–50, 174–82, 212–13, 294, 297, 316–17, 362
Civitalba, 310
clans, 3–4, 6, 44–6, 214, 215, 239–42, 246, 257, 283–7; *see also* elites
Claudius Caecus, Appius (censor 312), 5, 317, 319, 339–40, 343, 354
Claudius, Appius (consul 495), 213, 219, 242, 251, 274, 285
Claudius, Appius (decemvir 450), 248, 254–5, 258
Claudius, emperor, 120–4, 266
clay beds (Velabrum) 66, 139, 154–5, 160, 199
Cleisthenes, 128, 290
clients, *clientela* (patronage), 105, 120, 213, 214, 218–20, 257, 285–6
Cloaca Maxima, 132, 186, 282, 362
Cloelia, 134, 225–6
Coarelli, Filippo, 78, 187, 211, 214, 281
coinage, Italian, 266, 352
coinage, Roman, 97, 128–9, 194–5, 209–10, 234, 338, 352–3

collective memory, 13, 16, 103, 117, 262, 348, 355
colonies, colonisation, 15, 195, 206, 218, 252–3, 261, 270–1, 287–90, 300, 301, 302, 305, 311–12, 314, 315–20, 324
colonies, Etruscan, 270–1
colonies, Latin, 261, 280, 287–90, 300, 302, 315–20, 344
colonies, Roman, 316
Colonna, Giovanni, 63, 68, 86, 143, 154
comitia centuriata, 106, 127–31, 133, 237, 211, 239, 242
comitia curiata, 106, 114–15, 237, 242
comitia tributa, 133, 136, 237
Comitium, 151–2, 154, 156, 183, 344
commercium, 273, 303
concilium plebis, 248, 254, 261, 341
consular tribunes, 14, 237, 259
consulship, 3, 94, 107, 127, 242, 259, 260, 337–8, 364
conubium, 273, 303
Corinth, 7, 27, 49, 66, 71, 72, 74, 109, 111, 118, 162, 186, 191, 197, 199, 203, 208, 238
Coriolanus *see* Marcius Coriolanus
Cornelius Scipio Africanus, P., 324
Cornelius Scipio Barbatus, L., 348–9, 350
Cornell, Tim, 8, 108, 123, 124
Corsica, 300
Coruncianus, T., 338
cremation *see* funerary culture
Cremera, 285–6, 294
crisis, fifth century, 212, 290–2
cults, female participation, 230, 258, 358

cults, plebeian, 249, 254, 258, 260, 339, 345, 352
Cumae, 51, 64, 137, 158, 160, 199, 203, 269, 290, 291, 292, 303
Cumaean Chronicle, 112, 134
Curia Hostilia *see* Senate house
curiae, 105–9, 130, 344
Curius Dentatus, Manius, 311, 314, 338, 343

debt, 14, 220, 246, 249, 251, 256–7, 259, 263, 283, 337, 339
debt bondage, 209, 216, 217–18, 220, 256–7, 261, 353
decemviri, 227, 242, 247–8, 254–9, 328
Delian League, 323
Delphi, Delphic Oracle, 271, 310, 346, 352, 353, 359, 361
Demaratus of Corinth, 27, 74, 111, 118–19, 120, 126, 162, 191, 197, 222–3, 231, 258
Demetrius Poliorcetes, 206, 352
demography, population, 210–14, 320
Diana, 183, 278; *see also* temples
Diana, sanctuary at Lake Nemi (Aricia), 272–3, 278–9
dictatorship, 14, 15, 135–7, 328, 349, 364
  Latin, 135, 278–9
Diodorus Siculus, 22, 248, 265, 300, 310, 343
Diomedes, 83
Dionysius of Halicarnassus, 5, 18, 21–2, 23, 82, 86, 90, 91, 103, 105, 108, 111, 112, 127, 167, 206, 219, 228, 239, 241, 246, 251–2, 267, 279, 292, 314–15, 329, 356
Dioscuri (Castor and Pollux), 27, 86, 184, 357; *see also* temples

Domus Regia, 146, 150, 151
drama *see* historical drama
Duris of Samos, 16, 310

economy, 21, 27, 29, 30, 34, 35, 40, 43, 51, 64–5, 129, 192–210, 243, 257, 263, 282, 290, 295, 326–7, 341, 364
elite, elites, 23–4, 30–3, 43, 51–61, 68–9, 70, 80, 124, 135, 143, 187, 190, 197, 215–20, 221–4, 230, 239–45, 251, 260–1, 282, 285, 291, 293, 324, 332, 334–9, 341, 347–50, 358, 363–4
elogia, 4, 6, 112, 268, 348–50
Elogia Tarquiniensia, 6, 112, 268
emporia, 49, 69–78, 86, 124, 161, 204–5, 232, 269, 357, 359
Ennius, 18, 101
Ephesus, 183
Esquiline cemetery, 24, 26, 143–5, 148, 176, 187, 197–8, 207, 218, 224, 350–1, 361
Esquiline hill, 24, 139, 162, 174, 184, 198–9, 201
ethnicity, ethnic identity, 17, 27, 33, 35, 36, 83, 89, 99, 116, 124, 222, 224, 324, 330, 354
  Etruscan, 39, 224, 268
  Latin, 39, 271–3, 293, 359
  Roman, 90, 99, 104, 107, 224, 231–6, 273–4, 295, 359, 362–3
Etruria, Etruscans, 39, 50, 63, 71, 74, 78–9, 89, 107, 233, 265–71, 291, 292, 295, 309–11, 325, 352; *see also* Tyrrhenians
Etruscan epigraphy, 74, 76–7, 124, 218, 222, 231, 240, 235, 269, 270, 291, 293
Etruscan League, 265–8, 271
Etruscan religion, 72–7, 109, 357

Etruscans at Rome, 124, 191, 233, 235–6, 245–6, 361
Evander, 16, 82–3, 84, 87, 89, 90, 98, 103, 161, 233, 234
evocatio, 295, 343, 357
exempla, 20, 31–2, 132, 225–6, 248
exiles, 7, 82, 84, 111, 132, 133, 160, 218, 234, 256, 278, 282, 295, 298

Fabii, 17, 219, 220, 224, 241, 285–6, 287, 294, 338, 340
Fabius Maximus, Q., 337, 340–1, 350
Fabius Pictor, 6, 17, 31, 93, 98, 100, 211, 228
Fabricius, C., 31, 338, 347
fabulae pratextae, 5; see also historical drama
family records, 3–4, 6, 17, 348
Fanum Voltumnae, 218, 233, 266
Fasti, 10, 133, 137, 245, 260, 261, 282, 337
Fasti Antiates Maiores, 355–6
federal cults, Latin, 183–4, 233, 273, 359
Feriae Latinae, 9, 39, 233, 272, 359
festivals, 5, 13, 39, 87, 103, 104, 106, 112, 183, 193, 194, 195, 218, 229, 233, 235, 266, 268, 274, 329, 355–6, 358–9
Festus, 23, 92, 109, 129, 220, 224, 238, 256, 280, 335
Ficoroni cista, 201, 357
Fidenae, 294
Filippi, Dunia, 154, 161
flamines, flaminicae, 229, 355
Flavius, Gnaeus, 340–1, 358
floods, 139–40, 148, 152, 186
Fordicidia, 106, 195
formula togatorum, 323
Fortuna, 117, 163, 183, 184, 343

Forum Boarium, 25, 78, 87, 135, 141, 142, 156, 160–6, 195, 198, 199, 204–5, 207–8, 232, 357, 359, 360, 361, 362; see also temples: Sant'Omobono
Forum, Roman, 24, 25, 26, 139–40, 142, 143, 145, 146–8, 151–5, 156, 158, 186, 210, 330, 344–6
foundation myths, 12, 17, 28, 81–102, 103–8, 234–5, 347
freedmen, freedwomen, 104, 256, 257, 314, 340, 354, 359
Fregellae, 307, 308, 319
funerary culture, 26, 35, 39–43, 44, 50–1, 53–61, 68–9, 142–5, 148, 194, 221–2, 240, 257, 269, 293, 347–50
  female, 51, 57, 61, 221–2, 224, 230
Furius Camillus, M., 31, 101, 220, 261, 294–6, 298, 327, 347

Gabii, 7, 9, 26, 35, 43, 46, 61, 63, 136, 158, 275, 278, 320, 368
Gallic sack of Rome, 12, 16, 206, 296–9, 300, 304, 331
gates, Rome, 149, 150, 184, 186–7, 301, 346
Gellius Egnatius, 309–10
gender, 30, 31, 50–1, 222
genocide, 304, 322, 330
gens, gentes see clans
Giglio shipwreck, 71, 77, 79, 204
grain imports, 203, 212, 282
grave goods, 35, 40, 43, 49, 57, 68, 201, 216, 222, 240, 293; see also funerary culture
Graviscae, 71–3, 74, 77, 78, 124, 205, 232, 261
Greek artists at Rome, 98, 163, 199, 201, 254
  in Italy, 54, 64, 69, 201, 232

Greek influence on Rome and Italy, 47–51, 54–5, 61–4, 66–79, 81–90, 98–9, 108–9, 118–19, 125–6, 129, 132, 161–5, 171–3, 184, 190–1, 199–201, 204–9, 210, 216–18, 232–3, 254, 256, 291–2, 318, 343–8, 350–3, 356–7, 360–2
Greek parallels for events at Rome, 7, 33–4, 183, 249, 250
Greek rites at Rome, 90

Hannibal, 17, 312, 314, 317, 332
Hannibalic War *see* Punic Wars
Hecateus of Miletus, 16, 84
Hellanicus of Lesbos, 16, 84, 87
Heraion of Samos, 171, 191, 361
Hercules, 74, 81, 83, 87, 89, 90, 98, 161, 163–4, 167, 230, 346, 357, 358
Herdonius, Appius, 218, 285
Herodotus, 7, 72
Hersilia, 104, 224, 230
Hesiod, 84, 233
Hispellum, 233
historians, early, 15–19, 83–5
historical drama, 5, 93, 117, 227, 255
historiography, 1–34, 81–102, 103–4, 115–18, 263–5
Horatia, 225
Horatii, 225
Horatius Cocles, 134, 345
houses, 25, 66, 135, 145–6, 187, 188, 199, 283, 332

identity, Roman *see* ethnicity: Roman; self-image, Roman
imperialism, 192, 292, 324–32, 339
infantry, 129, 245, 251, 286, 325–6, 331
   allied, 323–4

intermarriage, 222–4, 255, 257–8, 259, 273, 303; *see also* marriage
interregnum, interrex, 14, 14, 114–15, 242
iteration, 337–8

Janiculum, 174, 248, 260, 286
Janus, 19, 183
Junius Brutus (plebeian leader), 252
Junius Brutus, L. (consul 509), 117, 126, 132–4, 227, 347
Juno, 167, 254, 297, 357; *see also* temples
Juno Regina, 295, 343, 357
Jupiter, 112, 173, 233, 347, 355; *see also* temples
Jupiter Indiges, 27
Jupiter Latiaris, 173, 359

kings, 20, 31, 54, 100, 101, 103–38, 152, 155, 163, 173, 174, 183, 226–7, 235, 244, 267, 274–8, 285, 335, 338
Kleikos, 207, 218, 361, 362

Lake Regillus, 278–80, 356
landholding, 195–7, 241, 259, 260, 261, 273, 282, 288, 295, 303, 312–14, 315, 317, 319, 325, 353
Lapis Niger, 8, 10, 112–13, 208, 357
Lapis Satricanus, 220, 284–5, 287
Latin League, 271–4, 275, 278–80, 288, 301, 303, 315, 316
Latinus, 83, 84, 91, 97, 224, 272
Lavinia, 83, 224, 226
Lavinium, 38, 46, 77, 83, 85, 86–7, 124, 180, 226, 272, 278, 303

laws, legislation, 8, 9, 197, 254–6, 258–9, 260, 261, 334, 336, 337, 339–41, 352, 353
leges regiae, 255
Lex agraria (368 BC), 259–60, 368
Lex agraria (111 BC), 261, 323, 368
Lex Atilia Marcia, 339
Lex Canuleia, 258, 259
Lex Genucia, 260
Lex Hortensia, 260, 341
Lex Licinia, 197, 259–60, 261, 353
Lex Ogulnia, 260, 339
Lex Ovinia, 238, 335–6, 339
Lex Poetelia-Papiria, 217, 218, 261, 353
Lex sacrata (plebeian), 249
Licinio-Sextian laws, 197, 259–61, 353
Valerio-Horatian laws, 258
see also XII Tables
Liber, 184, 199, 345
liber linteus (Etruscan ritual text), 13
libertas, liberty, 217, 345, 338
Licinius, C. (tribune 367), 259–60
Licinius Macer, 13, 18, 19, 135
linen books, 13, 18
literacy, 8–15, 63, 65, 222, 354–5; *see also* alphabet; writing
literary evidence, 1–34, 81–102, 103–4, 109–11, 115–18, 131–5, 197, 237–8, 248–50, 255, 261–2, 263–5, 275–8, 328–9, 334–5, 354–5
and archaeology, 26–7, 33–4, 119, 138, 150–1, 156, 163, 168, 174, 190, 191, 214–15, 224, 238–9, 283, 361–2

Livy, 1, 18, 19–21, 22, 24, 29, 82, 90–1, 120, 127, 132, 133, 134, 135, 211, 217, 242, 248, 252–3, 259, 260, 261–2, 275–6, 279, 282, 285–6, 291, 294, 296, 306, 311, 315, 316
Lucretia, 132, 134, 225, 227, 230
Lulof, Patricia, 163, 184
Lupercal, 90, 139, 359
Lupercalia, 103, 195, 235, 359

Maelius, Sp., 338
Maenius, C., 347
magistracies, 14, 106, 135–6, 137, 219, 237, 239, 245, 254–5, 260, 261, 314, 328, 334, 337, 341
Magna Graecia, 49–51, 137, 173, 180, 209, 216, 238, 254, 256, 260, 291, 292, 334, 344, 346–7
Magna Mater, 203–4
maiores gentes, 242; *see also* clans
Mamertini, 253, 336
Manlius Capitolinus, M., 297, 338
Manlius Torquatus, T., 301, 328–9
Marcius Coriolanus, C., 5, 23, 225, 258, 261, 282–3
marriage, 69, 115, 222–4, 228, 229, 230, 242, 255, 257–8, 259, 373, 306, 355
confarreatio, 228–9, 355
see also intermarriage
Mars, 90, 220, 229, 284, 346, 355
Marsyas, 345
Marzabotto, 270
Massilia, 71, 72, 183–4, 206, 236, 296, 298, 300, 318, 320, 359, 361
Mastarna, 120–3, 126, 136, 213, 285; *see also* Servius Tullius
Mater Matuta, 163, 228, 283, 284
meddices, 291

Mediterranean world, 29, 34, 51–3, 61, 69–79, 81, 83–5, 89, 99, 101–2, 109, 118, 137, 173, 180, 183, 190–1, 192, 201–10, 216, 232, 236, 255, 290, 296, 300–1, 318–19, 325, 359, 360–2, 364
Messana, 253, 336
Metellus, L., 349–50
Metellus, Q., 349–50
Mevania, 309
Minerva, 163, 167, 254, 357; *see also* temples
mobility, 34, 69, 124, 230, 231, 232, 236, 250, 271, 290, 297, 299, 362
  social mobility, 30, 116, 124, 131, 216, 245–54, 282, 287, 364
Momigliano, Arnaldo, 2, 85, 124, 130, 211, 212, 251
Mommsen, Theodor, 2, 250, 317
monarchy *see* kings
monarchy, fall of, 20, 126, 131–7, 237–9, 278
Mura Sommella, Anna, 169, 171
Murlo, 66–7, 68, 158, 184, 240, 360
myth, 28, 81–102, 117, 122, 161–85, 228, 230, 233, 273–4, 345, 357, 360
  Etruscan, 74, 75, 85–6, 123, 265, 268, 270
  Latin, 86–7, 272
myths, aristocratic, 214–15, 241, 244

Narnia, 309
Navalia, 204, 209
Neptune, 203
Nestor, cup of, 84, 88
networks, 34, 39, 51, 78, 119, 137, 230, 232, 271, 285, 290, 306, 356, 361, 363

new men, 4, 338
nexum, *nexi see* debt bondage
Niebuhr, Barthold, 2
nobility *see* elite
nostalgia, 29, 30–1, 32, 335
Numa Pompilius, 23, 110, 112, 115, 120, 125, 183, 198, 235, 355

Odysseus, 83–5
Ogulnii, brothers, 94n, 97, 167
olives, olive oil, 54, 192–4, 195
Olympia, 173, 357
oral tradition, 4–8, 31, 81, 89, 90, 91, 93, 101, 117, 134, 228, 255, 264, 282, 338, 355
Ostia, 205–6, 275, 300, 316

Palatine, 25, 26, 83, 90–1, 139, 142, 143, 146, 148–50, 155, 174, 186, 332, 359
Papirius Cursor, L., 345
pastoralism, 103, 192, 193, 194–5
patres conscripti, 133, 242
patricians, 30, 105, 106, 114, 216, 220, 239–45, 255, 257, 258, 259–61, 335, 337, 340, 358
patronage *see* clients
Penates, 83, 86, 235
Philinus, 309
Philip V of Macedon, 314, 315
Phocaeans, 184, 204, 206
Phoenicians, 47, 49, 50, 54, 61, 77, 124, 161, 232, 362
Pietrabbondante, 345
piracy, 206–7, 209, 308, 352, 362
Pithecusae, 49–51, 63, 64, 69, 70, 78, 84, 158, 199, 222
Plautus, 31, 229
plebeians, 105, 106, 130, 133, 213, 216–18, 219, 239, 242, 243–62, 263, 290, 295, 297, 298, 318, 332, 337–8, 339–41, 345, 352, 353, 363

Polybius, 3, 10, 17, 23, 27, 31, 134, 203, 206, 207, 264, 270, 277–8, 301, 307, 323–4, 326, 330, 335, 336, 339, 348
Pomptine Plain, 281–3, 286
Pontecagnano, 40, 43, 55, 268–9
Pontius, Gaius, 308
Pontius, Herennius, 308
population *see* demography
pottery, 55, 143, 154, 197–8, 205, 207–9, 361
  Apennine, 38, 141
  Attic, 77, 201, 208, 266, 271, 290
  bucchero, 53, 70, 71, 207, 208
  Corinthian, Etrusco-Corinthian, 49, 71, 78, 119, 207
  Euboean, 49, 161, 293
  Genucilia plates, 201
  Mycenaean, 38
  Red figure, 201
Praeneste, 57, 93, 94, 124, 201, 221–2, 234, 280, 282, 303
priesthoods, 13, 39, 87, 90, 106, 107, 114, 133, 225, 229–30, 237–8, 242–3, 257, 260, 267, 273, 274, 287, 297, 298, 337, 339, 355, 357, 358
proconsul, 338
prorogation, 14, 338
Publilius Philo, Q., 338
Punic Wars, 17, 18, 22, 98, 210, 312, 314, 324, 326, 332, 349
Punicum, 77, 205
Pyrgi, 72, 74–7, 78, 124, 205, 232, 311, 316, 361
Pyrgi tablets, 27, 55, 76–7, 135, 277–8
Pythagoras, 5, 346

quaestors, 337
queens, 118, 120, 125, 132, 226–8, 230; *see also* Hersilia; Lavinia; Tanaquil; Tullia
Quirinal hill, 25, 139, 142, 145, 148, 174, 198, 208, 258
Quirinus, 104

Realism, 331–2
Regia, 66, 87, 135–6, 146, 150, 158, 182, 183–5, 187, 199, 227, 357, 360, 361
Regisvilla, 77, 205
religion, 30, 67, 72, 75, 76, 81–2, 86–7, 99, 115, 133, 150, 154, 161, 167, 173, 183, 233, 249, 254, 266, 272–3, 278–9, 295, 331, 343, 345, 352, 354–9
Remus, 7, 31, 81, 85, 88, 90–9, 100, 103, 225
rex sacrorum, 114, 133, 135, 136, 238, 243
Rhea Silvia (Ilia), 90, 225
Rhodes, Rhodians, 309, 352
Rhome (Trojan woman), 84
roads, 141, 150, 186, 187, 208, 255, 270, 293, 311, 317–19, 341, 343; *see also under individual viae*
Robigalia, 194
Romanocentrism, 33, 264
Rome, foundation date, 7, 100–2, 151, 187
Romulus, 7, 8, 17, 31, 81–109, 112, 114, 146, 150–1, 174, 183, 202, 219, 228, 234, 237, 239, 273, 362, 363
Romulus and Remus, statue group *see* wolf and twins
Rostra, 204, 279, 344

Sabine Women, 104, 106, 224, 228, 233, 235, 273–4
Sabines, Sabinum, 7, 63, 89, 104, 107, 120, 167, 195, 207, 208, 218, 224, 231, 235, 239, 246, 285, 292, 311, 314, 315, 327, 338

Sacra Via, 25, 142, 187, 199, 226
Sacred Mount, 246, 248, 252, 258
Salian Virgins, 229, 358
Salii, 107
salt, salt pans, 70, 141, 205, 207, 208, 293–4
Samnites, Samnium, 29, 249, 264, 269, 270, 280, 291, 301–2, 304, 306–11, 316, 319, 323, 325–6, 327, 330, 332–3, 345, 347, 348–50, 352
Sardinia, 39, 49, 70, 77, 97, 236, 277, 300–1, 311, 361
Satricum, 46, 66, 124, 163, 166, 220, 234, 272, 275, 280–4, 287, 330
secession, 216, 245–55, 258, 260, 341, 362–3
self-image, Roman, 27–33, 89–90, 99, 104, 107, 215, 220, 273, 331, 350; *see also* ethnicity: Roman
Senate, 13, 104, 105, 114, 125, 133, 237, 238, 239–40, 241–2, 261, 334–9, 340, 341
Senate house, 158, 199, 226, 239, 340, 344
Senones, 296, 299, 311, 331
Sentinum, 16, 309, 310, 311, 326
Sepulcretum, 24, 142, 146, 148, 160, 187
Servian reforms, 127–31, 180, 209, 286, 325, 364; *see also* centuriate system
Servian walls, 174–82, 212–13, 294, 297, 300, 362
Servius Tullius, 128, 130, 132, 136, 163, 174, 182, 168, 182, 183, 198, 210, 218, 226, 233, 237, 273, 285
Sextius, L. (tribune 367), 259–60
ships, 47, 71, 203–5, 206, 209, 277
Sibylline Books (Oracles), 14, 355

Sicily, Sicilians, 16, 49, 50, 51, 83, 84, 98, 137, 171, 173, 199, 201, 203, 206, 235, 236, 244, 254, 277, 301, 311, 336, 346, 348, 352
Sicinius Dentatus, L., 328
single combat, 301, 305, 328–9, 331
slaves, slavery, 123, 192, 209, 217–18, 255, 256–7, 267, 295, 314, 327, 353–4
Smith, Christopher, 262
social differentiation, 40, 190
society, social institutions in Rome, 214–20
Solon, 129, 256
Sora, 281, 316, 319
Spina, 207, 271
state formation, 46, 65, 80, 155, 190, 241, 354–5, 360
statues, 94–7, 134, 163, 167, 183, 226, 228, 345, 346, 347
Stesichorus, 16, 84, 87, 98, 233
stipendium, 294
Struggle of the Orders, 217, 243–62, 329, 337, 339
Suessa Pometia *see* Satricum
Summanus, 167
synoecism, 155

Tabula Iliaca Capitolina, 84
Tabula Veliterna, 281
Tanaquil, 118, 120, 125, 224, 226–8, 230
Tarentum, 207, 344, 346, 350–2
Tarpeia, 225, 230
Tarquin dynasty, 118, 122, 123, 124–6, 132, 162, 186, 191, 227–8, 235, 257, 355–6
Tarquinii, 6, 43, 69, 72, 74, 118–19, 137, 180, 201, 204, 222, 224, 231, 265, 268, 274, 292, 309, 322, 330, 362

Tarquinius, Sextus, 7, 132, 227
Tarquinius Priscus, L., 27, 105, 110, 111, 115–19, 163, 167, 174, 186, 191, 193, 226, 231, 241, 244, 274, 362
Tarquinius Superbus, L., 7, 110, 124–6, 131–7, 160, 163, 167, 168, 174, 183, 216, 227, 244, 255, 275, 278–9, 281, 283, 320
Tarracina, 77, 281, 283
taxation, 209, 294, 300, 323, 326, 353
temples, Rome, 12, 15, 182–5, 190, 199, 239, 341–3, 357, 358–9
  Castor, 27, 66, 86, 184, 239, 327, 357
  Ceres, Liber and Libera, Aventine, 13, 184, 199, 249, 254, 352
  Diana, Aventine, 8, 9, 183–4, 233, 273, 359
  Dius Fidius, 9, 185, 320
  Jupiter Feretrius, 9, 105, 183, 199
  Jupiter Optimus Maximus, Juno, and Minerva, 24, 27, 123, 133, 136, 156, 167–73, 180, 239, 254, 263, 277, 282, 346, 357, 358, 361
  Mater Matuta, 228; *see also* Sant'Omobono (below)
  Mercury, 10, 184, 198, 203, 275
  Moneta, 13
  Sant'Omobono, 67, 87, 160–6, 183, 184, 361, 362
  Saturn, 184, 239, 357
  Vertumnus, 343
  Vesta, 25, 148, 150, 183, 189, 355
  Victoria, 343
terracottas *see* architectural terracottas
territory, Roman, 212, 214, 274–8, 294, 303, 311, 312–15
tesserae hospitales, 218, 232
Tiber, 24, 78, 90, 138–41, 148, 152, 203–6, 208, 275, 293
Tibur, 93, 234, 278, 303
Timaeus, 16, 17, 85, 86, 100, 212, 352
Titus Tatius, 104, 107, 110, 235
Tolumnii, 9, 293
tomb paintings, 57, 69, 201, 204, 221, 293, 350
tombs
  Bernardini Tomb, 222
  Bocchoris Tomb, 222, 223
  François Tomb, 121–2
  Heroon of Aeneas, Lavinium, 86
  Isis Tomb, 222
  Regolini Galassi Tomb, 57, 221–2
  Tomb AA1, Veii, 43
  Tomb XV, Castel di Decima, 60–1
  Tomb 70, Acqua Acetosa Larentina, 57–60, 224
  Tomb 98, Esquiline, 143
  Tomb 193, Esquiline, 207
  Tomb of the Fabii, 350
  Tomb of the Leopards, 222
  Tomb of the Scipios, 350
  Tomb of the Ship, 204
  Tumulus 2, Caere, 56
  see also funerary culture
topography, of Rome, 138–41
Torelli, Mario, 86, 130, 154, 213, 234
trade, 35, 36, 38, 49, 53, 63, 65, 69–80, 118, 137, 141, 154, 197–210, 269, 270, 271, 277, 290, 293, 301, 361
treaties, 8–9, 13, 134, 308, 320–4, 361
  Cassian Treaty, 9, 273, 279–80, 320

Rome and Massalia, 206, 298n, 300
Rome and the Samnites, 302, 307, 330, 350
Rome-Carthage, 9, 10, 27, 98, 277–8, 281, 301, 309, 311, 362
tribes, Roman, 180, 274, 275, 312–15, 339–40, 354; *see also* territory, Roman
tribunes, 14, 15, 106, 244n, 247–8, 249, 254, 258, 259–60, 337, 339, 352
tributum, 209, 294, 315, 326
Triumph, 3, 10, 15, 31, 183, 186, 235, 264, 310, 328, 330, 345, 349, 358–9
Trojan War, 83, 88, 100–1, 122
Tullia, 125, 132, 226–8, 230
Tullus Hostilius, 112, 115, 158, 174, 274, 275
XII Tables, 9, 14, 194–5, 198, 201, 218, 219, 254–9, 345, 353
tyrants, Greek, 8, 125, 132, 181, 191, 255
Tyrrhenians, 16, 84, 233; *see also* Etruscans

Umbria, Umbrians, 108, 232, 266, 270, 271, 281, 309–11, 318n, 319, 322, 323, 332
Uni, 74, 76, 173, 295, 357; *see also* Juno Regina
urbanisation
  in Etruria and Latium, 39–47, 64–9, 360–1
  Rome, 138–92, 212–13, 341–7, 361–2

Valerius Antias, 18, 19, 249
Valerius Corvus, M., 301, 328–9

Valerius Publicola, P., 116, 132, 284–5, 287–8
values, Roman, 30, 31, 32, 282, 350; *see also* self-image, Roman
Varro, 23, 31, 100, 105, 110, 335, 356
Veii, 27, 43, 44, 57, 78, 86, 88, 96, 119, 123, 163, 176, 214, 218, 219, 220, 224, 234, 235, 256, 267, 285, 297, 300, 309, 310, 312, 315, 342, 357, 361, 363
  sack of, 292–6, 299, 304, 327, 330, 353, 363
  see also architectural terracottas
Velabrum *see* clay beds
Velitrae, 162, 224, 280, 281, 289, 302, 303; *see also* architectural terracottas
Verginia, 227, 248, 255, 258
Vesta, 235; *see also* temples
Vestal Virgins, 39, 90, 225, 229, 238, 257, 355, 358
Vetulonia, 43, 55, 286
Veturia, 225
Via Appia, 210, 270, 314, 317, 319, 339, 343, 352
Via Aurelia, 311, 317
Via Campana, 141, 208
Via Flaminia, 311, 317
Via Salaria, 141, 195, 208, 293
Via Valeria, 317, 343
Vibenna, Aulus, 27, 122–3, 126, 293
Vibenna, Caelius, 90, 120–4, 126, 136, 213, 227, 285
Villanovan culture, 39–47, 70, 145, 268–9, 360
Vitellia, 286, 287
Volsci, 217, 225, 234, 243, 246, 252, 275, 278, 279, 280–3, 284, 289–90, 291, 292, 302, 304, 307, 316

Volsinii, 69, 119, 218, 233, 234, 266, 309, 310, 327, 338, 343, 357, 363
Volumnia, 225
votive dedications and deposits, 72, 74, 78, 149, 198, 207, 208, 215, 257, 282, 292, 293
Vulca of Veii, 167, 218, 293
Vulci, 43, 77, 78, 121–3, 198, 222, 309, 338

walls *see* city walls
war economy, 326–7
warfare, 43, 309
  archaic, 283–7
  mid Republican, 324–32
  and calendar, 329
weights and measures, 209–10
wine, 31, 53, 54, 57, 71, 193–4, 222, 224, 228–9, 257
Winter, Nancy, 184, 199
Wiseman, Peter, 5, 32, 94, 105, 134
wolf and twins, 90–9, 225, 345, 346–7
women, 30–1, 50–1, 57–60, 69, 220–30, 361, 362
  as kingmakers, 120, 125, 227–8
  legal position, 257
  literacy, 222
  participation in cults and sacrifice, 230, 358
  prohibition on drinking wine, 31, 228–9, 230
  Trojan, 84, 97
  see also Sabine women
woolworking, 198, 221, 230
world system, 34, 36, 192, 203
writing, 65, 83, 84, 222; *see also* alphabet; literacy
written records, 8–15

EU representative:
Easy Access System Europe
Mustamäe tee 50, 10621 Tallinn, Estonia
Gpsr.requests@easproject.com

www.ingramcontent.com/pod-product-compliance
Lightning Source LLC
Chambersburg PA
CBHW052054300426
44117CB00013B/2114